THE WORLD ALMANAC OF THE
AMERICAN WEST

THE WORLD ALMANAC OF THE
AMERICAN WEST

Introduction: Alvin M. Josephy, Jr.
General Editor: John S. Bowman

World Almanac
An Imprint of Pharos Books
New York, New York

A Bison Book

First published in hardcover in 1986.
All rights reserved. No part of this book may be
reproduced in any form or by any means without
permission in writing from the publisher.

Distributed in the United States by Ballantine
Books, a division of Random House, Inc., and in
Canada by Random House of Canada Ltd.

Library of Congress Catalog Card Number 87-61053

Pharos Books
ISBN 0-88687-323-1
Ballantine Books ISBN 0-345-34973-3

Printed in the United States of America
Printed in 1987

World Almanac
An imprint of Pharos Books
A Scripps-Howard Company
200 Park Avenue
New York, NY 10166

10 9 8 7 6 5 4 3 2 1

Pages 2-3: *A solitary horseman against a Western sky.*
This page: *Celebrating completion of the Great
Southern Pacific Railroad.*
Following pages: *Ruins of the original Spanish
mission at San Juan Capistrano, California.*

CONTENTS

INTRODUCTION

Americans, the poets say, are a westering people, drawn onward by the sun and a western star. 'It's an old Spanish custom gone astray, a sort of English fever, I believe, or just a mere desire to take French leave,' wrote Steven Vincent Benét.

Certainly, it is an ancient inheritance, as old as the time of Columbus. The land he discovered was 'the best and most fertile and temperate and level and excellent that is in the world,' he announced, where spring was perpetual and the nightingale sang so sweetly 'that a man might never wish to leave.' Conquistadors and commoners sailed eagerly in his wake, their minds aflame with visions of an earthly paradise beyond the western horizon. Over the centuries, their successors kept coming – pressing on, in waves, to the mainland, the Appalachians, the plains, the Rockies, and the Pacific.

In a unique way, this book unifies the many colorful and dramatic threads of that grandest of all American epics, the westering movement that Columbus began five hundred years ago. At the same time, it provides a fresh perspective of American history, for it focuses on the challenges, heartbreaks, and achievements of our ancestors, men, women, and children, who steered toward the setting sun and, in doing so, created the foundations of the present-day United States. Interwoven with the human chronicles is the unfolding narrative of the West itself, but as the almanac's topical essays, biographies, and detailed chronology make clear, it is important to recognize that to the people who moved on, there was always, in each generation, a new 'West.' Moreover, wherever the West was at any point in time, it never stood alone in history, detached from the main centers of life – which had once been frontiers themselves – but was a profound contributor to the culture and historic course of its age. In short, though the many Wests revealed in this volume lay along the outer fringe of civilization and conjure up vivid images of their own, they were always an integral part of the essence and flavor of our total national experience.

What were the dreams that impelled men and women to move westward? Escape, adventure, the pursuit of fortunes in gold, furs, land, and other natural resources were some of them. Others were a new start in life, an improvement in health, spiritual solace in an unspoiled, virgin land, and, not the least, freedom. To many, the urge was clear and simple, a return to what mankind, in its unfettered youth, had possessed and lost. 'Every sunset which I witness inspires me with the desire to go to a West as distant and as fair as that into which the sun goes down,' wrote Henry David Thoreau. 'Eastward I go only by force; but westward I go free.' Thoreau's West were the woods, rivers, and ponds of the Northeast, but to this day, silent wildernesses with no trace of man's works continue to comfort those who share his yearnings for oneness with nature.

In every generation, in addition, there were lures for the more materialistic-minded. Listen to one of the earliest of them, the promotional report of the British seafarer Arthur Barlowe, who in 1584 explored the Outer Banks of North Carolina. 'We found such plentie,' he said, 'both on the sande, and on the green soil on the hils, as in the plaines, as well as on every little shrubbe ... that I thinke in all the world the like aboundance is not to be founde; and my selfe having seene those partes of Europe that most abound, find such differences, as were incredible to be written.' Like the song of a siren, his words inspired many English families to sail west, some of them vanishing without trace as members of the Lost Colony of Roanoke Island.

Western history is full of other Barlowes: Manasseh Cutler, who attracted colonists to the Ohio Valley; Stephen Austin, who enlisted settlers for Texas; and the Reverend Jason Lee, who stumped the Northeast for emigrants to Oregon, were only a few of many hundreds. All of them promised opportunities, a new start, and material rewards, and all helped to populate the continent.

Not entirely dissimilar were those who had a driving need to know what lay across a river or over the next fog-covered ridge. 'It was on the first of May, in the year 1769, that I resigned my domestic happiness for a time, and left my family and peaceable habitation on the Yadkin River, in North Carolina, to wander through the wilderness of America, in quest of the country of Kentucke,' Daniel Boone told his biographer. His western gropings were followed by those of scores of others, who brought knowledge of the country to the armies of emigrants who came after them. Boone found the Cumberland Gap that opened the first Great American

Boom and bust: Horace Tabor's Denver mansion and a Dust Bowl farm in Oklahoma.

West. A half century later, in a different clime farther west, Bible-toting Jedediah Smith and his fellow trappers found the South Pass that provided a route for wagons across the Rocky Mountains to Oregon and California. Behind such men came civilization.

If the West was a golden land of opportunity, however, it was also a dark land of savagery and hardship, where reality often blotted out the promotional myths. The romance and drama, with which the history of the westward movement glows, reflect the presence of unceasing conflict: of man against the frightening forces of a strange and stupendous land; man against wild creatures, loneliness, nameless terrors, harsh climate; man against his fellow men. Embedded in the journals and tales of travel and homemaking are everyday accounts of starving times, thirst, ferocious blizzards, tornadoes, and storms, epidemics of sickness, droughts, plagues of crop-destroying insects, and persons becoming lost and disappearing in uncharted wilds. To be sure, the challenges and trials called daily for resource, initiative, and the best a person could offer, and inevitably had much to do with molding the independence, self-reliance, and rugged individualism that contributed to the American character. But on each frontier, for many, the western star that had drawn them there flickered out in the blackness of dashed hopes.

Though the dreams and lures that drew people west were often well seasoned with myth, the awesomeness of the western land and the drama of real life had a tendency, at the same time, to breed new myths. Writers and artists, in particular, often envisioned what they expected to see, rather than what was actually there, and delineated landscapes and humans – scouts, mountian men, Indian fighters, cowboys, and others – bigger and better than life. Their Natty Bumppos and Currier and Ives prints, evoking the spirit of Manifest Destiny and Westward the Course of Empire that overcame all odds, became part of the national culture, as did captivity stories, dime novels, Wild West shows, pulp romances, and movies that departed so far from fact that it became difficult ultimately, even for Westerners, to separate truth from fiction.

The distortions and unrealities had many sides. Domestic life, the humdrum routines of everyday people, and whatever was undramatic faded away in favor of outsized heroes and villains and heart-pounding events. The West became a province of unending action and stereotypical deeds and figures. We have long known the stock image of the hardy frontiersman. But what of the roles and trials of the equally hardy frontier women who were with him, and of the blacks and other minorities who also populated the West? Familiar as the Indian is, for instance, we still know little of him as a real person, who resisted patriotically for his people, his religion, his land, life, and freedom. Stereotyped, treated by history like a tree to be cleared out of the way of advancing whites, he was so shrouded in myth that his present-day status and needs, all stemming from the past, can barely be understood by the rest of the American people.

In addition, the very terms that long defined the westward movement – winning the West, conquering the wilderness, taming the mountains, making the desert bloom – now give us pause. In an age of concern for the environment and the wise husbanding of non-replenishable resources, we see once-desirable realities turning also into myths. Inseparable from the westward movement were greedy speculation, cut-and-run exploitation of resources, and mindless development that left ruin in its wake. What they entailed – the damming and silting of rivers, the polluting and waste of water, the spoliation and salinization of land, the disappearance of wildlife and depletion of fish runs, the ravaging of grasslands, the creation of dust bowls, and the poisoning of air – are subjects for rethinking and new perceptions.

The West, it is said, never ends; both in myth and reality, it only changes. And so it does. Today, there is a new West, with new hopes, new problems, and new struggles. The migrations into it, larger than ever before in history, are fast overspreading its empty spaces. The surges themselves expose ironically the ultimate myth of the westering movement, for we now recognize that while it was occurring in the past, there was also a significant flow of people from south to north. Today, it is a flood, with signs that the migrations from Mexico and Central and South America will grow larger in the

years ahead, giving tomorrow's West an increasingly Hispanic coloration. Meanwhile, the traditional farming-ranching economy of much of the West is giving way to one based on industry and technology. Stock-raising, lumbering, mining, and fishing, all mainstays of yesterday, are in a crisis from which they may never fully recover. Facing dispossession like the Indians whom their homesteading fathers once dispossessed, irrigation farmers are also threatened, not only by falling watertables, but by the competing water needs of the new industries, the increased population, the burgeoning housing and recreation developments, and the belatedly observed waterrights claims of Indian reservations. These are just some of the issues that will give new character to the ongoing history of the West, as it evolves into the twenty-first century.

A Santa Fe freight train crosses the Colorado.

Finally, as we read in this volume of those whom history remembers, let us not forget the multitudes of whom we know nothing – other than that they, too, followed the sun and a western star and helped to found a nation. *'Hear the wind blow through the buffalo grass,'* wrote Benét,

Blow over wild-grape and brier.
This was frontier, and this,
And this, your house, was frontier.
There were footprints upon the hill
and men lie buried under,
Tamers of earth and rivers.
They died at the end of labor,
Forgotten is the name.

ALVIN M. JOSEPHY, JR.

CHRONOLOGY

Nebraska homesteaders of the late 1800s.

CHRONOLOGY

Christopher Columbus, discoverer of the New World.

3 AUGUST 1492
Exploration Christopher Columbus, a Genoese sea captain in the employ of the Spanish Crown, sets sail from Spain to 'discover islands and mainland in the Ocean Sea.' 'Islands' refers to the numerous tracts of land (many of them imaginary), depicted on maps of the time, in particular, Cipangu – present-day Japan; 'mainland' refers to Cathay (China). Columbus was setting forth to find a direct sea route westward from Europe to the Far East. For at least another hundred years, most voyages to the New World will be undertaken by men who seek a sea road to the Orient.

12 OCTOBER 1492
Exploration Columbus first sets foot on the New World, an island of the Bahamas that he names San Salvador. He believes he has arrived at some island belonging to the East Indies, or in any case off the coast of Asia.

15 MARCH 1493
Exploration Columbus arrives back in Spain with news of his discoveries, which spreads throughout Europe. The race to the West has begun.

3-4 MAY 1493
International In two papal bulls (edicts), Pope Alexander VI grants to Spain all lands not now under Christian rule that fall west of a demarcation line 100 leagues west of the Azores; Portugal is to have sole rights to newly discovered lands east of that line.

11 JUNE 1493
Exploration Columbus sets sail, with more than 1200 men on 17 ships, on his second voyage to the New World – which he still believes to be the Indies. In a trip that lasts almost three years, Columbus will explore the Leeward Islands, Puerto Rico, Jamaica, Hispaniola, and Cuba, assuming throughout the voyage that these islands lie off the coast of Asia.

7 JUNE 1494
International Portugal and Spain sign the Treaty of Tordesillas, moving the demarcation line established by the papal bulls of 1493 to 370 leagues west of the Cape Verde Islands. It is not clear whether Portuguese mariners have already discovered the coast of Brazil, but in any case this treaty will now give Portugal the right to claim Brazil. Other European countries will soon choose to ignore both the papal bulls and this treaty.

MAY-6 AUGUST 1497
Exploration John Cabot, an Italian sea captain commissioned by the English King Henry VII to find a sea route to the Indies, sails from Bristol (probably on 20 May); he first sights the land mass of the North American continent on 24 June – probably Newfoundland – and claims the area for England. He continues to sail southward along the coast of Newfoundland, then returns to Bristol on 6 August. Cabot believes he has reached some extension of the Eurasian land mass.

1497-1499
Exploration Vasco da Gama, a Portuguese sea captain commissioned by his king, sails down the coast of Africa, rounds the Cape of Good Hope, and sails on to India. When he returns (July 1499), his report will open up a new route to the Indies, but it will not stop others from seeking the westward passage.

MAY 1498
Exploration John Cabot leaves on his second voyage in search of a sea passage to the Indies; he will be lost at sea with four ships. Nothing is known of his whereabouts on this voyage.

30 MAY 1498
Exploration Columbus sets sail on his third voyage, this time taking a more southerly route and arriving at Trinidad; eventually, he will spot the coast of Venezuela. In 1500 Columbus will be sent back to Spain in chains – because of conditions in the Spanish colony at Hispaniola.

27 JUNE 1499
Exploration Amerigo Vespucci, an Italian navigator sailing on a Spanish expedition led by Alonso de Ojeda, first sights the South American coast around the mouth of the Amazon River. On this and a second expedition, 1501-02, Vespucci

Charles V, King of Spain and Holy Roman Emperor.

will explore thousands of miles of the South American coastline. It is his name, Latinized as America, that will first be applied to what is now recognized as a new continent (on the 1507 map of Martin Waldseemüller).

1500

Exploration João Fernandes and Pedro Maria de Barcelos, Portuguese from the Azores, sail westward seeking some of the real and imaginary islands reported to be in the distant ocean. They discover a large land mass that they name *Tierra del Lavrador* – 'Land of the Farmer,' in honor of Fernandes, a farmer. In fact, they have sighted Greenland, but mapmakers will eventually shift the name 'Labrador' to eastern Canada.

1500-1502

Exploration Two Portuguese brothers, Gaspar and Miguel Corte-Real, make three voyages that bring them at least to Newfoundland, but both are lost at sea.

11 MAY 1502-JUNE 1503

Exploration Columbus sails on his fourth voyage; this time he will explore the coast of Central America from Honduras to Panama.

1504

Commerce It is believed that French fishermen may have been visiting the Grand Banks off Newfoundland for some time, but the earliest authentic records name Jean Denys of Honfleur, France.

20 MAY 1506

Exploration Christopher Columbus dies in Valladolid, Spain. Although increasing numbers of Europeans are now realizing that the discoveries to the west comprise a New World, Columbus seems to have believed to the end that the region he had visited was part of the Indies or Asia.

25 APRIL 1507

Discovery The German-born geographer Martin Waldseemüller publishes his *Cosmographiae Introductio*: its maps are the first to show North and South America as separate from Asia – and the first to name the New World 'America,' after Amerigo Vespucci, whom Waldseemüller credits with discovering this New World.

1508-1509

Exploration Sebastian Cabot, son of John, sails west in search of a passage across the northern edge of the New World. Although there is no absolute proof of his destination, he seems to have reached the area around Newfoundland, possibly even what would later be known as Hudson Strait.

2-8 APRIL 1513

Exploration Juan Ponce de Leon, who has conquered Puerto Rico for the Spanish, sights Florida and lands near the site of St Augustine. He will sail

The sword of a conquistador, *forged in Toledo.*

CHRONOLOGY

south along the Florida coast to Key West, then up the west coast, always assuming that the peninsula is an island.

26 SEPTEMBER 1513
Discovery Vasco Nuñez de Balboa, his Indian guide, and 65 Spaniards arrive at the last mountain ridge on the Isthmus of Darien (Panama) before the ocean. Balboa calls a halt and goes up to the peak alone – to become the first European to view the Pacific from this shore. Four days later, standing on the Gulf of San Miguel, he will claim for the Spanish King 'all this sea and the countries bordering it.'

1519
Exploration Alonso de Pineda, on behalf of the Spanish governor of Jamaica, sails up the western coast of Florida – establishing that it is not an island – and around the edge of the Gulf of Mexico.

20 SEPTEMBER 1519-27 APRIL 1520
Exploration Ferdinand Magellan, a Portuguese navigator in the service of the Spanish King, sets sail with five ships and about 265 men in an effort to reach the East Indies by sailing westward. On 21 October he enters the strait named for him; on 28 November he reaches the Pacific. In the Philippine Islands, Magellan will be killed on 27 April 1520 (while fighting with one group of natives against another).

1521
Commerce João Alvares Fagundes, a Portuguese shipowner, has already made one voyage – probably in 1520 – to Newfoundland and into the Gulf of St Lawrence. Now he returns with a shipload of people he hopes to establish in a fishing (and soap-making!) colony. They settle on Cape Breton, but meeting hostility from the local Indians and from French fishermen, the colony fades away within the next few years. Although this is the end of the first attempt to colonize the New World, it is the beginning of hostilities among the various peoples who will try to possess it.

17 JANUARY-8 JULY 1524
Exploration Giovanni de Verrazzano, an Italian mariner commissioned by Francis I of France to find a northwest passage to Asia, sails from the Madeiras in *La Dauphine*. He will make his first landfall in the New World about 1 March along the coast of North Carolina; sailing northward along the Outer Banks off North Carolina, he will see water on the other side – and report that he has sighted 'the Eastern Sea ... the same that flows around the shores of India and China.' (This error will be perpetuated for a century or more, starting with a map made by Verrazzanno's brother, Girolamo.) On 17 April Verrazzano will sail into the Upper Bay of present-day New York Harbor and view the mouth of what will be called the Hudson River. He will then sail north to New-

Henry Hudson receives his commission from the Dutch East India Company.

foundland and arrive back in France on 8 July 1524. Although he had failed to find the northern passage, Verrazzano confirms that there is a continuous body of land between Newfoundland and Florida.

1524
Discovery A Congress, or Commission, meets at Badajos, Spain, and discusses, among other topics, the state of geographical knowledge about the New World.

10 JUNE 1527
Exploration Two English ships, the *Sampson* and the *Mary Guilford*, depart Plymouth for North America; the *Sampson* is soon lost at sea in a storm, but the *Mary Guilford*, captained by John Rut, reaches Newfoundland, and eventually sails all the way down to the West Indies, before returning to England in the spring of 1528. More important than the voyage was its inspiration: a proposal by Robert Thorne – prosperous English merchant living in Seville, Spain – to King Henry VIII that he should seek out a passage to Asia via the northerly route. Thorne even suggested that a ship might go right up over the North Pole and down into the Eastern Ocean, halving the distance traversed by the Spanish and the Portuguese. Thus the search for the Orient still motivates most voyages that are slowly making the New World more accessible.

JUNE 1527
Exploration Pánfilo de Narváez sets sail from Spain with a royal commission to conquer and colonize the land between Florida and Rio de las Palmas in eastern Mexico.

14 APRIL 1528-1536
Exploration Pánfilo de Narváez leads his party of 300 ashore at Tampa Bay, Florida. Told by the Indians that there is much gold in a locale called Apalache, Narváez sends the ships along the coast of the Gulf and proceeds to march inland. Arriving near the site of present-day Tallahassee and finding no riches, the men return to the Gulf and construct five crude ships; on 22 September 1528, the 242 survivors set sail. One by one, the ships are wrecked along the coast, until only one of them, captained by Cabeza de Vaca, treasurer of the expedition, is cast up on the coast of Texas (probably in Matagorda Bay). The 80 Spaniards are captured by the Indians and made to work for them; after several years, Cabeza de Vaca and three of his shipmates, including Estevan, an African slave, manage to escape. Making their way westward across Texas, they eventually reach the Rio Grande, then proceed west across Sonora, Mexico, and down the Yaqui River to the Pacific Coast. There they make contact (1536) with a group of slavehunters sent out by Niño de Guzman, the governor of New Galicia, the northern province of New Spain, or Mexico.

FRANCISCO VÁSQUEZ DE CORONADO, 1510-1554

Francisco Vásquez de Coronado was of that mythic breed of Spanish *conquistador* who went out lusting for gold and, to his astonishment, discovered merely a new world. Born in 1510 in the old university town of Salamanca, Coronado went to Mexico with its first viceroy in 1535. He was industrious, married well, and in 1538 became governor of Nueva Galicia. Then one Fray Marcos appeared from the Zuñi area of present New Mexico with tales of fabulous cities of gold. The viceroy named Coronado to mount an expedition to find and conquer these cities.

In early 1540 Coronado set out with 200 mounted men, a company of footsoldiers, and some 1000 Indian allies, plus a gigantic pack train. This expedition, destined to fail in finding gold, was to prove one of the most productive exploring parties of all time.

The column moved along the Sierra Madre to the Rio Sonora, then north to the upper Gila and present-day Arizona, where the first of the 'golden cities' proved to be the adobe pueblos of the Zuñi Indians. From there Coronado sent García López de Cárdenas northwest in search of riches. Instead, Cárdenas found the Hopi Indians and the Grand Canyon, which he was the first white man to behold. Meanwhile, Coronado had pushed on to the Rio Grande, contacting the Pueblo Indians.

After a winter among the Pueblos in 1541, Coronado headed east upon hearing Indian tales of the golden land of Gran Quiera. He marched his men across parts of present-day Texas, Oklahoma, and Kansas before turning back in disgust. In 1542 he was back in Mexico to report his 'failure' to the viceroy. After returning to political affairs, Coronado died in Mexico City in 1554.

1530-1533
Exploration Hernán Cortés, the conqueror of Mexico, has returned from a visit to Spain and now sets up a shipyard at Zacatula on the Pacific Coast of Mexico; he will send out a series of maritime expeditions in search of a water route back to the Atlantic. On one of these, in 1533, Cortes will discover the southern tip of the peninsula of California, or Baja California, which he will believe to be an island.

APRIL-AUGUST 1534
Exploration Jacques Cartier, a mariner sponsored by Francis I of France, sails to seek a new route to China. He makes his first landfall at Newfoundland, then proceeds along the coast of Labrador to Prince Edward Island and the Gaspé Bay until he sails for France on the first of August. Once again, a mariner has failed to find a Northwest Passage to the Orient but has returned with increased knowledge of the New World that lies to the west.

19 MAY 1535-15 JULY 1536
Exploration Jacques Cartier makes his second voyage to North America. This time he proceeds up the St Lawrence River until he arrives, on 8 September, at an Indian village called Stadaconé,

which will become the site of Quebec City. On 2 October a small party of longboats led by Cartier arrives at another Indian town, known as Hochelaga, on the site of present-day Montreal. When Cartier returns to France – with 10 Indians – he will bear news of this great river that offers the prospect of penetrating the New World (but he will have named the rapids below Montreal *La Chine*, in the belief he had reached the edge of Asia!).

APRIL-OCTOBER 1536
Westward Movement The first 'tourist cruise' to the New World is led by Richard Hore, a merchant of London, who takes two ships with Englishmen to Newfoundland with the double purpose of fishing for cod and simply seeing the wonders of North America. They are so desperate for food that some resort to cannibalism before the survivors arrive back in England.

1536
Discovery Cabeza de Vaca and the other three survivors of the epic trek across southwest America – which began after their arrival in Florida in 1528 – arrives in Mexico City and tells of the wonders he has seen during his years in the unknown territories. He has probably been the first European to see buffalo, for instance, and he may have seen the Pueblo Indians. He also reports stories of large and prosperous Indian cities to the north of where his travels had taken him – these will soon be transmuted into the Seven Golden Cities of Cibola. Cabeza de Vaca will repeat his stories upon his return to Spain, which will inspire several major expeditions into North America, including the crucial ones led by de Soto and Coronado.

7 MARCH-AUGUST 1539
Exploration Don Antonio de Mendoza, Viceroy of New Spain, has failed to persuade Cabeza de Vaca to lead an expedition back into the territory he has recently left. However, Mendoza has bought the African slave Estevan, and trained some of de Vaca's Indian companions as interpreters. Today they set out on an expedition headed by Fray Marcos, a Franciscan monk. Estevan will be killed by Indians in May (although he will survive in Zuñi Indian lore into the twentieth century). Fray Marcos will go on to see the 'city' the Indians call Cibola – in fact, the Hawikuh Pueblo in west-central New Mexico – and then turn back and, in his own words, 'with far more fright than food,' return to Mexico. Fray Marcos's report will further whet the appetites of the Spaniards for the golden cities that await them.

28 MAY 1539-1543
Exploration Hernando de Soto, governor of Cuba, lands on the Florida coast – probably at Tampa Bay, possibly at Charlotte Harbor – with

Queen Elizabeth I, 1533-1603. England became a world power during her long and autocratic reign.

600 men and 213 horses, fighting hounds, and a herd of swine. His party explores the western area of Florida, spending the winter of 1539-40 at Apalachee (which Narváez had visited in 1528). In the spring, the expedition marches north to the Savannah River region, then west to the Blue Ridge Mountains, then back to the Gulf of Mexico near Mobile where the party winters. In the spring of 1541, de Soto leads his men north across the Mississippi River near Memphis; they move west through the Ozark Mountains and spend their third winter in eastern Oklahoma. On returning to the Mississippi in the spring of 1542, de Soto dies of an illness, and Luis Moscoso de Alvarado assumes command. He leads the group westward to the Red River in Texas, then to the upper Brazos River; they spend their fourth winter, 1542-3, by the Mississippi, near the mouth of the Arkansas River. In the summer of 1543, they sail down the Mississippi and into the Gulf, eventually making their way to the mouth of the Rio de Panuco, in eastern Mexico. Of the original 600, 311 return.

8 JULY 1539
Exploration Hernán Cortés, the governor of Mexico, dispatches Francisco de Ulloa from a point near Acapulco to explore the coast to the north. Ulloa sails to the head of the Sea of Cortés (Gulf of California), then south around the tip of Baja California – establishing that it is a peninsula, not an island.

23 FEBRUARY 1540-1542

Exploration Viceroy Mendoza has organized another expedition, this one under command of Francisco Vasquez de Coronado, who sets out in February 1540 with some 300 young Spaniards and many Indians; their immediate goal is to find the fabled Seven Cities of Cibola. On 7 July Coronado's men capture the Zuñi pueblo of Hawikuh, which Fray Marcos had identified as the principal city of Cibola; the Spanish rename it Granada-Cibola and make it their base camp. Coronado then sends out two secondary expeditions. One, led by Don Garcia Lopez de Cardenas, goes west in search of the great river of which the Indians speak; thus Cardenas becomes the first European to see the Grand Canyon, and perhaps southern Utah. The other expedition, led by Hernando de Alvarado, heads east; its members see the great Acoma Pueblo and move on into the Texas Panhandle. They meet a Plains Indian they nickname 'The Turk,' who tells of a wealthy kingdom named Quivira that lies to the northeast. Alvarado brings word of this back to Coronado, who will spend the winter of 1540-41 near Albuquerque before going in search of Quivira. Passing through the Texas Panhandle, Coronado heads up into Oklahoma and finally comes to Quivira – which turns out to be an unimpressive Indian settlement (probably near Wichita, Kansas). The Spanish garrot 'The Turk' for lying, then head back. After wintering on the Rio Grande, they arrive in Mexico.

25 AUGUST 1540

Exploration In conjunction with the overland expedition under Coronado, Hernando de Alarcon sets out from Acapulco to explore the Sea of Cortés (the Gulf of California) and seek out a possible water route inland to Cibola. Alarcon will enter the Colorado River and make his way up the valley for several weeks, but will fail to make contact with Cardenas, who has reached the Grand Canyon.

1541

Exploration Melchior Diaz is sent by Viceroy Mendoza on another expedition to Cibola; he crosses the Colorado River by raft and moves down onto the barren land of Baja California.

Indian Wars Niño de Guzmán had conquered the Indians of northwestern Mexico, known by the Spaniards as New Galiciia, and ruled the territory with great harshness. When Coronado's expedition into the north drew off many men, the Indians, led by one Texamatli, revolted against the Spanish. Since the rebellion centered around the town of Mixton, it is known as the Mixton War. The Spaniards call in all available forces and soon re-establish their authority.

JUNE 1542-JANUARY 1543

Exploration Juan Rodrigquez Cabrillo, a Portuguese employed by the Spanish, is sent by Viceroy Mendoza to continue the explorations along the coast north of Mexico (the former leader of the expedition, Alarcon, having been killed in the Mixton War). Cabrillo sets out from Acapulco in June and sails along the western shore of Baja California; he discovers San Diego Bay and lands at Point Loma Head (now Cabrillo National Monument). Then he sails up to the Northwest Cape beyond San Francisco (but fails to discover the Bay). Cabrillo returns to winter on San Miguel Island, off Santa Barbara, where he dies in January, 1543.

FEBRUARY-APRIL 1543

Exploration With Cabrillo dead, Bartolome Ferrelo assumes command of the expedition into Upper California and takes two ships north along the coast. They will claim to have reached the latitude of 44°N – just above the southern border of present-day Oregon – before turning back to Mexico.

1543

Discovery A temporary lull settles over the exploration of North America, as the first heroic phase comes to an end. Viceroy Mendoza retires this year, and de Soto's and Coronado's expeditions have failed to discover the fabulous golden cities that they had believed to exist among the Indians of the Southwest. Although the Spanish had discovered many major geographical features of North America, from the eastern coast of Florida all the way around the Gulf of Mexico and then along the western coast – including the Mississippi and Colorado Rivers – they had not found the rivers they hoped would link the Atlantic to the Pacific. Meanwhile, Jacques Cartier had returned to France in 1542 from his third expedition, this time carrying barrels of alleged gold, silver, and precious stones that he had found in Canada – all of which were quickly shown to be other minerals (the 'gold' was iron pyrite, the 'diamonds' were quartz crystals). The French had also failed to find any shortcut to China across the northern route. The true riches of the American West still remained to be discovered.

1559-1560

Exploration Don Tristan de Luna y Arrellano, one of Coronado's former captains, sails from Vera Cruz, Mexico, with 1500 settlers in an attempt to establish a colony on Pensacola Bay in Florida. The colony fails, but Arrellano, lured by tales of the riches of Quivira, follows the Alabama River up toward the Mississippi before turning back.

8 SEPTEMBER 1565

Settling Pedro Menendez de Aviles founds the first permanent European colony in North America at St Augustine, Florida, where he and his party of 1500 had arrived on 28 August. Although King Philip II of Spain had issued an order (23

CHRONOLOGY

September 1561) forbidding any more attempts at establishing settlements in the Florida region, the Spanish have changed their policy now that the French have begun to colonize the Atlantic coast from North Carolina to Florida.

1565

Philippines Miguel Lopez de Legazpi, a Spanish general, founds the first permanent Spanish settlement on Cebu Island and begins the conquest of the Philippines. Shortly thereafter the Spanish begin to send at least one ship back to Mexico each year with trade products. Prevailing winds and currents dictate that the best route takes them northeast to the northern coast of California: over the years many of these ships will put into harbors along the coast, as they make their way south to Mexico.

1566

Exploration Menendez, the founder of St Augustine and now victorious over the French along the south Atlantic coast, sends Captain Juan Pardo with a small party to 'discover and conquer the interior country from there to Mexico.' Pardo will build a series of blockhouses as far inland as the slopes of the Blue Ridge Mountains, but within two years most of the Spanish will have been killed by the Indians.

1576

Exploration Sir Humphrey Gilbert, a respected English soldier and navigator, publishes his *Discourse ... to prove a passage by the north-west to Cathaia and the East Indies*, in which he asserts that North America is an island (formerly known as Atlantis, in fact).

1576-1578

Exploration Inspired by Gilbert's book and claims, Martin Frobisher, an Englishman, will make three voyages during these years to find a northern sea route to Asia. He will reach Baffin Land, Frobisher Bay, and Hudson Strait and bring back some black ore and an Eskimo to prove he has found gold and 'Cathay.'

DECEMBER 1577-26 SEPTEMBER 1580

Exploration Francis Drake, the English sea captain, sets out with five ships to raid the Spanish along the Pacific coast of the Americas. He becomes the first Englishman to pass through the Straits of Magellan; then, with only his *Golden Hind*, he moves north along the coast of South and North America, arriving at San Francisco Bay on 17 June 1579. Drake sails still farther north, possibly to the coast of Washington, and claims all this territory for England as New Albion. Finding no sea passage that would take him back to the Atlantic, he sets off across the Pacific and finally arrives at Plymouth in September 1580 after almost three years at sea.

1581

Exploration Three Spanish missionaries – Franciscan Friars Rodriguez, Lopez, and Santa Maria – set out from Mexico to convert the Pueblo Indians described by Coronado and Fray Marcos. They proceed down the Conchos River, and then up the Rio Grande, until Santa Maria is killed by Indians. Rodriguez and Lopez continue with their party to Puaray, a central pueblo; they visit the nearby salt mines, and see the buffalo and the great pueblo of Acoma before they are killed by Indians.

1582

Exploration David Ingram, an old English sailor, claims that in 1568 he and two others set out from the Rio Panuco, on Mexico's east coast, and walked all the way across North America to a Canadian river near Cape Breton Island. His tales of geographical features and Indians are vague and confusing, but close enough to lead some to believe that he actually accomplished this feat.

1582-1583

Exploration Before word of the death of all three friars reaches Mexico, another missionary, Fray Beltran, decides to go in support, accompanied by a wealthy citizen, Antonio de Espejo. They arrive at Puaray and learn of the murder of the other friars, but go on to visit additional pueblos. Fray Beltran then turns back, but Espejo continues, led on by reports of a large lake to the west where people wear gold ornaments. Espejo never finds this Lake of Gold (as it was called on many maps, probably referring to the Gulf of California), but he sees the turquoise mines in Arizona and gets to the buffalo plains before making his way back to Mexico.

1583

Exploration Sir Humphrey Gilbert is lost at sea off the Azores while returning from his second voyage in search of a Northwest Passage. This will not deter other Englishmen from seeking this route: John Davis will make three voyages (1585-7), George Weymouth will go in 1602 (bearing a letter from Queen Elizabeth to the Emperor of Cathay!), John Knight departs in 1606, Thomas Button in 1612 (carrying letters from King James to the Emperor of Japan and other Oriental kings), and still others will follow. They will not find the desired route, but will add to that knowledge of northern lands and waters which will finally make a Northwest Passage possible.

21 JULY 1586-10 SEPTEMBER 1588

Exploration Thomas Cavendish, an English mariner, sets out from Plymouth with three ships to repeat Drake's circumnavigation of the globe. After passing through the Straits of Magellan, he moves up the coast of South America; off California, he seizes a Spanish treasure ship, the *Great St Anne*. Cavendish arrives back with one ship.

The landing at Roanoke Island, North Carolina, by John White, a member of the expedition of 1585.

1587
Discovery Pedro de Unamuno, a Spanish captain of a ship from the Philippines, lands at Morro Bay on the California coast.

1590
Discovery Richard Hakluyt, an English geographer who has accompanied Sir Walter Raleigh on his Roanoke expedition, publishes an anthology of reports of the most notable voyages of discovery by Englishmen: *The Principall Navigations, Voyages and Discoveries of the English Nation at any Time within the Compasse of these 1500 years*. Between 1598 and 1600, a second and greatly enlarged edition appears, including accounts of the most recent voyages by such men as Drake, Frobisher, Gilbert, and Raleigh. The publication of Hakluyt's work is both a milestone and an inspiration for opening up the New World in the west.

1593
Exploration Inspired by the reports of Espejo and hoping to find the riches still promised by Quivira, the Spaniard Sosa sets off from Mexico without royal permission; he gets as far as Taos, New Mexico, before he is arrested and brought back to Mexico.

1593-1594
Exploration Another unauthorized expedition sets out from Mexico in search of Quivira and riches, this one led by a rough freebooter, Antonio Guiterrez de Humana. He will reach the Arkansas River in Kansas, proceed to the River Platte in Nebraska, and murder his partner before turning back.

1595
Discovery Sebastian Cermeño, the Spanish captain of a ship from the Philippines, comes into Drake's Bay, which he names San Francisco Bay. He trades with the local Indians before he runs his ship aground, then makes his way back to Mexico in a small boat from the ship.

1598-1608
Settling The Spanish Council of the Indies has decided to colonize the new lands north of Mexico. It appoints Don Juan de Oñate, a wealthy citizen of the mining town of Zacatecas, in northern Mexico, to be the new governor of the territory. (Oñate's wife is the granddaughter of Cortés and a great-granddaughter of Montezuma.) Oñate sets off with his large party in 1598: as they cross the Rio Grande near El Paso, they hold an impressive

CHRONOLOGY

ceremony. On the east bank of the river, Oñate establishes his first 'capital,' San Juan de los Caballeros (near Bernalilo, north of Albuquerque) New Mexico, later moving it to San Gabriel on the west bank. The Catholic missionaries set about establishing churches and converting the peublo Indians, but the Indians cannot accede to all demands. At one point Oñate's nephew, Zaldivar, is killed; in revenge, the Spaniards virtually destroy the great pueblo of Acoma. (The Indians will attempt a revolt in 1599, but will soon be suppressed.) The Acoma Pueblo, on top of a steep mesa some 357 feet high, had been founded about ad 1150; since its inhabitants revived it after the Spanish destruction, it is regarded as the oldest continuously inhabited community in North America. Oñate will send out exploring parties and will himself embark on two major expeditions: one, in 1601, takes him up to Oklahoma and over to the Quivira region (around Wichita, Kansas). It is this expedition that apparently introduces the horse to the Indians of the American Plains, greatly changing their way to life. On his second expedition, Oñate heads west and reaches the Colorado River, which he follows down to the Gulf of California. In his absence, both the Spanish colonists and the Indians have grown increasingly discontented, and in 1609 Oñate will be replaced as governor and will return to Mexico to face various charges (including the use of undue force against the Acoma Pueblo). Eventually (1624) Oñate will be pardoned.

1602-1603
Exploration Sebastian Vizcaino is commissioned by King Philip III of Spain to seek out a strait that might lead northward from the great western sea (the Pacific) and thence to the east and Quivira. The three ships under Vizcaino sail with Fray Ascension, a 'cosmographer' who will write a full account of the voyage. The expedition heads up the coast of California, discovers Monterey Bay, then proceeds up to Drake's Bay and beyond it to the coast of Oregon. One ship will report a great river coming down from the east, perhaps connecting with the legendary Strait of Anian. By the time Fray Ascension writes his account in 1620, he will claim that this strait in turn connects with the body of water known as the Gulf of California – proving that California is an island. Mapmakers will perpetuate this error for many years.

1603
Exploration Samuel de Champlain, a French mariner, has already sailed to the West Indies with the Spanish fleet. On returning in 1601, he had written a *Brief Narrative* in which he proposed, among other things, that a canal be constructed at the isthmus of Panama. King Henry IV of France has appointed him royal geographer, and now Champlain makes his first voyage to North America. He ascends the St Lawrence to the site of

Montreal and the Lachine Rapids, gathering much geographical knowledge about the lands immediately north and west from the Indians. He seems to have heard of Lake Ontario, Lake Huron, and even Niagara Falls, but he has no sense of the distances involved (and in fact confuses Lake Huron with the South Sea, or Pacific). However, Champlain's report on this first voyage will inspire both his own subsequent journeys and settlements and other generations of French expansion westward across North America.

24 MAY 1607
Settling English colonists land at Jamestown, Virginia, and begin English settlement of this part of North America.

1607-1608
Exploration Henry Hudson, an English navigator, makes two voyages for the English Muscovy Company to find a north*east* passage to Asia – up around the northern coast of Eurasia. He fails, and this effectively ends English interest in such a route.

25 MARCH 1609
Exploration Henry Hudson, now in the employ of the Dutch East Indies Company, sets forth to the west to find a short route to the Orient for the Dutch. On 11 September he will enter what is now Upper New York Bay, then sail up the river that bears his name to the site of Albany before returning to the Atlantic and Europe.

1610
Settling Pedro de Peralta, the new governor of the Kingdom and Province of New Mexico, establishes its new capital at Sante Fe, which will remain continuously occupied to the present day.
Arts/Culture Gaspar Villagra, who accompanied Oñate on the ambitious expedition that set forth in 1598 to explore New Mexico, publishes in Spain *History of New Mexico*, his epic poem on this event; it is considered a fairly reliable account, as well as one of the first works of poetry written in North America.

17 APRIL 1610-SUMMER 1611
Exploration Henry Hudson, back in the employ of the English, sails again to search for a Northwest Passage; on 25 June he enters the strait that leads to the great inland sea that bears his name. After wintering over on James Bay, Hudson's men mutiny on 21 June 1611 and set Hudson, his son, his first mate, and five others (including the ship's carpenter, who refuses to leave his leader) adrift in a small boat. They are never seen again (but then only eight of the mutineers make it back to England).

1611-1612
Discovery Etienne Brulé, at the age of about 18,

had gone to live with the Algonquin Indians (1810) to learn their language and their country. Now he spends several years with the Huron Indians, becoming probably the first European to see Lake Huron.

1613
Exploration Samuel de Champlain, newly returned to Canada from France, sets out once more to seek the western lakes; he gets only as far as Allumette Island in the Ottawa River.

1615-1616
Discovery Samuel de Champlain goes with Etienne Brulé and a party of Huron Indians to Georgian Bay on Lake Huron. Champlain then accompanies some Hurons in an attack on enemy Iroquois near Oneida Lake in New York; Champlain is wounded and winters with the Hurons.

AUGUST 1619
Life/Customs On 9-14 August, the Virginia House of Burgesses – the first representative assembly in America – sits for its first session in Jamestown. Its decisions are subject to approval by the Virginia Company in London. This same month, 20 African blacks are brought to Jamestown on a Dutch ship and bought as indentured servants – which will lead to the introduction of black slavery in North America. (The Spanish have already brought African slaves with them to Central and South America.)

Above: *Starting the settlement at Jamestown.*
Below: *Henry Hudson and his ship, the* Half Moon.

CHRONOLOGY

21 DECEMBER 1620
Settling After exploring the coast since their arrival in the New World on 9 November, the Pilgrims have chosen to settle at Plymouth and now begin to disembark. Santa Fé, New Mexico, is a village of 50 residents at this time.

22 MARCH 1622
Indians The Opechancanough Indians attack and massacre some 350 colonists in the English colony of Virginia. The colonists retaliate with a series of raids on the Indians. The Spanish are already pressing the Indians from the west; now increasing pressure from European colonists on the east will create a pincer effect that will continue for another 270 years, until the Indians are forced out of their native lands.

1623
Exploration Etienne Brulé, now one of Champlain's main agents, is asked by Champlain to continue his explorations north and west. Brulé goes out along the north shore of Lake Huron, possibly reaching Lake Superior on this trip.

1629
Missionary Work Spanish missionary Fray Juan Ramirez arrives at the Acoma Pueblo to make another attempt to convert the Southwestern Indians to Christianity.

1630
Population There are now some 3000 colonists in Virginia and 300 in the Plymouth Colony; the next decade will see 16,000 additional colonists in the Massachusetts Bay Colony alone. Although the Spanish in the Southwest and the French in Canada have had almost a 100-year head start on the English, their few settlements do not comprise nearly this many permanent settlers.

1632
French Canada Etienne Brulé, one of the pioneers in living among the Indians, is killed – and

---

FORGOTTEN DISCOVERERS OF THE WEST

Not all explorers were of the conquistador type – bold conquerors impelled by personal glory or gain. Others were cut from a different cloth, often that of the Roman Catholic Church – the *Frays* and *Pères* who were in the vanguard of Spanish and French forays into the west. These men were missionaries, come to convert the natives, and their zeal often resulted in amazing feats of endurance and courage. One such was Fray Marcos, a Franciscan born in Nice, France, who had first spent time in Peru before coming to Mexico. In 1539 he made a major expedition up into the Zuñi pueblo territory. Although Marcos exaggerated, it was his account of the seven cities of Cibola that inspired the important expedition of Coronado. In 1581 Friars Augustin Rodriguez, Lopez, and Santa Maria went back up into the pueblo Indian territory via the Conchos River and Rio Grande Valleys. Fray Bernardino Beltran sought to trace them in 1582, but the three had been killed by the Indians.

Far to the north, Champlain brought the first Catholic missionaries to French Canada in 1615 – four members of the Récollets, a branch of the Franciscans. These men lived among the Indians and soon contributed knowledge of the new lands and peoples. The Jesuits arrived in French Canada in 1625; men like Isaac Jogues and Jacques Marquette would make notable contributions to opening up the western territory as they spread their faith. Many kept valuable written records of their travels.

Another group who received little publicity were the French *coureurs du bois* ('frequenters of the forests') and *voyageurs* – scouts and guides, trappers and traders who penetrated the western reaches of French Canada and led the way into the Pacific Northwest. Many chose deliberately to live among the Indians, learning their languages and their ways. Some married Indian women and spent their whole lives in the wilderness. Etienne Brulé, Nicolas Vignau, and Jean Nicolet are only three of the better known *voyageurs*.

HEMING.
COUREUR DE BOIS.

evidently eaten – by Huron Indians who had come to hate his overbearing ways.

SEPTEMBER 1633

Westward Movement Massachusetts Bay Colony settler John Oldham leads a group inland to the Connecticut Valley; they spend the winter at Wethersfield, Connecticut. Meanwhile, William Holmes of Plymouth Colony has been commissioned to erect a trading post on the river, above the Dutch post at Hartford. The movement west is underway.

1638

Exploration Jean Nicolet, one of Champlain's young assistants, sets out to visit the Winnebago Indians said to reside 300 leagues to the west. Nicolet expects that he may also find the reported sea route to China, so he packs a ceremonial robe 'made of China damask, all strewn with flowers and birds of many colors.' Nicolet makes his way along Lake Huron to Sault Ste Marie, then down through the Straits of Mackinac to the Green Bay of Lake Michigan, where he meets the Winnebagoes, or 'People of the Sea.' Nicolet seems to believe that some great ocean lies not far to the west – that a water route to China may yet be found.

1641

Westward Movement A group of traders in the Virginia colony petitions the Assembly for permission to extend its activities farther west into the Appalachians.

Early settlers of New England face privation (shown by the rationing of 'five kernels of corn') and attack by hostile Indians.

Massachusetts colonists lay a foundation for their settlement.

CHRONOLOGY

MIS-MAPPING THE NEW WORLD

From the first voyages of discovery and exploration, maps and reports began to give Europeans a surprisingly immediate image of the New World to the west. (Almost all expeditions included a professional chart- or map-maker, often a Portuguese; they were regarded as experts at this.) On the one hand, these early depictions were surprisingly detailed and helpful; at the same time, numerous errors were introduced – understandably, since the discoverers had no way of knowing the dimensions of the new lands. Thus the first printed map to show any part of the New World, the Contarini map of 1506, shows the West Indies floating off in the Atlantic, with only Japan to the west and the Asian mainland to the north. The Cantino map of 1502 shows not only the 'hip' of South America but parts of what are evidently intended to be the peninsula and Keys of Florida. As Spanish, Portuguese, French, and English ships – often captained by Italians – made further contacts with the shores of the Gulf of Mexico, Central and South America, and the eastern coast of North America to Labrador, maps became quite accurate about the coastal features – although they were long thought to be the coasts of Asia!

In 1529 a map made by Jerome Verrazzano, brother of the great explorer Giovanni, showed a large bulge or gulf of the Pacific Ocean jutting into North America at about the point where North Carolina lies, thus reducing North America to two relatively small bodies of land linked at that point by a narrow isthmus. It has been suggested that Verrazzano sailed down along the Outer Banks and looked across to the sounds off North Carolina and assumed he was looking at the Pacific Ocean. (By this time, everyone knew that the Pacific Ocean existed west of the New World; they even knew the approximate size of the earth: what they didn't know was how far west North America extended.)

Other errors persisted in early maps, particularly of the Far West, the last region to be explored. California was reported to be an island in 1602. Even though this was refuted by the explorations of Eusebio Kino in 1698, the misconception remained on maps well into the eighteenth century. Many early maps show the legendary lands of Cibola and Quivira. The often-cited Strait of Anian was believed to breach a narrow isthmus between the northernmost reaches of North America and Asia. Appearing first on Zaltierri's map of 1566, this body of water was actually found and named by Vitus Bering in 1728. In many cases, the search for non-existent places and features led explorers to discovery.

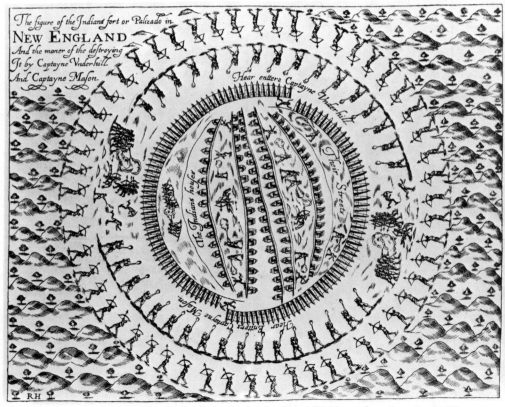

An Indian fort under attack by New England colonists in John Underhill's Newes from America *(1638).*

SEPTEMBER 1641-SUMMER 1643

Exploration The Jesuit Fathers Isaac Jogues and Charles Raymbault set off from the French post on Georgian Bay, Lake Huron, and head west to Sault Ste Marie, where they are perhaps the first Europeans to get a true sense of the relative locations of Lakes Superior and Michigan. Father Raymbault will die in the summer of 1642, and Father Jogues will be taken by the Iroquois. After enduring a terrible captivity, he will be rescued by Dutch traders a year later.

Isaac Jogues, SJ, who was canonized as a martyr.

1643

Indian Wars The Iroquois, who have been opposed to the French from their first appearance, begin a war against them and their Indian allies – principally the Hurons – that will go on for some 20 years. At the end of that time, the Iroquois will be the dominant Indians across all of eastern Canada.

1647

Discovery Although several Frenchmen have undoubtedly been aware of a great waterfall between Lakes Erie and Ontario, the first explicit reference to Niagara Falls – 'a waterfall of a dreadful height' – is made by the Jesuit priest Ragueneu this year.

1650

Westward Movement The Englishman Edward Williams, in a pamphlet published this year to promote the great potential of the Virginia colony, says that it also offers 'a most compendious passage to the discovery of these more opulent kingdoms of China, Cochin-China, Cathay, Japan, the Philippines, Sumatra, and all those beauteous and opulent provinces of the East Indies which beyond dispute lie open to those seas which wash the southwest parts of Virginia, through whose bosom all those precious commodities will flow.' Williams is simply repeating the still commonly held notion that the South Sea, or Pacific Ocean, does not lie too far west of the Atlantic seaboard.

27 AUGUST 1650

Exploration Abraham Wood, commander of Fort Henry, which the Virginian English have established near the mouth of the Appomattox River, leads a small party to explore the unknown lands to the southwest. They penetrate only about 100 miles, but bring back word of the possibilities of fur trading and new land.

JUNE 1653

Indian Wars Having defeated the Hurons in numerous encounters and terrorized many of the French across eastern Canada, the Iroquois appear at Montreal and negotiate a truce. This will last only for some five years, during which time the French will effectively cease their explorations westward.

1654-1657

Exploration Médard Chouart, Sieur de Groseilliers, and his brother-in-law, Pierre Esprit Radisson, French 'woodsmen' or explorers, travel extensively in the area around Lakes Huron, Michigan, and Superior, getting to know regional Indians and resources perhaps better than any previous Frenchmen.

1658-1666

Indian Wars The Iroquois, backed by the Dutch and later by the English, all but wipe out the French in Canada (total population only about 3000). Not until the Marquis de Tracy arrives in Quebec (June 1665) do the French launch an organized military campaign, and the Iroquois are finally curbed. They will ask for peace in 1667.

1659-1660

Exploration Groseilliers and Radisson set off on another exploratory expedition, possibly becoming the first Europeans to reach Minnesota.

1666

Missionary Work Father Jacques Marquette, a French Jesuit, arrives in New France and sets about learning the Indian languages when he settles at Trois Rivieres, Quebec.

1667

Discovery Although French Canadians have been vaguely aware of a large river to the west that runs southward, the first specific reference to it comes this year from a French missionary, Father Allouez. He reports 'people dwelling to the west of this place toward the great river Messipi.'

CHRONOLOGY

*The Dutch fort at Bowling Green (New York City)
around 1633; an imaginative re-creation.*

CHRONOLOGY

1668
Exploration The civil administrator of New France, Jean Talon, sends Jean Peré via Lake Ontario and Lake Simcoe to investigate reports of copper mines around Lake Superior.

1669-1670
Exploration John Lederer, a German physician, persuades Governor Berkeley of the Virginia colony to let him make a brief trial expedition farther west. He reaches the Blue Ridge Mountains and looks westward over the Shenandoah Valley to the Appalachians, through which he fails to find any pass.

1670
International By now, the three major European powers interested in exploiting the New World – England, Spain, and France – are engaged in increasingly hostile rivalry for the vast territory that they dimly realize lies west of the Atlantic seaboard.

14 JUNE 1671
French Canada The Sieur de St Lusson, acting on behalf of Jean Talon, the administrator of New France, raises the arms of France with great ceremony before a gathering of Louis Jolliet, a guide, many Jesuit missionaries, and various Indians. In addition to the known lands of New France, he claims 'all other countries, rivers, lakes, and tributaries . . . which are bounded on the one side by the Northern and Western Seas and on the other side by the South Sea.'

1 SEPTEMBER 1671
Exploration Abraham Wood, commander of the English Fort Henry, sends an expedition led by Thomas Batts and Robert Fallam to learn about the rivers and other features that lie beyond the Blue Ridge Mountains. They discover a stream that eventually will join the Kanawha River and flow into the Ohio, thence into the Mississippi.

1672-1673
Exploration Dr Henry Woodward of the English colony at Charles Town, South Carolina, has taken an active role in dealing with the Indians in order to hold off the Spanish to the south. During these years he explores the western reaches of South Carolina.

MAY-SEPTEMBER 1673
Exploration Louis Jolliet has been appointed (1672) to lead an expedition to investigate the Mississippi River; Father Jacques Marquette, who has been engaged in missionary work among the Indians of Canada since 1666, is asked to join him. With five other *voyageurs*, they set out from Green Bay on Lake Michigan. They ascend the Fox River, make portage to the Wisconsin River, and then go down to the Mississippi. When they reach the junction of the Arkansas and Mississippi Rivers, they realize that the Spanish are active on the lower reaches of the Mississippi, so they turn back, returning to Lake Michigan via the Illinois River in September.

4 DECEMBER 1674
Westward Movement Father Marquette establishes a mission at what is now Chicago.

1676
Indians The Apache Indians in New Mexico rise against the Spanish, but are quickly put down.

SEPTEMBER 1678-AUTUMN 1680
Exploration Daniel Greysolon, Sieur de Luth, or Duluth, sets out with a small party of Frenchmen and Indians to establish French rule west of Lake Superior. He tries to improve relations among the Indians of the region and gets as far west as Mille Lacs. There he sends off a small party that may have reached Dakota and hears tales of a great sea to the west (possibly the Great Salt Lake). Before he can explore farther west, he learns that Father Hennepin and his two companions, Michel Accault and Antoine de Gay Anguel – who had broken off from LaSalle's expedition in February 1680 to explore the Upper Mississippi – have been captured by the Sioux. Duluth demands their release from the Sioux and then returns to Lake Michigan.

1678-1680
Exploration Robert Cavelier, Sieur de LaSalle, has enjoyed a successful career since coming to New France in 1666. Now he sets out with his lieutenant, Henri de Tonti, to explore the Mississippi Valley. Father Hennepin is the chaplain of the expedition. They build a blockhouse at the outlet of the Niagara River, then cross the Great Lakes in *Griffon*, the first sailboat built by Europeans to travel on the lakes. They then erect Fort Miami on the site of St Joseph, Michigan, and in January 1680 build Fort Creve Coeur on the site of Peoria, Illinois. Father Hennepin is sent with Michel Accault to explore the Upper Mississippi; they will be captured by hostile Sioux in April 1680, but will be rescued by Sieur Duluth. LaSalle, meanwhile, has left Tonti in command of Fort Creve Coeur and returned to Fort Frontenac for supplies. As Tonti is forced to flee the fort when attacked by Iroquois, it will be 1681 before LaSalle joins up with him again at Mackinac Island.

1680-1692
Indians The Pueblo Indians of New Mexico have been unhappy under Spanish rule for many years now, and one of their medicine men, Popé, has been preaching the traditional religion and the need to be free of Spanish domination. In August 1680, he leads an uprising of the Pueblos (including the famed Acoma). The Indians attack Santa Fe and kill some 400 settlers and missionaries; the

JACQUES MARQUETTE, 1637-1675, AND LOUIS JOLLIET, 1645-1700

The first white men to traverse the upper Mississippi River were a dedicated missionary of the Society of Jesus and an intrepid explorer – Jesuit Father Jacques Marquette and Louis Jolliet. Marquette was born in Laon, France, on 1 June 1637, and educated at Jesuit schools in France. In 1666 he was sent to New France (now part of Canada) as a missionary to the Indians. Jolliet was born in Quebec, Canada, in September of 1645; after showing aptitude for studies, he set out to follow his yen for exploration.

The two met near Lake Superior in 1669, Marquette pursuing his missionary work and Jolliet on a supply expedition. (After their meeting, Jolliet accomplished the first traverse to Lake Erie from the upper Great Lakes, using the Detroit River.) The two had heard Indians talk of the Mississippi (Big River), and there was speculation that this river flowed into the Pacific. In 1672 the governor of New France ordered Jolliet to find the river and investigate its possibilities as a trade route. Since Marquette knew some Indian dialects, he was sent along with Jolliet.

In May 1673 the two partners and five companions set out from St Ignace in two birchbark canoes. They headed south along the coast of Lake Michigan to Green Bay, thence to the Fox River and a portage to the Wisconsin River, aided by Indian guides. From the Wisconsin they descended into the Mississippi, becoming the first white men to travel on it (17 June 1673). The expedition descended as far as the mouth of the Arkansas River; by that point it was realized that the river flowed into the Gulf of Mexico rather than the Pacific. Fearful of hostile Indians and the Spanish to the south, they turned back, returning to Lake Michigan by way of the Illinois and Kankakee Rivers and portaging across the wilderness that was to become Chicago. After a five-month journey, they arrived home in October 1673.

Marquette had only two years to live: his health impaired by the voyage, he died on a missionary trip to Illinois in 1675. Jolliet went on to explore the Labrador coast and Hudson Bay. He died in the Gulf of St Lawrence in 1700.

French Jesuit Jacques Marquette, who died on a missionary trip to Illinois in 1675.

survivors flee down the Rio Grande to El Paso. Popé now assumes the role of despot and attempts to wipe out all traces of the Spanish and their Christian religion. However, dissension among the Indians and attacks by the Apaches weaken the Pueblos; by the time Popé dies in 1692, the Spanish have reasserted their oppressive rule over the region.

1681

Missionary Work Father Eusebio Francisco Kino, a distinguished Jesuit astronomer, arrives in New Spain. He will soon accompany an expedition from Mexico that is intended to colonize Baja California. When that settlement is abandoned, Father Kino goes to a region that includes northern Sonora, Mexico, and southern Arizona. His base is

CHRONOLOGY

Nuestra Señora de los Dolores in Sonora, and in years to come he will teach the Indians much about agriculture and animal husbandry, while establishing many missions throughout the territory.

JANUARY-9 APRIL 1682
Exploration LaSalle, Tonti, and their party set out to trace the Mississippi to its mouth. Although held up by the ice at Fort Creve Coeur in February, they continue on a relatively uneventful journey and on 9 April reach the open sea of the Gulf of Mexico. After planting the cross and singing a hymn, LaSalle claims 'possession of the river and of all rivers that enter it and of all the country watered by them' for His Majesty, King of France, in whose honor he names the great region 'Louisiana.'

1682
Settling The first Spanish settlement in Texas is made at Ysleta, on the site of El Paso, by refugees from Santa Fe and New Mexico who fled the uprising by the Pueblo Indians.

1683-1686
Exploration Duluth launches a new expedition, hoping to discover the Western Sea that (like many French Canadians) he believes to lie not far west of the Great Lakes and the Mississippi. Duluth will set his brother up as a trader on Lake Nipigon and build a fort at Kaministikwia (1684) and another, Fort St Joseph (1686), on the St Claire River.

1684-1687
Exploration LaSalle has been in France since 1683 – leaving Tonti in command of Fort St Louis, which

they had built at Starved Rock on the Illinois River. This year, with royal authority to colonize and govern the whole Mississippi Valley from Lake Michigan to the Gulf of Mexico, LaSalle sets out with four ships to establish a French colony at the mouth of the river. Because the coastline of the Gulf is so unvarying, LaSalle can't locate the Mississippi's outlet. Finally, the party goes ashore on the Texas coast – probably at Lavaca Bay – and establishes Fort St Louis. LaSalle tries several expeditions in an effort to reach the Mississippi and return to Canada, but his men grow increasingly mutinous. In 1687 they will murder LaSalle.

1685
Exploration Dr Henry Woodward, who has already led several expeditions from Charles Town, South Carolina, goes as far west as the Chattahoochee Valley in Georgia.

1686
Exploration Henri de Tonti, worried because he has received no word from LaSalle, sets out down the Mississippi River to find him. He will fail, of course, but along the way Tonti founds the settlement of Arkansas Post at the mouth of the Arkansas River.

7 JANUARY-19 MARCH 1687
Exploration LaSalle sets out on his third attempt to go overland to the Mississippi and the Illinois country, where he knows Tonti to be. Disputes over the division of food, LaSalle's brooding stubbornness, and the generally exhausting conditions lead some of LaSalle's men to shoot him. Despite this failure of LaSalle's expedition, he has begun what becomes the great French colonization of Louisiana.

22 APRIL 1689
Discovery The Spanish in Mexico have been hearing reports that other Europeans were dealing with the Indians in eastern Texas – territory they consider their own preserve. Most, if not all, of these 'intruders' are survivors of Fort St Louis, which LaSalle had been forced to set up on Lavaca Bay in 1684. Spanish authorities have sent out several expeditions to track down the intruders, and today one of the expeditions finds the abandoned remains of the fort. Eventually the Spaniards will find about 10 of the French colonists scattered among the Indians. In the course of this search, the Spaniards will increase their knowledge of eastern Texas and its coast.

1690-1692
Exploration Henry Kelsey, a young man employed by the Hudson's Bay Company – the English trading company chartered in 1670 – is sent west from Hudson Bay to establish trading relations with the Indians. Eventually he makes his way to Lake Winnepeg and the Saskatchewan

---

JEAN LOUIS HENNEPIN, 1640-1705

Explorers of the American West were given to tall tales, and one of the first of those tale-tellers was garrulous Flemish missionary Jean Louis Hennepin. Born in Flanders on 7 April 1640, Hennepin became a curé (parish priest) in Canada in 1675. On the voyage from Europe, he had met Robert Cavelier de la Salle, who took the curé with him on a 1678 voyage to explore and colonize the Mississippi River Valley.

In his journeys with de la Salle, Hennepin made observations that led to the first account of Niagara Falls (whose size he managed to exaggerate), explored Illinois and the Midwest, named Lake St Claire, explored the upper Mississippi, discovered and named St Anthony's Falls at present-day Minneapolis, and spent several months as a prisoner of the Sioux.

After Hennepin returned to France, he wrote *Description de la Louisiane nouvellement découverte* (1683), followed in the next decade by two other books. These accounts, popular and translated into many languages, were a heterogeneous mixture of truth, exaggeration, good maps, plain lies, and plagiarism. Hennepin died in Utrecht in 1705, having fallen into obscurity after his moment of glory.

River; he is probably the first European to see the great open plains of Canada.

1690-1693

Missionary Work The Spanish cross the Trinity River Valley in eastern Texas and make their way northeast to the Red River during this period. While opening up this region, they establish missions, including the first Spanish mission anywhere in Texas, Francesco de los Tejas, near the Neches River. However, by 1693 all the missions will be abandoned due to the hostile climate and Indian attacks.

1692

Spanish Rule The Pueblo Indians, who have been ruled by Popé since their revolt in 1680, have lost their initiative: dissent has arisen among them, and the Apaches have attacked from without. Now Popé is dead, and with the arrival of Diego de Vargas Zapata this year, the Spanish reassert their control over New Mexico. Other Pueblo Indians, including the Hopi farther west, remain more independent of the Spanish. In 1696 there will be another uprising by the Pueblo Indians, but it is subdued by 1699.

OCTOBER 1698-MAY 1699

Settlement The French remain determined to establish a colony at the mouth of the Mississippi to counter the Spanish and English presence in this part of America. Pierre LeMoyne d'Iberville, a distinguished Canadian, sails from France in October 1698 with colonists and supplies in four ships. The party reaches the Gulf of Mexico early in 1699 and searches for the mouth of the Mississippi. D'Iberville goes ashore at Old Biloxi (now Ocean Springs), Mississippi, then locates the river with a party of canoes. D'Iberville builds Fort Maurepas, at Old Biloxi and, leaving his brother in charge, goes back to France to report success.

1698

Exploration Thomas Welch, a trader from South Carolina, sets out from Charles Town and proceeds due west until he reaches the mouth of the Arkansas River.

AUGUST 1699

International An English vessel from the Carolina colony makes its way some 100 miles up the Mississippi River before it is warned to turn back by the French. The competition for control of the American West is heating up.

1700

Exploration The French movement westward begins in earnest this year, both in the south (from Louisiana) and in the north (along the western tributaries of the Mississippi). In the Illinois territory, Canadian voyageurs begin to explore the Missouri Valley. Louis de St Denis explores the

---

EUSEBIO FRANCISCO KINO, 1645-1711

One of the most brilliant and industrious of American missionaries, Father Eusebio Kino was born at Segno, Italy, in 1645, and educated as a Jesuit in Germany. Though he had dreamed of missionary work in China, fate took him to Mexico in 1681. There Kino published a book on the comet of 1680, while pursuing an unsuccessful mission to Baja California. As would be his habit, he tirelessly wrote diaries and letters and made maps. In 1687 he began his life's work, among the Pima Indians of Pimería Alta.

Over the next 24 years, from his base at Nuestra Señora de los Polares, Kino labored in every direction at once: making converts; founding missions at San Miguel, Santa Cruz, Magdalena, and elsewhere (many of which would become towns); developing the farming skills of the Pimas; making several expeditions to the Gila and Colorado Rivers, including discovery of the Casa Grande; and studying, writing, and mapmaking (he was the first to realize that Baja was a peninsula, not an island, and his map of the area was used worldwide for a century). Kino died at Magdalena in 1711.

Red River, a tributary of the Mississippi, with an eye to trade possibilities with the Spanish and the Indians. At the same time, Jean Couture, a Canadian *coureur du bois*, explores the Mississippi Valley (for South Carolina) and the Tennessee River to the southern end of the Appalachians. His Carolinian employers call him 'the greatest Trader and Traveler amongst the Indians for more than 20 years.' Within a year, Couture is guiding traders up the Savannah into Tennessee and Ohio, to trade with the Indians.

Settling The Spanish found the mission of San Xavier del Bac near present-day Tucson, Arizona. In the north, the French build Fort Mackinac, overlooking the strategic Straits of Mackinac, between Lakes Huron and Michigan, to safeguard the passage from the Louisiana Territory to Canada. Control of the straits and of Mackinac Island, a center in the developing fur trade, is vital to French interests in the north. This same year, a group of some 500 French Huguenot colonists arrives to settle in coastal Virginia.

Westward Movement By 1700 the movement west reaches the edge of the Virginia Piedmont territory. It will be 60 more years before the Virginia Piedmont is tamed and settled.

Population The total population of New England is approximately 130,000; 65,000 live in the Middle Colonies (New York, New Jersey, Pennsylvania, and Delaware), and 88,000 in the Chesapeake Colonies (Maryland and Virginia). In the Carolinas, only 12,000 have established a foothold. The largest city is Boston, with 7000 inhabitants, while New York has some 5000 settlers. In 1700 most of the population hugs the seacoast and, inland, lives on isolated farms and in sparsely populated villages.

CHRONOLOGY

24 JULY 1701
Settling The French, under Antoine de la Mothe Cadillac, build Fort Pontchartrain on the Detroit River between Lakes Saint Clair and Erie. Like Fort Mackinac, Fort Pontchartrain (soon to be known simply as Detroit) guards important fur trade routes.

OTHER EVENTS OF 1701
Colonial Affairs In New York, the Assembly votes to maintain neutrality toward the French colonists across the border in Canada. New York sticks to this policy until 1709, during Queen Anne's War, when New York abandons her neutral stance.

4 MAY 1702
War Queen Anne's War (known in Europe as the War of the Spanish Succession) begins and lasts until 1713, when it is ended by the Treaty of Utrecht. The war breaks out upon the death of Charles II of Spain, who leaves no heir. France supports a grandson of Louis XIV for the throne, while England and Austria support an obscure Bavarian prince. England's real aim is to prevent the alliance of Spain and France. In the course of the 11-year war, the Bavarian contender dies, and the grandson of Louis XIV wins the throne by default. In the colonies, while there is nothing to rival England's victory at Blenheim and the capture of Gibraltar, the English and their colonists clash in a series of skirmishes with the French, the Spanish and their Indian allies throughout North America and the West Indies.

OTHER EVENTS OF 1702
Settling The French shift Fort Maurepas – founded in 1699 on Biloxi Bay (in present-day Mississippi) by Pierre Le Moyne, Sieur d'Iberville – to Mobile Bay; the new fort is known as Fort Louis and is designed to check the Spanish presence at Pensacola, Florida. Mobile will be the capital of French Louisiana until 1719.
Queen Anne's War D'Iberville has asked King Louis XIV for reinforcements for his fort on Mobile Bay, but the king sends instead a shipload of *filles de joie* to keep up troop morale. In despair, d'Iberville returns to France to put his case to the king; he leaves his brother, Jean Baptiste Le Moyne, Sieur de Bienville, in command. D'Iberville will win a commission and a fleet and return to the New World to fight France's enemies, but in Havana, Cuba, in 1706, he contracts yellow fever and dies.

1703
Exploration By this year, French explorers with pack trains, flat boats and canoes are heading west from Louisiana and from settlements on the Illinois River. They seek the 'River of the West' that was believed to flow from an undiscovered source near the Missouri or Mississippi to the Pacific.

ANTOINE DE LA MOTHE CADILLAC, c 1656-1730

As he founded Detroit, it was only fitting that one of its most elegant automobiles would be named for Antoine de la Mothe Cadillac some two centuries later. He was born to minor nobility in Gascony, France, around 1656. After military training he left for the New World in 1683, living for a time in Maryland and then in Maine before taking command of a post at Mackinac in 1694.

Cadillac returned to France in 1699 to propose a plan for a military post on the Detroit River, intended to protect the fur trade against the British and the Indians. His petition granted, he set out with grants and colonists, founding the post in 1701. Though the settlement prospered, his quarrelsome ways made enough enemies to land Cadillac in court in 1704. Acquitted, he returned in triumph to Detroit and brought his family from France to join him.

Despite his desire to live out his days in Detroit, 'the Paris of New France,' Cadillac was named governor of Louisiana. Taking the post in 1713, he proved once more a quarrelsome leader and his appointment lasted only three stormy years. He was recalled in 1716, cooled off in the Bastille after another political wrangle, and lived his last years in his native Gascony, where he died in 1730.

Settlement French Jesuits settle an outpost at the confluence of the Kaskaskia and Mississippi Rivers in the continuing French attempt to control the Mississippi and the trade that passes along it. Also this year, the Spanish open mines at Chihuahua and Santa Eulalia in Nueva Vizcaya and establish a chain of missions across the west Rio Grande into Texas.
Indians The Reverend Solomon Stoddard of Northampton, Massachusetts, urges his frontier-town parishioners to use dogs 'to hunt Indians as if they were bears.' In settlements like Northampton, Stoddard's injunction that Indians 'act like wolves and are to be dealt with like wolves' falls on sympathetic ears.

1-28 JULY 1704
Queen Anne's War South Carolina colonists and their Indian allies sweep through the Appalachian Indian territory and destroy 13 of 14 Spanish missions, in an attempt to gain access to the French-held Louisiana territory. A counterattack by the Choctaw Indians halts the successful South Carolina campaign.

28-29 FEBRUARY 1704
War French soldiers and Abenaki Indians attack the tiny frontier settlement of Deerfield, Massachusetts, massacring 50 colonists and abducting more than 100 others. Many of the 100 die on the forced march to Canada through bitter winter conditions. Of those who survive, many are ransomed, or redeemed, by surviving relatives, while a number of the children are raised as Indians.

A sketch of Philadelphia as it may have looked in the early eighteenth century.

OTHER EVENTS OF 1704

Settling The French establish an important new outpost, Fort Miami (near present-day Fort Wayne, Indiana), to help safeguard the trade route along the Mississippi.

1705

Settling The French build Fort Vincennes on the Wabash River, at a site where there had been a small settlement of trappers and traders since 1702. Vincennes is said to be Indiana's oldest town.

Life/Customs Robert Beverley's *History of Virginia* is published, with an account of hunting methods in the colonies. This is useful information for settlers moving west into less populous areas, where the wild turkey, raccoon and opossum described by Beverley abound.

1706

Exploration Juan de Urribarri explores the Arkansas River as far as the Colorado-Arkansas border and claims the territory for Spain. He also attempts (unsuccessfully) to ransom Christian captives from local Indian tribes, including the Osage and the Pawnee.

Settlement Jean Baptiste le Moyne, Sieur de Bienville, succeeds his brother, d'Iberville, as governor of France's Louisiana. The Spanish refound La Canada in New Mexico and establish Albuquerque.

Life/Customs On Long Island, a closed season on deer hunting is imposed, a sign that continuous hunting has seriously reduced the local deer population and a signal to hunters and settlers to think of moving west.

1707

Life/Customs John Williams, one of those abducted by the Indians from Deerfield in 1704, publishes a stirring account of his captivity and rescue entitled *The Redeemed Captive*. Williams's account of his salvation from the twin evils of heathenism (the Indians) and Catholicism (the French) makes his book the first American best-seller.

1708

Life/Customs Kings, Queens, and Suffolk Counties in New York declare 1 April to 31 July a closed season on hunting turkeys, heath hens, partridges and quail. This is another sign of overhunting on the east coast and the need to push west.

3 SEPTEMBER 1709

Settling The proprietors of Carolina grant a total of 13,500 acres to two new groups of immigrants, Germans from the Palatinate and Swiss from Berne. With the success of these first two groups, others from Switzerland and Germany soon follow to settle in the Carolinas.

1710

Settling German emigration to the colonies increases with the example set by German and Swiss settlers to the Carolinas. Germans now settle in New York, New Jersey and Pennsylvania, as well as the Carolinas.

CHRONOLOGY

22 SEPTEMBER 1711
Indians Tuscarora Indians massacre a settlement of North Carolinians in the first clash of the Tuscarora War, which continues until 1713; South Carolina comes to the aid of North Carolina. Ultimately, the entire Tuscarora tribe is removed to New York State (where some members still live, near Niagara Falls).

14 SEPTEMBER 1712
Colonial Affairs Sieur Antoine Crozat gains a 15-year monopoly of the fur trade in an enormous territory, extending from Illinois to the Gulf and from the Carolinas to New Mexico. The first governor of the territory is de la Mothe Cadillac, founder of Detroit.

11 APRIL 1713
Queen Anne's War The Treaty of Utrecht ends Queen Anne's War, with some clear gains for England in the New World, especially in matters of commerce. While the French keep Cape Breton Island, and some small islands in the Saint Lawrence River, the British hold Nova Scotia, Hudson Bay and Newfoundland. In addition, England gains Gibraltar and Minorca in the Mediterranean Sea. As the historian Samuel Eliot Morison would put it, 'Before Queen Anne's reign, England was *a* seapower; after 1713, she was *the* sea power, and long so remained.'

1714
Exploration Louis St Denis, backed by Governor de la Mothe Cadillac of Louisiana, sets off up the Red River on foot as far as present-day Natchitoches, thence continues to San Juan Bautista on the Rio Grande, with a party of 12 Frenchmen and 30 Indians. They explore vast tracts of Texas, arousing fears among the Spanish of the growing French interest in the area. The Spanish arrest, then release, St Denis, but determine to reclaim Texas for Spain.
Settling Bienville founds Fort Toulouse on the Alabama River, near the junction of the Coosta and Talapoosa Rivers, as a way station for furs en route to Mobile. In Virginia, German 'redemptioners' are sent by Governor Spotswood beyond the falls of the Rappahannock to work the iron mines. The Germans found a colony known in their honor as Germana.
External Affairs King George I succeeds Queen Anne on the English throne.
Life/Customs Tea is introduced into the American colonies, after it has become fashionable in England.

15 APRIL 1715
Indians Stirred up by the Spanish, members of the Yamassee Indian tribe attack and slaughter several hundred Carolinian settlers. In consequence, Carolinians attempt to settle the Georgia territory to the south, to create a buffer zone between themselves and the Indians.

OTHER EVENTS OF 1715
Settling Louis de St Denis returns to Louisiana from his exploration of Texas, then leads a party of Spanish missionaries and soldiers to East Texas, where they found the trading post of Natchitoches.

JANUARY 1716
Exploration A Spanish expedition of 9 friars, 26 soldiers, 6 women and 1000 head of cattle and goats leaves Saltillo, Mexico, for San Juan Bautista, thence north. En route, they found four missions near the Neches and Angelina Rivers, Texas, and reoccupy Eastern Texas for Spain.

OTHER EVENTS OF 1716
Settling Bienville founds Fort Rosalie at Natchez, in an attempt to subdue the Natchez Indians.
Indians South Carolina settlers attempting to occupy territory once held by the Yamassee Indians in the area northwest of Port Royal come into conflict with the native inhabitants. The South Carolinians, with their Indian allies, the Cherokees, attack the Yamassees and the allied Lower Creek tribe. Casualties are heavy on both sides, but by springtime the South Carolinians have the edge. At the same time, to the north, Indian activity along the Fox-Wisconsin Trail closes it, and trade is diverted to Lake Superior and the Wisconsin River.
Westward Movement Governor Spotswood of Virginia initiates the settlement of the Southern Piedmont Region by sending an expedition of local gentry known as the 'Knights of the Golden Horseshoe' to explore the rich Shenandoah Valley. As a result of this expedition, the interior of Virginia is charted for settlement.
Transportation The easy flow of trade between the Spanish in Texas and the French in Louisiana is increasingly curtailed by the Spanish network of border forts erected to protect their interests in anticipation of future western movement by the French. This will be the case for the next five years, interfering with transport of goods.

1717
Exploration Louis de St Denis makes a second trip of exploration from Louisiana to Texas, taking with him traders interested in opening the area. To the north, Zacharie Robutel, Sieur de la Noue, repeats the trip made by Jacques de Noyon in 1688 to the Lake of the Woods (upper Minnesota/Canada). He has to call off his search for the Western Sea at that point, due to hostile Sioux.
Settling New groups of settlers pour into the colonies: the Scotch and the Irish, first to New England, thence to Pennsylvania; and the Germans directly to Pennsylvania. Among the Germans are members of small religious sects like the Mennonites, the Moravians and the Dunkers, who will put their distinctive stamp on the life and culture of Pennsylvania.

A colonial kitchen of Revolutionary days.

NOVEMBER 1718

Settling Jean Baptiste le Moyne, Sieur de Bien-ville, Governor of Louisiana, founds New Orleans in the final stage of the French drive to gain an empire in the New World. Now the Mississippi is French-controlled for most of its length, with an important series of forts (begun in 1674) to guard it. Among the most important recent foundations are Fort Chartres in the Illinois country, and a permanent garrison at the Natchitoches trading post. Also in this year, the French explorer Claude Charles du Tisne explores the area around Galveston Bay and establishes a small outpost there. The Spanish are not idle: under Martin de Alarcon they found a mission and fort on the bend of the San Antonio River in South Central Texas; this settlement will become the important town of San Antonio. In South Carolina, colonists build forts at Columbia and Fort Royal, in an attempt to strengthen defenses against the French, the Spanish and hostile Indians.

Indians The Tuscarora Indians negotiate a formal close to the Tuscarora War, which had effectively ended in 1713.

Colonial Affairs The Illinois is formally annexed by Louisiana, cutting off an important trade route for Canada.

JANUARY 1719

War France and Spain declare war in Europe, with the immediate result that hostilities break out all along the border between French and Spanish spheres of interest in the New World.

OTHER EVENTS OF 1719

Exploration Bernard de la Harpe and Sieur du Rivage explore the Arkansas and Canadian River valleys as far as 100° west, pacifying local Indians and opening much of the land to trade. Du Rivage, a brilliant surveyor, charts the territory with great accuracy. De la Harpe, however, raises some eyebrows when his journals are made public; he reports frequent sightings of unicorns. At the junction of the Canadian and Arkansas Rivers, de la Harpe's horses are stolen and the explorers return on foot to Natchitoches. At the same time, du Tisne is sent by de Boisbriant, commander at Kaskaskia, to explore the mouth of the Missouri west into the Missouri Valley as far as the Osage River. Du Tisne hopes to reach Comanche territory to set up trade agreements, but he is turned back by hostile Pawnee Indians along the Osage.

1720

Exploration Don Pedro de Villasur leads a military expedition northwest over the mountains from Sante Fe, to extend Spanish influence along the eastern slopes of the Rockies. When his party is almost wiped out by a Pawnee attack, Sante Fe and Taos remain the northernmost outposts for Spain. This same year, Czar Peter the Great of Russia determines to send out an expedition to discover whether there is a land bridge between Siberia and the New World. This will be the first of several such expeditions.

CHRONOLOGY

Settling The French further safeguard the important trade routes from Canada to the Mississippi River Valley by building Fort Quiaton on the Wabash. This post will prove critical in the slave trade, with 20,000 slaves passing through here in its first decade. In addition, the French reinforce Fort Kaskaskia on the Mississippi, one of the last of the forts designed to protect the Mississippi trade routes. To the north, the French build Fort Niagara, as a defense against hostile Iroquois Indians, and Fort Louisbourg on Cape Breton Island. In Virginia, the legislature passes an act giving free homesteads of 1000 acres in its frontier areas to anyone who will settle there.

Finance The Mississippi Company, founded by the speculator John Law in 1717, collapses, bankrupting many who had invested in the Louisiana Territory. Law was a Scottish financier and gambler who had fled Scotland when condemned to death for killing a man in a duel. He opened a bank in Paris in 1716 issuing vast amounts of his own paper money. It was used to speculate in stock issued by his own trading company, which had trade monopolies with the French in Canada and Louisiana. Supposedly, Law was going to make profits through land sales and other enterprises, but when the investors began to demand gold for their money and he couldn't deliver, panic set in and the Mississippi Scheme, or Bubble, burst. Although hundreds of individual investors lost out, Law's scheme did serve to attract European attention to settling this part of the New World.

Population The population of the American colonies is approximately 470,000 by 1720, with Boston (12,000) still the largest city. Philadelphia has grown to 10,000, with New York City third at 7000.

1721

Exploration The French explorer de la Harpe sets off from Mobile and follows the Arkansas River, with an eye to checking Spanish influence in the area. He establishes posts at Little Rock, the mouth of the Canadian River, and near the Touacara Indian villages.

Education French missionaries found a Jesuit college at Fort Kaskaskia (in what is now Illinois), with a library deemed to be one of the finest in the colonies.

4 JUNE 1722

Settling More German colonists arrive in the territory of France, this time a group of 250, who settle at Mobile, Alabama.

OTHER EVENTS OF 1722

Exploration Etienne Veniard, Sieur de Bourgmond, explores and opens up for the French much of the land between the Arkansas River and the Platte River Valleys. He founds Fort Orleans, some 300 miles up the Mississippi, to guard these new trade routes for France. Veniard continues to explore the area for five years and gains much useful knowledge for French interests.

Settling At the newly founded site of San Antonio, Texas, the Spanish build the Alamo as a Franciscan mission; not until much later would the Alamo be converted into a fort. By 1722, thanks in large measure to the efforts of the Marquis of Aguayo, Texas is effectively held by Spain. This year the French make New Orleans the capital of their Louisiana Territory.

Indians By now the Tuscarora Indians have joined with the old League of the Iroquois – the Five Nations – to form the confederacy known as the Six Nations. The League of the Iroquois has long been friendly to the English, and this year the Six Nations negotiate a treaty with the colonists of Virginia, the Indians agreeing not to cross the Blue Ridge Mountains or the Potomac River without Virginia's permission.

Life/Customs Daniel Coxe publishes his *Description of La Louisiana, as also of the Great and Famous River, Meschacebe or Mississippi*, sparking interest in the west.

1723

Settling The French found Fort St Philippe in the Illinois territory and Fort Orleans, in Carol County, Missouri, at the mouth of the Grand River, in an attempt to secure the land route to New Mexico. In Missouri, the Company of the Indies opens lead mines for the French; Governor Cadillac inspects many of them.

Indians William and Mary College in Williamsburg, Virginia, builds Brafferton Hall as the first permanent school for Indians established in the colonies. Not until 1769, with the foundation of Dartmouth College, will an institute of higher learning for Indians be established.

21 NOVEMBER 1724

Exploration Pedro de Rivera, ex-governor of Tlascala, Mexico, journeys from Mexico City along the entire line of military outposts stretching to the north. The seven-month tour shows that Texas and New Mexico are securely in Spanish hands.

Settling The French fortify Fort Vincennes (established in 1705) on the Wabash to safeguard the all-important water route from Canada to the Mississippi River Valley. In Vermont, colonists from Massachusetts build Fort Dummer (at present-day Brattleboro) in an attempt to hold the Indians as far north of the Massachusetts border as possible.

Life/Customs Laws known as the Black Code are promulgated in Louisiana, establishing Roman Catholicism as the religion of the territory and establishing rules of conduct for black and white (in effect, for master and slave). Intermarriage between the races is forbidden.

1725

Exploration Czar Peter the Great appoints Vitus

Bering, Martin Spanberg and Alesei Chirikof to pursue the search for a land bridge to America. Bering will make two lengthy expeditions, 1725-28 and 1733-41. During the second expedition, Bering discovers the strait which bears his name and foresees the possibility of immense wealth from the Pacific Northwest fur trade.

Settling To counter the French Fort Niagara, English colonists build Fort Oswego on Lake Ontario, as French and English vie for control of the Great Lakes. At the same time, New England colonists hurriedly build a series of northern border forts to protect themselves against continuing attacks by the Abenaki Indians and their French allies.

Population The number of black slaves in the American colonies is now estimated at approximately 75,000.

1726

Settling The French continue to expand their system of forts in the Mississippi River Valley by adding a new outpost at the mouth of the Illinois River.

Colonial Affairs This year there are nearly 100,000 squatters in the Pennsylvania frontier land; their presence will be a source of conflict between colonial governments and land speculators.

Workaday life in Benjamin Franklin's Almanac.

1727

Settling Fort Beauharnois (now in Minnesota) is founded in Sioux territory on Lake Pepin as part of the new French effort to find a route to the Pacific. German and Scotch-Irish settlers, alarmed at the number of squatters and settlers in Pennsylvania and the northern colonies, begin to relocate to Virginia.

Indians Dr Cadwallader Colden publishes the first history of the Iroquois tribes, *A History of the Iroquois Nations*. Active in politics and letters, Colden, with his daughter, Jane, was also one of the colonies' first botanists to follow the new Linnaean system of classification. The English receive permission from the Oswego Indians to build a fort near Oswego, a major port site on Lake Ontario; the Oswego Indians also allow the English to trade directly with the western Indians.

1728

Exploration Vitus Bering, a Danish sea captain in the Russian Navy, heads the expedition commissioned by Czar Peter the Great in 1725 to find out whether Asia is connected by land to North America. Bering sets sail in the *Gabriel* from Kamchatka Peninsula in Siberia, sights St Lawrence Island and passes through the strait that will bear his name, but he is unable to sight the coast of North America, due to heavy fog. Bering deduces correctly, however, that the two continents are not connected.

Old Bruton Parish Church in Williamsburg, Virginia, completed in 1715.

CHRONOLOGY

Colonial Affairs The English Crown purchases the Carolinas from the proprietors for the sum of £17,500; in 1730, the territory will be divided as North and South Carolina.

Indians The Natchez Indians, joined by the Choctaws, attack Forts Rosalie and Natchez in an attempt to oust the French. After some initial victories, the Indians are defeated.

1730

Population The estimated population of the American colonies this year is 654,950, with 275,000 white colonists living in New England.

23 JANUARY 1731

Colonial Affairs This year sees the end of the personal monopolies (held first by Antonie Crozat, later by John Law) on trade rights in the Louisiana territory, and the reversion of those rights to the French Crown.

OTHER EVENTS OF 1731

Exploration Pierre de la Verendrye begins a series of western expeditions and explorations that will go on until 1744; as he moves west, he builds a chain of forts: Rainy Lake (Saint Pierre, 1731), Lake of the Woods (Saint Charles, 1731), Lake Winnipeg (Maurepas, 1732), Assiniboine River (La Reine, 1738), Saskatchewan (Fort Dauphin, 1741). De la Verendrye explores the Dakotas, Montana and Saskatchewan. In addition, the French build a fort at Crown Point on Lake Champlain to fortify the Saint Lawrence against possible English or Indian attacks.

28 FEBRUARY 1732

Settling In an attempt to create the Georgia Colony, a group buys Lord Carteret's one-eighth share of the grant from Carolina which gave Lord Carteret exclusive rights to settle.

20 JUNE 1732

Settling James Oglethorpe receives a Royal Charter to found the Georgia Colony, with rights of settlement for 21 years. Georgia becomes a refuge for all persecuted religious minorities save Roman Catholics, and for those who have endured debtors' prisons. The new colony's location makes it an ideal buffer against the Spanish in Florida and the French in Louisiana.

OTHER EVENTS OF 1732

Settling More Scotch-Irish settlers leave Pennsylvania for the south, especially Virginia, North and South Carolina and the new colony, Georgia.

Colonial Affairs The younger Sieur de Vincennes fortifies the important Vincennes settlement on the Wabash River in southwest Indiana.

Transportation Facilitating westward travel, the first regularly scheduled public stagecoach begins operation between Burlington and Amboy, New Jersey.

Life/Customs The first 'guide book' published in America appears this year: Dr Henchman and T Hancock's *Vade Mecum* for America, with information on roads and lodgings from Maine to Virginia. Also this year, Russians, while engaged in sporadic fighting with coastal Indians, map the northwest coast of America, succeeding where Bering had failed in 1728.

12 FEBRUARY 1733

Settling Oglethorpe founds Savannah, on the Savannah River, with the compliance of friendly local Creek Indians.

JULY 1733

Settling Some 40 Jews are allowed to settle at Savannah, in contrast to the French policy, which had expelled the Jews from Louisiana in 1724.

OTHER EVENTS OF 1733

Exploration Bering, Spanberg and Chirikof leave Saint Petersburg on a new expedition, financed by the Russian Academy of Science. Not until 1741 will they have gathered sufficient supplies to set off from Kamchatka, Siberia.

1734

Exploration The Mallet Brothers, explorers, ascend the Missouri to the Mandan Indian territory and open a trade route thence into western Canada.

Transportation At this time, use of Conestoga wagons – the 'wagons of Empire' or 'prairie schooners' built by German immigrants around Conestoga, Pennsylvania – becomes widespread. Many of the Germans leave Pennsylvania themselves, traveling in such wagons into Virginia and the Shenandoah range. Philadelphia builds a great road through Lancaster County for the wagons to travel.

1735

Settling French colonists from Canada cross into Illinois to settle in French territory there; in Missouri, French traders establish the first settlement at Sainte Genevieve. In Georgia, Oglethorpe fortifies the southern Georgia frontier with Fort Okfuskee and founds Augusta, on the Savannah River, as a trading post. The first Moravian community in America is established at Savannah by the Reverend Gottlieb Spangenberg. At the same time, Moravians settle in Pennsylvania (which will become one of their strongholds) at Bethlehem.

OTHER EVENTS OF 1735

Arts/Culture The Swedish-American painter Gustavus Hesselius paints a picture of the Indian chief Lapowinsa, commissioned by the Penn family. This is one of the first known portraits of an American Indian.

Life/Customs The New England colonies suffer a devastating epidemic of scarlet fever.

1736

Settling In the years 1736-41, the possibility of mining attracts many Spaniards to California. In Georgia, more Scottish immigrants arrive, founding New Inverness on the Altamaha River.

Indians In the Chickasaw War, Bienville founds Fort Tombecbe on the Tombigbee River in Choctaw County to control the Chickasaws and Choctaws. Skirmishing continues until 1740, when the Chickasaws cease hostilities against the French; they remain friendly to the English.

1737

Arts/Culture In one of the westernmost frontier posts, Cahokia, Illinois, a courthouse building is erected. It remains the oldest continuously used public building in the United States.

20 JULY 1738

Exploration The French explorer Pierre de la Verendrye heads westward from Michilimackinac (Mackinac Strait), arriving on 5 August at Kaministiquia, on the western shore of Lake Superior. He proceeds farther west and founds Fort St Charles on Lake of the Woods and Fort Maurepas on the Red River, near Lake Winnepeg in Manitoba, before arriving in Mandan Indian territory on 28 November.

OTHER EVENTS OF 1738

Settling In Virginia, the assembly votes to found Augusta and Fredericksburg, expanding settlement across the Blue Ridge Mountains. Also this year, the last wilderness town in Connecticut is sold to speculators.

Life/Customs The Pennsylvania Legislature restricts fishing in the Schuylkill River (a sign that the river is dangerously close to being fished out), and a riot ensues.

19 OCTOBER 1739

War England declares war on Spain in what comes to be known as the War of Jenkins' Ear; in Europe, the conflict is part of the wider War of the Austrian Succession (1740-48), and in the colonies it is part of King George's War (1743-8). Although the main issues are trade and territory, the immediate cause is English outrage at the Spanish assault on one Thomas Jenkins, a British seaman. During the war, colonial contingents first call themselves Americans, rather than provincials.

OTHER EVENTS OF 1739

Exploration The French explorers Pierre and Paul Mallet reach the headlands of the Arkansaw River with a small party of Canadians and sight the Rocky Mountains. In nine months, they cross Nebraska, Kansas, Colorado and New Mexico, returning on 22 July to Santa Fe, where they are welcomed and entertained as heroes. Spanish authorities try to convince them to seek China via the legendary Northwest Passage.

Settling Oglethorpe defends Georgia with new military posts on the islands of Amelia, Cumberland, St Andrew's and St Simon's, in addition to the major settlement of Augusta. Oglethorpe continues to conclude treaties with regional Indians, especially the powerful Creeks.

1 MAY 1740

Exploration The Mallet Brothers begin to explore the Pecos Valley and the countryside of New Mexico. By 14 June they find it necessary to abandon their 18 horses and build two elm-bark canoes (with knives as their only tools). They continue their explorations on the river which becomes known as the Canadian in their honor.

OTHER EVENTS OF 1740

Settling Irish immigration increases due to another potato famine, with the new wave of Irish settlers heading south, into the Shenandoah Valley, Virginia, Georgia and the Carolinas. In Alabama, Lachlan McGillivray, a Highland Scot, marries an Indian chieftain's daughter and settles at the Creek village of Otciapofa, near Montgomery, where their son will be educated. McGillivray's presence favorably disposes the Creeks to the English.

Colonial Affairs In Georgia, the size of an individual land grant is increased from 500 to 2000 acres in a measure that also allows seven-year tenancies on the new holdings.

British Policy Parliament passes a bill granting naturalization to immigrants to the American colonies after seven years of residency, with reciprocal rights of citizenship within the 13 colonies.

1741

Exploration The Mallet Brothers arrive in New Orleans with salted meat to sell. Impressed by their exploits, the Governor, Jean Baptiste Le Moyne, Sieur de Bienville, asks them to guide an expedition under Andre Fabry, Sieur de la Bryere, to trace the route from the mouth of the Mississippi to the mines of New Mexico. The expedition is a failure, in part because drought makes river travel virtually impossible. The Mallets are lost on the expedition, and are never heard of again. In the far north, the Danish explorer Vitus Bering leads a second Russian expedition to explore the coast of North America. The first Europeans to discover Alaskan land are actually Aleksei Chirikov and some of his crew from the *Saint Paul* who, on 15 July, sight Prince of Wales Island in the Alexander Archipelago. The next day, Bering and his ship, the *Saint Peter*, discover Kayak Island. Soon thereafter, the *Saint Peter* is wrecked on one of the Commander Islands (named for Bering). The Danish explorer dies on 8 December and is buried there with members of his crew. The survivors build a new ship and make their way back to Kamchatka with tales of the rich prospects for fur trade in the area. This sparks renewed interest in finding a

CHRONOLOGY

Northwest Passage among the English, French and Spanish. Also in this year, the sons of Pierre de la Verendrye, François and Louis-Joseph, revisit North Dakota and become the first Europeans to move into South Dakota and Montana.
Settling The French found Fort Cavagnolle on the Kansas River.
Arts/Culture Father Meurin, a Jesuit scholar, arrives in the Illinois territory to study the Indian dialects; a dictionary of local dialects results from his efforts.

1 NOVEMBER 1743
Exploration Pierre de la Verendrye sees the Rocky Mountains.

FEBRUARY 1743
Exploration De la Verendrye sees the Black Hills.

19 MARCH 1743
Exploration De la Verendrye returns to the Missouri from points west.

30 MARCH 1743
Exploration De la Verendrye reaches Pierre, South Dakota, where he buries lead plates attesting to the expedition's progress. On 16 February 1913, local schoolchildren will discover them.

2 JUNE 1743
Exploration De la Verendrye's party returns to Fort La Reine, after an expedition of 13 months; they have not found the Western Sea, but have explored much of the western continent.

OTHER EVENTS OF 1743
Settling Russian fur traders begin to exploit the rich supply of Alaska seal and sea otter in the Aleutians, on Bering Island, and to settle in the area for the purpose of trapping and trading.

15 MARCH 1744
External Affairs The conflict known in the colonies as King George's War, and in Europe as the War of the Austrian Succession begins, pitting France and Spain against England. It will last until 1748.

OTHER EVENTS OF 1744
Indians The Six Nations of the Iroquois, at Lancaster, Pennsylvania, grant to the English their lands in the northern Ohio territory; this is an immediate source of conflict with the French, who hold this territory.
Westward Movement Fur traders, primarily from Pennsylvania, led by George Croghan and Conrad Weiser, expand their posts in the Ohio territory, setting the stage for conflict with the French there.
Arts/Culture Arthur Dobbs, former governor of North Carolina, publishes a description of the North American interior as far north as Hudson Bay, suggesting the existence of a Western Sea.

28-29 NOVEMBER 1745
War In one of the major battles of King George's War, the French burn the English settlement at Saratoga in northern New York and attempt to seize the fort at Albany, New York. In part, these attacks are in retaliation against hostile Iroquois action, after an English trader, William Johnson, wooed the Iroquois away from their French allies.

1746
Settling The Arkansas Route is safeguarded for trade when the Comanche and eastern Indian tribes make a peace treaty; in the following years, French explorers and traders pour into the area.

1747
Westward Movement The Ohio Company is formed by a group of prominent Virginia families, including the Fairfaxes, Washingtons and Lees. The Company receives a grant of 200,000 acres from the Virginia Assembly to colonize land along the southern fork of the Ohio River.

20 OCTOBER 1748
Westward Movement Hugh Parker and Thomas Crescap, traders working for the Ohio Company, finally reach the Ohio territory.

OTHER EVENTS OF 1748
Settling The English settle at Drapers Meadow on the frontier of Virginia, the first settlement by the English west of the Allegheny Divide.
Westward Movement In the Ohio territory, the agents sent out from Pennsylvania, Croghan and

---

JOHANN CONRAD WEISER, 1696-1760

Born in Germany on 2 November 1696, Johann Conrad Weiser was to become one of the greatest experts on the North American Indians. After arriving with his family in New York in 1710, Weiser spent much of 1713-14 with an Iroquois chief, who taught the fascinated youth about Indian tongues and customs. After quarreling with his stepmother, Weiser took up residence in an Indian village near Schoharie.

For a decade beginning in 1719, he was active as a translator between Indians and whites. In 1729 he took his growing family to Tulpehocken, Pennsylvania, where he began to develop a large farm. There he befriended various leaders of the Six Nations and became a voice of understanding and moderation in Indian affairs. He helped dissuade the Six Nations from supporting the French, contributed to a 1742 treaty, and helped defuse tensions between the Iroquois and the state of Virginia in 1743.

Weiser's chief opponent in Indian matters was Sir William Johnson, who objected to Weiser's support of Six-Nation neutrality in King George's War. In 1748 Weiser's pacifying efforts extended to the Western tribes, and he helped promote trade with Indians all the way to the Mississippi. However, the aggressive policies of Johnson and others gradually gained the ascendancy. Weiser died at one of his farms in 1760.

Shipping tobacco from the Virginia colony in the mid-1700s.

Weiser, win a treaty with the Ohio River Valley Indians – an important first step to establishing a free flow of trade.

15 MARCH 1749
Westward Movement The English Privy Council increases the holdings of the Ohio Company with a grant of 200,000 acres between the Ohio and Kanawha Rivers and the Allegheny Mountains, requiring only that the land be settled and defended by at least one fort.

19 MAY 1749
Westward Movement King George II gives the Ohio Company another 500,000 acres along the Upper Ohio River, as well as a Royal Charter.

12 JULY 1749
Westward Movement The Loyal Land Company of Virginia receives from the Governor of Virginia a grant of 800,000 acres in the area west of the Virginia-North Carolina border.

6 DECEMBER 1749
Exploration Pierre de la Verendrye, the great French explorer, dies at 64, still searching for the Western Sea.

OTHER EVENTS OF 1749
Westward Movement The French, apprehensive at the English movement west due to expansion of the Ohio Company, take several defensive steps. First, they settle and defend Toronto, then they send Celeron de Bienville into the Ohio River Valley to establish France's claim to that territory. On behalf of France, de Bienville buries lead plates at the mouth of each river he reaches.

1750
Exploration Thomas Walker leads the first European exploration party through the Appalachians at the point where Virginia, Kentucky, and Tennessee meet: this pass will be called the Cumberland Gap, after the Duke of Cumberland,

FRONTIER FORTS

The first frontier forts, or stations, in North America were built as semi-permanent defense outposts for soldiers; as settlers arrived, the frontier fort became something of a military town, into which the settlers would retreat at times of Indian attack. Most began with a simple log building, to which several cabins might be added, connected by palisaded defense walls. As the fort grew, other buildings were added: often one wall of the rectangular fort would consist of adjacent houses. The outer defense wall was often a double row of pointed wooden stakes, their ends set deep into the earth for greater strength. But any fort, however strong its walls, was always vulnerable to surprise attack, to fire, and to siege.

Under various names – the military town of New England, the station of the southwest – the frontier fort was the characteristic first community of settlers in the New World. In Massachusetts, 11 military towns were designated by the legislature between 1694-5; their inhabitants were forbidden to flee during Indian attack except by permission of the governor and council. One such fort was Deerfield, Massachusetts, founded in 1667, the scene of an Indian massacre during Queen Anne's War (part of the French and Indian Wars, 1689-1763). When the Indians and French soldiers attacked the tiny settlement of Deerfield, the inhabitants retreated into the fort, which stood on a slightly elevated natural defense site. Nonetheless, the attackers broke through the wooden stockade walls, killed 50, and abducted 100.

Many American towns began, like Deerfield, as frontier forts: of these, Fort Duquesne, later Fort Pitt, today's Pittsburgh, is one of the best known. During the French and Indian Wars, frontier forts were of critical importance, and much fighting centered around them. Whoever controlled the fort controlled local trade routes and usually the local Indian tribes. Some forts, like Pitt, changed hands repeatedly during the eighteenth century.

Still other forts, like Fort Chipewyan, founded by Alexander MacKenzie in 1788 at the western end of Lake Athabasca, were critical as supply points, first for exploration and later in settling the west. From Fort Chipewyan, MacKenzie set off down the river which was to bear his name to the Arctic Ocean.

The importance of the frontier forts is clearly shown by the British unwillingness after the Revolutionary War to give up their forts on the Great Lakes: for 13 years after the Peace of Paris, the British clung to these four forts on the Great Lakes, along with two on Lake Champlain, two on the Saint Lawrence, and several others in the territory. When the British turned over the forts to the United States, it was a final acceptance of their loss of North America.

one of George II's sons. Dr Walker, one of the famous 'Long Knives' (explorers and trappers identified by the long hunting knives they carried) will report his discovery, and in 1769 Daniel Boone will lead a party of settlers through the Cumberland Gap (soon to be known as the Wilderness Road) into central Kentucky. This year Boone's father leaves southern Pennsylvania with his wife

CHRONOLOGY

and six of his eight children to head through the Shenandoah Valley into Yadkin County in North Carolina. There he hooks up with other 'movers,' as these pioneers are known, among them James Robertson, who will found Nashville. In the west, in 1750-51, Jacques Repentigny Legardeur de St Pierre, and Joseph Boucher, Chevalier de Niverville, explore the La Pas River as far as the Rocky Mountains and build Fort La Jonquiere. Along the Ohio, the scout and trapper Christopher Gist explores much of the Upper Ohio River for the Ohio Company, stopping at Pickawillany.

OTHER EVENTS OF 1750

Settling A new trading post is established at Cumberland, Maryland, one of the most remote frontier posts. In New Mexico, the French influence among the Indians has made New Mexico dependent on the French, to the dismay of the Spanish. In Massachusetts and Connecticut, densely settled at this time, people begin to concentrate on opening up Maine, New Hampshire and Vermont. By the time of the Revolution, 94 new towns will have been founded in Maine, 100 in New Hampshire and 74 in Vermont. New Yorkers, on the other hand, push farther into Pennsylvania and the southern colonies searching for new land to settle.

1751

Settling The Greenbriar Land Company of Virginia receives 900,000 acres on the Greenbriar River in what is now West Virginia for purposes of development. German Moravian settlers buy 100,000 acres of rich farm land in North Carolina near the Yadkin River. At the same time, more Irish and Scottish immigrants settle in the western Appalachian mountains, whence they move out along the Tennessee River, erecting forts as they progress.

Colonial Affairs Benjamin Franklin (a member of the Pennsylvania Assembly at this time) draws up a plan for unification of the colonies of New England, New York, Pennsylvania and Maryland. Franklin's plan to unite the English colonies is one of the first such formal proposals, and will be presented to the Albany Congress in 1754, to be approved with some modifications. Franklin's role in unifying the colonies will be major.

JULY 1752

Colonial Affairs The French, alarmed at the English presence in the Ohio River Valley, seize the English trading post of Pickawillany.

OTHER EVENTS OF 1752

Exploration French traders and trappers are entering the area of Wyoming, Kansas and Nebraska, and have reached the Rockies by every important stream between the Red River and Saskatchewan. John Finley, one of the 'Long Knives,' sees the Falls of the Ohio at the site of

present-day Louisville and returns with tales of a fertile virgin territory. Daniel Boone is one of those most interested.

Indians In a treaty between the Iroquois and Delaware Indians and the Virginia Colony, Virginia lays claim to land south of the Ohio River (the Treaty of Logstown). Under terms of the treaty, the powerful Ohio Company will erect a fort in the territory and take charge of settling and developing the region. In an attempt to control Indian uprisings in Arizona, the Spanish establish their first settlement in Arizona, a presidio, or fort, at Tabac.

10 SEPTEMBER 1753

Indians The Delaware and Iroquois Indians, at the Winchester Conference, revoke the year-old Treaty of Logstown and throw in their lot with the French, supporting their claim to the Ohio territory.

APRIL 1753

Westward Movement The Governor of French Canada, Marquis Duquesne de Menneville, orders the erection of a series of forts to strengthen the French position in the Ohio territory. Fort Presque Isle (at present-day Erie), Fort Le Boeuf (by a portage point on French Creek) and Fort Venango (at the confluence of French Creek and the Allegheny) are built at once.

13 OCTOBER 1753

Westward Movement Governor Dinwiddie of Virginia sends the 21-year-old George Washington, an excellent surveyor, into the Ohio territory with guide and frontiersman Christopher Gist to get a sense of French intentions in the region held by the Virginia-controlled Ohio Company.

21 DECEMBER 1753

Westward Movement Washington reaches the French fort of Le Boeuf in the Ohio territory and tells the commander that Virginia demands immediate French departure; the French refuse. When Washington returns next year to Virginia, Dinwiddie publishes the surveyor's journal, which includes the French admission that 'It was their absolute Design to take possession of the Ohio, and by G – they would do it.'

OTHER EVENTS OF 1753

Settling Moravians from the large German settlement at Bethlehem, Pennsylvania, leave their homes to settle in the western part of North Carolina.

Westward Movement While in the Ohio territory, Christopher Gist cuts a road through virgin territory to a point named Red Stone Creek, on the Monongahela River, where a small band of 11 families settles. Gist, a representative of the Ohio Company, is empowered to lead them.

George Washington captures Fort Duquesne.

JANUARY AND FEBRUARY 1754
Westward Movement Governor Dinwiddie receives Washington's report on French intentions to stay in the Ohio territory and orders construction of a fort at the confluence of the Allegheny and Monongahela Rivers. The French oppose this attempt successfully and establish their own Fort Duquesne (present-day Pittsburgh).

17 APRIL 1754
War The French sweep through the Ohio territory, capturing the strategic forks of the Ohio River.

28 MAY 1754
War Colonial troops led by George Washington meet French troops led by Jumonville near Fort Duquesne, and Washington's 150 Virginians rout the French. This is the first battle in the French and Indian War (1754-63), ending what the historian Samuel Eliot Morison has called the period of 'cold war maneuvering for the west.' Washington moves at once to consolidate his victory by building Fort Necessity at Great Meadows, 50 miles south of the French Fort Duquesne.

3 JULY 1754
French and Indian War Washington, after a long and successful siege by French forces from Fort Duquesne, has to surrender Fort Necessity, granting effective control of the Ohio Valley to the French.

9 AUGUST 1754
British Policy England counters the 'Plan of the Union' with a proposal that the colonies be united under a commander-in-chief for colonial affairs and a separate commissioner for Indian affairs. Nothing comes of this plan.

OTHER EVENTS OF 1754
Settling Virginia offers 1000 freehold acres (also free of quitrents for 10 years) to anyone who will settle in its western territory. By 1757, Virginia has settled an additional 2 million acres.
Colonial Affairs The Albany Congress approves Benjamin Franklin's Plan of the Union with some amendments; however, the individual colonies and the English Parliament reject the plan, which would have created a union of the English colonies (excepting Georgia and Nova Scotia) under a president-general appointed by England.
Westward Movement The Susquehanna Company of Connecticut purchases land from the Six Nations of the Iroquois in the area of the upper Susquehanna River; the same land is claimed by heirs of William Penn.

20 FEBRUARY 1755
French and Indian War With two of the British Army's worst regiments, understrength and ill trained, General Edward Braddock arrives in Virginia to take up his post as commander-in-chief of colonial forces against the French in the French and Indian War. Braddock recruits locals to

CHRONOLOGY

Braddock's defeat in the French and Indian War.

bring his regiments to full strength, and, in concert with colonial governors, plans a campaign against the French-held forts of Beausejour, Crown Point, Niagara, and Duquesne, of which the last is his immediate objective.

14 APRIL 1755
French and Indian War With an immense army train, utterly inappropriate for the bad roads, Braddock sets out from Virginia for Fort Duquesne, 110 miles from Fort Cumberland; his exhausted troops will arrive 32 days later after hacking a road through the virgin hardwood forest. George Washington is in charge of the 450 colonial troops which accompany Braddock.

9 JULY 1755
French and Indian War In what has been called the Pearl Harbor of the war, Braddock is decisively defeated at the Battle of the Wilderness, eight miles from Fort Duquesne. As a result of this defeat (during the course of which Braddock is killed, after having four horses shot out from under him), the Indians of the northwest desert the English, side with the French and attack English settlements the length of the New World frontiers. George Washington leads survivors of the Battle of the Wilderness back to Virginia; of the 1459 officers and men who had set out, only 462 return.

DECEMBER 1755
French and Indian War George Washington, arriving in Virginia after the Battle of the Wilderness, persuades the colonies to build more forts between the Potomac River and the James and Roanoke Rivers, thence into South Carolina. Washington hopes that these new forts will help counter the French strength emanating from Fort Duquesne.

9 JANUARY 1756
Indians The new Indian commissioner, Sir William Johnson, demands that all future land transfers from Indians to colonists have his approval in an attempt to eliminate double-dealing and misunderstandings. In April Johnson's term of office is extended.

16 JANUARY 1756
External Affairs The French and Indian War spreads to Europe, where it is to be known as the Seven Years' War; Prussia and England conclude a new treaty.

1 MAY 1756
External Affairs Alarmed by the English-Prussian pact, the French ally with Austria.

11 MAY 1756
French and Indian War The Marquis of Montcalm, Louis Joseph, arrives in Canada to assume command of French forces.

SCOUTS AND SURVEYORS

Before the pioneers could head west to farm and settle, scouts and surveyors had explored much of the vast new continent and brought back reports to the first settlers of where the Indians were most friendly, the rivers most fordable, and the soil most tillable. Although one tends to think of the early scouts – of whom Daniel Boone is the best known – as free-lance loners, in fact, most, like Boone himself for many years, worked for the great companies that opened the west to settlement. While Boone explored Kentucky and discovered the Cumberland Gap on his own, he blazed the Wilderness Trail for the Transylvania Company, which hoped to move settlers west along the new road. The early scouts – like the Indian scouts from whom they learned their craft – moved with an eye to the economic development and military security of the lands they explored.

If the first scouts learned their trade from the Indians, the early surveyors inherited a science that had been radically improved by the Dutch in the seventeenth century. Surveying skills were critical, first in the production of accurate maps and charts, and later in the construction of America's first roads, canals and, finally, railroad beds. In addition, surveying was necessary to establish property boundaries, whether for the great land-development companies, for new territories and states, or for individuals.

If Daniel Boone is the best known of the early scouts, George Washington is certainly the most famous 17th-century surveyor. In 1748 the young Washington helped with a property survey for the wealthy Baron Fairfax. Later, while working as a surveyor in the Virginia-controlled Ohio territory, Washington made a name for himself by warning Virginia's Governor Dinwiddie of the impending French attack.

Scouting and surveying skills came together in the great Lewis and Clark Expedition of 1804-06, initiated by President Jefferson to explore much of the land acquired in the Louisiana Purchase of 1803. Louis and Clark's surveying skills were put to use mapping the Northwest from Saint Louis to the Pacific. Their own scouting skills were aided by those of their translator-guide Sacagawea, a Shoshone Indian. Figures like the maiden Sacagawea and the hero Boone soon became legendary, spawning a host of fictional descendants, of whom Cooper's Natty Bumppo is the best known.

SIR WILLIAM JOHNSON, 1715-1774

The career of Indian-affairs superintendent and soldier William Johnson reflects the persistent ambiguity of Indian-white relations: although he was a student and admirer of Indian ways, and skillful at dealing with tribal leaders, the gentlemanly Johnson also coveted the land of his friends in the Six Nations.

Born in County Meath, Ireland, in 1715, Johnson emigrated to America around 1737, settling on a family tract in the Mohawk Valley, which he was to develop into a rich farming community. As a fur trader, he became close to the Six Nations, especially the Mohawks, who were to be friends and allies throughout his career. He first came to prominence as an Indian commissioner in King George's War during 1745-8; he secured the loyalty of the Six Nations and performed valuable service against the French.

In the ensuing years before the outbreak of the French and Indian War, Johnson expanded his trade and his holdings while exerting himself tirelessly in Indian affairs. When hostilities with the French were imminent in 1754, Johnson was enlisted to secure the loyalty of the Six Nations and, in 1755, was given command of a mixed force of colonial militia and Indians to attack the French stronghold at Crown Point. There, on 8 September, his force successfully turned back an attack of French and Indians and afterward built Fort William Henry at the head of Lake George. Having subdued the French in the northern colonies, Johnson was widely acclaimed. The King made him a baronet and overall Indian superintendent.

Johnson captured Niagara in 1759, founded Johnstown, and accompanied Lord Amherst in his successful operation against Montreal. After the French departure, Johnson negotiated with the Indians in Canada, returning home in 1761 with the reputation of a war hero and Indian manager par excellence.

Thereafter Johnson busied himself equally with his estate and with Indian affairs. He promoted the rational but unrealistic idea of fixed boundaries between Indian and white lands (though he was quite successful in bargaining for Indian land himself). He took two common-law Indian wives after the death of his German wife, and by them had 11 children. Johnson died on 11 July 1774, just before his efforts for the Crown and for white-Indian peace began to come apart in revolution.

15 MAY 1756
External Affairs War breaks out in Europe with the English declaration of hostilities against France.

23 JULY 1756
War John Campbell, Earl of Loudoun arrives in the colonies to lead the English forces against the French under Montcalm.

AUGUST 1756
French and Indian War In the opening battle of the expanded war, Montcalm destroys the English forts at Oswego and George (14 August). In consequence, the English yield the Mohawk Valley to the French, and settlers there flee to Schenectady and Albany. Many will return when hostilities are ended.

OTHER EVENTS OF 1756
Settling Benjamin Franklin proposes the establishment of two new colonies, one south of Lake Erie, another on the nearby Scioto River.

JULY 1757
Westward Movement English colonists, in an attempt to woo the Cherokee and Creek Indians (two of the Five Civilized Tribes) establish the outpost of Fort Loudoun on the Little Tennessee River.

CHRONOLOGY

9 AUGUST 1757
French and Indian War Montcalm captures the English Fort William Henry on Lake George; its surviving defenders are attacked by Indians as they make their way to Fort Edward. Some 1400 survive the arduous journey.

OTHER EVENTS OF 1757
Arts/Culture In Madrid, Father Andres Burriel publishes an account of Jesuit work around the Gulf of California; when this is translated into English, Dutch, French and German, it sparks renewed interest in finding a Northwest Passage.

MAY 1758
Indians Cherokee Indians raid throughout the frontier of Virginia; settlers retaliate.

1 JULY 1758
French and Indian War Loudoun's replacement as supreme commander of British forces, James Abercromby, attacks Fort Ticonderoga on Lake George; French forces of 3000 under Montcalm defeat Abercromby's 12,000 soldiers.

26 JULY 1758
French and Indian War In one of the first English

victories, a combined force of British and colonial soldiers under Major General Jeffrey Amherst and Brigadier General James Wolfe attack and seize the French-held fort of Louisbourg, Nova Scotia, near the mouth of the Saint Lawrence.

27 AUGUST 1758

French and Indian War In another victory, English troops seize Fort Frontenac near present-day Kingston, Ontario.

English forces under General Wolfe storm Quebec in 1759 and capture the city.

AUGUST 1758

Indians New Jersey establishes the first Indian reservation in America at Edge Pillock, in Burlington County, for the Unami Indians.

18 SEPTEMBER 1758

French and Indian War Abercromby, like his predecessor Loudoun, is replaced as supreme commander after his defeat by Montcalm at Fort Ticonderoga. Amherst takes over.

THE FRENCH AND INDIAN WARS

The French and Indian Wars (1689-1763) is an umbrella term for some 70 years of struggles in the colonies between the French, with their Indian allies, and the British, with their Indian supporters. Each great power sought to wrest control of America, Canada, and the West Indies from the other. Throughout the conflicts, the French and the British had two primary aims: to control the Eastern Seaboard by holding such important ports as Quebec, and to dominate the western frontier by controlling such strategic border posts as Fort Vincennes.

The first phase of the French and Indian Wars – known in Europe as the War of the Grand Alliance, and in the colonies as King William's War – lasted from 1689-97, and set the tone for much that was to follow. In short, the British sought to seize Canada from the French by attempting (unsuccessfully) to take Quebec, while the French harassed British frontier posts. The conclusion of conflicts in Europe brought the end, albiet briefly, of fighting in the colonies. Dismayed by the lackluster military performance of their English allies, the powerful Iroquois nation resolved to remain neutral in the future.

Hostilities broke out anew in 1702, with the onset of Queen Anne's War (to 1713), known in Europe as the War of the Spanish Succession. Once again, the British tried, and failed, to seize Quebec. Again, the French and their Indian allies harassed British frontier posts. The French and Abenaki Indian attack on Deerfield, Massachusetts, in February 1704 was a particularly bloody episode in this conflict. Under the terms of the Peace of Utrecht, which ended the war in both Europe and the colonies, French Acadia and the land dominated by the Hudson's Bay Company became British. (In 1755 and 1758, the British expelled the French colonists of Acadia, an event commemorated by Longfellow in his 'Evangeline.')

After 30 years of relative peace, King George's War – the colonial counterpart to the War of the Austrian Succession – broke out in 1744. Fighting was fierce but inconclusive, and relative peace was restored with the Treaty of Aix-la-Chapelle in 1748. Nonetheless, the final phase of the French and Indian Wars (known as such in the colonies) began almost immediately (1756-63); in Europe, where fighting began two years later, this was known as the Seven Years' War. Now fighting centered on control of the rich Ohio territory in the West, and the critical port of Quebec in the East. In 1758 the British seized strategic Fort Duquesne (present-day Pittsburgh), and in 1759 Wolfe seized Quebec for the British. When the conflict ended in 1763, under the terms of the Treaty of Paris, Britain held French Canada and stood supreme in the New World.

CHRONOLOGY

8-26 OCTOBER 1758
Indians Some of the Delaware Indians have been helping the French destroy settlements on the frontier of Pennsylvania; in an effort to keep other Delaware Indians from joining in such attacks, the government of Pennsylvania has held a series of conferences with the Indians. In the fourth, held at Easton, Pennsylvania, this month, the Iroquois Indians have also sent representatives. In the final Treaty of Easton, the Iroquois agree to abrogate a previous treaty made at the Albany Congress of 1754, by which they had ceded most of the land of western Pennsylvania to the English; instead, the Iroquois now give the Delaware the right to hunt and live in security in these lands – and the European colonists agree not to settle in this territory. This treaty will be violated within a month.

25 NOVEMBER 1758
French and Indian War In a major reversal, the French blow up Fort Duquesne to prevent it falling into English hands. A critical factor in the English victory is the creation of Forbes's Road, from Philadelphia to the forks of the Ohio, which opens the way west for both military and civilian travelers.

OTHER EVENTS OF 1758
Indians Settlers take the fall of Fort Duquesne and the opening of Forbes's Road as a signal to ignore the Treaty of Easton, and many move west to settle the Allegheny Plateau.

SUMMER 1759
French and Indian War In June, General Wolfe, with 9000 men, sails his fleet up the Saint Lawrence and joins Rear Admiral Durrell's land forces for the attack on Quebec. By July, Wolfe's troops hold the north shore of the Saint Lawrence above Quebec; Montcalm tries, and fails, to burn the British fleet, and by the end of August, Wolfe is ready to attack Quebec. Also this summer, on 25 July, the British attack and seize Fort Niagara. At Fort Ticonderoga (26 July) and Fort Saint Frederick (31 July), the French are forced to blow up their own outposts to prevent their capture.

12-13 SEPTEMBER 1759
French and Indian War Wolfe stealthily brings his men across the river, scales the cliffs and ranges his troops in the Plains of Abraham, where the English and French join battle. Both Wolfe and Montcalm are killed, but the English win the Battle of Quebec.

18 SEPTEMBER 1759
French and Indian War The French formally surrender Quebec to the English; never again will the French presence in North America be as strong, and gradually the French claim on the west will weaken before the vigorous onslaught of the Spanish and the English.

OTHER EVENTS OF 1759
External Affairs In what is known as England's 'wonderful year,' the French in India are defeated and Guadaloupe falls to England, which appears invincible after the great victory at Quebec..

1 APRIL 1760
French and Indian War Jeffrey Amherst sends aid (but not enough) to forts on the western frontier of Virginia under attack by Indians.

7 AUGUST 1760
French and Indian War Fort Loudoun on the Little Tennessee River surrenders to Indian attackers after a bitter siege. Many survivors are cut down by Indians as they flee from Loudoun to Fort Prince George.

8 SEPTEMBER 1760
French and Indian War English forces under Generals Amherst and Haviland meet at Montreal in sufficient strength to compel the governor of Quebec to surrender the entire province of Quebec (New France) to the English.

26 OCTOBER 1760
External Affairs George III comes to the English throne.

29 NOVEMBER 1760
French and Indian War In another defeat for the French, Detroit falls to the English, and the local Indians now ally with the British.

OTHER EVENTS OF 1760
Population The population of the 13 colonies is estimated at 1,600,000 in 1760. The Spanish population of New Mexico and Texas is already larger than the English population of Georgia, with Albuquerque at 1814, La Canada at 1515, Sante Fe at 1285. There are also 10,000 Christianized Indians in the area.

AUGUST 1761
Exploration Alexander Henry of New Jersey leaves Montreal for Michilimackinac and spends the next 16 years in the fur trade in competition with Montreal trappers and traders.

9 SEPTEMBER 1761
Indians In the opening stages of Pontiac's Rebellion, the Ottawa Indians protest the English refusal to supply them with ammunition. Pontiac, chief of the Ottawas, leads a general revolt against the English, due largely to Indian resentment of the behavior of General Amherst.

13 OCTOBER 1761
Westward Movement In an attempt to enforce the Treaty of Easton (1758), which forbade new settlement west of the Allegheny Mountains, the English Colonel Henry Boument issues a procla-

mation reiterating the terms of the Treaty of Easton; settlers ignore it and continue to pour into the western territory.

2 DECEMBER 1761
British Policy Lord Egremont, the English Secretary of State, issues a declaration requiring royal approval of all land grants in Indian territory; the proclamation is not enforced strictly.

OTHER EVENTS OF 1761
Indians The Cherokee Indians, after a series of defeats, are forced to surrender and cease hostilities against the frontier settlements.

2 JANUARY 1762
French and Indian War England declares war on Spain, which allies with France and Austria in the ongoing Seven Years' War.

3 NOVEMBER 1762
French and Indian War France signs a treaty with the English at Fontainebleau and a secret treaty with Spain, promising to give Spain all the French territory west of the Mississippi as well as the Isle of Orleans in Louisiana. This is the first step in ending the Seven Years' War, which the French are eager to do.

OTHER EVENTS OF 1762
Settling The last of the western Massachusetts towns in the Berkshires are sold to land speculators.
Westward Movement The Susquehanna Company, based in Connecticut, settles Pennsylvania's Wyoming Valley, despite Pennsylvania's objections.
Transportation Pennsylvania surveys a route for a canal from the Susquehanna at Middletown to the Schuylkill at Reading, as part of the effort to open the west to trade. Work on the canal will not begin until 1791.

10 FEBRUARY 1763
French and Indian War The Treaty of Paris ends both the colonial and European phases of the Seven Years' War, and marks the end of France as a North American power. France gives up her North American holdings, but retains the Caribbean islands of Guadeloupe, Martinique and St Lucia. Spain receives Cuba in compensation for the loss of all Spanish territory in Florida. Immediately, colonials ask the English Crown for land to settle in Illinois and West Virginia. The State of Virginia claims rights over today's West Virginia, Kentucky, Ohio, Indiana, Illinois, Michigan, Wisconsin and parts of Minnesota. The French threat to Spain's colonies in North America is now ended, although the Spanish must still worry about the English. In Texas, the Spanish turn from their missions in the east to strengthen their presence along the northern frontier and the Gulf.

PONTIAC, 1720?-1769

History has never quite decided whether Ottawa Chief Pontiac was a great fighter and forger of Indian alliances, or simply an eloquent leader whom white writers mythologized. In either case, the alliance of which he was nominal leader was one of history's most successful in resisting white encroachment on Indian land – up to the point at which the enterprise was doomed to fail.

Tradition says Pontiac was born along the Maumee River about 1720. The son of a Chippewa mother and an Ottawa father, he gained the allegiance of both tribes as the foundation of his power as chief. He was probably among the opponents of General Braddock at Fort Duquesne in 1755. The Peace of Paris effectively opened Western lands to white expansion; Pontiac saw this as a usurpation of Indian territory, and said so, eloquently, at a conference near Detroit in 1763. Thereafter his alliance (which included tribes from as far west as the Mississippi) laid siege unsuccessfully to Detroit, but annihilated eight other British forts and defeated several expeditions. In 1766 Pontiac finally signed a peace treaty with the British, and thereafter honored it despite French efforts to turn him against the British. By his death in 1769, he was already a romantic figure to the American imagination, the subject of plays and books. The historian Francis Parkman immortalized him in *The History of the Conspiracy of Pontiac*.

---

7 MAY 1763
Indians In the opening stages of Pontiac's rebellion, the Ottawa Indian chief's plan to capture Detroit fails; however, the Ottawa attack and in one month destroy all British garrisons from Detroit to Niagara. From May 1763 to early 1765, Pontiac virtually obliterates the string of frontier outposts. Massacres occur at Presqe Isle, Le Boeuf, Venango, Mackinac, Sandusky, St Josephs and Ouiatanon.

13 JULY 1763
Indians Lord Jeffrey Amherst, alarmed at Pontiac's destruction of seven English forts, suggests to Colonel Bouquet that blankets contaminated with smallpox be given to the Indians. The plan is rejected only because of concern that English troops distributing the blankets might contract the disease.

2-3 AUGUST 1763
Indians In a major setback for Pontiac's forces, the Indians are roundly defeated at the Battle of Bushy Run, near present-day Pittsburgh.

9 SEPTEMBER 1763
Westward Movement The Mississippi Company, led by George Washington, receives a grant of 2.5 million acres from the English Crown for settlement by Virginia soldiers who had served in the French and Indian War. The land lies between the Ohio and Wisconsin Rivers.

CHRONOLOGY

7 OCTOBER 1763
British Policy In another abortive attempt to control settlement, George III signs the Proclamation of 1763, which limits English settlement west of the Appalachians and orders those already there to return. The land is placed under control of a military commander.

NOVEMBER 1763
Indians Pontiac's forces abandon their siege of Detroit.

13 DECEMBER 1763
Indians Irate settlers, angered by Indian attacks to the west, attack the non-hostile Indians of Lancaster County; only Benjamin Franklin's efforts defuse the crisis.

DECEMBER 1763
Colonial Affairs A group calling themselves the Suffering Traders, assisted by Benjamin Franklin, seeks land in Indiana, Illinois and West Virginia from the English Crown. The Indiana Company is forced to facilitate their land claims.

OTHER EVENTS OF 1763
Discovery Russian fur trader Stepan Glotov discovers Kodiak Island, which will become vital in the fur trade. To date, the only result of Bering's two expeditions to North America has been the traffic of Russian private fur traders, who have developed a thriving trade in skins with the Aleutian Island natives. The Russians have mistreated the Aleuts, practically enslaving them, and the Aleuts rise in revolt. The heaviest fighting occurs between 1763 and 1766, when the Aleuts kill the entire crew of a Russian ship commanded by Denis Medvedev; they are avenged by another Russian sea captain, Ivan Soloviev.
Settling The first settlements in the Valley of the Greenbriar and the Monongahela spring up in West Virginia. At the same time, Washington and other Virginia aristocrats, including members of the Lee family, form the Mississippi Land Company to acquire land in the upper Mississippi Valley.
Life/Customs Jeremiah Dixon and Charles Mason begin to survey the boundary between Pennsylvania and Maryland, which will come to be known as the Mason-Dixon line.

12 APRIL 1764
Indians The English sign peace treaties with various former supporters of Chief Pontiac at the Treaty of Presque Isle. Pontiac himself fights on for two more years.

10 JULY 1764
British Policy The British Board of Trade attempts to reorganize administration of the Indian territory, dividing the trans-Appalachian country into districts along the line of the Ohio River.

17 NOVEMBER 1764
Indians Pontiac's forces surrender at the Muskingham River in the Ohio territory.

OTHER EVENTS OF 1764
Settling In defiance of the 7 October 1763 Proclamation, settlers push the frontier across the Alleghenies at a rate of 17 miles per year between 1764 and 1774. In Missouri, the French fur traders Pierre Laclede and Rene Auguste Chouteau found the settlement of Saint Louis, which will become the most important town in the area. In Oklahoma, the first European trading post is established at Salina by the Chouteau family of Saint Louis. Pittsburgh is laid out and surveyed as a town.

1765
Exploration Juan Maria Riviera, seeking gold, comes up into the San Juan Valley of Colorado. He explores and names La Plata (Silver) Mountains in the Utah Basin.
Settling Spain sends José de Galvez to serve as *visitador general* in New Spain and counter the renewed European interest in exploiting the area.
British Policy Parliament passes the Stamp Act (22 March 1765), one of the precipitating causes of the American Revolution. It is the first attempt at direct taxation of the colonies; with the Quartering Act, stipulating that colonials must house British troops, it is widely resented. By the time that the Stamp Act goes into effect (1 November 1765), the colonies are united in their determination to ignore it.

5 MARCH 1766
Colonial Affairs Don Antonio Ulloa arrives to take over as governor of Louisiana as Spain takes control of Louisiana from France.

MARCH 1766
Settling The Suffering Traders, who organized the Indiana Company in 1763, organize the Illinois Company.

17 APRIL 1766
Westward Movement The English Auditor General for North America overrules the Proclamation of 1763 and allows settlers who had held land grants prior to that date to keep their land. Confusion ensues, as settlers attempt to prove that they were in place before 1763.

24 JULY 1766
Indians Chief Pontiac formally surrenders to the English at Oswego.

OTHER EVENTS OF 1766
Westward Movement The fur trader and scout Benjamin Cutbird travels by river from Virginia to New Orleans, exploring virgin territory.
British Policy Parliament repeals the Stamp Act (18 March 1766), but affirms its absolute right to

William Bradford's Pennsylvania Journal *announces that it is ceasing publication due to the Stamp Act.*

legislate for the colonies. In the colonies, delight at the repeal of the Stamp Act is moderated by continuing anger at the Quartering Act.

11 SEPTEMBER 1767
Indians Frustrated by his dealings with the Indians, the Commissioner for the Southern District, Lord Shelburne, proposes revamping the administration of Indian affairs and the creation of three new colonies: Upper Ohio, Illinois and Detroit. The proposal is ignored by Parliament.

DECEMBER 1767
Westward Movement Daniel Boone makes his first trip beyond the Appalachian Mountains along the Virginia-Kentucky frontier.

OTHER EVENTS OF 1767
British Policy Parliament passes the Townshend Acts (29 June 1767), which replace the Stamp Acts as a means of raising taxes in the colonies to finance their defense. The Townshend Acts are no more popular than the Stamp Acts.
Exploration James Finlay of Montreal is the first English trader to get as far west as the Saskatchewan.
International The Jesuits are expelled from the entire Spanish Empire, and hand over their missions to the Franciscans. The Franciscans prove less effective in dealing with Indian unrest than had their predecessors.

MARCH 1768
Colonial Affairs The first Secretary for the Colonies, Lord Hillsborough, proposes wide-ranging reforms for the western territories, including shifting the 1763 line limiting settlement still farther west, and giving control over fur trade to colonial authorities.

14 AUGUST 1768
Westward Movement The Treaty of Hard Labor, negotiated at Hard Labor, South Carolina, moves the frontier west when the Cherokees agree to it.

3 NOVEMBER 1768
Westward Movement The Indiana Company expands with a purchase of 1,800,000 acres from the Iroquois Indians southeast of the Ohio River.

5 NOVEMBER 1768
Westward Movement The League of Iroquois at Fort Stanwix in the Mohawk Valley agrees to accept £10,460 for southwestern New York, western Pennsylvania and parts of West Virginia, as well as their claim to sections of Kentucky and Tennessee.

NOVEMBER 1768
Westward Movement The Creek Indians agree to border shifts westward affecting South Carolina and Georgia (whose new border becomes the Ogeechee River).

CHRONOLOGY

A Tory tax collector is tarred and feathered by irate colonists: 1774.

OTHER EVENTS OF 1768
Settling Settlers in great numbers have crossed the Appalachians now to occupy the center of the continent.
Indians At the Savannah Conference, the Creek Tribe agrees to allow settlement as far west as a line running from Mobile to western Florida.
Colonial Affairs Resentment of the Quartering and Townshend Acts increases throughout the colonies, and troops from Nova Scotia are moved to Boston to cope with possible unrest.

APRIL 1769
Settling Hordes of would-be settlers storm the land office in Pittsburgh seeking to purchase land in the newly opened western territories.

1 MAY 1769
Westward Movement Daniel Boone sets off from his home by the Yadkin River in North Carolina 'to wander through the wilderness of America in quest of the county of Kentucky.' With him go John Stuart and John Finley.

7 JUNE 1769
Exploration Daniel Boone sees the Kentucky territory from the Cumberland Gap. On 22 December, Boone, his brother and two friends are captured by the Shawnee Indians, released, then recaptured.

JULY 1769
Exploration Gaspar de Portola, the Spanish governor of the western territories the Spanish call 'the California,' leads an expedition up the Pacific Coast, and establishes the first colony in Upper California on San Diego Bay. De Portola's expedition includes the Franciscan missionary Father Junipero Serra, who founds the first permanent Spanish settlement on the West Coast, San Diego de Alcala mission. The Franciscans are to be as active in settling the West Coast for the Spanish as the Jesuits had been in settling Canada for the French.

27 DECEMBER 1769
Settling The Ohio Company procures a grant from the British Crown of 20 million acres under provisions of the Treaty of Stanwix.

OTHER EVENTS OF 1769
Exploration Fearing Russian expansionist plans, José de Galvez, the *visitador general* of New Spain, sends two land and three sea expeditions to secure Spanish control of San Diego and Monterey. 'Their loss would be irreparable,' de Galvez affirms. On 1 October, one group reaches Monterey Bay and heads north, discovering San Francisco Bay on 21 October. After an arduous return trip, having been reduced to eating their pack mules, they reach San Diego on 21 January 1770.

DANIEL BOONE, 1734-1820

One of the most enduring mythic heroes of the early American frontier, pioneer and Indian fighter Daniel Boone fit his legend better than most. Though he did not, as once claimed, found Kentucky, and though in his mature years he spent about as much time in legislative halls as in the wilderness, he was indeed a woodsman, heart and soul.

Born to a Quaker farming family near Reading, Pennsylvania, in November of 1734, Boone developed early into a crack hunter and trapper. In 1755 he joined General Braddock's ill-fated campaign against the French, escaping on horseback from a disastrous defeat in July. A resourceful leader, he headed two short expeditions into Kentucky (which had been explored two decades before) in 1767-9. Eventually, he set out with a group of settlers in 1775, establishing a fort at the site of what became Boonesborough. He spent the next two years developing the settlement and fighting Indians.

In the Revolution Boone was a militia officer, and he spent time as a captive of both the Shawnees and the British. He escaped from the latter and returned to Boonesborough in 1778, just in time to help fight off a major British attack. In 1779 he entered politics and in 1786 was elected to the legislature. Moving to West Virginia after losing his Kentucky land titles, he became a legislator there.

Around 1798 Boone moved to Missouri, where he settled on a land grant and was appointed district magistrate. He died in Missouri in 1820, already a legendary figure. Three years later, Lord Byron devoted part of his *Don Juan* to Boone and made his name known worldwide.

A romantic depiction of Daniel Boone protecting his family from Indian attack.

21 JANUARY 1770
Exploration A group under José de Galvez reaches San Diego and rests for some months. By May, however, the expedition is engaged in fortifying Monterey Bay.

18 OCTOBER 1770
Indians The Treaty of Lochabar with the Cherokee Indians revises the terms of the Treaty of Hard Labor (1768) and moves the Virginia boundary line west, adding another 9000 square miles to Virginia's domain.

OTHER EVENTS OF 1770
Colonial Affairs After the Boston Massacre (5 March 1770), the Crown moves to repeal the Townshend and Quartering Acts.

Westward Movement There is a steady stream of settlers from North and South Carolina across the Blue Ridge Mountains.

Population The population of the American colonies is now estimated to be 2,205,000.

APRIL 1771
Exploration Daniel Boone, John Finley and John Stuart return to North Carolina from their journey through the Cumberland Gap.

16 MAY 1771
Colonial Affairs Since 1768 a group who settled on the western frontier of the colony of North Carolina have been agitating against what they regard as extortion and oppression by the politically powerful in the eastern part of their colony. In

January the North Carolina assembly passed the 'Bloody Act,' making rioters guilty of treason, but this has not stopped the frontiersmen – known as the Regulators. Today some 120 militia defeat the Regulators at a battle at Alamance Creek, near Hillsboro, in north-central North Carolina; the leaders of the 'rebellion' are executed, and the survivors are forced to swear an oath of loyalty to the government of North Carolina. Many supporters of the Regulators flee and settle in Cherokee Land, where they form the Watauga Association to govern themselves. This was neither the first nor the last time that Americans on the western frontiers of colonies and states would feel oppressed by more urban inhabitants to the east – and when they failed to have their way by arms, they often simply moved farther west.

AUGUST 1771
Westward Movement Connecticut settlers in the Wyoming Valley of Pennsylvania resist local attempts to dislodge them.

OTHER EVENTS OF 1771
Exploration Surveyor John Donelson, drawing the boundary of Virginia for the Treaty of Lochabar, pushes the line as far west as the Kentucky River. In the west, the English trader Thomas Curry reaches Saskatchewan, opening more trade for England. In Spanish California, Fray Francisco Garces, a Franciscan, and Juan Bautista de Anza, commandant of the presidio of Tubac in the Santa Cruz Valley, plan for an expedition to open a road to Monterey. 'The plan is not repugnant to me, nor does it seem very difficult,' wrote Garces, who would spend the next five years in a vain attempt to attain his goal.

JUNÍPERO SERRA, 1713-1784

The fact that saints figure prominently in the names of California cities is due mainly to the efforts of an indomitable Franciscan friar named Junípero Serra, one of the most successful missionaries to the American Indians. Born on the Spanish island of Mallorca on 24 November 1713, Serra received his doctorate in theology from the University of Palma and became a noted teacher and orator. He resigned his brilliant university career to go to Mexico as a missionary, arriving there in 1750.

After nine years among the Indians of the Sierra Gorda, Serra was sent to California to establish missions. Despite a lame leg and frail health, Serra made the considerable journey and set about his work with extraordinary energy. First he founded the mission of San Diego in 1769; over the next 15 years of his life nine more followed, including San Luis Obispo, San Juan Capistrano, San Francisco de Assisi, and Santa Clara. Eventually there would be 21 missions along the coast of California. Respected by fellow missionaries and loved by the Indians, Serra converted some 6000 natives and made them successful farmers as well. Still immersed in his labors, Serra died at San Carlos on 28 August 1784.

---

9 APRIL 1772
Colonial Affairs An interpretation of the Camden-Yorke opinion of 1757 allows for legal purchase of Indian lands by colonials without patents from the Crown. The Camden-Yorke decision as applied in India had held that Indian princes retained title to their lands even after the British conquest. By analogue, the new interpretation maintains that American Indian tribes and their leaders in the colonies retain title to their lands.

OTHER EVENTS OF 1772
Settling Settlers from Virginia and North Carolina in East Tennessee establish the Watauga Association to govern their territory, which is outside the 13 colonies. This is the first formal act to govern territory outside the colonies.

SEPTEMBER 1773
Westward Movement Daniel Boone, in defiance of both Indian and colonial wishes, heads into Kentucky, where the Indians attack and rout his party.

16 DECEMBER 1773
Colonial Affairs The Boston Tea Party exacerbates the growing conflict between the British and the North American colonies.

OTHER EVENTS OF 1773
Settling Daniel Boone leads a party of family and neighbors toward the Cumberland Gap to settle Kentucky, but the party turns back after the Indians capture and kill Boone's oldest son, James. In violation of the Proclamation of 1763, the Philadelphia firm of David Franks and Co organizes the Illinois Wabash Company and buys huge tracts of land from the Illinois Indians.

8 JANUARY 1774
Exploration Garces and de Anza set off from the Santa Cruz Valley to find the best land route to Monterey Bay, with 20 men, 35 pack animals and 65 beef cattle.

7 FEBRUARY 1774
Exploration The party led by Garces and de Anza arrives at Gila Junction.

22 MARCH 1774
Exploration The Spanish explorers arrive and rest at Mission San Gabriel, California.

27 AUGUST 1774
Settling The Transylvania Company is founded by Judge Richard Henderson of North Carolina to allow for further land speculation in Kentucky; for £10,000, Transylvania is purchased from the Cherokees. Henderson then hires Daniel Boone to lead a group of woodsmen to improve the old Indian trails from Virginia into Kentucky – what becomes known as the Wilderness Road.

AUGUST 1774

War Lord Dunmore's War (also known as the Shawnee War) breaks out between the Shawnee Indians and Virginia. The immediate cause is Dunmore's construction of a fort in Shawnee and Delaware territory at the forks of the Ohio River the previous year.

10 OCTOBER 1774

War Lord Dunmore's troops defeat the Shawnees at Point Pleasant on the Great Kanawa and Ohio Rivers, ending the Shawnee War.

OCTOBER 1774

Indians In the treaty of Camp Charlotte between the Shawnees and Kentucky, more Kentucky land is opened for settlement by the Shawnees. However, the Cherokee Indians still claim some of the land ceded over by the Shawnees.

OTHER EVENTS OF 1774

Exploration Juan Perez leads a Spanish expedition that is the first to move up the Pacific Coast as far as present-day Washington State. Early this year, Virginia sent John Connolly to Fort Pitt to seize land claimed by both Virginia and Pittsburgh.

Settling The Illinois and Wabash land companies are organized to purchase and develop land in that region. In Kentucky, James Harrod of Pennsylvania founds Harrodsburg, the first permanent settlement in that colony.

Colonial Affairs Tensions between the English and the colonies culminate in the meeting of the First Continental Congress in Philadelphia.

16 MARCH 1775

Westward Movement Daniel Boone sets out with 30 woodcutters to mark out and hew the Wilderness Road through the Cumberland Gap to Kentucky. In the next quarter-century, some 200,000 pioneers will pass along this trail.

17 MARCH 1775

Indians In the Treaty of Sycamore Shoals, the Cherokees sell land in Kentucky to the Transylvania Company.

1 APRIL 1775

Westward Movement Daniel Boone founds Boonesborough by the Kentucky River in the present-day State of Kentucky.

18-19 APRIL 1775

War The American Revolution begins with the 'shot heard round the world' at Lexington and the skirmish at Concord.

23 MAY 1775

Settling In a meeting in Boonesborough between Henderson and the Cherokees, the Indians formally yield their claim to the land the settlers are occupying through land grants from the Transylvania Company.

OTHER EVENTS OF 1775

Exploration Bueno Heceta leads a second Spanish expedition up the Pacific Coast as far as the coast of Washington. Father Garces explores the territory around Yuma, searching for the best route to Santa Fe. In December he explores the mouth of the Colorado River and converts many Indians. The explorer de Anza leads 150 colonists from Sonora, on the Gulf of California, to San Francisco.

Arts/Culture James Adair, a trader, publishes his *History of the American Indians,* in which he contends that the American Indians are descendants of the 10 lost tribes of Israel.

14 FEBRUARY 1776

Exploration Father Garces arrives at a Mohave settlement near modern-day Needles on the Colorado River; he records that he was welcomed as 'the first Spaniard who has been in their land.' For much of the year, he explores villages of the Moquis (Hopi) Indians, between Needles and Santa Fe.

1 JULY 1776

Exploration English Captain James Cook sails on a voyage of discovery along the North Pacific, in the course of which he will (in 1778) discover Nootka Sound.

29 JULY 1776

Exploration The Franciscan explorer Father Silvestre Velez de Escalante, accompanied by Athanasio Dominguez, sets off on a six-month, 1500-mile expedition to map and explore the mountains of New Mexico, Colorado, Utah and Arizona, in the course of which they see the Great Salt Lake and the Grand Canyon – but do not find a Northwest Passage. Father Escalante's report of the 'inhospitable land' west of Utah (what will become Nevada) discourages exploration of that area for some time.

9 OCTOBER 1776

Settling Franciscan missionaries, led by Juan Batista de Anza, found the mission of San Francisco de Asis (present-day San Francisco) at the *presidio* (fort) on this site.

19 NOVEMBER 1776

Settling North Carolina annexes the Watauga settlement, until now self-governing, as Washington County.

DECEMBER 1776

Settling Virginia accepts George Rogers Clark's proposal and annexes Kentucky settlements in danger of Indian attack as Kentucky County, Virginia. It will become a state in its own right in 1792.

An American plantation painted by Paul Sandby and engraved for Scenographia Americana *(1768).*

CHRONOLOGY

OTHER EVENTS OF 1776

Settling Judge Henderson petitions the Continental Congress to accept Transylvania as a 14th state, but Congress, afraid of antagonizing states with rival claims to the land, does not act. In California, the mission of San Juan Capistrano is founded; its chapel is the oldest building still standing in California. In Arizona, the Spanish establish their second *presidio*, or fort, at Tucson, an Indian settlement. Juan Batista de Anza and Father Garces establish missions in the area of Yuma, Arizona.

Colonial Affairs The Continental Congress endorses the Declaration of Independence on 2 August. In heavy fighting, with great loss, Washington is forced to retreat across the Hudson River. However, in a surprise attack on Christmas Day, Washington crosses the Delaware and seizes Trenton and 1000 prisoners with the loss of only six men.

6 AUGUST 1777

Indians Mohawks led by Chief Joseph Brant assist British forces in ambushing colonial soldiers en route to the besieged Fort Stanwix, in upstate New York. During this year, the Shawnee, Miami, and Wyandot Indians enter the war on the side of the British, and complicate matters for revolutionary forces throughout Kentucky, Pennsylvania, and points farther west.

NOVEMBER 1777

Settling San Jose is founded as the first secular community of California. The rowdy behavior of San Jose's 66 inhabitants scandalizes the friars at the nearby Mission of Santa Clara.

OTHER EVENTS OF 1777

Settling The Articles of Confederation reassure the 13 states formed from the colonies by affirming that no individual state should be deprived of its territory for the benefit of the country as a whole.

Colonial Affairs Colonial fortunes improve with victories in the two Battles of Saratoga, and Washington winters at Valley Forge.

18 JANUARY 1778

Exploration Captain James Cook of the British Navy, on an exploratory voyage in the Pacific, rediscovers the Hawaiian Islands (earlier visits by Europeans have been completely forgotten). He stays about two weeks, trading with the Hawaiians, who evidently regard him as a god. Cook renames the islands the Sandwich Islands, in honor of Britain's First Lord of the Admiralty, the Earl of Sandwich.

6 MARCH 1778

Exploration Captain James Cook, seeking the award of £20,000 that Parliament has offered to the person who discovers the Northwest Passage, sails along the Pacific Northwest coast in *Resolution* and

Discovery, arriving off the coast of 'New Albion' (present-day Oregon) on this date. He names a promontory Cape Foul Weather, the name it retains to this day.

30 MARCH-20 APRIL 1778

Exploration Captain Cook's ships, battered by heavy seas, put in at a sheltered inlet, Nootka Sound. Cook assumes it to be on the mainland, but it is in fact on the west coast of Vancouver Island. After repairing their ships (and making the acquaintance of the native Eskimos), Cook and his ships put back out to sea.

20 APRIL-24 OCTOBER 1778

Exploration Cook's expedition sails north and proceeds along the coast of Alaska; he surveys, charts and names all the geographical and oceanographic features he encounters. Coming to Cape Prince of Wales, the most westerly point of the Americas, he passes through the Bering Strait and the Arctic Circle. Almost trapped by pack-ice in the Chukchi Sea, Cook finally makes his way south to Unalaska in the Aleutians; after repairs, the expedition sets out for Hawaii on 24 October.

30 MAY 1778

Indians More than 300 Iroquois Indians, allies of the British and Loyalists, attack and raze Cobleskill, New York, and raid settlements in Wyoming Valley, Pennsylvania.

3-4 JULY 1778

Indians Sixteen hundred Indians and British forces kill settlers in the Wyoming Valley of Pennsylvania, scalping 200. They put Fort Kingston to the torch.

7-17 SEPTEMBER 1778

Indians Shawnee Indians attack and lay siege to Boonesborough, Kentucky, but the town does not fall.

11 NOVEMBER 1778

Indians Chief Joseph Brant's Indians, with Loyalist troops, massacre settlers at Cherry Valley, New York.

26 NOVEMBER 1778

Exploration Captain Cook and his ships return to Hawaii after their 10-month expedition all the way into the Arctic Circle. The ships put in first at Maui Island, where Cook is treated with extraordinary ceremony. As he moves through the Hawaiian islands, it becomes apparent that he has been identified with the native god Lono.

9 DECEMBER 1778

Westward Movement Virginia annexes territory recently explored by George Rogers Clark and names it Illinois County. Captain John Todd is named governor.

A late eighteenth-century schoolroom.

OTHER EVENTS OF 1778
Settling Virginia attempts to mollify the Transylvania Company by giving it 200,000 acres near the Green and Ohio Rivers.
Indians George Rogers Clark organizes the colonial counterattack against the Indians who are supporting the British.
War The British carry their successful campaign against the colonials into the south and capture Savannah.

14 FEBRUARY 1779
Exploration Captain Cook and his men are still traversing the Hawaiian islands, where they have been victimized by thievery. Cook goes ashore today with a landing party to reclaim the various valuables which have been stolen. In the ensuing melee, the British begin to fire their guns and Cook is stabbed and beaten to death on the beach. Cook's body – or parts thereof – is not recovered and buried at sea until 22 February, when the British leave the island.

25 FEBRUARY 1779
Indians George Rogers Clark, with 150 men, persuades Indians assisting the British at Vincennes to desert, whereupon the British have to surrender.

FEBRUARY 1779
Settling James Robertson leaves Virginia with a small band to claim land in what is now Tennessee for the Transylvania Company.

15 MARCH-31 JULY 1779
Exploration Following the death of Captain Cook, his successor in command, Captain Charles Clerke, leads the expedition's two ships back into the Northern Pacific in search of the northern passage to the Atlantic that had been one of Cook's goals. The ships pass through the Bering Strait on 5 July and explore the North American coast. On 31 July they repass through the strait and head for Russian territory – effectively abandoning the search for the Northwest Passage.

29 AUGUST 1779
Indians American forces at Newtown defeat Indians and Loyalists led by Chief Joseph Brant and pursue the Indians northward, destroying a number of villages and considerable foodstores of potential use to the Loyalists.

OTHER EVENTS OF 1779
Exploration The Spanish explorer Anza explores the San Luis Valley and the Arkansas River, returning to Santa Fe over the mountains.
Settling The Spanish establish a permanent settlement in Texas, at Nacogdoches. The Illinois

CHRONOLOGY

Wabash Company is formed by merging the Illinois Company of 1773 and the Wabash Company of 1775.

War British forces continue their successful southern campaign, and Washington endures a harsher winter at Morristown than the winter of 1777 at Valley Forge.

1 JANUARY 1780

Settling Henderson and his little band meet the advance party led by Robertson into Tennessee, their progress slowed by the worst winter in the area's recorded history.

28 JANUARY 1780

Settling Henderson and Robertson found Nash-

THE REVOLUTION IN THE WEST

The shot fired on the 19th of April in 1775 at Lexington, Massachusetts may have been heard 'round the world,' but it did not make much of an impact on the western frontier of the colonies. While heavy fighting went on in the New England and Middle Atlantic area, the conflict was not carried to the 'west' until 1777. To a large extent, the story of the American Revolution in the west is the story of one man, George Rogers Clark (1752-1818), the older brother of William Clark, of Lewis and Clark fame.

In 1777 George Rogers Clark perceived the potential British threat to frontier posts in the Ohio and Illinois territories. If the British were to hold the string of frontier posts and forts, their defensive position would be greatly enhanced. Furthermore, with the forts in British hands, the colonials would have no defense against raids by Indians loyal to the British. To get information on British strength, Rogers sent two spies into the Ohio territory. Alarmed at their reports, he persuaded Virginia's Governor Patrick Henry to send an expedition against the British in the northwest.

With a band of 250 volunteers, Clark proceeded by river to Pittsburgh, and then to Louisville, Kentucky, whence he launched a successful surprise attack, first on Fort Massac and then – on 4 July – on Fort Kaskaskia. Both were important victories in the American struggle to secure the frontier. Later in the same year, Clark seized strategic Fort Vincennes and, in his boldest move, took Fort Sackville by surprise in the dead of winter in 1779. Only the ineptitude of the local frontier commander, John Bowman, thwarted Clark's most ambitious plan: the capture of Detroit.

The war in the west was largely a series of raids and counterraids for control of the border posts and forts. In Wisconsin, for example, the mixed-blood Charles Michel de Langdale, son of a French father and an Ottawa Indian mother, supported the British during the Revolution. De Langdale led numerous raids on frontier posts held west of the Alleghenies by the colonials. Nonetheless, Wisconsin today remembers de Langdale more as the founder of Green Bay, and has named a county in his honor.

After the Revolution, the frontier was steadily pushed west, thanks in large measure to the successful efforts of George Rogers Clark and his men in securing the frontier against the British.

---

borough (present-day Nashville, named for the Nash Brothers of North Carolina) on the Cumberland River.

MARCH 1789

Settling Robertson leaves Nashborough and heads for Boonesborough in an attempt to get supplies for his starving settlers. This month Indians attack and kill 30 of John Donelson's party, which is struggling to reach Nashborough. One who survives is the beautiful 13-year-old Rachel Donelson, who, at 22, will leave her husband for Andrew Jackson.

24 APRIL 1780

Settling Survivors of the Donelson party reach Nashborough. Soon afterward John Donelson plants Tennessee's first cotton crop near his claim.

10 OCTOBER 1780

Westward Movement Congress passes a resolution urging the states to cede their western territories to the Union, which will create new states from the territories. Connecticut does so at once.

OTHER EVENTS OF 1780

Settling In 1780-83 a major wave of 20,000 new settlers arrives in Kentucky. At the same time, North Carolina declares Henderson's claim to territory including Nashborough invalid, and claims the land for her soldiers. In return, the state grants the Transylvania Company 200,000 acres in the Powell's Valley area, on the border between Kentucky and Virginia. New York cedes to the Continental Congress her claims to lands held by the Iroquois.

Indians Spain, through Esteban Miro, Governor of Louisiana, enlists Indians to halt Anglo-American westward expansion.

1781

Settling The Act of 1781 permits poor settlers in Virginia to buy 400 acres for 80 shillings. Virginia cedes to the Continental Congress her claims to land north of the Ohio River. A report of Captain Cook's voyages is published in London, sparking interest in the Pacific Northwest.

Life/Customs More and more settlers build proper log cabins and have housewarming parties known as bran dances (a term later corrupted to barn dances), in which corn siftings are danced into the wood floors to seal the raw wood.

War In several costly victories, the British lose many men; in the south, Americans retake most of South Carolina.

7 MARCH 1782

Indians American soldiers massacre 96 peaceful Christian Delaware Indians at Gnadenhutten, Ohio, in retaliation for terrorist raids carried out by other Indian tribes. This pattern will repeat itself for a century.

Samuel Adams, a delegate to the First and Second Continental Congresses.

4 JUNE 1782
Indians In retaliation for Gnadenhutten, Indians and Loyalists kill Colonel William Crawford, who had commanded the soldiers at the massacre.

19 AUGUST 1782
Indians Indians and Loyalists raid settlements in Kentucky and win a battle at Blue Licks.

25 AUGUST 1782
Indians Chief Joseph Brant of the Mohawks continues to raid throughout the Pennsylvania and Kentucky territories.

OTHER EVENTS OF 1782
War In Paris, American and British representatives sign a preliminary peace treaty, granting American independence. In Hawaii, the various island chiefs, who have long fought among themselves and resisted unification, cease their hostilities after the battle of Mokuohai, at which Kamehameha establishes himself as Hawaii's most powerful chief.

3 SEPTEMBER 1783
War Britain and the United States sign the Treaty of Paris, formally ending the Revolutionary War. Under terms of the treaty, the United States receives all territory as far west as the Mississippi River. Florida is ceded by England to Spain.

15 OCTOBER 1783
Indians A Congressional committee issues a report on the status of the Indians, and urges a meeting between the Indians and the new government; this does not happen.

OTHER EVENTS OF 1783
Settling Georgia begins to appropriate lands belonging to the Creek Indians, but the Creeks, rallied by their Scot-Creek chief, Alexander McGillivray, raid settlements for several years. Kentucky petitions Congress for statehood, declaring that 'If our society is rude, much wisdom is

not necessary to supply our wants, and a fool can put on his clothes better than a wise man can do it for him.' In North Carolina, the territory which is present-day Tennessee is put up for sale in 100-acre plots at five cents per acre: in seven months, speculators lay claim to 4 million acres. By the end of the year, there are 25,000 American settlers in the Allegheny Plateau.

Blacks Virginia frees all blacks who served in the Continental Army, and the Northern states bar any future importation of slaves into the north.

20 FEBRUARY 1784
Settling Georgia forms the Tennessee Company to make land grants in the Tennessee Valley.

1 MARCH 1784
Settling Jefferson proposes that the western territories should ultimately be divided into 13 states and enter the union on an equal footing with the original 13. Jefferson's plan is adopted (23 April), but never enacted.

19 MARCH 1784
Indians Congress abandons the ideal of one meeting with all the Indians in favor of separate meetings with individual tribes. These are: 22 October 1784 with the six Iroquois Nations at Fort Stanwix; 22 January 1785 with the Wyandot, Delaware, Chippewa and Ottawa at Fort McIntosh; 31 January 1786 with the Shawnee at Fort Finley. At each meeting, the tribes present ceded their territories to the United States; this was immediately contested by those not present, and some signators said they had not understood the import of the documents.

2 JUNE 1784
Settling North Carolina cedes her western territories to the United States.

26 JUNE 1784
Settling Spain closes the lower Mississippi to navigation, interrupting trade and making settlement difficult in this area; however, in return Spain grants trade rights in many of her ports for 25 years.

23 AUGUST 1784
Colonial Affairs At Jonesborough, the people of East Tennessee declare an independent state of Franklin, named in honor of Benjamin Franklin.

1 SEPTEMBER 1784
Settling Pennsylvania allows Connecticut settlers in the Wyoming Valley area of Pennsylvania to return to their lands, thus ending a conflict.

22 SEPTEMBER 1784
Settling The Russians found their first permanent settlement in Alaska on Kodiak Island (Three Saints Bay). The group of 192 settlers is led by the

Russian fur trader Gregory Shelikov. Between 1784 and 1786, the little party is harassed by the local Eskimos, but the settlement is secure by the time Shelikov leaves two years later.

22 OCTOBER 1784
Indians The Six Iroquois Nations, in the Second Treaty of Fort Stanwix, cede all remaining territory west of the Niagara River; however, the Ohio Indians do not recognize this as binding.

1 NOVEMBER 1784
Westward Movement Georgia moves her boundary west from the Tugaloo to the Oconee River in a treaty with the Creek Indians.

OTHER EVENTS OF 1784
Settling James Wilkinson attempts to separate Kentucky from Virginia and to gain for himself rights to use the lower Mississippi for transport; in the latter, he is unsuccessful until 1787.

Colonial Affairs The 'citizens' of the new State of Franklin meet and select a governor, John Sevier, a Revolutionary War hero known as 'Nolichucky Jack,' because he was as swift on campaign as the tempestuous Nolichucky River.

Exploration Captain Charles Clerke publishes an account of Cook's voyages, as well as the discoveries of Samuel Hearne in the Northwest.

21 JANUARY 1785
Indians The Ottawa and Wyandot Indians cede their land in the present-day state of Ohio to the new government in the Treaty of Fort McIntosh.

7 FEBRUARY 1785
Westward Movement Georgia incorporates Bourbon County in territory now part of Alabama and Mississippi; however, the Spanish also claim this land and order the Georgians to leave in October of this year.

5 MAY 1785
Indians The Cherokee Indians cede most of their land to the new State of Franklin in the Treaty of Dumpling Creek; the United States does not recognize either Franklin or the treaty.

8 MAY 1785
Westward Movement Congress passes the Land Ordinance of 1785, which provides that the northwestern territories be surveyed and divided into six-mile-square townships, each divided into 36 lots of 640 acres. This is a great improvement over earlier, more haphazard systems, which allowed for endless border disputes.

20 MAY 1785
Westward Movement Thomas Hutchins, official geographer for the new nation, begins the survey ordained in the Land Ordinance with the first seven range lines west of the Ohio River.

10 OCTOBER 1785
Westward Movement Spain is still ordering Georgia to turn over Bourbon County; Georgia continues to resist.

28 NOVEMBER 1785
Indians In the Treaty of Hopewell, between the United States and the Cherokees, the legitimacy of the State of Franklin is denied again. The Cherokees are given back the land they had ceded to Franklin in the Treaty of Dumpling Creek.

OTHER EVENTS OF 1785
Exploration Benjamin Tupper explores the land beyond the Ohio for Massachusetts Governor Rufus Putnam, with an eye to development.
Settling Fort Hamar is built at the mouth of the Muskingum River to keep squatters out of the territory. In Hawaii, the first of the European trading ships begins to carry furs between the Pacific coast of North America and China, putting in at Hawaii.
Indians Joseph Brant, Chief of the Mohawks, attempts to form an Indian Confederacy. Throughout the Ohio territory, tribes harass settlers and ignore the governmental land grants and surveys. The English covertly assist the Indians by refusing to evacuate their border forts at Lake Champlain, Oswego, Niagara, Detroit and Michilimackinac.
Arts/Culture Peter Pond's excellent map of the north Pacific Coast is published.

1 MARCH 1786
Westward Movement The Ohio Company is formed in Boston to purchase land and settle New Englanders wanting homesteads in the 1.5 million acres acquired along the Upper Ohio River.

29 AUGUST 1786
International John Jay, for the United States, and Don Diego de Gardoqui, for Spain, work out a plan by which the United States formally revokes claims to navigate the lower Mississippi for 25 years; Congress rejects the plan.

OTHER EVENTS OF 1786
Transportation The Spanish seize and hold an American flatboat attempting to navigate the lower Mississippi.

25 MAY-17 SEPTEMBER 1787
National The Constitutional Convention meets at Philadelphia to frame the articles of government. On 13 July Congress passes the Northwest Ordinance to establish a government north of the Ohio. The Ordinance urges reconciliation with the local Indian tribes, and provides that the region should be divided into between three and five territories, each of which should become a state when it attained a population of 60,000. Eventually, 31 of the states will enter the union under the principles of the Northwest Ordinance..

OTHER EVENTS OF 1787
Exploration Charles William Barkley finds the inland channel that the British captain John Meares will name Juan de Fuca Strait in 1788 (after the sailor who is said to have discovered it).
Transportation James Wilkinson receives a monopoly on navigation of the Mississippi from Esteban Miro, Governor of Louisiana.

FEBRUARY 1788
Settling Rufus Putnam's advance party departs for Marietta on behalf of the Ohio Company.

7 APRIL 1788
Settling Rufus Putnam's group founds Muskingum, present-day Marietta, Ohio, as one of the first steps in settling the Northwest Territory under the terms of the Northwest Ordinance of 1787.

21 JUNE 1788
National The Federal Constitution is formally adopted today, when New Hampshire becomes the ninth state to ratify it.

15 JULY 1788
Westward Movement Arthur Saint Clair becomes the first governor of Ohio in ceremonies held at Marietta.

17 AUGUST 1788
Settling Losantiville (present-day Cincinnati) is founded at the confluence of the Ohio and Great Miami Rivers by New Jersey Judge John Cleves, who also founds Columbus.

OTHER EVENTS OF 1788
Westward Movement In Kentucky and Tennessee, there is considerable agitation between those who would join these territories with Spanish territory and those who would not. The issue is vexed, centering on access to navigation on the lower Mississippi River.

9 JANUARY 1789
Indians The governor of the Northwest Territory reaffirms the Treaty of Fort MacIntosh, with the Ohio Indians, in the Treaty of Fort Hamar. This treaty established the principle of payment to the Indians for land received.

17 FEBRUARY 1789
National John Sevier drops all claims to be governor of the state of Franklin and swears an oath of allegiance to North Carolina, whereupon he becomes the representative for the Franklin Territory in the North Carolina legislature.

21 NOVEMBER 1789
Settling Georgia sells 25,400,000 acres to speculative land development companies for $207,580. Settlers found Walnut Hills (today's Vicksburg).

CHRONOLOGY

22 DECEMBER 1789
Settling North Carolina cedes Tennessee to the United States to become a separate state.

OTHER EVENTS OF 1789
Exploration Alexander MacKenzie embarks on the long voyage of discovery along the river which today bears his name; it runs from the Great Slave Lake through Canada's Northwest Territory to the Arctic Ocean, a vital route in the fur trade in North America.
Settling The colony of New Madrid (Missouri) is founded at the juncture of the Ohio and Mississippi Rivers by Colonel George Morgan of Philadelphia, who had purchased the rights from the Spanish.
National George Washington is elected President in the first election held by the new nation.

1 MARCH 1790
Population Congress passes the Census Act, calling for routine censuses of the United States. The 1790 census shows a total population of 3,929,625, of whom 59,557 are free blacks and 697,624 are slaves. Philadelphia, with 42,000 inhabitants, is the largest city; New York has 33,000; Boston, 13,000.

MARCH 1790
Westward Movement Five ships, with more than 500 men, women and children, leave France to settle at Gallipolis, Ohio, deceived by promises that it is already the 'garden of the universe.' The settlement fails, and many settlers are left in dire straits.

26 MAY 1790
Westward Movement Congress establishes a government for Tennessee (formerly the State of Franklin).

7 AUGUST 1790
Indians In the never-implemented treaty of New York, Alexander McGillivray, the Scot-Creek chieftain, pledges loyalty to the United States on behalf of the Creek Indians; however, within months, McGillivray, in the pay of the Spanish, is leading attacks on frontier settlements.

18 OCTOBER 1790
Indians The Ohio Indians defeat an expedition of Americans near Fort Wayne, Indiana, beginning five years of hostilities in the Northwest Territory.

28 OCTOBER 1790
International England and Spain attempt to quell the crisis of Nootka Sound (off present-day Vancouver), in which Britain, Spain and the United States advance claims to the same territory.

OTHER EVENTS OF 1790
Hawaii Chief Kamehameha invades the island of Maui and becomes its sole ruler. An American merchantman, Simon Metcalfe, puts in at Maui with his ship *Eleanor* to barter for food and water. Violence soon breaks out, and when Metcalfe orders his men to fire, hundreds of Hawaiians are massacred. In an unrelated incident, Metcalfe's son Thomas is later killed by the Hawaiians.
Settling Alexander Baranof is sent to Alaska from Russia to conduct fur-trading activities and found outposts of trade.
Transportation Daniel Boone's Wilderness Road is heavily used, and estimates suggest that 90 percent of Kentucky's 75,000 inhabitants had traveled it. From the Wilderness Road, secondary roads fanned out throughout the territory.

30 MARCH 1791
Transportation Construction begins on the Knoxville Road, linking the Wilderness Road with Knoxville, south of the Ohio River. The road opens up frontier areas to settlement.

26 APRIL 1791
Indians The Cherokees, in the Treaty of Holston River, cede most of their land to the United States in return for a promise that their remaining land will be theirs in perpetuity.

10 SEPTEMBER 1791
Westward Movement Indian activity in the Ohio territory necessitates the construction of Forts at Hamilton, Saint Clair, Jefferson, Greenville and Recovery.

ROBERT GRAY, 1755-1806

Robert Gray began his nautical career as a young navigator in the Revolution. He was to put his skills to the highest test as explorer of the western coast of America, discoverer of the Columbia River, and the first captain to carry the American flag around the world.

Gray was born in Tiverton, Rhode Island, on 10 May 1755. After the Revolution he worked for far-sighted Boston merchants who planned to trade with the Indians of the Northwest for otter pelts, then use those pelts to barter for tea in China. Except for Gray, that might have remained a wild scheme. In 1787 Gray and another commander set out in two ships for the Northwest; Gray was promoted to command of the larger ship, the *Columbia*, during the voyage. He was to make that vessel as famous as *Old Ironsides*.

His ships picked up the pelts, took them to China, and continued on around the world with a load of tea, arriving in Boston Harbor in August of 1790 to a 13-gun salute. The voyage had carried the American flag around the world for the first time. The next year Gray repeated the accomplishment, this time discovering and exploring the Columbia River, named for his ship, which was later to divide Washington and Oregon. Gray returned to Boston from China, completing his second circumnavigation, in July 1793. His discovery of the river was later to bolster American claims to Oregon against the British.

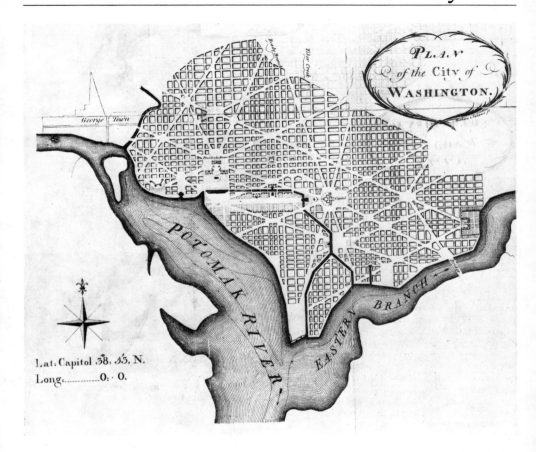

Plan for the city of Washington published in 1792.

4 NOVEMBER 1791

Indians Further fighting near Fort Wayne between local Indians and forces led by General Arthur Saint Clair, governor of the Northwest Territory, results in substantial loss of life among Saint Clair's forces.

OTHER EVENTS OF 1791

Exploration England sends George Vancouver to explore the area around Nootka Sound, off present-day Vancouver, named for him. Alexander Macomb, in what is known as Macomb's Great Purchase, buys 3,675,000 acres from local Indians on the eastern shore of Lake Ontario for 16 cents an acre.

Settling After several invitations from Gregory Shelikhov to head his trading activities in Alaska, Alexander Baranof, another Siberian-Russian fur trader, finally arrives on Kodiak Island. He will exercise strong control over both the Russians living in Alaska and the native Americans, bringing some order and permanency to Russian operations there. Baranof will constantly defy his superiors in Russia by trading with other Euro-

peans in Alaska, where the czar is determined to crowd out all competition. Baranof recognizes that it is a simple matter of survival to trade furs for items which the Europeans in the area can supply.

5 MARCH 1792

Indians General Anthony Wayne takes over as governor of the Northwest Territory from General Arthur St Clair, who has suffered several major defeats.

8 MAY 1792

Indians Congress passes the Militia Act, allowing states to draft all able-bodied men between 18 and 45, in an attempt to raise troops to counter Indian hostilities.

11 MAY 1792

Discovery Captain Robert Gray, the first American to circumnavigate the globe with his own command, discovers a great river in Washington-Oregon and names it after his ship, the *Columbia*.

CHRONOLOGY

OTHER EVENTS OF 1792

Exploration The American Philosophical Society grants $128 to the French explorer Michaus 'to find the shortest and most convenient route of communication between the United States and the Pacific Ocean.' George Vancouver, the British explorer, and Robert Gray, the American fur trader and explorer, are both navigating the coastal area of Washington and Oregon. Vancouver sails into Puget Sound and maps the area. In Hawaii, the merchant Captain Brown becomes the first American to discover the harbor of Honolulu during a voyage which takes place in 1792-3. Brown gets the local chief, Kahehili, to cede him the harbor, called Oahu, in return for providing assistance in ongoing hostilities against Chief Kamehameha.

Settling The Russian settlement on Kodiak Island is moved from Three Saints Bay to Kodiak Village, which is better situated for fishing and the fur trade.

22 JULY 1793

Exploration After a 75-day journey, Alexander MacKenzie and his party reach the Pacific, thus completing the first recorded continental crossing above Mexico, from Fort Chipewyan on Lake Athabasca, Saskatchewan, to Bella Coola at Dean Channel on the Pacific. MacKenzie commemorates his accomplishment by painting on a boulder: 'Alexander MacKenzie, from Canada, by land, the twenty-second of July, one thousand seven hundred and ninety-three' (these words are now chiseled there). MacKenzie's accomplishment deals a near death blow to the dream of a Northwest Passage by sea.

31 JULY 1793

Exploration Robert Gray returns to Boston after his second voyage around the world.

6 NOVEMBER 1793

War The British, as part of the war between England and France, order that any ship transporting French goods can be impounded. The United States is furious at this invasion of neutrality, and the countries drift toward war.

OTHER EVENTS OF 1793

Indians In the Treaty of Nogales between Spain and the Southern Indian tribes, Spain attempts to use the Indians to halt the American westward movement.

Settling By 1793 the Sir William Pultney Estate and the Holland Land Company own most of the land west of Lake Seneca in New York.

Arts/Culture Jedediah Morse publishes his *American Universal Geography*, in which he states that 'The Mississippi was never designed as the western boundary of the American Empire.' This is one of the first statements of America's 'Manifest Destiny.'

John Jay is burned in effigy by anti-Federalists hostile to his treaty with England (1794).

FEBRUARY 1794

Indians The British Governor of Quebec offers to return lands in Ohio to the local Indians, if they will assist England in any future war against the United States.

Hawaii Great Britain (through Captain George Vancouver) persuades Chief Kamehameha of Hawaii to cede the island of Hawaii to Britain. Kamehameha hopes for British support in any future local hostilities, and Britain hopes to secure Hawaii against the Americans.

20 AUGUST 1794

Indians General 'Mad' Anthony Wayne, the hero of Brandywine, decisively defeats the Indians at the Battle of Fallen Timbers and later constructs Fort Wayne to secure the territory of northwest Ohio.

19 NOVEMBER 1794

International Jay's Treaty mandates the withdrawal of British forces from their military forts in the Northwest Territory in return for repayment of debts owed to British subjects before the Revolution. The treaty is ratified by Congress on 24 June 1795, despite much public disaffection after its terms are made known.

7 JANUARY 1795

Settling The Georgia Legislature, heavily bribed, sells the state's western land holdings (some 35 million acres) to land speculators for a mere $500,000. Confusion arising from this transaction will linger until 1810, when the Supreme Court rules that Georgia cannot reverse this action.

3 MARCH 1795

Westward Movement The French settlers at Gallipolis, Ohio, receive deed to their land despite the counterclaims of the Scioto Company.

19 JULY 1794

Westward Movement The Connecticut Land Company buys land still known today as the Western Reserve beside Lake Erie, and, the next year, founds Cleveland. The bulk of the land in the Western Reserve will be sold by Connecticut to land developers at 40 cents an acre.

3 AUGUST 1795

Indians In the Treaty of Greenville, between Anthony Wayne and the local Indians, the Indians relinquish two-thirds of Ohio and part of Indiana to the United States, and grant permission for 16 forts to be built in the remaining Indian territory.

27 OCTOBER 1795

International In the Treaty of San Lorenz, Spain promises to abandon two forts recently built on the US side of the Mississippi, to relinquish claims north of the 31st parallel and to open the Mississippi to navigation.

OTHER EVENTS OF 1795

Settling In Alaska, the city of Mikhailovsk is founded by Baranof on the island that now bears his name (also known as St Michael's). This town is located six miles north of the modern city of Sitka.
Hawaii Kamehameha defeats his rivals at the Battle of Nuuanu Valley on Oahu, emerging as the chief of virtually all the major Hawaiian Islands. Only Kauai eludes his control, but it will be 15 years before he launches a campaign to secure it.

18 APRIL 1796

Indians Congress passes an 'act for establishing trading houses with the Indian tribes,' the first of which will be built in Georgia and Tennessee.

18 MAY 1796

Westward Movement Congress mandates the survey of all lands in the Northwest Territory preparatory to auctioning the land in tracts of 640 acres for $2 an acre; many speculators have to buy on credit, benefiting the wealthy land speculators.

11 JULY 1796

Westward Movement As the British withdraw from their frontier forts, American forces move in.

GEORGE VANCOUVER, 1757-1798

Born in Norfolk, England, on 22 June 1757, George Vancouver began his navy career at the age of 13 and spent most of the next three decades in extraordinary voyages of discovery. He was with Captain James Cook on his voyage around the world in 1772-5, and a few years later he accompanied Cook to the Arctic.

After nine years of sailing in the West Indies, Vancouver took command of Cook's old ship, the *Discovery*, and explored the coasts of Australia and New Zealand, making improved charts of their coasts. The year 1791 found him in Tahiti and the Hawaiian Islands. Next year he began an historic mapping of the western coast of America from San Francisco north to British Columbia. It was on that trip that he skirted the island that later bore his name and received the surrender of a Spanish settlement. After further surveys of the California coast and of Alaska, Vancouver retired to England. He died in Surrey in 1798.

---

29 OCTOBER 1796

Exploration Captain Ebenezer Dorr sails the *Otter* along the California coast and into Monterey Bay, the first American ship to explore this coast.

OTHER EVENTS OF 1796

Exploration A French spy, Victor Collot, steals the map of Missouri made by the explorer Truleau, one of the first accurate maps of the Missouri territory. Daniel Boone is turned down in his application to convert the Wilderness Trail into a road suitable for wagons. In his letter of application, Boone states, 'I think my Self intitled to the offer of the Business as I first Marked out that Rode in March 1775 and Never rec'd anything for my trubel.' Disenchanted with the state of affairs, in Kentucky, Boone will move in 1799 to Spanish Missouri.
Settling From this year on, great numbers of new settlers, on foot or with wagons, move along the Old Walton Road into north-central Tennessee; flatboats carry others into the Ohio Valley.

1797

Settling The main church at San Juan Capistrano is begun, the most ambitious of Spanish California's buildings to date.
International Relations between France and America worsen, as do relations between the United States, Spain and the Cherokees. French demands for a 'loan' evoke the response from Charles G Pinckney, 'Millions for defense, but not one cent for tribute.'

7 APRIL 1798

Settling Congress creates the Mississippi Territory out of lands ceded it by Spain; the territory initially contains parts of Alabama and Mississippi and later includes Tennessee and West Florida.

CHRONOLOGY

12 OCTOBER 1798
Settling The capital of the Mississippi Territory is situated at Natchez, and boundaries are drawn for the territory.

OTHER EVENTS OF 1798
Settling Daniel Boone receives a grant of 850 acres in Missouri from the Spanish Government in Louisiana.

14 DECEMBER 1799
Life/Customs George Washington dies at Mount Vernon at age 67 after an illustrious career which began when, as a young surveyor, he explored and surveyed the Ohio Territory in 1752.

OTHER EVENTS OF 1799
Settling Alexander Baranof establishes Sitka as the capital of Russia's trading operations in Alaska; Baranof is head of the Russian-American firm, a trading company that will prosper greatly. Baranof earns a bad reputation, however, among the native Alaskans, whom he treats cruelly, enslaving many. This year, Daniel Boone, now 65, moves west of the Mississippi into the area of Missouri to take up his land grant from the Spanish and to homestead anew. With his sons, Nathan and Daniel Morgan Boone, he continues to hunt, trap and explore until his death in 1820.

1 OCTOBER 1800
International The secret Treaty of San Ildefonso between France and Spain is signed. Spain, which has held the Louisiana area since 1762, agrees to return it to France, the original Old World owner. (The transfer is not to occur till 15 October 1802.) Two factors contribute to this. First, the Spanish feel increasing pressure from American pioneers and settlers who have moved into Kentucky, Ohio and Tennessee, and who are shipping their goods and produce down the Mississippi River to and through New Orleans. Second, the first consul of France, Napoleon Bonaparte, envisions a new French Empire in North America. The treaty meets the immediate needs of the two European powers, but its ramifications will eventually double the area of the young United States.

OTHER EVENTS OF 1800
Population Total US population stands at 5,308,483, including 869,849 slaves. The center of population is 18 miles southwest of Baltimore, a westward shift from the census of 1790.
National The western section of the Northwest Territory becomes the Territory of Indiana. William Henry Harrison becomes governor of the new Northwest Territory, with the capital at Chillicothe.

4 MARCH 1801
National Thomas Jefferson is inaugurated the third president of the United States, also the first to be inaugurated in Washington, DC. Jefferson calls for 'Peace, commerce, and honest friendship with all nations – and entangling alliances with none.'

MAY 1801
International President Jefferson learns from his agents that Spain intends to pass the Louisiana area to France. He is alarmed by this news, knowing that Napoleon is a formidable foe.

6 AUGUST 1801
Ideas/Beliefs The religious 'Great Revival' of the West begins at Cane Ridge, Kentucky, near the home of the Methodist itinerant preacher Peter Cartwright. Between 10,000 and 25,000 people are present.

5 DECEMBER 1801
International American ambassador to France Robert R Livingston meets French Foreign Minister Talleyrand for the first time. Talleyrand denies what has by now become common knowledge – that a secret treaty has provided for France to take Louisiana.

OTHER EVENTS OF 1801
Westward Movement There is now a postal office in Natchez, Mississippi, the farthest one west to date. There had been a post office in Memphis since 1800, but the route will not reach Detroit until 1806.

9 JANUARY 1802
Education Western University is chartered in Athens, Ohio. It will become Ohio University in 1804, and will grant its first degrees in 1815.

FEBRUARY 1802
Transportation Albert Gallatin, Secretary of the Treasury, proposes that an allotment be made from the sales of public lands for the construction of roads from the Atlantic Ocean to the Ohio River.

18 APRIL 1802
International Jefferson writes to Ambassador Robert Livingston in Paris that the secret cession of Louisiana to France 'completely reverses all the political relations of the U.S.' If France comes to hold New Orleans and threatens to strangle the United States economically, then 'We must marry ourselves to the British fleet and nation.' Livingston then writes a 12,000-word essay on the reasons why it will be disadvantageous to France to take possession of Louisiana, and distributes copies to Napoleon's advisers.

30 APRIL 1802
National The first Enabling Act is passed by Congress, authorizing any territory organized under the Ordinance of 1787 to hold a convention, frame a constitution and thus prepare for entry into the Union.

Curing tobacco in Virginia, from an engraving published in 1800.

The Mississippi River at New Orleans.

Agriculture John Chapman, better known as Johnny Appleseed, arrives at Licking County, Ohio, with a bag of appleseeds he has collected at cider mills in New York and Pennsylvania. His planting becomes a mission which yields perhaps 100,000 square miles of fruit-bearing trees.

Ideas/beliefs The Plan of Union between the Congregational and the Presbyterian Churches – devised by Jonathan Edwards the Younger – is agreed to. The Congregational churches will concentrate upon missions in the New England area, while the Presbyterians will focus their energies upon the western regions. The agreement will last for 30 years.

16 OCTOBER 1802

International In New Orleans, the Spanish intendant – who still holds authority, since the cession of territory to the French has not taken effect – suspends the American right of deposit within the city, revoking an important concession made in the Treaty of Lorenz in 1795 (27 October). This is particularly disturbing in light of information presented by the customhouse at Natchez – that cargoes of tobacco, flour, hemp, cider, and whiskey valued at more than $1 million descend the Mississippi River each year. Use of the port is vital to American commerce.

28 OCTOBER 1802

International Livingston writes to Jefferson that Joseph Bonaparte, brother of France's First Consul, has casually inquired whether the United States would rather purchase East and West Florida – present-day Florida and the southern parts of Alabama and Mississippi – or Louisiana. Livingston writes that, 'I told him that there was no comparison in their value, but that we had no wish to extend our boundary across the Mississippi.' However, Jefferson now begins to envision a continental United States.

29 NOVEMBER 1802

Territorial In Chillicothe, the Ohio constitutional convention approves a constitution.

OTHER EVENTS OF 1802

Settling Alexander Baranof, manager of the Russian-American Company, leads a group of Russian colonists in the task of rebuilding the town of Sitka, Alaska, which had been destroyed by the Tlingit Indians. Sitka becomes the capital of Russian Alaska in 1806, and will be called the 'New World Paris.'

12 JANUARY 1803

National A congressional committee report authorizes President Jefferson to effect negotiations with the French and the Spanish Governments to purchase New Orleans and the provinces of East and West Florida – there is no way of knowing that Spain refused to include the Floridas in the territorial cession at the Treaty of San Ildefonso. The report recognizes western movement and asserts US territorial desires: 'It must be seen that the possession of New Orleans and the

THE LOUISIANA PURCHASE

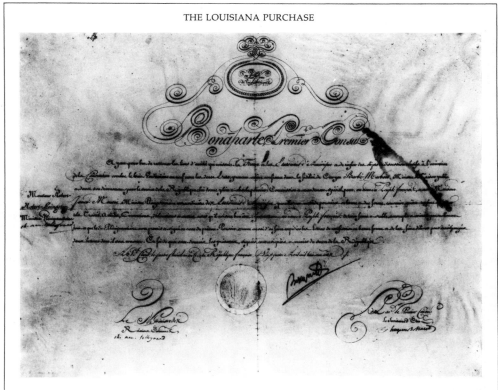

This territorial acquisition, which doubled the physical size of the United States, came as a surprise to both the Congress and President Thomas Jefferson. The roots of the purchase lay in Old World diplomacy. Close to the end of the Seven Years' War, France secretly gave all of its land west of the Mississippi River to Spain. Spanish authorities in New Orleans attempted to prevent encroachment upon this land by the young United States, but demography was against Spain. In 1800 there were only 12,000 French and Spanish settlers in present-day Louisiana, while 300,000 Americans had moved into Kentucky and Tennessee.

In view of this looming population threat, and under pressure from France, Spain transferred the title of the Louisiana Territory to France at the secret Treaty of San Ildefonso in 1800, although actual possession of the land did not change until three years later. What followed came as good fortune to the United States. President Jefferson and Congress recognized the centrality of New Orleans to the strategic, geographic, and commercial future of the nation, and sent James Monroe to Paris to negotiate for the purchase of the city of New Orleans and West Florida. Napoleon Bonaparte, the French first consul, wanted to create a new French Empire in North America, but his European wars were more important to him, and they cost a great deal of money.

Much to the surprise of Monroe and American Ambassador Robert R Livingston, Napoleon's repre-

Negotiating the Louisiana Purchase of 1803.

sentative offered to sell the entire Louisiana Territory to the United States. Negotiations lasted for three weeks. With the signing of an agreement on 2 May 1803, the United States gained 828,000 square miles of real estate for the small cost of $15 million. Referring to the boundaries of this land, French Foreign Minister Talleyrand said that the United States had obtained a noble bargain and could make the best of it. Most would agree that the nation has done so.

CHRONOLOGY

Floridas will not only be required for the convenience of the United States, but will be demanded by their utmost necessities. ... The Floridas and New Orleans command the only outlets [of the Mississippi and its tributaries] to the sea, and our best interests require that we should get possession of them.' James Monroe is named minister plenipotentiary to France and instructed to purchase New Orleans and West Florida for two million dollars. Monroe if authorized to pay as much as ten million dollars if necessary.

18 JANUARY 1803
National In a secret message to Congress, President Jefferson asks for an appropriation of $2500 to send an exploratory expedition west on a diplomatic mission to the Indians and to extend internal commerce. Congress grants the request, making possible what will become known as the Lewis and Clark Expedition.

1 MARCH 1803
National Ohio is admitted to the Union as the seventeenth state. Formerly the eastern section of the Northwest Territory (and still called the Northwest Territory after the western region became the Indiana Territory in 1800), Ohio has grown to a population of 70,000 since 1794. Slavery is prohibited by the state constitution from the start – the first such instance in US history.

3 MARCH 1803
Finance Congress provides for the sale of all uncommitted public lands in the Mississippi Territory.

11 APRIL 1803
International French diplomat Talleyrand asks American representative Livingston how much the United States might be willing to pay for the entire Louisiana area. Livingston replies that his country is interested only in New Orleans and the two provinces of Florida, but Talleyrand responds that without strategic New Orleans, the remainder of Louisiana would be of little value to France.

12 APRIL 1803
International James Monroe arrives in Paris and learns of the offer Talleyrand has made the day before. Initially, Monroe and Livingston concur that they do not have authority to bargain for all of Louisiana.

18 APRIL 1803
International In New Orleans, French Prefect Pierre Clement Laussat writes that 'If New Orleans has been peopled and has acquired importance and capital ... it is due to three hundred thousand planters who in twenty years have swarmed over the eastern plains of the Mississippi and have cultivated them and have no other outlet than this

river [the Mississippi] and no other port than New Orleans.' Laussat's recognition of the American population explosion occurring just west of the Appalachian Mountains comes just when his superiors in Paris have decided to sell the entire Louisiana area to the United States.

15-30 APRIL 1803
International Livingston and Monroe – while secretly feuding with each other – begin serious negotiations with François de Barbe-Marbois, Minister of the French Treasury.

19 APRIL 1803
International Spain restores the right of deposit to American traders at New Orleans.

2 MAY 1803
International The Louisiana Purchase is signed. Livingston and Monroe purchase 828,000 square miles of land – including New Orleans but not East or West Florida – between the Mississippi River and the Rocky Mountains for approximately $15 million.

7 JUNE 1803
Indians Governor William Henry Harrison of the Indiana Territory signs a treaty with nine Indian tribes to obtain Indian lands around Vincennes, along the Wabash River and beyond the border agreed to by the 1795 Treaty of Greenville.

JULY 1803
National President Jefferson suggests removing Indians to west of the Mississippi River: a bill to this effect passes in the Senate, but fails in the House.

31 AUGUST 1803
Exploration Meriwether Lewis and William Clark begin to descend the Ohio River, as the first step of their expedition across the continent.

30 NOVEMBER 1803
International Spanish Governor de Salcedo turns over New Orleans to the French prefect, Pierre Clement de Laussat, completing the process begun three years earlier in the Treaty of San Ildefonso.

20 DECEMBER 1803
International The French Prefect de Laussat turns over New Orleans and Lower Louisiana to US government representatives William C Claiborne and James Wilkinson.

OTHER EVENTS OF 1803
Transportation Road-building in the Midwest is spurred by an allotment of five percent of the net proceeds of sale of public lands within Ohio. The brig *Dean*, constructed on the Allegheny River, reaches Liverpool, England. Shipbuilding is an ever-growing industry.

9 MARCH 1804
International At Cahokia, opposite St Louis, Upper Louisiana is transferred from Spanish to French control and formally presented to the United States.

26 MARCH 1804
Finance The Land Act sets cash payment for western public lands at a minimum of 160 acres, at $1.64 per acre – down from the previous $2.00 price.
National The land acquired in the Louisiana Purchase is divided into the Territory of Orleans – present-day Louisiana west of the Mississippi River – and the District of Louisiana. The area that is now Missouri is placed under jurisdiction of the Indiana Territory.

14 MAY 1804
Exploration Meriwether Lewis and William Clark lead an expedition of 29 men (16 others will accompany them to the Mandan villages in present-day North Dakota) out of St Louis on a keelboat and two pirogue boats.

13 AUGUST 1804
Indians Governor Harrison purchases the land between the Wabash and the Ohio Rivers from the Delaware Indians.

29 SEPTEMBER 1804
Territorial Settlers in present-day Missouri hold a convention and send a memorial to Congress demanding a redress of grievances and a greater measure of self-government.

1 OCTOBER 1804
Territorial Governor Harrison of the Indiana Territory arrives in Missouri to institute territorial government there. Also, William C Claiborne is installed as the first governor of the Louisiana Territory.

MERIWETHER LEWIS, 1774-1809, AND WILLIAM CLARK, 1770-1838

Forever linked in history, Lewis and Clark were archetypal American frontiersmen. Their epochal journey of discovery across the wilderness to the Pacific was the most important of their age, and the first step in opening the country for settlement from sea to sea. Lewis was born in Albemarle County, Virginia, on 18 August 1774, a neighbor of Thomas Jefferson, with whom he maintained contact throughout his first career as an army officer. Clark was born in Caroline County, Virginia, on 1 August 1770. He grew up a frontiersman and something of a naturalist; joining the army in 1792, he spent several years as an Indian fighter.

The two men met as members of the same division in an Indian campaign of 1793. After the campaign they lost touch for several years, but in 1803, after President Jefferson secured Louisiana, he enlisted Lewis to lead an expedition to the Pacific; Lewis asked Clark to be co-leader. Their expedition sailed up the Missouri River in May 1804, and wintered in North Dakota. With the help of the Indian guide Sacagawea, they ascended the upper Missouri the following spring and continued across the Rocky Mountains and down the Columbia River, mapping the territory as they went and studying the wildlife and Indian tribes. After wintering on the Pacific coast, they retraced their route by land, descended the Yellowstone River, and arrived at St Louis in September 1806, to great acclaim.

Jefferson named Lewis governor of the Louisiana Territory in 1807. Chafing at the duties of the office, Lewis left for Washington in 1809 and on the journey died of gunshot wounds, possibly self-inflicted, in Tennessee. Clark became governor of the Missouri Territory in 1813 and served in the war with Britain. For a number of years thereafter he was an Indian agent. Clark died in St Louis in 1838. He and his partner had drawn the imagination of the country across the wilderness to the Pacific and contributed enormously to knowledge about the West.

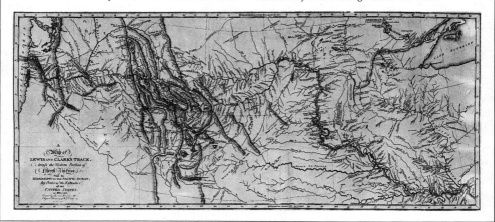

CHRONOLOGY

27 OCTOBER 1804
Exploration The Lewis and Clark Expedition reaches the Mandan Indian towns on the Missouri River – the explorers have traveled 1600 miles in 23 weeks. They set up winter quarters near present-day Bismarck, North Dakota.

OTHER EVENTS OF 1804
Exploration A government-sponsored scientific mission led by William Dunbar explores the lower Red River and the Ouachita River. In 1806 an expedition led by Thomas Freeman will produce the first accurate map of the lower Red River.
Westward Movement Elihu Stout, a printer for the *Kentucky Gazette* in Lexington, straps a printing press and type onto pack horses and takes the wilderness trails leading to Vincennes, capital of the Indiana Territory.
Population The population of Ohio is 120,000. Kentucky has 300,000 people, Tennessee 170,000, and the combined Alabama-Mississippi area around 20,000. These numbers are exactly what the Spanish officials in New Orleans had seen and feared as early as 1800.
Education The 'Coonskin Library' is founded in Marietta, Ohio. Settlers along the Ohio River barter coonskins for books from Boston merchants.

SACAGAWEA, c. 1784-1884

The story of Sacagawea is a good example of what the relationship between whites and Indians could be at their best. Without this indomitable young woman as a guide, the epochal Lewis and Clark Expedition might never have made it to the Pacific. She was born to the Shoshone tribe around 1784, but as a child was abducted by the Minnetares, who gambled her and another woman away to one Toussaint Charbonneau. This French Canadian, citing Indian custom, promptly married both of them.

Explorers Lewis and Clark met Sacagawea and her husband at Fort Mandan in 1804 and hired them as guides. The only woman in the expedition, she set out on the formidable journey with her two-month-old son strapped to her back. She proved an unerring guide, leading the expedition to the Shoshones and enlisting their aid (after she talked her brother out of killing the whole party). With Sacagawea leading the way, the expedition reached its goal of the Pacific in November of 1805. They headed back by way of the Yellowstone.

When they reached Minnetare country, Charbonneau had had enough, and Sacagawea remained with him. Thereafter her story is uncertain: by one account she died along the Missouri in 1812; by another she was identified at the Shoshone agency at the age of 100 and died there in 1884. In any case, like most Indian allies, she was used as long as needed and then dropped. Nonetheless, she became one of the most honored women in American history – a mountain, a river, and a pass bear her name, and there are memorials all along the route of her extraordinary journey.

Life/Customs The Hermitage (now a national shrine) is built by Andrew Jackson and his wife, Rachel, as a three-room cabin in the Tennessee wilderness.

11 JANUARY 1805
Territorial The Indiana Territory is divided; its northern section becomes the new Michigan Territory. General William Hull, a hero in the American Revolution, is named governor, and the capital is at Detroit. The District of Louisiana becomes the Louisiana Territory.

11 FEBRUARY 1805
Exploration Meriwether Lewis acts as the midwife at the birth of a child to Sacajawea, a Shoshone squaw who will act as a guide for the expedition.

2 MARCH 1805
National Congress enacts legislation confirming the French and Spanish land grants in Louisiana. Aaron Burr's term as vice-president ends. He leaves for Pittsburgh on 10 March, hoping to meet General James Wilkinson there, but the general has already left for St Louis. Wilkinson and Burr share a desire to use the West as a stepping-stone to more power – perhaps by provoking a war with the Spanish along the Sabine River boundary with Spanish Mexico.

4 MARCH 1805
National Thomas Jefferson is inaugurated for his second presidential term. His inaugural address calls attention to the discontinuance of internal taxes. George Clinton succeeds Aaron Burr as vice-president.

7 APRIL 1805
Exploration The Lewis and Clark Expedition breaks camp. The 16 men who had arranged to return to St Louis at this point do so, taking with them specimens and souvenirs of the wilderness they have seen. The expedition moves forward via two pirogue boats and six cottonwood canoes.

11 APRIL-13 AUGUST 1805
Exploration The Lewis and Clark Expedition will travel 1200 miles on the Missouri River without sighting an Indian.

26 APRIL 1805
Exploration The Lewis and Clark company reaches the mouth of the Yellowstone River.

26 MAY 1805
Exploration Lewis and Clark sight the Rocky Mountains.

2 JUNE 1805
Exploration Lewis and Clark encounter a river (the Marias) entering the Missouri River from the

north. After days of earnest deliberation, they decide that the south fork is the true Missouri River and move on.

13 JUNE 1805

Exploration Lewis and Clark reach the Great Falls of the Missouri River, which shows them that they had made the correct choice in following the south fork of the river.

MAY-SEPTEMBER 1805

National Aaron Burr and General Wilkinson, commander of forces in the Mississippi Valley, hold a secret conference whose subject was never made public.

9 AUGUST 1805

Exploration General Wilkinson sends Lieutenant Zebulon M Pike to find the sources of the Mississippi River. Pike leaves from St Louis.

15 AUGUST 1805

Exploration Lewis and Clark cross the Continental Divide.

17 AUGUST 1805

Exploration Good fortune comes to the Lewis and Clark Expedition when it encounters a band of Shoshone Indians whose chief is the brother of Sacajawea. The expedition spends the month of September wandering through some of the hardest terrain yet encountered – the Bitterroot Mountains.

23 SEPTEMBER 1805

Indians Lt Zebulon Pike, representing the US Army, purchases from the Minnesota Sioux for $2000 in wares a nine-square-mile tract at the mouth of the Minnesota River; here he helps set up a military post, Fort Snelling, the first United

A cross-section of the Mississippi River, printed in 1810.

States Government presence in this region. This is the first of many treaties and negotiations (to 1889) by which the Sioux lose their ancestral lands.

ZEBULON PIKE, 1779-1813

'Zeb' Pike had a desultory career as an army officer and explorer, but his place in history is secured by his namesake mountain, Pike's Peak. Born into a military family in what is now Trenton, New Jersey, on 5 January 1779, Pike became a frontier lieutenant at the age of 20. His first notable adventure came in 1805, when General James Wilkinson sent him to find the source of the Mississippi River. Pike and 20 men made a difficult winter journey up the river from St Louis; he reached what he mistakenly thought was the source before turning back in 1806.

Pike's next journey, also ordered by Wilkinson, was more ambitious: to explore the upper reaches of the Arkansas and Red Rivers and to scout Spanish settlements in New Mexico, about which Wilkinson seemed uncommonly interested. Leaving St Louis in summer 1806, Pike and his men parleyed with the Pawnees and moved up the Arkansas to the Rockies, which they explored for two months. It was then that Pike made his climb on what later became Pike's Peak – though he failed to reach the top.

Thereafter, the Spanish, curious about his doings in New Mexico, arrested Pike and took him to Chihuahua for questioning. It was a genteel arrest, however, and Pike used the time to study the countryside and settlements. He returned to the United States in 1807 to find himself suspected of complicity in Wilkinson and Aaron Burr's scheme for a Southwest empire. Pike managed to clear himself and made a valuable report on the New Mexico territory. Commissioned a brigadier general during the War of 1812, Pike was killed in April 1813 after leading a successful assault on the British at York (now Toronto), Canada.

CHRONOLOGY

10 OCTOBER 1805
Exploration The Lewis and Clark Expedition finds a west-flowing river – the Snake.

16 OCTOBER 1805
Exploration Zebulon Pike goes into fortified winter quarters at Little Falls in present-day Minnesota.

2 NOVEMBER 1805
Exploration The Lewis and Clark Expedition reaches the Cascade Mountains.

7 NOVEMBER 1805
Exploration Lewis and Clark record: 'Great joy in camp, we are in view of the Ocean, this great Pacific Ocean which we [have] been so anxious to see.' However, the expedition has actually reached the headwaters of the Columbia River, and will not reach the Pacific until the middle of November.

7 DECEMBER 1805
Exploration The Lewis and Clark Expedition settles in for the winter and builds Fort Clatsop in present-day Oregon. The winter is spent organizing and recording the data collected, especially maps of the terrain covered.

OTHER EVENTS OF 1805
Alaska Alexander Baranof, the governor of Russian Alaska, sends the ship *Juno* to set up a post at the mouth of the Columbia River. The attempt is frustrated by storms, and the ship takes refuge in San Francisco Bay, thereby missing a possible encounter with the Lewis and Clark Expedition.

19 FEBRUARY 1806
National President Jefferson issues a preliminary report on the Lewis and Clark Expedition entitled *Message from the President of the United States Communicating Discoveries Made in Exploring the Missouri, Red River and Washita by Captains Lewis and Clark, Doctor Sibley and Mr Dunbar*. The report is based heavily upon the material sent from Lewis and Clark to St Louis after the winter of 1804-5.

29 MARCH 1806
Transportation Congress authorizes construction of the Cumberland Road from Cumberland, Maryland, to Zanesburg, Virginia, on the Ohio River. The road will open the way to many pioneers, for at this time the great majority of Americans still live east of the Appalachian Mountains.

SPRING 1806
International Nicolai Petrovich Rezanov, the chamberlain of the czar and an official of the Alaska-based Russian-American Fur Company, enters San Francisco Bay aboard the ship *Juno*. He trades with the Spanish missions and inspects the harbor, noting that it is weakly defended. The Spanish military presence in California is ineffectual.

30 APRIL 1806
Exploration Zebulon Pike returns to St Louis. He has explored the upper Mississippi and reached Cass Lake in present-day Minnesota, but has not discovered the source of the Mississippi River.

15 JUNE 1806
Exploration The Lewis and Clark Expedition begins to ascend the Rocky Mountains from the western side.

15 JULY 1806
Exploration Recommissioned by General James Wilkinson – who is secretly in the pay of Spain – Pike goes to explore the Southwest. The expedition goes up the Missouri River through present-day Kansas and southern Nebraska to New Mexico and into the Rio Grande Valley.

23 SEPTEMBER 1806
Exploration The Lewis and Clark Expedition returns to St Louis, 36½ months after its departure.

11 OCTOBER 1806
National Wilkinson receives a coded letter from Aaron Burr, possibly saying that the time has come to provoke a war between Spanish and American forces along the Sabine boundary.

21 OCTOBER 1806
National Wilkinson writes to President Jefferson about Burr, exposing what he calls a 'deep, dark, wicked, and widespread conspiracy.'

15 NOVEMBER 1806
Discovery Zebulon Pike sights what will be called Pike's Peak in Colorado.

27 NOVEMBER 1806
National President Jefferson warns American citizens not to participate in any illegal campaign against Spanish-ruled territory – obviously a warning to Aaron Burr.

WINTER 1806
Exploration Pike's expedition makes a stockade on the upper Rio Grande in Spanish territory; he and his party are eventually taken prisoners by a Spanish force from Santa Fe, then led to the American border (July 1807) and sent across.

OTHER EVENTS OF 1806
Science/Technology Jesse Hawley projects a plan for what will become the Erie Canal.
Indians The US Government establishes an Office of Superintendent of Indian Trade; it centralizes the operations of the many government agents who largely control trade with the Indians. The office will be abolished in 1822, but it is a forerunner of the Bureau of Indian Affairs.

22 JANUARY 1807
National President Jefferson formally notifies Congress of Aaron Burr's alleged conspiracy to carve out a private empire in the Southwest. Burr is arrested in Alabama on 19 February.

3 MARCH 1807
National Jefferson removes General Wilkinson from his post as governor of the Territory of Upper Louisiana because of his alleged involvement with Burr.

19 APRIL 1807
Exploration Manuel Lisa leads a party of fur traders out of St Louis. Their destination is the Yellowstone River in eastern Montana.

17 AUGUST 1807
Science/Technology Inventor Robert Fulton takes his steamboat *Clermont* up the Hudson River from New York City to Albany in 32 hours.

3 AUGUST-1 SEPTEMBER 1807
National Aaron Burr and his associates are tried for treason on the charge of trying to separate the Western territories from the United States.

1 SEPTEMBER 1807
National Burr and his associates are acquitted of treason, due to a strict interpretation of the law on treason by Supreme Court Chief Justice John Marshall.

SEPTEMBER 1807
Exploration A large three-company expedition – including a military wing under Lieutenant Joseph Kimball and Ensign Nathaniel Pryor – leaves St Louis hoping to join Manuel Lisa.

21 NOVEMBER 1807
Settling Manuel Lisa is building Fort Raymond on the Yellowstone River, at the mouth of the Big Horn.

OTHER EVENTS OF 1807
Discovery John Colter, fur trapper, discovers the Yellowstone area in present-day Wyoming.
Westward Movement Fortescue Cuming, a writer, notes that the homogeneous frontier society in Ohio is beginning to break up.
Territorial Meriwether Lewis is appointed Governor of the Louisiana Territory. William Clark becomes its Indian agent and brigadier general of its militia; he holds these posts until his death on 1 September 1838.

APRIL 1808
Finance John Jacob Astor incorporates the American Fur Company: he is the only stockholder.
National Treasury Secretary Albert Gallatin submits his *Report on the Subject of Public Roads*

JOHN COLTER, c1775-1813

John Colter began his wilderness career with the party of Lewis and Clark, and abandoned it six adventurous years later upon deciding he'd just as soon hang on to his scalp. Born near Staunton, Virginia, about 1775, Colter first entered history when he signed on with Lewis and Clark in 1803, leaving the expedition on the return leg to join a trapping outfit. In 1807 his employer sent him to confer with the Indian tribes around the Yellowstone. Traveling alone through utter wilderness, Colter was credited with traversing present-day Yellowstone Park.

In 1808 Colter was hunting with a group of Crow Indians along the Missouri when they encountered a larger group of Blackfeet, who happened to be hunting Crows. During the ensuing bloodbath, Colter was seen killing a Blackfoot; thereafter he was a marked man among that tribe. A year later, Colter and fellow trapper John Potts were accosted by Blackfeet. Potts was riddled with arrows and scalped, Colter stripped and told to run. And run he did, outdistancing the tribe's fastest braves – except for one whom he disarmed and killed with the brave's own spear. In 1810 he returned with a large party of trappers and erected a stockade, but after the Blackfeet had killed and scalped five of his party, Colter determined to pursue less hazardous endeavors. He moved to the vicinity of St Louis, secured a young bride, and settled down to farming. He died peacefully, and with all his hair, in 1813. Unable to afford a funeral, his wife simply placed his pouch on his body and vanished. Colter's remains were discovered in 1926.

---

and Canals, in which he proposes $16 million in Federal expenditure for road building.

12 JULY 1808
Communications The *Missouri Gazette*, published in St Louis, becomes the first newspaper west of the Mississippi River.

16 JULY 1808
Finance William Clark, Manuel Lisa, Pierre Chouteau and others incorporate the Missouri Fur Company to compete for the thriving fur trade in the newly opened American interior.

10 NOVEMBER 1808
Indians The Osage Indians cede all of their lands in present-day Missouri and Arkansas north of the Arkansas River to the United States.

OTHER EVENTS OF 1808
Settling The US Army builds Fort Madison in Iowa.

9 JANUARY 1809
Indians President Jefferson authorizes a deputation of the Lower Cherokee Indians to visit lands west of the Mississippi to see if relocating is feasible. By 1840 Indian removal will be almost complete.

CHRONOLOGY

1 MARCH 1809
Territorial The Illinois Territory is created from part of the Indiana Territory.

4 MARCH 1809
National James Madison is inaugurated the fourth President of the United States.

30 SEPTEMBER 1809
Indians In the Treaty of Fort Wayne, Indians of southern Indiana cede three tracts of their land along the Wabash River to the US Government.

OTHER EVENTS OF 1809
Exploration Thomas Nuttal, a natural scientist, sets off for a two-year exploration of the Missouri River beyond the Mandan Indian villages.

JOHN JACOB ASTOR, 1763-1848

Intelligence and energy combined with opportunism characterized John Jacob Astor, the man who set the standard for the heyday of American capitalism. Born to a butcher's family in Heidelberg, Germany, on 17 July 1763, Astor migrated as a teenager to join a brother's business in London. In 1783 he took a ship for New York; on board he learned the secrets of the fur trade, and he stepped off the boat determined to make his fortune in that business.

In 1785 he married Sarah Todd, a well-connected lady with a good eye for furs, and made his first trading trip up the Hudson. By 1800 he had developed one of the leading fur businesses in the country. The next year he moved his family into the grand establishment that was to become New York's Astor House Hotel, and at the same time began buying large tracts in the city that would add considerably to his fortune.

A friend of Thomas Jefferson, Astor was to use that connection to his own ends. The Louisiana Purchase and the Lewis and Clark Expedition opened up immense trading territory, and he was quick to pounce on it. Appointed by Jefferson as Northeast executive agent, Astor formed the American Fur Company in 1808 to challenge the Hudson's Bay and other rival companies. The next years were spent in expanding and consolidating his operations in the new territory, buying out and suppressing competition, and plying the Indians with liquor. His frontier traders became a law unto themselves.

Astor's most extravagant idea was the founding of Astoria, a post for the China trade at the mouth of the Columbia River – the first permanent settlement in the Pacific Northwest. But the post succumbed to Indian depredations and the War of 1812. Nothing daunted, Astor made a killing in bonds during the war and helped establish the Second Bank of the United States. After the war he monopolized the fur trade on the Missouri.

Astor pulled out of the fur business in 1834 to concentrate on real estate and other investments. He died the richest man in America in 1848, leaving most of his $20 million estate to his son, although some half a million dollars went to New York libraries. The New York *Herald* observed that 'He has exhibited at best but the ingenious powers of a self-invented money-making machine.'

Settling David Thompson, trader, explorer and geographer for the Hudson Bay Company, establishes two trading posts in present-day western Montana and nothern Idaho, Salesh House and Kullyspell. Ivan Kuskof, a fur trader of the Russian North American Fur Company, creates a settlement north of Bodega Bay in California. In 1812 the Russians will set up Fort Ross here.

23 JUNE 1810
Finance John Jacob Astor organizes the Pacific Fur Company to capitalize on the rich resources of the Pacific Northwest.

8 SEPTEMBER 1810
Exploration Astor's ship *Tonquin* sails from New York as part of his bid to control the commerce of Oregon. *Tonquin* stops at the Hawaiian Islands, then arrives off the Columbia River in March 1811. Shortly after setting up the settlement of Astoria, the ship is destroyed by a gunpowder explosion following an Indian attack.

OTHER EVENTS OF 1810
Exploration Zebulon Pike's observations of Spanish territory in New Mexico are published in *An Account of Expeditions to the Sources of the Mississippi . . . and in the Interior Parts of New Spain.* These will prove useful to the Santa Fe traders and emigrants to Texas during the 1820s.
Population The total US populaton is 7,239,000, up 36.4 percent since 1800. The center of population moves north and west to a point 40 miles northwest of Washington, DC.
Life/Customs Alexander Wilson, an ornithologist, notes that the gap between the most prosperous and the least prosperous people is widening on the Ohio and Kentucky frontiers.
Hawaii King Kamehameha I extends his rule over the northernmost of the major Hawaiian Islands, Kauai, making himself the effective ruler of all Hawaii. He and his successors will derive much of their income from exporting sandalwood to China.

28 JANUARY 1811
Finance The South West Fur Company is formed, with John Jacob Astor as controller of two-thirds of the interest.

21 APRIL 1811
Westward Movement Wilson Price Hunt, Astor's principal partner in the Northwest venture, leaves St Louis for Oregon on the overland arm of Astor's colonization attempt (begun by the *Tonquin* on 8 September 1810).

18 JULY 1811
Westward Movement Hunt deviates from the Louis and Clark route by striking west from the Missouri River on horseback. He proceeds slowly and by 9 September has only reached the Bighorn River at a point southeast of today's Yellowstone.

JULY 1811

War The Shawnee Indian chief Tecumseh has taken the lead in opposing the encroaching European settlements in the Northwest. While his brother, Tenskwatawa, known as the Shawnee Prophet, tries to inspire Indians with a religious fervor, Tecumseh has been traveling among the tribes from Ohio to the Rockies in an effort to organize a confederacy that would resist the settlers. Now, angered by the series of treaties that the governor of the Indiana Territory, General William Henry Harrison, has signed with various Indian tribes to open up more land to the settlers, Tecumseh actively incites the tribes to resist. On 31 July the settlers of Vincennes in the Indiana Territory urge Governor Harrison to go on the offensive, specifically to attack the principal Indian settlement on the Tippicanoe Creek.

SEPTEMBER 1811

Transportation The steamboat *New Orleans*, built at Pittsburgh by Nicholas Roosevelt, is launched on the Ohio River: this is the first steamboat to appear on western waters; its maiden voyage will be memorable.

26 SEPTEMBER 1811

War General Harrison leads a force of 1000 well-trained men out of Vincennes to attack the Indian settlement known as Prophetstown, 150 miles north on the Tippicanoe Creek. After 65 miles, the men will stop and construct Fort Harrison, at Terre Haute, to serve as an advance base. Most of October will be given over to this project – indicative of Harrison's determination to subdue the Indians.

28 OCTOBER-6 NOVEMBER 1811

War Harrison sets out for the final approach to Tecumseh's settlement on the Tippicanoe; within a week the force has arrived near the edge of the settlement. Harrison agrees to confer with Tecumseh about a possible compromise and has his troops encamp about one mile from the settlement. Since Harrison believes he has agreement that neither side will engage in hostilities during the negotiations, his men go to sleep without much concern.

4 NOVEMBER 1811

National The national elections of 1810 bring into office a number of so-called War Hawks – Congressmen who advocate a hard line against all perceived threats to the nation's territory, including the British, Indians and Spanish. Those from the Northwest are especially aroused by the work of Tecumseh and his brother, the Prophet.

7 NOVEMBER 1811

War Before dawn, the Shawnee Indians steal into Harrison's sleeping encampment and attack his soldiers.

8 NOVEMBER 1811

War Seeking revenge for the surprise Shawnee attack, Harrison leads his troops onto the settlement along the Tippicanoe and razes it (most of the Indians having fled). Harrison will immediately be treated as a hero (and will eventually parlay Tippicanoe into the presidency); although in fact one-quarter of his men are dead or wounded and little has been done to rid the threat of Tecumseh and the Prophet. Tecumseh foregoes any immediate confrontation with the settlers, but he already knows that he will find ready allies among the British at need.

16 DECEMBER 1811

Environment The largest earthquake in American history occurs, with its center at New Madrid, Missouri. Tremors are felt over 300,000 square miles. The ground sinks or rises by as much as 5-25 feet within a 30,000-square-mile area. For several hours, the Mississippi River actually flows northward, and Reelfoot Lake in Tennessee is created by the overflow. The greatest loss of life is on boats navigating the Mississippi and Ohio Rivers, but, miraculously, the steamboat *New Orleans* survives.

OTHER EVENTS OF 1811

Discovery Wilson Price Hunt discovers an overland route to the Pacific Ocean via the Snake and Columbia Rivers.

Westward Movement The Cumberland Road, later known as the National Road, begins in Cumberland, Maryland. In 1840 it will reach Vandalia, Illinois. (Now it is known as Highway 40.)

Transportation The Kaskaskia and Cahokia Road is chartered in Illinois.

12 JANUARY 1812

Science/Technology Having survived the New Madrid Earthquake, the *New Orleans* reaches the city of the same name – becoming the first steamboat to make the passage from Pittsburgh to New Orleans.

15 FEBRUARY 1812

Westward Movement William Hunt arrives at Astoria, Oregon, on behalf of John Jacob Astor.

30 APRIL 1812

National Louisiana, formerly the Territory of Orleans, becomes the eighteenth state of the Union. The population exceeds 70,000, and slavery is permitted. New Orleans, the state capital, is America's fifth most populous city. Later, state government will move to Baton Rouge.

6 MAY 1812

Settling Astor's ship *Beaver* arrives at Astoria, Oregon, with supplies for the Pacific Fur Company settlement.

The Battle of Lake Erie, War of 1812.

CHRONOLOGY

1 JUNE 1812
War of 1812 President Madison asks both houses of Congress to declare war on Great Britain. The situation has been brewing for some years now, for Americans are aware that the British have been encouraging various Indian tribes, particularly those along the Canadian border, to attack American settlers. Meanwhile, because of their war with Napoleonic France, the British have unilaterally declared their right to interfere with American trade at sea, even to impressing seamen.

3 JUNE 1812
War of 1812 Sir George Prevost, Governor General of British Canada, realizes that war between Britain and the United States is likely and invites Tecumseh to confer with him at Amherstburg, in present-day Ontario. Athough the British had temporarily withdrawn their support of Tecumseh after the battle at Tippicanoe, they are now willing to work with any Indian allies they can get.

4 JUNE 1812
Territorial Because there is now a State of Louisiana, the remaining Louisiana Territory is renamed Missouri Territory.

19 JUNE 1812
War of 1812 President Madison proclaims a state of war between the United States and Great Britain. He had received the backing of the House of Representatives (79-49) on 4 June and of the Senate (19-13) on 18 June. No one knows yet that on 16 June the British had agreed to suspend (as of 23 June) the orders that authorized British ships to stop neutral ships, including American vessels. By now events have moved too far, and the United States proceeds to war. Those states that depend on maritime trade are antiwar, but frontier states tend to favor it.

12 JULY 1812
War of 1812 General William Hull, commander of American troops in the western territories, leads a force of 2200 men across the Detroit River to occupy Sandwich, Canada.

17 JULY 1812
War of 1812 The American post on Michilimackinac Island, between Lakes Huron and Michigan, surrenders to the British without firing a shot. This event will help win the Indians under Tecumseh over to the British side.

CHIEF JOHN ROSS, 1790-1866

John Ross was born into a genteel family and educated, but the fact that he was one-eighth Cherokee Indian was the fateful element in his birth and in his life as an Indian leader. He was born near Lookout Mountain, Tennessee, on 3 October 1790; his father was a Scotsman who had lived among the Cherokees, his mother one-fourth Cherokee. After completing his education, Ross became an agent to the Arkansas Cherokees. In the War of 1812, he fought for Andrew Jackson in the Battle of Horseshoe Bend, against the Creeks. Later he worked for the interests of the eastern Cherokees, becoming their chief by election in 1828.

Despite years of effort, Ross was unable to prevent the government's forced removal of his tribe from Tennessee. He accompanied them to Arkansas on the tragic 'Trail of Tears' to what is now Oklahoma. His Indian wife was among the casualties of the journey. Later he married a white Quaker and lived grandly in a plantation mansion, owning numerous slaves. In 1839 Ross helped draft a constitution for the united Eastern and Western Cherokees and served as their chief until his death in Washington in 1866. His last years were spent walking a difficult line between the Union and the Confederacy during the Civil War. Though he was often criticized for his genteel white lifestyle, he sought to make the best of a very bad bargain for his people.

Meriwether Lewis, explorer of the West.

Oliver Hazard Perry, hero of the Battle of Lake Erie.

The British burn Washington during the War of 1812.

8 AUGUST 1812
War of 1812 General Hull withdraws from Canada with his 2200-man force and returns to Detroit: he fears the alliance of the Indians with the British in this relatively remote region.

15 AUGUST 1812
War of 1812 Fort Dearborn, at the present site of Chicago, surrenders. The garrison is brutally massacred.

16 AUGUST 1812
War of 1812 General Hull surrenders Fort Detroit and 1400 men without fighting. The entire Northwest is now exposed to the alliance between the British and Tecumseh's Indians.

17 SEPTEMBER 1812
War of 1812 President Madison and Secretary of War Eustis make William Henry Harrison a brigadier general and give him command of the army in the Northwest.

OTHER EVENTS OF 1812
Settling Scottish and Irish families under Thomas Douglas, Earl of Selkirk, make the first settlement in present-day North Dakota, at Pembina. In 1823 they will move farther north after learning that they have been on American soil.
Finance Robert KcKnight leads a pack train to Santa Fe on the assumption that the revolution against Spain in Mexico will lift restraints upon trade. He and his men are imprisoned, and their goods are confiscated.
Ideas/Beliefs Samuel J Mills makes a tour of the hinterland to assess religious practice for the Connecticut and Massachusetts Missionary Societies. He reports that 'The Sabbath is greatly profaned, and but few good people can be found in any one place . . . within 30 miles of the falls of the Ohio.' As for New Orleans, the French Catholics there are 'destitute of schools, Bibles, and religious instruction.'
Exploration Robert Stuart leaves Astoria, Oregon, to take messages to John Jacob Astor in New York. Stuart spends the winter of 1812 in Wyoming, enters Nebraska early in 1813 and reaches the Missouri River that April. His route will become the Oregon Trail.

4 MARCH 1813
National James Madison is inaugurated for his second term as president.

27 MARCH 1813
War of 1812 Captain Oliver Hazard Perry arrives at Presque Isle, Pennsylvania, and starts to supervise the construction of a flotilla from materials brought from Pittsburgh.

President James P Monroe, as painted by Alonzo Chappell.

9 MAY 1813
War of 1812 General Harrison successfully defends Fort Meigs (in present-day Ohio) against Tecumseh and the British.

2 AUGUST 1813
War of 1812 Major George Croghan stops the British at Fort Stephenson on the Sandusky River.

AUGUST 1813
War of 1812 Captain Oliver H Perry moves his American flotilla out onto Lake Erie off the island of Put-in Bay.

10 SEPTEMBER 1813
War of 1812 Oliver H Perry defeats the British fleet on Lake Erie and sends a message to General Harrison: 'We have met the enemy and they are ours.' This decisive battle gives the United States control of Lake Erie.

5 OCTOBER 1813
War of 1812 Harrison defeats the British and their Indian allies at Moravian Town on the Thames River in Ontario, Canada. Tecumseh dies in the battle, the Indian confederacy is broken and the British threat to the Northwest is removed.

23 OCTOBER 1813
War of 1812 Americans voluntarily turn Astoria over to the British Northwest Company when they realize that a British armed force is on its way to take the settlement. The British arrive on 30 November.

OTHER EVENTS OF 1813
Arts/Culture Padre Narciso Duran, choirmaster of the San Jose Mission in California, compiles a choirbook for use in the Catholic missions of the Southwest. Most of the choir members are Indians who adapt the religious music to their own folk tradition.
Hawaii Don Francisco de Paula Marin, a Spanish settler in Hawaii, suggests that pineapple cultivation would be good for the islands economically. Commercial development of the pineapple will begin some 70 years later.

24-25 AUGUST 1814
War of 1812 British General Robert Ross's expeditionary force sets fire to the Capitol, White House and other government buildings in Washington, DC.

24 DECEMBER 1814
War of 1812 The Peace of Ghent is signed, ending the War of 1812. The treaty rests upon *status quo ante bellum* – restoration of prewar territorial conditions. This leaves the northwest border between the United States and British Canada open to some dispute. Maritime issues are not addressed.

CHRONOLOGY

OTHER EVENTS OF 1814
Exploration A full report on the Lewis and Clark Expedition is published. It had originally been written by Meriwether Lewis, but has been edited by Nicholas Biddle and Paul Allen since Lewis died in 1809. Thomas Jefferson writes the preface to the *History of the Expedition*.

8 JANUARY 1815
War of 1812 With both sides unaware that the war has ended with the Peace of Ghent, the British attack a 4500-man force of mainly Tennessee and Kentucky sharpshooters at New Orleans. The British are thoroughly defeated, and news of the victory makes the American commanding general, Andrew Jackson, a national hero.

JULY-SEPTEMBER 1815
Indians As a result of the British withdrawal after the War of 1812, American authorities are in a position to force new terms on various Indian tribes. During this period, General William Clark negotiates an important treaty at the Portage des Sioux in Missouri. The Sioux recognize US sovereignty in the region and agree to stop raiding white settlements.

NOVEMBER 1815
Westward Movement A committee of the North Carolina legislature reports that within the past 25 years, more than 200,000 inhabitants of the state have moved west and thousands more are leaving each year.

5 DECEMBER 1815
National President Madison asks Congress for improvements in the armed forces, creation of a national currency, construction of roads and canals and establishment of a national university. This is a significant departure from the previous Jeffersonian emphasis upon states' rights and powers.

OTHER EVENTS OF 1815
Transportation The Conestoga wagon remains popular with travelers to the West. It usually has a four-to-six-horse team festooned with bells and a length up to 60 feet; it carries a load of several tons.
Finance Government land offices report that they have sold around one million acres of public land this year.
Life/Customs John R Jewitt publishes *Narrative of the Adventures and Sufferings of John R Jewitt* at Middletown, Connecticut. It tells the story of how the Nootka Sound Indians captured the trading ship *Boston* off Vancouver Island in 1803 and killed all aboard except for the author and one other survivor.

10 MAY 1816
Settling At Green Bay, in present-day Wisconsin, Fort Howard is founded as a base for the Illinois Territory fur trade.

AUTUMN 1816
International Russian naval officer Otto Von Kotzebue arrives at San Francisco and notes the plenitude of sea otters, potentially valuable for the fur trade. The lethargy of Spanish rule in California is apparent to all observers.

11 DECEMBER 1816
National Indiana, originally part of the Northwest Territory, and territory in its own right since 1809, becomes the nineteenth state of the Union. Its population stands at 75,000; slavery is not allowed within its borders. Indiana permits the electors of each county to tax for the maintenance of schools, but few counties actually do this.

1 MARCH 1817
National Congress authorizes the Mississippi Territory to hold a convention as a necessary prerequisite to becoming a state.

3 MARCH 1817
Transportation The steamboat *Washington* initiates a commercial route between Louisville and New Orleans: the cost per passenger is $100-$125. On the Mississippi River, the rate of speed is 25 miles per hour downstream and 16 miles per hour upstream.
Territorial The Alabama Territory is organized from the eastern section of the Mississippi Territory. The capital is placed at St Stephens, near Mobile.

4 MARCH 1817
National James Monroe is inaugurated the fifth US President, ushering in what will be called the 'Era of Good Feelings.'

15 MARCH 1817
Transportation The New York State Legislature authorizes construction of the Erie Canal, a $7-million-dollar project that will connect New York City with the west by way of the Hudson River and the canal between Albany and Buffalo on Lake Erie.

28-29 APRIL 1817
International The Rush-Bagot Agreement is signed. Both the United States and Britain will limit their naval forces on the Great Lakes to no more than two vessels on any one of the lakes.

4 JULY 1817
Transportation Digging begins at Rome, New York, for the Erie Canal, a $7-million project to increase access to the West.

AUTUMN 1817
International The United States sends the sloop of war *Ontario* to the West Coast to reassert its claim to the Oregon country after the loss of Astoria to the British in 1813.

10 DECEMBER 1817
National The Mississippi Territory becomes the State of Mississippi, the twentieth state of the Union.

OTHER EVENTS OF 1817
Exploration Henry R Schoolcraft, geologist and ethnologist, explores southern Missouri and Arkansas.
Settling The US Government establishes Fort Smith in Arkansas to protect settlers from a feud between the Osage and Cherokee Indians there. French fur trader Joseph La Framboise starts the first settlement in present-day South Dakota, where Fort Pierre now stands.
Finance A P Chouteau and Julius de Mun move their trapping and trading enterprise on the Arkansas River across the Spanish border into New Mexico. Their goods are taken, and they are imprisoned briefly. Spain is jealously guarding her borders against American encroachment.
Education The American Tract Society begins to circulate large quantities of religious literature, via circuit riders, to families on the frontier.

An early nineteenth-century engraving of a grizzly bear and her cub in the wild.

8 JANUARY 1818
National Congress receives the first petition calling for the admission of Missouri to the Union.

20 OCTOBER 1818
International Richard Rush and Albert Gallatin sign the Convention of 1818 between the United States and Britain. The boundary between the United States and British North America is set at the forty-ninth parallel. The Oregon country is to be open to people of both nations for 10 years.

3 DECEMBER 1818
National Illinois becomes the twenty-first state. Its population is 40,000; slavery is prohibited.

OTHER EVENTS OF 1818
Indians The Quapaw Indians cede lands between the Arkansas and Red Rivers to the United States.
Westward Movement The Cumberland Road reaches Wheeling, Virginia, on the Ohio River.

CHRONOLOGY

13 FEBRUARY 1819
National The Missouri Bill is introduced in Congress. It would permit the people of the Missouri Territory to draft a state constitution and prepare to enter the Union. The issue of slavery complicates the procedure. New York Representative James Tallmadge proposes a two-clause amendment to the bill: the first would ban the further introduction of slavery into Missouri, and the second would free at the age of 25 children born to slaves after the admission of Missouri.

16-17 FEBRUARY 1819
Slavery The House of Representatives passes both clauses of Tallmadge's anti-slavery amendment to the Missouri Bill.

22 FEBRUARY 1819
International John Quincy Adams and Luis de Onis sign the Adams-Onis Treaty in Washington. Spain cedes East Florida to the United States and renounces any claim to West Florida, while the United States relinquishes any claim to Texas. The American-Spanish territorial boundary is set from the mouth of the Sabine River, north along the Red and Arkansas Rivers, then straight out to the Pacific Ocean along the 42nd parallel. Thus Spain cancels by default any claim she might have to the Pacific Northwest.

27 FEBRUARY 1819
Slavery The Senate turns down both clauses of the anti-slavery Tallmadge amendment to the Missouri Bill.

2 MARCH 1819
Territorial The Arkansas country of the Mississippi Territory is reorganized as the Arkansas Territory, with its capital at Arkansas Post on the Mississippi River.

6 JUNE 1819
Exploration Major Stephen H Long leaves Pittsburgh at the behest of John C Calhoun, the Secretary of War, to find the sources of the Red River. This is the first Federally sponsored expedition of this kind since the Lewis-and-Clark and Zebulon Pike expeditions.

14 DECEMBER 1819
National Alabama becomes the twenty-second state, with a population of 128,000. Slavery is allowed.

OTHER EVENTS OF 1819
Settling The US Army establishes Fort Atkinson on the Missouri River, 16 miles north of present-day Omaha.
Alaska Long-time Governor Alexander Baranof dies, and Russian prosperity in Alaska declines.
Science/Technology Stephen H Long takes the steamboat *Western Engineer* – the first on the

Missouri River – to the Council Bluffs area.
Finance The Panic of 1819 rises from commodity inflation and wild land speculation in the West. Many western states enact bills for debtors relief.
Commerce The Missouri Fur Company is reorganized with a number of new partners. Its founder, Manuel Lisa, dies the following year.

17 FEBRUARY 1820
National The Senate passes the Missouri Compromise Measure, which will bring Missouri into the Union as a slave state and Maine as a free state. Furthermore, there will be no slavery north of latitude 36°30'. There are now 12 free and 12 slave states.

MARCH 1820
Hawaii Kamehameha II has succeeded his father as king (1819). One of his first official acts was to abolish the traditional religion of his people, combining polytheism and human sacrifice. Now he welcomes a group of Protestant missionaries from New England, led by Hiram Bingham, who arrive on the *Thaddeus*. The Protestant missionaries are so successful in converting the Hawaiians, that by the time the first Roman Catholic missionaries arrive in 1827, they are not welcomed.

24 APRIL 1820
Finance The Land Act of 1820 abolishes credit provisions and reduces minimum purchase to 80 acres at a per-acre price of $1.25. Even so, far more speculators than farmers can afford to buy land.

15 JULY 1820
Exploration Edwin James leads two other members of the Long expedition on the first climb up Pike's Peak, which Zebulon Pike had first sighted on 15 November 1806.

2 SEPTEMBER 1820
Transportation The *Indiana Sentinel* rejoices that a line of stagecoaches now runs from Louisville to Vincennes and then on to St Louis.

26 DECEMBER 1820
Westward Movement In San Antonio, Moses Austin asks the Spanish governor for permission to settle 300 American families in Texas.

OTHER EVENTS OF 1820
Exploration Major Long and his 19 soldiers return east by way of the Arkansas River. Long has not found the headwaters of the Red River, and he reports that 'In regard to this extensive section of country between the Missouri River and the Rocky Mountains, we do not hesitate in giving the opinion that it is almost wholly unfit for cultivation.' Henry Schoolcraft, pioneer American geologist, is with an expedition that is prospecting for lead around Lake Superior.

Settling Colonel Josiah Snelling builds Fort Anthony where the Minnesota and Mississippi Rivers meet. The vast north-central region is attracting new settlers.

Population Total US population is 9,638,453, and the center of population is 16 miles east of Moorefield, West Virginia. The population west of the Appalachian Mountains is 2,236,000, but the most impressive population growth between 1800 and 1820 has been in Ohio: from 45,365 to 581,434. By 1840 the population of Ohio will reach 1,519,467, third only to New York State and Pennsylvania. Meanwhile, approximately 1,250,000 people have built homes on either the level land near the Great Lakes or the plains near the Gulf of Mexico.

17 JANUARY 1821
Westward Movement The Spanish governor of Texas grants a charter to Moses Austin to settle 300 families in Texas. Soon American settlers will far outnumber Mexicans there.

22 FEBRUARY 1821
International The Senate consents to the Adams-Onis Treaty for the second time (there had been a delay of ratification in Spain).

24 FEBRUARY 1821
International Mexico declares its independence from Spain.

2 MARCH 1821
Finance Congress passes the Relief Act, which allows price adjustments on unpaid-for land purchases in the West.

Steamboats became important in transportation early in the nineteenth century.

5 MARCH 1821
National President Monroe is inaugurated for his second term.

10 JUNE 1821
Westward Movement Moses Austin dies in Missouri, while preparing to move his group of families into Texas. His work will be continued by his son, Stephen Austin. Hugh Glenn and John Fowler leave Covington, Kentucky, with the goal of reaching Santa Fe, New Mexico. The recent declaration of Mexican independence leads them to hope that they will be allowed to trade with the Mexicans. Glenn eventually reaches Santa Fe, while Fowler reaches Taos, where he finds that the Mexicans there are extremely poor.

10 AUGUST 1821
National Missouri becomes the twenty-fourth state, the twelfth that permits slavery. The capital is at Jefferson City, and the 1820 census shows 66,856 people including 10,222 slaves.

12 AUGUST 1821
Westward Movement Stephen F Austin arrives at Bexar, Texas, to take possession of the land granted to his father, Moses Austin, by the Spanish governor.

1 SEPTEMBER 1821
Finance William Becknell leads a trading party out of Independence, Missouri, toward Santa Fe.

CHRONOLOGY

4 SEPTEMBER 1821
International Czar Alexander I issues an imperial *ukase* extending Russian claims on the Pacific Coast to the 51st parallel, which is in the Oregon country. It is now more than 15 years since Alexander Baranof sailed the ship *Juno* into San Francisco Bay from Russian Alaska.

SEPTEMBER 1821
International Augustin de Iturbide, an army officer, enters Mexico City and assumes leadership of the Revolutionary Government.

AUTUMN 1821
Settling Joshua Pilcher, successor to Manuel Lisa as head of the Missouri Fur Company, establishes Fort Benton at the mouth of the Big Horn in

Montana on the same site that the company had abandoned in 1810.

16 NOVEMBER 1821
Exploration William Becknell and his trading group arrive at Santa Fe, where they do a brisk trade with the Mexicans. By mapping their route, they define what will be the Santa Fe Trail. When they return to Franklin, Missouri, with their new-found riches, the trail will become well traveled.

OTHER EVENTS OF 1821
Settling Stephen F Austin's group makes its first settlement at Columbus and Washington-on-the-Brazos in southeastern Texas.
Arts/Culture Charles Taylor Caldwell sails to Europe with $10,000 allocated by Kentucky for the

Slavery came to Louisiana in 1716 and played an important role in development of the sugar industry.

purchase of a library for Transylvania University. By 1830 that university has the largest library west of the Alleghenies – 2000 volumes.

Finance Under provisions of the Relief Act of 1821, previous purchasers of government land can now pay off their debts at the reduced price set by the Land Act of 1820, with more time to meet payment installments.

Territorial The Iowa region – which has been part of the Missouri Territory since 1812 – becomes part of the unorganized territory of the United States.

20 MARCH 1822

Exploration Veteran fur trader William Henry Ashley publishes an advertisement in the St Louis *Missouri Republican* calling for 100 young men to ascend the Missouri River to its source and to develop the fur trade there.

22 MAY 1822

Finance William Becknell leaves from Franklin, Missouri, on what will be his second trip to Santa Fe. This time he takes 21 men and three wagons. The expedition pioneers the Cimarron Cutoff, a shorter but much more hazardous route than the better-watered 'Mountain Route' of the Santa Fe Trail.

4 MAY 1822

National President Monroe vetoes a Congressional bill that would authorize establishment of toll gates and collections on the Cumberland Road. The President declares that Congress does not have the right of jurisdiction and construction, but he recommends a Constitutional Amendment for a national system of internal improvements.

24 JULY 1822

International A strongly worded US diplomatic note protests the Russian Czar's *ukase* of 4 September 1821. The threat of war is implied.

3 SEPTEMBER 1822

Indians The Fox and Sauk Indians sign a treaty that permits them to live on the lands they had previously ceded in the Wisconsin Territory and Illinois.

27 OCTOBER 1822

Transportation A 280-mile section of the Erie Canal is opened, linking Rochester and Albany, New York. Although people have been leaving the New England area for some time, the Erie Canal makes their western migration easier.

12 DECEMBER 1822

International The United States extends official recognition to independent Mexico and its new emperor, Augustin de Iturbide.

OTHER EVENTS OF 1822

Finance John Jacob Astor organizes a branch of

JOHN McLOUGHLIN, 1784-1857

Along with his associate Peter Ogden, John McLoughlin was one of the most important of the Hudson's Bay Company fur traders of the Pacific Northwest in its British era. He was born in Rivière du Loup, Quebec, in 1784, and entered the fur trade in 1814 after gaining a medical degree. In 1821 he and Ogden became directors of Hudson's Bay Company activities in the Columbia River Department, which ranged down into Washington and Oregon Territory. McLoughlin was the moving force in erecting Fort Vancouver in 1825, a fur post which for years was the only white settlement in the area.

McLoughlin had an ambiguous position to maintain in engaging in business as a British subject in an area coveted openly by the United States. Though he had difficulty with both sides from time to time, in the main, he got along with American settlers and kept the furs flowing to Canada. However, as the American presence grew, McLoughlin's friendliness to the settlers precipitated something of a forced retirement from the company in 1846. In his last years, after Oregon became a US Territory, McLoughlin founded a town on the Willamette River and pursued his claim to the town with US authorities; it was settled in his favor only after his death in 1857. Throughout a difficult time, his had been a voice of moderation.

---

the American Fur Company in St Louis. Between now and 1834, Astor's company will dominate the fur trade west of the Mississippi. William Henry Ashley and Andrew Henry organize the Rocky Mountain Fur Company in St Louis.

Arts/Culture Mary Noah Ludlow, comedienne, sings 'Hunters of Kentucky' before an enthusiastic crowd in New Orleans. The song turns the Battle of New Orleans (1815) into a Jacksonian legend.

18 FEBRUARY 1823

Westward Movement Mexican Emperor Augustin de Iturbide confirms that the Texas land grant that had been made by Mexico to Moses Austin is transferable to his son, Stephen F Austin.

MARCH 1823

International Mexican Republicans, led by Antonio de Santa Anna, force Emperor Iturbide to abdicate.

14 APRIL 1823

Westward Movement The new Mexican Government grants confirmation to Stephen F Austin's settlement of Texas.

17 JULY 1823

International John Quincy Adams, US Secretary of State, informs the Russian Minister to the United States that 'We should contest the right of Russia to *any* territorial establishment on this continent.' America is becoming very assertive in its defense of territorial rights. This issue will be addressed by a US-Russian treaty in April 1824.

CHRONOLOGY

2 DECEMBER 1823
International President Monroe formulates the Monroe Doctrine in a speech to Congress. The doctrine opposes any future colonization or intervention in the sovereign states of the Western Hemisphere by European powers.

AUTUMN 1823
Settling Stephen F Austin begins to lay out San Felipe de Austin on the Brazos River as the colonial seat of government. Mexico responds by providing new land grants to American settlers in Texas.

OTHER EVENTS OF 1823
Indians Arikara Indians attack a trading party led by General William Ashley, lieutenant governor of the Missouri Territory. The Federal Government sends an army group under Colonel Henry Leavenworth to punish the Indians.

10 FEBRUARY 1824
National Both houses of Congress pass the General Survey Bill, which empowers the president to initiate surveys and estimates of roads and canals required for national, military, commercial, or postal purposes.

FEBRUARY 1824
Exploration Jedediah Strong Smith, a guide for the Rocky Mountain Fur Company, leads a group of explorers through the South Pass of the Rocky Mountains in Wyoming.

2 MARCH 1824
Transportation Federal control of interstate commerce is established by *Gibbons v Ogden*, a Supreme Court case dealing with a steamboat monopoly. On 16 March the *New Jersey Journal* declares that 'The navigable waters of this state, and of the United States, are again free.'

30-31 MARCH 1824
National Henry Clay applies the phrase 'American System' to a combination of the protective tariff and a national system of internal improvements as a means of expanding the domestic market and lessening dependence upon overseas resources.

17 APRIL 1824
International A US-Russian territorial treaty is signed by which Russia acknowledges that 54°40' is the southern limit of her territory in the Pacific Northwest. A major competitor for the Northwest has been removed.

7 MAY 1824
International Texas and Coahuila are organized as one of the states of the Mexican Federal Republic, now the single most important rival to US dominance of North America. Thousands of Americans have already settled in this region.

JEDEDIAH STRONG SMITH, 1799-1831

The short but eventful career of Jedediah Smith typifies the early days of Western exploration, which was often a fatal adventure. Born in Bainbridge, New York, on 6 January 1799, Smith gravitated to the adventurous life of the Rocky Mountain fur trade in the early 1820s. In 1826 he determined to try to reach Oregon territory through California.

Toward the end of 1826, Smith led a party of 17 men from the Great Salt Lake to the San Gabriel Mission in California. Unable to cross the mountains, he left most of his men camped in the wilderness on the American River and returned with two others across the desert to Great Salt Lake (they were the first whites to cross this formidable desert). Upon setting out again to rejoin their camp, Smith's party of 18 was ambushed by Mohave Indians, who killed ten. The rest made it to the American River camp, where the two parties spent a difficult winter in the Sacramento Valley. In spring 1828 they headed up the coast toward Oregon, but ran tragically afoul of Indians again – Umpquas this time – who killed all but three of the party. Smith returned to the supposedly safer fur trade in Santa Fe. In May 1831 he was killed by Comanches along the Cimarron River.

---

17 JUNE 1824
Indians Secretary of War John C Calhoun establishes, without authorization from Congress, the Office of Indian Affairs. It will be 1832 before this bureau is backed by Congressional enactment of a bill creating a Commissioner of Indian Affairs.

4 OCTOBER 1824
International The Mexican Congress adopts a constitution making Mexico a republic.

OTHER EVENTS OF 1824
Discovery Fur trader James Bridger discovers the Great Salt Lake, which he believes is an ocean because of its saline water.

Settling The Hudson's Bay Company (English) builds Fort Vancouver on the Columbia River in Oregon. Under the leadership of Dr John McLoughlin, this post becomes a formidable foe in the bid for control of the fur trade in the Northwest.

Indians The US Government creates Forts Gibson and Towson in present-day Oklahoma to prepare for relocation of the Five Civilized Tribes from east of the Mississippi. Between 1820 and 1846, the Creek, Chickasaw, Choctaw, Seminole and Cherokee Indians are moved to Oklahoma. The lands they are settled on are granted to them for 'as long as grass grows and rivers run.'

Finance The first annual rendezvous for the fur trappers of the Rocky Mountain area is held at Green River, Wyoming, under supervision of the company of General William Henry Ashley. The rendezvous becomes an annual event, with the site changing nearly every year. The trappers bring in enormous numbers of animal skins, which they trade for whiskey, new supplies and money.

Finance A party of 180, with 26 wagons, realizes a profit of $190,000 carrying needed goods along the Santa Fe Trail.

27 JANUARY 1825
National Congress approves a frontier line that marks off an official Indian territory – in the area of the so-called Great American Desert, in present-day Oklahoma and Kansas. The effect of this boundary will be similar to that of the line which the British had established in 1763: settlers will face an additional challenge, but will continue to move west. When the country just north of the Red River is allocated to the Choctaw Indians, squatters in that area are forced to move south into Texas.

12 FEBRUARY 1825
Indians The Creek Indian Treaty is signed. Tribal leaders agree to turn over all their lands in Georgia to the Federal Government, and promise to migrate west by 1 September 1826. Many of the Creeks reject the treaty, but it foreshadows the American Government's policy of moving Indian tribes even farther westward.

3 MARCH 1825
Exploration Congress authorizes a Federal survey to mark the Santa Fe Trail between the Missouri River and New Mexico.

7 MARCH 1825
International The first American minister to Mexico is named: Joel R Poinsett.

24 MARCH 1825
Westward Movement Mexican law opens the state of Texas-Coahuila to American colonization.

4 JULY 1825
Transportation Construction resumes on the Cumberland Road, to extend it from Wheeling, West Virginia, to Ohio. From Wheeling on, it will be called the National Road.

10 AUGUST 1825
Indians A treaty is signed between government commissioners and the Osage Indians at Council Grove, Kansas. The Osage agree to give up still more of their land.

19 AUGUST 1825
Indians Tribal representatives of the Chippewa, Iowa, Potawatami, Sauk, Fox, Sioux, and Winnebago Indians sign a treaty settling their territorial boundaries among themselves – arranged by the Federal Government at the request of the Chippewa and Sioux tribes in Prairie du Chien, Wisconsin.

DAVID 'DAVY' CROCKETT, 1786-1836

The myth of Davy Crockett started well before his death, aided by his formidable talents as a hunter and frontiersman, his yen for the public eye, and his gift for good old-fashioned American hokum. Crockett was born near Greeneville, Tennessee, on 17 August 1786. After running away from home at 13, he drifted for some years, then married and settled down to desultory farming in various parts of backwoods Tennessee. For a while he served ably as a scout for Andrew Jackson in the Creek War of 1813-14. After the death of his first wife and his remarriage, Crockett moved into the political arena and was elected to the state legislature in 1821.

In 1827 Crockett acted on a joking suggestion that he run for Congress and parlayed his lively and homespun public style into the first of three terms in the House. Practically illiterate and with scant understanding of government, Crockett made little headway as an anti-Jackson Whig, but he certainly enlivened the Washington scene with his personality – he was already the grizzled 'b'ar hunter' of his self-created legend. Despite his speaking tour of the North in 1834, the Jackson juggernaut defeated Crockett's campaign the following year. In 1836 he arrived in Texas to lend a hand with the revolution there, and met his end in a hail of bullets during the last stand of the Alamo.

---

26 OCTOBER 1825
Transportation The Erie Canal opens for traffic. It is 363 miles long, making the water route from New York City to Lake Erie 550 miles long.

6 DECEMBER 1825
National President John Quincy Adams makes the first annual presidential address to Congress. He recommends road and canal construction, and exploration of the interior and the Pacific Northwest. Western Congressmen approve, and are affiliated in an uneasy alliance with New England legislators based on support for the American System.

OTHER EVENTS OF 1825
Exploration Peter S Ogden leads a party for the Hudson's Bay Company into the northwest area of present-day Nevada, exploring the Humboldt River Valley, and traveling to what is now Winnemucca, Nevada.

National By now it is clear that the United States is committed to a 'removal policy' – the relocation of most Indians living east of the Mississippi to the west of it. Many will be settled in present-day Oklahoma and Kansas by 1835 – until the demand for land displaces them again.

International The Republic of Mexico declares that California is a territory, and sends José Maria de Enchenadia to set up a territorial government there. He is not very well received by the residents of California; there will be an unsuccessful revolt against him in 1828.

CHRONOLOGY

James Fenimore Cooper's novels of frontier life were a major contribution to the mythos of the West.

Indians The US Government makes Kansas an Indian territory. Between 1825 and 1842, nearly 30 tribes give up lands east of the Mississippi River and resettle on small reservations in Kansas. The largest groups are the Shawnee, Delaware, Potawatami, Chippewa, Munsee, Iowa, Sauk, Fox, Wyandot and Kickapoo tribes.

Transportation It is reported that half the nation's mails are carried by horse and rider.

Arts/Culture Guidebooks for travel become available. Stagecoach travelers can now purchase a guide to the entire country, *The American Traveler* by Daniel Hewett. A popular literary theme of the 1820s is the romantic 'noble savage' treatment of the Indians, as in *Frontier Maid* (1819), *Yamoyden* (1820), *Logan, an Indian Tale* (1821), and *Ontwa, Son of the Forest* (1822). In 1826 James Fenimore Cooper's *The Last of the Mohicans* sells over two million copies.

22 AUGUST 1826
Exploration Jedediah Strong Smith leaves a rendezvous point on Bear River, east of the Great Salt Lake, with 14 companions.

NOVEMBER 1826
Exploration Smith and his men cross the Mohave Desert.

27 NOVEMBER 1826
Exploration Smith and his company arrive in San Diego, the first Americans to take this route into California.

16 DECEMBER 1826
International Benjamin Edwards, the brother of a corrupt American *empresario* in Texas, rides into Nacogdoches, Texas, and declares that he is the ruler of the Republic of Fredonia, which he defines as extending from the Sabine to the Rio Grande Rivers. Stephen Austin raises a small army and squelches the Fredonia Revolt, but the seeds of distrust are sown between the American Texans and the Mexicans.

OTHER EVENTS OF 1826
Arts/Culture Timothy Flint, novelist, publishes *Francis Bervain*, a sentimental story of a New Englander involved in the Mexican revolt of 1822. The book portrays accurately the Southwest border regions of the United States.

MAY 1827
Settlement Fort Leavenworth (in present-day Kansas) is built on the Santa Fe trade route to provide protection for this flourishing commercial artery.

3 JULY 1827
Exploration Jedediah Strong Smith returns to the Great Salt Lake with three of his original party.

13 JULY 1827
Exploration Jedediah Strong Smith sets out to reunite with the men he had left in California, following the same route used in 1826.

6 AUGUST 1827
International A joint occupation of the Oregon country is agreed to by the United States and Great Britain. This renews the Convention of 1818, which Richard Rush and Albert Gallatin had concluded on 20 October. Its effect will continue to be a state of undeclared war between the competing financial interests in the Oregon country, beginning with the Hudson's Bay Company and the American fur companies.

OTHER EVENTS OF 1827
Transportation Government commissioners present their report on the Santa Fe Trail. Unfortunately, they have not mapped the important Cimarron Desert, which traders prefer to the route via Chouteau Island.

Finance The American Fur Company absorbs the Columbia Fur Company and dominates the fur trade on the upper Missouri River,

Arts/Culture James Fenimore Cooper's *The Prairie* is a best seller.

1827-1829
Exploration Jedediah Strong Smith and his party follow roughly the same route they had used in 1826 from the Great Salt Lake to Southern California via the Sevier, Virgin and Colorado Rivers. They cross the Mohave Desert to the San Bernardino Mountains and the mission farms of San Gabriel, California – a route which will later become famous as 'the Mormon outlet'

21 FEBRUARY 1828
Indians A printing press arrives at Cherokee Council headquarters in Echota, Georgia, where Indian linguist Sequoyah has developed an 86-symbol alphabet to render his people's language. Publication of the *Cherokee Phoenix*, the first US newspaper in an Indian language, will begin this year.

9 JULY 1828
Exploration Smith and his men reach the Umpqua River in Oregon. On 14 July 1828, they are attacked by the Umpqua Indians. Only Smith and three of his men escape.

OTHER EVENTS OF 1828
Settling Massachusetts schoolteacher Hall J Kelley writes to Congress asking that the Federal Government assist in founding a colony on the Northwest Coast. This comes 18 years after John Jacob Astor's original attempt at colonization (at Astoria); private efforts are still more prominent than governmental in the Northwest.
California A rebellion breaks out in California against Mexican rule, represented by the territorial governor who has been in place since 1825. Secularization of the Catholic missions to the Indians, like the one at San Gabriel, is sought by the rebellious Spanish-Mexican settlers, who are known as *Californios*. Secularization is achieved by 1833, but nine more rebellions between 1828-43 weaken Mexican rule in California and encourage the movement of non-Hispanic settlers into the region.
Environment Franklin, Missouri, where the Santa Fe Trail begins, is washed away by flooding along the Missouri River. The trail head is relocated to Independence, Missouri.

JANUARY 1829
National The House of Representatives defeats a bill that calls for creation of a territorial government in Oregon.

4 MARCH 1829
National In his first inaugural address, President Andrew Jackson calls for a just and liberal policy toward the Indians; he fails to clarify his position on the important issue of internal improvements – road-building, surveying, map-making. This ambivalence will be manifested throughout his two terms in office.

26 JULY 1829
Indians In the Michigan Territory, the Chippewa, Ottawa and Potawatami Indians cede lands to the US Government.

25 AUGUST 1829
International President Jackson offers to purchase the Texas area from the Mexican Government and is refused. By 1830 the population of

Stephen F Austin's colony in Texas will rise to 4428. Other Americans are either settling or squatting on Mexican land in Texas.

6 NOVEMBER 1829
Exploration Thirty-one men leave the Mexican village of Abiquiu to pioneer a trade route to Southern California. They are led by Antonio Armijo, who will become the last Mexican territorial governor of New Mexico.

2 DECEMBER 1829
Slavery Mexican President Guerrero proclaims Texas exempt from the ban on slavery in Mexico.

8 DECEMBER 1829
Exploration Antonio Armijo's party of Mexicans makes the difficult 'Crossing of the Fathers,' as it will become known, in present-day Utah. The name is given in honor of two Franciscan friars, Silvestre Velez de Escalante and Francisco Athanasio Dominguez, who pioneered this passage in 1776.

OTHER EVENTS OF 1829
Transportation There are now 104,521 miles of postal road operating throughout the United States.
Indians A large trade caravan – 60 men and 36 wagons, led by Charles Bent and Colonel Marmaduke – is attacked by Comanche Indians when its military escort turns back at the Mexican border of the Santa Fe Trail. After reaching New Mexico, it is escorted back by a Mexican cavalry force, which is also attacked by Comanches during its return by way of the Cimarron Cutoff.

The Choctaw Indians of the Southeast were among the Five Civilized Tribes relocated to the West.

CHRONOLOGY

Westward Movement A Massachusetts school-teacher, Hall J Kelley, establishes a society 'for the encouragement of the settlement of Oregon by Americans.' In 1830 he will publish *A Geographical Sketch of That Part of North America called Oregon*, in which he describes the area as a large valley 'nourished by a rich soil and warmed by a congenial heat.' A trend that has prevailed throughout the nineteenth century continues: individual pioneering and exploration lead the way west. This year the Federal Government assigns an armed force under command of Major Bennet Riley to escort caravans on the Santa Fe Trail. Bennet uses oxen rather than mules or horses as draft animals, a decision that has lasting consequences for the development of the Great Plains.

1830

Exploration Beginning in 1829, Peter S Odgen of the Hudson's Bay Company has led a party of fur trappers from the mouth of the Snake River to the Humboldt Sink, thence to the Colorado River and Sacramento, California. Their trail-blazing effort ends on the Columbia River, where a boating accident leads to the loss of most of the beaver skins they had collected, as well as the records of the expedition, near the Dalles River. Nevertheless, such explorers as Odgen, Smith and the Mexican Antonio Armijo are pioneering trails that will become familiar to the settlers who follow them in the 1840s and 1850s.

JANUARY 1830

Exploration Antonio Armijo's pack train reaches the Virgin River (draining present-day Arizona and Nevada) and proceeds to the San Gabriel missions in Lower California via the Mohave River and the Cajun Pass. This expedition opens what will be called the Old Spanish Trail.
National The Webster-Haynes Debate in the Senate revolves around the proposal that all land sales and surveys be discontinued. The debate leads to a possible alliance between Southern and Western Senators against those from the Northeast.

6 APRIL 1830

International A revolutionary government in Mexico forbids further American colonization of Texas and prohibits the importation of black slaves into the area.
Ideas/Beliefs The Church of Jesus Christ of Latter Day Saints – popularly called the Mormon Church – is founded at Fayette, New York, by Joseph Smith and 30 followers. Smith will publish his *Book of Mormon* this same year.

10 APRIL 1830

Transportation William L Sublette leads 10 loaded wagons, each drawn by five mules, and two one-mule Dearborn carriages out of St Louis. These are the first wagons to travel on the Oregon Trail. The caravan proceeds to the annual fur trappers' rendezvous at the head of the Wind River, and on 16 July arrives at present-day Casper, Wyoming. There, Sublette sells his business to the Rocky Mountain Fur Company and returns to St Louis. He sends a report to John H Eaton, Secretary of War, on his experience with the wagon train, saying that the 'ease and safety with which it was done proved the facility of communicating overland with the Pacific Ocean.'

28 MAY 1830

National President Jackson vetoes the Maysville Road Bill on ground that the project lies wholly within the State of Kentucky and Federal support would require a constitutional amendment.
Indians Jackson signs the Indian Removal Act, which grants subsidiary authority to move eastern Indians to the lands west of the Mississippi River.

29 MAY 1830

National The Pre-emption Act, allowing purchase of public land at a minimum $1.25 per acre by persons who have cultivated the land within the previous year, is enacted. Its provisions are renewed at intervals until 1862, when the Homestead Act replaces them.

15 JULY 1830

Indians At Prairie du Chien, Wisconsin, Indians of the Sioux, Sauk and Fox tribes sign a treaty that gives the United States most of present-day Iowa, Missouri and Minnesota.

OTHER EVENTS OF 1830

Exploration William Wolfskill blazes a caravan route along the Old Spanish Trail.
Settling The town of Chicago is laid out at Fort Dearborn.
National The Postmaster-General (a cabinet member since 1829) reports that there are 8000 post offices and 115,000 miles of postal route in the country – extending as far west as the Rocky Mountains.
Population The total population is 12,866,000, 8.8 percent of whom live in cities of 2500 or more. The center of population has moved to a point 19 miles southwest of Moorefield, West Virginia. More than one-fourth of the American people now live west of the Appalachian Mountains. Louisiana, Indiana, Mississippi, Alabama, Missouri, Kentucky and Ohio have a combined population of 3,700,000. Finally, more than one half of the people who live in what is called the Old Northwest are in Ohio, but there are still unsettled areas in that state.
Transportation About 200 steamboats are operating on the Ohio and Mississippi Rivers. The nation has 1277 miles of canals. Its 73 miles of railroad are mostly in New York and Pennsylvania.
Arts/Culture The frontier man first appears on the

stage in James K Paulding's *The Lion of the West*, performed at the Park Theater in New York City. The play has not survived, except for a speech that was printed in several periodicals. Timothy Flint publishes his last novel, *Shoshonee Valley*, which centers on pioneer ways and mores.

Life/Customs Morgan Neville writes 'The Last of the Boatmen' for *The Western Souvenir*, memorializing the frontier exploits of Mike Fink. Born at Fort Pitt in 1770, Fink had been an Indian scout and became known as 'the king of the keelboatmen' on the Mississippi and Ohio Rivers. The mythos of the American West is becoming explicit.

5 APRIL 1831
International The United States completes negotiations on a commercial treaty with Mexico; it appears that the two nations will be able to cooperate.

27 MAY 1831
Exploration Comanche Indians kill Jedediah Strong Smith along the Santa Fe Trail.

27 JUNE 1831
Indians An agreement is reached between Chief Black Hawk of the Sac (or Sauk) and General Gaines of the US Army. The tribe agrees to move west to the Mississippi River, but begins to starve when separated from their land.

AUGUST 1831
Ideas/Beliefs Joseph Smith chooses Independence, Missouri, as the Holy City of Zion for the Mormon Church.

OCTOBER 1831
Indians Indians of the Nez Percés and Flathead tribes arrive at St Louis from Oregon to learn more about the religion of the white man. This will lead to an increase in missionary activity.

OTHER EVENTS OF 1831
National In *Cherokee Nation v Georgia*, the Supreme Court rules that the Cherokee Indians are a domestic, dependent nation, not a foreign nation. This is another step in the government policy of relocating eastern Indians west of the Mississippi River.

International After clashes between California natives and Mexican soldiers, the Mexican Government sends a new governor, Manuel Victoria, to California.

Science/Technology Cyrus McCormick invents the mechanical reaper, which will revolutionize prairie farming.

Transportation The steamboat *Yellowstone* arrives at Fort Tecumseh – now Fort Pierre – on the Missouri River.

Finance Two hundred men and 100 wagons, carrying goods worth $200,000, make the journey to Santa Fe.

Arts/Culture James Ohio Pattie, who had trapped in the Taos (New Mexico) area, been to California and spent time in a Mexican jail there, returns to Kentucky and writes his *Personal Narrative* (which is edited by Timothy Flint). Parts of it seem fanciful, but recent evidence has established its basic veracity. For instance, Pattie says that in return for being paroled from the Mexican prison, he had vaccinated some 20,000 people in California in 1829.

Hawaii The native Hawaiians have become such dedicated Protestants that this year they drive out the Roman Catholic missionaries who have been here since 1827. Many of the Hawaiians who have converted to Catholicism will be imprisoned. It will be July 1839 before the Catholic French intervene.

6 FEBRUARY 1832
Transportation The first printed suggestion for a transcontinental railroad appears in *The Emigrant*, published in Ann Arbor, Michigan.

6 APRIL-2 AUGUST 1832
War In 1804 some Sauk and Fox tribal chieftains had accepted a treaty with the United States and ceded their lands east of the Mississippi. But Black Hawk, a Sauk chief since 1788, had refused to recognize the treaty (claiming, among other things, that the signators had been made drunk). Over the years some skirmishes had been fought by those adhering to Black Hawk's position, but by 1830 most of the Sauk and Fox Indians had moved west of the Mississippi. In 1831 another treaty was simply imposed upon the Indians still in the Wisconsin territory and Illinois to force them to leave. Now, in April 1832, Chief Black Hawk leads about 400 of his braves and their families back into Illinois. When he sees that few Indians are willing to rally to his cause, he sends an emissary to negotiate with the white man; the emissary is shot down, and the angry Black Hawk attacks a large force of white troops. This is the Black Hawk War, in which the youthful Abraham Lincoln and Jefferson Davis will have small roles. After this attack, Black Hawk leads his forces over into the Wisconsin Territory, while the US Army assigns General Henry Atkinson to command a force, largely of volunteers, that engages in several encounters with the Indians.

1 MAY 1832
Exploration Captain Benjamin Louis Eulalie de Bonneville leads a wagon train out of Fort Osage on the Missouri River. The caravan reaches the Columbia River and Bonneville explores the West for three years. Several place names there will commemorate his activities.

13 JULY 1832
Discovery Henry R Schoolcraft finds Lake Itasca in Minnesota, the source of the Mississippi River.

Yosemite Valley, California.

Chief Black Hawk of the Sauk tribe.

2 AUGUST 1832
War The final battle of the Black Hawk War takes place on the Bad Axe River in Wisconsin. Black Hawk is overpowered not only by Atkinson's forces, but also by a Sioux war party; he raises a white flag, but his enemies ignore this and massacre most of his people, women and children included. Black Hawk escapes and goes to hide among the Winnebago Indians. The war has ended.

27 AUGUST 1832
Indians The Winnebago Indians give Black Hawk over to the US authorities. He will be imprisoned for about a year, then released to live out his days (till 1838) with the remnants of his family and people in Iowa.

15 OCTOBER 1832
National Congress passes a measure authorizing the War Department to enlist mounted troops, known as dragoons, for use on the Western plains to protect caravans on the Santa Fe Trail.

25 OCTOBER-7 NOVEMBER 1832
Disease The first Asiatic cholera epidemic occurs in the United States. It appears in New Orleans, where 6000 people perish in this two-week period.

2 DECEMBER 1832
Mexican War: Approach Samuel Houston – a former governor of Tennessee who has been living among the Cherokee of Oklahoma – crosses the

Red River and enters Texas for the first time. On 13 February he had written his old comrade in arms, Andrew Jackson, now President, that the Texans are allegedly planning to draw up a constitution and seek statehood.

28 DECEMBER 1832
Education St Louis University, in St Louis, Missouri, charters under Roman Catholic (Jesuit) auspices. This is the first Catholic university west of the Alleghenies. Its first degree is awarded in 1834.

OTHER EVENTS OF 1832
Settling Hall Kelley, who has been propagandizing for settlement of the Oregon country, goes to California by way of Mexico. After joining Ewing Young in San Diego, Kelley proceeds to Oregon, where Dr John McLoughlin of the Hudson's Bay Company gives him a cold reception.,
International Governor Manuel Victoria of California returns to Mexico City, and the Mexican Government promises California a voice in self-government if it remains a territory within the Republic of Mexico. California agrees to the arrangement.
Westward Movement Massachusetts merchant Nathaniel J Wyeth – roused by Hall Kelley's booklet about the Oregon country – recruits young men to go West. From St Louis, they reach the annual fur trappers' rendezvous at Pierrés Hole in the Teton Mountains of Eastern Idaho. Wyeth eventually reaches Oregon, but finds that his planning is inadequate, and returns east.
Finance A Congressional report says that the Santa Fe trade has increased steadily for nine years, and that the 'circulating medium of Missouri now consists principally of Mexican dollars.'
Transportation The steamboat *Yellowstone*, owned by the American Fur Company, makes its way up the Missouri River to Fort Union at the mouth of the Yellowstone. Next year she will carry the German Prince Maximilian of Wied and the Swiss painter Karl Bodmer as far as Fort McKenzie, just east of the Great Falls. Maximilian's *Travels* and Bodmer's drawings preserve a picture of life on the upper Missouri. The Chicago Road, a military highway facilitating settlement of southern Michigan and upper Indiana, is completed. By 1840 Michigan will have 212,267 people, Indiana, 685,866. The north-central section of the country is filling up.
Exploration Mountain men of the Hudson's Bay Company make their way south through Oregon, over unmapped trails, to trap in the Sacramento Valley. They will do this annually until the fall of 1840, when John Sutter will inform James Douglas, the chief factor of the Hudson's Bay Company, that all hunting and trapping rights in the Sacramento were granted solely to him, Sutter, by the Mexican Government.

1832-1835
Exploration A Rocky Mountain trapping and hunting expedition is led by Captain Bonneville. The expedition discovers oil east of the Wind River Mountains in Wyoming and becomes the subject of Washington Irving's *The Adventures of Captain Bonneville* (1837).

JANUARY 1833
Ideas/Beliefs William Walker, an educated Wyandot Indian, writes a story about Indians living in the Oregon country who desire to learn about the white man's religion, according to the 'Book of Heaven.' Walker's story, published in the Methodist *Christian Advocate and Journal* on 1 March, incites missionaries to travel to Oregon.

4 MARCH 1833
National Andrew Jackson is inaugurated for his second presidential term.

1 APRIL-13 APRIL 1833
Mexican War: Approach A convention of Texan settlers at San Felipe votes to separate from Mexico.

OTHER EVENTS OF 1833
Settling Chicago is incorporated as a village. The Bent and St Vrain Fur Company builds a fort near present-day La Junta, Colorado. Bent's Fort (or Fort William) is used as a trading post for beaver skins, replacing the annual fur trappers' rendezvous. Noted frontiersmen, Kit Carson among them, will use Bent's Fort as a base for expeditions.
International Mexico's Secularization Act in California opens mission lands there to lay settlement. The main effect is that the ranch succeeds the mission as the focus of California life.
Westward Movement Settlement of the Iowa country begins with conclusion of the Black Hawk War, which opens the Black Hawk Purchase, a 50-mile-wide strip of land on the west bank of the Mississippi River.
Science/Technology Samuel Colt perfects a revolver and begins production of the weapon at Patent Arms Manufacturing Company in Paterson, New Jersey.
Transportation The pioneer clipper ship *Ann McKim*, built for speed, is constructed in Baltimore. It will carry emigrants from New York and Boston to San Francisco by way of Cape Horn.

3 JANUARY 1834
Mexican War: Approach Stephen F Austin is arrested and imprisoned by Mexican authorities for eight months after he presents resolves to Mexican President Antonio Lopez de Santa Anna. These resolves ask for separate statehood for Texas – apart from Coahuila.

APRIL 1834
Westward Movement Nathaniel J Wyeth leaves

Independence, Missouri, with the Rocky Mountain Fur Company. Upon reaching the Idaho rendezvous, Wyeth finds that the trappers will not buy his goods. The determined Yankee merchant builds Fort Hall on the Snake River between 15 June and 5 August.

30 JUNE 1834
Indians An Act of Congress establishes a Department of Indian Affairs, but it remains under the War Department until 1849.

14 SEPTEMBER 1834
Westward Movement Wyeth reaches the Pacific Coast just one day before his ship, the *May Dacre*, arrives bearing supplies. Wyeth builds Fort William on an island at the mouth of the Willamette River in Oregon.

16 SEPTEMBER 1834
Ideas/Beliefs The Reverend Jason Lee, a Methodist missionary, arrives at Fort Vancouver. He accepts advice from Dr John McLoughlin and sets up the first American farming settlement in Oregon near present-day Salem.

OTHER EVENTS OF 1834
Settling Forts Boise and Hall are built in present-day Iowa. Fur traders William Sublette and Robert Campbell establish Fort William, the first permanent trading post in Wyoming, at the site of today's Fort Laramie National Monument.
Westward Movement Some 80,000 people leave the city of Buffalo, New York, for the West by way of Lake Erie. The majority head for Michigan, which has become known as the land of opportunity. Their route will be smoothed by the opening of the Territorial Road, which facilitates settlement in southern Michigan.
Science/Technology Cyrus McCormick patents the early model of his reaper. In 1841 he will sell his first two machines.
Finance At the annual rendezvous at Ham's Fork of the Green River, it becomes apparent that the competition between the Rocky Mountain Fur Company and the American Fur Company has led to the Rocky Mountains being trapped out – the two companies have less than 80 beaver packs combined. The latter company buys out the interests of the former, but even so, the best days of the fur trade are over.
Territorial The area known as the Black Hawk Purchase is attached to the Territory of Michigan.
Exploration Joseph Reddeford Walker leads an expedition from Salt Lake down the Humboldt River. They cross the Sierra Nevada Mountains to the California coast, by way of the Walker Pass to the Mohave-Colorado basin. The expedition returns through the unknown Owens Valley. These are the first white men to see and describe the Yosemite Valley and the giant redwoods of the Tulumne Grove. They also find the first relatively

---

STEPHEN FULLER AUSTIN, 1793-1836

Perhaps it was Stephen Austin himself who best summed up his career when he said: 'My ambition has been to succeed in redeeming Texas from its wilderness state by means of the plough alone, in spreading over it North American population, enterprise, and intelligence. ... My object is to build up, for the present as well as for future generations.' He was, indeed, the man who virtually built Texas from wilderness. Austin was born in present Wythe County, Virginia, on 3 November 1793. Well-educated despite his frontier background, he was appointed as a young man to office in the territorial legislature.

In 1821 he followed his father in immigrating to Texas. By the next year he had taken Mexican citizenship and with that country's sanction founded the first Anglo-American colony. Soon he gained virtual dictatorial powers from Mexican authorities, and thereafter pursued his efforts at colonization with remarkable energy and skill: holding the Indians at bay, building services, keeping the stream of immigrants coming in without arousing the animosity of Mexico, and maintaining good relations with the United States as well.

As agitation grew for independence, Austin gradually shifted his stance from maintaining the tie with Mexico to favoring a semi-independent state. However, in 1835 he returned from frustrating negotiations in Mexico to find that revolution was growing beyond his control. When fighting broke out in the fall of 1835, Austin gave in to the inevitable and went north to negotiate with the United States about annexation. In 1836 he returned to the new Republic of Texas to be defeated by Sam Houston for its presidency. Austin served briefly as its secretary of state before his death at the age of 43 in December 1836. With strength of purpose and political acumen, he had helped populate a vast wilderness in America's Southwest.

---

easy route around the southern end of the high Sierra Mountains – Walker Pass.

30 JUNE 1835
War Texans led by Colonial William B Travis capture the Mexican garrison at Anahuac. Later, in the fall, other armed clashes will occur, and American settlers of Texas will grow increasingly resistant to the strong centralized government envisioned for them by Mexican President Santa Anna.

SEPTEMBER 1835
War Stephen Austin returns to Texas after being freed from a Mexican prison. Austin now favors war between Texas and Mexico as the only possible recourse for the American settlers in Texas.

OCTOBER-NOVEMBER 1835
Mexican War: Approach A convention of Texans rejects Mexican rule, favors self government, and claims the right of secession from the Republic of Mexico.

George Catlin's portrait of Keokuk, leader of the Sauk and Fox alliance.

24 NOVEMBER 1835
Territorial The provisional government of Texas authorizes creation of the Texas Rangers, which will be one of the earliest state police forces in the nation.

9 DECEMBER 1835
War The Texan Army, inspired by the courageous leadership of Colonel Benjamin Milan, captures San Antonio.

15 DECEMBER 1835
International President Santa Anna announces a constitution for all Mexican territories.

29 DECEMBER 1835
Indians A minority of Cherokee Indian leaders sign the Treaty of New Echota, in Georgia; the terms call for Cherokee surrender of lands east of the Mississippi and movement to the area that is now Oklahoma. Most Cherokee, led by Chief John Ross, will repudiate this treaty, but 'The Trail of Tears,' during the winter of 1838-9, makes relocation to the Indian Territory reservation inevitable. The Cherokee Nation gives up all its land in Georgia for five million dollars compensation. Meanwhile, the Seminole Indians of Florida have rebelled against their scheduled removal to the West, setting off the Second Seminole War. It will last until 14 August 1843, six years after the capture of Seminole leader Osceola.

JOSEPH REDDEFORD WALKER, 1798-1876

One of the lesser known of the great guides, explorers, and mountain men of his era – perhaps due to his modesty and solitary tendencies – Joseph Walker was a living exponent of the West that was his home. Born in Virginia in 1798, he was reared in Tennessee. By 1819 he was in Missouri, where he began over a decade of trading and trapping, with the Indians as his main companions.

The decline of the fur trade and increase in settlers brought Walker out of the mountains to become a guide. In 1833 Benjamin Bonneville sent him and a party of 50 men on an exploratory expedition west. From the Great Salt Lake, Walker and his party crossed Utah, Wyoming, and Nevada and became the first white men known to traverse the Sierra Nevada. From Monterey, California, they made their way back by another route to rejoin Bonneville in Utah.

From that experience, Walker became a guide to wagon trains en route to California; he guided John C Frémont's third expedition there in 1845-6. Walker revisited California with the Gold Rush of 1849, and for nearly two decades traded there. In this period he also discovered gold deposits near present-day Prescott, Arizona. His last few years were spent in quiet retirement in Contra Costa County, California, where he died in 1876.

CHRONOLOGY

OTHER EVENTS OF 1835
Indians Colonel Dodge of the US Army leads a party of Indians on an expedition on the Platte and South Platte and returns by way of the Arkansas River.

Finance Failure of the wheat crop in western farming areas causes a severe economic crisis, with a strain upon banking and lending facilities. The firm of Ladd and Company starts the first sugar plantation in Hawaii, on Kauai Island.

Ideas/Beliefs Samuel Parker and Dr Marcus Whitman go west for missionary work, parting at the rendezvous at Ham's Fork in Wyoming. Parker goes on but fails to establish a mission, and returns east by way of Honolulu in 1838. Whitman returns to New York State, where he marries Narcissa Prentiss and prepares to go west again in 1836.

23 FEBRUARY-6 MARCH 1836
War The siege of the Alamo is carried out by a Mexican Army, 6000 strong, led by Mexican President Santa Anna. The defenders refuse to surrender and are all killed when the fort falls. Well-known frontiersmen like Davy Crockett, Jim Bowie, and William B Travis end their trails at the Alamo.

2-4 MARCH 1836
War Declaration of Texan independence is made in Washington-on-the-Bravos, where David G Burnet is chosen as provisional president and Sam Houston as Army commander.

An isolated frontier settlement, drawn by Hervieu.

JAMES BOWIE, 1796-1836

The invention of a lethal-looking knife for hunting and fighting is an unusual claim to immortality, but 'Jim' Bowie is remembered largely for the weapon that bears his name. His real claim to greatness is in his contribution to Texas independence. Born in Logan County, Kentucky, in 1796, Bowie gravitated to New Orleans to pursue various trades – lumber, sugarcane, slave-dealing. Moving to Texas in 1828, he took on Mexican citizenship and acquired vast landholdings by the clever device of getting Mexicans to apply for free grants and then buying those grants cheaply. In 1831 he married the daughter of the Mexican vice-governor.

Bowie's connections with Mexico notwithstanding, he became active in the Texas independence movement: in the revolution that ensued, he proved to be a leader of great courage and strength (it was claimed that in earlier years he liked to rope and ride alligators). He ended up in the fatal Alamo siege of 1836, felled by a serious illness rather than the battle. As to his invention – tradition has it that Bowie cut himself while killing an Indian with a butcher knife. Thereafter he had a friend make him a big knife with a guard. Thus the Bowie knife – though it is as likely that it was his brother's invention. In any case, the knife became a treasured part of the equipment of Texas roughnecks for decades.

16 MARCH 1836
National Texas' revolutionary government sends George Childress and Robert Hamilton as commissioners to Washington, DC, but their authority is not accepted by the US Government.

27 MARCH 1836
War Three hundred and thirty defenders of Goliad, a Texan outpost, are captured and shot to death by order of Santa Anna. Although this episode never becomes as famous as the Alamo, 'Remember Goliad' becomes a rallying cry.

21 APRIL 1836
War Sam Houston's Texan force surprises and defeats the Mexican Army and captures Santa Anna at the Battle of San Jacinto. Texas' independence is now a reality through military victory.

1-4 JULY 1836
National A Congressional resolution calls for recognition of Texas, but President Jackson declines.

15 JULY 1836
National Arkansas becomes the twenty-fifth state, and the thirteenth that permits slavery.

SEPTEMBER 1836
Territorial Settlers of the Republic of Texas decide that they wish their area to become a part of the United States.

12 SEPTEMBER 1836
Settling Marcus Whitman reaches Vancouver, leading a party that includes the first white women to cross the North American continent. Whitman's wife, Narcissa Prentiss Whitman, and Eliza Spaulding have traveled from Utica, New York, since March. The Whitmans start a mission at Waiilatpu for the Cayuse Indians, while Henry and Eliza Spaulding establish one at Lapwai for the Nez Percés. By 1840 it becomes apparent that the three Indians who went to St Louis in October 1831 asking to learn about the white man's religion were not very representative of their fellow Indians in the Oregon area.

22 OCTOBER 1836
International Sam Houston is sworn in as the President of Texas and will serve until 1841. There is speculation that President Andrew Jackson and Houston have worked together secretly, but Jackson's wish was for a State of Texas within the United States, not an independent nation.

7 NOVEMBER 1836
International California declares independence from Mexico. Juan Bautista Alvarado becomes the governor, with the capital at Monterey. There is no military reaction from Mexico, which instead confirms Alvarado as the governor, opening an uneasy truce between Mexico and California.

OTHER EVENTS OF 1836
National A famous map, known as Albert Gallatin's map, is published in Washington. Significantly, the 'J E Smith Route' appears on it. Even

A nineteenth-century milliner displays her wares.

though Jedediah Strong Smith's trails are incorrectly traced, this is an indication that exploration of the Far West is being noticed.
Indians During President Jackson's two terms in office, 94 Indian treaties have been concluded under coercion.
Arts/Culture Washington Irving publishes *Astoria*. Based almost totally upon oral testimony, this book recounts the original attempt to settle Oregon in 1811-13.
Population Thirty thousand emigrants from the United States have arrived in Texas since 1821.
Science/Technology The steamboat *Beaver*, Hudson's Bay Company, goes from Fort Vancouver down the Willamette River, but cannot penetrate beyond the Dalles River.
Transportation Construction begins on the Illinois and Michigan Canal, which will connect Chicago with the Illinois River and the transportation on the Mississippi River system. There are now 1000 miles of railway track in 11 states.
Finance President Jackson announces that in the future public land will be sold only for hard money or notes of specie-paying banks. Between 1835-7, nearly 40 million acres are sold – three-quarters of them to speculators, the rest to settlers.
Territorial The Wisconsin Territory is formed from that part of the Territory of Michigan that lies west of the present-day state of Michigan. The Platte Country is purchased from the Indians and added to Missouri in 1837. The Indian Country now extends from Wisconsin to Arkansas.

CHRONOLOGY

WINTER 1836-1837
Finance William A Slacum, official agent of President Jackson, helps the settlers in Oregon to organize the Willamette Cattle Company, which raises money and sends Ewing Young to California to buy several hundred head of cattle. The object is to give the American missions economic independence from the Hudson's Bay Company.

26 JANUARY 1837
National Michigan becomes the twenty-sixth state, the thirteenth free state. It has a population of roughly 175,000, largely emigrants from New England and New York who have come since the Erie Canal was opened in 1825.

3 MARCH 1837
National As the last act of his presidency, Andrew Jackson recognizes the independent Republic of Texas. The President nominates Alcée La Branche of Louisiana as US chargé d'affaires to the Republic of Texas.

4 MARCH 1837
National Martin Van Buren is inaugurated the eighth president of the United States. He is the first US president to be born after the Declaration of Independence of 1776.

18 MAY 1837
Ideas/Beliefs The first Methodist reinforcements for the Oregon missions arrive by sea. Among the party are Anna Pitman, Susan Downing, and Elvira Johnson, who become the wives of Jason Lee, Cyrus Shepherd, and H K W Perkins, respectively.

SUMMER 1837
National Six thousand people cross the Sabine River into Texas by way of Gaines Ferry: the US recognition of Texas has dispelled fear of a possible reconquest by Mexico. Between 1836-46, the population of Texas rises from 30,000 to 142,000.

4 AUGUST 1837
National Texas petitions to be annexed by the United States, but the US Government refuses (25 August).

OTHER EVENTS OF 1837
Indians The people of Chihuahua, Mexico, adopt the notorious *Proyecto de Guerra*, which offers to pay $100 for the scalp of a male Indian, $50 for that of any squaw, and $25 for that of a papoose, to discourage Apache Indian raids upon the caravans on the Santa Fe Trail. This year the Sioux and Chippewa Indians surrender their claim to the St Croix Valley of Minnesota. A land boom follows, consisting of lumbermen and settlers from England.
Population Chicago, incorporated as a city, has 3000 inhabitants, but it has been laid out to

A wooding station for Mississippi steamboats.

accommodate 300,000. St Louis has 10,000 people, New Orleans, 60,000. There are 35,000 in Pittsburgh and 5000 apiece in Detroit and Cleveland.
Science/Technology Blacksmith John Deere invents the first plow with steel moldboard. This improvement upon wooden and cast-iron blades will revolutionize prairie farming.
Finance The Hudson's Bay Company purchases Fort Hall (Idaho) from Nathaniel J Wyeth.

1837-1840
Westward Movement A lumber industry begins operating in Minnesota and northern Wisconsin; the new market for crops induces farmers to move into the timber country.
Arts/Culture Alfred Jacob Miller, a painter from Baltimore, makes the first pictorial representations of such natural wonders of the West as Chimney Rock, Devil's Gate, Independence Rock, the Wind River Mountains, and the Tetons.

12 JANUARY 1838
Ideas/Beliefs Joseph Smith flees Kirtland, Ohio, to escape arrest after the failure of a Mormon bank. With his associate Sydney Rigdon, Smith relocates in the far west of the Missouri frontier.

23 MAY 1838
Arts/Culture Samuel Parker returns to Ithaca, New York, having traveled for two years and 28,000 miles, including a trip to Hawaii. Parker's *Journal of an Exploring Tour Beyond the Rocky Mountains*, published the same year, gives vivid and apparently accurate descriptions of Indians, buffalo, the gateway through the Rocky Mountains at South Pass, Wyoming, the mountains, the frontiersmen – whom Parker accuses of decivilizing the Indians – and the activities of the Hudson's

Bay Company in the Oregon country. Thus the pioneers of the 1840s will have foreknowledge of what the Far West is really like.

4 JULY 1838
Territorial The Iowa Territory is formed by separating off the western reaches of the Wisconsin Territory, with the Mississippi River as the border. The new territory includes all of present-day Iowa, most of Minnesota, and two-thirds of North and South Dakota. The capital is placed at Burlington temporarily; next year it is moved to Iowa City. The area is named for the Iowa River, which takes its name from the Iowa Indians.

WINTER 1838-1839
Indians The US Government is now actively engaged in forcing many Indian tribes east of the Mississippi, especially those in the southeastern United States, across the Mississippi to the western territories. Under the treaty of 1835, the Cherokees had allegedly agreed to go, but most have refused to do so. Therefore, the State of Georgia has obtained a court order for their removal, and US Army troops, commanded by General Winfield Scott, hero of the Mexican War, have been rounding up the Cherokees and driving them into concentration camps. In October and November, the troops lead the Indians westward in 15 detachments of about 1000 each. The journey from Georgia through Kentucky, Illinois, and Missouri to Oklahoma is made mainly on foot; as winter deepens, many of the Indians become sick and die. The logistics of the operation are mismanaged, with a shortage of food and constant pressure from the soldiers, who do not allow the Indians to minister to their sick or bury their dead properly. Some 4000 Cherokees die on what becomes known to them as the Trail of Tears. (About 1000 are able to escape removal and stay in the Great Smoky Mountains of North Carolina.)

OTHER EVENTS OF 1838
Arts/Culture Alexander Forbes, a Scot, publishes *A History of Upper and Lower California*, which receives favorable notice in the London *Times* and is widely read on both sides of the Atlantic. California is becoming a focus of both American and international attention.

11 FEBRUARY 1839
Education The University of Missouri charters in Columbia as the University of the State of Missouri.

11 APRIL 1839
International US citizens are granted arbitration rights on claims that they have against Mexico, in a treaty concluded in Texas.

SPRING 1839
Settling Thirteen men, led by Thomas J Farnham, leave Peoria, Illinois, and make their way to the Willamette Valley in Oregon with a train of pack horses. They are the advance guard of the settlers of the 1840s.

JULY 1839
Hawaii The Protestant missionaries have been very successful thanks to the patronage of Kamehameha III, who has been ruling since 1825. They have developed an alphabet for the Hawaiian language, translated the Bible into it, and founded many schools. They have considerable influence with the king – and have shown no tolerance for Roman Catholics. This month, the French frigate *L'Artémise* blockades Honolulu and threatens to destroy it unless all imprisoned Catholics are released and the Hawaiians extend religious freedom to all, including Roman Catholics. The Hawaiians accede.

AUGUST 1839
Settling John Augustus Sutter, a Swiss-immigrant trader, arrives in the upper Sacramento Valley, the first white pioneer in that area.

23 SEPTEMBER 1839
International France recognizes Texan independence, the first European nation to do so.

OTHER EVENTS OF 1839
International James Treat, confidential agent of the Republic of Texas, seeks to gain recognition of Texan independence and acceptance of the Rio Grande boundary between Texas and Mexico, but the Mexican Government refuses to negotiate with him.
Arts/Culture Ornithologist John K Townsend writes *Narrative of a Journey across the Rocky Mountains to the Columbia River*, based on his travel with Nathaniel J Wyeth in 1834.
Indians The infamous Trail of Tears takes Cherokee, Choctaw, Chickasaw, Creek, and Seminole Indians on a forced march from their lands in the south – Alabama, Georgia, Florida, and Tennessee – to the Indian country in present-day Oklahoma. Several thousand Indians die en route.

APRIL 1840
Mexican Policy Governor of California Alvarado arrests over 100 foreigners, most of them Americans, in California.

OTHER EVENTS OF 1840
Indians Forty thousand Indians from the Five Civilized Tribes are resettled in Indian Territory in Oklahoma by this time. Most of them are organized in self-governing republics with constitutions and laws.
Population The population of the United States is 17,069,453, up 33 percent since 1830. The center of US population is 16 miles south of Clarksburg, West Virginia.

CHRONOLOGY

Transportation There are 3326 miles of canals and 2818 miles of railroad track in the United States. (The figure for railroad miles is greater than that for all of Europe.)

Education There are approximately 50 colleges and universities west of the Allegheny Mountains; the student population of those institutions is around 5000.

Arts/Culture Richard Henry Dana publishes *Two Years Before the Mast*, with physical descriptions of the coast of California, giving many Easterners their first accurate knowledge of that area. George Catlin has visited more than 40 Indian nations from the Great Lakes to the Rocky Mountains (1832-40). He returns with over 500 oil paintings, which constitute a classic portrait of the West.

Hawaii The island kingdom becomes a constitutional monarchy and adopts a constitution based loosely on that of the United States. It calls for a supreme court and a bicameral legislature, the upper house being a council of chiefs and the lower an elected house of representatives.

4 MARCH 1841

National William Henry Harrison has campaigned for the presidency on his image as a 'man of the frontier': his campaign slogan was 'Tippicanoe and Tyler, too!,' from his role at the Battle of Tippicanoe, which pushed the Indians farther west. Today he is inaugurated as the ninth president, at the age of 68. However, Harrison catches a cold at his inauguration ceremony, which develops into pneumonia. One month later he is dead.

4 APRIL 1841

National John Tyler takes the oath of office as the tenth president of the United States. He is the first vice-president to succeed to the presidency upon the incumbent's death. As a Southerner, Tyler supports states' rights; as an expansionist, he will work toward the annexation of Texas.

6 APRIL 1841

Settling Joseph Smith, after being driven from Kirtland, Ohio, in 1838 and spending time in Missouri Territory, had moved to Nauvoo, Illinois, and made this town the center of his Church of Jesus Christ of Latter Day Saints. Today, he and his followers lay the cornerstone of a temple here. In the next few years, the town will come to have a population larger than that of contemporary Chicago.

4 SEPTEMBER 1841

National Congress passes the Distribution-Preemption Act, which will have the immediate effect of encouraging settlement of frontier territory. The act has two parts (the result of a compromise among various members of Congress). 'Preemption' refers to the original Preemption Act of 1830, which allowed settlers who had already cultivated public land to pre-empt it by purchasing up to 160 acres at $1.25 per acre; this becomes permanent law. 'Distribution' refers to the fact that 500,000 acres of public land in the western territories will be distributed to each new State for the construction of internal improvements; proceeds of the sale of pre-empted lands will also be distributed among the States. This distribution element will be repealed in 1842, but the net effect of the act of 1841 is to throw open much of the West to independent settlers, or squatters.

16 DECEMBER 1841

Westward Movement Senator Lewis Linn of Missouri seeks protection for settlers moving west along the Oregon Trail in his bill to construct forts along the trail. The bill would also offer land grants to males over 18 years of age.

OTHER EVENTS OF 1841

Settling The first large wagon train of settlers reaches Sacramento, California, via the Oregon Trail. There are 48 wagons in the train. Subsequent trips will have a more manageable number of vehicles. Father Pierre Jean de Smet opens St Mary's Mission in the Bitterroot Valley of Montana. It will close in 1850 and be sold to John Owen for use as a trading post. De Smet and Antonio Ravalli also set up missions among the Couer d'Alene Indians of Northern Idaho.

War An expedition from the Republic of Texas invades Mexican territory to enforce its claim on the land (New Mexico) westward to the Rio Grande. The invasion is repelled by Mexican soldiers.

Education Russians open a theological school in Sitka, Russian America (Alaska), the first attempt at higher education here. By 1849 the school assumes the status of seminary; in 1858 it is moved to Kamchatka, Siberia.

MAY 1842

Exploration Colonel John C Frémont of the US Army Topographical Corps heads the first of several expeditions through the West to open up new territory for development. On this first expedition, he surveys the Wind River chain of the Rocky Mountains in southern Wyoming, guided by a man he meets in the western territory, Kit Carson, who will also guide Frémont's 1843 and 1844 expeditions.

JULY 1842

Hawaii Two ambassadors from King Kamehameha III leave Hawaii for Washington, London, and Paris to obtain recognition and guarantees for the kingdom of Hawaii from the Great Powers, who are showing increasing interest in imposing their own authority.

9 AUGUST 1842

International Several outstanding border disputes between Britain and the United States are

JOHN C FRÉMONT, 1813-1890

As a leading explorer of the American Far West, John C Frémont was his own best publicist, but in his later military career he proved to be his own worst enemy. Born to a French emigré's family in Savannah, Georgia, on 21 January 1813, Frémont spent his early years in the South, where he was finally expelled from Charleston College. After that unpromising start, he pursued work as a teacher and then as a surveyor of the South and West.

In 1841 Frémont initiated both success and failure by marrying the daughter of the powerful Senator Thomas Hart Benton. Jessica Benton Frémont was to become an ardent promotor of her husband's interests and a collaborator in his writings. The senator helped get Frémont his first big expedition – to find the best overland route to Oregon. In 1842 Frémont took a party that included guide Kit Carson to the South Pass of the Continental Divide, ascending Frémont Peak en route. His report, read widely, laid the foundation of the great migration to Oregon.

The following year Frémont set out on an expedition to Oregon Territory, in the course of which he explored the Rockies, Great Salt Lake, Oregon itself, the Cascades, and the Sierra Nevada. Upon returning to St Louis in 1844, he was hailed by the nation: his account of the trip is a classic of American exploration. In his own time, Frémont was called the Pathfinder. An 1845-6 expedition explored the same area more fully, but ended in Frémont's expulsion from California by Mexican authorities. California was about to become a major field of the Mexican War.

In 1846 Frémont helped lead a premature revolt proclaiming independence from Mexico. In ensuing battles and machinations, he ran afoul of cavalry commander Stephen Watts Kearny, which resulted in Frémont's court-martial for insubordination in 1847. President Polk canceled his sentence. He became one of California's first senators in 1850-51, thereafter leading another expedition to the Pacific. In 1856 he ran for President on the first Republican ticket, against James Buchanan. Through Senator Benton's influence, he was named to several military posts during the Civil War. It was his downfall: leading parties on the plains and mountains, Frémont was magnificent; as a military and political leader, he was overly impulsive, high-handed, and slow to take direction. Two years into the war, he was maneuvered out of the army.

CHRONOLOGY

CHRISTOPHER 'KIT' CARSON, 1809-1868

Beginning as an illiterate trapper and mountain man, Kit Carson became in his own lifetime and thereafter a legendary Western guide. Born in Kentucky on 24 December 1809, Carson grew up in a stockade in Mississippi, where fear of marauding Indians was unremitting. In 1829 he joined an expedition across the Mohave Desert to California.

In 1831 Carson teamed up with Thomas Fitzpatrick, the renowned guide the Indians called 'Broken Hand,' on a trapping venture to the north. For over a decade, Carson was a trapper in the Rockies and environs, making the acquaintance of Jim Bridger, fighting Indians and rival trappers, and marrying an Arapaho woman who bore him a daughter.

In 1842 Carson met John Charles Frémont, 'the Pathfinder,' who enlisted him as a guide on his first two expeditions. During the Mexican War, Carson served in the army in California, guided Kearny's cavalry from New Mexico to California, and fought in the disastrous Battle of San Pascual. Arriving in Washington with despatches in the summer of 1847, he found himself famous, due largely to Frémont's writings.

Carson returned to Taos, New Mexico, and became Indian Agent there in 1853. Commissioned at the outset of the Civil War, he suppressed the native Apaches and Navahos in the area. At Adobe Walls, in Texas, Carson held off an attack of some 4000 hostile Indians with 400 men and two cannon. The last years of his life brought him to various military posts, during which he finally learned to read and write. An acquaintance called the mild but fearless Carson 'One of Dame Nature's gentlemen.'

resolved by signature of the Webster-Ashburton Treaty. Britain cedes the area south of a line from Lake Superior to the Lake of the Woods (where in 1866 the rich Mesabi iron deposits will be discovered). This treaty provides an important precedent for the resolution of similar border disputes between Britain and the United States.

11 SEPTEMBER 1842
War Mexican soldiers invade and capture San Antonio in the Republic of Texas. It is the beginning of several months of hostilities against this independent nation-state.

3 OCTOBER 1842
Settling American missionary Marcus Whitman leaves Oregon for Boston and Washington, DC, to generate public interest in his mission in the western territory and to encourage further settlement.

20-21 OCTOBER 1842
War Commodore Thomas ap Catesby Jones, commanding a fleet of the US Navy in the Pacific Ocean, seizes Monterey, the capital of the Mexican Province of California, when he hears that the United States and Mexico are at war. Catesby Jones had feared that the British would take advantage of the hostilities to seize California. He returns the post the following day when he learns of his mistake. Apologies and reparations are made to Mexico by President Tyler.

19 DECEMBER 1842
Hawaii The two Hawaiian ambassadors have been in Washington, DC, for about two weeks, when they receive a letter from Daniel Webster, secretary of state. It declares 'as the sense of the government of the United States, that the government of the Sandwich Islands [Hawaii] ought to be respected; that no power ought either to take possession of the islands as a conquest or for the purpose of colonization, and that no power ought to seek for any undue control over the existing government, or any exclusive privileges or preferences in matters of commerce.' Armed with this informal recognition of independence by the US Government, the two ambassadors soon set off for London and Paris. Meanwhile, various Americans have already assumed positions of some influence in the Hawaiian Government, and increasing numbers of American whaling ships are putting into Hawaii for supplies.

OTHER EVENTS OF 1842
Settling Some 130 people in 18 wagons leave Independence, Missouri, to join Whitman's mission in Walla Walla, Oregon.
Arts/Culture Theatrical burlesques become popular in America. Their repertories include parodies of frontiersmen, Indians, Irishmen, and Yankees.

3 FEBRUARY 1843
Territorial The Oregon Bill passes the Senate, but Senator Linn's bill to encourage migration to the Northwest Territories will die in the House.

25 FEBRUARY 1843
Hawaii Captain Lord George Paulet has been at Honolulu since 10 February with the British frigate *Carysfort*. He has threatened to attack the town unless certain demands made by the British in the islands are met. The Hawaiian king is powerless, so he signs today a provisional cession of the Hawaiian Islands to Captain Paulet as representative of the Queen of England. Captain Paulet justifies this on the grounds that a French fleet is on its way to take over the islands. A commission is to govern the islands, to which the king appoints as his deputy Dr Gerrit P Judd, an American medical missionary who plays an influential role in the royal government. The commission raises the British flag over all the islands and begins to set aside Hawaiian laws and to impose British rule. The king will send a trusted American on a ship to Mexico (11 March) with news of what the British are doing.

8 MAY 1843
National Secretary of State Daniel Webster resigns over the ongoing dispute about the annexation of the Republic of Texas.

10 MAY 1843
Hawaii Dr Judd, the Hawaiian king's deputy on the British-imposed commission running the government, resigns. Secretly, he takes government records and hides them in a royal tomb. He continues to work on behalf of Kamehameha III.

22 MAY 1843
Westward Movement The first of 1000 pioneers leaves Elm Grove, Missouri, bound for Oregon.

29 MAY 1843
Exploration John C. Frémont and guide Kit Carson set off for a second exploration of the West. They explore the Snake and Columbia River Valleys, as well as the San Joaquin Valley in California. The journey takes 14 months.

15 JUNE 1843
War A truce is declared between Mexico and the Republic of Texas.

JULY 1843
Territorial A convention in Cincinnati calls for adoption of a resolution to make 54° 40' the American line for the Oregon Territory; this would push the boundary north to encompass present-day Washington State.

5 JULY 1843
Settling Organic Law is adopted by settlers meeting in Champoeg, Oregon. The constitution, based on the laws of Iowa, will serve until the United States extends its jurisdiction, establishing the Oregon Territory.

24 JULY 1843
National President Tyler appoints Abel Upshur to succeed Daniel Webster as Secretary of State. Upshur favors annexing Texas.

31 JULY 1843
Hawaii British Admiral Thomas sailed from Mexico as soon as he heard of the action of Captain Paulet; on arrival in Honolulu, he tells the king that independence will be restored. The formal ceremony takes place today as the British flag is lowered and the Hawaiian flag raised. At an afternoon thanksgiving service, King Kamehameha III says '*Ua mau ke ea o ka aina i ka pono*' ('The life of the land is preserved by righteousness.'), which becomes the motto of Hawaii. The British Government will approve of Admiral Thomas's actions. Indeed, since the arrival of the two Hawaiian ambassadors in London in February 1843, the British have shown considerable willingness to guarantee Hawaii's independence; their primary concern is to make sure that the French do the same. Throughout the months between February and November, negotiations continue between the Hawaiian ambassadors and these two countries.

23 AUGUST 1843
National American officials are showing renewed interest in the annexation of Texas, as the Republic continues to develop alliances with Britain and other European countries. Mexico's President Santa Anna warns the United States that annexation would be tantamount to declaring war against Mexico.

16 OCTOBER 1843
National Texas President Sam Houston, concerned about losing Great Britain's support, refuses annexation negotiations with high-level US officials. Houston knows the Senate will not support the annexation, and he will not gamble his country's British alliance by encouraging such talks.

28 NOVEMBER 1843
Hawaii Representatives of the British and French Governments sign a joint declaration in London recognizing the independence of Hawaii and agreeing never to try to take possession of the islands. Although the United States did not go beyond Secretary of State Webster's letter of December 1842, this serves as official recognition: the first commissioner representing the US Government will soon arrive in Hawaii.

OTHER EVENTS OF 1843
Settling Famous trapper and guide James Bridger

CHRONOLOGY

Slave dealers plying their trade.

opens Fort Bridger on the Black Fork of the Green River in southwest Wyoming; it becomes an important way station on the Oregon Trail.
Arts/Culture William H Prescott publishes his *History of the Conquest of Mexico* in three volumes; he has spent four years writing this work.

16 JANUARY 1844
National Secretary of State Abel Upshur continues to push for annexation of Texas. Upshur asks the US representative to the Republic to assure President Houston that there is two-thirds-majority support in the Senate for an annexation treaty.

MARCH 1844
Exploration Frémont arrives at Sutter's Fort in Sacramento via the Sierra Nevada.

6 MARCH 1844
National John C Calhoun becomes secretary of state, replacing Upshur, who died 28 February in an explosion on the warship *Princeton.*

12 APRIL 1844
National The Republic of Texas moves closer to annexation when it signs a treaty with the United States ceding public lands in the Republic to the US, which extends $10 million to the Republic for assumption of public debts. The treaty, negotiated by Calhoun, goes to the Senate (22 April), where President Tyler urges its adoption.

24 MAY 1844
National 'What hath God wrought!' is the rhetorical question Samuel F B Morse relays over his invention the telegraph, when he sends his first message from Washington, DC, to Baltimore, Maryland.

27-29 MAY 1844
National American expansionism is formally expressed as the Democratic platform of presidential candidate James K Polk. The platform stresses 'reannexation' of Texas and 'reoccupation' of Oregon. The slogan 'Fifty-four Forty or Fight' asserts the US right to the land that will become the State of Washington. That land, north of Oregon, is at present occupied by the British by mutual agreement.

8 JUNE 1844
National The Senate rejects the proposed Texas treaty by a vote of 35-16. At the heart of the dispute is the issue of slavery: the anti-slavery forces in the Senate convince the majority that admitting Texas as a slave state will lead to another confrontation between North and South.

27 JUNE 1844
Ideas/Beliefs Joseph Smith, leader of the Church of Jesus Christ of Latter-Day Saints – the Mormons – and his brother, Hyrum, are killed by an angry mob, after being jailed in Carthage, Illinois. They had been accused of destroying the printing press of the Nauvoo *Expositor*, which was printing

stories critical of Smith's teachings on the Mormon practice of polygamy.

7 AUGUST 1844
Exploration Frémont returns to St Louis, Missouri, bringing maps and journals of his trips which, when published, will guide a generation of westward-bound settlers.

8 AUGUST 1844
Idea/Beliefs The leaders of the Mormon Church choose Brigham Young as their new leader and prophet; Young had hurried to Nauvoo, Illinois, from his missionary preaching in New England as soon as he heard of Smith's death. Hostilities between the Mormons and their neighbors will intensify over the next year, and Young will decide to move the Holy City of Zion still farther west.

1 NOVEMBER 1844
Territorial At a convention in Iowa City, voters adopt a constitution for Iowa, which is expecting statehood.

3 DECEMBER 1844
National President Tyler, in his annual message to Congress, suggests that Congress annex Texas by a joint resolution instead of trying to adopt a treaty. A Joint Resolution requires only a majority vote; a treaty requires two-thirds majority.

4 DECEMBER 1844
National James K Polk, with his frankly expansionistic platform, is elected President of the United States, defeating Henry Clay. Polk favors acquiring Texas, California, and Oregon as US territories.

12 DECEMBER 1844
National Anson Jones succeeds Sam Houston as President of the Republic of Texas.

OTHER EVENTS OF 1844
Science/Technology Babbitt's Best Soap, the first soap powder, becomes nationally known. Its inventor, appropriately, is Benjamin T. Babbitt.
Arts/Culture The forerunner of the popular Gold Rush song 'Buffalo Gals' is copyrighted by Cool White.

Benjamin Franklin Reinhart's idealized painting of a wagon train halting for the night.

CHRONOLOGY

23 JANUARY 1845
National Congress unifies national elections to the first Tuesday following the first Monday in November in all states.

25 JANUARY 1845
National By a vote of 120 to 98, the House of Representatives votes to annex the Republic of Texas in a Joint Resolution.

1 FEBRUARY 1845
Education The Texas Baptist Education Society receives a charter from the Congress of the Republic of Texas to open a college at Independence. The Institute merges with the University of Waco in 1886 to become Baylor University.

3 FEBRUARY 1845
National The House passes a bill to establish a government for Oregon with a northern border of 54° 40'. The Senate refuses to consider the bill because it would prohibit slavery.

27 FEBRUARY 1845
National The Senate passes the Joint Resolution on the annexation of the Republic of Texas by a vote of 27 to 25. The resolution is amended to provide for negotiating a new treaty, which may be presented as a Joint Resolution. The House passes the amended resolution on 28 February.

1 MARCH 1845
National President Tyler signs the Joint Resolution annexing the Republic of Texas, the first use of this procedure to acquire a territory or accept a treaty. Four states will eventually result from the Texas territory. In the new treaty, slavery is restricted to south of the Missouri Compromise line of 30° 30'; Texas will reserve its public lands and must pay its own debts.

4 MARCH 1845
National James Knox Polk, perhaps the most frankly and aggressively expansionistic president to date, is inaugurated. In his address he reaffirms his agenda, proclaiming that the United States has 'clear and unquestionable' title to Oregon and that the annexation of Texas is a matter between the Republic and the United States.

6 MARCH 1845
Mexican War: Approach The Mexican Minister to the United States, General Juan Almonte, in Washington, DC, protests President Polk's reference to Texas and demands his passport to leave the United States.

28 MARCH 1845
Mexican War: Approach The Mexican Government, in protest of the Texas annexation treaty, notifies US Minister Wilson Shannon that diplomatic relations have been severed.

Let this Poke manage two stools if he can, I'll cut my stick, and be off for the sunny south.

Dad ... I've lo... give me ...

Calhoun

Follow me brave soldiers, strike but one blow, and Oregon is ours!

MAY 1845
Exploration The third expedition to the West under John C Frémont begins.

25 MAY 1845
Hawaii The first meeting of the legislature is held in Honolulu.

28 MAY 1845
Mexican War: Approach President Polk sends US Army troops to the southwest border of Texas to guard the Republic against an invasion by Mexico. This signals a change in the US position. Polk, believing Texas will agree to annexation, decides to treat the Republic as a state.

11 JUNE 1845

Mexican War: Approach General Zachary Taylor is ordered to position his troops on or near the Rio Grande River, the disputed border of the Republic of Texas and Mexico. Taylor positions his troops on the south bank of the Nueces River, the border Mexico recognizes. By 31 July he will have 1500 untried troops at his side. The United States is interested in showing its support of the Republic to further the annexation treaty.

15 JUNE 1845

Mexican War: Approach Texas is formally guaranteed protection by US troops if the Republic consents to the terms of the treaty.

The newly elected President Polk watches calmly as expansionists threaten Oregon, Calhoun leaves the Cabinet and spoilsmen and reformers clash.

23 JUNE 1845

Mexican War: Approach A special session of the Republic of Texas Congress meets to vote for annexation to the United States.

4 JULY 1845

Mexican War: Approach A convention, called by President Anson Jones, meets in San Felipe de Austin to accept annexation of Texas by the United States under the terms of the Joint Resolution signed by President Tyler on 1 March 1845.

Springfield, Illinois, where Lincoln practiced law.

12 JULY 1845
National The British, who had been working steadily to get Mexico to recognize the independence of the Republic of Texas, are now faced with the Oregon boundary question. Secretary of State James Buchanan offers to extend the 49th parallel for the boundary. On 29 July British minister Sir Richard Pakenham refuses the offer. Months later he will ask the United States to reconsider.

27 AUGUST 1845
Mexican War: Approach At a constitutional convention, Texans adopt a formal state-oriented constitution.

30 AUGUST 1845
National President Polk, true to his campaign pledge of '54°40' or fight,' orders Secretary of State Buchanan to withdraw the US offer of the 49th parallel for the territory of Oregon.

16 SEPTEMBER 1845
Mexican War: Approach President Polk, with the support of his cabinet, is prepared to pay as much as $40 million to Mexico for the territories of New Mexico, California, and the land from the Nueces River south to the Rio Grande, the boundary preferred by Texans for their Republic.

OCTOBER 1845
Hawaii The first of several Organic Acts is passed, initiating reorganization of the government. Many native Hawaiians will object to the prominence of foreigners in the new government.

13 OCTOBER 1845
National Annexation and a new state constitution are approved by a majority of Texan-American voters.

17 OCTOBER 1845
Mexican War: Approach The US Consul in Mexico City, John Black, reports that the Mexican Government is willing to negotiate once the United States withdraws its naval ships from the coast of Vera Cruz. The ships are withdrawn immediately when Washington learns of the interest in negotiations.
National President Polk appoints Thomas Larkin US Consul in Monterey (California). Larkin has a secret mission to prepare the territory for annexation by the United States and also to block any foreign designs on the territory.

10 NOVEMBER 1845
Mexican War: Approach John Slidell, commissioned to negotiate a settlement with Mexico, receives amended instructions en route to Mexico City. He is to offer $5 million for New Mexico and $25 million for California, if Mexico agrees to the Republic of Texas boundary at the Rio Grande.

2 DECEMBER 1845
National President Polk, in his first annual message to Congress, reaffirms the Monroe Doctrine when he opposes any European colonization of North America. Enunciating what will become known as the 'Polk Doctrine,' the president also opposes any European attempt to maintain a balance of power. Polk specifically calls for an end to the joint occupation of Oregon.

6 DECEMBER 1845
Mexican War: Approach Slidell arrives in Mexico City and is informed on 16 December that the government will not receive him because his mission lacks the consent of Congress, his appoint-

ment has not been confirmed by the Senate, and the Mexican agenda is specifically limited to discussions of the boundary of the Republic of Texas. Slidell sends a report to Washington.

27 DECEMBER 1845
National British Minister Richard Pakenham asks the US Government to renew the 49th-parallel offer and submit it to arbitration. He is refused by President Polk.
Ideas/Beliefs The phrase 'manifest destiny' assumes a life of its own today when it is used in a New York *Morning News* editorial on the Oregon dispute. It originated in the July-August issue of *United States Magazine and Democratic Review*, where editor and founder John L O'Sullivan described foreign governments as trying to prevent the annexation of the Republic of Texas to stop 'the fulfilment of our manifest destiny to overspread the continent allotted by Providence for the free development of our yearly multiplying millions.' The phrase will spread, as it is picked up by elected officials and other journalists to justify all continental expansion.

29 DECEMBER 1845
Mexican War: Approach Texas becomes the twenty-eighth state of the union.

OTHER EVENTS OF 1845
Settling *The Report of the Exploring Expedition to the Rocky Mountains in the Year 1842 and to Oregon and Northern California in the Years 1843-44* is published by John C Frémont. The book will encourage a generation of pioneers to travel west.
Arts/Culture Caroline M Kirkland publishes a collection of short stories about Western life called *Western Clearings* under the pen name of Mrs Mary Clavers.

4 JANUARY 1846
Mexican War: Approach General Mariano Paredes, who overthrew the Herrera Government on 31 December, assumes the presidency. Paredes asserts the primacy of Mexico by announcing that he will defend all territories he regards as Mexican.

5 JANUARY 1846
National The House of Representatives passes a resolution to end the Anglo-American joint occupation of the Oregon Country, expressing 'the right of our manifest destiny to spread over our whole continent,' in the words of Massachusetts Representative Robert C Winthrop during the debate.

13 JANUARY 1846
Mexican War: Approach President Polk receives Slidell's December report and orders General Taylor to move his troops to the left bank of the Rio Grande River. Slidell's appointment is confirmed by the Senate on 20 January, but he is still refused

an audience in Mexico. In a second report to President Polk (dated 6 February), Slidell states that Mexican intransigence is founded in part on the belief that the United States will fight with Great Britain over the Oregon country.

27 JANUARY 1846
Mexican War: Approach Captain John C Frémont reaches Monterey, in Mexican California, during another exploratory expedition to the West. It is suspected, though still disputed, that he is under secret orders to prepare the territory for acquisition.

3 FEBRUARY 1846
Mexican War: Approach General Taylor receives his orders to advance to the Rio Grande. Heavy rains delay him until 8 March.

10 FEBRUARY 1846
Westward Movement Twelve thousand Mormons begin their exodus from Nauvoo, Illinois, led by Brigham Young. They travel to Council Bluffs on the Missouri River and wait there to learn of their final destination.

19 FEBRUARY 1846
National The State of Texas establishes its capital in Austin.

26 FEBRUARY 1846
National The British are asked to take the initiative if they want the 49th-parallel question reopened.

John Slidell, US negotiator with Mexico in 1845-6.

Expulsion of the Mormons from Nauvoo, Illinois, in September 1846.

CHRONOLOGY

24 MARCH 1846
Mexican War: Approach Taylor arrives at the strategic Point Isabel, just north of the mouth of the Rio Grande, to find that the Mexicans have burned the fort to the ground. His second in command, General William Worth, pushes on to the north bank of the Rio Grande.

27 MARCH 1846
National A bill to provide free homesteading in the Northwest is defeated in the House.

28 MARCH 1846
Mexican War: Approach Four thousand American soldiers under General Worth build Fort Texas; across the river, at Matamoros, 5700 troops under General Pedro de Ampudia fortify the town.

12 APRIL 1846
Mexican War: Approach General Ampudia warns Generals Taylor and Worth to retreat from Mexican territory and go back across the Nueces River; otherwise, 'Arms alone must decide the question.' Taylor refuses and asks instead for a US Navy blockade of the mouth of the Rio Grande.

24 APRIL 1846
Mexican War General Mariano Arista, replacing Ampudia, sends his cavalry 30 miles upriver with orders to cross to the north bank of the Rio Grande. The Mexican soldiers, about 1600, meet and surround a reconnoitering party of 63 American dragoons. Eleven Americans are killed, five wounded, and the remainder captured. On 26 April Taylor sends a message to President Polk: 'Hostilities may now be considered as commenced.'

27 APRIL 1846
National President Polk signs a joint resolution of Congress authorizing termination of the Anglo-American treaty of 1827 on the occupation of Oregon. It had passed both houses by 23 April. Polk now insists that the British make a formal proposal to fix the boundary at the 49th parallel.

1 MAY 1846
Mexican War General Taylor heads back to his supply base at Point Isabel and calls upon the governors of Texas and Louisiana to send a total of 5000 volunteers. The Mexicans cross the Rio Grande in force and lay siege to Fort Texas, under command of Major Jacob Brown (30 April to 3 May).

8-9 MAY 1846
Mexican War General Taylor is thrown into the Battle of Palo Alto, even as President Polk first hears about the 24 April skirmish. Taylor, who has hastened the construction of defense works at Point Isabel, is marching back to relieve Fort Texas. At the water hole called Palo Alto, on May 8, with some 2000 troops and 200 supply wagons, he meets 6000 Mexican soldiers blocking the route. The Mexicans are overpowered by superior

Gathering at a country store in Natchez, Mississippi, from a nineteenth-century engraving.

American weaponry: as many as 400 Mexican soldiers are killed, compared to about 9 Americans. Meanwhile, in Washington, Polk has called an emergency session of his cabinet (evening of 9 May) to seek support for a declaration of war.

11 MAY 1846

Mexican War 'Mexico has passed the boundary of the United States, has invaded our territory and shed American blood on American soil,' Polk tells Congress. In declaring war against Mexico, the United States is assuming legitimate the declared Rio Grande boundaries the Republic of Texas claimed for itself when it voted annexation as a state.

13 MAY 1846

Mexican War Congress authorizes $10 million and the recruitment of 50,000 soldiers when it votes to declare war on Mexico.

18 MAY 1846

Mexican War 'Old Rough and Ready,' as Taylor is now called, crosses the Rio Grande to occupy the Mexican town of Matamoros. Taylor's troops had chased the Mexicans out of a ravine just north of Matamoros in continued fighting on 9 May. In this fighting, during which the siege of Fort Texas was lifted, the Mexicans suffered severe losses even though they outnumbered the Americans, be-

Pictures like A Scene in the West *added to the attractions of frontier life in the 1850s.*

cause their weapons were old and inferior. Fort Texas is renamed Fort Brown to celebrate its commander.

3 JUNE 1846

Mexican War Colonel Stephen Watts Kearny, commanding 'the Army of the West,' is authorized to take possession of California with naval support from Commodore John D Sloat, who is to blockade Mexican ports in the Pacific and seize the San Francisco Bay. Commodore David Conner sets up blockades of enemy ports on the Gulf of Mexico.

14 JUNE 1846

California Rivalry among Mexican leaders helps foster 'the Bear Flag Revolt.' A handful of settlers takes over the city of Sonoma, led by William B Ide; they raise a flag with the emblem of a bear and declare the Republic of California, independent of Mexico. The group is joined by Frémont, who is chosen to lead the new republic on 5 July.

15 JUNE 1846

National The Senate consents to a new treaty with Great Britain abolishing co-habitation of the Oregon territory by the two countries and setting the US-British boundary at the 49th parallel.

CHRONOLOGY

7 JULY 1846
National Commodore John Sloat lands at Monterey and claims possession of California for the United States as he hoists the Stars and Stripes.
Mexican War General Santa Anna, in exile in Cuba, promises the United States he will help them win the war, co-operate in US wishes for a Rio Grande boundary for Texas, and even insist on a California boundary through the San Francisco Bay in return for $30 million and safe passage through the Gulf of Mexico blockade. He wins safe passage and goes back on his agreement by denouncing former President Herrera and leading an expeditionary force north to fight General Taylor's troops. All hopes of an early peace fade when Santa Anna is elected President of Mexico on 6 December.

9 JULY 1846
California Commander John B Montgomery seizes San Francisco and Lt James W Revere occupies Sonoma. The Stars and Stripes replace the Bear Flag, and Mexican infighting is interrupted by a common enemy. Within days, a US Naval party takes possession of Sutter's Fort on the Sacramento River. Mexican forces unite for a stand at Los Angeles.

24 JULY 1846
California The California Battalion is organized under Frémont. Occupation of Santa Barbara and Los Angeles is accomplished by 13 August.

15 AUGUST 1846
Life/Culture The first newspaper in California, the *Californian*, begins publication in Monterey.
Mexican War Colonel Kearny arrives in Las Vegas and announces annexation of New Mexico by the United States. By 18 August a temporary government is established in Santa Fe.

17 AUGUST 1846
California Commodore David Stockton announces that California has been annexed by the United States and establishes himself as governor.

19 AUGUST 1846
Mexican War General Taylor begins his month-long advance to the Mexican city of Monterrey with a force of 3080 regulars and 3150 volunteers.

14 SEPTEMBER 1846
Mexican War Santa Anna becomes Commander-in-Chief of the Mexican Army.

22 SEPTEMBER 1846
Mexican War One month after Stockton reports that 'peace and harmony' have been restored to California, Mexicans led by José Maria Flores revolt against US authorities and drive Americans from Los Angeles, Santa Barbara, San Diego, and other towns.

25 SEPTEMBER 1846
Mexican War After four days of fighting, General Taylor's army succeeds in taking the Mexican city of Monterrey. Estimated losses: US 120 killed, 368 wounded; Mexico 367 killed and wounded. Taylor consents to an eight-week armistice pledging no advances farther south unless the truce is broken. Colonel Kearny, with a reduced Army of the West, heads for California, leaving a temporary territorial government under Governor Charles Bent in New Mexico. On the trail, he runs into Christopher 'Kit' Carson just east of the Colorado River. Carson, unaware of the turn of events in California, is on his way to Washington to report the successful US occupation of the territory. Kearny, hearing the good news, sends 200 of his 300 dragoons back to New Mexico and continues west.

19 OCTOBER 1846
Mexican War The Mormon Battalion, no longer needed to help secure California as a result of the Bear Flag Revolt, is mobilized by Captain George Cooke to blaze a trail from Santa Fe to San Diego. Cooke chooses only the most fit for this arduous venture, selecting 397 of the original 500 recruited from the winter camp of the Mormons at Council Bluffs. Of the trek – which took almost two and a half months to complete, and required dismantling of the wagons to get them through a narrow gorge – Captain Cooke said, 'History may be searched in vain for an equal march of infantry.' At one point his men had to go for three days and two nights without water.

2 NOVEMBER 1846
Mexican War Word reaches General Taylor that President Polk is unhappy about the truce: Polk wants to keep the pressure on Mexico. Taylor informs Santa Anna that the truce will be terminated on 13 November.

NOVEMBER 1846-FEBRUARY 1847
Westward Movement The Donner Party, as it will become known from two of its prominent families (mainly from Illinois and Iowa), is snowbound on Alder Creek and what will be named Donner Lake in the Sierra Nevada. One of the group's 81 members, Patrick Breen, writes in his journal in November that 'No liveing (sic) thing without wings can get about.' At Fort Bridger, in July, the group had decided to take what seemed to be a more expeditious route to California. Described in the *Emigrants' Guide*, by Lansford W. Hastings (1843), as the Hastings Cut-off, the route has proven to be cruelly difficult. By October the party is caught by early snow. Dissension and ill will divide the party: one group will try to proceed through the passes in December, but will suffer terrible losses. The remaining members begin to eat the flesh of those who die. It will be 19 February 1847 before the first of several rescue expeditions from the Sacramento Valley reaches the survivors

near Truckee Pass. Of the original 89 who had set out in July, only 45 come down from the mountains alive.

16 NOVEMBER 1846
Mexican War General Taylor captures Saltillo, the capital of Coahuila.

25 NOVEMBER 1846
Mexican War Colonel Kearny crosses into Southern California, where Flores' insurrection is in progress, unaware of the situation there. Kearny's men defeat the Mexicans at the village of San Pascual on 6 December and move to occupy San Diego on 12 December.

12 DECEMBER 1846
National The United States signs a treaty with the Republic of New Granada (Colombia) establishing commercial access across the important Isthmus of Panama, which connects the Atlantic and Pacific Oceans. The US guarantees the sovereignty of New Granada and the neutrality of the isthmus. The Senate will consent to the treaty on 3 June 1848.

28 DECEMBER 1846
National The non-slave state of Iowa joins the Union as the twenty-ninth state.

29 DECEMBER 1846
Mexican War General Taylor occupies Victoria, the capital of the Mexican state of Tamaulipas. Kearny and Stockton leave San Diego with 559 dragoons, sailors, marines, and volunteers to march north toward Los Angeles.

OTHER EVENTS OF 1846
Hawaii The Board of Commissioners to Quiet Land Title begins its deliberations on how to divide the Hawaiian Islands among the king, the chieftains, and the commoners – in effect, how to abolish the feudal system, under which most of the land has always been regarded as the property of the king. What is estimated as a two-year job ends up taking some nine years, but the commission will finally accomplish what is known to Hawaiians as The Great *Mahele* (division). Essentially, it is a clearing of land titles through payment of fees (as late as 1906, there will still be negotiations over such clearance). Although commoners are allowed to purchase the land they have been working as tenants, relatively few do so at first. One of the more immediate effects of the *mahele*, in fact, is that it allows non-Hawaiians to purchase land.
Arts/Culture *Mince Pie for the Millions*, the first collection of 'tall tales' from the frontier, is published anonymously. It contains stories like 'A Sensible Varmint,' about Davy Crockett and the 'rakkoon.' Such tales will become very popular components of American folklore and increase the attraction of the frontier.

3 JANUARY 1847
Mexican War General Winfield Scott, backed by President Polk, orders the transfer of 9000 of General Taylor's men to join Scott in an expedition against Vera Cruz. Polk, largely because of the truce called last fall, is convinced that Taylor cannot bring the war to a successful conclusion; thus he backs Scott's proposal to attack Vera Cruz. Taylor, who knows he is considered a presidential candidate by the Whig Party, is suspicious of military intrigue backed by the Democratic Polk.

10 JANUARY 1847
Mexican War Kearny, Stockton and their small army retake Los Angeles, which ends fighting between Mexicans and Americans in California.

13 JANUARY 1847
Mexican War The Treaty of Cahuenga, giving generous terms to the defeated Mexicans, is signed in the San Fernando Valley with Captain Frémont representing the United States and Andres Pico, Mexico.

16 JANUARY 1847
California Confusion over orders leads to a conflict about setting up the civil government of California: both Stockton and Kearny think they should be responsible. Frémont is appointed governor by Stockton, who relieves Kearny of all command duties except those involving his dragoons. Kearny warns Frémont that he is guilty of disobedience to a superior officer.
National The Oregon Bill passes the House. It excludes slavery through restrictions in the Northwest Ordinance and will be tabled by the Senate.

20 JANUARY 1847
Mexican War A bloody rebellion occurs in Taos, New Mexico, where Mexicans, angry at the way bored American soldiers are behaving and at the lack of respect they have received, attack Governor Bent at the home he is visiting. First the sheriff and guards are killed, then the governor. His mangled body, paraded through the streets, becomes an open invitation to retaliation. By the end of the evening, 15 Americans are dead, and many flee to Santa Fe to sound the alarm. By 4 February, with more bloodshed, the rebellion is quelled.

5 FEBRUARY 1847
Mexican War General Taylor refuses to communicate with General Scott, as he has been ordered to do by President Polk. Instead, Taylor goes west from Saltillo, 18 miles to Agua Nueva.

13 FEBRUARY 1847
California General Kearny receives fresh orders confirming his mandate to set up the government of California, which he announces will be located in Monterey. Frémont refuses to give up his governorship in Los Angeles.

CHRONOLOGY

15 FEBRUARY 1847
Mexican War The House passes a bill authorizing $3 million for negotiations with Mexico in anticipation of an end to the war. Attached to the bill is the Wilmot Proviso, which would ban slavery from the territories acquired from the war. In the end (3 March), and after much debate, the Senate version, without the Proviso, will become law.

18 FEBRUARY 1847
Mexican War General Scott establishes his headquarters at Tampico to prepare for the battle of Vera Cruz.

22-24 FEBRUARY 1847
Mexican War Santa Anna, with 15,000 men, demands an unconditional surrender from General Taylor with his 4800 troops just three miles north of the hacienda of Buena Vista. Taylor refuses, and the battle of Buena Vista, which will end in American victory, ensues. Santa Anna returns to Mexico City to take the oath as President of Mexico. The war in northern Mexico is over, but Taylor remains in command of the forces there until he is relieved, at his own request, in November.

28 FEBRUARY 1847
Mexican War Colonel Alexander Doniphan, with his regiment of Missouri Mounted Volunteers, defeats the Mexicans in the Battle of Sacramento (Mexico) on his way to the state of Chihuahua to join and support General Wool. The pressure against Santa Anna intensifies.

9 MARCH 1847
Mexican War The first amphibious invasion in US military history takes place when General Scott's troops land on the beaches south of the city of Vera Cruz. The expedition had been delayed by an outbreak of smallpox among Scott's troops. Inside the fortress, 5000 Mexican soldiers wait. Two weeks are spent building fortifications on the beach, and a Mexican demand for surrender is turned down on 22 March. By 29 March, the city is under US occupation and Scott is looking toward Mexico City.

8-17 APRIL 1847
Mexican War Scott leaves Vera Cruz and is stopped at Cerro Gordo by Santa Anna's men on 9 April. During the battle of 17 April, US Engineer officers Captains Robert E Lee and George B McClellan provide distinguished reconnaissance. By 15 May, Scott and his victorious army are within 80 miles of Mexico City.

16 APRIL 1847
Settling Brigham Young, Prophet of the Church of Jesus Christ of Latter-Day Saints, leads a small group of Saints (Mormons) from Council Bluffs to their new Zion – the Great Salt Lake Basin.

31 MAY 1847
California Kearny attempts some resolution of the conflict over civilian leadership in California when he appoints Colonel Richard B Mason governor and travels to Washington with Frémont.

6 JUNE 1847
Mexican War A hopeful President Polk authorizes Nicholas P Trist to negotiate a truce with the Mexican Government of Santa Anna. However, British Minister Charles Bankhead's services are required as liaison between Trist and General Scott before any discussions are held with the enemy. Scott regards the Trist mission as an invasion of his business, and armistice as a military question.

22 JULY 1847
Settling Although their leader is sick with 'mountain fever,' the 143 Mormon Saints push on, hacking a path through the canyon wide enough for their wagons with picks and shovels. On the other side of the Wasatch Range, the group sees 'a broad and barren plain hemmed in by mountains, blistering in the burning rays of the midsummer sun. On all sides, a seemingly interminable waste of sagebrush ... the paradise of the lizard, the cricket and the rattlesnake,' according to one witness. Earlier on their travels, the trapper Jim Bridger had suggested a more hospitable place; seeing their determination he had offered $1000 for the first bushel of corn raised from the desert. Brigham Young's wagon will arrive on 24 July. Legend has it that he raised himself on his elbow and, pointing to the arid expanse, said 'This is the place.' Thus was the State of Deseret (later Utah) established.

27 AUGUST 1847
Mexican War Peace talks begin between Trist and former Mexican President Herrera, after an armistice is declared by Scott. By 7 September, Mexicans have rejected the terms proposed and the truce is ended.

8 SEPTEMBER 1847
Mexican War General Worth's army of 3447 is deployed to Molino del Rey for what was supposed to be a diversionary attack. After a serious day-long battle, Worth's forces retreat: US losses, 117 dead, 653 wounded; Mexican losses, about 2000 killed and wounded, some 700 captured.

11 SEPTEMBER 1847
Arts/Culture 'Oh, Susanna' by Stephen Foster is performed for the first time at the Eagle Saloon in Pittsburgh. The song will be carried West, with gusto, by the '49ers.

13-14 SEPTEMBER 1847
Mexican War After hacking their way through the walls around Mexico City and fighting past

becoming a journeyman house painter and glazier. Encountering *The Book of Mormon* soon after its publication, Young studied the book assiduously for two years before joining the new Church of Jesus Christ of Latter-Day Saints. He was soon given important responsibilities, leading a group to Ohio in 1833 and traveling around the eastern United States and later England as a missionary. After going to Missouri with Smith, 'the Prophet,' to challenge the Mormon persecution there, Young became a senior member of the administrative body called the Twelve Apostles. In the wake of Smith's murder by an Illinois mob in 1844, it was inevitable that the fiery Young would take over leadership of the Church, rallying the devastated congregation, leading an exodus to Nebraska and, in 1847, bringing a vanguard of 148 to their 'promised land' at Great Salt Lake, Utah.

For the next three decades, Young led the community in the authoritarian style of Smith, but unlike the founder, he was a pragmatist, not a visionary. Young brought in new settlers by the thousands, organized farming and business operations, consolidated control of the entire territory, irrigated the desert, created what became the University of Utah, and laid the foundations of an enduring economic organization.

The genius of Young was to turn even hardship and persecution to the Church's advantage. During two decades of hostility with the US Government, Mormon solidarity increased. The Utah Territory was created in 1850, posing a threat to Mormon independence and Young's dictatorial power. When a US Army expedition under Johnston arrived in Salt Lake City in 1858, the Mormons were gone, and the party had to occupy an empty capital. Soon Young and his people returned, with their power undiminished.

Determined as he was in public, in private Young was a genial man, not at all averse to merrymaking – which must have been an asset in a family that numbered, in that polygamous era of Mormonism, some 27 wives and 56 children. By the time Young died in Salt Lake City in 1877, the Mormon community numbered 140,000; it would continue to thrive into the twentieth century, and remains an influential force in American life..

BRIGHAM YOUNG, 1801-1877

The fact that the Mormon Chuch survived and even prospered through the extraordinary rigors of its first decades was largely due to the indomitable will of Brigham Young, who forged a community out of the visions of its founder, Joseph Smith. Young was born into an indigent farming family in Whitingham, Vermont, on 1 June 1801 and soon moved with his family to the Revival-charged atmosphere of western New York State. He grew up virtually uneducated,

several fortresses in their path, Scott's troops raise the American flag over 'the halls of Montezuma.' For the second time in US military history, Scott issues a military order – General Order No. 20 – that establishes a military government and orders of discipline for soldiers and citizenry.

22 NOVEMBER 1847

Mexican War With Santa Anna out of the country, interim President Pedro Maria Anaya signals Trist that the Mexican Government is interested in talking peace based on the original terms proposed in late August.

29 NOVEMBER 1847

Settling The usual fate of the medicine man who lost a patient was death: so it is that missionary Marcus Whitman, Narcissa, his wife, and others are killed at their mission near Walla Walla. An outbreak of measles among the Cayuse, brought by settlers travelling west, could not be cured.

6 DECEMBER 1847

National Abraham Lincoln takes his seat in the House of Representatives as the new Congressman from Illinois.

OTHER EVENTS OF 1847

Science/Technology Cyrus McCormick opens a new reaper factory in Chicago.

Settling The American Fur Company establishes Fort Benton in northern Montana, at the head of the Missouri River.

Agriculture George Page patents his revolving disc harrow, an implement that will prove a boon to farmers faced with the back-breaking task of cultivating the prairie sod of the Nebraska and Kansas Territories.

MARCUS WHITMAN, 1802-1847

Marcus Whitman and his fellow Protestant missionaries pursued their work among the Indians with unquenchable determination, but events beyond their control turned their zeal into martyrdom. Whitman was born in Rushville, New York, on 4 September 1802, and was trained as a doctor. After years of practicing medicine, he followed his conscience to become a missionary to the Indians of the Northwest. He and his wife, Narcissa, also a missionary, traveled to Oregon with a party that reached the Walla Walla River in 1836. Narcissa and another missionary wife were the first American women to reach Oregon overland.

Establishing a series of mission stations in Oregon and Idaho, the group settled down to converting, teaching, and civilizing the Indians. Things went well until 1842, when internal dissension threatened the work. Whitman thereupon made his legendary 3000-mile ride to Boston to arouse public interest in continuing the work of the missions. He returned to Oregon to find that tensions with the Indians had increased. Matters came to a head with the outbreak of a measles epidemic in 1847. Concluding that Whitman had somehow caused the disease, the Cayuses brutally massacred the Whitmans and 12 others in November. The result was the collapse of the missions and a war of vengeance against the area's Indians. The Whitmans' efforts had come up against the tragic cycle of violence and retribution in Indian-white relations.

---

24 JANUARY 1848
Westward Movement Gold is discovered at Sutter's Creek, a branch of the American River in the lower Sacramento Valley. New Jersey mechanic James Marshall, building a sawmill for John A Sutter, makes the discovery. As word spreads throughout the year, the prospect of riches renews the impetus toward Western settlement. Stories of the Donner Party, the fate of the Whitmans, and dejected pioneers who turned back defeated had slowed interest. By late 1849, the population of California will have grown by 100,000.

31 JANUARY 1848
National For his conduct in California, John C Frémont is found guilty of mutiny, disobedience, and prejudicial conduct by a court-martial that deliberates for two months. President Polk approves the sentence, except for the charge of mutiny, but cancels the penalty and orders Frémont restored to duty. Frémont, however, resigns his commission.

2 FEBRUARY 1848
Mexican War The United States and Mexico sign the treaty of Guadalupe Hidalgo, ending the Mexican-American war. The United States gets the territories of New Mexico, California, and the Rio Grande border of Texas, an addition of 1,193,061 square miles 'for our yearly multiplying millions.' The US agrees to pay $15 million for the land and assumes payment of $3.25 million in claims Americans have brought against Mexico. The Senate consents to the treaty in March, but without the Wilmot Proviso – slavery is left an open question.

APRIL 1848
National The Pacific Mail Steamship Company is founded to deliver mail to the West by way of the Isthmus of Panama.

29 MAY 1848
National Wisconsin – a non-slave state – becomes the thirtieth to join the Union.

MAY 1848
Agriculture Clouds of seagulls sweep in to feast on the crickets that are consuming the second crop of some 4000 Mormons in Zion. This is seen as a sign from Providence, but the Saints are admonished by their leader for relying too much on God and too little on their own efforts. Irrigation work begins this year, and Young institutes an organizational plan integral to the settlement's survival and eventual prosperity.

14 AUGUST 1848
National The territory of Oregon is formally organized when Polk signs the Oregon Bill. The debate in Congress surrounds the question of

---

JOHN AUGUSTUS SUTTER, 1803-1880

It was John Sutter's peculiar fate to see the outbreak of the Gold Rush in his own yard, and thereafter to see it drive him from wealth to bankruptcy. Sutter was born in Baden, Germany, on 15 February 1803. He emigrated to the United States at the age of 31 and ended up in California in 1839. With energy and enterprise, he wooed the Mexican authorities there and built his own almost baronial estate, complete with fort, livestock, fields, and a small army of workers. With status as a Mexican citizen and minor official, Sutter presided over his estate with almost complete power. He was a benevolent dictator, however, and a friend to settlers coming over the Sierra.

So it went until 1848, when Sutter's little empire began to crumble before his eyes. One of his hands, who was building a sawmill on the property, discovered gold. Galvanized by that immemorial glitter, events followed fast. Within a few days, Mexico had ceded California to the United States in the wake of the Mexican War. Shortly thereafter, the discovery at Sutter's Mill had triggered the great Gold Rush of 1849. Meanwhile, despite Sutter's support of statehood, authorities contested his Mexican land title, giving him no recourse when hordes of prospectors squatted on his property. Within four years he was bankrupt. He began a long and unsuccessful struggle with state and national authorities to gain compensation for his loss, and clear title to his property, but he was consistently blocked in his efforts. Still petitioning, he died in Washington in 1880, one of the saddest victims of gold fever.

slavery, not only in Oregon, but throughout the territories newly acquired from Mexico. Attempts to have the Missouri Compromise line extended to the Pacific fail, and the bill the President signs prohibits slavery only in the Oregon Territory.

19 AUGUST 1848
Life/Customs The news is spreading: today reports in the *New York Herald* describe the discovery of gold at Sutter's Mill, California.

7 NOVEMBER 1848
National Mexican War hero Zachary Taylor is elected president; his running mate is Millard Fillmore. True to his statement of four years ago, Polk has declined a nomination from his Democratic Party. The issue of slavery – specifically, who has the right to decide whether an area will hold slaves – dominates the national discussion.

5 DECEMBER 1848
National President Polk takes the opportunity, in his last annual message to Congress, to confirm the discovery of gold in California.

OTHER EVENTS OF 1848
Immigration The first group of Chinese immigrants reaches San Francisco on board the *Eagle*. By 1852 about 18,000 Chinese will have immigrated to the United States.

12 FEBRUARY 1849
National San Franciscans gather to set up a temporary government for their region. The need for an established authority will become more pressing as thousands arrive to search for gold.

28 FEBRUARY 1849
Westward Movement The *Californian* docks in San Francisco Bay with the first load of gold hunters. Thousands more are on the way, from as far off as Australia, to seek their fortunes.

3 MARCH 1849
National Congress establishes the Home Department (Department of the Interior) to set policies on public lands, settlement and Indians. The Bureau of Indian Affairs is transferred into it from the War Department.

5 MARCH 1849
National Zachary Taylor is inaugurated – the third Whig President – with his vice-president, Millard Fillmore. Taylor is the twelfth President of the United States.
Territorial A convention of all citizens in 'Upper California east of the Sierra Nevadas' is called in Salt Lake City to discuss organizing a territorial government. The need for a secular organization becomes apparent to Church President Brigham Young, as the number of gentiles (as all non-Mormons are called) increases in the city and the

territory. Salt Lake City is on one of the main routes to California.

10 MARCH 1849
Territorial The Mormons vote to form the State of Deseret, with boundaries set and provision for elections. The new state will support the US Constitution.

2 JULY 1849
Territorial The legislature of the State of Deseret meets to elect a delegate to Congress and adopts a resolution petitioning Congress for admission into the Union as a state.

1 SEPTEMBER 1849
National A constitutional convention convenes in Monterey, California. A resolution prohibiting slavery is adopted as part of the constitution, which will be ratified by popular vote on 13 November, when the 'state' requests admission to the Union.

4 DECEMBER 1849
National In his first annual message to Congress, President Taylor urges admission of California to the Union. Congress remains at odds over the issue of slavery. Southern Congressmen resist the idea of another free state – which will leave the slave states in a minority. Secession is mentioned as a possibility.

BENJAMIN L E DE BONNEVILLE, 1796-1878

Benjamin Louis Eulalie de Bonneville came to America from his native France to pursue a dream of America as a place of unlimited opportunity and high adventure. In a lifetime of soldiering and exploration, however, Bonneville was to find more notoriety than real success. Born near Paris on 14 April 1796, Bonneville gained from his family democratic ideals and the friendship of the Marquis de Lafayette and Thomas Paine. He followed Paine to the United States in 1803, attended the Military Academy at West Point and was assigned to Fort Smith, Arkansas Territory, in 1821.

After years of routine service in the West, Bonneville took an extended leave to pursue fortune and adventure in the fur trapping business. Funded by John J Astor and others, Bonneville headed into the Wyoming mountains with a large company in 1832. Due to general inexperience, this endeavor proved fruitless. Bonneville returned to military service in 1835 to find himself cashiered for overstaying his leave. After his restoration to military command, he went on to fight with distinction in the Mexican War, becoming a lieutenant colonel. Despite failing health, he was also an active commander in the Civil War. Bonneville died at Fort Smith in 1878. His primary fame came from his travel journals, which were edited and published by his friend Washington Irving. Historians have tempered Irving's glowing portrait of Bonneville as an explorer, while agreeing that he was an effective officer and a true friend of the Indians.

CHRONOLOGY

20 DECEMBER 1849
California With the population increased by 100,000, the need for civil order is intense. In San Francisco and other communities, vigilante committees form to take these matters in their own hands.
National A treaty of amity, commerce, and navigation is concluded between the islands of Hawaii and the United States in Washington, DC.

OTHER EVENTS OF 1849
Arts/Culture *The California and Oregon Trail*, by Francis Parkman, is published, a recollection of the author's trip in 1846. This book becomes a classic of Western literature.
Settling Mormon Station is settled in Nevada, one of many settlements established by Brigham Young to offer succor to Mormon converts arriving from nations around the world. Founded in the Carson Valley of Nevada, it will be called Genoa after 1855. It is the first white settlement in the state.
Transportation The Pacific Railroad is chartered in Missouri with plans to link St Louis and Kansas City. A stagecoach line opens to carry mail between Independence, Missouri, and Santa Fe, New Mexico.
National The US Government buys Fort Laramie, a fur trading post, to convert it into an army post.

29 JANUARY 1850
National Senator Henry Clay of Kentucky offers eight resolutions, the Compromise of 1850, in an attempt to organize the territories while still dealing with the tortuous issue of slavery. The resolutions include admitting California as a free state and allowing territorial governments for New Mexico and Utah without reference to slavery. By the Compromise's terms, the boundaries of Texas would be adjusted and the United States would assume Texas' public debt. The last resolutions involve slavery: that the fugitive slave law would be strengthened, but no slavery would be allowed in Washington, DC.

10 FEBRUARY 1850
Transportation The Illinois Central Railroad is chartered with a grant of 2.7 million acres of land from Cairo to Galena, by Governor Augustus C French.

12 MARCH 1850
California California requests statehood.

15 APRIL 1850
National The Senate consents to the Clayton-Bulwer treaty. It guarantees that neither the United States nor Great Britain will ever fortify or control the proposed Nicaraguan Canal. In the end, American diplomats had more interest in the canal (to facilitate east-west travel) than did American investors, for the canal is never built.

8 MAY 1850
National Clay's resolutions go to a committee made up of seven Whigs and six Democrats. The result is two compromise bills, an 'Omnibus bill' covering the territories and a second bill prohibiting slave trade in the nation's capital.

25 MAY 1850
Territorial The New Mexican Convention adopts a state constitution establishing its boundaries and prohibiting slavery.

3-10 JUNE 1850
National A convention of the 'slave' states advocates extending the Missouri Compromise line to the Pacific. This would include the Southwest and Monterey (southern) California in the area open to slavery. The irony is that the land involved is primarily suited for cattle grazing and ranching, activities that are incompatible with slave labor.

1 JULY 1850
Transportation The first overland mail service west of the Missouri River is established, with monthly deliveries between Independence, Missouri, and Salt Lake City, Utah.

8 JULY 1850
Population In the overland gold rush to California, over nine-tenths of the population is male. By 1859 the ratio of men to women will be 6:1.

9 JULY 1850
National President Zachary Taylor dies of Asiatic cholera, which is sweeping the nation. Travelers going west for gold die by thousands and are buried along the trail.

10 JULY 1850
National Millard Fillmore, of New York, is sworn in as the thirteenth President of the United States.

31 JULY 1850
Territorial A territorial government is established for the Mormon State of Deseret, now renamed the Utah Territory. Extending from the Rocky Mountains to the crest of the Sierra Nevadas, its northern border is the Oregon Territory, its southern border the territory of New Mexico. No restrictions are made on slavery. Brigham Young is to be the governor.

25 JULY 1850
Westward Movement Gold is discovered in the Rogue River of Oregon, providing new territory for the overflow of miners in California.

9 AUGUST 1850
Territorial The boundaries of New Mexico and Texas are adjusted; $10 million goes to Texas for assumption of debts.

13 AUGUST 1850
California The Senate approves admission of California as the thirty-first state, a non-slave state.

15 AUGUST 1850
Territorial The Senate approves the territory of New Mexico, with boundaries that include the present state of Arizona, the southern tip of Nevada, and part of southern Colorado.

6-9 SEPTEMBER 1850
National The House approves the Texas, New Mexico, and Utah bills, based on Clay's resolutions, and statehood for California. President Fillmore signs the bills on 9 September.

28 SEPTEMBER 1850
National Brigham Young is formally appointed Governor of the Utah territory by President Fillmore.

OTHER EVENTS OF 1850
Life/Customs Five hundred ships in San Francisco Bay are deserted by sailors intent on instant riches from the gold mines. Gold fever is at its height.
Communications The *Weekly Oregonian* begins publication in Portland.
Life/Customs Indians watch in dismay and anger, as 50,000 prospective miners swamp the Oregon Trail and the wild game begins to disappear.
Settlement Fargo, North Dakota, is established as an outfitting post for the Wells Fargo Express Company, owned by William G Fargo.

The Old Capitol at Vandalia, Illinois, before Springfield became the seat of state government.

Education The University of Deseret, forerunner of the University of Utah (1892), opens as a secular and normal school in Salt Lake City.
Ideas/Beliefs *The Deseret News,* owned by the Church of Jesus Christ of Latter Day Saints, begins publication in Salt Lake City as the first newspaper in Utah.

3 MARCH 1851
Finance Congress authorizes the Department of the Treasury to begin coining three-cent silver pieces.
National The postal rate for a half-ounce letter traveling up to 3000 miles drops to three cents, reflecting improvements in transportation.

10 JULY 1851
Education The College of the Pacific is chartered in Santa Clara, California, under its original name, California Wesleyan College, by Methodist missionaries. The school is renamed University of the Pacific in 1852 and offers its first degree in 1858.

23 JULY 1851
Indians The Treaty of Traverse des Sioux is signed. The Sioux give up their land in Iowa and most of their Minnesota holdings. Another pact is signed at the Great Treaty Council, with about 10,000 members representing several tribes: it agrees that the nations will allow settlers to pass peacefully through their lands in return for a $50,000 annuity and goods for 50 years.

CHRONOLOGY

PETER SKENE OGDEN, 1794-1854

One of the greatest frontier fur traders, Peter Ogden showed all the qualities demanded by that enterprise – the ability to deal with both Indians and whites, imperviousness to danger and hardship, and a great interest in exploring. He was born in Quebec, Canada, in 1794, the son of an American Tory who had emigrated after the Revolution. Schooled in the law, Ogden succumbed to a yen for adventure and joined the fur trade, ending up with the Hudson's Bay Company in 1821. For the rest of his life he would pursue that firm's business all over the American Northwest and southwestern Canada.

In those days a fur man was inevitably an explorer: Ogden named Mount Shasta and was among the first whites to see the Great Salt Lake. Other relics of his journeys include names all over the West – for example, Utah's Ogden City, River, Valley, and Canyon. Throughout his career, Ogden had close and mutually trusting relationships with the Indians. Thus he was the logical person to bargain for the release of white women and children made hostages during the 1847 Cayuse massacre of the Marcus Whitman missionary group in Washington. Like many fur traders, Ogden had several Indian wives. His rapport with the Indians was reflected in his book *Traits of American Indian Life and Character*.

22 OCTOBER 1851

National President Fillmore enjoins Americans to cease and desist all hostilities against Mexico.

OTHER EVENTS OF 1851

Labor The first group of Chinese indentured laborers arrives to work the plantations in Hawaii. They are paid three dollars per month plus room and board.

Westward Movement At least 32,984 English converts to the Church of Jesus Christ of Latter-Day Saints prepare to leave their country for Utah. The Mormon missionaries also have a successful tour of the Scandinavian countries, as they seek converts to their church. A Perpetual Immigration Fund has been established in Utah to provide loans for those needing cash to travel.

Ideas/Beliefs 'Go West, young man, Go West,' writes John B L Soule, editor of the *Terre Haute Express*. This expression of enthusiasm about the opportunity of starting a new life while helping the country grow is appreciated by Horace Greeley, who reprints the editorial in the *New York Tribune*. Greeley gives Soule credit, but as the better-known personage, Greeley himself is associated with the phrase.

Transportation David McKay arrives in San

Francisco, the destination of his record-setting sail aboard the clipper ship *Flying Cloud*. McKay had sailed from New York to San Francisco Bay in 89 days and 8 hours, a time that will never be beaten by sailing ships.

3 JULY 1852

National Congress establishes a branch of the United States Mint (Bureau of the Treasury) in San Francisco.

2 NOVEMBER 1852

National Franklin Pierce, a Democrat, easily defeats Winfield Scott – the last national candidate of the Whig Party. Pierce, a lawyer, had left politics 10 years before. He was the fourth candidate considered by the Democrats in the party's attempt to find a compromise position on free- and slave-state issues. Pierce, who supported the Compromise of 1850 in his campaign, will not hold to it when it comes to the test, leading to the strife known as 'Bloody Kansas.'

24 NOVEMBER 1852

International Commodore Matthew C Perry sails for Japan from San Francisco on the steamship *Susquehanna*, accompanied by a small navy squadron. Perry seeks to open the Pacific to US trade, secure better treatment for shipwrecked Americans, and end Japan's exclusion of the western world.

OTHER EVENTS OF 1852

Ideas/Beliefs The Church of Jesus Christ of Latter-Day Saints officially sanctions 'plural marriage' as a means of increasing the population of Zion. This doctrine will later be the target of federal laws and an impediment to Utah's admission as a state.

Communications The *Columbian* begins publication in Olympia (Washington).

Arts/Culture *Expedition to the Great Salt Lake* is published in London. Written by Howard Stansbury, Captain of the Corps of Topographical Engineers, US Army, the book is a report of more than 200 pages detailing a possible route for the proposed transcontinental railroad through the Black Hills and south of Salt Lake City. Stansbury, who made his survey in 1849 and 1850, wrote favorably about the Mormons, with whom he wintered. His book, widely read in England, encouraged many converts to the Church of Jesus

Great Salt Lake and Salt Lake City, Utah, in 1853.

The buffalo-skin teepee of the plains Indians.

Christ of Latter-Day Saints to travel to Zion. The book also represents the first careful scientific survey of the Great Salt Lake Valley.
Labor The National Typographics Union is formed, the result of a convention of journeymen printers in Cincinnati.
Utah As President of the Church of Jesus Christ of Latter-Day Saints, and Governor of the Territory of Utah, which is settled almost entirely by Mormons, Brigham Young consolidates his and the Church's power. He establishes a theocracy by urging the legislature to create courts with first jurisdiction over civil and criminal cases. His action supplies the generally impoverished community with ready access to free arbitration of disputes, while depriving the Federal Courts of any business.

12 JANUARY 1853
Education Williamette University is chartered in Salem, Oregon. The first degree from this Methodist school will be granted in 1854.

21 FEBRUARY 1853
Finance The Coinage Act, passed by Congress, authorizes the minting of three-dollar gold pieces.

2 MARCH 1853
National The Washington Territory is organized from the Oregon Territory by Congress, using the 46th parallel as the southern boundary. The geographical boundaries for the new territory are the Columbia River to the south, and the Rocky Mountains to the west. Still to be negotiated are

treaties with the Nez Percé, the Cayuse, the Chinook and other native landholders.

3 MARCH 1853
Transportation Congress appropriates $150,000 to pay for a survey by the War Department of various routes for a transcontinental railroad. The best route will be recommended by the surveyors.

4 MARCH 1853
National Franklin Pierce is inaugurated as the fourteenth President of the United States. The first to commit his inaugural address to memory, Pierce pledges more peaceful expansion and support of the Compromise of 1850. His cabinet is composed of men who favor expansion. Pierce hopes to acquire Hawaii and Cuba.

8 APRIL 1853
National Exploration begins for a railroad route between the 47th and 49th parallels.

19 MAY 1853
National Negotiations begin with Mexico to purchase land along the southern border of the New Mexico Territory. The United States wants the strip for a proposed railroad route from Texas to California.

8 JULY 1853
National Commodore Perry and his naval squadron reach Yedo Bay in Japan. Perry presents letters of introduction and intent to the Japanese Emperor.

8 OCTOBER 1853
National William Walker and 45 others set sail from California for Guyamas, Sonora, on the Mexican mainland in the Gulf of California, ostensibly to stop Apaches from raiding against southern California settlers.

22 OCTOBER 1853
National US Minister James Gadsden, in Mexico City, receives instructions to negotiate the purchase of a thin strip of land extending south of the Gila River, west to the 37th parallel boundary of California, and east to the Rio Grande border of Texas.

25 OCTOBER 1853
National Captain John W Gunnison and a party of eight surveyors are attacked and killed by Indians in the Utah Territory, where they were surveying possible sites for the transcontinental railroad. Officials from the US Government refused to believe that the Mormons had nothing to do with the attack, although no connection could be proved. Investigations indicated that the Indians had attacked to avenge the murder of one of their own the previous month. Tensions will erupt into the Mormon War.

3 NOVEMBER 1853
National The Walker Expedition lands at La Paz, captures the Mexican Government, and declares the Republic of Lower California. Walker is a filibuster – an independent adventurer who engages in private military action in a foreign country.

24 DECEMBER 1853
Transportation The steamer *San Francisco* founders on its way to California. Two hundred and forty passengers and crew members die, of the 700 aboard.

The flourishing port of San Francisco, as seen in a lithograph from 1851.

30 DECEMBER 1853
National Cession of 29,640 square miles of desert is secured from Mexico by Gadsden for a purchase price of $10 million. The land completes the southern boundary of New Mexico and Arizona. It also yields some of the most enduring gold and silver fields of the century (discovered in 1856). Gadsden himself views the strip as important for a southern transcontinental railroad route.

THE TEXAS QUESTION

American settlers began to drift across the Sabine River into Mexico as early as 1815. Before that, it is possible that Aaron Burr and General James Wilkinson had planned to provoke a war with Spain over the Sabine boundary between the United States and Spanish Mexico. In the Adams-Onis Treaty of 1819, the United States consolidated its hold on both East and West Florida, while relinquishing any claim it might have to the area of present-day Texas – between the Sabine and Rio Grande Rivers. However, some Americans believed that the Louisiana area – claimed by de la Salle in 1689 and incorporated into the United States in 1803 – included the land up to the Rio Grande River, rather than ending at the Sabine River. Here was the crux of the problem. Due to American infiltration, both authorized and secret, Americans (perhaps better called Texan-Americans) began to outnumber Spanish settlers in the Texas area. Most notable was Stephen F Austin's settlement on Washington-on-the-Bravos, which flourished even though the land grant had to be confirmed, made transferable, and then reconfirmed by rapidly succeeding governments in Mexico. The United States wanted the Texas area, and pursued negotiations with Mexico in 1825

and again in 1829, to purchase the land. Both times, the American effort failed, and the Mexican Government began to regret having allowed Americans to settle in Texas.

In April 1830, Mexico forbade the importation of black slaves, and began to enforce its Sabine border. When General Santa Anna became president – and then dictator – of Mexico, the Texan-Americans began to agitate for greater freedoms, first, for separation from the joint Mexican state of Texas-Coahuila, then for independence from Mexico. They won their freedom at the battle of San Jacinto in April 1836. In September of that year, they voted in favor of annexation by the United States. President Jackson refused, but recognized Texan independence on 3 March 1837. Thus the Republic of Texas was born. Although it was annexed in 1845, there were for a short time three nations involved in the Texas area. As had been important in the Spanish cession of Louisiana to France, and subsequently in Napoleon's move to sell the Louisiana Territory to the United States, American settlers were moving ahead of legislative mandates and were relentlessly pushing the frontier farther west.

OTHER EVENTS OF 1853

Education   The City of San Francisco establishes the California Academy of the Sciences, the first such institution in the West.

Life/Customs   'It opened up with a saloon to supply the necessities of life and later added a grocery store and a Chinese restaurant,' recalls one visitor to Gila City. The mining boom town is settled by about 1200 prospectors near Fort Yuma (1850) at the confluence of the Gila and Colorado Rivers (Arizona). By 1864 the mines will be exhausted, but during their lifespan they yield $2 million in gold. The city boasted all the amenities of civilization 'except a church and a jail.'

13 JANUARY 1854

Education   Pacific University is chartered in Forest Grove, Oregon, as Tualatin Academy and Pacific University. It was founded in 1849 by Congregationalist and Presbyterian churches. The first degree will be granted in 1863.

18 JANUARY 1854

National   William Walker adds Sonora, Mexico, to his Republic of Lower California by proclamation.

23 JANUARY 1854

National   The Chairman of the Senate Committee on Territories, Stephen A Douglas, introduces a bill to organize the country west of the Missouri River, north of the 37th parallel, into the territories of Kansas and Nebraska. Douglas's bill would allow the territorial governments to decide whether to be slave or free states, thus challenging the Missouri Compromise, which stated that no

---

JAMES BRIDGER, 1804-1881

Grizzled, illiterate, garrulous, and familiar with the land from Idaho to New Mexico, Jim Bridger was a quintessential mountain man. Born in Richmond, Virginia, on 17 March 1804, he was orphaned at 13 and in 1822 answered a newspaper ad for trappers along the Missouri. Over the next 20 years, Bridger trapped all over the West. In 1824 he discovered the Great Salt Lake, and in later years explored the Yellowstone region, whose considerable wonders he embellished in the telling. When the fur business fell prey to changing fashions, Bridger established Fort Bridger in Wyoming, a waystation on the Oregon Trail. There his hospitality, wit, storytelling, and intimate knowledge of the area made him indispensable to travelers on the trail – who included John C Frémont and Brigham Young. Nonetheless, the Mormons drove Bridger from his place in 1853. After a brief retirement, he returned as a government scout. One of his jobs was that of guiding Johnston's expedition against the Mormons in 1857-8. Until his retirement in 1868, Bridger was an unerring guide for scores of parties. By then he had also acquired three Indian wives and four children. A legend in his own time, Bridger died near Kansas City in 1881.

CAUTION!!

COLORED PEOPLE OF BOSTON, ONE & ALL,

You are hereby respectfully CAUTIONED and advised, to avoid conversing with the

Watchmen and Police Officers of Boston,

For since the recent ORDER OF THE MAYOR & ALDERMEN, they are empowered to act as

KIDNAPPERS AND *Slave Catchers,*

And they have already been actually employed in KIDNAPPING, CATCHING, AND KEEPING SLAVES. Therefore, if you value your LIBERTY, and the *Welfare of the Fugitives* among you, *Shun* them in every possible manner, as so many *HOUNDS* on the track of the most unfortunate of your race.

Keep a Sharp Look Out for **KIDNAPPERS, and have TOP EYE open.** *APRIL 24, 1851.*

Boston abolitionists warn fugitive slaves.

states organized from the Louisiana Purchase north of 36°30' could allow slavery.

28 FEBRUARY 1854

National   Opponents of the Douglas proposal of popular sovereignty meet in a Ripon, Wisconsin, schoolhouse. The 50 Democrats assembled there form the Republican Party.

8 MARCH 1854

National   William Walker, his group now reduced to 34, is chased to the US border by the Mexican Army and surrenders to the US military commander in San Diego. He will be tried in San Francisco in May on charges of violation of neutrality laws, and acquitted.

31 MARCH 1854

International   The Treaty of Kanagawa is signed by Commodore Matthew C Perry and the Emperor of Japan. The treaty allows the United States to open a consulate, makes available the ports of Shimoda and Hakodate for refueling of American ships, and establishes a limited trade. Japan had been closed for two centuries to all Western trade except for strictly limited exchanges between the Dutch and the Chinese at Nagasaki. US interest in opening relations with the Japanese had rested primarily on the need for a coaling station.

4 APRIL 1854

National An American Commission to Hawaii, headed by David L Gregg, seeks meetings with King Kamehameha III to discuss possible annexation of Hawaii by the United States to prevent any threat from foreigners. By the end of the year, though, the king receives reassurance that the major powers will guarantee Hawaii's freedom, so the issue of annexation dies.

26 APRIL 1854

National Alarmed at the potential for the spread of slavery if the Kansas-Nebraska Act is passed, a group of abolitionists in Boston form the Massachusetts Emigrant Aid Society to settle Kansas with anti-slave pioneers.

22-30 MAY 1854

National After months of debate and negotiations, the Kansas-Nebraska Act is passed by the House of Representatives (22 May) and the Senate (25 May) and signed by President Pierce (30 May). The act establishes two territories, with the settlers to decide the question of slavery in each. The Kansas Territory comprises all of present-day Kansas and most of present-day Colorado. The Nebraska Territory comprises present-day Nebraska and parts of South and North Dakota, Wyoming and Colorado. Existing treaties, with the Osage, Cherokee, Cheyenne, Chippewa and other nations, which conferred land from these territories on their members in perpetuity, are ignored. Senator Douglas's reported interest in the act is a central route – favoring Illinois – for the transcontinental railroad; he also hopes to improve his chances for the presidency by winning over Southern states.

29 JUNE 1854

National Pennsylvania lawyer Andrew Reeder is appointed the first territorial governor of Kansas (the first of seven territorial governors in the next seven years).

JULY 1854

National The Federal Government opens a land office in the new Kansas Territory to distribute property. Pro-slavery forces are already taking claims and fighting each other without regard for the law. Meanwhile, in Michigan, anti-slavery men are meeting to join the Republican Party. Whigs, Free-soilers, and anti-slavery Democrats hold meetings demanding repeal of the Kansas-Nebraska Act and the Fugitive Slave Law.

3 AUGUST 1854

National The Graduation Act passes Congress with strong support from the West. It provides for disposal of public lands which remain unsold for a period of 10 to 30 years at sale prices ranging from $1 per acre for 10-year-old land to 12½ cents per acre for 30-year-old land.

MARK HOPKINS, 1813-1878

Mark Hopkins was one of the four visionary men who built the Central Pacific Railroad that made the American West accessible to the long-settled East. He was born to a merchant family in Henderson, New York, on 1 September 1813. After studying law, Hopkins gravitated to business endeavors. With the discovery of gold in California in 1848, Hopkins formed a mining company and headed west. As it turned out, though, rather than mining gold he mined the California prospectors, supplying their needs in a series of businesses that grew in 1854 to an iron and hardware establishment formed with his friend Collis P Huntington.

Concerned about abolitionism and other political questions, Hopkins and Huntington entered a discussion group that included Leland Stanford and Charles Crocker. Then Theodore Judah appeared with his plan for a railroad to the East, and the four entrepreneurs formed the Central Pacific Railroad in 1861. During the construction period, Hopkins served as treasurer of the company and was considered the moving intelligence of the enterprise. He remained treasurer until his death in 1878, and left a fortune of $20 million.

11 NOVEMBER 1854

Hawaii The draft of a proposed treaty for annexation of the Hawaiian Islands is received in Washington. The treaty calls for immediate statehood, and $300,000 in annual payments to King Kamehameha IV and his chiefs.

29 NOVEMBER 1854

National John W Whitfield, a pro-slavery candidate, is elected territorial delegate to Congress in an election marred by fraud and violence, caused by some 1700 armed men from western Missouri.

CHRONOLOGY

28 DECEMBER 1854
Transportation William H Russell, Alexander Majors, and W B Waddell form a partnership to provide regular overland freight service from Fort Leavenworth, Kansas, to California. The company is subsidized in part by the Federal Government.

OTHER EVENTS OF 1854
Hawaii Kamehameha IV succeeds his uncle as King of the Islands of Hawaii. During his reign (1854-63) he will encourage the spread of sugar plantations, development of ranches, and other agricultural experiments – which will lead to immigration from various countries. English is introduced in Hawaiian schools. The attempted treaty for reciprocity with the United States fails.
Mining With ratification this year of the Gadsden Purchase by the Senate, the West's first copper mine opens at Ajo (Arizona).
Communications The *Nebraska Palladium and Platte Valley Advocate* is started in Bellevue, Iowa, by Thomas Morton.
California Sacramento is designated the capital of California.
Education The first territorial legislature in Washington passes legislation providing for the establishment of common schools in the territory.

16 JANUARY 1855
Territorial The first territorial legislature of Nebraska meets at Omaha City. The government organizes smoothly under Governor Thomas B Cuming, appointed by President Pierce. Slavery is

Bactrian camels imported from Egypt for cavalry use.

not an issue in the territory, since there are very few slaves present (only 15 in 1861 when slavery is outlawed).

28 JANUARY 1855
Transportation An alternative to traveling all the way across North America by land and water, or sailing around the tip of South America, is now available with completion of a railroad across the Isthmus of Panama, built with US financing.

31 JANUARY 1855
Hawaii Secretary of State William Marcy rejects the draft treaty to annex Hawaii. Marcy says US policy is not to cause important changes in the government of Hawaii.

20 FEBRUARY 1855
Territorial The second territorial Governor of Nebraska, Mark W Izard, reaches Omaha.

3 MARCH 1855
Transportation At the suggestion of Secretary of War Jefferson Davis, $30,000 is appropriated by Congress to introduce camels into the South-western desert. Thirty-three camels are ordered from Egypt.

30 MARCH 1855
Territorial Elections of a territorial legislature in Kansas are marred by fraud and violence, as 5000

Missouri 'Border Ruffians' participate. The Missouri men act, and even vote when necessary, to ensure election of a pro-slavery legislature. The armed Missourians intimidate Governor Reeder, so that he will not declare the election invalid. With fewer than 3000 registered voters, 6300 ballots are cast.

31 APRIL 1855
Education The College of California is chartered in Oakland. It is the first Western institution to offer a curriculum comparable to that of Eastern colleges. Established under Congregational and Presbyterian auspices, the college grants its first degree in 1864.

2 JULY 1855
Territorial The Kansas Legislature disregards Governor Reeder's plea for conciliation when it meets at Pawnee and adopts strict laws protecting slavery and meting out punishment to anti-slavery agitators. A few anti-slavery legislators are expelled.

16 JULY 1855
Territorial The Kansas Legislature moves from Pawnee to Shawnee Mission and authorizes a test oath for future elected officials.

31 JULY 1855
Territorial Kansas Governor Reeder is removed from office. Charged with land speculation, his real offense is opposing the pro-slavery legislature.

SEPTEMBER-OCTOBER 1855
Territorial Mass conventions are held by anti-slavery colonists in Kansas to organize the Free State Party. Arms are shipped in by Northern sympathizers. James H Lane is appointed military commander of the Free State militia.

3 SEPTEMBER 1855
Territorial Wilson Shannon is appointed by President Pierce to succeed Reeder as territorial governor of Kansas.

5 SEPTEMBER 1855
Territorial Anti-slavery colonists convene at Big Springs, Kansas, to repudiate the pro-slavery legislature. They ask admission to the Union as a Free State.

30 SEPTEMBER 1855
Transportation Faced with a serious cash-flow problem, the Mormon Governor of the Utah Territory, Brigham Young, establishes a hand-cart brigade to cut expenses of overland migrants to Zion. Instead of wagons drawn by teams of animals, two-wheeled carts pulled by men and women will be used. 'Fifteen miles a day will bring them through in 70 days,' writes Young.

THE GOLD RUSH

It was almost a year from the time that James Marshall found gold at the sawmill he was building for his boss John Sutter to the first rush of Easterners for the gold fields. Although there were reports of fantastic riches to be had just by looking down and picking nuggets off the ground, many newspapers were skeptical; editors wondered at the hyperbole and questioned the motives of miners inviting attention to such a great find. In that first mining season, the so-called forty-eighters, about 5000 men, averaged a $1000 profit. (A good Eastern laborers' wage was a dollar a day, and soldiers' pay amounted to $7 per month, plus room and board.)

By the end of 1849, however, about 80,000 men had 'rushed' to California to get rich. Half came by sea, many starting in December of 1848 after the Eastern newspapers and President Polk waxed enthusiastic about the reports of gold. These men either took a ship around Cape Horn, or caught steamers to the Isthmus of Panama, hiked and boated across the swampy isthmus, and steamed up the Pacific to San Francisco. The other half took one of several overland trails. Young men flocked to Independence, Missouri, by the thousands and headed west as soon as the grass had grown high enough on the western banks of the Missouri River – grass that would be the food for their livestock and teams along the overland trails.

The work was hard, and got harder as the competition grew and the easy gold had been carted away. Miners stood in cold rivers with water to their hips for hours at a time. At other locations they hacked away at quartz deposits for veins of gold. 'Gold fever' came to mean scurvy, dysentery, and other illnesses resulting from poor food and the roughest living conditions. The rudiments of civilization followed the miners in the form of gambling tents, saloons, and shopkeepers. Everyone charged what the market would bear – with prices as high as $16 for a box of sardines, $3 for a half pound of cheese – and the price of gold was set at $16 an ounce by the merchants of San Francisco. Foreigners became the target of Anglo-Saxon bigotry, as frustrations over the hard work and elusive profits increased. A murder a day became common, with Latins and Indians the chief targets. Rapes occurred among the handful of women in the territory.

Ironically, most of the miners left the fields poorer than when they'd arrived. It was the merchants and developers who made their fortunes. Many a man took his broken spirit and headed home; others stayed, choosing a trade, or starting a farm, seeking, perhaps, to restore the values they had helped destroy in the gold rush.

1 OCTOBER 1855
Territorial John W Whitfield is re-elected as Congressional delegate from Kansas by the pro-slavery legislature.

9 OCTOBER 1855
Territorial Ex-Governor of Kansas Reeder is elected Congressional delegate by the Free State men. Tensions in the territory are building to the point where armed conflict will become inevitable.

CHRONOLOGY

23 OCTOBER-2 NOVEMBER 1855
Territorial The Free State Party of Kansas holds a constitutional convention in Topeka and produces a document prohibiting slavery in the territory.

14 NOVEMBER 1855
Territorial Governor Shannon organizes a 'Law and Order' party at a pro-slavery meeting at Leavenworth.

26 NOVEMBER-7 DECEMBER 1855
Territorial The 'Wakarusa War' breaks out near Lawrence, Kansas, along the Wakarusa River. Some 1500 border ruffians from Missouri participate, refraining from a direct attack on Lawrence because the town is strongly held by well-armed Free Staters. Fighting subsides with the intervention of Governor Shannon.

15 DECEMBER 1855
Territorial Kansas Territory now has two constitutions, as the Topeka Constitution of the Free Staters is adopted by popular election. The constitution includes ordinances prohibiting entry of Negroes into the territory. The ordinances pass along with the constitution.

OTHER EVENTS OF 1855
Indians The Utes and Jicarilla Apache are subjugated by the US Army, lifting the threat of attack along the western portion of the Santa Fe trail. Native Americans of Northern California and Southern Oregon are forced to live on reservations following the Rogue River Wars.
Settling A gold rush to the Columbia River in the Washington Territory is halted by warriors of the Yakima Nation in the spring of 1855. A Mormon mission is established in Fort Lemhi, Idaho. The settlement represents part of Brigham Young's plan to populate the State of Deseret. Mormons establish a short-lived support post for emigrants at the present site of Las Vegas. An attempt to mine lead nearby also fails due to a lack of manpower and essential equipment.
Territorial Three federal judges are appointed to the Utah Territory by President Pierce to reestablish some federal authority in the area. Two of the judges are apostates from the Mormon Church. They will preside over empty courtrooms.

JANUARY-MARCH 1856
Territorial Settlers in the Black, Walla Walla, and Yakima River Valleys erect blockhouses at the urging of Oregon Territorial Governor Issac I Stevens to protect themselves from the Yakima and other nations who resent their intrusion.

8 JANUARY 1856
Mining Borax is found at a California spring by D John Veatch, the first discovery of this mineral in the United States. The crystalline compound will be used in medicine and industry.

Frederick Douglass, spokesman for black freedom.

15 JANUARY 1856
Territorial Kansas now has two governments for the same territory, as the Free State Party elects its own governor and legislature in Topeka.

11 FEBRUARY 1856
Territorial President Pierce issues a proclamation warning both the Free State men and the 'border ruffians' in Kansas to cease and desist their disruptive activities. Because Pierce had earlier (24 January) delivered a special message to Congress condemning the Topeka government as an act of rebellion, he is recognized as supporting the pro-slavery government of Kansas.

4 MARCH 1856
National The Topeka legislature formally requests statehood for Kansas and elects Andrew Reeder and James Lane Senators.

17 MARCH 1856
National Stephen A Douglas introduces a bill for a constitutional convention in Kansas, denouncing the anti-slavery Topeka government.

19 MARCH 1856
National The House of Representatives appoints a committee to study charges of voter fraud in the Kansas elections. The Committee confirms the fraud and violence of the elections, citing the discrepancy between 2905 registered voters and 6000 votes cast.

A woodcutter's cabin on the Mississippi.

21 APRIL 1856
Transportation The first bridge across the Mississippi is completed. It extends from Davenport, Iowa, to Rock Island, Illinois, and is open for railroad traffic.

15 MAY 1856
California The editor of the San Francisco *Daily Evening Bulletin*, James King, is found murdered. 'Committees of Vigilance' are formed to keep order in the streets.

21 MAY 1856
National Civil war erupts in the Kansas territory. The Free State Party has a fresh shipment of arms from the north (so-called Beecher's Bibles). They lose the first round, as the Border Ruffians, aided by pro-slavery men, including the Kickapoo Rangers of Colonel Jefferson Buford, sack Lawrence. The Free State Hotel is burned, printing presses for *The Herald of Freedom* and *The Kansas Free State* are destroyed, homes are pillaged, and one man is killed. Exaggerated accounts of the fighting inflame Northern sympathizers.

24-25 MAY 1856
National In the Kansas Territory, abolitionist John Brown, accompanied by his four sons and two others, execute the Pottawatomie massacre – the midnight murders of five pro-slavery colonists living near Dutch Hanry's Crossing at Pottawatomie Creek. Free State men disavow any connection with Brown's actions. Militias of the warring Kansas factions are alerted to stand by.

4 JUNE 1856
National Kansas Territorial Governor Shannon orders all irregular armed units to disperse.

9-11 JUNE 1856
Westward Movement The first of 10 handcart brigades leaves Iowa City for Salt Lake City. Two companies totaling 497 persons drawing 100 carts head out singing – all are newly converted to the Mormon faith. They reach Zion on 26 September.

SPREADING THE WORD

The West was alive in literature during the early 1800s. The written word spread knowledge that was both informative and misleading. Zebulon Pike and Stephen Long's official reports created the fiction of a great desert on the southern plains west of the Mississippi, but a particularly prescient Congressional report in 1803 recognized the population explosion that was about to occur in the Mississippi River Valley. Meriwether Lewis and William Clark's journals constitute a classic work of observant exploration; in fact, they were so carefully detailed that Western historians have been able to trace most of that famous journey mile for mile, word for word. Hall J Kelley, the most famous popularizer of the Oregon country, described that land as lush, fertile, and protected by mountains from the winds off the Pacific Ocean. Joseph Smith's *Book of Mormon* (1830) sparked the Church of Jesus Christ of Latter-Day Saints, which colonized Utah in its effort to escape religious persecution. William Walker's article in the *Christian Advocate and Journal* (1833) inspired missionaries to concentrate their efforts in Oregon, where it was said that the Indians wanted to learn about the 'White Man's Bible.' Americans and Europeans alike learned about California through two significant books – Alexander Forbes's *A History of Upper and Lower California* (1838), and Richard Henry Dana's *Two Years Before the Mast* (1840), which gave considerable physical description of the California coast. These publications helped to legitimize the West for Eastern readers. After all, it was one thing to hear an oldtimer say that he had trapped for furs west of the Rocky Mountains, but it would be equally dramatic, and possibly more accurate to read an account such as *Journal of an Exploring Tour Beyond the Rocky Mountains* (1838) by Samuel Parker, who traveled for two years and 28,000 miles – and returned to Ithaca, New York, to write his story. Such reports encouraged increasing numbers of Americans to make their way west.

A third company arrives in October. However, the next two companies are delayed until August while their carts are built. Caught by early snows, and ill-equipped for a winter trek 1200 miles across the plains, 225 of 1000 die before reaching Salt Lake City. 'We soon thought it unusual to leave a campground without burying one or more persons,' wrote one emigrant. Stopped finally by heavy drifts, the settlers await rescue. President Young, on learning of the disaster, decides to set up more settlements for the next five handcart-company crossings.

3 JULY 1856
National The House of Representatives passes a bill to admit Kansas as a Free State under the Topeka Constitution. The bill fails in the Senate.

31 JULY 1856
Settling Fort Lookout is established on the Missouri River in the Nebraska Territory (South Dakota). It is built near the Fort Lookout of the

A flotilla of elegant Mississippi steamboats.

CHRONOLOGY

THE MORMONS

The Mormons settled the West in the pursuit of a common ideal – the establishment of their faith. This distinguishes their settlement from others of the exodus west that began in the 1840s. For the majority, the way west was taken for personal interest. Families and single pioneers may have banded together for safety, comfort, and thrift, but they did not cross the deserts, face their fears of the unknown, or make the painful goodbyes to friends in search of a common good.

The Mormon settlement is also notable for the history of friction and persecution they tried to leave behind, and the land they chose to be their Zion. Brigham Young, Prophet and second President of the Church of Jesus Christ of Latter-Day Saints, chose the arid land of the Great Basin, territory nobody else seemed interested in. The Mormons are the only one of many American experiments in religious communities, or utopias, to survive. The Shakers were comparable in their commitment, and flourished for years after their American founding by Mother Ann Lee in 1774. But their practice of celibacy made it inevitable that their communities would dwindle in the absence of significant numbers of converts.

In terms of development of the west, the Saints, as they called themselves, faced and solved many problems of basic survival and logistics that would benefit future newcomers. Brigham Young, with his genius for leadership and organization, asked that the Saints give over any self-directed ambitions to devote all energies to the good of the church, which would mean survival for its members. They established an irrigation system and a method of distributing valuable natural resources with little more than necessity, as opposed to experience, for a guide. Water was owned by all, and sent through a network of ditches to grow the necessary crops. The land was distributed by need and capability. No man was given more acres than he could husband.

The need for sacrifice was constant in the early years. Men were called from their families to highly successful missions in Europe to gather more Saints for the church. Others were sent to establish settlements in far-flung areas in and out of the territory, both for the benefit of all church members and to offer help to overland converts emigrating to Utah.

Brigham Young, President of the Church and the first Governor of the territory, established even the width of the streets. He chose Saints for new communities for the skills that would be needed to make the community self-sufficient. The policy of polygamy was encouraged by Young out of the need to bring more children into the faith to allow an entrance to Zion for the spirits of those who had died before the birth of Mormonism.

The Mormons could not leave history behind. Conflict soon caught up with them: they were perceived as a theocracy that set itself above the good of the country. Their self-assuredness, their total dedication to the church and its leader – these would always be a source of discomfort and conflict for those on the outside, the gentiles. This does not diminish the contribution of the determined and self-sacrificing people who made the desert bloom and established for themselves the State of Deseret, which became the territory and finally the State of Utah.

Columbia Fur Trading Post. The military installation seeks to protect settlers from attacks by natives of the land.

1 AUGUST 1856
National The House of Representatives refuses to seat either the Free State or the pro-slavery delegate from the Kansas Territory.

4 AUGUST 1856
Settling Fort Randall takes the place of Fort Pierre in keeping the peace between the Sioux and the Ponea. (Fort Pierre was abandoned because of insufficient grass, timber and hay. Fort Randall is on the Missouri River in the Nebraska Territory (southern South Dakota).

8 AUGUST 1856
Settling Fort Simcoe, in the Simcoe Valley of the Washington Territory is established as a base of operations for the war against the Yakima.

13 AUGUST 1856
National The town of Franklin, a pro-slavery stronghold in the Kansas Territory, is seized by members of the Free State militia.

16 AUGUST 1856
Industry Gail Borden, recognizing the plight of mothers and their children on long sea journeys, works on a process for 'the concentration of milk.' His patent, received on this day for the process, leads to condensed milk.

18 AUGUST 1856
National Governor Shannon resigns his post in the Kansas Territory. President Pierce replaces him with Daniel Woodson, a pro-slavery man, as Acting Governor.

25 AUGUST 1856
National Acting Governor Woodson issues a proclamation declaring that the Kansas Territory is in a 'state of insurrection,' and calls out the pro-slavery militia.

30 AUGUST 1856
National Kansas militiamen (300) attack Osawatomie, a town defended by John Brown and 40 other Free State supporters. The militia prevails, drives out Free Staters, and pillages the settlement. Guerrilla warfare rages throughout the territory.

9 SEPTEMBER 1856
National Former Mayor of San Francisco John W Geary arrives in the Kansas Territory as the presidential appointee to assume the governorship.

13 SEPTEMBER 1856
Ideas/Beliefs The Doctrine of Blood Atonement – that there are some sins that can only be atoned for by the letting of blood – is revived in the Utah

Territory, as Mormons undergo a reformation. The last two years have been marked by poor harvests and other troubles. Sermons preached by President and Prophet Brigham Young and others in the Church hierarchy inflame the Mormons with devastating future results.

15 SEPTEMBER 1856
National Kansas Territory Governor Geary uses Federal troops to intercept a band of 2500 Border Ruffians. He is successful in convincing them to go home instead of launching a planned attack on the Free State stronghold of Lawrence. 'Peace now reigns in Kansas,' declares Geary. The battle over slavery in the territory (November 1855-December 1856) will cost 200 lives and $2 million in property damage.

4 NOVEMBER 1856
National Democratic candidate James Buchanan defeats Republican John Frémont in presidential elections. The country has virtually split along pro-slavery and anti-slavery lines; Buchanan has won in 14 slave states.

17 NOVEMBER 1856
Settling The first military post in the Gadsden Purchase territory, Fort Buchanan, is located on the Sonoita River (Arizona) to control the Apache and protect southern emigration routes.

2 DECEMBER 1856
National In his final message to Congress, President Pierce laments that the Kansas Territory 'was made the battlefield, not so much of opposing factions, or interests within itself, but of the conflicting passions of the whole people of the United States.'

Currier and Ives print of a riverside cotton plantation.

FEDERAL EXPLORATORY EXPEDITIONS

Shortly after 1800 the US Government saw the need to learn about the west. President Thomas Jefferson had long been interested in what lay beyond the Appalachian Mountains. Even before the Louisiana Purchase was concluded, Jefferson initiated the process that sent the Lewis and Clark Expedition west. This was perhaps the most successful of all the federal expeditions: it demonstrated the feasibility of crossing the continent and opened the way for a large number of private individuals to explore the land west of the Mississippi River.

In 1805-07, Lieutenant Zebulon Pike explored the upper Mississippi River Valley and the Southwest. While under arrest by Spanish authorities, Pike made observations that were published in 1810 and later served as a reference for explorers of the Southwest, particularly along the Santa Fe Trail. Pike's negative contribution was to originate the myth of the Great American Desert, on the southern and central plains west of the Mississippi River. The legend was reinforced by the federal explorations of Major Stephen H Long in 1819-20. Sent by the War Department to find the source of the Red River of the southwest, Long found the Canadian River – named for its original French-Canadian discoverers – and many previously unknown animals, insects, and plants. Long reiterated the idea of a vast desert that was totally unfit for agriculture. The main result was that the plains were among the last areas to be settled – after large sections of California and Oregon.

Twenty-two years after Long's expedition, John Charles Frémont led a federal expedition to the Wind River Chain of the Rocky Mountains. Frémont's *Exploring Expedition to the Rocky Mountains* established his reputation, and in 1843-4, he led another officially sponsored expedition, this one to the Columbia River country and the Carson River in Nevada. Frémont returned to St Louis by California, the Old Spanish Trail, and the Arkansas River. His charting of present-day Wyoming, Utah, Oregon, California, and Nevada legitimized the Far West as a territory to be settled and exploited.

CHRONOLOGY

OTHER EVENTS OF 1856

Communications The Western Union Telegraph Company is formed to take advantage of the increasing system of telegraph wires across the country.

Arts/Culture Commodore Perry publishes the *Narrative of the Expedition of an American Squadron to the China Sea and Japan Performed in the Years 1852, 1853, and 1854.* Despite its cumbersome title, the book will play a role in the attraction to things Oriental in coming decades.

Alaska With the end of the three-year Crimean War waged by Russia against Britain, France, and Turkey, the Russian Government, under Czar Alexander II, which has been forced to assume responsibility for much of the Russian-American Company's fur trade in Alaska, will begin to lose interest in its Alaskan holdings.

12 JANUARY 1857

National The Kansas pro-slavery legislature meets in Lecompton to begin deliberations on a state constitution, in defiance of Governor Geary's recommendation of a thorough revamping of the laws, new elections, and genuine self-government. The Lecompton legislature calls for June elections of delegates to a constitutional convention. Geary vetoes the bill. His personal pro-slavery sympathies are offset by the desire to see impartial justice done.

3 MARCH 1857

Communications The Postmaster General is authorized by Congress to secure bids for an overland stagecoach service for mail and passengers from the Missouri River to San Francisco.

4 MARCH 1857

National Governor Geary resigns as Kansas' third territorial governor, because he finds no support in the Pierce Administration for his attempts to bring true self-government to Kansas.

National James Buchanan is inaugurated the fifteenth President of the United States. Buchanan, a Democrat, supports the policy of popular sovereignty on the question of slavery, but condemns the violence in Kansas.

6 MARCH 1857

National The United States Supreme Court declares (*Dred Scott v Sandford*) that the Missouri Compromise of 1820 and all laws banning slavery in the territories are unconstitutional. In the Dred Scott decision, the Court finds that Congress has no right to deprive persons of their property without due process of law according to the Fifth Amendment to the Constitution.

26 MARCH 1857

National President Buchanan appoints Robert J Walker, former Secretary of the Treasury, Territorial Governor of Kansas. Walker's inaugural address (26 May) will request co-operation from both pro-slavery and Free-State factions. Walker promises that any constitution adopted will be submitted to a fair vote.

29 MARCH 1857

Westward Movement The Fancher Wagon train, led by Captain Alexander Fancher, leaves northwest Arkansas for California. The wealthy, well-equipped group comprises 50 men, 40 women, and 50 children. They will never arrive at their destination.

20 MAY 1857

National President Buchanan, after hearing reports from Utah's territorial judges in Washington, sends a US Army contingent to the territory; he is convinced that the region is in a 'state of rebellion.' Many of the reports he has heard are exaggerated.

10 JUNE 1857

Communications The XY Company (Brigham Young Carrying and Express Company) wins a contract from the United States to carry mail and freight. The company has a second purpose: to facilitate migration to Utah. Staging points are set up with settlements along the way; missionaries are installed to aid emigrants. The first mail delivery, from Independence, Missouri, to Salt Lake City is accomplished in only 26 days. The United States cancels the contract in less than six months, another reflection of tension between the Mormons and the Federal Government.

15 JUNE 1857

National The Kansas pro-slavery legislature meets in Lecompton, calling for elections to the constitutional convention. Free Soilers refuse to participate, as this would mean recognizing the legitimacy of the Lecompton legislature.

13 JULY 1857

Territorial President Buchanan appoints Alfred Cummings to replace Brigham Young as territorial governor of Utah. It will take Cummings several months to arrive in the territory. Young responds by saying, 'My power will not be diminished. No man they can send here will have much influence with this community.'

15 JULY 1857

National Governor Walker persuades Free Staters to participate in a new election for the Kansas Territory. The elections will be held on 5 October.

18 JULY 1857

Territorial Federal troops under command of Colonel Albert Sidney Johnston leave Fort Leavenworth, Kansas, for Utah. News of this reaches the territory, where Brigham Young calls for Mormons throughout the territory, and in outlying areas, to abandon their homes and come to Salt Lake City in defense of Zion. The Nauvoo Legion is dispatched to harass Colonel Johnston's troops, while other Saints are sent into the Wasatch Mountains to defend the passes.

28 AUGUST 1857
Westward Movement Fort Abercrombie is established on the banks of the Red River of the North, at Graham's Point (North Dakota) to protect settlers of the Red River Valley from attack by Sioux.

SEPTEMBER 1857
Territorial Brigham Young declares martial law in the Utah Territory. The atmosphere is tense, as many Saints remember the murder of their first prophet in Nauvoo, Illinois, and the subsequent exodus to Council Bluffs.

7-11 SEPTEMBER 1857
Territorial The Fancher train, encamped in Mountain Meadows (southern Utah), is attacked by warriors of the Paiute Nation. Some charge that the Indian attack is encouraged by the Mormon Church – that the Fancher train was chosen for destruction the moment it entered the territory. A contingent of Mormons, including John D Lee, approaches the camp with a flag of truce. They declare that the Indians can be pacified if the travelers will submit to Mormon custody and safekeeping. Children under the age of eight are put into one wagon, the sick and the injured into another. Women, some with infants in their arms, are next, and finally the men and boys of the train file out of the meadow, walking single file between the Mormons. As the wagons and women move ahead, the Mormons turn on the men and murder them at point-blank range. Paiute warriors kill the women; Mormons kill the sick and wounded in the second wagon. The young children are taken to Mormon homes, until they are located by federal officials. Early investigations are stymied. Whether the massacre was a deliberate act of the Mormon Church to avenge the blood of its prophets, or an act initiated by angry Paiutes and facilitated by fanatical Mormons, may never be known. In the end, only John D Lee is brought to trial (1877) and condemned to be shot for the murders.

15 SEPTEMBER 1857
Territorial With the territory under martial law, President Young forbids any US armed forces to enter Utah. In October Major Lot Smith of the Nauvoo Legion will attack unguarded army supply wagons in advance of Colonel Johnston's troops: 72 federal wagons and many animals are destroyed, leaving the troops without provisions.

16 SEPTEMBER 1857
Transportation The Butterfield Overland Mail

ISAAC INGALLS STEVENS, 1818-1862

Isaac Stevens gained success as both a soldier and a politician; his ruthless dealings with the Indians, however, threw a shadow over his career. Born in Andover, Massachusetts, on 28 March 1818, Stevens graduated first in his class from West Point and served as an engineer in the Mexican War. He resigned from the military in 1853, when he was appointed governor of Washington Territory. That year he headed a large exploring party that did pioneering work in looking for a Pacific railway route.

As governor of Washington Stevens extracted over 100,000 square miles of territory from the Indian tribes of the area in a series of treaties. When the tribes rose in revolt in 1855, Stevens called out 1000 volunteers and ruthlessly suppressed the rebellion. In the process he jailed any whites who spoke for the Indians, including a chief justice who was arrested in his own courtroom. Stevens resigned the governorship in 1857, after which he served in Congress for two terms and gained approval of his Indian treaties. In the Civil War, he resumed his military career, becoming a major general in 1862. He was killed at the battle of Chantilly, Virginia, that same year.

Company is awarded a federal contract to provide mail and passenger service from St Louis and Memphis to Arkansas, thence to Texas, Los Angeles, and San Francisco. The company will make runs every two weeks, averaging about 25 days per run. They receive a federal annual mail subsidy of about $600,000.

5 OCTOBER 1857
National Elections are held in the Kansas Territory under strict supervision; thousands of fraudulent votes cast by pro-slavery supporters are thrown out, and the Free State Party wins a majority in both houses of the legislature.

19 OCTOBER-8 NOVEMBER 1857
National At the meeting of the pro-slavery Lecompton legislature to plan for a state constitution, it is decided to offer for vote an article recognizing citizens' right to have property in slaves. Should this article be rejected, reason the participants, the territory would still have its original constitution, allowing slavery.

5 NOVEMBER 1857
Territorial Johnston's US Army troops, unable to cross into the Utah Territory before winter, decide to winter over at Fort Bridger (Wyoming). They have no supplies, or extra animals, having been raided repeatedly by the Mormon Nauvoo Legion.

8 DECEMBER 1857
National President Buchanan, in his annual message to Congress, requests money for soldiers and supplies to suppress the revolution in the Utah Territory.

CHRONOLOGY

Above: *Mormon converts cross the Rocky Mountains en route to Salt Lake City.*
Left: *The Mississippi as Mark Twain knew it.*

17 DECEMBER 1857
National Kansas Governor Walker resigns because of Buchanan's decision to uphold the Lecompton Constitution. Frederick P Stanton becomes Acting Governor. Buchanan's about-face to Walker was an attempt to preserve party unity: it will have the opposite effect.

21 DECEMBER 1857
National In territorial elections, the Lecompton Constitution, with provisions for owning slaves, passes by 6226 to 569. Almost 3000 of these votes are later shown to be fraudulent. The Free State men refuse to vote.

OTHER EVENTS OF 1857
Settling Squatters settle around the present-day site of Sioux Falls, South Dakota.
Transportation The last length of track is laid connecting New York City to St Louis, Missouri. Celebrations abound, with many Americans dreaming of the day when the country might be connected by rail from coast to coast.
Environment Mt Saint Helens, in present-day Washington State, erupts. It will then remain calm until 1980.

Life/Customs In San Francisco, an eccentric dressed in the style of Napoleon III of France appears on the streets claiming to be 'Emperor Norton.' He issues proclamations, demands free meals, and appears at public occasions. He is, in fact, Joshua Norton, originally from South Africa, a failed businessman who has apparently become a harmless madman. San Franciscans will humor him until his death in 1880, and he will live on in their memories as the subject of numerous books, plays, and operas, the most notable being Henry Mollicone's 1981 opera *Emperor Norton*.

4 JANUARY 1858
National Urged by the Free Staters of Kansas, Acting Governor Stanton calls for an unequivocal vote on the Lecompton Constitution, permitting a vote only for or against it. The results: 10,226 against the constitution, 138 for the constitution with slavery, and 24 for the constitution without slavery. This results in the removal of Stanton as Acting Governor by President Buchanan.

7 JANUARY 1858
National William Walker, the Western adventurer who has been filibustering in Nicaragua, is chided by President Buchanan for his activities. In 1860 the government of the Honduras will step in, and Walker will be arrested, tried, and shot for his attempts to take over governments in Central America.

2 FEBRUARY 1858
National President Buchanan recommends to Congress admission of the territory of Kansas as a state under the unpopular Lecompton Constitution.

25 FEBRUARY 1858
National Philadelphia lawyer Thomas Kane, self-appointed ambassador to the Mormon Saints from President Buchanan, arrives in Utah to persuade Brigham Young to accept Alfred Cummings as territorial governor. Young agrees, provided the US Army does not enter the territory.

23 MARCH 1858
National The Senate approves admission of Kansas as a state under the Lecompton Constitution. On 1 April the House will vote to resubmit the constitution to the people of Kansas.

12 APRIL 1858
National Governor Alfred Cummings is received warmly in Salt Lake City, while Federal troops remain at Fort Bridger. In one of his first addresses to the people of Salt Lake City, Governor Cummings states that they must allow the federal troops into the city. In a panic, some 30,000 Saints pack their household goods and desert the area north of Salt Lake City for the town of Provo to the south. The exodus, which takes several weeks, leaves the northern territory deserted except for a few men who are directed to burn the towns if they are to be taken over.

4 MAY 1858
National Compromise in Congress on Kansas statehood: the Lecompton Constitution will be sent back to the voters. If it is approved, statehood will follow. If it is rejected, statehood will be deferred until the population reaches about 93,000 (the average number of people represented by each Congressman in the House at this time).

11 MAY 1858
National Minnesota is admitted to the Union as a non-slave state. It is the thirty-second state of the Union.

JUNE 1858
National Commissioners from President Buchanan arrive at Camp Scott in Utah and proceed south to Provo. They bring a full pardon from the president 'to all who will submit themselves to the just authority of the federal government.' The pardon had been signed by the president two months earlier, and the commissioners admonished 'to bring those misguided people to their senses.' Only after the pardon is signed is the US Army allowed to march through Salt Lake City – still deserted – into an area southwest of the city, where they will construct Camp Floyd.

12 JUNE 1858
Mining Nineteen Georgians and 46 Cherokee Indians reach Bent's Fort on the Arkansas River, in south-central Kansas Territory. Many of the prospectors become discouraged and quit early, but those who stay on will find their gold many miles north, along the Cherry Creek, near the site of Denver.

24 JUNE 1858
Westward Movement Fort Garland, in the San Luis Valley (Colorado), is established to curb the Utes and Jicarilla Apache.

4 JULY 1858
National Following their leader, Mormons return to their homes in Salt Lake City and farther north. Governor Cummings declares peace in the territory.

2 AUGUST 1858
National Kansas voters reject the Lecompton Constitution again, by a wide margin: 11,812 to 1926. The area remains a territory.

24 AUGUST 1858
National Camp Floyd, in the Cedar Valley west of Utah Lake, is established to support US troops in the territory. It will become Fort Crittendon in 1861, when the man for whom it was named,

Secretary of War John B Floyd, joins the Confederacy.

SEPTEMBER 1858
Mining A band of about 50 men, the Lawrence Party from Lawrence, Kansas, arrives at Dry Diggins (Colorado) and establishes Montana City. Lean pickings result in an early abandonment, with many of the party moving on to Cherry Creek, where some 1000 prospectors are converging. Two towns, the Denver City Company and the Auraria Town Company, are established.

16 SEPTEMBER 1858
Transportation The Butterfield Overland Mail Company starts its first run from St Louis to San Francisco. Destination is reached on 10 October, just 23 days, 23 hours, and 3000 miles later.

20 SEPTEMBER 1858
Westward Movement Camp Walbach on the Lodgepole Creek, east of the Cheyenne Pass, is established to protect emigrants traveling through this dangerous pass (between Nebraska and Wyoming).

6 DECEMBER 1858
National In his second annual message to Congress, President Buchanan asserts that the authority of Constitutional law has been fully restored and peace prevails throughout the territories.

20 DECEMBER 1858
National Abolitionist John Brown conducts a raid from Kansas Territory into Missouri, where he frees 11 slaves and kills a man in the process. The former slaves are taken to Canada.

OTHER EVENTS OF 1858
Westward Movement With the opening of the Columbia River area to settlers, members of the Yakima Nation are aroused. They become particularly angry when 2000 prospectors head for the Fort Colville mines near the Columbia (present-day Washington) seeking gold. The miners are repulsed by attacks from the Yakima at first, but in the summer, the Indians sue for peace. The mines, however, are a disappointment, and the camps formed to make men rich become supply stations for a much larger strike along the Fraser River in British Columbia.

Indians Yankton Sioux leaders cede Southeastern Dakota to the United States.

Transportation George M Pullman begins building sleeping cars for use on the transcontinental railroad.

Science/Technology Lewis Mill patents his modern mowing machine; Charles Wesley March patents a harvester that can gather grain into bundles. These inventions will make radical changes in the agricultural sector.

WINTER 1859
National The financial panic continues.

14 FEBRUARY 1859
National Oregon is admitted to the Union as the thirty-third state, the eighteenth non-slave state. The state has 50,000 inhabitants and elects as its first governor Democrat John Whiteaker.

WAGONS WESTWARD

'Old America seems to be breaking up and moving westward.' Morris Birbeck's statement, made in 1818, has long been considered a classic literary description of westward movement. Birbeck was writing about a journey he had made from Virginia to Illinois. He noted that around 12,000 wagons passed through Philadelphia and Baltimore in 1816, heading toward Ohio. Many of these were Conestoga wagons, which had been created and over time adapted to meet the harsh demands of pioneer travel. The Conestoga was usually 60 feet long and employed a team of four to six horses. The sides of the wagon flared outward; the wheels had broad tires, heavy spokes were 'toed in' with strong nails, and hoops supported a canvas cover.

Road building began at a tremendous pace in approximately 1795. The Cumberland Road, later the National Road, was the most famous emigrant turnpike, but two turnpikes connected the Hudson River with Buffalo, New York, as early as 1802. Large numbers of settlers traveled through New York and Pennsylvania on their way to Ohio, while the Cumberland Gap was the gateway for emigrants to Kentucky and Tennessee. Numbers illustrate the results of the great migrations in 1815-40. In 1800 Indiana had 5641 people, Mississippi had 8850, and Ohio had 45,365. By 1840 the respective populations had risen to 685,866 (gain of 1021 percent), 375,651 (rise of 4200 percent), and 1,519,467 (rise of 3300 percent)! These people moved west because of dissatisfaction with the traditional, settled way of life in the original 13 colonies, and with the expectation of buying cheap land. Connecticut, in particular, lost large numbers of its people to western movement. The pioneers left few written records, and it is difficult to know how many found satisfaction in the new western states. But westward movement had begun in full force by 1820 and would continue throughout the nineteenth century.

Abolitionist John Brown on his way to execution.

MARCH 1859

Mining Even before the grass has grown to feed horses, the '59ers rush for the gold fields of Colorado, near the Rocky Mountains. The slogan 'Pike's Peak or Bust' left many busted, as farmers and laborers ruined in the financial panic of 1857 (which had its start in San Francisco in 1855) turned back. Many find all the claims near Denver already staked. Returning east, they alert about half of the 100,000 miners-to-be whom they meet on the trails. By late spring the rush is over, only to begin again once the real strike is made.

18 APRIL 1859

Transportation The Leavenworth and Pike's Peak Express Company has a trial run between Fort

Slow progress toward a new home in the West.

Leavenworth and the gold fields of the Kansas Territory with its stagecoach service.

19 APRIL 1859
Westward Movement Fort Mojave is built on the banks of the Colorado River (Arizona) for the purpose of controlling the Mojave and Paiute at Beal's Crossing.

6 MAY 1859
Mining John H Gregory hits pay dirt at Gregory's Gulch on the north branch of Clear Creek, when he finds a quartz vein rich in gold. Journalist Horace Greeley is traveling in the West and attests to the riches to be found in this part of the Rockies. Thus a series of strikes begins in the western part of the Kansas territory (present-day Colorado), most of them requiring tunneling and rock-crushing equipment. Such Colorado towns as Boulder, Golden, Canon City and Colorado Springs all owe their existence to mining activity. By 1860 as many as 5000 miners a week pour into the western Kansas Territory.

9 MAY 1859
National Utah Territorial Governor Cummings declares any assemblage of armed men in the territory illegal, in an attempt to handle the presence of both federal troops and armed Mormons.

12 MAY 1859
National 'Where, under our Declaration of Independence, does the White Saxon man get his

Opposite: *Theater-goers at Natchez, Mississippi.*

THE LURE OF THE WEST

Long before Horace Greeley would promote the slogan 'Go West, young man!' the image of fabulous prospects in the west was deeply ingrained in the European consciousness. From ancient times, the West had been regarded as the abode of favored peoples – from the Isles of the Blest, where the dead might spend eternity, to the Lost Continent of Atlantis, which Plato had located west of his known world. Thus it is not surprising that soon after Columbus brought back reports of the more or less naked innocents he had found living in the unknown lands to the west, some speculated that he had discovered the original Garden of Eden; by 1512 Pope Julius II was declaring that the Indians were directly descended from Adam and Eve. Meanwhile, others were seeing America as the lost continent of Atlantis. The first man to voice this idea in print was a Spanish historian, Francisco López de Gómara, in his *General History of the Indies* (1553). Some Europeans were soon suggesting that the newly discovered continent be called Atlantis, and the image remained powerful.

The maps Columbus used showed numerous other islands off to the west, including one called Antillia, sometimes known as the Island of Seven Cities. This island seemed to move about the Atlantic during the 1400s, but in all cases it was regarded as a prosperous and fortunate locale. When early trans-Atlantic voyagers did not encounter it, the island's existence was questioned, but the image of seven rich cities resurfaced in the Southwest. The first report was made by Friar Marcos, a Franciscan missionary-explorer, who in 1539 journeyed from Mexico into the Zuñi Indian territory of New Mexico. There he saw the great pueblo of Hawikuh, described to him as one of seven such great cities in this region he called Cibola. When he returned to Mexico, the Seven Cities of Cibola became ever larger and richer with the telling. They were, in fact, the objective of Coronado's great expedition of 1540-42. When he failed to find them, he was deceived by an Indian from the Great Plains, 'The Turk,' into believing that there was yet another fabulous land: Quivira, where 'everyone had their ordinary dishes of wrought plate, and the jugs and bowls were of gold.' Both the Seven Cities of Cibola and Quivira would persist on maps and in reports for many decades, part of the mystique of the American West.

---

power to deprive all women and negroes of their inalienable rights?' queries Susan B Anthony, at the opening of the Ninth National Women's Rights Convention in New York City. Her theme will soon be picked up by pioneering women west of the Mississippi.

10 JUNE 1859
Mining It's the richest mining discovery in US history – the Comstock Lode in the Washoe Mountains (Nevada) of the Utah Territory. The original discovery is made by Peter O'Riley and Patrick McLaughlin, digging in Six Mile Canyon. 'Old Pancake' (he was too lazy to bake his bread) Henry Comstock comes upon the miners and insists on a

share, since it is his water they use to wash away the dirt. Over a 20-year period, the mine yields $300 million in gold and silver. All the mine's discoverers die poor; the only ones to make and keep a fortune from it are men like George Hearst, who buys the prospectors out. Virginia City is built to house the miners who come pouring over the mountains to get rich.

12 AUGUST 1859
Arts/Culture F H Conway's play *Pike's Peak or, The Search for Riches* premieres at the Old Bowery Theater in New York City.

Harriet Tubman of the Underground Railroad

SAMUEL HOUSTON, 1793-1863

The man who brought Texas to statehood, Sam Houston, was a remarkable success in nearly everything he did – as trader, lawyer, soldier, governor, and senator. But this bigger-than-life figure, who was instrumental in creating a bigger-than-life state from a former desert, could not master the forces that finally tore Texas out of the Union. Houston was born near Lexington, Virginia, on 2 March 1793. Moving to Tennessee after his father's death, he pursued small businesses and spent much of his time living with the Cherokee Indians. During the War of 1812, he fought alongside Andrew Jackson and was wounded at the Battle of Horseshoe Bend.

After the war Houston was an Indian agent briefly, then went on to study and practice law. In 1823 he was elected to Congress; four years later he became Tennessee's governor. But after his new wife left him in 1829, he resigned abruptly and spent the next years drinking, despairing, and living again among the Cherokees, who adopted him into the tribe. This led to a series of efforts on behalf of Indians, which in turn led, in 1832, to a commission from President Andrew Jackson to parley with Indians in Texas.

Houston was soon caught up in the independence movement, becoming commander of the Texas Army. On 21 April 1836, his forces overwhelmed the Mexican army of Santa Anna, and Texas was independent. Houston was elected first president of the Republic, serving in the legislature between his two terms. As president, he was remarkably successful in organizing the government apparatus, managing the Indians, keeping the Mexicans at bay, and preparing the way for statehood. When Texas entered the Union in 1845, Houston was elected to the US Senate, where he served for 13 years, returning home to become governor in 1859. But in 1860 the tides of secession began to roll, and Houston was torn between his love for his state and for the Union. He fought secession, but when it was voted in 1861 he acquiesced and was peacefully deposed – he refused to call in federal troops to maintain his position. Houston died in Huntsville in 1863.

SEPTEMBER 1859
National The Merchants Grain Forwarding Association is organized to help farmers sell their grain. This co-operative tendency will strengthen and spread in coming decades.

22 SEPTEMBER 1859
Ideas/Beliefs In the Fort Scott *Democrat* (Kansas), an article on a suffragette speech in a local hospital reports that Clarina Nichols, pioneer and lecturer on women's rights, urges that women be given the right to vote: 'If men didn't give them their rights, they would revolt – wouldn't marry. What a row that would make.'

4 OCTOBER 1859
National An anti-slave constitution, drawn up by the Free Staters, is ratified by Kansas Territory voters 10,421 to 5530.

Top: *The landing of Columbus at San Salvador, 12 October 1492, from a lithograph by Currier & Ives.*
Above: *Henry Hudson sights 'a great lake of water,' New York Bay, in a painting by George Wharton Edwards.*
Left: *Vasco Nuñez de Balboa claims dominion over the Pacific Ocean in the name of Spain.*

Top: *De Soto's discovery of the Mississippi.*   Above: *The British surrender at Vincennes, 1779.*

Top: *France salutes the Stars and Stripes (1778)*.   Above: At Concord Bridge, *by N C Wyeth.*

Top: *Wimar's* The Buffalo Hunt.
Above: *George Catlin's portrait of White Cloud.*
Above right: *Catlin's* Mint, *a Mandan woman.*

Opposite top: *Lindneux's* Sand Creek Massacre.
Opposite below: Geronimo, *by Henry Cross.*

The siege of Vicksburg, Mississippi, 1863.

Opposite: *A C M Russell painting.*
Above: *Frederic Remington's watercolor* Cavalry Man.
Left: *Remington's bronze* The Bronco Buster, *c1905.*

PONY EXPRESS!

CHANGE OF TIME!

REDUCED RATES!

10 Days to San Francisco!

LETTERS

WILL BE RECEIVED AT THE

OFFICE, 84 BROADWAY,

NEW YORK,

Up to **4 P. M. every TUESDAY,**

AND

Up to **2½ P. M. every SATURDAY,**

Which will be forwarded to connect with the PONY EXPRESS leaving ST. JOSEPH, Missouri,

Every WEDNESDAY and SATURDAY at 11 P. M.

TELEGRAMS

Sent to Fort Kearney on the mornings of MONDAY and FRIDAY, will connect with **PONY** leaving St. Joseph, WEDNESDAYS and SATURDAYS.

EXPRESS CHARGES.

LETTERS weighing half ounce or under............ $1 00
For every additional half ounce or fraction of an ounce 1 00
In all cases to be enclosed in 10 cent Government Stamped Envelopes,
And all **Express CHARGES** Pre-paid.

☞ **PONY EXPRESS ENVELOPES For Sale at our Office.**

WELLS, FARGO & CO., Ag'ts.

New York, July 1, 1861.

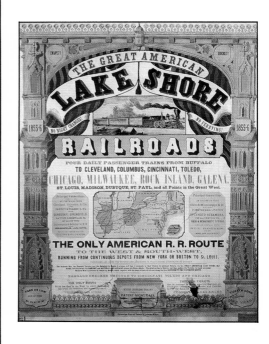

Top: On the Oregon Trail *by Albert Bierstadt.*
Above: *An 1855 advertisement for the Lake Shore Railroad from New York and Boston to St Louis.*
Left: *The Pony Express captured the public imagination during its short term of service.*
Opposite top: *Cave-in Rock on the Ohio River.*
Opposite bottom: The Great West, *Currier & Ives.*

Top: *The Grand Canyon.*
Above: *The American Bison – a survivor.*
Right: *The geyser Old Faithful at Yellowstone.*
Opposite top: *Crater Lake, Oregon.*
Opposite below: *The Mendenhall Glacier, Alaska.*

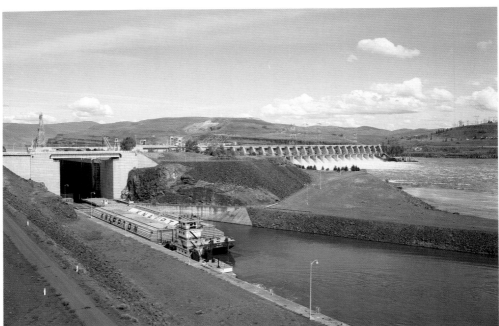

Opposite top: When Winter Comes
Opposite bottom: *The Dalles Dam, Oregon.*

Top: *Grain barges on the Columbia River.*
Above: *Drilling an oil well in Oklahoma.*

Great cities of the West (clockwise from top) Las Vegas, Nevada; San Francisco and Los Angeles, California; Seattle, Washington.

24 OCTOBER 1859

National 'Congregate a hundred Americans anywhere beyond the settlements, and they immediately lay out a city, form a State Constitution and apply for admission to the Union, while 25 of them become candidates for the United States Senate,' notes one traveler. For the second time in less than a year, the more than 100 miners at Pike's Peak petition Congress to establish the Territory of Jefferson. Unwilling to wait (until 1861 for the Colorado Territory), the miners establish a functioning government, with elected officials, by the summer of 1859.

OTHER EVENTS OF 1859

Communications The *Rocky Mountain News* begins publication at the Cherry Creek digging site of Denver. Its publisher is William N Byers. The *Weekly Arizonian* begins publication in Tubac, south of Tucson.

23 FEBRUARY 1860

National Legislators in the Kansas Territory pass the free-state Wyandotte Constitution over the veto of Governor Samuel Medary.

3-13 APRIL 1860

Transportation The first relay riders of the Pony Express carry 49 letters and a special newspaper edition from St Joseph, Missouri, to Sacramento, California, in only 10 days. The service is organized by William H Russell and Alexander Majors, owners of an overland freight and coach-line service.

9 JUNE 1860

Arts/Culture *Maleska: The Indian Wife of the White Hunter* is the first of Irwin P Beadle's Dime Novel Series, published in New York City. The novel is written by Mrs Ann Sophia Stevens.

22 JUNE 1860

National President Buchanan vetoes a homesteading act that was passed by both houses of Congress.

6 NOVEMBER 1860

National Abraham Lincoln is elected President of the United States.

OTHER EVENTS OF 1860

Indians Fort Churchill is located on the north side of the Carson River, about 30 miles south of Carson City, following a Paiute uprising in western Nevada. A war begins at Williams Station when the Paiute avenge the kidnap and rape of two of their girls by white men at the station: all the men at the Station are killed. From Virginia City, 105 volunteers march down the Carson River to avenge the death of fellow-miners. Most of them are killed too. A later attack by whites, 750 from Virginia City, at Pinnacle Mountain, achieves the white objective of pushing back the Paiute.

Settling At Franklin, Idaho, the first permanent agricultural settlement is made.

Mining Arizona mining at Tubac, and in the Santa Rita, Cuerro Colorado, and Santa Cruz Mountains is halted when US Army troops pull out of the area to prepare for the Civil War. The Apache in the area take back control. Gold is discovered in the Orofino Creek (northern Idaho) in Nez Percé country. The miners, largely from the West, arrive from gold fields in British Columbia, prospect in Idaho, then move farther east to Montana.

Life/Customs In Union (now Arcata), California, a youthful new member of the staff of the *Northern Californian*, Bret Harte, writes an editorial criticizing white Californians for participating in the killing of Indians; the citizens become so angry that Harte is forced to resign, but he will resurface years later as a prominent editor and author on Western subjects.

29 JANUARY 1861

National Kansas is granted statehood. Southern opposition has been obviated by the departure of many Southern States to join the emerging Confederate States of America, and the Republican-dominated Congress accepts the anti-slavery constitution of Kansas.

13-14 FEBRUARY 1861

Indian Affairs The nation's first Medal of Honor action takes place at Apache Pass in New Mexico Territory (present-day Arizona), when Colonel Bernard John Dowling Irwin, an assistant surgeon, 'voluntarily took command of troops and attacked and defeated the hostile Indians (Chiricahua) he met on the way.' (The action actually occurs before the medal is authorized by Congress on 12 July 1862.) The medal will be officially awarded on 21 January 1894.

18 FEBRUARY 1861

Indian Affairs Leaders of the Cheyenne and Arapaho tribes agree to abandon their claims to most of Colorado, which is guaranteed to them under an 1851 treaty. The tribes agree to move to a small reservation between the Arkansas River and Sand Creek in eastern Colorado. It is their understanding that they retain their freedom to roam and to hunt buffalo. This belief will lead to many conflicts over the next few years, as Cheyenne and Arapaho hunting parties come increasingly into contact with white settlers and Union soldiers.

23 FEBRUARY 1861

Civil War: Approach A referendum in Texas formally ratifies the ordinance of secession adopted by a state convention on 1 February 1861, and Texas leaves the Union. The day before, President-elect Abraham Lincoln had been warned of a plot on his life.

CHRONOLOGY

HORACE GREELEY, 1811-1872

Journalist Horace Greeley looms large over the history of communications in America during the mid-nineteenth century. In his role as polemicist, reformer, and abolitionist, Greeley's impassioned writings were among the most powerful forces of that eventful time.

Born in Amherst, New Hampshire, on 3 February 1811, Greeley arrived in New York in 1831, a pious and ragged refugee from a hardscrabble farming family who was determined to make his fortune as a newspaperman. After a few false starts, Greeley connected himself with powerful Whigs and founded the historic New York *Tribune*. With his fiery editorials, marked by down-home humor and lucidity of style, Greeley chastised slavery, fought for the rights of immigrants, deplored the Mexican War, and made himself both admired and – especially in the South – abhorred. He was widely but erroneously credited with originating the popular exhortation 'Go West, Young Man!' although he endorsed the idea.

In 1854 Greeley broke with the Whigs and a few years later became a founding member of the Republican Party. His political machinations (usually inept) helped secure Lincoln's nomination in the tumultuous Republican convention of 1860. At the beginning of the Civil War, Greeley was at the height of his influence, a force with whom Lincoln had to reckon on several occasions. But as the war went on, Greeley succumbed to waffling: he was no match for Lincoln's political skills, but neither did he get along with his supposed allies, the Radical Republicans.

After the war Greeley's essential humanitarianism came to the fore in his unpopular support of universal amnesty for the South (he even signed a bail bond for Jefferson Davis) and his advocacy of black suffrage. After a disastrous challenge to Ulysses S Grant's second presidential campaign in 1872, Greeley died, broken in spirit and influence, in Pleasantville, New York, in November of that year.

28 FEBRUARY 1861
National Congress creates the Territory of Colorado. The population of the area has expanded rapidly to 35,000, since the Pike's Peak gold rush of 1859. The territory is created from parts of Utah, New Mexico, Nebraska territories, and the new state of Kansas.

2 MARCH 1861
National Congress creates the Territory of Nevada. Recent discoveries of silver and gold along the eastern slopes of the Sierra Mountains in western Utah Territory have attracted a population of over 20,000. The action is mainly in response to local demands for establishment of a government closer to and more compatible with mining-camp needs. The territory created at this time is a little more than half the size of the present state. The section lying south of 37 degrees north latitude will be added by a Congressional act in 1866. The eastern boundary of Nevada will be moved eastward to the 38th meridian in 1862, then to the 37th meridian in 1866, at the expense of Utah Territory. Congress also creates the Territory of Dakota. Detached from Nebraska Territory, it comprises an area between the 43rd and 49th parallels and extends from the Minnesota border to the Continental Divide.

4 MARCH 1861
National Abraham Lincoln is inaugurated the sixteenth President of the United States. Lincoln hails from the 'prairie state' of Illinois and represents the Republican Party, which is steadfastly opposed to the extension of slavery in the West but would allow it to remain in the South.

18 MARCH 1861
Civil War: Approach A state convention having turned down a move to secede by a vote of 39-35, Arkansas agrees to an election later in the summer which will allow for public voting on the secession issue.

31 MARCH 1861
Civil War: Approach Another Federal outpost, Fort Bliss in Texas, surrenders to state troops.

12 APRIL 1861
Civil War Confederate forces fire on Fort Sumter in Charleston Harbor, South Carolina, and the Civil War begins. Seven states have seceded from the Union. West of the Mississippi River, Texas and Louisiana have seceded, and Arkansas will follow next month. Missouri remains tentatively in the Union as a border state. California and Oregon, despite pockets of Confederate sympathy in southern California, remain strongly pro-Union.

22 APRIL 1861
Civil War Arkansas Governor H M Rector refuses

to send troops to support the Union. The Federal arsenal at Fayetteville, Arkansas, is taken over by North Carolina state troops.

30 APRIL 1861

Civil War Complying with orders from President Lincoln, Federal troops evacuate Indian Territory forts, leaving the Five Civilized Nations – Cherokees, Chickasaws, Choctaws, Creeks, and Seminoles – virtually under Confederate jurisdiction and control.

MAY-OCTOBER 1861

Civil War The Confederacy negotiates alliance treaties with five Indian nations residing in Indian Territory (present-day Oklahoma). They are the Cherokee, Seminole, Creek, Choctaw, and Chickasaw. Each treaty terminates all relations with the United States and accepts each nation as a dependent territory of the Confederacy. Each Indian nation pledges to support the Confederate cause by raising an army: their aggregate population is nearly 100,000.

8 MAY 1861

Civil War At Little Rock, Arkansas, the state legislature votes 69-1 in favor of secession.

JULY 1861

Life/Customs Orion Clemens is appointed secretary of the recently created Territory of Nevada, the number two post in the territory. He brings along as an assistant his younger brother, Samuel Clemens, who has just ended a brief career as a Confederate volunteer. The two depart for Carson City, where the younger Clemens will change his name to Mark Twain, become 'smitten with silver fever,' and work as a reporter and traveling lecturer. Intending to stay in the Far West a few months, Twain will remain there until 1867, and will publish his experiences in a humorous memoir entitled *Roughing It* in 1872.

8 JULY 1861

Civil War The Confederacy, anxious to remove all Federal presence from the New Mexico Territory, places General Henry Hopkins Sibley in command of all Southern forces in the area.

25 JULY 1861

Civil War Confederates in the New Mexico Territory clash with Union troops from Fort Fillmore. The Southerners, under Captain John Baylor, hope to force the Federals from the Southwest, which would open up the area to Confederate control. Union soldiers, however, are able to push their opponents back. The following day, the same Union troops, under command of Major Isaac Lynde, are confronted at Fort Fillmore by Baylor's forces and Lynde abandons the fort. This occurs despite the fact that Lynde's Union troops outnumber Baylor's by 500 men to 250.

1 AUGUST 1861

Civil War Captain John Baylor, who routed Union troops from Fort Fillmore, decrees that all territory in Arizona and New Mexico south of the 34th parallel belongs to the Confederate States of America.

2 AUGUST 1861

Civil War Another fort in the Southwest, Fort Stanton, in New Mexico Territory, is evacuated as a result of attack by Baylor's Confederates.

10 AUGUST 1861

Civil War In the Battle of Wilson's Creek, in southwestern Missouri, a 5000-man Union force led by Brigadier General Nathaniel Lyon is defeated by a much larger Confederate force led by Major General Sterling Price and Brigadier General Ben McCulloch. Each side suffers approximately 1200 casualties. Lyon is killed in the engagement, but succeeds in buying time for the Union to establish greater control over Missouri.

30 AUGUST 1861

Civil War General John Frémont declares martial law throughout Missouri, and announces that he is confiscating the property, including slaves, of those who take up arms against the United States.

24 OCTOBER 1861

Communications Crews constructing a transcontinental telegraph line link up in Salt Lake City, and the first telegraph message is sent between San Francisco and Washington, DC, over a line 3595 miles long. Completion of the transcontinental line renders the Pony Express obsolete, and it ceases service.

21 FEBRUARY 1862

Civil War Confederate forces under Colonel Henry H Sibley, comprising 2600 infantry and cavalry, defeat 3800 Union troops under General E R S Canby, commander of the Department of New Mexico, at Valverde. Sibley then proceeds up the Rio Grande River and easily captures Albuquerque and Santa Fe. This Confederate victory threatens Union control of the entire Southwest region.

7 MARCH 1862

Civil War Federal forces under General Samuel Curtis are surprised by Confederates led by General Earl Van Dorn at Pea Ridge (also known as Elkhorn Tavern), Arkansas. About 17,000 Confederates, including some Indian troops, make valiant attempts to rout the Union soldiers, but the North is victorious.

8 MARCH 1862

Civil War The battle of Pea Ridge, Arkansas, the most significant Civil War battle in the trans-Mississippi West, brings the deaths of Generals

CHRONOLOGY

Jefferson Davis, President of the Confederacy.

McCulloch and McIntosh, depriving the Confederacy of two able commanders. Union troops under General Curtis hold out during a second day of fighting, which ends as Van Dorn and his men retreat to the Arkansas River. Van Dorn has orders to leave the state of Arkansas and to remove to the Mississippi River to aid in the defense of Confederate positions there. Despite the victory, Union losses are 1384 dead and wounded, while Confederate casualties are approximately 800 men.

26 MARCH 1862
Civil War In Colorado Territory an encounter between Southern cavalrymen and Union forces near Denver City results in the capture of 50 Confederates.

28 MARCH 1862
Civil War The First Colorado Volunteer Regiment, comprised mainly of miners and trappers, engages Colonel Henry H Sibley and his Confederate force near Glorietta Pass, 20 miles southeast of Santa Fe, following a forced march through heavy snowstorms. The battle is fought around a 23-room stagecoach stop known as Pigeon's Ranch on the Santa Fe Trail. The Confederate troops overrun the Union right flank, capture the ranch house, and appear to have won a significant victory. However, a Colorado detachment, led by Major John M Chivington, gets behind the Confederate position and destroys the Southern supply train of 73 wagons. The Confederates, chased by General Canby's cavalry, are forced back down the Rio Grande River into Texas. The engagement is officially known as the Battle of Glorietta Pass and represents the last serious Confederate threat to Union control of the Southwest. Later, due to its significance, the battle is dubbed by some the 'Gettysburg of the West.'

20 MAY 1862
National The Homestead Act is signed by President Lincoln. It offers to any citizen, or person who intends to become one, who is the head of a family and over 21 years of age, 160 acres of public land following five years of continuous residence and the payment of a registration fee of between $24 and $34. As an alternative, land under the act can be acquired after only six months at $1.25 per acre. Such homesteads are to be exempt from attachment for debts.

21 MAY 1862
Civil War The First California Volunteer Regiment – soon to be known as the California Column – reaches the mining settlement of Tucson in New Mexico Territory after crossing from southern California. The small Confederate garrison there flees eastward. The California volunteers are commanded by General James H Carleton, who establishes martial law over the mining camps in the area and declares himself military governor. The action restores to the Union the territory between Mesilla and Fort Yuma, thereby ending the Confederacy's 'grand design' for the Southwest.

2 JUNE 1862
National An act of Congress forbids slavery in the Federal territories, but President Lincoln refuses to endorse emancipating the slaves in those states either in rebellion or still loyal to the Union.

1 JULY 1862
Transportation Congress passes the Pacific Railway Act, authorizing the Union Pacific Company and the Central Pacific Company to construct the nation's first transcontinental railroad over a central route between Sacramento and Omaha on the Missouri River in Nebraska Territory. The Central Pacific, building east, is granted permission to build to the California-Nevada border. The Union Pacific will build west. It is hoped that the line will be completed in time for the nation's centennial in 1876.

2 JULY 1862
Education President Lincoln signs the Morrill Land Grant Act, which provides 30,000 acres to each loyal state for every senator and representative then in Congress, for the purpose of endowing at least one agricultural college. The act will lead to a vast expansion in the number of agricultural and engineering schools, particularly in the Middle and Far West.

Civil War cavalry general Philip Sheridan, who later became commanding general of the US Army.

Top: The Freedmen's Bureau *by A R Waud.*   **Above:** *The siege of Vicksburg, July 1863.*

17 AUGUST-26 SEPTEMBER 1862

Indians Peace with the Indians in Minnesota is broken when the Santee Sioux, led by Chief Little Crow, begin a six-week rampage against the white man. Many of the younger warriors in favor of the uprising counsel Little Crow that it is a good time to go to war, since many soldiers are away fighting in the white man's Civil War. Some 400 whites are killed, including many women and children. The Santee Sioux are finally defeated and forced to surrender by Colonel Henry H Sibley and the Sixth Minnesota Regiment. More than 600 male Indians are taken prisoner and held for trial.

5 NOVEMBER 1862

Indians Following a series of trials in Minnesota, 303 Santee Sioux are sentenced to death and 16 to long prison terms for crimes committed against white people in the state.

6 DECEMBER 1862

Indians President Lincoln commutes the death sentence of all but 39 of the convicted Santee Sioux in Minnesota.

26 DECEMBER 1862

Indians Thirty-eight Santee Sioux are hanged before a vengeful crowd of white settlers. One Indian is given a last-minute reprieve.

THEODORE DEHONE JUDAH, 1826-1863

While other men speculated about the grandiose notion of building a railway across America, it was Theodore Judah who made the first practical plan, convinced the right people it would work, and initiated the stupendous project that he would not live to see completed. He was born in Bridgeport, Connecticut, on 4 March 1826, and attended Rensselaer Polytechnic Institute. After graduation he worked for various railroads and planned and built the Niagara Gorge Railroad.

Various jobs had taken Judah to California, where he became caught up in speculation about a transcontinental railway. In 1857 he wrote a pamphlet on the subject that was read in Washington. By 1860 he was convinced he had found a workable route across the Sierra Nevada, and began raising money. With Leland Stanford and Collis P Huntington, he formed the Central Pacific Railroad Company and in 1862, in the midst of the Civil War, began laying track east toward the mountains.

Guided by Judah's expertise, the road pushed into the Sierra Nevada. However, business wrangles developed, and Judah was in danger of being bought out. Sailing East to raise money, he caught typhoid fever and died on arrival in New York in 1863. The great project he had begun was finished in 1869, when the roads of the Central Pacific and the Union Pacific were joined by a golden spike.

JANUARY 1863

Indians General P E Connor and 700 California volunteers conduct the Bear River Campaign near Salt Lake City against Shoshoni and Bannock raiders who have been attacking mining camps and Mormon agricultural settlements. More than 350 Indians are killed and 160 women and children taken captive. This military action destroys Indian power in northern Utah and southern Idaho and removes the threat to the Oregon Road.

1 JANUARY 1863

Agriculture The first claim under the Homestead Act of 1862 is filed by Daniel Freeman, a few miles west of Beatrice, Nebraska.

10 JANUARY 1863

Civil War At Galveston, Texas, Union gunboats bombard the city. Union forces led by General McClernand surround Fort Hindman on the Arkansas River, as Federal gunboats there effectively silence Confederate artillery from the fort.

11 JANUARY 1863

Civil War Fort Hindman, Arkansas, is seized by Federal troops under General John A McClernand and Admiral David Porter. During the battle, the Union loses 134 men and suffers 898 wounded and 29 missing. Confederate losses are 28 killed and 81 wounded, with 4720 taken prisoner.

President Abraham Lincoln in 1864.

24 FEBRUARY 1863
National Congress creates the Territory of Arizona from the western section of New Mexico Territory. The action is taken mainly to reward local Union support and to follow up the reconquest and occupation of the Southwest by the California Column.

MARCH 1863
Indians Almost 500 Mescalero Apache surrender following a relentless campaign waged by New Mexico volunteer companies commanded by Colonel Kit Carson along with California volunteers. They are assigned to an Indian reservation at the dreaded Bosque Redondo on the Pecos River, which has been established by General James Carleton, commander of the Department of New Mexico.

3 MARCH 1863
National Congress creates the Territory of Idaho in response to the movement of more than 20,000 miners into the Clearwater and Salmon River gold fields during the previous year. An area larger than Texas, Idaho will be reduced twice with the establishment of Montana Territory in 1864 and Wyoming Territory in 1868. Many prospectors who are unsuccessful in their search for gold will settle in the area as farmers and merchants.

26 MAY 1863
Mining Bill Fairwether and three companions, returning from Bannack City in eastern Idaho Territory empty-handed after a week of prospecting, strike gold in what they will call Alder Gulch. In response to this newest mining bonanza, Virginia City springs up with a population of 15,000 gold-fevered men and women.

4 JULY 1863
Civil War Vicksburg, the most important Confederate stronghold on the vital Mississippi River, falls to Union forces under General Ulysses S Grant. The loss of Vicksburg and the capture of 30,000 Confederate soldiers threatens Confederate supply routes west of the Mississippi River.

8 JULY 1863
Civil War Port Hudson, Mississippi, the only remaining Confederate fortress on the Mississippi River, falls to Union forces. The Union has split the Confederacy in half, thereby realizing one of its main objectives.

21 AUGUST 1863
Civil War Approximately 450 irregular Confederate raiders under William Clarke Quantrill stage a dawn terrorist raid on the town of Lawrence, Kansas, leaving 150 civilians dead, 30

CIVIL WAR AND THE WEST

Would slavery be allowed to expand into the Far West? This was one of the fundamental questions underlying the American Civil War. With the overthrow of the venerated Missouri Compromise of 1820, and enactment of the Kansas-Nebraska Act (1854) with its doctrine of 'popular sovereignty,' the question of slavery in the West was reopened. The Northern response to this action was the rise of the Republican Party, which opposed any further extension of slavery and which wished to preserve the West for 'free soil, free labor, and free men.'

During the war the West played a key role in the overall strategies of both Union and Confederacy. Controlling the Mississippi River and severing the Confederacy was a vital part of the Union objective. This goal was accomplished with the fall of Vicksburg in July 1863, which interrupted Confederate supply routes through Mexico and Texas and cut off the traffic in foodstuffs, beef, hides and horses from Texas farms and ranches. The Confederacy, for its part, fought hard to keep that supply route open. Moreover, in the early stages of the war, through its 'grand design' for the Southwest, the Confederacy sought to create a land corridor from Texas across New Mexico Territory to California and the Pacific Ocean. The Confederacy ambitiously sought to absorb this region for expanding slavery and to acquire the gold and silver mines of Nevada and Colorado. The Union wanted to retain these same valuable mining regions for its own war effort. Regular army troops had been recalled to the East or had joined the South, so volunteer forces had to be raised to man the forts, guard the freight and mail routes, and deal with Indians. When a Con-

federate military threat up the Rio Grande River toward Colorado was turned back at the Battle of Glorietta Pass in March 1862, the Confederacy's grand design effectively ended.

During the Civil War, the Far West began to develop at a rapid pace. In 1861 the only significant population concentration between eastern Kansas and Sacramento was the Mormon settlement of Salt Lake. However, following gold and silver strikes in Colorado and Nevada, these areas were organized as territories in 1861. Additional mining strikes and the spread of settlement led to the creation of Idaho Territory in 1863 and Montana Territory in 1864. In the context of the war, the Union Government was eager to organize these sparsely settled areas under federal control.

After the war, thousands of young men, from both North and South, were unwilling to return to the mundane life of farm chores or bustling cities. They went west to work the mines, build the railroads, ride the range and kill Indians, buffalo, and each other. 'Wild Bill' Hickok, a former Union army scout, brought his talents to the cattletowns of Kansas and Dakota Territory where, by a conservative estimate, he killed at least 36 men. Jesse James brought his dubious skills, acquired as a Confederate 'bushwhacker,' to a career of robbery and murder. Finally, the Indian tribes of the Great Plains would succumb to the same kind of brutal warfare that Generals William T Sherman and Philip Sheridan, commanding US Cavalry troops in the West after the Civil War, had so recently practiced against the Confederacy. By 1880 that war, too, would be over.

wounded, and much of the town a smoking ruin. In 1862 Quantrill had been denied a commission by Confederate Secretary of War J A Seddon, who termed his notions of warfare 'barbarism.' For some time the town of Lawrence has been strongly Unionist and abolitionist, thus earning Quantrill's enmity.

25 AUGUST 1863

Civil War In the wake of Quantrill's terrorist raid on Lawrence, Kansas, the Federal commander in Kansas City issues a misguided and ineffective anti-guerrilla directive ordering many citizens in the area out of their homes. Property and crops are destroyed, and 20,000 persons are left homeless.

1 SEPTEMBER 1863

Civil War Union forces under James G Blunt capture Fort Smith in western Arkansas, bringing an end to major military engagements in that area. The bulk of the Confederate and Union forces in the area are reassigned to the Eastern Theater. The Arkansas-Canadian River line becomes the boundary separating Union and Confederate forces, as a stalemate ensues in the region, characterized by guerrilla warfare. Confederate raiders have the advantage of familiarity with the terrain and covert support from the local population. They use these assets to keep the invading forces off base.

SIDNEY EDGERTON, 1818-1900

As the godfather of Montana Territory, Sidney Edgerton brought to his entire career a high degree of energy and integrity. Born in New York on 17 August 1818, Edgerton earned his law degree in Ohio in 1846. Among the most determined of Abolitionists, he quickly entered politics as a Free-Soil man and a delegate to the first Republican Convention in 1856. In 1858 he was elected to the first of two terms in Congress. In Washington, he pursued two interests above all – Abolition and a transcontinental railroad.

Lincoln appointed Edgerton chief justice of Idaho Territory in 1863, but Edgerton soon took up the cause of the counties in the area who wanted to form a separate territory. Due largely to his efforts, Montana Territory was formed in 1864, when Lincoln named Edgerton governor. He returned there to deal with a chaotic situation of widespread lawlessness and anti-Union sentiment. Over the next year he made considerable progress, but then resigned on the coming of Andrew Johnson. Having been an Abolitionist and an agnostic despite the dangers of such convictions, Edgerton was perhaps not sufficiently political to see his labors to their conclusion. After years of private law practice, he died in 1900.

Confederates evacuate the Cumberland Gap, giving Union forces control of Kentucky and Tennessee.

CHRONOLOGY

8 SEPTEMBER 1863
Civil War Federal transports and three gunboats from New Orleans enter the Sabine Pass in Texas to attack a small Confederate fort. Within an hour two Union ships have been disabled and another forced to surrender with the loss of some 70 men. The Union soon abandons this military operation.

10 SEPTEMBER 1863
Civil War Federal forces occupy Little Rock, Arkansas, after Confederates evacuate the state capital.

JANUARY 1864
Territorial A gang of holdup men and murderers known as 'road agents,' led by Sheriff Henry Plummer, have been preying on traveling miners who have found gold near Bannack and Virginia

---

INDIAN REMOVAL

Westward movement demanded a formal policy for handling the Indian tribes that stood in the way of settlers. In 1802 a Georgia state law began a process of agitation for the removal of the Indians to west of the Mississippi River. Some preliminary activities took place during the presidency of Thomas Jefferson. In 1804 Congress organized the Territory or Orleans – present-day Louisiana – as a possible Indian area, but General James Wilkinson discouraged that idea by promoting the claim that there were already large numbers of white settlers there. Westward movement was already outstripping a possible removal policy.

Jefferson sent a deputation of Cherokee Indians west in 1809 to see if relocation was feasible, but an actual Indian Territory was not created until 1825, when Congress approved a frontier line that blocked off all of present-day Oklahoma as Indian land. Treatment of Indians to be removed varied by geographic regions. In the Northwest the government sometimes purchased lands that overlapped one another in an effort to be fair to the Indians. The plight of the Five Civilized Tribes of the Southeast – Cherokee, Choctaw, Chickasaw, Creek, and Seminole – was harder. In 1838 the tribes were forced to leave their lands, and some 4000 Indians perished on the 'Trail of Tears' to Oklahoma.

By 1824 the secretary of war estimated that there were still approximately 77,000 Indians living east of the Mississippi River. Their removal was essentially completed by 1840. Ironically, however, westward movement was as frustrated as ever. In 1840 the west was strangely subdivided. Explorers, fur trappers, missionaries, and government agents had gone as far as New Mexico, Oregon, and California, but the majority of American settlers were still in the Mississippi Valley basin. One large impediment to their progress was the Indian country, which had been created to solve just that problem. One indication of the land hunger of the settlers was the rapid colonization of the Black Hawk Purchase, a 50-mile land strip on the west bank of the Mississippi in Iowa, opened in 1833. Year by year, through purchases, 'treaties,' wars, and other means, the Indians were pushed ever westward and then into smaller and smaller reservations.

City, in eastern Idaho Territory. A Committee of Vigilance is formed in haste and the gang is destroyed, as more than two dozen outlaws are hanged in accordance with 'hemp justice.'

JANUARY-MARCH 1864
Indians Following the destruction of their homes and peach orchards in the Canyon de Chelly (northeastern Arizona Territory) by volunteer troops under Colonel Kit Carson, almost 3000 Navajo Indians surrender and begin a 300-mile trek – known as 'The Long March' – to their assigned reservation at Bosque Redondo. Hundreds die during the forced march from cold, hunger, and disease.

18 MARCH 1864
Civil War A convention in Arkansas ratifies a pro-Union constitution and abolishes slavery in that state.

8 APRIL 1864
Civil War At Sabine Crossroads, Louisiana Confederate troops under General Richard Taylor turn back a Union force of 12,000 under General Nathaniel Banks. The Union objective is to reach Shreveport by advancing up the Red River. Union losses are 113 killed, 581 wounded, and 1541 missing. Southern losses are approximately 1000 killed and wounded from a force of almost 9000.

11 APRIL 1864
Civil War A pro-Union state government is established in Little Rock, Arkansas, during the Red River campaign.

26 MAY 1864
National Congress creates the Territory of Montana from Idaho Territory. Thousands of miners have swarmed into the area during the past year, creating population centers at Bannack, Virginia City, and Helena. The new territory adopts a seal depicting a miner's pick and shovel and a farmer's plow against a mountain background.

24 JUNE 1864
Indians Citing recent raids and attacks by hostile Indians, John Evans, the governor of Colorado Territory, orders all 'friendly Indians of the Plains' to report to their reservation at Sand Creek near Fort Lyon.

30 JUNE 1864
Conservation Yosemite Valley Park is authorized as the nation's first state park, when an area embracing the valley itself and the Mariposa Grove of Big Trees some miles south of it is granted to the state of California by an act of Congress. Actual control of the area and its development is delayed 10 years by the claims of settlers in the area. Yosemite will become a national park in 1890.

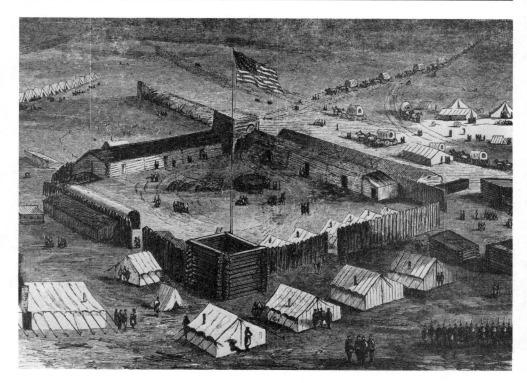

4 JULY 1864
Immigration Congress passes the Immigration Act, allowing importation of contract labor (the increasing demands of the Civil War have created a severe labor shortage). The Central Pacific Railroad will recruit thousands of Chinese from Shanghai and other cities to help build the transcontinental railroad toward the east. The Union Pacific Railroad will use thousands of Irish immigrants and other European nationalities as it builds west.

27 SEPTEMBER 1864
Civil War After crossing into Missouri from Indian Territory, General Sterling Price leads a Confederate cavalry force of 12,000 against a Federal garrison at Pilot Knob under the command of Thomas Ewing Jr. The Union forces, though badly outnumbered, beat off the attack, inflicting some 1500 casualties, and then escape under cover of darkness. Meanwhile, a small band of Confederate guerrillas, led by William 'Bloody Bill' Anderson, ride into Centralia, Missouri, looting and burning many of its buildings. Anderson and his men then capture a train as it pulls into town and kill more than 20 unarmed Federals on board. Later the band ambushes a column of Union cavalry sent out to intercept the raiders, killing another 100 Union soldiers. Massive Union reinforcements will arrive next month.

US Cavalry stockade of the Indian Wars era.

28 SEPTEMBER 1864
Indians Seven chiefs from the Cheyenne and Arapaho tribes, led by Black Kettle and White Antelope, meet with Colorado military and civilian officials at Camp Weld, near Denver. Governor Evans, Colonel John M Chivington, commander of the Third Colorado Regiment, and Major Edward Wynkoop, the commandant of Fort Lyon, are present. The governor accuses the Indians of numerous hostile attacks throughout Colorado. The Indians either deny responsibility for initiating hostilities, or blame the Sioux. Chivington warns the chiefs that 'My rule for fighting white men or Indians is to fight them until they lay down their arms and submit to military authority.' At the order of Colorado officials, the Cheyennes and Arapahoes move to Sand Creek near Fort Lyon and report to Major Wynkoop. Wynkoop issues the Indians rations, makes them feel welcome, and assures them of their safety.

23 OCTOBER 1864
Civil War In the Battle of Westport, Missouri, 20,000 Federal troops attack 8000 Confederate cavalry led by Generals Price and Shelby. The Confederates are forced to retreat southward along the Missouri-Kansas border. The battle ends the Confederate threat to Missouri.

CHRONOLOGY

26 OCTOBER 1864
Civil War Union troops ambush and kill the notorious Confederate raider 'Bloody Bill' Anderson near Richmond, Missouri.

31 OCTOBER 1864
National Nevada, with a population of fewer than 40,000, is admitted to the Union. Throughout 1864 national Republican leaders have pressured a constitutional convention to complete its work so that Nevada citizens could participate in the November election. President Lincoln is anxious to have Nevada's support for the proposed Thirteenth Amendment to the Constitution, which calls for the banning of slavery. Time is so short that in the longest telegram on record up to that time, the entire text of the proposed state constitution is telegraphed to Washington, DC, at the then staggering cost of $3416.77.

29 NOVEMBER 1864
Indians Colorado volunteers, led by Colonel Chivington, attack a Southern Cheyenne and Arapaho village at Sand Creek in southeastern Colorado. The village is 30 miles from Fort Lyon, whose commandant, Major Wynkoop, has been relieved of duty for being too friendly with the Indians. Numerous atrocities are committed by

---

THE FIRST WESTERNERS

Estimates vary considerably, but it is thought that there were from one to two million Indians living in North America when the first Europeans arrived – presumably at least half of them west of the Mississippi. These native Americans were probably descended from immigrants who had begun to come over from Asia into the land we know as Alaska sometime after 40,000 bc. (Most experts reject recent claims that tools from a much earlier date have been found in California.) The earliest migrants from Asia apparently crossed the Bering Strait land bridge at a time when the ocean level was low – because so much water was in great ice sheets – but others may have island-hopped along the Aleutians, or even used their crude boats to make their way across Lake Agassiz, the postglacial lake that once covered much of Manitoba and North Dakota. As hunters and food-gatherers, these bands of migrants moved south and east in search of more food and resources. Bone implements and crude stone tools dating from at least 20,000 bc have been found all the way from Alaska and the western United States down through Mexico to Peru. Although it is known that by 9000 bc ancestors of the later Indians were as far east as Massachusetts, most of the settlements were still west of the Mississippi. The discovery of human-made projectile points in prehistoric bison bones near Folsom, New Mexico (1927), showed that Stone Age hunters had roamed the American West by 9000 bc. Since then, many finds have established that the ancestors of the Indians were moving throughout North America in the millennia before and after that date.

In response to different environmental and other conditions, these first Americans began to develop particular cultures, both material (such as clothing and tools) and non-material (such as religion and government). When the Europeans arrived, the Indians had already split up into hundreds of tribes speaking as many as 300 distinct languages in North America alone. The languages have since been classified into several major groups – from 10 to 20, depending on the system – but the distribution of related languages does not always coincide with geographical proximity: thus the dialects spoken by the Arikaras of South Dakota, the Pawnees of Kansas, and the Wacos of Texas were closely related to the Iroquois language spoken by Indians of upstate New York.

What the Europeans saw, when they arrived, were exotic natives who, if they did not possess gold and jewels – in North America, that is – at least had vast tracts of land and numerous animals. They had not discovered iron and did not use wheeled vehicles, horses, or cattle until a later date. Most Europeans saw the native peoples as primitive savages, and soon realized how powerless they were in the face of firearms, iron tools, and European diseases to which they had no immunity. The outcome was inevitable.

The once-powerful Sioux are confined to reservations.

The 8th US Cavalry, formed after the Civil War for Mexican border patrol and Indian control.

the ill-disciplined soldiers, mostly against women and children. Chivington claims in his official report to have killed 400-500 Indian warriors: the actual number killed is 105 Indian women and children and 28 men. The soldiers' losses are nine killed and 38 wounded, many of the casualties caused by wild firing among the soldiers themselves. Chief White Antelope is killed, but Chief Black Kettle escapes. The incident, which causes a furor in the East, becomes known as the 'Chivington Massacre.'

JANUARY 1865

Indians Outraged Cheyenne, Arapaho, and Sioux warriors launch a series of attacks all along the valley of the South Platte River in Colorado. The Indians strike at wagon trains, stage stations, and military outposts. The town of Julesburg, in northeast Colorado, is burned, and its white residents scalped in retaliation for the massacre at Sand Creek. Denver is threatened. Communications and supplies throughout the area are halted.

9 APRIL 1865

Civil War Confederate General Robert E Lee surrenders to General Ulysses S Grant at Appomattox Court House, Virginia. This is the official end of the Civil War, but isolated resistance will continue for a short time, particularly in the West. Many experienced Union officers and troops will now be available for military duty against the Indian tribes of the Great Plains. General William T Sherman will soon assume command of all US military forces west of the Mississippi River.

15 APRIL 1865

National President Abraham Lincoln dies after being shot by an assassin the previous evening. Andrew Johnson of Tennessee takes the oath of office and is sworn in as President of the United States.

12-13 MAY 1865

Civil War At Palmitto Ranch, on the Rio Grande River in Texas, Federal troops attack and expel a Southern encampment. Later in the day, however, Confederates led by Colonel John S Ford launch an attack on the Union force there and force them to withdraw. The Battle of Palmitto Ranch is the last battle of the American Civil War.

20 MAY 1865

Civil War Confederate General E Kirby Smith, commander of Confederate forces west of the Mississippi River, surrenders. This action ends all organized Southern resistance.

24 MAY 1865

Science/Technology The first railroad rails of Bessemer steel are rolled in Chicago, Illinois. They are a significant improvement over iron rails and will become the standard for railroad construction.

10 JULY 1865

Transportation Although it has been three years since passage of the Pacific Railway Act, the Union Pacific Company only now lays its first rail out of Omaha, Nebraska. Progress is extremely slow at first, averaging only one mile per week.

14 OCTOBER 1865

Indians Federal commissioners and leaders of the Southern Plains tribes conclude a council and sign treaties at the mouth of the Little Arkansas River in western Kansas. Thomas Murphy, head of the Central Indian Superintendency, John B Sanborn, and General William S Harney represent the United States. Tribal leaders present include Black Kettle for the Southern Cheyennes, Ten Bears for the Comanches, and Satanta for the Kiowas. The objective of the US Government is to create a railroad corridor between the Platte and Arkansas Rivers. By the Little Arkansas Treaties, the signatory tribes cede to the United States their claims to the territory north of the Arkansas River and agree

to settle on diminished territories south of that stream. However, the Senate refuses to consent to the pacts, and federal officials refuse to protect the tribal territorial rights guaranteed by the treaties.

25 DECEMBER 1865

Industry The Union Stockyards open in Chicago. This will help develop a number of associated industries, principally stockraising and railroads, which will spread across the entire West. More than anything else, this development will help make Chicago the hub of transcontinental commerce.

OTHER EVENTS OF 1865

Transportation The first comfortable Pullman sleeping railroad car is built by George Mortimer Pullman in Chicago at a cost of $18,000. The car is longer, higher, and wider than the original 1859 Pullman sleeping car. It has the first raised upper-deck and folding upper-berth, and is heated by hot air furnaces under the floor, lighted with candles, and ventilated through deck windows. It is fully carpeted and its seats are covered with plush French upholstery.

Opposite: *An early Union Pacific train in Oregon.*
Below: *First engine used in the Pacific Northwest.*

Completion of the first transcontinental railroad.

Inventor George M Pullman.

JUNE 1866

Indians A delegation of Brule and Oglala Sioux, led by Red Cloud, meet with American officials at Fort Laramie. The Americans present demands to the Northern Plains tribes that include the improvement and fortification of the Bozeman Road, which runs from Fort Laramie to the mines near Virginia City in Montana Territory. The route runs along the Powder River east of the Bighorn Mountains and traverses some prime buffalo-hunting range of the Sioux. At the same time, Colonel Henry B Carrington arrives at Fort Laramie with 700 soldiers after marching from Fort Kearny, Nebraska. Carrington is under orders to establish a chain of forts along the Bozeman Road. Red Cloud considers the presence of the soldiers a threat to use force. He breaks off negotiations and departs.

28 JUNE 1866

Indians Colonel Carrington and his regiment of soldiers relieve two companies of hard-pressed soldiers near the headwaters of the Powder River. The post is enlarged and renamed Fort Reno. One-fourth of Carrington's soldiers remain there.

13 JULY 1866

Indians US Army soldiers under Colonel Carrington begin constructing Fort Phil Kearny, north of Fort Reno, near the mouth of the Tongue River.

Opposite: *Oglala Sioux leader Red Cloud.*

GRENVILLE MELLEN DODGE, 1831-1916

One of the pioneers in the glory days of American railroading, Grenville Dodge was a driving force behind the realization of his dream of a transcontinental railroad. Born in Danvers, Massachusetts, on 12 April 1831, Dodge developed an early interest in engineering and received a science degree from Norwich University in Vermont, in an era when railroading had the same fascination as aviation would have for the youth of a later age.

Dodge first became a railroad builder with the Illinois Central in 1852. Soon another job took him surveying in Iowa, and he settled in Council Bluffs, where he occupied himself with railroad and business ventures. He volunteered for the Civil War and became both a distinguished officer of Iowa volunteers (wounded twice in battle) and a resourceful railroad builder in a time when rails first became important in warfare. In one three-day period he built a 710-foot bridge across the Chattahoochee River.

After the war Dodge plunged into the long-dreamed-of project of building a transcontinental railway. Beginning in 1866, he planned and supervised the Union Pacific road forging west while the Central Pacific moved east. As the whole country waited for the news, the two roads met on 10 May 1869: when the golden spike was driven home, Dodge's ambition was realized. He went on to build thousands of more miles of roads in the United States and in Cuba until his death in 1916.

16 JULY 1866

Indians The First Sioux War begins in the Powder River country, as Oglala Sioux disrupt and drive off horses belonging to Carrington's soldiers.

SUMMER 1866

Indians Sioux warriors and allies from other Northern tribes engage in intermittent warfare along the Bozeman Road and against the newly constructed forts designed to protect it. Travel along the road is difficult and dangerous, and soldiers stationed at the forts are often deprived of supplies and isolated. By the end of summer, Red Cloud has gathered a force of 3000 Indian warriors.

The First Vote *by A R Waud.*

AUGUST 1866
Indians Colonel Carrington, under orders from the War Department, sends 150 soldiers to build Fort C F Smith, 90 miles north of Fort Phil Kearny.

21 DECEMBER 1866
Indians Captain William J Fetterman and 80 soldiers are ambushed and killed near Fort Phil Kearny. The soldiers leave the fort to go to the aid of a wood-cutting party, which is under attack by Indian decoys. Almost 2000 Sioux, Cheyenne, and Arapaho warriors take part in what becomes known as the Fetterman Massacre. This is the worst defeat the US Army has suffered in Indian warfare. Colonel Carrington is recalled from his command and reinforcements are sent to the Powder River area.

OTHER EVENTS OF 1866
Industry Dynamite is manufactured in San Francisco by Julius Bandmann, using the Nobel patents, under the name of Bandmann Neilson and Company. In 1867 the Great Powder Company will grow out of this concern. Dynamite will prove essential for blasting tunnels through the Sierra Nevada, as the Central Pacific builds the transcontinental railway line eastward. Dynamite will also be used in mining operations throughout the West.

31 JANUARY 1867
National Congress grants the right to vote to all males over the age of 21 in all US territories.

MARCH 1867
Indians In reaction to the Fetterman Massacre, a bill passes Congress which calls 'for establishing peace with certain Indian tribes now at war with the United States.' A Peace Commission consisting of four civilians and three US Army generals is formed. A plan is developed to confine all Indians of the Great Plains to two reservations: the northern tribes will be granted the Black Hills in the extreme western portion of the Dakota Territory, and the southern tribes will be moved to the western section of Indian Territory.

Transportation The Kansas Pacific Railroad reaches Abilene, Kansas. Joseph McCoy establishes the town as a terminus for Texas cattle to be shipped by rail to the East.

1 MARCH 1867
National Nebraska is granted statehood as the thirty-seventh state admitted to the Union.

30 MARCH 1867
International In the Alaska Purchase Treaty, concluded by American Secretary of State William H Seward and Russian Minister to the United States Edouord de Stoeckl, Russia transfers Alaska to the United States for $7,200,000. However, some unhappy Congressmen, with references to 'Seward's Folly,' voice opposition to the treaty and its ratification is delayed. The House of Representatives must approve the appropriation to conclude the treaty.

APRIL 1867
Indians General William T Sherman has devised

Secretary of State William H Seward.

THE RUSSIANS IN AMERICA

The Russian explorations of the New World were initially an extension of explorations in the vast wilderness of Siberia and the wastelands of Russia's outermost Asian territories. The first explorers of Siberia – known as *zemleprokhodsy*, or 'crossers of land' – traversed the barren eastern wastelands in search of the area's one great natural resource: fur-bearing animals, such as the seal, sea otter, beaver, and fox.

By 1725 Czar Peter I had decided that a more systematic exploration of the area was called for; he chose the Danish explorer Vitus Jonassen Bering (1681-1741) for the job. In 1728 Bering sailed through the strait that now bears his name, but did not recognize its importance, as foul weather prevented him from seeing the coast of Alaska.

In 1741 Bering, on the *Saint Peter*, and the Russian explorer Aleksey Ilich Chirikov, on the *Saint Paul*, set sail from Kamchatka on their ill-fated voyage of discovery. Miserable weather soon separated the two ships, and Bering headed east, past the Aleutian Islands. On 16 July he sighted the Saint Elias Mountains in Alaska, and sent a party ashore to reconnoiter. Shortly thereafter, the expedition ended in disaster, with a shipwreck on Bering Island and the leader's death. Survivors managed to fashion a new craft from the wreck and made their way back to Kamchatka in 1742. There they learned that Chirikov had also sighted the Aleutian Islands and had explored one of them, perhaps Attu.

These voyages sparked Russian and international interest in the fur trade of North America's far west. In 1784 the Shelikhov-Golikov Company established a trading post on Kodiak Island, and in 1799 was chartered by Czar Paul I as the Russian American Company. The company had a virtual monopoly over the fur trade in Russian America, including the Aleutians and Alaska. Its empire was farflung: it refounded Sitka, which had been destroyed in a skirmish with the Tlingit Indians, and founded a post at far-off Fort Ross, north of San Francisco, California. The fur trade was also given impetus by the discovery in 1786, by G G Pribilov, of the islands that bear his name and are the breeding grounds for countless seals.

The race to capture a share of the rich fur trade was often to the swiftest – and at the expense of the peaceful Aleut Indians and the Alaskan Eskimos of the area. The eighteenth century also saw extensive Russian mapping of the Pacific coastline and charting of the local waters. Russian exploration, settlement, and domination of the area continued until 1867, when the United States purchased Alaska and the Aleutian Islands.

---

a plan to drive all of the Plains Indians either north of the Platte or south of the Arkansas River, leaving a broad belt of territory for the transcontinental railroad and the Kansas Pacific Railroad. General Winfield Scott Hancock leads a large cavalry and infantry force across western Kansas. At Pawnee Fork, his troops capture and burn a Cheyenne village of 250 lodges. The Indians, fearing another massacre like the one at Sand Creek in 1864, flee before the advancing troops. In retaliation the Indians halt almost all travel across western Kansas. Surveying parties for the Kansas Pacific Railroad come under attack, and progress on that line is halted for over a month.

1 AUGUST 1867
Indians The Sioux and Cheyenne continue their war against the US Army forts stationed along the Bozeman Road. More than 500 Cheyenne warriors, led by Dull Knife and Two Moon, attack about 30 soldiers and civilians working in a hayfield near Fort C F Smith. In what becomes known as the Hayfield Fight, the defenders drive off the Indian attack with breech-loading Springfield rifles.

2 AUGUST 1867
Indians About 800 Sioux warriors, under Red Cloud, force a group of woodcutters working near Fort Phil Kearny to flee to a line of wagon boxes, which are then overturned and used for cover. In what becomes known as the Wagon Box Fight, these defenders are also equipped with repeating rifles and inflict 200 Indian casualties against five for the white defenders.

28 AUGUST 1867
National The first territory outside the North American continent, Midway Island in the North Pacific Ocean, is claimed by US Navy Captain William Reynolds for the United States.

5 SEPTEMBER 1867
Industry The first shipment of 20 cattle cars leaves Abilene, Kansas, on the Kansas Pacific Railroad bound for the East.

OCTOBER 1867
Life/Customs William F Cody is hired to kill 12 buffalo per day along the path of the Kansas Pacific Railroad as it progresses westward through Kansas. Cody is paid $500 per month, and over the next eight months kills more than 4000 buffalo. In so doing he becomes widely known as 'Buffalo Bill.'

21 OCTOBER 1867
Indians Some 7000 Indians gather, as the leaders of the Southern Plains tribes conclude a series of treaties with members of the new Peace Commission established by Congress. The signings take place on Medicine Lodge Creek in southwestern Kansas. US representatives include the Commissioner of Indian Affairs, Nathaniel G Taylor, and General Alfred H Terry. Indian leaders include Stumbling Bear, Satank, and Satanta for the Kiowas; Ten Bears and Little Horn for the Comanches; and Black Kettle and Tall Bear for the Southern Cheyennes and Arapahoes. The Kiowas and Comanches are assigned a 3,000,000-acre re-

Kit Carson (left) with Buffalo Bill Cody.

servation between the Red and Washita Rivers in western Indian Territory. A week later the Southern Cheyenne and Arapaho tribes are assigned an area between the Cimarron and Arkansas Rivers. Several newspaper correspondents cover the proceedings, including Henry M Stanley of the *Missouri Democrat*, who will later gain prominence by trekking through Africa to find Dr David Livingston.

18 OCTOBER 1867

International Following approval by the House of Representatives of a $7,200,000 appropriation for the purchase of Alaska from Russia, the United States assumes control of the territory in ceremonies at Sitka. President Andrew Johnson places Alaska under control of the War Department, where it will remain until 1877.

4 DECEMBER 1867

Agriculture The Patrons of Husbandry, popularly known as the Grangers, is founded in Washington, DC, to support agricultural interests. The organization is created by Oliver Hudson Kelley, who resigns his post in the Department of Agriculture. At first Kelley has little success in recruiting members, but after 1871, amid mounting resentment, hundreds of thousands of small farmers and businessmen will join: by early 1874 the Grangers will claim 1,500,000 members. The movement will take over many state legislatures in the Midwest and draft laws opposed to exorbitant prices and monopolistic practices undertaken by railroads and grain elevator operators.

29 APRIL 1868

Indians Sioux and Northern Cheyenne tribal leaders meet with US peace commissioners at Fort Laramie. A treaty is concluded which calls for an end to US Government attempts to improve the Bozeman Road and abandonment of the three forts recently constructed in the Powder River region. In return, the Indians agree to accept fixed reserva-

tions in Dakota Territory west of the Missouri River, but are promised the use of their old hunting grounds east of the Bighorn Mountains in southern Montana Territory.

25 JULY 1868

National President Johnson signs an act of Congress creating the Territory of Wyoming. Most of the area for the newly created territory is detached from the huge Dakota Territory. To square the western section of this new entity, small areas are taken from the Utah and Idaho Territories. This action by the Federal Government is mainly in response to demands by citizens who have already created a local government. The passage of the transcontinental railroad through the southern section of the territory, and the growth of population centers like Cheyenne and Laramie along its route, create the conditions for this move.

28 JULY 1868

National The Fourteenth Amendment to the US Constitution is ratified. It grants full citizenship to blacks and all other persons either born in the United States or naturalized with the notable exception of the native North Americans, who are denied citizenship.

International A treaty regulating commerce and immigration is signed between representatives of the United States and China. It calls for a free flow of immigration and travel between the two countries and is commonly known as the Burlingame

---

STATEHOOD

The Western states became part of the Union through an involved process. The constitution had not directly specified how new states should be added to the Union. Vermont (1791), Kentucky (1792), and Tennessee (1796) were authorized by acts of Congress, and Maine separated from Massachusetts in 1820. The Western regions became states on the basis of the Northwest Ordinance of 1787. Under its provisions, there was a four-step process to statehood. First, there had to be an organized territory, which developed and maintained a system of self-government and grow in population to between 20,000 and 40,000 people. Congress then would pass a specific act authorizing residents of the territory to form a constitutional convention. The third step was the writing of a constitution and its approval by the territorial residents. When an approved document was submitted to Congress, the territory would usually become a state in the Union, equal to all other states, regardless of date of entry. Western regions became states throughout the first third of the nineteenth century: Ohio (1803), Louisiana (1812), Indiana (1816), Mississippi (1817), Illinois (1818), Missouri (1821), Arkansas (1836), Michigan (1837). In 1840 there were two blocks in the way to future new states – the Indian country in Oklahoma and Kansas, and the unorganized territory in present-day Iowa, Nebraska, North and South Dakota, and Montana. Before the century was over, these, too, would gain statehood.

Treaty, after Anson Burlingame, a former American ambassador to China, who is chiefly responsible for its conclusion.

Above: *Battle of the Washita, November 1868.*

Below: *George Armstrong Custer (standing right).*

SEPTEMBER 1868

Indians General Philip Sheridan recruits a special company of frontier scouts at Fort Hays and orders them to track down and kill any Indians sighted along the path of the Kansas Pacific Railroad. Colonel George A Forsyth and 50 scouts are surrounded (17 September) by many Sioux and Cheyenne warriors at the Arickaree Fork of the Republican River, in eastern Colorado Territory. Forsyth's men set up sand-pit breastworks on an island in the river and come under siege for eight days: they are nearly wiped out before the arrival of a relief column. The battle is notable because Roman Nose, a fierce Northern Cheyenne chief, who had earned a reputation for skill and invincibility in battle, is killed. The fight is called by whites the Battle of Beecher's Island, in memory of Lieutenant Frederick Beecher, who is killed during the siege. The Indians record it as The Fight When Roman Nose Was Killed.

27 NOVEMBER 1868

Indians The Seventh Cavalry, led by Lt Colonel George Custer, attacks a large Cheyenne camp on the upper Washita River in western Indian Territory. Custer splits the regiment and attacks from four directions. The dawn attack in heavy snowstorms catches the sleeping Indians completely by surprise. Chief Black Kettle, who had narrowly escaped death at Sand Creek in 1864, is among the 103 Indians killed, 92 of whom are women, children, and old men. Nineteen US Army soldiers are killed when they are led down a trail into a trap.

Captain Louis McLane Hamilton, grandson of Alexander Hamilton, is another casualty. Custer's troopers slaughter the village herd of 800 ponies, burn every lodge, and gather more than 50 women and children as prisoners.

CHRONOLOGY

Building the Union Pacific Railroad.

OTHER EVENTS OF 1868
Arts/Culture Bret Harte assumes editorship of the *Overland Monthly* in San Francisco. Over the next three years he will print several of his own stories with Western settings – 'The Luck of Roaring Camp,' 'The Outcasts of Poker Flat,' and 'Tennessee's Partner' – which will make both Harte and the West familiar to many Americans.

2 FEBRUARY 1869
Science/Technology James Oliver patents a chilled-iron plow equipped with a smooth-surfaced moldboard that can slip through the hardened prairie soil without clogging. Other inventors will improve on his basic implement by covering the blade with an edge of tempered steel that can be removed for sharpening. By 1877 completely modern plows will be in use.

4 MARCH 1869
National Civil War hero Ulysses S Grant is inaugurated the eighteenth President of the United States. Grant appoints William T Sherman General of the Army, and Philip Sheridan Lieutenant General in charge of military forces west of the Mississippi River. Grant also chooses the first Indian Commissioner of Indian Affairs: his name is Ely Samuel Parker, or Donehogawa of the Iroquois. Parker appoints so many Quakers to posts as Indian agents that the Grant Administration policy toward the Western tribes becomes known as the 'Quaker' or 'peace policy.'

13 APRIL 1869
Science/Technology The air brake is patented by George Westinghouse Jr under the description of 'steam power brake.' It demonstrates immediately its value for making railroad transportation safer and eliminates the need for separate brakemen for each railway car. However, because it takes longer for the air to reach the last cars of the train, these often stop at different times. A 'triple air brake,' which corrects this fault, will be patented by Westinghouse in 1872.

10 MAY 1869
Transportation At Promontory Point in Utah Territory, the nation's first transcontinental railroad is completed, as the Central Pacific's *Jupiter* and the Union Pacific's *No 119* touch after gold and silver spikes are driven. Telegraph wires flash the news to an expectant nation, touching off a continent-wide celebration. Regular train service begins five days later, with average traveling time from coast to coast eight to ten days. However, until a bridge is completed across the Missouri River in 1872, travelers must still take a ferry boat from Council Bluffs, Iowa, to Omaha, Nebraska.

24 MAY-19 AUGUST 1869
Exploration The first exploration of the Grand Canyon is made by Major John Wesley Powell, who leaves Green River City, above the Colorado River head, on 24 May and emerges from the lower end of the Grand Canyon on 29 August, with five of the nine men who had started with him. The following year, Powell will be appointed chief of the US Topographical and Geological Survey of the

Colorado River of the West. Lake Powell, on the Colorado River in southern Utah, is named for him.

11 JULY 1869

Indians Eight companies of the US Fifth Cavalry attack the summer encampment of Tall Bull and his Cheyenne 'Dog Soldiers' at Summit Springs, in northeast Colorado Territory. The Dog Soldiers are a separate self-appointed warrior order that has refused to concur with earlier treaties. Tall Bull and 52 Indians are killed. The fight is recorded as the Battle of Summit Springs and is the last in that section of the Great Plains; it frees Kansas and the surrounding country from the threat of Indian attack. 'Buffalo Bill' Cody, while not participating directly in the battle, plays a key role in scouting out the village's location and later incorporates the battle as a showcase performance in his Wild West Show.

10 DECEMBER 1869

Social Change The legislature of the Territory of Wyoming grants the right to vote and hold office to women over 21 years of age, the first state or territory in the nation to do so. This move reflects the increased duties and responsibilities that frontier women have assumed as compared to women in the more settled East.

2 FEBRUARY 1870

Social Change After Wyoming, Utah Territory becomes the second territory or state in the nation to grant full suffrage to women.

COLLIS P HUNTINGTON, 1821-1900

It was Collis Potter Huntington and his business partner, Mark Hopkins, who first seriously took up engineer Theodore Judah's dream of building a transcontinental railroad. These two originated the Central Pacific Railway, linking the country from coast to coast. Huntington was born in Harwinton, Connecticut, on 22 October 1821. His early working years were spent in small trade; in 1850 he headed for gold-booming California and started a hardware business with Mark Hopkin as his partner. The business prospered in meeting the needs of supply-hungry prospectors.

After studying Judah's plan, the founding partners convinced Leland Stanford and Charles Crocker of its merit, and the Central Pacific was in business. Huntington was dispatched to Washington to seek federal assistance, and secured it handsomely in grants of cash and land. With Crocker to oversee the construction work across the desert, and the other three partners taking care of business matters, the job was finished in May 1869, when the Central Pacific connected with the Union Pacific in Utah. By then Huntington and his partners had begun creating the Southern Pacific, which became an equally successful venture. A philanthropist as well as a businessman, Huntington had a special interest in black colleges, donating considerable funds to the Tuskeegee and Hampton Institutes. He died in New York State in 1900, leaving his large collection of paintings to the Metropolitan Museum of Art in New York City.

Shooting buffalo on the southern route of the Oregon Trail.

CHRONOLOGY

JAMES BUTLER 'WILD BILL' HICKOK, 1837-1876

In an era when fiction and reality overlapped to a degree rarely seen since, 'Wild Bill' Hickok worked both as an effective lawman and as a caricature of himself on the stage. He was born in Troy Grove, Illinois, on 27 May 1837, and left the family farm to make his fortune in the West. In the mid 1850s, Hickok was a stagecoach driver on the Santa Fe and Oregon Trails. It was around this time that he was attacked by a cinnamon bear and killed it with a Bowie knife. In 1861 he survived a shootout with the McCanless gang in Nebraska; three of the outlaws were killed.

During the Civil War Hickok was a Union scout and spy; captured and sentenced to hang several times, he escaped in every case. In Missouri, in 1865, he gunned down his former partner Dave Tutt, who had turned traitor. After the war he was a sheriff and gambler in Fort Riley, Hays City, and finally Abilene, Kansas. His exploits became the stuff of legend in that already-romanticized era of the Wild West. It was every bit as wild as its reputation, and Hickok's adventures, involving many close scrapes and numerous notches on his gun, scarcely needed exaggerating. Having become a dime-novel hero, he played himself on the stage in the early 1870s and toured with Buffalo Bill's show. After going to Deadwood, Dakota Territory, Hickok was shot dead from behind by Jack McCall during a poker game in 1876; since then his last deal of two pairs, aces and eights, has been called the 'Dead Man's Hand.'

15 FEBRUARY 1870

Transportation Construction of a second transcontinental railroad, the Northern Pacific, begins in Duluth, Minnesota, on Lake Superior. The railroad will go bankrupt during the Panic of 1873, and the route will not be completed until 1883.

30 MARCH 1870

National Texas is readmitted to the Union.

31 MAY 1870

Transportation The first organized transcontinental railroad excursion, undertaken by the Boston Board of Trade, arrives in San Francisco. The group left Boston on 23 May carrying their own printing press, with which they published a daily newspaper titled *Trans-Continental*. Public interest is stimulated.

3 MARCH 1871

Indians The Indian Appropriation Act is passed by Congress: it declares that henceforth no Indian tribe or nation will be treated or recognized as a sovereign power with which the Federal Government must contract by treaty. The act declares that the Indian tribes shall be subject to all the laws of Congress and the administrative decrees of executive officials, particularly the Commissioner of Indian Affairs. All treaties negotiated before 1871, however, are to remain in force.

ALBERT PIKE, 1809-1891

In a lifetime of tireless endeavor, Albert Pike made a name for himself as a poet, lawyer, soldier, and Mason, but today he is best remembered for the least of his efforts – writing some verses for 'Dixie.' Pike was born in Boston on 29 December 1809 and left school as a teenager to study on his own and write poetry. Heading west in 1831, he taught school, wrote for an Arkansas newspaper, published a book of prose and poetry, and was admitted to the bar in 1837. Having built a considerable law practice, he left to command a cavalry troop in the Mexican War, at which time he had the first of his chronic problems with superiors.

Returning to Arkansas, Pike involved himself in pro-slavery politics and the Know-Nothing Party. When the Civil War began, he took a commission as a Confederate officer in command of Indian Territory, and led a force of Indians to take part in the Battle of Pea Ridge, Arkansas (7-8 March 1862). However, wrangles with superiors ended his military career within two years. After the war he secured a presidential order restoring his civil rights, and by 1868 was practicing law in Washington, DC, where began the involvement with Masonry that went on for the rest of his life (he died in Washington in 1891). His greatest effort was in rewriting the Masonic rituals, which were published in several editions between 1872 and 1905. He knew half a dozen languages, ancient and modern, and won considerable acclaim as a poet. Today, however, only his verses for 'Dixie' are read.

Chinese-American relations in flux (Thomas Nast).

30 APRIL 1871

Indians Another Apache war begins in New Mexico and Arizona Territories with the massacre of more than 100 Indians at Camp Grant, Arizona. The conflict will continue sporadically until the capture of the Apache leader, Geronimo, in 1886.

8 MAY 1871

International In the Treaty of Washington, between the United States and Great Britain, a joint commission is established to settle fishing and boundary disputes off the Pacific Coast. The question of jurisdiction over the San Juan Islands is to be settled by the German Emperor. The treaty is consented to by the Senate on 24 May.

2 OCTOBER 1871

Ideas/Beliefs Brigham Young and several other Mormon leaders are arrested and tried on charges of 'lascivious cohabitation' in pursuance of an 1862 Congressional act making bigamous marriages a federal offense in the territories. This is an attempt to proceed against polygamy by attacking the Mormon church law. Mormon leaders are convicted in the lower courts but, on appeal, the territorial supreme court rules that the defendants should be released because of lack of jurisdiction.

24 OCTOBER 1871

Civil Rights The bloodiest outbreak in a series of riots against Chinese on the West Coast occurs in Los Angeles, where 22 Chinese are killed by mob violence. There are 120,000 Chinese residing in the United States, mostly on the West Coast. The Orientals are regarded as a threat to desirable wage and working standards because of their willingness to work long hours for low wages. Because federal law bars the naturalization of Chinese

---

COCHISE, c 1812-1876

Chiricahua Apache chief Cochise became a byword for terror among settlers in the Southwest. Born around 1812 in southeastern New Mexico, Cochise raided only the Apache's old enemies, the Mexicans, for much of his life. But after a false accusation of kidnapping in 1860, and an arrest by American authorities while under truce, Cochise escaped into the mountains for a life of vengeance against American settlers.

With his father-in-law, Mangas Coloradas, Cochise became the scourge of whites in Arizona, swooping down to murder, rape, and kidnap settlers in countless raids. In one battle, Cochise and Mangas Coloradas, with some 500 braves, stood off 3000 California volunteers for a full day before artillery drove them away. More frequently, Cochise used the hit-and-run tactics of Indian guerrilla-style warfare, against which the whites were nearly powerless – at least until the arrival of the great Indian fighter General George Crook. His troops consisted mainly of Indians, including Apaches experienced on the warpath. In 1871 Crook and his Apaches ran Cochise to ground. Then a series of broken promises by the US Government gradually evicted the Apaches from their land. Returning peacefully after a breakout in 1872, Cochise died on an Arizona reservation in 1876.

immigrants, their lack of civil rights makes them vulnerable targets for legal and extralegal discrimination.

1 MARCH 1872
Conservation President Grant signs an act of Congress creating the Yellowstone National Park in the extreme northwestern section of Wyoming Territory, with a small section taken from Montana Territory. It is the nation's first national park. The tract of land set aside is 2,142,720 acres, and Nathaniel Pitt Langford is designated the park's first superintendent. The Act of Dedication declares 'That the tract of land in the Territories of Montana and Wyoming lying near the headwaters of the Yellowstone River ... is hereby reserved and withdrawn from settlement, occupancy, or sale under the laws of the United States, and dedicated and set apart as a public park or pleasuring ground for the benefit and enjoyment of the people.'

21 OCTOBER 1872
International By authority of the 1871 Treaty of Washington, the German Emperor, William I, awards the San Juan Islands to the United States. The archipelago lies east of Vancouver Island, off the northwest coast of Washington.

28 NOVEMBER 1872
Indians The Modoc Indians have been living away from their assigned Klamath Reservation in southern Oregon for several months, in defiance of

First black Congressmen – 41st and 42nd Congresses.

the US Government. Captain James Jackson and 38 soldiers of the First Cavalry attempt to move the Modocs and their leader, known as Captain Jack, back to the Klamath Reservation. Shooting breaks out, and the Modocs take refuge in the lava beds south of the Tule Lake, in northern California. In the course of their flight south, the Indians kill at least a dozen settlers.

12 FEBRUARY 1873
Finance Congress passes the Coinage Act of 1873. Silver is demonetized and dropped as a coin; gold is made the sole monetary standard. Advocates of silver, particularly Western mine operators, refer to the action as the 'Crime of '73' for decades.

3 MARCH 1873
Conservation Congress passes the Timber Culture Act. Under its terms a person can obtain an additional 160 acres of government land in return for planting 40 acres of trees. At the end of ten years (later reduced to eight), final title would be granted if the person could prove that the specified number of trees had been planted. The purpose of the law is to promote the preservation of timber on the Western prairie. Proponents of the act argue that groves of trees will reduce wind, attract increased rainfall, halt soil erosion, and provide lumber for building and fuel. By virtue of this legislation, over 65,000 homesteaders receive 10 million acres of land.

11 APRIL 1873
Indians A peace council with the Modoc Indians, who have been holed up in the lava beds in northern California, turns into a massacre. Modoc leader Captain Jack fires a pistol, killing Brigadier General E R S Canby; another Indian kills the Reverend Eleazer Thomas. A B Meacham, a former Indian agent for the Modocs, is shot but survives. A fourth member of the peace commission, Leroy S Dyar, escapes unharmed. This episode begins a month-long chase of 50 Modoc Indians by almost 1000 soldiers, before Captain Jack and his dwindling band are forced to surrender.

21 JULY 1873
Life/Customs Jesse and Frank James, with other members of their gang, derail and hold up their first train on the Rock Island Line, between Adair and Council Bluffs, Iowa. The James gang halts a load of transcontinental passengers. During the derailment the engineer and a number of passengers are killed.

18 SEPTEMBER 1873
Finance The brokerage firm of Jay Cooke and Company fails, plunging the country into a severe depression. Many other banks and thousands of businesses fail shortly thereafter. Unchecked railroad speculation, particularly with respect to Western lines, is a chief underlying cause of the Depression. The Northern Pacific Railroad, whose financial agent is Jay Cooke, is forced to abandon construction for five years at Bismarck in Dakota Territory.

3 OCTOBER 1873
Indians Four Modoc Indians, including their leader Captain Jack, are hanged at Fort Klamath in Oregon for the murders of General Canby and Reverend Thomas.

1 NOVEMBER 1873
Science/Technology Joseph F Glidden begins the manufacture of barbed wire in De Kalb, Illinois. The barbs are cut from sheet metal and inserted between two wires, which are then twisted. This invention answers the need for fences on the open prairie, where timber is sparse and expensive. The expansion of the cattle industry to the upper West creates the need to confine valuable livestock. Glidden obtains a patent for his product on 24 November 1874.

OTHER EVENTS OF 1873
National The administration of the Territories of the United States is shifted from the Department of State, where it has resided since 1789, to the Department of the Interior.

Mining Four miners strike the 'Big Bonanza' while digging through the rock of Davidson Mountain, near Virginia City, Nevada. At a depth of 1167 feet, the miners discover a vein of ore 54 feet wide filled with silver and gold. The richest strike in the history of mining produces a fortune estimated between $150 million and $200 million.

Science/Technology Oliver F Winchester develops the Winchester .44-40 (or Winchester '73).

The Indian remains an outsider in his own land.

This gun represents a vast improvement over Winchester's 1866 model, which could fire rapidly but lacked impact and range; it features a center-fire cartridge, which contains 40 grains of powder compared with 28 in the earlier model. This weapon becomes popularly known as 'the gun that won the West.'

23 MARCH 1874
Industry The first legislation sponsored by the rapidly growing Grange movement is passed in Iowa and provides for the regulation of railroad freight rates in the state. Wisconsin passes similar legislation on 11 March.

27 JUNE 1874
Indians In the Battle of Adobe Walls, in the Texas Panhandle, 29 buffalo hunters hold off 700 Kiowa, Comanche, Cheyenne, and Arapaho warriors with the aid of rapid-fire Sharps .50-caliber rifles. One of the defenders is William Barclay 'Bat' Masterson, later a famous peace officer in Dodge City.

AUGUST-DECEMBER 1874
Indians Over a period of several months, hundreds of Kiowas and Comanches come into Fort Sill, Texas, to surrender. This event finally breaks the power of the Indians on the north Texas plains and ends the Red River Wars. To guard against further Indian violence, 72 warrior chiefs are placed in irons and hauled under heavy guard to a military prison in St Augustine, Florida.

NOVEMBER 1874
Hawaii King Kalakaua of Hawaii visits the United States as a guest of the US Government. Kalakaua is the first king to visit from any country and is received in state by President Grant. The purpose of the visit is to strengthen ties between the two countries and aid the negotiation of a reciprocity treaty. After an extended tour of the United States, Kalakaua will return to Honolulu on 15 February 1875.

'CALAMITY JANE' CANNARY, 1852-1903

A living legend in her day, Calamity Jane was born on a farm in Missouri in 1852 and named Martha Jane Cannary. When she was 13, her family moved to a Montana gold-mining town. An expert rider from an early age, Jane went out on hunting parties during her family's five-month move west, which strengthened her sense of adventure and independence – few young girls did such things, even in those frontier days.

The death of Jane's parents when she was 15 left her to take care of herself. For some years she drifted from place to place in the Dakotas, Wyoming, Montana, and Colorado, taking odd jobs and getting into minor trouble with the law. While in Deadwood, South Dakota, for the gold rush of the 1870s, Jane befriended the legendary Wild Bill Hickok and found her way into Western lore in the Wild West Shows of her time. No one knows for sure just how much of her life's story was tall tales and how much was the truth, for Calamity Jane made numerous claims to fame. She said she had been a gold miner, a stagecoach driver, an Indian fighter, an army scout, an ox whacker, a nurse, and a Pony Express rider. Her audience accepted these tales uncritically, as one more manifestation of the popular frontier spirit. Reduced to poverty by a long illness, Jane Cannary died in South Dakota in 1903 and was buried in a pauper's grave next to Wild Bill Hickok. Her funeral was attended by thousands.

OTHER EVENTS OF 1874
Agriculture The worst grasshopper plague in history spreads devastation from Texas to the Canadian border. Clouds of grasshoppers attack crops, trees, and even farm equipment. The locusts block railroad tracks and obscure the sun. This combines with severe drought and the recent Depression to wreak havoc across the Great Plains. Western migration is reduced by half, as thousands of families forsake the frontier for the more settled regions of the Midwest and the East.

Rounding up cattle in Lone Cove, Colorado.

30 JANUARY 1875

Hawaii A treaty of commercial reciprocity is signed between the United States and Hawaii. The treaty allows Hawaiian raw materials and certain other products to be brought into the United States duty-free. Hawaii promises that it will not allow any of its territory to be turned over to a third power. The agreement leads to a vast expansion of the Hawaiian sugar industry, the importation of immigrant labor, and an influx of American capital.

AUGUST 1875

Exploration A military expedition led by Lt Colonel George A Custer confirms reports of gold in the Black Hills in western Dakota Territory. In response to these reports, the trickle of miners into the Sioux preserve turns into a flood. Outraged Indians and eager miners will come into conflict increasingly during the next few months.

OCTOBER 1875

Indians The US Government attempts to buy Indian lands north of the Platte River, but the Indians do not wish to sell their last holdings and refuse the money.

9 NOVEMBER 1875

Indians In his annual report, Indian Inspector E C Watkins identifies hundreds of Hunkpapa Sioux, under Sitting Bull, and Oglala Sioux, under Crazy Horse, as hostile Indians. On his recommendation it is ordered 'that these Indians be informed that they must remove to a reservation before the 31st of January, 1876, and that in the event of their refusal to come in by the time specified, they would be turned over to the War Department for punishment.'

DECEMBER 1875

Indians The US Government orders all Indians in the Black Hills of Dakota and Wyoming Territories to move to reservations or face military action.

OTHER EVENTS OF 1875

Industry Montana prospectors in the Butte district open the world's richest copper mine, the Anaconda.

1 FEBRUARY 1876

Indians Secretary of the Interior Z Chandler, noting that the Sioux Indians under Sitting Bull have refused to return to their reservations or report to agency posts, turns the Indians 'over to the War Department for such action on the part of the Army as you may deem proper under the circumstances.'

3 FEBRUARY 1876

Indians Secretary of War William Belknap acknowledges the receipt of Interior Secretary Chandler's letter and reports that 'immediate mea-

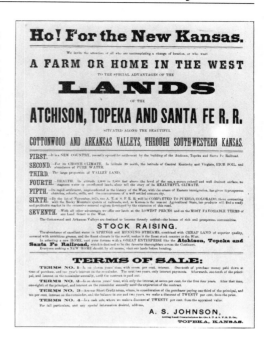

Railroad land in southwest Kansas is advertised.

sures' are being taken 'to compel the Indians to remain upon their reservation, as requested by your department.'

10 FEBRUARY 1876

Indians Brigadier General Alfred H Terry, commander of the Department of Dakota, receives orders for military action against the Sioux and Cheyenne tribes.

2 MARCH 1876

National Secretary of War William Belknap is impeached by the House of Representatives for receiving bribes in exchange for the sale of lucrative trading posts in Indian Territory. Belknap resigns the same day to avoid a trial by the Senate.

APRIL 1876

Life/Customs In response to the discovery of gold in the Black Hills, the notorious town of Deadwood is founded in western Dakota Territory. It is occupied by 7000 miners who rapidly turn it into a center of frontier lawlessness.

17 MAY 1876

Indians General Terry leaves Fort Abraham Lincoln in Dakota Territory with a force that includes Lt Colonel George Custer and 12 companies of the Seventh Cavalry. As part of a three-pronged maneuver planned by General Sheridan, Terry will move west until he reaches the Yellowstone River, then move upstream in a southwesterly

CHRONOLOGY

direction and locate the Indians. Colonel John Gibbon is moving east from Fort Ellis, Montana Territory, and General George Crook is moving northward from Fort Fetterman in Wyoming Territory. These Army units have been informed that they can expect to encounter no more than 500 Indians gathered at one time.

4 JUNE 1876
Transportation In celebration of the nation's centennial, a special *Transcontinental Express* arrives in San Francisco from New York in a record-breaking 83 hours and 39 minutes. It will be 50 more years before such service is instituted on a daily basis.

17 JUNE 1876
Indians On the Rosebud River, General Crook unexpectedly encounters the southern fringe of a huge Indian encampment. He is attacked by almost 1500 Sioux, led by Crazy Horse. The Indians are forced to retreat. Crook suffers only nine soldiers killed but is forced to regroup southward at Goose Creek.

21 JUNE 1876
Indians Aboard the steamer *Far West*, on the Yellowstone River near Rosebud Creek, Colonel John Gibbon, General Alfred Terry, and Lt Colonel George Custer meet to plan strategy. They are unaware of General Crook's encounter with Sioux Indians. It is decided that Custer and the Seventh Cavalry will ride south along Rosebud Creek to the headwaters of the Little Bighorn River, and then

Crook's cavalry at the Rosebud River.

reverse direction and ride north. Gibbon and Terry are to follow the Yellowstone to the Bighorn River, then ascend that river to the Little Bighorn.

22 JUNE 1876
Indians Lieutenant Colonel George Custer leaves Colonel Gibbon and General Terry with 12 companies of the Seventh Cavalry comprising more than 675 officers and troopers.

25 JUNE 1876
Indians Lieutenant Colonel George Custer and the Seventh Cavalry, having shortened by 20 miles the route mapped out by General Terry up Rosebud Creek, are 12 miles southeast of a huge Indian encampment on the west bank of the Little Bighorn River. Custer decides to split the regiment. Captain Frederick Benteen, with three companies, is ordered to search to the west. Major Marcus Reno is told to take three companies, cross the Little Bighorn, move down the valley and attack. Custer takes five companies and moves along the east bank of the Little Bighorn with the intention of supporting Reno's attack by striking the flank side of the village. One company of troopers is detailed to the pack train. On the opposite side of the Little Bighorn is the largest gathering of Indians ever seen in North America. Different tribes comprise six circles, with the Cheyenne encampment standing at the extreme north edge of the village. Southward from the Cheyennes, the Sans Arcs, Miniconjoux Sioux, Oglala Sioux,

Above: *Remington's* Signalling the Main Command.
Below: *Chief Low Dog, who fought against Custer.*

Blackfeet, and Hunkpapa Sioux are strung out for at least three miles. Altogether there are approximately 10,000 to 15,000 Indians. Reno and his three companies attempt to move against the south end of the village, but are nearly overwhelmed. These troopers are thrown back toward a cluster of cottonwood trees near the riverbank. This position is also untenable, and the remnant of Reno's command flees across the river and up an embankment to relative safety. Custer, having moved four miles upstream, is attacked and surrounded by Sioux and Cheyenne warriors streaming out of the village. The fight lasts only half an hour: Custer and his entire command are killed. Their bodies are stripped naked, their possessions taken. Most of the soldiers are mutilated beyond recognition. Meanwhile, Captain Benteen and his three companies, realizing it is futile to attempt to join Custer, move to Reno's position on the hilltop near the river. They are unaware of what has happened to Custer.

26 JUNE 1876
Indians The remainder of the Seventh Cavalry remains pinned down on their hilltop. Toward nightfall, the huge Indian encampment is dismantled and the warriors depart.

27 JUNE 1876
Indians The US Army column under General Terry and Colonel Gibbon discovers Lt Colonel

CHRONOLOGY

Custer and his men. The column also reaches Reno and Benteen. No exact count of the number of troopers who died is possible, because many of the bodies have been dismembered, or dragged away by the Indians. Most estimates are between 220 and 225. Including those killed in Reno's attack, fatal casualties at the Battle of Little Bighorn are usually listed at 265.

4 JULY 1876
National In the midst of centennial festivities, news of Custer's defeat reaches the East, and an outraged and patriotically charged public demands revenge.

Above: *Battle of the Little Big Horn.*
Below: *'Custer's last stand' was mythologized.*

1 AUGUST 1876
National President Grant issues a proclamation admitting Colorado to the Union as the nation's thirty-eighth state. In the previous five years, the population of the territory has grown from 40,000 to 150,000, and Republican leaders hope to have the support of Colorado's electoral votes for the November election. The proclamation issued by Grant allows the people of Colorado to participate in that election. Colorado's three electoral votes later prove crucial in Rutherford B Hayes's vic-

tory over Democrat Samuel J Tilden. Although Congress, since the 1840s, had regularly delegated to the President the authority to admit a territory when, in his judgment, it had met the conditions of the Congressional Enabling Act, a constitutional controversy breaks out over the admission process for new states. The Constitution provides that Congress shall be the sole judge of elections, returns, and qualifications of its members, and that Congress has the power to exclude or expel members. A new state can enter the Union only if its representatives are received by Congress. Subsequently, Democrats in Congress challenge Colorado's admission on ground that Congress has no power to delegate its authority to admit a state. In early 1877 the House Democrats contest the seating of Colorado's Republican Congressmen, arguing that Colorado is still a territory. This Democratic challenge is rejected, the representatives from Colorado are seated, and Rutherford Hayes's victory is upheld.

2 AUGUST 1876

Life/Customs James Butler 'Wild Bill' Hickok is shot and killed from behind while playing poker in Saloon No 10 in Deadwood, Dakota Territory. Hickok is holding two pair, aces and eights, a legendary combination known ever since as 'the dead man's hand.'

7 SEPTEMBER 1876

Life/Customs The James gang attempts to carry out a bank robbery in Northfield, Minnesota. This town of 500 people has been alerted, and many are lying in wait to ambush the gang, three members of which are shot and killed. Two others are wounded; only Jesse and Frank James escape. This marks the end of a long string of successful bank robberies for the James brothers. A $25,000 reward is posted for Jesse James, dead or alive, and $15,000 is offered for his brother Frank.

25 NOVEMBER 1876

Indians As part of an intensified campaign, following Custer's defeat, to drive all Indians from the Bighorn and Powder River region, Colonel Ranald Mackenzie attacks the Cheyenne village of Dull Knife. More than 200 lodges and hundreds of Indian ponies are destroyed. Numerous items belonging to deceased members of the Seventh Cavalry are discovered.

1 MARCH 1877

Judicial In the case of *Munn v Illinois*, the US Supreme Court, by a vote of 7-2, upholds an 1871 Illinois law that establishes maximum rates for the storage and handling of grain. The decision represents the first test for a series of laws, passed by the growing Grange movement, that are designed to curb the power of the railroads and grain-elevator operators throughout the West and Midwest. Corporation lawyers argue that the due-process

SITTING BULL, c 1834-1890

An implacable foe of the white man and his designs on Indian land, Sitting Bull was romanticized and admired by some whites while others were dispossessing his people. Sitting Bull was born to a subchief of the Sioux in present-day South Dakota around 1834. As a warrior in his early years, he became chief of the northern Sioux in 1866; his vice-chief was the great Oglala Sioux leader Crazy Horse.

After 1868 there was a period of peace when the US guaranteed the traditional Dakota lands of the tribes. But on discovery of gold in the Black Hills in 1874, the signs of white encroachment became unmistakable. Sitting Bull and Crazy Horse assembled a confederation of up to 4000 Sioux, Cheyenne, and Arapahoe warriors and went on the warpath in 1876. The high tide of their rebellion was in June of that year, when Crazy Horse stymied Crook in the battle of the Rosebud River, then, with Chief Gall, annihilated Custer at the Little Bighorn.

Soon thereafter the Indian confederacy dissolved in the face of increasing military pressure, and Sitting Bull took his remaining people to Canada in 1877. After several years of starvation, they surrendered in the United States in 1881. Imprisoned for two years, Sitting Bull then tried reservation life and even toured with Buffalo Bill Cody's Wild West Show for a year, despite his continuing antipathy to the white man. He was arrested in the wake of the Indian Ghost Dance agitation of 1889, although he had little to do with it. Despite efforts on his behalf by Cody and others, he was murdered by Indian police in December of that year, shortly before the Wounded Knee massacre that was the last action of the Indian wars. To whites and Indians alike, he had been a legendary figure in a hopeless cause.

clause of the 14th Amendment guarantees certain private rights of property against legislative invasion, particularly in such matters as prices, rate schedules, and labor laws. Chief Justice Morrison Waite, however, sustains the Illinois law as a proper exercise of the police power.

3 MARCH 1877
Agriculture The Desert Land Act is passed by Congress. The act offers to sell any person 640 acres of land at $1.25 per acre if the person undertakes to irrigate some portion of it. Twenty-five cents per acre is to be paid at the time of filing and the other dollar per acre within three years. The intent of the law is to promote establishment of individual farms in the arid and semiarid West, where the environment rules out the traditional homestead of 160 acres. The average settler, however, is in no financial position to undertake the expense of irrigation to bring arid land into production. Consequently, the law proves to be of little value to actual farm settlers in the 11 Western states and territories where it applies. Almost all of the claims made under the law are fraudulent, the work of land speculators and ranchers who acquire cheap land by tossing a bucket of water on the ground and calling it irrigation.

5 MARCH 1877
National Rutherford B Hayes of Ohio is inaugurated as nineteenth President of the United States.

14 JULY 1877
Labor A handful of enginemen on the Baltimore and Ohio Railroad walk out to protest a series of wage cuts. Within two weeks a chain of spontaneous and unorganized uprisings, directed mostly against railroads and railyards, spreads across the country.

23 JULY 1877
Labor As strikes and riots spread nation-wide, laborers gather at city hall in San Francisco to hear speeches calling for an eight-hour workday and the nationalization of railroads. Frustrated over economic conditions, the crowd breaks into and destroys about two dozen Chinese wash houses. While the Chinese population in California as a whole has dropped slightly, the percentage of Chinese in San Francisco has climbed from 8 percent to almost 30 percent. With rainfall in California the lowest in a quarter of a century, and almost one-fourth of the labor force unemployed, the Chinese offer a visible and convenient target for labor unrest.

24 JULY 1877
Labor Rioting against the Chinese community in San Francisco continues. Several Chinese are murdered and fires spread to many sections of the city.

Peter Cooper of the Greenback Party.

25 JULY 1877
Labor The lumberyard near the docks of the Pacific Mail Steamship Company in San Francisco is set ablaze, and firemen come under attack by rioters. Several men are killed and many injured. The steamship company and the Central Pacific Railroad are chiefly blamed for the large influx of Chinese into the city. The state militia is mobilized as federal gunboats stand by.

29 AUGUST 1877
Ideas/Beliefs Brigham Young, the leader of the Mormon Church in Utah Territory, dies. The US Government has refused to accept Utah as a state until the Mormon Church, the dominant force in the area, changes its religious practices to forbid polygamy. After Young's death, the changes will slowly be made.

SEPTEMBER-OCTOBER 1877
Labor Denis Kearney helps give rise to the Workingmen's Party in California. Kearney gives many fiery sandlot orations directed against the Chinese and in support of white laborers. Although the Chinese are only about 8 percent of the population of California, they comprise one-fourth of all workingmen available for hire in the 1870s. The Chinese are frequently hired by employers in manufacturing and construction, because their willingness to work long hours for low wages seems to provide an answer to the more advanced techniques and cheaper production costs of the East. Kearney is imprisoned again and again for his incendiary rhetoric, but he quickly becomes a hero and martyr for thousands. By

January 1878 the Workingmen's Party will be a major force in California politics.

5 SEPTEMBER 1877

Indians Crazy Horse, chief of the Oglala Sioux, is bayoneted by a soldier at Fort Robinson in Nebraska after pulling a knife upon learning he was to be imprisoned. Crazy Horse dies of his wounds a few hours later. He is about 35 years old.

5 OCTOBER 1877

Indians Chief Joseph of the Nez Percé surrenders his tribe of 4–500 in the Bear Paw Mountains in northern Montana Territory. The surrender takes place only 30 miles from the safety of the Canadian border and follows a 1300-mile flight from four different US Army columns during which a dozen separate battles are fought.

OTHER EVENTS OF 1877

Industry The first year-round, long-distance shipments of dressed beef are made by Gustavus Swift of Swift and Company, who ships meat from Chicago in ten refrigerated cars built to his own specifications.

CRAZY HORSE, c 1849-1877

One of the greatest leaders of the Indian struggle against white encroachment, Crazy Horse, was born into the Oglala Sioux tribe around 1849. He earned distinction as a warrior at an early age, and was an important leader in Red Cloud's successful war against the Bozeman Trail in 1865-8. After marrying into the Cheyenne tribe, Crazy Horse formed an alliance of Sioux and Cheyenne in resisting white efforts to confine the Indians on reservations. His people had been at peace for some years when the government guaranteed them their ancestral lands in the Dakota Black Hills. But when gold was discovered there in the mid-1870s, it became increasingly clear that the Indians were going to be forced out. This betrayal brought about the great Sioux-Cheyenne uprising of 1876-7, under the joint leadership of Crazy Horse and Sitting Bull.

In March of 1876, General George Crook's cavalry destroyed the village of Crazy Horse, but three months later the Sioux leader nearly swamped Crook by the use of masterful tactics in the battle of the Rosebud River. Eight days later, 25 June 1876, came the Battle of Little Big Horn; there two detachments under Gall and Crazy Horse annihilated the entire force of General George Custer. Thereafter the confederacy fell prey to the inevitable Indian deficiencies in long-range tactics. By 1877 the alliance was dissolved. At the urging of the now-peaceful Red Cloud, and having been promised limited freedom, Crazy Horse and his people surrendered in Nebraska in May 1877. In September the Sioux leader was arrested and killed under mysterious circumstances. One of his white adversaries later wrote this testament to Crazy Horse: 'He was a born soldier whose talents for warfare and leadership were of the highest order . . . one of the bravest of the brave and one of the subtlest and most capable of captains.'

JANUARY 1878

Industry In response to the discovery of silver-bearing carbonate-of-lead ores at the headwaters of the Arkansas River, a town is organized in central Colorado under the name of Leadville. The mining discoveries in 1878 and 1879 will exceed all previous finds in the area. The Robert E Lee Mine will pour forth $118,500 worth of silver in a single day. In Colorado it quickly becomes known that 'all roads lead to Leadville,' and the city becomes the most important influence in Colorado for more than a decade, inaugurating an era of prosperity.

17 JANUARY 1878

International Congress ratifies a treaty between the United States and Samoa. The harbor of Pago Pago is given to the United States Navy for use as a refueling station.

18 FEBRUARY 1878

Life/Customs An English rancher, John Tunstall, is shot and killed in New Mexico Territory, igniting what will be known as the 'Lincoln County War.' Tunstall's friends, including William Bonney, who is soon to be better known as Billy the Kid, or simply 'the Kid,' vow to avenge his death. Two warring factions are quickly organized between this group and Tunstall's killers. The ensuing violence attracts scores of gunmen, rustlers, and other desperadoes seeking to join one side or the other, some simply taking advantage of the general lawlessness. The subsequent fighting includes pitched battles fought in the town of Lincoln itself, leaving many dead.

28 FEBRUARY 1878

Finance Congress passes the Bland-Allison Act over the veto of President Hayes. A bill sponsored by Representative Richard P Bland of Missouri calls for the unlimited coinage of silver, but an amendment introduced by Senator William B Allison restricts monthly purchases of silver to between $2,000,000 and $4,000,000. Since the middle 1870s, silver has been found in large quantities in Nevada, Utah, and Colorado. In light of the expansion of silver production, Western silver mine operators, in alliance with inflationist-minded agrarian and labor groups, have come to view the demonetization of silver in 1873 as the 'Crime of '73': they call for unlimited coinage of silver. These groups view the coinage of silver as a means of raising farm prices and labor wages and pulling the country out of its economic depression. The resumption of silver coinage appears to be a victory for the silverites, but the Secretary of the Treasury uses his discretionary powers to limit silver purchases to the $2,000,000 minimum, thereby reducing overall demand for silver and inflationary pressures.

4 MARCH 1878

Arts/Culture Central City, Colorado, a small

CHRONOLOGY

mining town in the mountains outside Denver, inaugurates its handsome little opera house with an evening by local amateur musical groups. In subsequent years, many notable stars of the theater and opera will appear in productions here until Central City's boom times end and the town goes into decline.

3 JUNE 1878
Conservation   The Timber and Stone Act is

Black cavalrymen in action against the Utes, by Frederic Remington.

passed by Congress. It allows the cutting of timber on public land to increase farm acreage. Most of the land is given or sold cheaply to timber interests, with only a small percentage used for actual farming. Like many of its agricultural and conservationist predecessors, the Timber and Stone Act fails to solve the problem or help those who need it, but instead is used by Western big business to acquire still more property and wealth.

30 SEPTEMBER 1878
Life/Customs   In response to continuing violence in Lincoln County, New Mexico Territory, President Hayes appoints Civil War hero General Lew Wallace governor. On 7 October Hayes will declare that Lincoln County is in a state of insurrection. Wallace will succeed in bringing some semblance of order by means that include a general offer of amnesty and a clandestine meeting with Billy the Kid. Wallace is a writer of historical novels and will compose parts of his classic saga, *Ben Hur*, while residing in the old adobe Governor's Palace in Santa Fe.

3 MARCH 1879
National   The US Geological Survey is established by an act of Congress. Clarence King is appointed its first director.

29 MARCH 1879
Industry   The Wyoming Stock Growers Association is formed from the Stock Association of Laramie. Creation of this organization reflects the importance of the cattle industry in the territory; the group rapidly becomes the most influential political and economic power in Wyoming Territory, and later, in the state. From this the National Stock Growers Association will evolve.

RED CLOUD, 1822-1909

A number of Indian leaders won battles against whites: Chief Red Cloud was the only one who won a war. Even so, his cause and the traditional ways of his people were doomed – a fate that Red Cloud could not evade despite his years of struggle as a warrior and then as a peacemaker. Born into the Oglala Sioux of Nebraska in 1822, Red Cloud gained fame as a young warrior and became chief of his tribe in the 1860s. He led Sioux and Cheyenne resistance to the US Army's forts and emigration route on the Bozeman Trail. After besieging the forts and killing settlers for nearly three years, Red Cloud gained his point: in 1868 the government abandoned the trail.

Thereafter Red Cloud went off the warpath for the rest of his life. He lived for some time at the agency named for him in Nebraska, and was an active campaigner not only against white corruption, but also against Indian hostiles (he gave no support to Crazy Horse's rebellion). More than once he went to Washington as a negotiator for Indian interests. In the end his people were evicted to South Dakota (1878), and three years later Washington supported a corrupt agent in deposing Red Cloud from chieftainship. Though he kept up his attempts to secure peace and justice, his health and influence declined in his last years. Cavalryman Crook had described Red Cloud as 'a magnificent specimen of physical manhood' in his prime: he died sick and defeated at the Pine Ridge Reservation in 1909.

MAY 1879

Labor Chiefly under pressure from the Workingmen's Party, the State of California adopts a clause for its new constitution that outlaws employment of Chinese and bars granting suffrage to any 'native of China.'

SUMMER 1879

Indians The last Indians with a reservation in Colorado, the Utes, come under increasing pressure from greedy whites. A newspaper campaign is launched under the slogan 'the Utes must go.' During this period the Ute Indians are blamed for any regional malady, including a series of forest fires.

29 SEPTEMBER-5 OCTOBER 1879

Indians Fighting breaks out between the Ute Indians and 250 US Army soldiers led by Major Thomas Thornburgh at Milk Creek, in northwestern Colorado Territory. Twelve soldiers including Major Thornburgh, are killed, and 43 are wounded in a week-long battle. In what they believe is a last stand to save their reservation, 37 Utes are killed. Meanwhile, at the White River Agency, the Ute Indian agent, Nathaniel Meeker, and several other whites are also killed. In response, a call is issued to the people of Colorado to 'wipe out the red devils,' and militia units are organized across the state. The Utes are forced to surrender and relocated to Utah; their former reservation of 12,000,000 acres is thrown open for settlement and development – a pattern that has long prevailed.

Call for blacks to move west – 1878.

Hunkpapa Sioux chief Gall.

OTHER EVENTS OF 1879

Black Experience In the 'Exodus of 1879' between 20,000 and 40,000 blacks from the South seek homesteads in Kansas, after word spreads that they would be welcome there. Most of them are forced to turn back due to lack of capital, inexperience, and white hostility.

12 FEBRUARY 1880

Indians President Hayes issues a warning to illegal settlers, ranchers, and trespassers who have been stealing lands in Indian Territory.

18 FEBRUARY 1880

Labor In San Francisco, depressed economic conditions continue, and the anti-Chinese movement remains at fever pitch. During this month masses of unemployed have forced factory and mill owners to discharge hundreds of Chinese laborers. The *San Francisco Examiner* states that 'Every country owes its first duty to its own race and citizens. This duty properly observed on this Coast will cause much riddance of the Chinese pest.' Before the end of March, however, federal courts will strike down those clauses of the state constitution that bar the employment of Chinese.

17 NOVEMBER 1880
International In the Chinese Exclusion Treaty, between the United States and China, the United States may restrict, but not exclude, the immigration of Chinese.

19 FEBRUARY 1881
Life/Customs The Kansas state legislature passes a law prohibiting the sale of liquor except for medical or scientific purposes. Kansas is the first state to pass such a law.

4 MARCH 1881
National James A Garfield is inaugurated the twentieth President of the United States.

8 MARCH 1881
Transportation A second transcontinental railroad line is completed when the Southern Pacific, building eastward, joins the Atchison, Topeka and Santa Fe Railroad at Deming in New Mexico Territory.

14 JULY 1881
Life/Customs Having escaped from jail by killing both of his guards (he was waiting to be hanged for murder), William Bonney, popularly known as Billy the Kid, is cornered and killed in a dark room by Sheriff Pat Garrett in Fort Sumner, New Mexico Territory.

19 JULY 1881
Indians The Sioux Chief Sitting Bull returns from Canada after a four-year exile with 186 companions: he surrenders at Fort Buford, Dakota Territory.

20 SEPTEMBER 1881
National Vice-President Chester A Arthur is inaugurated the twenty-first President of the United States. James Garfield has died (19 September) after being wounded by a disgruntled office-seeker in Washington DC on 2 July.

26 OCTOBER 1881
Life/Customs In Tombstone, Arizona Territory, Marshal Virgil Earp, accompanied by his recently deputized brothers, Wyatt and Morgan, along with Doc Holliday, ambush and kill three men at the OK Corral, sending two others fleeing. The Earps and Holliday have attacked these men in order to cover up a stagecoach robbery of 18 March in Tombstone, involving Doc Holliday, during which the driver and a passenger were killed. The Citizen's Safety Committee in Tombstone considers the killings an act of murder. Virgil Earp is fired as town marshal on 29 October, but Tombstone's hell-raising days are not over yet.

1 DECEMBER 1881
National Secretary of State James G Blaine declares that the Hawaiian Islands are part of the Americas, falling within the Monroe Doctrine.

The Union Pacific depot, Omaha City.

The legendary gun fighters of Dodge City.

Transportation A third transcontinental railroad line is completed, when the Southern Pacific joins the Texas and Pacific at Sierra Blanca, Texas.

OTHER EVENTS OF 1881

Indians Helen Hunt Jackson publishes *A Century of Dishonor*, an account of the atrocities committed against Indian tribes in the West and an indictment of the nation's reservation policy. Jackson sends copies of the book to every member of Congress and to most federal officials.

22 MARCH 1882

Ideas/Beliefs In an attempt to break the power of the Mormon Church in Utah Territory and to force its members to renounce the practice of polygamy, Congress passes the Edmunds Act. The act declares the practice of polygamy to be a felony having a penalty of up to five years' imprisonment and/or a $500 fine upon conviction. Polygamous living, or unlawful cohabitation, is declared to be a misdemeanor punishable by six months' imprisonment and/or a $300 fine. In addition, all registration and elective offices in Utah Territory are declared vacant and a five-member board of commissioners, to be appointed by the President, is created and empowered to temporarily assume all duties pertaining to supervising elections in the territory. The commissioners are directed to make up a new list of eligible voters, denying suffrage, holding of office, and jury duty to polygamists. The courts move slowly at first to enforce this law, but ultimately more than 1300 persons are found guilty of practicing polygamy and sent to prison. Many Mormons go into hiding or flee the territory to escape prosecution under the law.

NATHAN COOK MEEKER, 1817-1879

Like many people caught up in visions of social reform, Nathan Meeker was more conversant with words and ideas than with the practical business of motivating people. That limitation was to cost him his life. Born on 12 July 1817, in Euclid, Ohio, Meeker was an idealistic youth who took up a wandering existence that he would pursue for most of his days (despite his marriage at 24). He drifted in and out of newspaper work, teaching, and small business for some years before becoming an agricultural writer for Horace Greeley's *New York Tribune* after the Civil War.

Pursuing his interest in co-operative farming, Meeker wrote for the *Tribune* a much-noted series on the Oneida Community. Then, in 1870, Meeker founded the Union Colony near Denver, with the support of Greeley and others. This co-operative farming community eventually covered over 20,000 acres, sharing much of its resources and having its own school and library (land was privately owned). Overtaken by restlessness again after eight years in the community, Meeker took an appointment as a Ute Indian agent, determined to transform the natives into small farmers. (The US Government had attempted to implement this policy with many of the Western tribes, no matter how unsuited they – or their land – might be to farming. It was one way of keeping the Indians on their reservations and off the warpath.) Unfortunately, Meeker's customary tactlessness in dealing with people carried over into his relations with the Utes and finally precipitated the massacre of Meeker and the entire agency in September 1879.

WILLIAM H 'BILLY THE KID' BONNEY, 1859-1881

Billy the Kid charmed many who knew him during his short but destructive career as an outlaw. Born William Bonney in New York on 23 November 1859, Billy accompanied his widowed mother to the Southwest as a child: they settled in Silver City, New Mexico, in 1868. By the age of 12, he had left school for a career of drifting and gambling and loitering; legend has it that at that age he killed his first man. In 1876 Billy and some friends robbed and murdered three Indians in Arizona, and from there set off in search of excitement, money, and notches on their guns. In the New Mexico cattle war of 1878, Billy worked as a gunman for one of the factions; among his victims on that job was Sheriff Jim Brady.

When Governor Lew Wallace arrived, he offered provisional amnesty to Billy and others involved in the cattle war. Declining the offer, Billy and his friends went on a rampage of cattle rustling and murder. Fulfilling a campaign promise, his one-time friend Sheriff Pat Garrett ran Billy to ground in 1880; in the ensuing trial the young outlaw was sentenced to hang for the murder of Sheriff Brady. But despite shackles and leg irons, Billy escaped in April 1881, killing two deputies. On 15 July Garrett found Billy again, and this time shot him dead. Many had admired his handsome smile and his youthful bravado. They were less inclined to admire the fact that he had killed a man for every year that he lived – most of them in cold blood.

CHRONOLOGY

3 APRIL 1882

Life/Customs The notorious bank and train robber and murderer, Jesse James, is shot and killed in his own home in St Joseph, Missouri, by Robert Ford. Bob Ford and his brother, Charley, have been guests of James for the past several weeks, planning another series of bank holdups. Ford has previously arranged for immunity from prosecution by Missouri authorities for past crimes in return for killing James. These arrangements include a secret meeting with Missouri Governor T T Crittenden, with whom Ford had met personally in Kansas City. After shooting James in the head, the Fords go to the nearest telegraph office, where Robert Ford sends Crittenden the one-line message: 'I have got my man.'

6 MAY 1882

Immigration Since his veto of 4 April has been overriden by Congress, President Arthur signs the Chinese Exclusion Act, which suspends immigration of Chinese labor for a period of 10 years. The act also declares that 'Hereafter no state court or court of the United States shall admit Chinese to citizenship.' The act violates the spirit of earlier treaties signed between the United States and China and creates anger and resentment in China, which will find its outlet in American xenophobia and attacks against Americans in China in the near future.

Jesse James, who was killed by a fellow outlaw.

THE FIRST TRANSCONTINENTAL RAILROAD

The Pacific Railway Act of July 1862 authorized two companies, the Union Pacific and the Central Pacific, to construct a transcontinental railroad between Sacramento, California and Omaha, Nebraska. Under the act's terms, the two companies were each granted ten alternate sections of public land on each side of the track for each mile constructed. This was doubled to 20 alternate sections in 1864. Each firm was to receive between $16,000 and $48,000 in government loans for each mile of track constructed, depending on the terrain.

Both companies got off to a slow start, as Civil War demands reduced the available supply of men and materials. The Union Pacific did not even lay its first rail until July of 1865. With the end of the war, construction moved ahead at a rapid pace. The Central Pacific, building east from Sacramento, discovered the value of Chinese labor and began importing great numbers of workers from Shanghai and Canton. Within a year 7000 Chinese were working on the line, as it crossed the formidable Sierra Nevada. In May 1866 General Grenville Dodge joined the Union Pacific as chief engineer, and construction of that end of the line assumed the characteristics of a military operation. Thousands of Irish immigrants and discharged soldiers made up what was known as the 'work train.' The surveying parties came first, followed by the graders, bridge gangs, tracklayers, track-ballasting crew, and train crews. Forty carloads of supplies were required to build each mile of track. The

Union Pacific only made it 40 miles out of Omaha in 1865, but the pace quickly accelerated as 260 miles of track was laid in 1866, 240 in 1867, and almost 500 miles in the peak year of 1868. In 1866, when Congress granted permission to the Central Pacific to build beyond the California-Nevada border, completion of the railroad became an all-out race with valuable public land and lucrative government loans at stake for each mile completed. As the Union Pacific moved westward, the raucous "hell on wheels" towns moved with them. Most were short-lived and disappeared quickly, while others, like Cheyenne and Laramie, became important permanent communities.

The two lines finally met at Promontory Point, Utah, on 10 May 1869 and the transcontinental railroad was a reality – but at a high price. During construction, the Central Pacific and the Union Pacific had acquired 33 million acres of public land for free. Both had developed phony construction companies, like the infamous Credit Mobilier, and then proceeded to sell supplies and equipment to themselves at inflated prices. The construction itself was often poor and wasteful. Tracks and bridges for hundreds of miles had to be reconstructed and paid for all over again due to the initial emphasis on speed.

The builders of the railroads, with their driving energy and their exploitation of human, material, and capital resources, established patterns that were emulated in other industries, including steel and oil, during the remainder of the nineteenth century.

SUMMER 1882

Industry Prominent Coloradoans, notably Horace Tabor and William Loveland, builder of the Colorado Central Railroad and owner of the *Rocky Mountain News*, organize the National Mining and Industrial Exposition in Denver. Its purpose is to advertise and promote the state of Colorado, its resources, and its potential for future growth.

OTHER EVENTS OF 1882

Mining A J Pritchard locates a quartz claim near Coeur d'Alene Lake in the panhandle of northern Idaho. Pritchard is able to keep the knowledge of the find from the general public until the fall of 1883, when the Northern Pacific Railroad floods the country with circulars advertising the strike to attract miners and settlers to the Northwest. The lead-silver district that results from Pritchard's find becomes the largest in the nation, as more than $2 billion worth of lead, silver, and zinc will be extracted from the hills of the Coeur d'Alene. Near Butte, Montana, at a depth of 300 feet, the first copper in any substantial quantity is found in the Anaconda mine in the form of a five-foot vein. This find signals the beginning of the copper era in Montana. As a result of this find, Marcus Daly purchases a site near the banks of Warm Springs Creek for construction of a copper smelter. The site is selected because of the scarcity of water in Butte. Maneuvering for possession of this water site contributes to a feud between W A Clark and Marcus Daly; this flames into a struggle known as the 'war of the copper kings.' By early 1883 the Anaconda shaft reaches a depth of 600 feet, where the copper vein widens to 100 feet across and consists of 55 percent pure copper sulphide. At Warm Springs Creek, 26 miles west of Butte, Daly will build the city of Anaconda, soon to be one of the classic 'company towns' of the American West.

1882-1883

Indians The Apaches of Arizona and New Mexico rebel at life on the reservation and go on the warpath. General George Crook, the experienced Indian fighter, is assigned to stop them. He persuades most of the Indians to return to the reservation, but one group, including Chief Geronimo, flees into Mexico. Under a recent treaty that allows Americans to enter Mexico when on the 'hot trail' of Indians, Crook takes his forces into Mexico in May 1883. The Apaches surprise everyone by surrendering and are taken back to the reservation, where even Geronimo seems to settle down to farming.

5 FEBRUARY 1883

Transportation The Southern Pacific Railroad, building eastward from New Mexico, completes its 'Sunset Route' as it reaches New Orleans, having absorbed the Galveston, Harrisburg and San Antonio Railway.

US Cavalry General George Crook.

3 MARCH 1883

National Having bridged the continent by railway, the United States begins to cast its glance toward the Pacific Ocean and such island possessions as Hawaii and Samoa. However, the US Navy consists entirely of wooden ships, and the nation has fallen to twelfth place among the world's naval powers. To support its new maritime interests, Congress now authorizes construction of three steel cruisers, inaugurating what will become known as the Steel Navy.

4 JULY 1883

Life/Customs The first Wild West Show by William F Cody, popularly known as Buffalo Bill, is presented as part of a Fourth of July celebration in North Platte, Nebraska. The following year, Cody commercializes the show and takes it to various parts of the United States.

8 SEPTEMBER 1883

Transportation A northern transcontinental railroad route is completed between Duluth, Minnesota, and Portland, Oregon, as the Northern Pacific Railroad drives the traditional golden spike at Independence Creek, 60 miles west of Helena, Montana Territory. Completion of the line is largely due to the efforts of German-born Henry Villard, who gained control of the Northern Pacific's board of directors and became its president in 1881. In 1883 the Northern Pacific Railroad also sends agents to Europe to encourage immigration to the American Northwest.

18 NOVEMBER 1883

Transportation Effective at noon, North American railroads adopt four standard time zones for the continent in order to standardize travel schedules. The dividing lines for the different zones are located at the 75th, 90th, 105th, and 120th meridians west of Greenwich, England.

WILLIAM FREDERICK 'BUFFALO BILL' CODY,
1846-1917

The world's romantic image of the cowboys and Indians of the plains is largely due to 'Buffalo Bill' Cody, who became a great scout and went on to reveal an even greater talent for publicizing himself and his Wild West show. He was born on an Iowa farm on 26 February 1846, and grew up mainly in Kansas. His father died when he was 11, and Cody supported the family working for wagon trains on the Plains. For a brief period he rode for the Pony Express.

During the Civil War, Cody was a scout for the Kansas Cavalry in operations among the Kiowas and Comanches. It was after the war, while hunting buffalo for railroad workers, that he earned his nickname with his exceptional marksmanship. He returned to scouting with the 5th Cavalry in 1869 and proved a fearless Indian fighter. At War Bonnet Creek in 1876, he was victorious in a much-heralded duel with the Cheyenne Yellow Hand.

By then Cody had already launched his show-business career, which was initiated by his friend E Z C Judson, who wrote thrillers under the name of Ned Buntline. The first of the Buntline dime novels with Cody as hero was an instant success: the series would run to some 1700 titles by various authors. Buntline made his first novel into a play, which Cody produced with himself as the leading man (among his supporting actors was 'Wild Bill' Hickok). Between stints of real-life action on the Plains, Cody appeared on the stage for 11 seasons.

In 1883 he created his most spectacular production: Buffalo Bill's Wild West Show. In its 30 years on the road, this outdoor extravaganza played all over the nation, and appeared before Queen Victoria and at the 1893 Chicago World's Fair. Among its stars were Annie Oakley and, for one curious season, Chief Sitting Bull of Little Big Horn fame. The show featured real cowboys and Indians in various acts, and also had roping and bronco-riding contests which developed into the modern rodeo. Cody remained a showman, horseman, and marksman almost until his death in Denver in 1917. His legacy was a dramatic image of the Wild West that has intrigued the world ever since.

OTHER EVENTS OF 1883

Industry Cattlemen meet at Caldwell, Kansas, and establish the Cherokee Strip Live Stock Association. Its membership consists of over 100 individuals and corporations owning more than 300,000 head of cattle. A five-year lease at $100,000 per year is negotiated with the Cherokee Nation for exclusive use of 6,500,000 acres of the Cherokee Outlet in Indian Territory. The lease will be re-negotiated in 1888 for $200,000 per year.

Industry The year 1883 represents the high-water mark for growth of the range-cattle industry in the West. In Wyoming alone, 20 stock-raising corporations, capitalized at $12 million, are formed. Most are created by the consolidation of smaller ranches already in existence. The most prominent of these is the Swan Land and Cattle Company, which uses $3,750,000 raised through stock sales in the East to combine three eastern Wyoming cattle ranches into a huge estate comprising 100,000 head of cattle.

17 MAY 1884

Alaska An Organic Act that applies the laws of Oregon to Alaska is passed by Congress. The region had been under administration of the War Department since its acquisition from Russia in 1867.

OTHER EVENTS OF 1884

Settling This year represents the height of the land boom in Dakota Territory, in progress since 1879. In 1884 alone, 11,082,818 acres are filed for claims under public land laws. This total is almost 40 percent of all the land disposed of in the nation by the Federal Government in 1884.

30 JANUARY 1885

Settling The Secretary of the Interior, Henry M Teller, recommends the opening of Indian lands in the Indian Territory to homesteaders. Since 1880 homesteaders, known as 'boomers' and led by David L Payne and William L Couch, have been crossing into Indian Territory from Kansas and Arkansas and settling on what is known as the 'Unassigned Lands' in the center of Indian Territory. Their actions are drawing increasingly favorable public opinion and placing increasing pressure on the Federal Government to take action. President Arthur, however, does not have sufficient time to act before the expiration of his term.

1 FEBRUARY 1885

Ideas/Beliefs In response to increasing federal pressure on and persecution of Mormons in Utah Territory, the president of the Mormon Church, John Taylor, goes 'underground,' taking with him the administration of Church affairs. During the next two-and-a-half years, Church affairs will be directed from a series of hideouts in and around Salt Lake City known only to a handful of trusted

Aberdeen, South Dakota, homesteaders in 1882.

members. Despite the efforts of hordes of US marshals, Taylor will continue to escape capture until his death on 25 July 1887.

25 FEBRUARY 1885
National An act of Congress forbids the fencing of public lands in the West. In Wyoming Territory alone, the Commissioner of the General Land Office has identified 125 large cattle companies that have fenced public lands. Under a crusading commissioner, William A J Sparks, many fences will come down during the next few years, but the General Land Office will, for the most part, find effective enforcement of this law hampered by lack of funds and extended litigation. Sparks will be forced to resign on 17 August.

3 MARCH 1885
Conservation The first permanent state forest commission, the Board of Forestry of California, is established. The first meeting is held in San Francisco on 1 April.

4 MARCH 1885
National Grover Cleveland is inaugurated the twenty-second President of the United States. Thomas A Hendricks is Vice-President.

CHARLES CROCKER, 1822-1888

One of the principals in the creation of the first transcontinental railway, Charles Crocker was the partner who spurned paperwork and took his extraordinary energy into the field to oversee construction. Born to a merchant's family in Troy, New York, on 16 September 1822, Crocker moved to Indiana with his family at the age of 14. After years of menial work and the start-up of a modest business, he caught the gold fever of 1849 and headed for California. He found no gold, but opened a store in Sacramento that prospered handsomely, bringing him enough notice to take him to the California legislature in 1860.

While Crocker was serving in the California legislature, he met Leland Stanford, Mark Hopkins, and Collis P Huntington, his future partners. In 1861 they formed the Central Pacific Railway Company with the intention of building east to connect with the Union Pacific, which was then heading west from Omaha. Thus began a remarkable odyssey. Crocker took charge of the actual work, living with his crews, sharing their hardships, driving the work forward. The result was one of the fastest construction jobs in history, sometimes averaging three miles of track per day in rough terrain. The whole job was finished an incredible seven years ahead of deadline. Crocker went on to be an officer of the Central Pacific, an organizer of the Southern Pacific, and a participant in other railroads and assorted businesses. He died a very rich man in Monterey, California, in 1888.

CHRONOLOGY

THE COWBOY

The original Texas cowboy was a synthesis of Spanish, Mexican and Anglo-American cultures. The conquistadors and early Spanish colonists introduced cattle and horses into the New World, with profound consequences for both the natives and the settlers of the Far West. The first cowboys in the Far West were Mexican *vaqueros* (from *vaca*, cow) who herded hardy Longhorn cattle descended from animals originally brought from Spain. They settled largely in what is now Texas, establishing their *ranchos* in the triangle of land between the Nueces River, the Rio Grande, and the Gulf of Mexico. The Americans who began to supplant them even before the Mexican War of 1846-8 assumed their methods of free-range stockraising, allowing the cattle to wander over the unfenced range to graze and breed. Hired cowboys guarded the animals from cattle thieves, or rustlers, and branded them to show ownership when they mingled with other herds. From their Mexican forerunners, the Americans also borrowed the wide-brimmed *sombrero*, leather 'chaps' to protect their legs from the thorny chaparral brush, and the *reata*, or lariat.

With the railroads, during the 1860s, came the 'cattle kingdom' of the Great Plains, extending from the Rio Grande all the way north to Oregon. The cattle were rounded up by the thousands in the fall and driven to the railroad 'cow towns' for shipment East. Up to 4000 animals were taken on 'the long drive,' surrounded by cowboy outriders, along several major routes, including the Chisholm, Shawnee and Western Trails. Abilene, Kansas, was a major railhead for cattle shipment, as were Kansas City and Dodge City, Kansas.

Whether on the range or on the trail, the cowboy had to contend with heat, dust, predators, stampedes by panicked animals, and the depredations of rustlers and Indians. He relied on the skill and strength of his horses, changing mounts often from the *remuda*, or pool, of wiry cattle ponies, which was tended by a wrangler. There was constant feuding with the sheepowners and farmers, who began fencing the land with barbed wire in the 1870s, blocking trails and access to waterholes. Eventually, barbed wire put an end to the open range – and to the cowboy's way of life. Overstocking and overgrazing were other factors in the decline of the cattle kingdom, which was ended by the 1890s. But the cowboy's colorful and exciting role in winning the West had already passed into legend, to remain an integral part of the American heritage.

Scenes from the 'cattle kingdom' days on the Great Plains.

7 MARCH 1885

Industry The Kansas state legislature passes an act to prohibit the driving of Texas cattle into or through the state between 1 March and 1 December. This legislation is passed in an attempt to curb the disastrous effects of Texas cattle fever and hoof-and-mouth disease.

17 MAY 1885

Indians Led by Geronimo, Nana, and Mangas, more than 100 Apache Indians flee their reservation at San Carlos in Arizona Territory and head for Mexico. A wave of panic seizes the area, as newspaper editorials and citizens call for the dispatch of thousands of federal troops.

4 JULY 1885

Ideas/Beliefs On this Independence Day, in reaction to what most Mormons consider continued persecution for their religious beliefs and deprivation of their constitutional rights, American flags are lowered to half-mast over Mormon buildings throughout Salt Lake City. The reaction nationwide is one of outrage and only hardens the determination of the Federal Government to break the power of the Mormon Church in Utah Territory.

2 SEPTEMBER 1885

Civil Rights Following a decade of smoldering resentment against Chinese mine laborers, white men at Rock Springs in Wyoming Territory go on a rampage, killing 28 Chinese and wounding 15 others. Several hundred more Chinese are chased from the town. Governor Francis E Warren requests federal troops from President Cleveland. These soldiers arrive and escort the Chinese who have fled back to Rock Springs. Federal troops will remain nearby, at Camp Pilot Butte, for 13 years. The fears of many whites in Rock Springs that it will become a 'Chinatown' are not realized. Chinese laborers are increasingly difficult to find following the decision by Congress in 1882 to suspend their immigration.

3 NOVEMBER 1885

Civil Rights Violence against Chinese communities in the West spreads, as white mobs, aided by local authorities, expel 200 Chinese from their homes and burn their property in Tacoma, Washington Territory. The riot follows almost six weeks of continuous anti-Chinese agitation, mass meetings, and newspaper propaganda whose theme is the now-familiar slogan 'The Chinese must go!' On 7 November President Cleveland warns the people of the area against further violence and dispatches federal troops to the scene.

11 NOVEMBER 1885

Education Leland Stanford Junior University is founded and incorporated by railroad magnate Leland Stanford as a memorial to his only son following his death. Generally known as Stanford University and located at Palo Alto, California, Stanford will become the most richly endowed university in the West and will quickly gain early prominence through the efforts of its first president, David Starr Jordan.

OTHER EVENTS OF 1885

Arts/Culture Mark Twain's classic novel *Huckleberry Finn* is published. The book is a portrayal of regional character and frontier experience along the Mississippi River. It is a milestone in American literature.

Indians In May 1885 Geronimo, retired to the Apache reservation since May 1883, goes on a drinking binge and deserts with a few braves; they head for Mexico. Before they cross the border, they have killed 73 civilians and soldiers. General George Crook is assigned again to capture Geronimo, and in December 1885 he sets out to cross into Mexico; in January 1886 he corners the Apache leader, but in a confused battle Mexican soldiers – who are themselves Indians and enemies of the Apaches – end up fighting the American troops. Geronimo will refuse to surrender until the end of 1886, when he is deported to Florida as a prisoner of war. Many of his companions in exile will die there before Geronimo and fellow survivors finally return to the Southwest.

Thomas Nast comments on anti-Chinese racism.

CHRONOLOGY

7 FEBRUARY 1886
Civil Rights Violent riots directed against ethnic Chinese continue, as 400 people are driven from their homes in Seattle, Washington Territory. Many flee as far away as San Francisco. Federal troops are dispatched to restore order.

14 FEBRUARY 1886
Agriculture The California orange groves send the first trainload of fruit to Eastern markets – the beginning of Western 'agri-business.'

6 MARCH 1886
Labor The Knights of Labor strike against Southwestern railroads controlled by Jay Gould, principally the Missouri-Pacific system and the Wabash and Pacific. A successful strike the previous year had reversed wage reductions, encouraging this contest for power between the Knights of Labor and the railroads. The strike is initiated by 3700 shopmen, switchmen, and yardmen, but more than 6000 workers are forced out of their jobs by the labor action. All freight traffic running east across the Mississippi River is suspended between 8 and 29 March. The strike is led by Martin Irons, a fiery regional leader of the Knights, who disable locomotives, pull pins from trains and ditch them by displacing rails, break into round-houses and machine shops, open water tanks, tear up tracks, and intimidate and assault employees willing to work. More than 400 of the 600 locomotives in service are disabled at one time or another during the strike. The strike sends out shock waves paralyzing economic life in Missouri, Kansas, Texas, and Arkansas. Public opinion at first sides with labor, but rapidly turns against the Knights in the wake of strike violence. The strike is broken by early April and results in a total defeat for the Knights of Labor. Shortly thereafter they lose their effectiveness as a representative for the rights of the working man and cease to function.

12 APRIL 1886
Indians General Nelson A Miles assumes command of the Department of Arizona, succeeding General George Crook. The renowned Indian fighter has resigned following rejection by the War Department of his promise to the Apache chief, Geronimo, that upon surrender he would be allowed to return to the reservation in Arizona after only two years of exile.

10 MAY 1886
Judicial In *Santa Clara County v Southern Pacific Railroad*, the Supreme Court rules that a corporation is a person under the 14th Amendment and therefore cannot be deprived of profits by government regulation without due process of law.

Above: *Apaches hunting in the desert*.
Below: *Cavalrymen of the Geronimo Campaign, 1885.*

For the first time the Court provides a substantive, as well as a procedural, interpretation of the due-process clause of the 14th Amendment. The ruling is an important retreat from an earlier ruling by the Court in 1877: *Munn v Ilinois* had allowed state legislatures to regulate corporate practices if the business of the corporation was 'affected with a public interest.' This ruling is the first in a series of blows to the Granger movement in the Midwest and West, which had sought to regulate unfair business practices by large corporations such as railroads and grain elevator operators.

30 JUNE 1886

Conservation By act of Congress, the US Forest Service is organized as the Division of Forestry. Dr Bernhard Eduard Fernow is appointed the first chief and serves until 1898.

4 SEPTEMBER 1886

Indians Returning from their sanctuary in Mexico, Apache Indians, led by Geronimo, surrender to General Nelson Miles at Skeleton Canyon in Arizona Territory. Geronimo and several other Apache leaders are sent into exile at Fort Marion, Florida, where they will remain until 1894.

25 OCTOBER 1886

Judicial In the case of *Wabash, St Louis and Pacific Railway Company v Illinois*, the Supreme Court strikes down an Illinois statute prohibiting railroads from charging more for a short haul than for a long haul over the same line. The Court rules that a state cannot regulate commerce within its own borders if that commerce is part of interstate traffic and invalidates the law as an infringement of Congress's exclusive control over interstate commerce. Because Congress has not acted to regulate interstate commerce of this kind, a 'twilight zone' has evolved wherein neither the states nor the Federal Government are supervising the unfair business practices of increasingly large and powerful trusts and corporations, in particular the nationwide railroads.

NOVEMBER 1886-FEBRUARY 1887

Industry The most devastating winter in memory sweeps across the Great Plains from the Canadian border to Texas. The snow begins falling in November and rarely ceases, freezing cattle and burying their grasslands. A short thaw in the middle of January is followed by a blizzard (28 January) of unprecedented proportions, lasting 72 hours. Afterward temperatures plunge to 50 degrees below zero Fahrenheit. Entire herds die, with losses for some ranchers between 75 and 85 percent of their livestock. The severe winter ends the cattle boom and the open-range method of raising cattle. As a result two important new industries are born: the cultivation of corn feed and hay to support cattle ranching.

GERONIMO, 1829-1909

One of the wiliest and most dangerous Apache raiders of all time, Geronimo survived to become a harmless 'decorative' Indian at the inauguration of Theodore Roosevelt. He was born Goyathlay, to the Apaches of southern Arizona, in June 1829. After Mexicans killed his wife and children in 1858, Geronimo took up the old Apache trade of raiding with a vengeance. As a young man he was a cohort in the raids of Cochise, and eventually became chief of the Chiricahua Apaches.

Like many renegades of the time, Geronimo was in and out of reservations, on and off the warpath. When the Apaches were forcibly evicted to New Mexico in 1876, he took to the Mexican mountains and raided across the border. Then, returning to the reservation, he took up farming with surprising success before the whites' duplicity drove him off again. In May 1885 he mounted a fierce campaign against white settlers in New Mexico and Arizona, pursued by Indian fighter General George Crook. In March 1886 Geronimo surrendered to Crook, but quickly bolted again, an episode that ended Crook's remarkable career. His replacement, General Nelson A Miles, brought Geronimo to bay in 1886. After some years as a prisoner, Geronimo settled at Fort Sill, Oklahoma, converted to Christianity, and became a successful farmer. In later years he was something of a local tourist attraction, appearing at fairs. After riding in Roosevelt's inaugural parade, he died at Fort Sill. His name survives as a jumping call of US paratroopers.

Scout Kit Carson was a frontier legend.

CHRONOLOGY

THE TRAIL DRIVES

The end of the Civil War found about 5 million head of cattle wandering the plains of Texas unchecked and unclaimed. Locally each animal was worth only about $4.00, but the war had drained sources of Eastern livestock and created a critical beef shortage there. In Chicago and Cincinnati, buyers were paying up to $40 per head of cattle. There was money to be made for those who could bring the cattle to the nearest railhead for shipment east. Thus the first 'long drive' began in 1866. The goal that year was Sedalia, Missouri, a railroad town on the Missouri Pacific Railroad. Few cattle reached Sedalia that year. Settlers and farmers objected to the thousands of cattle seeking to traverse their fields and farms, to the point of fighting a few pitched battles with the Texas 'drovers.'

The following year an Illinois stockman, Joseph McCoy, founded Abilene on the Kansas and Pacific Railroad and attracted almost 35,000 head of cattle. Abilene became the first in a series of booming 'cowtowns' that stretched west with the building of rail lines across Kansas. Newton, Ellsworth, Wichita, Hunnewell, Caldwell, and Dodge City each had its heyday. In the peak year of 1871, more than 600,000 head of cattle moved north along the trails.

Herds of every size made the 'long drive,' but it was generally agreed that 2500 animals was a manageable

number. About a dozen men, each equipped with about half-a-dozen horses, would move the herd at an average of about 10 to 15 miles per day over a four-month period. The most famous of these cattle highways was the Chisholm Trail, which extended from the mouth of the Little Arkansas River near Wichita, Texas, crossed the Red River and then closely followed the 98th meridian across Indian Territory.

After 1875 Dodge City was the main railhead for shipping cattle eastward: 1 million head were shipped over the next four years. By 1880 Texas was no longer the only source of cattle; stock-raising on a large scale had moved northward. During the 1870s the number of cattle in Kansas and Nebraska increased from 500,000 to 2,500,000; in Colorado from 71,000 to 791,000; in Wyoming from 11,000 to 520,000; in Montana from 36,000 to 430,000. In these areas heavier Angus and Hereford bulls were crossed with Texas Longhorns. As settlement and farming spread across Kansas, there was increased opposition to the huge herds and the raucous cowtowns they spawned. Finally, the rapidly expanding railway network in the West had moved down into Texas, eliminating the need for the long overland routes even from that region, and barbed wire had fenced off the open range. The trail drives were at an end.

20 JANUARY 1887

Hawaii The Hawaiian Reciprocity Treaty of 1875, which had been renewed in 1884 but not consented to by the Senate, is finally ratified when it is amended to give the United States the exclusive right to build a naval base at Pearl Harbor, near Honolulu.

4 FEBRUARY 1887

National The Interstate Commerce Act is passed

by Congress and signed into law by President Cleveland. The act applies only to railroads passing through more than one state and stipulates that all charges made by railways must be reasonable and just. Pooling operations, discriminatory rates, drawbacks, and rebates are prohibited. Railroads are required to post their rates, and it is illegal to charge more for a short haul than for a long haul over the same line. The act also creates the Interstate Commerce Commission, the first

West-Coast railway office, Atlantic & Pacific.

regulatory commission in US history. It is authorized to investigate the management of railroads, to summon witnesses, and to compel railroad companies to produce their financial books and papers for inspection. The vagueness of the statute produces difficulties in interpretation as to what constitutes 'reasonable' charges, rendering the act a weak vehicle for the regulation of railroads. The commission itself will soon be converted into a pawn of the railroad interests.

8 FEBRUARY 1887
Indians President Cleveland signs the Dawes Severalty Act. It provides for the dissolution of Indian tribes as legal entities and authorizes the President to divide the lands of any tribe, giving each head of a family 160 acres, with lesser amounts to single individuals. Instead of being legally tranferred directly to the Indians, the plots are to be held in trust by the Federal Government for 25 years. After this period, full ownership will be conferred and US citizenship granted. Reservation lands remaining after the distribution of the allotments are to be declared surplus and open for settlement by white homesteaders. As a result of this act, Indian tribes in the West forfeit 86 million acres of land, or 62 percent of their possessions prior to 1887. The act is the result of efforts by reformers, who argue that reservation life has produced indolence among the Indian tribes and has prevented their assimilation.

2 MARCH 1887
Agriculture To help farmers with land and crop management, Congress passes the Hatch Act. Farmland is being destroyed and soil depleted through bad management, intensive farming, and over-grazing of cattle. The act is designed to begin development of a science of agriculture by providing funds for agricultural experiment stations to be located in most states.

3 MARCH 1887
Ideas/Beliefs In a measure designed to plug loopholes in the Edmunds Act of 1882, Congress passes the Edmunds-Tucker Bill. Directed against the Mormon Church in Utah Territory, the bill abolishes woman suffrage in the territory. Voting, serving on juries, and holding elective office are made conditional upon signing a test oath pledging obedience to and support of all anti-polygamy laws. The Mormon Perpetual Emigrating Fund Company is declared dissolved to curtail the influx of foreign converts who are adding to Mormon

strength in the territory. Finally, to accomplish the destruction of Mormon political and economic power in Utah, the Church itself is disincorporated and its property impounded by the Federal Government.

MAY 1887
Industry The Swan Land and Cattle Company of Wyoming, only four years old, declares bankruptcy following the devastating winter of 1886-7. The demise of the huge livestock corporation is symbolic of the Depression that will grip the cattle industry on the Great Plains during the next 10 years. Over this period the number of cattle in Wyoming alone will decline from 9 million head in 1886 to only 3 million by 1895.

OTHER EVENTS OF 1887
Population California is experiencing a flood of new immigrants that reaches its peak this year. The Atchison, Topeka, and Santa Fe Railroad has reached Los Angeles, touching off a fierce rate war with the Southern Pacific Railroad. Passenger fares from the Midwest to southern California drop from $125 to as low as $1 in some instances. In all, more than 200,000 people will come to California by rail during 1887, as Los Angeles, in particular, embarks on a period of enormous growth.

JANUARY 1888
Conservation The Boone and Crockett Club for the protection of big game and wilderness areas in the American West is formally organized in New York City, with Theodore Roosevelt as its first president. The club is named after Daniel Boone and Davy Crockett, two of Roosevelt's heroes, and will be an effective lobbying agency for numerous conservationist acts in the years to come.

12 MARCH 1888
Immigration Secretrary of State Charles F Bayard and the Chinese Minister in Washington sign a treaty excluding Chinese laborers from the United States for 20 years. The United States agrees to pay the Chinese Government an indemnity of $276,619 for the losses of Chinese immigrants through mob violence, but admits no responsibility for the riots. China refuses to ratify the treaty.

4 JULY 1888
Sport The first organized rodeo competition is held at a racetrack at Prescott, Arizona Territory. Juan Leivas is awarded a medal 'for roping and tieing' a steer which had a 100-yard start in a time of 11.75 seconds. This rodeo develops into an annual competition.

1 OCTOBER 1888
Immigration President Cleveland signs the Scott Act, calling for the total exclusion of Chinese laborers for an undefined period. The Act also prohibits Chinese who go home for a visit from

---

THE INDIANS' LAST STAND

Early travelers westward crossed the Great Plains only as a means of reaching the California gold fields, or to settle in Oregon and the Great Basin of Utah. The dominant tribes of the area, the Sioux and Northern Cheyenne to the north, the Southern Cheyenne and Arapaho through the center, and the Kiowa and Comanche to the south, remained, for the most part, passive spectators. By the 1860s, however, the mining frontier had moved into Colorado and the rest of the Rocky Mountain region, and railway building followed quickly across Kansas, Nebraska, and Wyoming. The 200,000 Indians of the Great Plains and Rocky Mountains found themselves pushed northward to the Black Hills and the Yellowstone, Bighorn, and Powder River country and southward to the Texas panhandle and the western section of Indian Territory. The 'Iron Horse' and the flood of homesteaders drove away the precious buffalo and other wild game, as the native Americans came under the tremendous pressure of a totally different way of life backed by the energy of its 40 million pursuers.

Many Indian tribes and leaders reluctantly accepted their ever-dwindling reservation areas, but soon discovered that neither the United States Government nor their assigned reservations provided adequate food and other necessities. Moreover, there was the constant encroachment on reservation land by white miners and homesteaders, while the federal government turned a blind eye toward these depredations. Bands of younger warriors would often leave their reservations in search of buffalo, or the cattle, horses, guns, and ammunition possessed by the white man. Inevitably conflict followed.

After 1865 the US Army fought nearly 1000 battles and skirmishes against the Indians in the West involving about 25,000 troops. The total number of casualties suffered by the Army was 1944 – far less than in a single major Civil War battle. Most of these encounters were small affairs involving only a company or two, or cavalry attacks on unprepared Indian villages. Indian warriors were usually at a tremendous disadvantage, since they were trying to protect their women and children as they fought. Village lodges would be destroyed, food and clothing burned, and pony herds shot. The attitude of the white man toward the Indian was succinctly summed up by General Philip Sheridan who, in 1869, replied to the Comanche chief Tosawi's assertion that he was a 'good Indian' by saying: 'The only good Indians I ever saw were dead.' This was widely misquoted as 'the only good Indian is a dead Indian,' perhaps as a rationale for the fact that by 1880, the Indian way of life had been destroyed forever.

---

returning to the United States. By the spring of 1889, Chinese-American relations are at a low point, as diplomatic ties are almost severed.

OTHER EVENTS OF 1888
Arts/Culture The famous Western painter and illustrator, Frederic Remington, first gains public recognition with publication of his drawings in a book by Theodore Roosevelt, *Ranch Life and Hunting Trails*.

9 FEBRUARY 1889

Agriculture The Department of Agriculture becomes the eighth executive department and gains full cabinet status. The spread of farm settlement across the West and the growth of farm production was turning agriculture into a major sector of the nation's economic life, demanding full-time government supervision.

22 FEBRUARY 1889

National President Cleveland signs an Omnibus Bill providing for the admission of North Dakota, South Dakota, Montana, and Washington as states of the Union. Since the Democrats had come to power in the election of 1884, they had seen no advantage in admitting additional states, since it was assumed that the territories in the Northwest were Republican. However, with the election of Benjamin Harrison in November 1888, the Democrats are faced with the prospect of enabling acts for the admission of new states sponsored by a Republican Administration: they have decided to sponsor such legislation to their own advantage. The Democrats prepare an onmnibus bill that includes Democratic New Mexico, in addition to Dakota, Montana, and Washington; the bill invites those territories to draw up constitutions for statehood. The Republican Senate, however, revises the bill to exclude New Mexico and divides Dakota Territory into northern and southern sections. The four territories in this bill, signed by Cleveland, will be admitted to the Union in the fall by President Harrison.

2 MARCH 1889

National After providing for final Indian claims, Congress authorizes transfer of the Unassigned Lands in Indian Territory to the public domain.

4 MARCH 1889

National Benjamin Harrison is inaugurated the twenty-third President of the United States.

23 MARCH 1889

Settling President Harrison announces that the part of Indian Territory known as Oklahoma will be opened for settlement on 22 April and that existing United States land laws will be in force.

22 APRIL 1889

Settling Tens of thousands of eager settlers crowd the borders of the Unassigned Lands in central Indian Territory waiting for the 12 o'clock signal to rush in and stake their claims. The 1,920,000 acres in the area had formerly belonged to the Seminole and Creek tribes, but has been purchased by the Federal Government for $4 million. Rumor has it that many have already sneaked across the border to establish the town of Guthrie hours ahead of schedule, thereby earning the name 'sooners.' The future state of Oklahoma will be known as the Sooner State. Precisely at noon, the real rush

Outdoorsman Theodore Roosevelt in 1885.

HORACE A W TABOR, 1830-1899

The story of Horace Tabor, with its romance, its booms and busts, is the stuff of bad novels and folk opera – and in fact has appeared as both. Tabor was born in Holland, Vermont, on 26 November 1830 and migrated to Kansas in 1855. The next year he married another emigrant from Vermont. Unable to make a go at farming in Kansas, Tabor and his family headed for California in 1859, dreaming of gold. Things went well for a while in Tabor's mine on the Arkansas River, but then his lode played out. It was around 1878 when he discovered that the black sludge that had appeared in his sluice boxes contained a great deal of silver.

After that, money flowed Tabor's way in rivers, and he dispensed it with equal prodigality at the gaming tables and upon extravagant projects – notably the Leadville Opera House (by then he was mayor of the town) and the Tabor Grand Opera House in Denver, a city to which he contributed much. His prominence, not to mention his money, brought him political office, and finally a seat in the US Senate, where he filled out an unexpired term (1883). By then he had abandoned his first wife for the glamorous divorcée Elizabeth ('Baby') Doe. President Chester A Arthur was a guest at their wedding. However, over the next decade Tabor lost his silver touch. A series of swindlers and bad investments siphoned off his fortune, and his mines played out. By 1893 he was penniless: in his last year, friends got him a job as postmaster in Denver, where he died in 1899. Baby Doe sank into a destitute life in Leadville. In 1935 she was found frozen to death in her shack.

begins, resulting in such towns as Guthrie, Oklahoma City, Kingfisher, Stillwater, and Norman. By sunset, every available homestead lot has been claimed. Oklahoma City alone boasts an instant population of 10,000.

JUNE 1889

Arts/Culture The first two volumes of Theodore Roosevelt's *The Winning of the West* are published. Roosevelt's action-packed drama traces the spread of the United States across the continent, from the day Daniel Boone first pierced the Cumberland Gap in 1765 to the day Davy Crockett died at the Alamo in 1836.

14 JUNE 1889

International In Berlin, the United States, Great Britain, and Germany agree to establish a three-power protectorate over Samoa, in the southern Pacific Ocean. Earlier in the year, German and American warships were on the brink of hostilities when a hurricane descended on the Samoan

Top: *Nebraska homesteaders in 1887.*
Above: *Main Street, Coburg, Nebraska.*

Islands, destroying all three German and all three American warships at Apia Harbor on 16 March. The Senate will consent to the treaty on 4 February 1890.

20 JULY 1889

Life/Customs A group of big cattlemen, frustrated over what they consider to be unlawful depredations by small homesteaders and ranchers on their land and livestock, lynch James Averell and Ella Watson near Independence Rock in Wyoming Territory. Watson is the the only woman ever hanged in Wyoming. The six accused cattlemen are released on bail, but are never brought to trial — to no one's surprise.

2 NOVEMBER 1889

National North Dakota and South Dakota are admitted to the Union as separate states. During the past 10 years, the population of Dakota Territory has grown from 135,177, according to the census of 1880, to more than 500,000. This period is known as the Great Dakota Boom, as almost all of the land east of the Missouri River is claimed by settlers during this period.

An Indian cowboy in Montana.

8 NOVEMBER 1889
National Montana is admitted to the Union. Completion of the Northern Pacific Railroad and the discovery and mining of copper in large quantities have brought rapid population growth to the territory (from 21,000 in 1870 to over 140,000 by 1889).

11 NOVEMBER 1889
National Washington is admitted to the Union. During the past decade the territory has developed railway connections with the Great Lakes and the Mississippi Valley. The population has grown from almost 25,000 in 1870 to more than 350,000. Lumbering, shipbuilding, and commercial fishing are rapidly expanding industries.

17 NOVEMBER 1889
Transportation Daily railroad service to the Pacific Coast is inaugurated by the Union Pacific Railroad between Chicago and Portland, Oregon, and between Chicago and San Francisco. The Far West is increasingly accessible.

3 FEBRUARY 1890
Judicial The Supreme Court affirms the constitutionality of Idaho's Test Oath Law of 1885, which disenfranchised all Mormons living in that territory.

10 FEBRUARY 1890
Ideas/Beliefs As part of the continuing power struggle in Utah Territory, the Liberal Party, consisting entirely of non-Mormons, captures almost all of the elective offices, including that of mayor, in Salt Lake City. This is the first time that Mormons have lost election contests for these offices; it is another severe blow to the influence of the Mormon Church in the territory.

Holding down a claim in Oklahoma – 1889.

11 FEBRUARY 1890
Indians About one-half of the Great Sioux Reservation of 22 million acres is thrown open for settlement by President Harrison's proclamation. The reservation stretches from the Missouri River on the east to the Black Hills on the west, and from the Nebraska border almost as far north as Bismarck, North Dakota.

2 MAY 1890
National Congress adopts the Oklahoma Organic Act, which establishes territorial government for what was formerly Indian Territory. All reservations in western Indian Territory, when opened for settlement, are to be annexed to the new Oklahoma Territory. The so-called No Man's Land is also attached to the territory and becomes the Oklahoma panhandle.

19 MAY 1890
Judicial The Supreme Court delivers another crushing blow to the Mormon Church by sustaining the provisions of the Edmunds-Tucker Law, by which the church was dissolved and its property confiscated.

2 JULY 1890
National Congress passes the Sherman Anti-Trust Act. It bars conspiracy or contracts by trusts or corporations designed to further 'restraint of trade or commerce among the several states or with foreign nations.' The act is designed to end monopolistic practices in the oil, steel, and railroad industries. However, due to the ambiguous phrasing of such terms as 'trust,' 'combination,' and 'restraint,' the act does little to slow the continentwide growth of these industries and their

CHRONOLOGY

Railway bridge and tunnel construction in Arizona.

WOVOKA, c 1856-1932

Born into the Paiute tribe of Nevada about 1856, Wovoka gave little early indication of the visionary power that would bring the Indian peoples their last desperate hope and their last convulsive tragedy. For his first 30 years, he lived as a medicine man and ranch-hand for white settlers, who called him Jack Wilson.

Around 1889 Wovoka had one of those transforming visions that marked the lives of many Indian leaders – his was of a messiah who would come to save the Indians. As a result of his impassioned preaching, Wovoka's ideas spread over the West like wildfire, becoming the Ghost Dance cult, a mixture of Christian and Indian traditions. Its adherents believed that by dancing and purification they would prepare the way for their savior and from their despair bring a new era of peace and plenty; by donning Ghost Shirts, they would become immune to the white man's bullets.

The brutal massacre of Wounded Knee, South Dakota, in the winter of 1890 ended these hopes. There 150 Indians, many of them Ghost Dancers, were gunned down by the US Cavalry in the wake of agitation surrounding the cult (a few days before, Sitting Bull had been murdered). After that, the Ghost Dance cult faded away, and Wovoka died in obscurity in Schurz, Nevada, in 1932.

corrupt business practices. The weakness of this act, and the need to regulate the large corporations and trusts, will lead to the growth of a progressive movement, centered in the Midwest and the West, during the 1890s.

3 JULY 1890
National Idaho enters the Union as the forty-third state.

10 JULY 1890
National President Harrison signs an act of Congress granting statehood to Wyoming. Women retain the right to vote that they had held with territorial status: thus Wyoming becomes the first state in the nation to have women's suffrage. One of the main objections in Congress to admitting Wyoming to the Union is the relatively small population of the area – only 60,000.

14 JULY 1890
Finance Congress passes the Sherman Silver Purchase Act, which supplants the Bland-Allison Act of 1878. The Sherman Act calls for government purchase of 4,500,000 ounces of silver each month.

The steady decline in the price of silver bullion, coupled with the economic recession, has strengthened the political weight of silver and pro-inflation forces. Another factor is the recent addition of senators from silver-producing states like Montana and Idaho, who have strengthened silverite forces in Congress. The pro-silver Senate had passed a bill in June for the free and unlimited coinage of silver, but the House blocked its passage. A compromise is reached when the Senate agrees to support high tariff barriers contained in the McKinley Tarriff Bill; the House reciprocates with support for the Sherman act.

24 SEPTEMBER 1890

Ideas/Beliefs Wilford Woodruff, president of the Mormon Church, issues a proclamation known as the Manifesto. The proclamation denies that the Church still approves of plural marriages and declares Woodruff's intention to submit to federal law and to influence all Mormons to do likewise. The Manifesto is considered the final capitulation of the Mormon Church to Federal Government authority in Utah Territory. It is approved at a convention held by the Mormon Church on 6 October. The People's Party, the political organization of the Mormon Church, is abolished.

1 OCTOBER 1890

Conservation Yosemite National Park in California is created by an act of Congress. The act is chiefly the work of the naturalist John Muir and Robert Underwood, one of the editors of *Century Magazine*. Muir has recently written a series of articles for the magazine dramatizing the destruction of the area by herds of sheep, whom he calls 'hoofed locusts.' The sheep have been engaged in indiscriminate grazing and trampling in the area.

15 DECEMBER 1890

Indians Sitting Bull is arrested and killed by army troops at his lodge just south of the border between North and South Dakota. Alarmed federal officials had ordered the arrest of the Sioux chief for encouraging what they call the 'Ghost Dance Craze.' Many Indians across the West, particularly the Sioux, have become obsessed with this religious dance, which they believe will rid them of the white man, bring back the buffalo, and restore their old way of life. In response to the killing of Sitting Bull, and fearing for their own lives, hundreds of Sioux flee their reservations and Indian agencies in South Dakota.

29 DECEMBER 1890

Indians At Wounded Knee Creek, South Dakota, 350 Sioux Indians, led by Chief Big Foot, are under guard by the Seventh Cavalry, commanded by Colonel James W Forsyth. The Indians are ordered to surrender what weapons they have and guns, knives, axes, and tent stakes are placed in a pile on the ground. A shot is fired, which is followed by a volley of rifle fire by the Seventh Cavalry troopers. Rapid-firing Hotchkiss guns, stationed on a hill overlooking the encampment, open up firing almost a shell per second. When the fighting stops, Chief Big Foot and more than half the Sioux are dead. Many wounded Indians crawl away to die in the bitter cold of an oncoming storm. One estimate puts the final death toll at nearly 300 of the original 350 Indians. Losses for the Seventh Cavalry are 25 dead and 39 wounded. This is the last major engagement between Indians and US Army soldiers in American history.

US Seventh Cavalry officers after the Battle of Wounded Knee.

CHRONOLOGY

8 JANUARY 1891

Nebraska The confused election situation leads the Young Farmers' Alliance to try to prevent the governor's clerk from taking office. The Alliance conducts a fully armed session of the legislature, which is recessed when a sheriff's posse appears. But the plight of the farmers in Nebraska remains desperate: drought and falling crop prices have left the state's farmers overwhelmed by debts. The Populist Party and William Jennings Bryan will be among the offspring of this crisis.

CHIEF JOSEPH, c1840-1904

To his people, the Nez Percé, he was Hinmaton-Yalakit; to whites he was Chief Joseph, who would live in history as one of the great heroes of the foredoomed Indian resistance to white encroachment. He was born in the ancestral Wallowa Valley lands of his tribe, where Oregon, Washington, and Idaho meet. Joseph became chief of the Nez Percé in 1873, when his homeland was already threatened by a forced treaty of 1863 requiring eviction of the tribe to Idaho. When the government determined to enforce the treaty, Joseph led his people, who had never killed a white man, onto the warpath (1877).

Aware that he could not resist the US Army, Joseph decided to escape to Canada. As forces under General Oliver O Howard closed in, the Nez Percé melted into the hills. With a force of some 200 warriors and nearly 600 women and children, Joseph began a retreat of over 1000 miles, fighting 13 engagements with 10 army divisions. He could not avert defeat: army forces besieged the Nez Percé at Bear Paw Mountain, only 30 miles from the Canadian border. After five days, Joseph capitulated, his immortal words reflecting the whole tragedy of the Indian peoples: 'Hear me, my chiefs: My heart is sick and sad. From where the sun now stands, I will fight no more forever.' Despite years of joint effort by Joseph and his erstwhile enemy General Howard, he and much of his tribe never saw their homeland again. In 1903 Joseph visited President Theodore Roosevelt in Washington and was given a hero's welcome. The great fighter died in Nespelim, Washington, in 1904.

14 JANUARY 1891

Indians General Nelson A Miles, commander of the US troops at the massacre at Wounded Knee in December 1890, announces that the Sioux are finally returning to their reservation. Ghost Dancers have appeared from as far away as Oklahoma, and Indians from Montana have joined the camping Sioux – who made the last successful attack on a wagon train on 6 January – but by the 19th all the Sioux will be back at the Pine Ridge Reservation. The Ghost Dance movement will survive here and there throughout the year, however, and continue to cause some concern.

20 JANUARY 1891

Hawaii King Kalakaua dies in San Francisco, where he had gone in November 1890 to see if he might improve his health. He is immediately succeeded by his sister, Liliuokalani, already over 50 years old and a woman of considerable attainments and tenacity.

28 JANUARY 1891

Montana Because of allegations of election fraud, the state has both parties claiming control of the House; the dispute is resolved by giving the Republicans a majority of the House with a Democrat for Speaker.

Oklahoma Thousands of Oklahomans illegally occupy sections of the so-called Cherokee Strip, land set aside for Indians, after a rumor circulates that the area is open for settlement.

3 MARCH 1891

Conservation Congress passes the Forest Reserve Act: under its provisions, President Harrison will set aside 13 million acres of public lands for a national forest reserve, most of them in the West.

Immigration Congress establishes the office of Superintendent of Immigration. Frontier land is almost gone, Depression threatens the land, job security is non-existent, yet millions of foreigners continue to emigrate to America, so it is felt that some control on newcomers must be exercised.

5 MARCH 1891

Indians The city government of Phoenix, Arizona Territory, alarmed by the Federal Government's abandonment of nearby military forts, offers a $200 reward for every dead Indian.

11 MARCH 1891

Indians The US Congress begins what will be an unsucceessful attempt to enlist 2000 Indians as infantry and cavalry – rather than just as scouts, as they have been – for the US Army.

30 MARCH 1891

Populism The various farmers' alliances that have been forming due to deteriorating conditions for Western farmers are beginning to move toward direct action. Today the Kansas Farmers' Alliance, which has been the most active, organizes a corporation for the purpose of supporting farm families who are going hungry. Simultaneously, one of their leaders, 'Sockless' Jerry Simpson, calls on the Farmers' Alliance to work toward a takeover of the state government in the 1892 election and to nominate a candidate for President of the United States.

Conservation Congress establishes the first National Forest, Shoshone, and the first National Forest Reserve, Yellowstone Park Timberland Reserve.

5 APRIL 1891

California An investigation reveals widespread corruption in the California legislature. The powerful Republican Party reportedly paid $2000 per vote to elect Senator Falton in March (Senators are not yet elected by direct popular vote).

7 APRIL 1891

Labor Nebraska passes one of the first laws limiting the required working day to eight hours.

30 APRIL 1891

Agriculture The Kansas Board of Agriculture accuses members of the Farmers' Alliance of neglecting their lands, thereby causing their own problems.

1 MAY 1891

Discovery E Hazard Wells, chief of the Alaskan Exploratory Expedition, reports the discovery of the source of the Yukon River.

17 MAY 1891

Western Lore Money and various other items buried near Truckee, California, by the Donner Party is discovered by an itinerant prospector. (The Donner Party was the group from Illinois and Iowa who became trapped in the mountains by the winter weather in 1846-7 and resorted to cannibalism).

19 MAY 1891

Populism At a convention in Cincinnati, Ohio, representatives of various farmer, labor, and reform groups found the People's Party, which will become generally known as the Populist Party. It calls for such reforms as government ownership of the railroads, free coinage of silver, a graduated income tax, the eight-hour day, the secret ballot, popular election of Senators, and government warehouses where farmers could deposit grain against Treasury notes. The Populists will hold a national convention in 1892 and nominate their own presidential candidate, but the base of their support tends to remain in a few Midwestern and Western states. Their antipathy toward Big Business and focus on agrarian issues limits their appeal in the eastern part of the country.

Apache brothers Nalta and San Carlos, 1880s.

LELAND STANFORD, 1824-1893

Unlike his partners in the Central Pacific Railroad, Leland Stanford has two other claims in history – as governor of California and founder of the university that bears his name. Stanford was born in Watervliet, New York, on 9 March 1824, and studied law as a young man. After a few years of practice in Wisconsin, he moved to California in 1852, another settler heading for the gleam of gold, and began selling supplies to miners. Such was his success and prominence that nine years later he was elected governor. In office, he saw to it that the state remained firmly Unionist.

Stanford made the acquaintance of Collis Huntington, Mark Hopkins, and others interested in building a railroad east to link up with the Union Pacific. After leaving office in 1863, he took over the presidency of the Central Pacific, and held that position for the rest of his life. The two roads met to form the first transcontinental railroad in May 1869 at Ogden Point, Utah. Later, Stanford became president of the Southern Pacific for five years. Another lasting involvement came in 1885, when he founded the Leland Stanford Junior University in Palo Alto, named for his deceased son. In time, it became simply Stanford University. That same year he was elected to the US Senate, and he remained a senator until his death in Palo Alto in 1893.

Buffalo bones in a sod house dooryard.

WESTWARD THE WOMEN

In all the research and writing that has been done about the women who traveled west in the 1800s, the fact that emerges most clearly is that of individuality. The frontier experience was individual to each woman who set out with her family, or without; newly married, or alone. Such historic stereotypes as the 'gentle tamer' and the 'soiled dove' reflect more of the popular Victorian idea of women and the way these female pioneers captured the public imagination in literature and the newspapers than they reflect the actual pioneers.

In *Westering Women and the Frontier Experience, 1800-1915,* Sandra L Myres points out the stereotypes that have been perpetuated because historians have not gone back to the diaries and letters left by frontier women to describe their experience. Instead, they have relied on historical accounts that contain the fond stereotypes. Other scholars have used selected accounts by women to prove certain socialist or feminist points of view. Once primary sources are consulted in large numbers, it becomes clear that the stereotypes do great injustice to the individual women who went west.

First of all, most of the westering women enjoyed their adventures. Journals and diaries were popular pastimes, and many women wrote detailed descriptions of the landscape, the sky, the Indians they saw. Most of the women were deeply committed to their new way of life and had a sense of participation in a movement of historic importance.

Certainly, there were fears, sickness, deaths, and all the elements that make up what we today consider to have been the excitement of traveling west. These experiences, however, do not constitute the bulk of what has been left as a record by the westering women. Yes, there were hard times, hot dusty days where traveling was fatiguing and even boring, but these women were leaving an Eastern society that was quite confining to take part in establishing a society where the rules would have to be more accommodating to the needs of survival. The sky was wider, the landscape more open, and the challenges invigorating.

4 JULY 1891

Mining Winfield Scott Stratton, a carpenter who has been prospecting for gold in his spare time for 20 years, stakes a claim where he has discovered gold in the Cripple Creek field of the Rockies, south of Denver, Colorado. The claim, which Stratton names Independence in honor of the day, turns out to be a rich vein of gold; soon Stratton is staking out other claims that prove equally valuable. Stratton himself will eventually make millions and become one of the legendary Bonanza Kings of Cripple Creek, where since January 1891 – when Bob Womack struck the El Paso lode – many have taken fortunes from the field.

26 AUGUST 1891

Science/Technology An early attempt at rain-making is successful in bringing rain to Midland, Texas, dry since 1888.

22 SEPTEMBER 1891

Indians President Harrison proclaims another 900,000 acres of Indian land in Oklahoma open to settlers. This land has been owned by the Sauk, Fox, and Potawatomi Indians but was ceded by disadvantageous treaties to the United States.

25 DECEMBER 1891

Western Lore Catarino Garza, a Mexican outlaw and revolutionary, attempts to capture Fort Ringgold, in Texas; his attempt fails, but his forces continue to skirmish with US troops along the Rio Grande for several weeks, until Garza is forced by the weather to retreat south.

OTHER EVENTS OF 1891

Alaska The US Department of Interior's Education Bureau imports 16 Siberian reindeer into Alaska to help provide food, clothing, and export materials for the Eskimos. (Over the decades the herd will grow to close to 1 million.)

Texas Governor James Hogg establishes a state railroad commission empowered to regulate railroad rates and other functions. The bill will be confirmed by the US Supreme Court in 1894 and will be one of a number of such attempts to curb the abuses of the railroads.

Utah The Mormon People's Party, up to now the sole political force in the territory, dissolves, providing a chance for the Democrats and Republicans to organize within Utah.

Conservation The Timber Culture Act of 1873, which had offered 10 million acres of federal land – limited to 160 acres per person – to anyone who would plant 40 acres with trees, is repealed. In practice, the law had helped large cattle ranchers and land speculators at the expense of small farmers, but its repeal is seen as a setback to the growing conservation movement.

Education Leland Stanford Junior University opens in Palo Alto, California; it has been founded by the railroad magnate Leland Stanford in honor of his late son. Stanford will gradually become the equal of the finest Eastern colleges, and will provide the base for the advanced scientific-technical complexes that become known as 'Silicone Valley.'

Arts/Culture Hamlin Garland publishes his second book, *Prairie Folks*, a collection of short stories about farmers of the Great Plains region. The book's bleak tone and bitterly realistic portraits clash with popular romanticizing of the frontier and enhance Garland's reputation.

8 JANUARY 1892

Mining A coal mine explosion in McAllister, Oklahoma, kills 100 men and injures many more.

11 JANUARY 1892

Conservation The Pecos Forest Reserve in New Mexico is created by presidential order.

14 FEBRUARY 1892

Conservation The Department of the Interior issues a report showing that for years the timber from the US forest reserves has been cut without restraint by US, Canadian, and Indian foresters.

26 FEBRUARY 1892

Colorado Following discovery of rich veins of silver in southern Colorado by N C Creede, there is a minor rush to the area, as land grants are auctioned off. The town that springs up overnight on this site is named Creede and soon becomes one of the typically wild mining towns of the era. It is here, this year, that Robert Ford, who had killed Jesse James in 1882, will be killed in his own saloon.

29 FEBRUARY 1892

International A controversy has long been brewing over hunting rights in the Bering Sea, which

Kwakiutl Indian village, Northwest Coast.

America has claimed as its own, seizing Canadian vessels that come to hunt seals there. Today the United States and Great Britain agree to submit their dispute to arbitration by a commission formed of representatives from Italy, France, and Sweden. The commission will announce its decision on 15 August 1893: that the area is international water and that Canadian vessels must be free to enter, although there are limits placed on hunting. Britain is awarded damages.

1 APRIL 1892

Labor The first episode of ongoing labor unrest at the Coeur D'Alene lead and silver mines in Idaho begins as miners go out on strike. This first phase will turn into a small-scale guerrilla war and will end in July only when federal troops are called in.

3-9 APRIL 1892

Johnson County War Since becoming a state in 1890, Wyoming has attracted many new settlers, who have begun to build their homes and fence off small ranches on land where long-established cattlemen have been grazing their great herds. Furthermore, the big cattlemen are convinced that the small ranchers are building up their own herds by rustling. They have no proof of this, but they draw up a list of 70 persons whom they decide to kill – including some sheriffs and county commissioners, as well as suspected rustlers and small ranchers. The cattlemen have hired 25 gunmen from Texas, more than doubling their force; calling themselves the Invaders, they set out on 3 April to raid the KC Ranch, near Buffalo, in Johnson County, north-central Wyoming. They kill one alleged rustler and besiege his companion, Nate Champion, a Texan who had been hired by the small ranchers to serve as foreman of their independent cattle drive. After four hours, the

CHRONOLOGY

POPULISM IN THE WEST

Beginning with the Grange movement of the 1870s – formally founded by Oliver Hudson Kelley in 1867 as the Patrons of Husbandry – the farmers of the Great Plains were involved in an ongoing attempt to cope with the huge burdens of supporting themselves by farming. Floods and locusts were only two of the many plagues the farmers had to contend with; others included drought, erosion, unproductive land, over-production, overambition, and heavy costs. Banks, loan offices, grain elevators, and railroads all posed obstacles to the farmers' security. All this gave rise to a generic populism that played an important role in American life, especially in the West, in the last quarter of the nineteenth century.

The Grangers had taken the lead in fighting these problems, especially those caused by the avarice of the railroad kings. The single greatest accomplish-ment was enactment of the so-called Granger Laws, regulating the railroads to some extent and, more important, establishing the principle that states are empowered to regulate any business when it involves 'a public interest.' The Granger movement was by no means limited to Western concerns. It brought North-erners and Southerners together and helped to heal sectional wounds after the Civil War. It helped raise the Department of Agriculture to cabinet level and obtain rural mail delivery. Conservation and pure food laws were among its goals, and it admitted women to membership and fought for women's suf-frage. By 1880, however, the Grangers had lost their militant momentum – and most of their members – and settled back into an educational and social role. Their early recognition of the dangers of huge in-dustries going totally unregulated won them general approval. They also set an example for subsequent formal and informal organizations of laborers and producers to co-operate for the common good. One of the most important of these was the Populists.

The People's Party, better known as the Populists, held its first convention of sorts at Topeka, Kansas, in 1890, and attracted a disparate group. 'Sockless' Jerry Simpson spoke for the farmers; Ignatius Donnelly advocated a utopian society; James Weaver called for 'greenbacks' as the solution to people's debts; and Mary Elizabeth Lease, a Kansan, put it most succinctly when she cried, 'What you farmers need to do is raise less corn and more Hell!' The Populists' demands and goals were varied, but they centered on freeing the farmers of their crushing debts and making money more available to them.

By 1892 the Populists had won the governorship and legislature of Kansas, taken control of four Midwestern States, and nominated their own presi-dential candidate, James Weaver. Four years later, they claimed over one million members and promised to become a truly influential third party. However, William Jennings Bryan made an irresistible appeal with his 'cross of gold' speech and gained the nomi-nation of the Democratic Party. By promoting the goal of free silver coinage, it undercut the power of the Populists. With Bryan's loss, the rise of farm prices, and a general prosperity, the Populists lost their appeal. But if they collapsed as a formal political force, many of their concerns and reforms came to be adopted by other American political parties and by American society in general.

cattlemen set fire to the house: as Champion runs out, they shoot him down. When word of all this reaches Buffalo, another group of men arm them-selves and set out to confront the Invaders. They meet at the TA Ranch, but the new telegraph lines have been put to use, and federal troops arrive and put a stop to the imminent 'war.' The Invaders will be taken to Cheyenne for trial, but when crucial witnesses fail to appear, they are released. So ends the Johnson County, or Rustler, War, by no means the last time that Westerners decide to take the law into their own hands.

15 APRIL 1892
Settling Some 3000 people participate in a land rush at the Sisseton Indian reservation in South Dakota.

18-19 APRIL 1892
Indians The last formal Ghost Dance of the Cheyenne Indians takes place in the camp of Chief Left Hand in Oklahoma on the 18th. The next day, by order of President Harrison, some 3 million acres of land belonging to the Cheyenne and Arapaho Indians is opened to settlement by 30,000 waiting homesteaders. Chief Left Hand's camp is part of that land: the Ghost Dance has proven powerless against the white man's ways.

5 MAY 1892
Immigration Congress passes the Geary Chinese Exclusion Act, which requires all Chinese in the United States to register within the year or to face deportation. Pressure to pass such a law has come primarily from the West Coast, especially from California.

15 JUNE 1892
Education New Mexico, still a territory, opens its university; Congress will later grant over 300,000 acres to support the school.

2-4 JULY 1892
Populism The People's Party holds its first national convention in Omaha, Nebraska. James B Weaver of Iowa, a long-time fighter for populist causes, is nominated for president, with James G Field of Virginia for vice-president.

11 JULY 1892
Labor The striking silver miners in Coeur D'Alene, Idaho, fight with the strikebreakers called in by the owners.

23 JULY 1892
Indians Congress bans the sale of alcohol on all Indian lands.
Labor Federal troops are sent to the Coeur D'Alene mines in Idaho to force the strikers back to work.

5 OCTOBER 1892
Western Lore The infamous Dalton Gang raids

Arapaho perform the Ghost Shirt Dance – c 1893.

Coffeyville, Kansas, and tries to rob two banks; four gang members and four local men are killed in the shootout. Emmett Dalton might have gotten away but turns back to aid his brother and is shot repeatedly. He survives and is sentenced to life in prison in 1893, but will be pardoned in 1907 and live to become a prosperous citizen of California who helps make movies about his gang's exploits.

15 OCTOBER 1892
Settling President Harrison opens 1,800,000 acres of Crow Indian land in Montana to settlement.

8 NOVEMBER 1892
National Grover Cleveland defeats Benjamin Harrison by only some 360,000 popular votes, although his electoral vote is 277-145. James Weaver of the People's Party wins a surprising 1,027,329 votes – about 9 percent of the total cast – enough to send a message to some politicians about the appeal of the populist agenda. Among those elected to office is Charles Curtis, a popular figure in the Kansas Prohibition movement. Curtis is the grandson of a Kaw Indian chief and had spent three years on an Indian reservation before studying law; elected as a Representative on the Republican ticket, he will eventually serve as Herbert Hoover's vice-president.

OTHER EVENTS OF 1892
Conservation The Sierra Club is founded in California by a group led by the Scottish-American conservationist John Muir. Originally organized to combat the destruction of Western forests by lumber companies and farmers, the club will help create the National Park Service and the National Forest Service and expand its goals to work for all kinds of environmental and conservation causes.

Industry The first oil strike in California is made in Los Angeles, near Second and Glendale Streets.
Agriculture The Colorado Irrigation Company is founded to irrigate California's Imperial Valley; a small canal is built near the Mexican border, but Boulder Dam is still many years in the future.
Arts/Culture Robert Louis Stevenson publishes *Across the Plains*, an account of a journey across the United States during which he examines American attitudes, especially toward the Chinese.
Life/Customs The Barrett Scott case begins as Mr Scott, treasurer of Holt County, Nebraska, disappears after being charged with embezzlement. His capture, return, kidnapping, and lynching – the vigilantes are acquitted – will bring temporary notoriety to the town of O'Neill, Nebraska.
Agriculture The boll weevil, a cotton-eating beetle, first appears in southern Texas from Mexico or Central America; it will spread throughout the cotton-growing South and Southwest relatively quickly and soon threatens to wipe out the crop. It will never be eliminated entirely, despite the expenditure of vast amounts of money and insecticides. It has the side effect of forcing many states to diversify their agriculture.

1 JANUARY 1893
Communications The Reverend J L Prevost of the St James Mission, near the Tanana River of Alaska, establishes the *Yukon Press*, the first newspaper in the Alaskan interior. This territory is still very sparsely settled on account of the difficulty of building roads here.

WYATT EARP, 1848-1929

In the wildest and most lawless period of the Old West, it was often difficult to tell which side of the law a given gun was on. This is well illustrated by the career of gunfighter Wyatt Earp, who was either one of the heroes or one of the villains in the legendary shootout at the OK Corral. Earp was born in Monmouth, Illinois, on 19 March 1848, and in his early years moved to California to pursue various jobs on the plains – stagecoach driver, buffalo hunter, and small-time gambler. In 1874 he became a peace officer in Wichita, Kansas. Two years later he moved to Dodge City, where, with his friend the dandified sheriff and gambler Bat Masterson, Earp pursued trades in the hazy areas between sides of the law – a trigger-happy deputy and a faro dealer.

Moving to the wide-open cattle town of Tombstone, Arizona, in 1878, Earp teamed up with his two brothers as freewheeling peacekeepers and gamblers. A row between Wyatt and Ike Clanton's gang led to the gunfight at the OK Corral in October 1881, in which the Earp brothers were joined by the hard-drinking Doc Holliday. In one minute of flying lead, three of the Clanton gang fell dead and both Wyatt's brothers were wounded. Legend called it a victory of law and order; at the time, the town nearly lynched the Earps and Holliday: the Earps were out of the lawman business. After years of wanderings, Wyatt Earp died peacefully in Los Angeles in 1929.

CHRONOLOGY

Liliuokalani (left) was Queen of Hawaii at the time of American annexation.

14-17 JANUARY 1893
Hawaii Since succeeding to the throne in January 1891, Queen Liliuokalani has shown little liking for the constitutional restraints that her brother Kalakaua had accepted. On the morning of the 14th, she dismisses the legislature and discloses her plan to proclaim a new constitution with greater powers for the monarch. The opposition Reform Party holds an impromptu meeting that afternoon and appoints a 13-member Committee of Safety – made up of non-Hawaiians whose real goal is to have Hawaii annexed by the United States. This committee holds several meetings and by 16 January decides that it is time to get rid of the monarchy, set up a temporary government, and apply for admission to the United States. On 17 January the Committee of Safety takes possession of the government's main building and reads a proclamation that sets up a Provisional Government, with Sanford B Dole – a judge of American descent, but born in Hawaii – as president. Queen Liliuokalani – claiming that the American troops who came ashore on the 16th, ostensibly to protect American lives and property, are essentially supporting the rebels – surrenders her authority. She appeals to the US Government to restore her throne, while the Provisional Government dispatches commissioners to Washington to negotiate a treaty of annexation.

21 JANUARY 1893
Johnson County War The case against the Invaders is dismissed due to the failure of crucial witnesses to appear. It is also stated that the court has been able to find only 11 men in all of Wyoming deemed sufficiently free of bias to serve as jurors.

14 FEBRUARY 1893
Kansas The Kansas legislature all but comes to blows as the incumbent Republicans arrest the elected Populists, including Ben Ricky, the Populists' chief clerk. A crowd of farmers then storms the hall and occupies it overnight before Republicans batter down the doors. On the 25th, the Supreme Court will recognize the Republicans as the ruling party of Kansas.

9 MARCH 1893
Hawaii The newly inaugurated President Grover Cleveland withdraws the Hawaiian Annexation Treaty from consideration by the US Senate pending an inquiry into the events leading up to the January overthrow of the monarchy.

1 MAY 1893
Life/Customs The World's Columbian Exposition opens in Chicago with President Cleveland officiating. The fair commemorates the 400th anniversary of the discovery of America. In one of the lesser-known events of the fair, nine men will begin a horse race on 13 June from Chadron, Nebraska, to the gate of Buffalo Bill's Wild West Show in Chicago; the winner, who arrives almost two weeks later, will be John Berry.

27 JUNE 1893
Finance With silver hitting an all-time low of 77 cents per ounce, the Colorado producers unanimously agree to a complete shutdown of mines and smelters until the government takes steps to support the silver miners. However, the whole stock market has all but collapsed today, and the nation enters into what will be a four-year Depression.

5 AUGUST 1893

Indians The Osage Indians refuse to sell their 2 million acres in Oklahoma to the Federal Government; the acreage is adjacent to the Cherokee Strip, which will be opened to settlers on 16 September.

16 SEPTEMBER 1893

Settling The greatest opening of Indian lands in the West occurs today when the Cherokee Strip, or Outlet, in north-central Oklahoma, and the Tonkawa and Pawnee reservations, are opened to homesteaders – a total of some 6,500,000 acres. Some 50,000 people claim land on this first day.

1 NOVEMBER 1893

National The Sherman Silver Purchase Act is repealed after a bitter Congressional fight, but with the support of President Cleveland. The act has been in force only since 14 July 1890, when in return for supporting the Eastern states in high tariffs, the Western pro-silver states had gotten a bill calling for government purchase of large amounts of silver. The repeal will bring a collapse of the silver-based settlements and fortunes of Colorado and other Western states; one who loses in this is Horace Tabor, who will leave his wife, 'Baby Doe,' little more than a worthless mine when he dies penniless in 1899.

7 NOVEMBER 1893

Social Change Colorado adopts woman's suffrage by popular vote.

NOVEMBER 1893

Hawaii A new American ambassador, Albert S Willis, arrives in Honolulu, to replace the former ambassador, John L Stevens, who has been found overtly supportive of the revolutionary group that seized the government in January. Willis will try to give a fair hearing to both sides, but he mistakenly believes that Queen Liliuokalani will decapitate leaders of the coup if she is restored to power. In any case, Dole and his provisional government simply reject the role of the US Government in Hawaii. Thus President Cleveland will decide to take no action on Hawaii, and Dole's provisional government will remain in place for the next five years, even after the Republic is declared on 4 July 1894.

OTHER EVENTS OF 1893

Indians Congress establishes the Dawes Commission (named for Massachusetts Senator Henry L Dawes, its sponsor and chairman) to find ways of reorganizing the Indian Territory (which will eventually be absorbed into the State of Oklahoma). Its approach will be to gain assent from the chiefs of the Five Civilized Tribes, who have already been relocated here, to abandoning tribal titles to the land so that it could be allotted to individuals. The ultimate goal, of course, is to take the land from the Indians and absorb the whole territory into one state.

Social Change President Harrison offers amnesty to polygamists among the Mormons. But the Mormon Temple, ordained by Brigham Young in 1847 and dedicated this year, is still accessible only to 'worthy Mormons.'

Agriculture Robert Reid, an Iowa farmer and developer of Reid Yellow Bent, or Iowa, Corn, is honored at the Chicago World's Fair. This strain of corn is the backbone of Iowa's farms until hybrid corn arrives about 1925.

17 JANUARY 1894

Finance In an effort to restore the vanishing gold reserve behind US currency, the US Treasury floats a bond issue of $50 million, but the public's response is almost nil and banks end up buying most of the bonds.

22 FEBRUARY 1894

Life/Customs Governor James S Hogg of Texas is arrested for poaching on government land.

4 APRIL 1894

Indians Rustling leads to skirmishing as Cheyenne Indians near El Reno, Oklahoma, are caught taking cattle that white ranchers are illegally grazing on Indian land. The US Third Cavalry is dispatched to restore order.

17 APRIL 1894

Science/Technology Percival Lowell ushers in an era of astronomy in the West by founding the Lowell Observatory at Mars Hill, near Flagstaff, Arizona. It is the first of several notable observatories that will be based in the West to take advantage of the lack of atmospheric pollution.

APRIL 1894

National Coxey's Army is on the march! Jacob S Coxey – a laborer turned businessman who feels strongly about the plight of the many unemployed through the Depression – wants the government to spend millions of dollars in employing men on highway construction. To dramatize his demands, he has called on all the unemployed to march on Washington. He sets out on Easter Sunday from Massillon, Ohio, at the head of about 100 men. Meanwhile, other 'industrial armies' have been organized to march on Washington, perhaps the most notable being that led by 'General' Kelly, which sets out from San Francisco. Getting free train rides and meals, it is making its way east; among its members is a young Jack London. Other armies include the Montana Commune, one from North Dakota commanded by John Shuler, and another from Sacramento, California, led by Anna Smith. As these armies move eastward, they encounter hostility from some communities, and National Guard and US Army units are sometimes called out to keep them in line.

CHRONOLOGY

1 MAY 1894
Labor Jacob Coxey leads his 'Industrial Army' on a parade down Pennsylvania Avenue in Washington, DC – but there are only about 500 men instead of his predicted 100,000. Coxey is arrested for trespassing on the lawn of the Capitol, and his 'army' will gradually drift away. Meanwhile, several of the other industrial armies are still making their way east.

9 MAY 1894
Labor Kelly's Army has made it to Des Moines, Iowa, and the townspeople have helped them build boats to move downriver; setting out today, they will eventually get as far as Quincy, Illinois, where the army begins to drift away: Jack London hops a freight to Chicago. Kelly and a few of his supporters do make it to Washington eventually.

11 MAY-3 AUGUST 1894
Labor One of the most significant labor actions in American history takes place during this time, beginning with a strike called by workers at the Pullman Palace Car Company outside Chicago; the company has reduced its payroll and wages, but has not reduced rents for its worker's homes nor prices in the company store. Before the strike ends, there will be loss of life and of millions of dollars in property and wages. US troops will be called in.

31 MAY 1894
Hawaii In a unanimous decision, the US Senate declares that Hawaii must be allowed to keep its own government and that the United States will regard any nation that attempts to interfere there as hostile to itself – in effect, bringing Hawaii under the Monroe Doctrine.

21 JUNE 1894
National William Jennings Bryan, a US Representative from Nebraska, arouses 1000 delegates to a Democratic Silver convention in Omaha and bursts onto the national scene with his simple solution to all the economic problems besetting the nation – free silver.

26 JUNE 1894
Labor Eugene Debs, who had established his American Railway Union on 20 June 1893, calls for a general strike by all railway workers to show sympathy with the striking Pullman workers.

2 JULY 1894
Labor President Cleveland issues an injunction against the railroad strikers on the grounds of 'interference with interstate commerce and postal service' and orders Debs to call it off. US troops are sent to Chicago on 4 July to enforce the injunction, even though Illinois Governor Altgeld protests that this is a violation of the US Constitution and interference in the internal affairs of a state.

4 JULY 1894
Hawaii The Republic of Hawaii is declared under a new constitution, its government organized something like that of the United States, but with elements from other nations. Sanford Dole remains as president, but the flag of the former monarchy is still the republic's flag. The leading nations of the world will soon recognize the new government, although supporters of Queen Liliuokalani will continue to seek ways to restore her to power.

13 JULY 1894
Labor The railroad strike called by Eugene Debs has spread to California, but the state militia has refused to disperse the rioters in Sacramento and Oakland. Martial law is proclaimed, and the US Marines have been called in: today they fire on strikers in Sacramento. The trains in California will continue to operate under guard by the US Marines for another week.

27 JULY 1894
Western Lore Tom Smith, a fugitive horse thief, kills three US marshals and wounds two in a gunfight in Muskagee, Oklahoma.

SUMMER 1894
Agriculture A combination of heavy winds and drought is making this year's harvest the worst in memory for such states as Iowa, Kansas, and Nebraska.

3 AUGUST 1894
Labor The railway union calls off the Pullman strike, having gained nothing from management.

18 AUGUST 1894
Conservation Congress passes the Carey Desert Land Act, calling for the Federal Government to give each state up to 1 million acres of public land if the state will irrigate them.

1 SEPTEMBER 1894
Disaster A hurricane whips a fire that devastates Hinckley, Minnesota, and neighboring towns, killing some 500 people and leaving thousands more homeless. Hundreds of people take refuge in a railroad train that barely outruns the flames; parts of the train's rear cars are in fact aflame by the time it reaches a lake.

27 SEPTEMBER 1894
Indians The Bureau of Indian Affairs enacts a plan to place Indian children in the public school system with white children.

14 DECEMBER 1894
Labor Eugene Debs, the radical founder of the American Railway Union, is sentenced to six months in prison for his role in the Pullman strike. His defense attorney is Clarence Darrow, who

A chuckwagon on the plains.

resigns as a lawyer for the railroads to take on his first case as a defender of those who challenge the establishment.

OTHER EVENTS OF 1894

Indians Geronimo, the Apache chief who led federal troops on a chase through Mexico in 1885-6, is returned from federal prison in Florida to a guard house at Fort Sill, Oklahoma. He will convert to Christianity, settle down to farming, and eventually become something of a national icon.

Apache warrior Geronimo in his last years.

Mining The largest nugget of silver known to this time is found in the Smuggler Mine at Aspen, Colorado; it weighs 1840 pounds.

Finance A self-schooled economist, William Hope Harvey, publishes his *Coin's Financial School*, in which he explains the money problems of the day in simple terms, calling for the monet-ization of silver at the ratio of 16:1 to gold. His ideas will have considerable influence on the Populists, especially on William Jennings Bryan.

Western Lore Lobo, a giant wolf that has been terrorizing the area around Clayton, New Mexico, is finally trapped; a price of $1000 had been put on his head. He will be given new life by the writer-naturalist Ernest Thompson Seton, born in England and raised in Canada, who wrote and illustrated a popular series of nature books for boys after he settled in New York.

Life/Customs A group of Omaha businessmen who have attended the Mardi Gras in New Orleans decide that Nebraska needs a similar festival: they found the order of Ak-Sar-Ben (try it backward), complete with a coat of arms and various ceremonies.

ELISHA PEYRE FERRY, 1825-1895

As a political leader of Washington Territory for decades, and its first governor after statehood, Elisha Ferry made valuable contributions toward turning a near-wilderness into a functioning part of the United States. He was born in Monroe, Michigan, on 9 August 1825, to the family of a French emigré who had been an officer under Napoleon. Ferry studied law in Michigan and in 1846 moved to Waukegan, Washington, to take up his practice. That career brought him considerable acclaim, so much so that he moved quickly into public office – first as mayor of the town, then as an elector and a bank commissioner of Illinois.

During his service as a staff officer in the Civil War, Ferry made the acquaintance of General Ulysses S Grant, who in 1872, as president, named his old friend governor of Washington Territory. After two terms in the post, Ferry returned to private practice in Seattle. Upon Washington's elevation to statehood, he was the logical choice as its first elected governor. Ferry died in 1895 at the age of 70.

CHRONOLOGY

6 JANUARY 1895
Hawaii Supporters of Queen Liliuokalani, mostly native Hawaiians but including about 30 foreigners, attempt a coup against the Dole government; fighting goes on for about 10 days, and several men are killed, but the coup fails. The Queen is arrested and held for almost eight months in a room where she is denied all comforts and visitors. Under the threat that her supporters will be executed, she finally signs papers formally abdicating and abolishing the monarchy.

27 FEBRUARY 1895
Agriculture Nebraska's farmers are in such desperate straits that the state asks the Federal Government for a loan of $1,500,000 to help 100,000 farmers in their drought-stricken conditions. Farmers are selling their horses for as little as 25 cents each, and hay is going for $2 a ton.
Western Lore The Hughes Gang, which in January had robbed the Texas Pacific Railroad of $100,000 – one of the largest train robberies of the time – is arrested by US marshals in Muskagee, Oklahoma.

5 MARCH 1895
Finance The Democrats in the House of Representatives, led by Richard Bland of Missouri and Bryan of Nebraska, call for the free coinage of silver at the ratio of 16:1 to gold. The proposal will be rejected, but there will be further calls for the monetization of silver throughout the year.

13 MARCH 1895
Life/Customs Anti-immigrant rioting occurs in the coalfields of Colorado, and six Italians are lynched by masked men and mobs.

8 MAY 1895
Utah The territory of Utah submits a new constitution to the US Congress in its sixth attempt to gain statehood. This one differs in that it outlaws polygamy and prohibits control of the state government by any church. It also includes suffrage for women.

6 JULY 1895
Populism Mary Lease (or Yellin), the controversial populist, is ousted from her post on the Kansas State Board of Charities by the state Supreme Court, which cannot tolerate her outspoken stand on silver and other populist causes.

25 JULY 1895
Indians Bannock Indians – angered at the ambush of an Indian hunting party near Jackson Hole, Wyoming, on 26 June, that left two Indians dead – have surrounded 250 white settlers at Jackson Hole. Ute and Shoshone Indians are in the area and are believed ready to attack the Bannocks, but the US Army's 9th Cavalry is sent to drive off the Bannocks. The settlers have killed several unarmed Bannock prisoners.

ABIGAIL SCOTT DUNIWAY, 1834-1915

In the story of the long and bitter fight for women's rights in the United States, the name of Abigail Scott Duniway is written prominently. She was born near Groveland, Illinois, on 22 October 1834. At 18 she and her large family journeyed over the Oregon Trail in an oxcart; in the new territory she taught school before marrying Benjamin Duniway. Their farming life ended when he was disabled, and thereafter she supported her husband and their six children as a schoolteacher and storekeeper.

Distressed at the legal barriers against women that she found in business, Duniway determined on her life's work. After organizing an Equal Rights Society in Albany, Oregon, she soon started a feminist newspaper called *The New Northwest* and embarked on a decades-long round of organizing, lecturing, and writing. After years of frustration, the wall began to crack in 1883, when Washington Territory enacted her draft of a suffrage law. Moving to Idaho, she saw the same progress there in 1896. Finally, the vote for women came in her home state of Oregon in 1912. During her career she had written two novels and a book of verse; the year of her death saw publication of her autobiography, *Path Breaking*. It had been a long and hard path indeed from the Oregon Trail to political power for women, but she lived to see the end of it.

AUTUMN 1895
Agriculture Despite the rain and windstorms that did severe damage to Western crops in July, a surprisingly large harvest will lead to a near-record abundance of wheat and corn. However, this will only drive prices down and not particularly benefit individual farmers.

OTHER EVENTS OF 1895
Science/Technology Daniel David Palmer, Canadian born, introduces chiropractic in Davenport, Iowa. Chiropractic ('doing by hand' in Greek) is a branch of medicine based on the theory that disease and ailments result from the disruption of nerve functions and are best relieved by hand massage.
Conservation The US Army engineer Hiram Chittenden publishes *Yellowstone National Park*, outlining his ideas on a national policy to preserve the wilderness. It will be influential in helping to extend the National Park system, which began with Yellowstone in 1872.
Communications William Allen White buys the Emporia (Kansas) *Gazette* for $3000; he will edit it for the rest of his life and make both the paper and himself spokesmen for grass-roots and small-town America. Long before he becomes known as 'the Sage of Emporia,' White will have an impact on Republican Party politics after his 1896 editorial, 'What's the Matter with Kansas?,' attacks the Populists, whose main base is in his state.

4 JANUARY 1896
Utah Utah enters the union as the forty-fifth state.

WESTERN ARTISTS

The vast and colorful Western landscape inspired many American artists, both before and after the Far West was opened to settlement. In the early nineteenth century, painters like Albert Bierstedt and George Catlin worked in oils on large, panoramic canvases that depicted a West that was largely ideal, populated by a red-skinned 'noble savage' in the mode of Jean Jacques Rousseau. Later in the nineteenth century, as American artists explored the West first-hand, a more realistic, less idealized style evolved. Frederic Remington, the best-known exponent of this style, painted and drew over 2700 pictures of the Old West during his years on the frontier – an imperishable record of the vanishing Indians, cowboys, cavalrymen and settlers and their way of life.

Charles Marion Russell left his native St Louis for the West at the age of 16 and found work herding cattle, whence his nickname 'the Cowboy Artist.' He captured the life of the Old West in oil and bronze, portraying the people and animals of the region in such works as *Waiting for a Chinook* and *The Bucking Bronco*, even as the 'cattle kingdom' was coming to an end.

Early in the twentieth century, Wisconsin-born Georgia O'Keefe arrived in the Southwest and began to paint her surroundings in a highly personal and monumental style that was both symbolic and abstract. Her enlarged and isolated natural forms, as in the painting *Yellow Cactus Flower*, seemed to overflow the confines of her canvas. Another native Midwesterner, abstract expressionist Jackson Pollock, acknowledged his debt to the Navaho sand painters in evolving a style characterized by subjectivity and improvisation. He was a pupil of Thomas Hart Benton, whose artistic legacy included Western Americana. Such writers as Will James, Tom Lea, and Ross Santee also contributed to the genre with illustrations for their enduring books on the West – personal testaments to a vanished era.

Remington's evocative Riding Herd in the Rain.

The Bronco Buster.

6 JANUARY 1896
Finance With gold reserves at a dangerously low level, President Cleveland authorizes still another sale of bonds; this time the public will buy them up, indicating a return of confidence.

12 FEBRUARY 1896
National The Territories Committee of the House of Representatives, a body dominated by anti-silver Easterners, refuses to accept Arizona for statehood; the undeclared reason is that this would strengthen the influence of pro-silver forces in Congress.

22 MARCH 1896
Indians An executive order empowers the Bureau of Indian Affairs to appoint native Indians to positions at reservation schools and agencies, but not outside the reservations.
Life/Customs Ira Terrell, the author of Oklahoma's death penalty statute, becomes the first man executed under it after he is revealed as a convicted felon.

10 APRIL 1896
Social Change The people of Ellis, Kansas, elect to municipal office a ticket composed almost entirely of women.

29 APRIL 1896
Mining The second fire inside of a week rages through the center of Cripple Creek, Colorado, the gold-mining center; three people are reported dead, two of whom are described as looters.

22 MAY 1896
Finance Pro-silver Senators attempt to get a measure passed that would forbid the government from issuing any more bonds: this would force the nation to coin silver or face bankruptcy. The attempt is unsuccessful.

27 MAY 1896
Disaster One of the worst tornadoes in US history sweeps through St Louis and East St Louis, leaving some 500 dead, thousands homeless. Damages amount to $13 million.

CHRONOLOGY

7 JULY 1896
National The Democratic Party convention is meeting in Chicago, as the Eastern 'Bourbon' powers have wished, but they are in a minority and in danger of losing control of the party to the pro-silver delegates should these become unified. The unifying force comes in the person of Nebraskan William Jennings Bryan, who concludes his mesmerizing speech with: 'Having behind us the producing masses of this nation and the world, supported by the commercial interests, the laboring interests, and the toilers everywhere, we will answer their demand for a gold standard by saying to them: You shall not press down upon the brow of labor this crown of thorns, you shall not crucify mankind upon a cross of gold.' Pandemonium breaks loose, and Bryan ends up receiving the Democratic nomination (although the gold-Democrats will bolt the party and nominate their own candidate).

22 JULY 1896
National The Populist Party, convening in St Louis, nominates William Jennings Bryan for President, but to show their independence from the Democratic Party, they nominate a different vice-presidential candidate, Thomas Watson, a leader for Southern farmers' interests. Meeting this same day in St Louis, some Republicans also nominate Bryan to express their opposition to the Republicans' choice, William McKinley, regarded as a front man for big-business interests personified by Mark Hanna.

SUMMER 1896
Discovery W A Dickey discovers a high mountain in Alaska – he estimates it to be 20,000 feet – and names it Mount Denali. On returning to the towns of Alaska, however, and hearing of the presidential election, he will rename it Mount McKinley.

12 AUGUST 1896
Mining Gold is discovered near Klondike Creek in northwestern Canada, near Alaska. It will be almost a year before word of this rich lode reaches the United States, but this will trigger off a great 'gold rush' that brings 100,000 prospectors and 'boomers' into the Klondike area over the next three years.

1 OCTOBER 1896
National Rural free delivery is established throughout the country by the Federal Post Office; this will be especially appreciated by residents of the West, where distances between settlements are so great.

3 NOVEMBER 1896
National William McKinley is elected president, with 7,104,799 votes to Bryan's 6,502,925 – but the Republicans, backed by the nation's business and established interests, spent at least $7 million to Bryan's $300,000. Bryan's emotional position on silver simply couldn't win over enough voters, despite his charismatic appeal.

Social Change Although it is overshadowed by the McKinley victory, women's suffrage advances, as Idaho adopts an amendment to allow women in Idaho to vote.

Ideas/Beliefs William 'Billy' Sunday, a former professional baseball player and since 1891 a worker for the YMCA, sets forth on his career as an evangelist. In his crusades against drink and other evils, he will convert about 1 million people in the next 40 years.

Communications W H Simpson establishes the advertising department of the Atchison, Topeka, and Santa Fe Railroad. It becomes one of the first railroads to promote the scenery along its routes and even commissions over 500 original paintings of the Western genre.

Life/Customs 'Judge' Roy Bean – self-proclaimed 'Law west of the Pecos' – promotes what he bills as the world heavyweight championship between Maher and Fitzsimmons. As such fights are illegal in every state except New York – which only legalized them this year – the fight takes place on a sandbar in the Rio Grande.

19 JANUARY 1897
Labor The Colorado miners' strike, begun in June 1896, ends today as the owners agree to increase wages; the strike is estimated to have cost about $3 million.

2 FEBRUARY 1897
California The 'Six Companies,' the leading Chinese Tong (gang) in America, which claimed to control and protect America's Chinese communities, especially in San Francisco, is dissolved on the Chinese New Year due to internal politics.

FEBRUARY 1897
Mining A deserted mineshaft in Leadville, Colorado, is reopened, and miners discover a rich vein of lead and silver ores. Other old mines are being reopened at this time, as the economy begins to pick up. At Cripple Creek, Colorado, the Caves of Aladdin are soon yielding $2000 worth of gold a day.

7 MARCH 1897
Ideas/Beliefs Kansas State Representative Walters attempts to get the Biblical Ten Commandments recognized as state law. Meanwhile, in nearby Oklahoma, Lucy Factor, an Indian, is accused of witchcraft and shot.

28 APRIL 1897
Indians The Dawes Commission, established in 1893 to acquire the Indian Territory lands, reaches an agreement with the Choctaw and Chickasaw Nations dissolving tribal government, dividing

common lands into 40-acre homesteads, abolishing liquor sales, and granting coal concessions to the Federal Government.

APRIL 1897
Industry The first oil strike in Oklahoma is made at Bartlesville. Over the next several decades, with major strikes elsewhere, oil becomes the state's largest industry.

23 MAY 1897
Judicial The Supreme Court declares Nebraska's maximum shipping rate for railroads to be unconstitutional, a major setback for farmers.

16 JUNE 1897
Hawaii The Hawaiian Government and the US Secretary of State, John Sherman, sign a Treaty of Annexation, an acknowledged goal of the Hawaiian Government for many years. Non-native commercial interests are finding US tariffs on sugar disastrous for the Hawaiian economy. There is also a fear that the increasing numbers of immigrants from Japan may instigate Japanese interference in the islands' politics. Submitted to the US Senate, the treaty will not get enough votes to go into effect this year.

Panning for gold in the Yukon, 1898.

14 JULY 1897
Mining Confirmation of the fabulous new gold find in the Klondike comes with the arrival in San Francisco of *Excelsior* with $750,000 worth of gold aboard. Thousands of men head north – over 100,000 will emigrate to Alaska over the next three years. (Among those who go off to seek their fortunes is Jack London, who will strike paydirt with his writings about Alaska.)

1 SEPTEMBER 1897
Finance Democrats, Populists, and silver-Republicans meet in Lincoln, Nebraska, to form a triparty alliance dedicated to the monetization of silver, even though this had been effectively rejected by Americans when they elected McKinley.

2 NOVEMBER 1897
Transportation Edward Harriman, highly regarded for his management of the Illinois Central Railroad, takes over operation of the Union Pacific Railroad. Reorganizing it after its 1893 bankruptcy, he will soon turn it into a major line and begin to acquire other railroads.

OTHER EVENTS OF 1897
Agriculture James Wilson becomes Secretary of Agriculture: from now through 1913, he will transform the department from a cabinet back-

water to a major force for research and advanced agricultural practices.

Labor Iowa passes its first Child Labor Law, forbidding the employment of any child under the age of 14 in coal mines.

Finance Gold discoveries in Colorado, Washington, Wyoming, and other states; the Klondike gold rush; and increasing prosperity in the farming states of the West effectively undermine the appeal of the Populists with their commitment to the monetization of silver.

Life/Customs Jefferson Randolph 'Soapy' Smith begins his career in the Skagway, Alaska, district among the goldminers – the same career for which he was run out of Creede, Colorado: his racket is to sell cakes of soap for $5 after claiming that many of them were wrapped in $50 and $100 bills. Some were, but they always went to his 'shills,' or come-on men. Smith is famous for his saying, 'The way of the transgressor is hard – to quit.' By June 1898 Soapy will be forced to quit.

1 JANUARY 1898

Indians An act of Congress, requiring approval by the president of all acts passed by the Indian reservation councils, goes into effect today.

13 JANUARY 1898

Mining A relatively mild winter, reports of the discovery of another rich vein of gold in the Yukon, and the claim that reports of famine in the Yukon are untrue – all combine to touch off another wave of gold rushers to the north.

15 FEBRUARY 1898

Spanish-American War An explosion rocks the US battleship *Maine* in the harbor of Havana, Cuba, killing 260 of the crew. 'Remember the Maine!' becomes the battle cry of those who since 1896 have been trying to get America to confront Spain over its policies in Cuba. (The cause of the explosion is never proven: American experts claim it was an external explosion, but the ship is towed off and sunk in deep water, so that no one can conduct further investigations.) War fever overtakes many Americans, including some in high governmental positions.

28 FEBRUARY 1898

Labor The Supreme Court, in *Holden v Hardy*, upholds a Utah statute that limits daily working hours in mining industries to eight. This will be an important victory for labor and will set a precedent for negotiations over many contractual terms.

28 MARCH 1898

National The Supreme Court, in *United States v Wong Kim Ark*, rules that US citizenship is without respect to race or color; thus a child born in the United States cannot be deported under the Chinese Exclusion Act, according to this landmark ruling.

JUNE 1898

Life/Custom Soapy Smith, now practicing his scam on the men of Skagway, Alaska, is challenged to a gunfight by one Frank Reid: both Smith and Reid are killed.

19-25 APRIL 1898

Spanish-American War Congress adopts a resolution that is essentially an ultimatum to Spain: unless Spain evacuates its armed forces from Cuba and recognizes the island's independence, the President will be allowed to use American armed forces to effect this. Not unexpectedly, Spain breaks off diplomatic relations with the United States on the 21st. Congress then passes the Volunteer Army Act, authorizing such units as the 'Rough Riders.' Spain declares war on the 24th; next day the United States declares that a state of war has existed since the 21st.

1 JULY 1898

Spanish-American War Theodore 'Teddy' Roosevelt, former Assistant Secretary of the Navy, leads a charge up Kettle Hill, Cuba – a charge that will carry him all the way to the White House. (It was little noted then or since that the troops who followed and suffered heavy casualties were the all-black 9th and 10th US Cavalry regiments.) Although even Teddy had to dismount to get up the hill, the image of the Rough Riders – the last elite US Cavalry regiment – seemed to epitomize all that was most dashing about the American West.

7 JULY 1898

Hawaii President McKinley signs a joint resolution of both houses of Congress that annexes Hawaii to the United States. (This joint resolution is a means of avoiding the need to have the two-thirds majority required for a treaty.) Many Americans are opposed to this move, seeing it as an unwanted step toward imperialism. However, Spanish-American war actions in the Philippines have convinced other Americans of the need for a reliable base in the Pacific.

SUMMER 1898

Exploration The War Department's Abercrombie Expedition explores between Valdez and the Alaskan interior, discovering the Keystone Canyon and Thompson Pass, a route used by gold-seekers for the next two decades.

9 AUGUST 1898

Spanish-American War Spain accepts the peace terms offered by the United States and effectively surrenders this afternoon. The 'splended little war' has ended, and overnight the United States finds its western boundaries pushed halfway around the world to embrace Hawaii, Guam, and the Philippines. The latter will prove an acquisition that entails many problems.

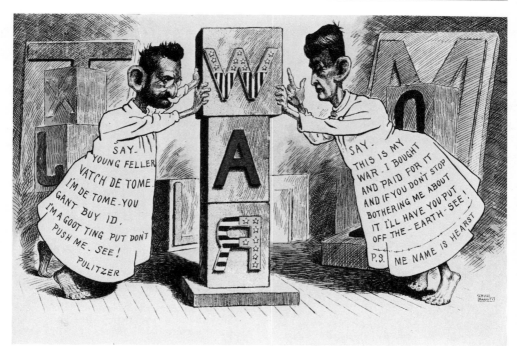

Hearst and Pulitzer caricatured as 'yellow journalists.'   *The Spanish-American War.*

CHRONOLOGY

IMMIGRANTS FROM THE ORIENT

The Japanese who began to arrive in California early in the twentieth century, like the Chinese who had appeared several decades earlier, faced a culture, social system, and language radically different from their own. Underlying much of the hostility they encountered was a fear of economic competition from the hard-working and frugal newcomers. The living standards of Japanese laborers were considered so low that 'No White man can compete with them,' according to California Governor William Stephens in 1920. He also declared that 'The Japanese operate 623,752 acres of the very best lands in California.' That state was notorious for discriminating against Orientals during the first decades of this century. Laws were passed to prevent them from owning and leasing land for farming. Weeks after the devastating San Francisco earthquake of 1906, the city passed ordinances requiring Japanese, Chinese, and Korean children to attend segregated schools for Orientals. This move provoked anti-American demonstrations in Japan and embarrassed President Roosevelt's administration. Roosevelt summoned San Francisco Mayor James Duval Phelan to Washington and pressured him into rescinding the order, but the president accomplished this only by promising to get the Japanese to reduce immigration (the so-called gentleman's agreement of 1907).

This did not prevent Mayor Phelan from expressing his views. He told the *San Francisco Chronicle* that 'The Chinese and Japanese are not bona fide citizens. They are not the stuff of which American citizens can be made. Personally I have nothing against the Japanese, but they will not assimilate with us and their social life is so different from ours, let them keep at a respectful distance.' These views were probably accepted by many people on the West Coast. Japanese men, for instance, were stereotyped as sexually aggressive in speeches by Grover Johnson, the father of California Governor and then Senator Hiram Johnson. The *San Francisco Chronicle* propagandized in a 1920 editorial that 'The Japanese boys are taught to look upon . . . American girls with a view to future sexual relations.' A 1920 movie, *Shadows of the West*, depicted two white girls kidnapped by a group of Japanese men; audiences cheered as the girls were rescued by a posse of American Legionnaires. The stage was being set for the internment of the Japanese in 1942 and the seizure of their land and property.

12 AUGUST 1898

Hawaii The formal ceremony transferring sovereignty of Hawaii to the United States takes place in Honolulu at noon.

AUTUMN 1898

Arts/Culture Bert Phillips and Ernest Blumenschein, two artists on a sketching trip from Denver to Mexico City, stop at the Taos Pueblo in New Mexico. They are so inspired by the landscape that they remain, sell their horses, and found what is known as the Taos Art Colony. Taos soon begins to attract artists of many kinds, from many countries.

OTHER EVENTS OF 1898

Mining Western Nevada's Comstock Lode – perhaps the richest-ever silver deposit in the United States, worked since the 1860s and the source of vast fortunes for 'silver kings' – is effectively abandoned this year due to the decline in its productivity and the price of silver in the world market.

Social Change A coalition of farmers and laborers in South Dakota pushes through the right to 'initiative': this gives voters the power to submit laws to the legislature and to vote on them directly if the legislature ignores them. This is regarded as an early accomplishment of the Progressive movement.

Arts/Culture Thomas Edison's moviemaking division creates a short film, 'Cripple Creek Ballroom,' the first 'Western.'

15 JANUARY 1899

Arts/Culture Edwin Markham publishes a poem entitled, 'The Man With the Hoe' (inspired by the French artist Millet's painting): it is a moving protest against the bleak lives of the laboring masses and is reprinted in newspapers across the country within a week.

3 MARCH 1899

National Congress establishes the Isthmian Canal Commission – actually the third such group (the first was in 1895, the second in 1897) to study the best possible route for a canal through Central America. There is increasing pressure to build one, as America sees itself extending its interests ever farther west.

APRIL 1899

Labor Miners in Idaho go out on strike, bringing a return to the violence that marked the Coeur D'Alene strikes of 1892. Governor Frank Steunenberg calls in federal troops to repress rioting strikers. In 1905 he will pay with his life for this act.

2 JUNE 1899

Western Lore The so-called Wild Bunch, led by Butch Cassidy and his sidekick, the Sundance Kid, rob a Union Pacific train at Wilcox, Wyoming. They blow up a freight car along with the safe.

AUGUST 1899

Politics Democrats meeting in Iowa and other states to prepare for the next presidential election begin to split. The pro-silver Populists insist that theirs is the true platform, while more moderate Democrats want to drop the silver issue and take up other causes. To some extent, this is merely a continuation of the struggle between the new West and the old East.

SEPTEMBER 1899

Environment An earthquake in Disenchantment Bay, Alaska, shatters the Muir Glacier, throwing tons of ice into Glacier Bay and cutting off the regular tourist steamers from visiting this natural wonder.

15 OCTOBER 1899

Transportation The 'Overland Limited' makes its first run from Chicago to Oakland, California. This luxury train stops in Reno, Nevada, helping to make it convenient for gamblers; the train will remain in service till 1947.

AUTUMN 1899

Mining Deposits of gold are found along the coast near Nome, Alaska, and a new gold rush is under-way.

Butch Cassidy and his gang re-created on film.

OTHER EVENTS OF 1899

Social Change Carry Nation and several tem-perance-minded associates hold a prayer meeting in front of a saloon in Medicine Lodge, Kansas. Nation rushes at the saloon with an umbrella, but fails to gain admittance. This will only inspire her to more determined efforts to drive out liquor in the years ahead.

Industry The Guggenheim family begins its attempt to gain control of the American Smelting and Refining Company, which will be accomplish-ed in 1901. Meyer Guggenheim had been a suc-cessful merchant in Philadelphia until, in the late 1880s, he acquired interests in mining properties in Colorado. Moving into smelting and refining, he is now on the verge of becoming one of the great industrialists of the twentieth century.

Transportation After a seven-year battle between the city of Los Angeles and private railroad interests, the Federal Government begins building the city's main harbor at San Pedro.

Conservation Mount Rainier National Park in Washington is established by Congress.

Arts/Culture Frank Norris publishes his first novel, *McTeague*, which naturalistically portrays the side-effects of the greed of modern industry on the poor and lower middle class of San Francisco. Norris will go on to become a noted novelist and journalist whose works portray the post-frontier West with unsparing realism.

Author Jack London as a young sailor in port at Yokohama.

14 MARCH 1900
Finance The increase of the world's gold supply in recent years has considerably weakened the arguments of pro-silver forces. Today the US Congress passes the Gold Standard Act, which establishes the US dollar as backed by 25.8 grains, nine-tenths fine; all forms of US money are put on a parity with gold. Since the nation now has a gold reserve of $150 million, national banks with a minimum capital of $25,000 are established in towns of 3000 people or less with the goal of meeting the farmers' need for capital.

3 APRIL 1900
Agriculture The first of several major irrigation projects in the Imperial Valley of California is begun.

30 APRIL 1900
Hawaii President McKinley signs the Organic Act that sets up the new government of the Territory of Hawaii. Not unexpectedly, the government is structured much like that of the US Federal Government, and its laws are to be consonant with those of the US Constitution. All citizens of Hawaii automatically become citizens of the United States. Sanford Dole is appointed governor of the territory, having served as president of the Hawaiian republic.

19 JUNE 1900
National The Republicans nominate McKinley for a second term as president. Less expected is their vice-presidential nomination of Theodore Roosevelt, who appears in his Rough Rider hat and kerchief – not the last time that an American will appeal to the voters as a cowboy.

25 JUNE 1900
Life/Customs Oliver Lippincott drives an automobile into Yosemite National Park and proceeds to the top of Glacier Point. It is the beginning of the age when the automobile will take Americans to the remotest parts of their land.

4 JULY 1900
National The Democratic National Convention, meeting in Kansas City, nominates William Jennings Bryan again for president. He has already received the nomination from one wing of the Populists, but despite his appeals to farmers and labor, and his denunciations of big business, he will fail to convince Americans of a need for fundamental changes.

29 JULY 1900
Transportation The White Pass and Yukon Railway is completed, connecting Skagway, Alaska, with Whitehorse, in Canada's Southern Yukon Territory. The railroad will begin to provide a route out of the Yukon for many disappointed gold-seekers.

8 SEPTEMBER 1900
Disaster A terrible hurricane sweeps through Galveston, Texas, leaving 6000 dead and causing some $20 million in property damage. Because of the looting that follows and the city government's failure to deal with the aftereffects, the first commission government is established in Galveston.

18 SEPTEMBER 1900
National Minnesota holds the nation's first direct primary for elective officials: it will inspire other Americans to go over to the direct primary system for most elective offices.

6 NOVEMBER 1900
National McKinley is re-elected president with 292 electoral votes to Bryan's 155. The causes and problems of the West are again to take second place to those of the East.

DECEMBER 1900
Alaska Several diseases are now epidemic among the miners and Eskimos who have descended on Nome, and most of the game in the area has been killed by hungry 'boomers.' Approximately 30,000 men are stranded on the beaches at Nome, of whom only a few hundred are even trying to find gold.

28 DECEMBER 1900
Social Change Carry Nation uses an iron rod in her campaign against drink and licentiousness, charging into a hotel bar in Wichita, Kansas, to break a mirror and furniture and throw rocks at a painting, 'Cleopatra at the Bath.' The painting, by John Noble, had already been accepted by the National Academy of Design.

OTHER EVENTS OF 1900
Population The national census reveals a total population of 76,303,387. The center of population continues to move west, about 45 miles southwest since 1890, to a point near Seymour, Indiana. Attempts to take a true census in Alaska have been frustrated by the lack of roads and navigable streams, by disappearing boomtowns, and by the fact that a large part of the population is on the trail at any given moment.

Alaska Juneau becomes the official capital of the Alaska Territory, although it will be six years before the executive offices move there from Sitka. Congress has passed a criminal law code for Alaska (in 1899) and a civil law code is passed this year, but it is hard to impose much law and order on this remote land. At Nome, for instance, Judge Arthur Noyes is assigned as district judge, but after declaring all gold below the high-water mark to be in the public domain, he will proceed to loot the fields for his own profit until he is dismissed in 1902.

Labor William Dudley Haywood, a miner since the age of 15, becomes national secretary-treasurer of the Western Federation of Miners, headquartered in Denver. Haywood will become known as 'Wild Bill': as a founder of the Industrial Workers of the World in 1905, he will be regarded as a dangerous radical by many Americans.

Mining Silver and gold are discovered at Tonopah, Nevada, touching off a new rush and rejuvenating the state, whose population has fallen from 62,000 to 42,000 in the last 20 years.

Communications *Chung Sai Yat Po*, the first Chinese newspaper in the United States, is published in San Francisco.

Arts/Culture Jack London's first collection of short stories, *The Son of the Wolf: Tales of the Far North*, is published to general acclaim, both critical and public. (Up to now, London's stories had been reaching a limited public through the *Overland Monthly*, published in San Francisco.

Lyman Frank Baum, who has worked as a newspaper editor in South Dakota, publishes *The Wonderful Wizard of Oz*, which will go on to become one of the most popular – and controversial – children's books in America. (Some will later insist it was Baum's allegory on the role of Populism: Oz is said to stand for ounces of precious metals; the Wizard is the cynical and deluding President; the blustering, cowardly lion is Bryan; the Scarecrow is the farmer and the Tinman the industrial laborer; the Wicked Witch is a powerful capitalist; while Dorothy represents the average, wholesome American.)

Life/Customs One of the early precursors of the 4-H Club movement is founded at the Macoupin County Fair, in Illinois. Such clubs spread throughout rural America and are soon being supported by state governments and by the US Department of Agriculture. They will eventually spread to over 50 foreign countries.

10 JANUARY 1901

Industry The oil boom is launched with the find in Beaumont, Texas. Anthony F Lucas owns the Spindletop claim, which starts the flow of black gold in the region.

4 MARCH 1901

National William McKinley is inaugurated for his second presidential term. Theodore Roosevelt is vice-president.

9 MAY 1901

Finance A struggle of giants emerges over control of the Great Pacific and Northern Pacific railway lines. The Hill Morgan group collides with the comparatively new Harriman, Kuhn, Loeb and Company. Stock prices soar from $100 to $1000 a share, throwing the financial community into turmoil. When a settlement is forced upon the two contestants to preserve the entire banking structure, they form a new corporation in New Jersey. The new Northern Securities Company almost monopolizes transportation between the Great Lakes and the Pacific Coast. Theodore Roosevelt later makes a move against this corporation when, as president, he campaigns against Big Business; in February 1902, Roosevelt will successfully bring a suit against the titan, signaling an improved atmosphere in industrial relations.

MAY 1901

Agriculture Sheepmen in Sweetwater County, Wyoming, employ a band of well-armed men to resist attacks from cattle ranchers.

14 MAY 1901

Agriculture The California Development Company completes a canal to bring water from the Colorado River to the Imperial Valley in California. As the first waters arrive, a number of settlement and ecological problems begin.

JULY 1901

Agriculture Willie Nickell, 13 years old, is shot to death in an ambush between Laramie and Wheatland, Wyoming. Nickell's father had introduced sheep into cattle country.

6 SEPTEMBER 1901

National President McKinley is shot by anarchist Leon Czogosz, as the president attends a reception for the Pan-American Exhibition in Buffalo, New York.

14 SEPTEMBER 1901

National Theodore Roosevelt rises to the presidency following the death of President McKinley at 2:15 AM. The forty-two-year-old Roosevelt takes the oath of office at 3:00 PM. By asking McKinley's cabinet to remain, Roosevelt calms the fears of Big Business and party bosses that the administration change will radically alter national politics.

OTHER EVENTS OF 1901

Industry The Red Folk-Tulsa oil field opens, as Oklahoma becomes an oil center.

Education Oklahoma City University is founded in the city of the same name. Southwest State College opens at Weatherford, and the University Preparatory Schools begin at Tonkawa, Oklahoma.

Life/Customs In Utah, Joseph Fielding Smith is elected president of the Mormons. The Wyoming state legislature passes an anti-gambling law that will become effective in 1902.

MARCH 1902

International Roosevelt plans possible military action to handle the Alaska boundary dispute with Canada. The president orders the secretary of war to have 'additional troops sent as quietly and unostentatiously as possible to Southern Alaska.'

2 JUNE 1902

Regional Oregon becomes the first state to adopt the initiative and referendum on a general scale.

These progressive reforms are subsequently adopted by most states. Under the leadership of William S U'Ren, Oregon later introduces primary voting and the recall of elected public officials. These measures, which aim at enhancing political participation, are the cornerstone of the Progressive movement. Other state-led reforms during the Roosevelt Administration include women's suffrage, labor legislation, minimum wage, and workmen's compensation.

17 JUNE 1902

Conservation The National Reclamation Act (sometimes called the Newlands Act) sets aside proceeds from land sales in 16 Western and Southwestern states to finance construction and maintenance of irrigation projects in arid areas. During his tenure, Roosevelt will also form a 150 million-acre forest reserve and withdraw from sale 85 million acres of prime Alaskan land until its mineral value can be assessed. Roosevelt will endear himself to the public by his concern for conservation. A renowned hunter, Roosevelt will make headlines by refusing to shoot a baby bear: the result of this incident is one of the most popular children's playthings – the Teddy Bear.

SUMMER 1902

Mining Another large gold discovery is made in Alaska, this one at Fairbanks. Alaska is soon overrun by 'sourdoughs' (miners and prospectors) in rough mining camps.

JULY 1902

Agriculture One hundred and fifty armed men stop fifteen herds of sheep that cross a 'deadline' in New Fork country of the Green River Valley, Wyoming. The cattlemen shoot a herdsman, kill 2000 sheep, and scatter others.

4 DECEMBER 1902

Mining Harry Stimler and William Marsh make a gold discovery on Columbia Mountain, Nevada, about 30 miles south of an earlier discovery at Tonopah. This will lead to the famous Goldfield, Nevada, Mining District.

OTHER EVENTS OF 1902

International The United States submits the first international case to the Hague Court of Arbitration. The US case against Mexico concerns arrears of interest on the Pious Fund of the Californias.
Conservation Crater Lake National Park is established in Oregon.
Arts/Culture Investigative reporter Ida Tarbell exposes the oil monopoly in her *History of the Standard Oil Company*. Her *McClure's Magazine* reports join other exposés of current business practices and social conditions. Notable works in this genre include *The Octopus* and *The Pit* by Frank Norris and *The Iron Heel* by Jack London. These carefully researched works will make a

Top: *Western genre author Owen Wister.*
Above: *Novelist Frank Norris, an unsparing realist.*

definite imprint on political discourse and legislation. Owen Wister publishes his novel about Wyoming cowboys, *The Virginian*, which will serve as the epitome of much that is written and filmed about the American West for decades to come. Wister himself was born in Philadelphia and educated at Harvard; it was ill health that forced him to travel to the West – not unlike his friend Theodore Roosevelt, the subject of a 1930 biography by Wister.

1 JANUARY 1903

Nevada Democrat and Silverite John Sparks becomes governor. Sparks will be involved in the Goldfield, Nevada, mining strike in 1907-08.

CHRONOLOGY

24 JANUARY 1903
International Great Britain and the United States sign an agreement establishing a joint commission to decide boundaries between Canada and the Alaska Panhandle.

FEBRUARY 1903
Agriculture A gang of masked men kill sheepman William Minnick and slaughter 200 of his sheep between Thermopolis and Meeteetse, Wyoming.

16 MARCH 1903
Hawaii Sanford B Dole, the first governor of the territory of Hawaii, approves a joint resolution passed by both houses of the territorial legislature, which requests the US Congress to pass 'an Act

---

THE ALASKA BOUNDARY SETTLEMENT

The Anglo-Russian treaty of 1825 left boundaries between Canada and Alaska ambiguously defined. At the time of the treaty, the vast wilderness separating the regions seemed of little economic importance. The discovery of gold in the Klondike changed all that and brought the United States into a heated confrontation with its northern neighbor. Canada wanted to gain access to a direct water route into the gold fields. With this gold in mind, the Canadians claimed that the boundary extended to the heads of important inlets from the sea. The United States considered this an extravagant claim. As tensions increased, US Secretary of State John Hay, in 1899, worked out a temporary modus vivendi. US, British, and Canadian officials agreed to work out a permanent settlement, through the use of a tribunal composed of 'six impartial jurists of repute.'

Three of these men were to be appointed by the United States and three by the British. The actual tribunal consisted of two prominent Canadians, one of whom had judicial experience; Lord Alverstone, lord chief justice of England; and three Americans. President Theodore Roosevelt appointed Secretary of War Elihu Root, Senator Henry Cabot Lodge of Massachusetts, and ex-Senator George Turner of Washington. None of these men had acquired much repute in a judicial capacity, and there were grave doubts as to their impartiality. Lodge, for example, was one of the country's leading 'anglophobes' and had already publicly committed himself against the Canadian claim. The tribunal met in London in 1903, and by a vote of four to two sided with the United States. The equal division of four small islands and other adjustments suggest that the decision was more a compromise than a strict judicial decision.

President Roosevelt was pleased with the advantageous settlement, reached on the eve of a national election. In a letter to Henry White, American ambassador in London, he exclaimed, 'The Alaska and Panama settlements coming in one year make a very good showing, do they not? I shall get Cuban reciprocity through, too.' Canadian-American relations, however, were strained for decades, despite Roosevelt's assertion that the settlement 'furnished a signal of proof of the fairness and good will with which two friendly nations can approach and determine issues.'

---

enabling the people of this Territory . . . to meet in convention to frame and adopt a state constitution, whereby and whereunder this Territory may be admitted as a State into the Union.' With a few exceptions, succeeding Hawaiian legislatures will undertake to adopt similar resolutions.

MARCH 1903
Agriculture Seven masked men tie up a sheepherder, kill his horses, and slaughter some 500 sheep 40 miles north of Lusk, Wyoming.

JULY 1903
Agriculture National guardsmen rush to Thermopolis, Wyoming, where sheepmen threaten to lynch a man held for the murder of William Minnick in February.

4 JULY 1903
Science/Technology The first cable across the Pacific is laid between San Francisco and Manila. President Roosevelt sends the first message to the Philippines. The message comes back to Roosevelt from around the world in 12 minutes.

1 AUGUST 1903
Transportation The first cross-country automobile drive is completed. The 52-day journey in a Packard from San Francisco to New York opens a new era in American travel. By 1905, some 80,000 cars will be running, and in 1906 Princeton's President Woodrow Wilson will proclaim that 'Nothing has spread socialistic feeling in this country more than the use of the automobile.'

10 AUGUST 1903
Labor Unions in Cripple Creek, Colorado, go out on strike, beginning the most disastrous labor war in Colorado history. The showdown is between the Mine Owners' Assocation and the Western Federation of Miners. On 6 June 1904, the Florence & Cripple Creek depot in Independence is blown up; thirteen non-union miners are killed and six others are crippled. The explosion effectively ends the hopes of the Western Federation of Miners in the Cripple Creek District, and in 1904 the miners will return to work. The loss is shared between management and labor, however, because the district never booms again as it had before the strike.

20 OCTOBER 1903
International The commission that has investigated the Alaska boundary dispute rules in favor of United States interests.

22 OCTOBER 1903
Industry The Amalgamated Copper Company announces the shutdown of all its enterprises in Montana except its newspapers. Ten thousand men are laid off on the first day of this show of strength; within a week, an estimated four-fifths

Pioneer Western movie The Great Train Robbery

of the wage earners in Montana are unemployed.
Agriculture Tom Horn is hanged in Wyoming for the murder of Willie Nickell in July 1901.

18 NOVEMBER 1903
International The long sought-after sea link between the east and west coasts comes closer to realization through a treaty for the Panama Canal. The Hay-Buneau-Varilla treaty gives the United States permanent rights to a ten-mile-wide strip of land in return for $10 million and an annual charge of $250,000 after nine years.

OTHER EVENTS OF 1903
Conservation Following passage of the Federal Reclamation Act on 17 June 1902, the state of Utah furthers this action by passing an act vesting ownership of water with the state.
Arts/Culture One of the earliest movies that tells a story is made by the American director, Edwin S Porter, his 11-minute *The Great Train Robbery*. Aside from his pioneering techniques in filming and editing, he also started Americans, and the world, on their love affair with 'the Western.'

30 APRIL-1 DECEMBER 1904
Life/Customs The Louisiana Purchase Exposition is held in St Louis, Missouri. Six years of preparation have gone into this celebration of the Louisiana Purchase and dramatization of Missouri's economic growth. The 1240-acre area is the largest of all international expositions to date; the exposition costs more than $31,500,000, and is attended by nearly 20,000,000 persons. The automobile is popularized: more than 100 cars are on display – including one that has traveled from New York State to the exposition.

29-30 JUNE 1904
National Texan George W Carroll is nominated as the vice-presidential candidate of the Prohibition Party, which is very active in Texas and other states in the Southwest.

JUNE 1904
Agriculture State newspapers report that a sheepman has been shot to death south of Tensleep, Wyoming.

8 NOVEMBER 1904
National Theodore Roosevelt is elected president. Referring to the fact that he has already served for three years following McKinley's death, Roosevelt vows that he will not run for the office again – a statement which will haunt him in 1908 and 1912.

Above: *The first oil well, Titusville, Pennsylvania.*
Right: *Texaco derricks at Sour Lake, Texas, 1903.*

OTHER EVENTS OF 1904
Agriculture The Kinkaid Act provides grants of 640 acres of desert land in Nebraska. The legislation stipulates a five-year residency and improvements valued at $800.
Conservation Idaho's first reclamation project – the Minidoka on the Snake River – is authorized.
Civil Rights The Arkansas Supreme Court invalidates the poll tax amendment.

3 MARCH 1905
Settling Congress opens nearly 1,500,000 acres of the Wind River Reservation in Wyoming for settlement and entry under the Homestead Act.

10-13 APRIL 1905
Agriculture The Wyoming Wool Growers Association is organized.

7 MAY 1905
Immigration Racism results in the founding of the Japanese and Korean Exclusion League on the West Coast.

11 MAY 1905
Disaster A tornado strikes Synder, Oklahoma. Nearly 100 persons are killed, and 141 others are injured.

CHRONOLOGY

1 JUNE-15 OCTOBER 1905
Life/Customs The Lewis and Clark Centennial Exposition is held in Portland, Oregon. The event occupies 402 acres on the site of Willamette Heights. Twice the anticipated number of visitors attend, making the exposition a conspicuous financial success. Although it has been less than 100 years since permanent settling began here, and only 50 years since statehood, Oregon now leaves its frontier past behind.

27 JUNE-8 JULY 1905
Social Change The Industrial Workers of the World union is organized in Chicago, with William D Haywood as one of its leaders. The union advocates class struggle, mass action, and no compromise with the ruling class. Side by side with this type of militant unionism is a roused electorate that will experiment with the initiative, referendum, and recall – political devices being adopted in Western states.

30 JUNE 1905
Mining An explosion at the Union Pacific company's Mine Number One at Hanna, Wyoming, kills 171 men.

3 OCTOBER 1905
Arts/Culture David Belasco exploits 'Wild West' themes in a play that captures the imagination of East-coast audiences: *Girl of the Golden West.*

30 DECEMBER 1905
Labor Former Idaho Governor Frank Steunenberg is killed by an explosive device at his home, in revenge for his calling in federal troops in the Coeur D'Alene strike of 1899. The trial, in 1907, will attract international attention.

OTHER EVENTS OF 1905
Education Kearney State College is founded as a normal (teacher-training) school in Kearney, Nebraska.
Arts/Culture Jack London's *White Fang* is published.
Life/Customs Will Rogers begins his vaudeville career. He will go on to fame in the Ziegfeld Follies of 1916 and a motion-picture career. Born in Oklahoma in 1879, Rogers will die in 1935 in a plane crash near Point Barrow, Alaska. Statues of the much-loved cowboy philospher stand in Washington, DC, and Claremore, Oklahoma.
Environment Flood waters from the Colorado River will begin to fill a large depression in southern California; in the next two years, the water will be replenished to form the Salton Sea, still existent.

16 APRIL 1906
Arts/Culture Enrico Caruso, the famous Italian opera singer, storms out of the Grand Opera House in San Francisco before the final curtain rings down on *The Queen of Sheba.* Caruso is angered by audiences who 'talk animatedly to each other right to the final curtain.' He has toured the United States from New York City to San Francisco, where the Italian community has organized a relief committee for victims of the recent eruption of Mount Vesuvius. Caruso offers to perform a charity concert for the cause, explaining to the press that Vesuvius is a terrifying sight (he was born nearby).

18 APRIL 1906
Environment At 5:13 am, San Francisco is rocked by a massive earthquake. Fires spread for three days. Five hundred persons are killed, and half a million are made homeless. Remarkably, the city will be rebuilt quickly: in 1915 the new city will display itself to the world at the Panama-Pacific International Exposition.

7 MAY 1906
National Congress passes the Alaska Delegate Bill. Alaska may now elect one delegate to Congress who will not have the power to vote, but will serve as a 'board of information' on Alaskan affairs.

21 MAY 1906
International The United States and Mexico sign a treaty providing for equal distribution of the waters of the Rio Grande River between the two countries. Last year Congress had authorized the Rio Grande Project to bring flood control, power and irrigation to southern New Mexico and Texas.

FRANK STEUNENBURG, 1861-1905

Frank Steunenburg reached political power as a newspaperman. He was born to a Dutch immigrant family in Keokuk, Iowa, on 8 August 1861. After graduating from Iowa State Agricultural College, he became a typesetter for newspapers, then a reporter, first for the Knoxville, Iowa *Express,* of which he was part owner, and then for his and his brother's *Caldwell Tribune* in Idaho.

Steunenburg made the *Tribune* a major voice of the region, crusading for Idaho statehood, and joined the constitutional convention in 1889. After serving in the new state legislature, he was elected Idaho's fourth governor in 1896. During his four-year term, he firmly suppressed the Coeur-d'Alene riots, earning himself both national and the enmity of organized labor. In 1900 he made a bid for the Senate, but was rejected by his own party's convention.

Retired from politics by 1905, Steunenburg was killed by a bomb that had been attached to his front gate. A member of the miners' union confessed to having placed the bomb, but implicated union officials, including radical labor organizer William 'Big Bill' Haywood. Idaho Senator William Borah represented the State, and union officials were represented by Clarence Darrow, in a trial that attracted world-wide attention: only the union man who had placed the bomb was found guilty.

11 JUNE 1906

Agriculture The Forest Homestead Act allows the secretary of the interior to open forest land for agricultural exploitation.

16 JUNE 1906

National President Roosevelt signs the Enabling Act providing for combination of the Twin Territories (Oklahoma and Indian) into a single state. The Act provides for a constitutional convention. On 17 September 1907, the people of the two territories accept the work of their convention, and on 16 November 1907, Oklahoma will become the forty-sixth state in the Union.

29 JUNE 1906

Mining An executive order withdraws all coal claims on federal land to permit reassessment of their value. The lands are later reopened at $35-$100 an acre.

1 AUGUST 1906

Discovery John M Huddleston finds diamonds near Murfreesboro, Arkansas, the only diamond mine in North America.

SEPTEMBER 1906

Immigration The California Republican state convention adopts a resolution favoring exclusion of the Japanese and all other Asiatics from the United States. BY 1907 California will have a Japanese population of over 30,000.

11 OCTOBER 1906

Immigration The San Francisco school board orders Japanese, Korean, and Chinese children to attend an Oriental school. President Roosevelt explodes when he hears about the action. Anti-American feeling runs high in Japan, and Roosevelt is compelled to intervene because of the international consequences of the issue. He invites the mayor of San Francisco to the White House and persuades him to rescind the order. In return, the president agrees to discourage further Japanese emigration to the United States. In 1907-08, the president concludes the famous 'Gentlemen's Agreement' with the Japanese Government, by which Japan agrees to discourage laborers from moving to the United States mainland and Hawaii.

20 NOVEMBER 1906

National A constitutional convention meets at Guthrie, Oklahoma.

6 DECEMBER 1906

California Abraham Ruef, a lawyer who has effectively dominated the city of San Francisco through Mayor Eugene Schmitz since 1901, is arraigned with Schmitz on extortion charges. Schmitz will be found guilty on 13 June 1907, and Ruef on 10 December 1908. Neither man will be required to serve his full sentence.

WESTERN HUMORISTS

Artemus Ward (Charles Farrar Browne) was in the vanguard of Western humorists who had their roots in the lecture circuit and in journalism. He began a story about Artemus Ward, a traveling showman who exhibited waxworks, when he worked for the *Cleveland Plain Dealer* in the mid-nineteenth century. A native of Waterford, Maine, Ward delivered his humorous lectures all over the country, and encouraged the young Mark Twain (Samuel Langhorne Clemens) whom he met on the Pacific Coast.

Clemens chose his pen name from his days as a Mississippi Riverboat pilot, when the sounding call 'Mark Twain' indicated a shallow place in the channel. He tried his hand, unsuccessfully, at gold mining in 1861 and settled in San Francisco as a journalist in 1864. His satirical *Innocents Abroad* (1869) established his reputation as a humorist, which was confirmed by his account of his gold-mining days in *Roughing It* (1872). Works of increasing maturity and perception culminated in *Tom Sawyer* (1876) and *Huckleberry Finn* (1884), classics of American literature and graphic portrayals of the nineteenth-century scene.

One of the best-loved American figures of his time (1879-1935) was Will Rogers, who was born to prosperous Irish-Cherokee parents in what would become Oklahoma. He left school to become a cowboy and then a 'rope artist and rough rider' in various Wild West shows, where audiences responded warmly to his Southwestern drawl and timely comments on current affairs. He was a *Ziegfeld Follies* regular for several decades and grew in popularity as 'the cowboy philosopher' who had 'never met a man I didn't like.' In the middle 1920s, he wrote a daily syndicated column on the news and he remained in demand as a lecturer, film star, and radio commentator until his death in a plane crash in 1935.

Mark Twain (Samuel Langhorne Clemens).

CHRONOLOGY

OTHER EVENTS OF 1906

Discovery The Northwest Passage is finally accomplished by Norwegian explorer Roald Amundsen. Since the 1500s explorers have tried to sail north of Canada from the Atlantic Ocean to the Pacific. Sir Martin Frobisher began a series of English expeditions in 1576. However, the closest to success was Sir Robert McClure in 1850. McClure forced a passage to the northern shore of Banks Island, anchored his ship in a bay which he

---

THE NORTHWEST PASSAGE

As early as 1525, those in the best position to know were accepting the idea that the Atlantic route to the Orient was blocked by one continuous land mass of great size. There was, to be sure, the sea route to the south, which Magellan's expedition had traversed between 1519-22, and in 1513 Balboa had revealed that there was a relatively narrow isthmus between the Atlantic and the Pacific. But after the Cabots' voyages of 1497 and 1509 and Verrazzano's travels in 1524, it was clear that there was land from Labrador and Newfoundland all the way to the Strait of Magellan. Thus emerged the quest that would occupy many centuries – for an unobstructed sea route from the Atlantic to the Pacific along the northern edge of North America.

The first mariner to seek the Northwest Passage despite knowledge of the obstructions was Jacques Cartier. In his voyages of 1534 and 1535-6, he got sidetracked down the St Lawrence River as far as the site of modern-day Montreal. The next major thrust toward this route was made by Sir Humphrey Gilbert, whose *Discourse ... to prove a passage by the north-west to Cathaia and the East Indies* (1576) directly inspired the three voyages of Martin Frobisher. (Gilbert, not so incidentally, brought all his geographical and other knowledge to the assumption that the new America was the old Atlantis.) In Frobisher's wake came many daring voyagers – John Davis, George Weymouth, James Hall, Henry Hudson, William Baffin, Luke Foxe, Jens Munck, Thomas James, and others. However, their progress was limited, as seen from the location of such features as Hudson and Baffin Bay. After Thomas James's failure of 1632 – his account provided Coleridge with graphic matter for *The Rime of the Ancient Mariner* – the search came to a temporary halt. (William Baffin had mistakenly reported Baffin Bay to be landlocked, thus discouraging navigation by such a route for some 200 years).

For many decades after 1632, seekers after a northwest sea route to the Pacific tended to think in terms of the various lakes and rivers across the northern United States and southern Canada. In 1778 James Cook revived interest by his attempt to find a passage from the Pacific side; he failed, but the British were already committed to extending their knowledge of this Arctic region. William Edward Parry navigated from the east as far west as the Viscount Melville Sound in 1819-20; when another Englishman, Robert McClure, reached the same sound in 1854 from the west, the existence of the Northwest Passage was established. But it would be 1906 before the great Norwegian explorer Roald Amundsen made the first complete transit by ship.

---

named God's Mercy, and tried, unsuccessfully, to continue on foot. Amundsen's ship, *Gjoa*, completes the first trip through the Northwest Passage in 1906, traveling from east to west. The first west-to-east voyage will be completed in 1942 by the Royal Canadian Mounted Police schooner *St Roch*.

Alaska Juneau begins to function as the capital of Alaska.

Life/Customs The Antiquities Act of 1906 empowers the president to preserve landmarks, structures, and objects of historic or scientific interest as national monuments.

Conservation In 1864 Congress had granted Yosemite Valley to the state of California for public use. State administration had proved inadequate, and trees were felled in vast quantities. Now the valley is returned to the Federal Government to become the heart of a 1200-square-mile park.

1906-1912

North Dakota 'Honest' John Burke serves as governor for three terms. A Democrat, Burke is nevertheless elected with many Republican votes.

12 JANUARY 1907

National President Roosevelt urges Congress to reimburse the Southern Pacific Railroad for a major portion of the $3,100,000 it had spent fighting flooding from the Colorado River in the Imperial Valley of California.

10 FEBRUARY 1907

Conservation After 52 days of work, the Colorado River is diverted to its old channel to empty into the Gulf of Mexico. The river has flooded many times – interfering with plans to exploit California's Imperial Valley.

14 MARCH 1907

Immigration Japanese laborers are excluded from entering the United States by a presidential order.

Conservation Members of the Inland Waterway Commission are appointed by President Roosevelt. They are required to study and report on rivers, lakes, and their relation to forests, traffic congestion, and other matters. During Roosevelt's time in office, five national parks are established, including Crater Lake in Oregon and Mesa Verde in Colorado. As a result of the National Monuments Act of 1906, the president sets aside 16 national monuments and 51 wildlife sanctuaries. The Devil's Tower in Wyoming is the first monument to come under this legislation. Later, Arizona's Petrified Forest will be designated a monument in an effort by Roosevelt to protect the area from souvenir hunters and gem collectors.

11 JUNE 1907

Conservation A protest meeting is organized in Denver against the land reservation policy. Western grazing interests succeed in having the Forest Reserve Act of 1891 repealed.

Naturalist John Muir, 1838-1914.

SUMMER 1907
Hawaii Fort Shafter is completed and occupied as the first permanent post for US Army troops in Hawaii. The Army had set up the post as the Kahauiki Military Reservation in 1899. Fort Shafter will serve as the focus for defending the harbor and city of Honolulu.

16 NOVEMBER 1907
National Oklahoma, formerly the Oklahoma and Indian Territories, is admitted to the Union as the forty-sixth state. Citizens had voted to name the state Sequoya, after the Indian creator of the Cherokee alphabet, but Congress has refused. The new state constitution allows for initiative and referendum. The state's population is 1,414,000.

27 NOVEMBER 1907
Labor A major union strike is called at the mines of Goldfield, Nevada. Governor John Sparks calls for federal troops, and in early January 1908 the mines will reopen under military protection. This labor disturbance signals the end of the economic boom in southern Nevada.

OTHER EVENTS OF 1907
National Three leaders of the Western Federation of Miners union – Charles H Moyer, William D Haywood, and George A Pettibone – are tried for the murder of former Idaho Governor Frank Steunenberg in 1905. Through questionable extradition proceedings, the men are brought from Colorado to Idaho. A jury of farmers and ranchmen acquit Haywood and Pettibone, while Moyer is released without a trial. William E Borah was the trial prosecutor and Clarence Darrow the defender.

Education Fort Wright College is founded in Spokane, Washington.

Nebraska The legislature requires that candidates for public office be nominated by primaries.

Arts/Culture Robert Service's *Songs of a Sourdough* appears. The poems include 'The Shooting of Dan McGrew,' which will remain a favorite for many years. The poet, English by birth, had moved to Canada at the age of 23.

18 FEBRUARY 1908
International The Gentlemen's Agreement with Japan is reached through a diplomatic note sent to the American ambassador acknowledging Roosevelt's order of 14 March 1907, and agreeing not to issue any more passports to Japanese laborers for emigration to the United States.

28 MARCH 1908
Mining A second major accident strikes the Wyoming coalfields. More than 60 miners are killed by an explosion and cave-in at Union Pacific Coal Company's Mine Number One at Hanna.

13 MAY 1908
Conservation A White House Conservation Conference announces that the conservation of forest and water resources is now a matter of vital national importance. Among those in attendance are cabinet members, Supreme Court justices, congressmen, and the governors of 34 states.

8 JUNE 1908
Conservation The National Conservation Commission is established. Gifford Pinchot, chief of the Forest Service and of the new commission, has a mandate to submit reports on water, timber, soil, and mineral resources.

7 JULY 1908
National The Democratic Party holds its national convention in Denver. Populist William Jennings Bryan is nominated for president.

3 NOVEMBER 1908
National William Howard Taft wins the presidential election over William Jennings Bryan. Theodore Roosevelt had put himself out of the 1908 presidential race on the night of his election in 1904. Taft will not enjoy the kind of public support that Roosevelt has had.

OTHER EVENTS OF 1908
National Congress authorizes the US Army and Navy to establish a naval station at Pearl Harbor, Hawaii. For many years the US Government has been working to improve the facilities at Pearl Harbor, but this authorization marks the begin-

ning of a major US naval presence in the Pacific Ocean. The new station has been given an added impetus by the visit of the Great White Fleet to Hawaii.

National In *Muller v Oregon*, the Supreme Court upholds an Oregon law limiting working hours for women. The Court denies that the state violated the fourteenth amendment by limiting the liberty to enter into contracts.

Civil Rights The poll tax is readopted in Arkansas.

Education A teacher's college is established at the University of Nebraska.

11 JANUARY 1909
Conservation Gifford Pinchot, chairman of the National Conservation Commission, submits to President Roosevelt the first inventory of US Natural Resources. The commission's systematic study of mineral, water, and forest resources lays the foundation for much subsequent legislation affecting mining, forests, and agricultural expansion in the West.

19 FEBRUARY 1909
National The Enlarged Homestead Act increases the maximum permissible homestead to 320 acres in parts of Colorado, Montana, Nevada, Oregon, Utah, Washington, Arizona, and Wyoming. Its provisions stipulate that 80 acres should be cultivated; timber and mineral rights are still excluded.

4 MARCH 1909
National William Howard Taft is inaugurated as the twenty-seventh president.

22 MAY 1909
National President Taft authorizes opening to settlement 700,000 acres of land in Washington, Montana, and Idaho.

27 SEPTEMBER 1909
Conservation President Taft puts aside 3 million acres of oil-rich land for conservation purposes, including Teapot Dome, Wyoming. Although Taft continues the conservation policies which Roosevelt began, he receives little recognition.

13 NOVEMBER 1909
National Scandal hits Washington. Louis R Davis, a special assistant in the field division of the Interior Department, charges in *Collier's* Magazine that Secretary of the Interior Richard A Ballinger has favored the Guggenheims and other vested interests in patenting claims to Alaskan coal lands. Earlier, Ballinger had infuriated conservationists by reopening public lands in Wyoming and Montana that had been withdrawn during the Roosevelt Administration. A joint congressional committee in the Republican-controlled Congress exonerates Ballinger from wrongdoing, but public

Frederic Remington in his studio.

feeling against him is so great that he resigns to relieve the Taft Administration of further embarrassment.

26 DECEMBER 1909
Arts/Culture Frederic Remington, 48, the creator of over 2700 works of art on such Western subjects as *The Bronco Buster* and *The Last Stand*, dies in Ridgefield, Connecticut.

OTHER EVENTS OF 1909
Civil Rights Homer Lea publishes *The Vale of Ignorance*, a diatribe against the Japanese in California. Lea argues that 'A nation can be kept intact only so long as its ruling element remains homogeneous,' and urges removal of the Japanese.

Arts/Culture Robert Service's *Ballads of a Cheechako* is published.

Life/Customs The Alaska-Yukon-Pacific Exposition is held from June to October in Seattle. It is designed to exhibit the resources of Western America.

Conservation Olympia National Park and Zion National Park are established.

7 JANUARY 1910
National President Taft dismisses Gifford Pinchot as head of the Forest Service: Pinchot had accused Interior Secretary Ballinger of misusing public lands. Taft is the largest loser in these controversies. Although he has reserved oil-rich lands, the public decides that he is not doing as much as Roosevelt had done for public land conservation.

16 MAY 1910
National The Bureau of Mines is set up as part of the Interior Department.

FEMALE SUFFRAGE IN THE WEST

Suffrage leaders including, seated, Susan B Anthony (second left) and Elizabeth Cady Stanton (third right).

At first it might seem contradictory that the Old West, still portrayed as essentially 'a man's world,' should have taken the lead in extending political rights to women. The apparent contradiction diminishes, however, when the West is considered as a frontier region, receptive to breaking the old social molds. Initially, the woman's suffrage movement in the United States was led by women from the East – Lucretia Mott, Elizabeth Cady Stanton, Susan B Anthony, and others – who fought for a broad spectrum of social reforms, from the abolition of slavery and imposition of prohibition to female property rights and access to higher education and the professions. For the women in the Western territories and states during these years – roughly the 1840s to 1900 – many of these goals did not seem too pressing.

However, it was a Western territory, Wyoming, that became the first American political entity to give women the right to vote (1869). (They were also granted the right to hold office and to serve on juries.) The territory of Utah extended the right to vote to women in 1870. When Wyoming entered the Union in 1890, it was the first state to have female suffrage; Colorado became the second; Idaho was third in 1896;

and Utah joined the Union in 1896. After a lull in the movement for woman's suffrage, it was another Western state, Washington, that adopted it next, in 1910; then came California in 1911. In 1912, three more states were added – Oregon, Arizona, and Kansas. When the 19th Amendment finally became the law of the land, requiring every state to adopt female suffrage, only 15 states had already enacted such legislation, most of them west of the Mississippi.

In many others ways, too, women in the Western states achieved political rights. In 1870 Wyoming Territory had the first American women on juries. That same year Mrs Esther H Morris became the first woman justice of the peace – in Wyoming. And it was Nellie Tayloe Ross of Wyoming who became the first woman to serve as governor of a state, while Miriam A 'Ma' Ferguson became the second woman, in Texas, both in 1925. However, these women essentially 'inherited' their office from their husbands. The first woman to be elected to Congress in her own right was Jeanette Rankin, who was a Representative from Montana in 1917-19 and 1941-3; on both occasions, she voted against American participation in the world wars that were underway.

25 JUNE 1910
Conservation Congress authorizes President Taft to withdraw public lands subject to new legislation. The legislators also prohibit creation of further land reserves in Oregon, Idaho, Colorado, and Washington.

3 OCTOBER 1910
National A constitutional convention meets in Santa Fe, New Mexico.

8 NOVEMBER 1910
California Hiram Johnson is elected governor of California. He will break the political domination of the Southern Pacific Railroad in the state and initiate reform legislation. Johnson will also help to found the Progressive Party and will be its vice-presidential candidate, on the ticket with Theodore Roosevelt, in 1912. Progressive Party ideals will last into the present in the enlargement of government for social and economic purposes.

1910-1911

Environment South Dakota experiences a severe drought, which leads many people to leave the state, abandoning their farms. Before this the state's population had increased by more than 180,000 between 1900 and 1910. Those who remain in South Dakota turn toward more radical politics and policies.

OTHER EVENTS OF 1910

Population The census figures show that 1,141,990 people live in Washington. The population of Utah is now 373,351. Oklahoma reaches 1,657,155 inhabitants. Nevada – which has a population smaller than that of some cities – checks in at 81,875 residents, and Wyoming at 145,965. Arkansas records 1,574,449 people, and Idaho counts 325,549. South Dakota passes half a million with a census population of 583,888; North Dakota is nearly equal at 577,056. Oregon begins the new decade with 672,765, while Texas has 3,048,710 people and Nebraska 1,192,214.

Transportation The first US Army airplane is flown at Fort Sam Houston in Texas.

Arts/Culture Robert Services's novel *The Trail of '98* is published.

San Francisco-born Isadora Duncan was in the forefront of the modern dance movement.

Life/Customs Joe Hill joins the International Workers of the World local in San Pedro, California. Hill becomes an activist and writes such union songs as 'Casey Jones – the Union Scab.' Hill was born Joel Hagglund in Gaule, Sweden, in 1879 and emigrated to the United States in 1902.

The state capital of Oklahoma moves from Guthrie to Oklahoma City.

Agriculture Engineers complete the Shoshone Dam in Wyoming. Later the name will be changed to the Buffalo Bill Dam.

21 JANUARY 1911

National The National Progressive Republican League, representing the progressive wing of the Republican Party, is organized by US Senator Robert M LaFollette of Wisconsin.

26 JANUARY 1911

National Nevada's state legislature ratifies the sixteenth amendment to the Constitution. Nebraska and North Dakota follow suit on 9 and 17 February.

24 FEBRUARY 1911

National President Taft sends a message to the Senate and the House concerning the New Mexico constitution and state government. 'I transmit hereby a copy of the constitution, which I am advised has been separately submitted to Congress, according to provisions of the act, by the authorities of New Mexico, and to which I have given my formal approval. I recommend approval by Congress.'

7 MARCH 1911

International Twenty-thousand troops are sent to the border with Mexico to protect the interests of US citizens during the Mexican Revolution. Fighting in Mexico has been so close to the border that US citizens have gathered to observe it.

18 MARCH 1911

Science/Technology Theodore Roosevelt presides at the opening of the Roosevelt Dam on the Salt River in Arizona. This federally financed project will allow major irrigation projects that will open up large areas of the Southwest.

SANTA FE, ARIZONA?

New Mexico and Arizona were admitted to the Union as the 47th and 48th States, respectively, in 1912, but had a little-known referendum of 1906 turned out differently, there might have been only 49 states at this writing. During 1905 and 1906, Congress had been asked to consider several bills that provided for one large state to be formed from the territories of Arizona and New Mexico. Finally, on 16 June 1906, the Senate passed a resolution, 42 to 29, calling for a referendum on the question: 'Shall Arizona and New Mexico be united in one state?' Citizens of the territories would be allowed to vote on merging first into one territory, later into one state. Although New Mexico was by far the more populous territory, the prospective territory-state would be called Arizona, but to compensate, its capital was to be Santa Fe.

Support for this political entity was encapsulated in an oratorical masterpiece entitled 'Arizona the Great.' This speech, delivered by Senator Beveridge, visualized a great Southwestern border state, 'second in its size and eminent in wealth among the states of the greatest of nations.' The prospects of this new Arizona pleased the editorial writers of *The New York Times*, who concluded that the joint state was a foregone conclusion. But one Dwight D Heard led opponents of the merger to Washington. According to Heard's group, 'Opposition of at least 95 percent of the people of Arizona was proved by written protests from nearly every social, religious, political, and business organization within our Territory, and petitions of protest signed by thousands of our citizens.'

Finally, in November 1906, the issue was put to the test. Of the 40,930 people in New Mexico who voted, 26,195 favored joining the two territories. But in the far less populated Arizona territory, where 19,406 votes were cast, only 3141 favored joining the two territories. The opposition prevailed by the narrow margin of 1664 votes.

---

15 AUGUST 1911

National President Taft vetoes statehood for Arizona, because it will permit the recall of judges. In his veto message Tafts says that the recall provision is 'so pernicious, so destructive to the independence of the judiciary, that it is likely to subject the rights of individuals to possible tyranny.' Arizona removes the recall provision.

21 AUGUST 1911

National President Taft affixes his seal of approval to the resolution admitting both New Mexico and Arizona as states at 3:08 PM. Bonfires blaze in every New Mexico town from Folsom to Columbus. In town meetings, joyous citizens let out the enthusiasm built up during a 58-year struggle for statehood. After it has been accepted into the Union, Arizona provides again for the recall of judges.

OTHER EVENTS OF 1911

International Union activist Joe Hill takes part in the Mexican Revolution with an international brigade.

6 JANUARY 1912

National New Mexico becomes the forty-seventh state. Its capital city (Santa Fe) is 300 years old, and its population is more than 325,000.

14 FEBRUARY 1912

National On St Valentine's Day, President Taft signs the proclamation admitting Arizona to the Union. Seated at his desk in front of movie cameras, Taft affixes his signature at 10:02 AM and hands the golden pen to Delegate Ralf Cameron. A few minutes later, the president sends a telegram to Arizona Governor Sloan, congratulating 'the people of this our newest commonwealth upon their realization of their long cherished ambition.'

24 FEBRUARY 1912

National Theodore Roosevelt throws his hat into the political ring again, announcing that he is a candidate for the Republican presidential nomination.

18 JUNE 1912

National The Republican convention in Chicago nominates Taft, but the party is badly split between Taft and his conservative supporters and Roosevelt's progressive followers. Roosevelt and his delegates walk out of the convention – setting the stage for one of the most complicated election years in US history.

25 JUNE-2 JULY 1912

National In Baltimore, Maryland, the Democratic convention nominates Woodrow Wilson, the governor of New Jersey, for president on the forty-sixth ballot. William Jennings Bryan has thrown his votes to Wilson.

5 AUGUST 1912
National The Progressive Party nominates Roosevelt for president, Hiram Johnson of California for vice-president.

24 AUGUST 1912
Alaska Local government is formally established, as Alaska becomes an organized US Territory. The first territorial legislature is elected on a non-partisan basis. The first act of the legislative body gives women the right to vote, seven years before adoption of the nineteenth amendment in the United States.

5 NOVEMBER 1912
National Democratic candidate Woodrow Wilson wins the presidential election by a landslide in electoral votes. The popular vote is 6,293,454 for Wilson, 4,119,538 for Roosevelt, and 3,484,980 for Taft.

OTHER EVENTS OF 1912
Transportation The Voluntary Wyoming Highway Association is organized to promote highway routes across the state.
Social Change Female suffrage is granted by the Oregon state legislature.
Education Southern Methodist University is founded in Dallas.
Labor The International Workers of the World union probably peaks in strength at about 30,000 members, most of whom are in lumber camps, wheat fields, textiles, or dock work. By 1930 the estimated membership will decline to fewer than 10,000.
Environment Mount Katmai, on the Alaska Peninsula, erupts, hurling six cubic miles of rocky matter into the air. The volcano discharges gases and volcanic ash over most of northwestern America and kills virtually all of the animal and plant life on the Alaska Peninsula.

25 FEBRUARY 1913
National The sixteenth amendment to the Constitution is adopted by the nation; it will provide the legal basis for a graduated income tax.

4 MARCH 1913
National Woodrow Wilson is inaugurated president. His inaugural address forecasts a broad-based program of conservation of both human and natural resources. The former university president and governor of New Jersey brings a sense of noblesse oblige to the presidency. Whereas Roosevelt's administration emphasized optimism and adventure, and William Howard Taft resembled a good public steward who did not receive credit for his work, Wilson will demonstrate intellectual force in the pursuit of his goals.

A Shoshone irrigation project on arid farms lands near Cody, Wyoming (1907).

CHRONOLOGY

5 MARCH 1913
National William Jennings Bryan of Nebraska becomes secretary of state in Wilson's cabinet. Albert Sidney Burleson of Texas is postmaster general.

19 APRIL 1913
California Governor Hiram Johnson signs the Anti-Alien Land Act, which prohibits Japanese ownership of land or tenancy of agricultural land in California. The Japanese Government protests, as does President Wilson, who is concerned with the act's ramifications for international relations.

4 JULY 1913
Transportation Special excursion rates are offered on trains running in Alaska. On 2-6 July, the round-trip fare for a trip from Chatanika to Fairbanks is $4.00.

OTHER EVENTS OF 1913
Industry Salmon production along Puget Sound in Washington reaches its height: over 2,500,000 cases are packed during 1913. When runs become much smaller, the canneries will have to look to Alaskan fishing grounds for the largest percentage of their catch. However, Seattle remains the base for the fishing fleet and industry.
Transportation Arkansas establishes its state highway department.
Conservation Utah's first major reclamation project is completed when the US Bureau of Reclamation finishes construction of the Strawberry River Reservoir.

20 APRIL 1914
Labor Strikers at the Colorado Fuel Iron Company have been harassed continuously, but today brings violence. Some 200 company guards attack an encampment of striking workers; the private army rakes the strikers' tents with gunfire, then spikes them with kerosene and sets them on fire. At least 21 of the strikers are killed and 100 others wounded. The strike will continue for eight months, but the operators will prevail eventually.

30 MAY 1914
Environment Lassen Peak in California's Sierra Nevada range has long been considered extinct, but now it proves to be an active volcano as steam and ash come forth. On 8 June, and again on 14 June, steam rises to the height of 10,000 feet above Lassen's crest.

15 AUGUST 1914
International The United States formally declares its neutrality in World War I, which has begun in earnest with declarations of war between Germany, Russia, France, and Great Britain.

29 AUGUST 1914
National President Wilson appoints a Texan as attorney general. Thomas Watt Gregory assumes the cabinet post on 3 September.

24 DECEMBER 1914
Conservation John Muir, explorer, naturalist, and discoverer of the Alaskan glacier that bears his name, dies in Los Angeles at the age of 76. Muir was born in Dunbar, Scotland, and his family moved to Wisconsin when he was eleven. He grew up on a farm and developed a great love of nature. As explorer and discoverer, Muir tramped through many regions of the United States, Europe, Asia, Africa, and the Arctic. Muir was the first to explain the glacial origin of Yosemite Valley. His efforts on behalf of forest conservation influenced both the US Congress and President Theodore Roosevelt.

26 JANUARY 1915
Conservation Congress establishes Rocky Mountain National Park.
Life/Customs Nevada Governor Emmet D Boyle signs an 'easy divorce law' that will make Nevada the divorce capital of the United States. Nevada now requires only a six-month residency to end a marriage.

6-20 FEBRUARY 1915
Life/Customs The San Francisco Panama-Pacific International Exposition is held to mark the opening of the Panama Canal. Some 13 million visitors attend the exposition during its run, of which public airplane rides are a prime feature. The first ship passed through the canal on 3 August 1914.

APRIL 1915
Transportation President Wilson announces the selection of a route for the projected Alaska Railroad. Government funds will pay for the railroad from Seward to Fairbanks via the Kenai Peninsula. Construction is begun in 1915, using the well-worn equipment and rolling stock that has recently built the Panama Canal. In the summer of 1923, President Harding will tour the completed railroad.

30 APRIL 1915
Conservation President Wilson creates Naval Petroleum Reserve No 3 out of 9481 acres in Teapot Dome, Wyoming.

19 OCTOBER 1915
International President Wilson recognizes Venustiano Carranza as President of Mexico. Carranza's former associate, Mexican revolutionary general Francisco 'Pancho' Villa, is annoyed by this recognition of his rival. Villa will create serious disturbances along the US border in an attempt to draw the United States into Mexican conflicts. Unfortunately, Carranza will be unable – or perhaps unwilling – to police the border effectively. Next spring the United States will send troops into Mexico.

WESTERN ARCHITECTURE

The architecture of the American West reflects the ethnic diversity of its inhabitants and an abiding feeling for the land. The settlers of colonial times had built log cabins, frame houses, and eventually more elaborate constructions of dried brick in the style of their homelands. As the frontier moved farther west, these materials were often in short supply, and new modes of building evolved.

The first man-made structures in the Far West were the Indian pueblos, an indigenous style from which the Spanish borrowed when they built their adobe missions. Spanish colonial architecture was characterized by thick walls for protection against the desert heat; low, simple lines; and flat roofs that could serve as reservoirs for infrequent rainfalls. A scarcity of both wood and native stone dictated the use of sun-dried brick made from earth.

The typical 'Texas house' of the nineteenth-century land and cattle boom consisted of two cabins joined by a roofed space, which developed into the still-popular ranch house style of today. Originally, the rancher used one cabin for working and eating, the other for sleeping. Farmers on the Great Plains, lacking wood for building, constructed their homes of sod blocks roofed with thatch.

On the West Coast, where wood was plentiful, the redwood bungalow, with low, sweeping lines and a wide verandah, came into use. Its original design was Oriental, and Chinese and Japanese immigrants contributed other Eastern influences, including the landscaping concept by which man-made structures did not obtrude upon the setting, but seemed an integral part of the environment. American architects like Chicago's Louis H Sullivan and his pupil Frank Lloyd Wright (1869-1959) shared this sensitivity to the relationship between setting and structure. Wright's horizontal 'Prairie Style' houses, with their rooms freely interconnecting, had a major influence on contemporary architecture. The complex he called Taliesin West, near Phoenix, Arizona, is characteristic of his best work.

The West Coast offers a microcosm of Western architecture in evolution, from the Spanish and Moorish-style mansions of Hollywood to the sheet-glass skyscrapers of San Francisco. In between is an eclectic mixture of bungalows, ranch houses, Chinese and Japanese styles, and the occasional castle, like that of San Simeon, built by newspaper magnate William Randolph Hearst. All reflect the energy, the enterprise, and the excitement of America's romance with its frontier.

Top: *Spanish mission, San Luis Rey, California.*
Center: *Frank Lloyd Wright's Barnsdall House.*
Above: *Modern Tulsa, Oklahoma.*

---

19 NOVEMBER 1915

Labor Joe Hill, union activist and songwriter, is executed by a firing squad after being found guilty in the slaying of a Salt Lake City grocer. Some 30,000 persons attend his funeral in Chicago and his ashes are scattered in every state except Utah. Hill becomes a hero of radical labor.

7 DECEMBER 1915

World War I: Approach President Wilson asks for a standing army of 142,000 and a 400,000-man reserve.

OTHER EVENTS OF 1915

Population Chena, Alaska, once a boom town, now has only 50 inhabitants. Some settlers are moved by sledge to Fairbanks. Buildings are used for firewood by the people who remain.

Agriculture The Nonpartisan League originates among radical Scandinavian and Russian wheat farmers of North Dakota, led by ex-Socialist Arthur C Townley. The League's basic premise is that farmers' problems can best be solved by political action. The organization is strongest in North Dakota and Minnesota, but it spreads across the

CHRONOLOGY

Western wheat belt from Wisconsin to Washington. The league will obtain state ownership of grain elevators and mills in North Dakota.

Mining There are major labor strikes at the copper mines in Clifton and Morenci, Arizona.

Wyoming After bitter political fighting, progressives in Wyoming establish a state utilities commission that has been opposed by the railroads and other interests. A workmen's compensation law is also passed.

Transportation Yellowstone Park is officially opened to automobiles.

Finance The South Dakota state legislature passes a law guaranteeing the safety of bank deposits.

Education Texas passes a school-attendance law.

Life/Customs The Wyoming legislature passes a law limiting application of the death penalty.

1 JANUARY 1916
Life/Customs State-wide prohibition goes into effect in Arkansas.

10 JANUARY 1916
International Mexican revolutionary general Pancho Villa orders the deaths of 18 American mining engineers in Chihuahua, Mexico.

9 MARCH 1916
International Pancho Villa leads an army of approximately 1500 guerrillas across the US border and attacks Columbus, New Mexico. Seventeen Americans are killed. US troops pursue the guerrillas, killing 50 of them on US soil and 70 more in Mexico. Brigadier General John J Pershing is ordered into Mexico to capture Villa. On 15 March Pershing leads 6000 men across the border.

General John J Pershing in Mexico.

9 MAY 1916
International President Wilson orders the militia of Texas, New Mexico, and Arizona to mobilize along the Mexican border.

7 JUNE 1916
National Progressive Party delegates nominate Theodore Roosevelt for the presidency. Roosevelt declines to run again, and puts his support behind Charles Evans Hughes, who is nominated by the Republican Party on 10 June.

28 JUNE 1916
Wyoming All candidates who have been endorsed by the Nonpartisan League win nomination on the Republican ticket during the primary elections.

5 NOVEMBER 1916
Labor A large group of deputized policemen carrying rifles fires on some 250 International Workers of the World (Wobblies) supporters coming off a chartered steamboat in Everett, Washington. The Wobblies are protesting the treatment of their fellows, who were forced to run a gauntlet as they left Everett.

7 NOVEMBER 1916
National Hiram Johnson is elected to the US Senate from California. Johnson first came into political prominence in 1909, when he secured the conviction of San Francisco boss Abraham Ruef. As governor of California (1911-17) Johnson has shattered the domination of the railroads in state

politics. He will remain in the Senate until his death in 1945. On this same day Jeannette Rankin of Montana becomes the first woman elected to the US House of Representatives.

29 DECEMBER 1916
National The Stock Raising Homestead Act is revised to permit homesteads of up to 640 acres of grazing or forage land. The previously available land was not suitable for irrigation and does not include rights to mining coal or minerals.

OTHER EVENTS OF 1916
Labor The International Workers of the World union calls out miners in the Mesabi range in Minnesota.
Conservation The US Congress authorizes the Hawaiian National Park, which will be dedicated in 1921.

1 JANUARY 1917
Utah Simon Bamberger, elected in 1916, becomes the first non-Mormon governor of Utah. He serves until 3 January 1921.

28 JANUARY 1917
International General Pershing is ordered to return to the United States from Mexico after almost a year of fruitless searching for Pancho Villa in the northern mountains.

19 FEBRUARY 1917
International American troops stationed along the border with Mexico are recalled.

24 FEBRUARY 1917
World War I: Approach British secret service agents have intercepted a telegram sent by German Foreign Minister Arthur Zimmermann to the German ambassador in Mexico on 16 January 1917. The British now turn over the telegram to President Wilson. According to its contents, Zimmermann believes that US entry into the war is inevitable, despite Wilson's desire to remain neutral. Zimmermann instructs his ambassador to approach Mexican President Venustiano Carranza with the suggestion that if Mexico enters the war on Germany's side, Germany will endeavor to have New Mexico, Texas, and Arizona returned to Mexico. Wilson releases the contents of the cable to the American public on 1 March. Public opinion begins to consolidate in favor of the Allied cause.

2 APRIL 1917
World War I: Entry President Wilson asks Congress to declare war on Germany: 'The world must be made safe for democracy.' Congress grants the president's request. Politicians and statesmen in Washington may not fully appreciate that the war will have a second front of sorts – labor issues in the West will conflict with national duty in some cases. In fact, the mobilization of American society for war will divide the country to a degree that has not been seen since the Civil War, and will not be repeated until the Vietnam War.

APRIL 1917
Labor A lumber strike occurs in Washington just as US entry into World War I has made the national demand for lumber skyrocket. The strike is called to secure a working day of eight instead of ten hours. As the strike continues throughout the year, the Federal Government grows desperate for lumber, and the War Department assigns Colonel Brice Disque to the task of sending soldiers into the forests to cut timber. Most of the troops have never used lumbering equipment, and the effort fails. In March 1918 Colonel Disque will be forced to instruct the lumber companies to rehire the striking loggers on an eight-hour-day basis.

8 JUNE 1917
Disaster A fire breaks out in the Speculator Mine in Butte, Montana. Flames and superheated fumes boil up to the surface from the 2400-foot level. Rescue crews and machinery are rushed from as far away as Red Lodge, Montana, and Colorado Springs, Colorado, in an attempt to rescue trapped miners, but the heat is too intense to permit rescue operations. One hundred and sixty-two miners are found dead – many are discovered piled against cement bulkheads. Surviving miners know that Montana state law requires metal bulkheads which can be opened, and that this law has never been enforced in Butte. Accordingly, the Metal Mine Workers Union is formed three days later; by 29 June, more than 15,000 men are on strike in Butte, Anaconda, and Great Falls. By midwinter of 1917-18 however, the labor rebellion is over; at every turn, the Anaconda Company has prevailed.

1 AUGUST 1917
Labor Frank Little, an agitator for the International Workers of the World, is dragged from his room by six masked men and hanged from a railroad trestle on the outskirts of Butte, Montana. The Butte *Bulletin* declares that 'Every man, woman and child knows that [Anaconda] Company agents perpetrated this foulest of all crimes.' Little's murder is neither solved nor forgotten.

25 AUGUST 1917
Texas Lieutenant Governor William P Hobby becomes governor upon the removal of James E Ferguson. Elected in 1914, and re-elected in 1916, Ferguson has championed tenant and independent farmers. Soon after his second inauguration, Ferguson was impeached, found guilty on 10 charges of corruption, and removed from office. He will attempt to vindicate himself in 1924, but will be refused admission to the primary elections. His wife takes up his cause: she is nominated for governor and elected in 1924, re-elected in 1932. Both of the Fergusons fight the Ku Klux Klan.

CHRONOLOGY

SEPTEMBER 1917
Labor William Dudley Haywood is one of many International Workers of the World leaders and members arrested for sedition – they have denounced World War I as a capitalist attack on the worldwide working class. In 1918 Haywood will be convicted and sentenced to 20 years in prison. While free on bail in 1921, he escapes to the Soviet Union, where he remains until his death on 18 May 1928.

OTHER EVENTS OF 1917
Transportation Puget Sound and Lake Washington are connected by completion of the Lake Washington Ship Canal.
Labor A strike at the Bisbee mines in Arizona results in the deportation of 1200 miners by railroad to New Mexico.

1917-1921
South Dakota Peter Norbeck serves as governor. He regulates railroad rates, raises assessments of corporate property, and has the state government take over certain businesses.

22 FEBRUARY 1918
National The Montana legislature passes the Montana Sedition Law, which will be seized upon by the Judiciary Committee and used in creation of the federal Sedition Act, passed on 16 May 1918. This law, which is probably more restrictive than any legislation since the Alien and Sedition Act of 1798, is directly traceable to violence and conflict in Montana and the lynching of IWW agitator Frank Little in Butte, Montana, on 1 August 1917.

11 NOVEMBER 1918
International The German Government signs an armistice, and hostilities end six hours later. The relatively short period of US involvement in World War I has cost the nation over $41 million, 130, 174 lives, and some 203,000 wounded soldiers.

14 DECEMBER 1918
Arkansas The new state constitution is rejected by voters, 37,187 to 23,280.

OTHER EVENTS OF 1918
Arts/Culture Willa Cather broadens her canvas and creates a masterpiece of prairie life in her novel *My Antonia*, the story of Antonia Shimerda and her community of Bohemian, Scandinavian, French, and Russian settlers.
Life/Customs Women are allowed to vote in Democratic primaries in the state of Arkansas.

6 FEBRUARY 1919
Labor Sixty thousand workers stay home in Seattle, in a general strike that paralyzes the city. In January the Washington state legislature had passed a bill making it a crime to advocate or practice violence or terrorism in working for social or political reforms. Following the general strike's beginning, Mayor Ole Hanson threatens martial law, to no avail. The strike will end only when strikers begin returning to work on their own after a long absence.

18 MARCH 1919
Life/Customs General John Joseph Pershing is honored when the Nevada legislature establishes Pershing County with its seat at Lovelock. Pershing fought in the Philippine campaign and led the punitive expedition against Pancho Villa, before commanding American Expeditionary Forces in World War I. Following the war, he has received the highest rank ever given an American army officer to date: General of the Armies of the United States.

1 JULY 1919
Social Change The Wyoming state legislature tries to stop consumption of alcohol by instituting Prohibition. This movement has gained strength in the aftermath of World War I.

14 JULY 1919
Agriculture The Montana Federation of Farm Bureaus meets in Billings and asks the governor to deal with 'a very serious situation . . . unusual and without precedent.' Drought has hit Montana, beginning late in 1917. By the summer of 1918, it has become disastrous to the state's agriculture and even its population. Farmers are leaving in empty freight cars. A mass exodus continues through 1920. The drought will denude two million acres of land and partially devastate millions more.

WILLIAM C McDONALD, 1858-1918

Beginning as one of the great cattle barons of the Southwest, William C McDonald went on to ride herd as a Democrat over the new Republican-dominated state of New Mexico. McDonald was born in Jordanville, New York, on 25 July 1858. After taking a law degree, he moved to New Mexico and started a store in White Oaks. About 1890 he got into the beef business, and over the next two decades put together a considerable cattle empire.

Looking for a candidate for the first New Mexican state governor in 1911, the Democrats seized on McDonald as the best man to challenge prevailing Republican power. Having never sought elective office, McDonald held out to the last minute before accepting the nomination. In the campaign he paid his own way, promised nothing, and was elected owing nothing to anyone. During his highly successful years as governor, he was a tireless political and tax reformer, promoter of education, and overseer of land development. His office was open to any and all; his tendency to deal with people directly brought protests from the Democratic organization. Nonetheless, the Republican-dominated legislature never managed to override his veto. After leaving office, McDonald died at El Paso, Texas, in 1918.

NELLIE TAYLOE ROSS, 1876-1977

Nellie Tayloe Ross was elected governor of Wyoming on the same day that 'Ma' Ferguson was elected to the same office in Texas. Ross took office first, however, so she is credited with being the first woman governor in the United States. Like Ferguson, Ross gained office in the wake of her governor husband. She was born in St Joseph, Missouri (on a date she refused to name). In 1900 she married lawyer William Ross and accompanied him to Cheyenne, Wyoming, where he practiced law. William Ross was elected governor in 1922; on his death in 1925, his wife was elected to complete his term. Unlike Miriam Ferguson, Ross was an active and astute politician, though that was not enough to get her re-elected – women in government were still far from being taken seriously. After 1926 Ross was active in Democratic politics, becoming a strong FDR supporter. She was rewarded by being named the first female director of the US Mint, and served in that capacity from 1933 until 1953.

---

25 SEPTEMBER 1919
National President Wilson collapses with a stroke in Pueblo, Colorado. He has been campaigning nationwide for acceptance of his plan for US inclusion in a League of Nations that would work to prevent war. Although he never truly recovers from his collapse, Wilson remains in office throughout his second term.

2 OCTOBER 1919
National The Utah state legislature ratifies the nineteenth amendment – voting rights for women – to the Constitution.

11 NOVEMBER 1919
Labor A group of American Legionnaires in Centralia, Washington, drags International Workers of the World agitator Wesley Everest from jail, then castrate and hang him. Public opinion in the state has turned against the IWW union because of the hardships brought about by the general strike in Seattle.

OTHER EVENTS OF 1919
Agriculture The governor of Utah organizes a conference in Salt Lake City to discuss the use of water from the Colorado River. Representatives of Wyoming, Utah, Colorado, New Mexico, Nevada, Arizona, and California attend the meeting. They lay the groundwork of planning for the future Boulder Dam.
North Dakota The Nonpartisan League gains control of the North Dakota legislature and enacts nearly its entire political platform – state ownership of terminal elevators and flour mills, state inspection of grain and grain dockage, relief of farmers' improvements from taxation, rural credit banks operated at cost, and establishment of an industrial commission to manage state-owned enterprises.

5 JULY 1920
National The Democratic Party holds its National Convention in San Francisco and nominates the little-known James M Cox for president and Franklin Delano Roosevelt for vice-president.

21-22 JULY 1920
National The National Convention of the Prohibition Party meets in Lincoln, Nebraska. Aaron S Witkins of Ohio is selected as its presidential candidate.

26 AUGUST 1920
National The nineteenth amendment to the Constitution is enacted. Women now have the same voting rights as men.

2 NOVEMBER 1920
National Republican presidential candidate Warren G Harding defeats Democrat James M Cox by a substantial margin in the presidential election.

OTHER EVENTS OF 1920
Population National population stands at 105,710,620. The center of population is near Spencer Owen County in Indiana. For the first time in census-taking, the population of rural areas drops to less than 50 percent of the total population. The actual number of farm residents has dwindled to less than 30 percent. Washington state has 1,563,396 people, Utah has close to half a million, Oklahoma passes the two million mark. Nevada's population declines to 77,407, while Wyoming's increases to 194,402. Texas now has nore than 4,500,000 people. South Dakota grows to 636,547, and North Dakota keeps pace with 646,872. Alaska now has 55,036 persons and Hawaii has 255,881.
Industry The Osage County oil fields in Oklahoma begin pouring out black gold.
Communications Station KFBL (now KRKO), the first in Washington State, begins to broadcast. WRR, the first in Texas, begins broadcasting in Dallas.

22-23 FEBRUARY 1921
Transportation Completion of radio towers between the east and west coasts to facilitate night flying permits overnight transcontinental air mail service. Air mail is now transported coast to coast in 48 hours. Before this, air mail had to be transferred to trains at night.

28 FEBRUARY 1921
Agriculture The Supreme Court unanimously declares unconstitutional the profiteering and hoarding sections of the World War I-era Food Control Act; about 2500 prosecutions are nullified by this decision. The Court also rules the Farm Loan Act unconstitutional. After the war, agriculture enters a decade of severe depression.

CHRONOLOGY

4 MARCH 1921
National Ohio Republican Warren G Harding is inaugurated the nation's twenty-ninth president. To uphold his campaign promise of a 'return to normalcy,' Harding appoints such highly regarded men as Charles Evans Hughes to the post of Secretary of State, Herbert Hoover as Secretary of Commerce, and Andrew Mellon as Secretary of the Treasury. Other choices are less fortunate, as the trusting Harding appoints such dubious cronies as Harry Daugherty to the post of Attorney General, speculator and oil man Albert Fall as Secretary of the Interior, and a former US Army deserter, Charles Forbes, to head the Veterans Bureau.

APRIL 1921
Industry In Fort Worth, Texas, the first helium production plant is completed under auspices of the US Navy Department. On 1 July 1925, the Bureau of Mines takes control of the plant, which operates until 1929, when it closes due to a dwindling supply of the gas.

11 APRIL 1921
Iowa The legislature levies the nation's first state cigarette tax, to become effective 4 July 1921. This act repeals the current law prohibiting the sale of cigarettes in Iowa.
Oklahoma/Texas In a suit pursued by Texas, the US Supreme Court upholds the Oklahoma-Texas boundary line.

25 APRIL 1921
Nebraska The legislature passes a law denying aliens the right of land ownership in the state.

MAY 1921
Agriculture In an attempt to deal with the growing woes of the nation's agricultural community, members of Congress organize the Bipartisan Farm Bloc.

6 MAY 1921
Indians A Tulsa, Oklahoma, court rules in favor of Mary Partridge, an Indian woman, in her suit to recover Crosbie Heights, a Tulsa residential district. Over 100 property owners are defendants in the suit, in which $1.5 million is involved. In the decision, Partridge is granted title to all the property in question.

31 MAY 1921
National In the first step of what will become known as the Teapot Dome scandal, Navy Secretary Edwin Denby removes the naval oil reserves at Elk Hills, California, and Teapot Dome, Wyoming, from his control to jurisidiction of the Department of the Interior, under the leadership of Albert Fall. Fall will claim that the oil fields are unnecessary to the nation's strategic reserve. The transfer is almost unnoticed at the time, but it will have major repercussions.

1 JUNE 1921
Black Experience Race riots in Tulsa, Oklahoma, result in the death of 9 whites and 21 blacks, numerous injuries, and the destruction of ten blocks of homes in the black ghetto. The trouble began the previous night when police arrested a black for attacking a white girl. Martial law is imposed and enforced by four National Guard companies.

3 JUNE 1921
Environment The flood waters of the Arkansas River, swollen by a cloudburst, destroy a large part of Pueblo, Colorado. Over 1500 persons are killed or missing, and the state militia and home guard take charge. Property damage is estimated at $25 million. More rain and floods follow in other parts of Colorado and Kansas.

20 JUNE 1921
National Oklahoma's Alice Robertson is the first woman to preside over the US House of Representatives in a half-hour session.

25 JUNE 1921
Industry In the Los Angeles area, an important oil discovery is made at Signal Hill, Long Beach. With the earlier discoveries at Huntington Beach and Santa Fe Springs, and the 1922 find at Torrance, the wealth of oil in the Los Angeles Basin will help to make California, in 1923, a world leader in crude oil exports. The quality of the oil found there is also very good for making gasoline, an advantage that may well have something to do with the development of California as an automobile-centered culture.

23 JULY 1921
Life/Customs In Beaumont, Texas, the Ku Klux Klan claims responsibility for several recent cases of tarring and feathering. The KKK revival has yet to reach its peak, as members continue to terrorize the South and West, and to spread into the North and Midwest. The KKK now supports not only white supremacy, but religious fundamentalism, anti-Semitism, anti-Catholicism and militant patriotism.

10 AUGUST 1921
Transportation The first major battleship built on the Pacific Coast, the *California*, is commissioned. The vessel was launched on 20 November 1919 at the Mare Island Navy Yard in California.

15 AUGUST 1921
Agriculture The Packers and Stockyards Act outlaws monopolistic practices in the sale of livestock, poultry, and dairy products. The act, to be enforced by the Department of Agriculture, also bans price manipulation and control, and discriminatory and unfair practices; it requires stockyard owners and packers to submit their schedule of charges to the Department of Agriculture.

24 AUGUST 1921

Agriculture The Grain Futures Trading Act regulates the sale of grain by contract markets for future delivery. A substantial tax levied on certain future deliveries seeks to do away with speculative transactions, market manipulation, and monopolistic practices. In the following year, the Supreme Court invalidates the act, and the second Grain Futures Act, of 21 September 1922, will regulate the trade under the interstate-commerce power.

30 AUGUST 1921

International The Mexican Supreme Court annuls President Carranza's decrees confiscating American and other oil rights obtained prior to 1 May 1917, declaring that the nationalization cannot be retroactive.

5 SEPTEMBER 1921

Life/Customs At a riotous party in a San Francisco hotel, the host and famous comedic actor 320-pound Roscoe 'Fatty' Arbuckle allegedly rapes starlet Virginia Rappe, who dies four days later. The Arbuckle case raises a storm of controversy and results in three trials, in September 1921, January 1922, and April 1922, in which Arbuckle is finally acquitted. As a result of the unfavorable publicity created by the Arbuckle case and by the sordid unsolved murder of director William Desmond Taylor, Hollywood comes to be seen as a latter-day Sodom and Gomorrah. Consequently, the movie industry begins self-censorship of films by creating a body headed by Will Hays. This self-censorship helps to redeem the film capital's image and to protect what has become in a few short years a highly profitable industry.

10 SEPTEMBER 1921

Civil Rights The California Supreme Court declares the state Alien Poll Tax Law unconstitutional, holding it in violation of the Fourteenth Amendment and of the agreements between the United States and Japan.

16 SEPTEMBER 1921

Ideas/Beliefs Western communities begin to strike back, as El Paso, Texas, bans masked parades by the Klu Klux Klan. On 20 September the University of Nebraska forbids KKK membership among its student body. During a 1 October KKK parade in Lorena, Texas, 10 persons are wounded in a gunfight between the sheriff's posse and the paraders.

29 SEPTEMBER 1921

New Mexico Rancher and state Republican Party leader Olaf Bursum wins the special election for the unexpired Senate term of Albert Fall, now Secretary of the Interior. During the next four years, Bursum will lead an unsuccessful attempt to reduce the land holdings of the Pueblo Indians.

21 NOVEMBER 1921

Education In Ames, Iowa, the nation's first educational radio station is established with the call letters WOI. The station, at Iowa State College, receives a license on 28 April 1922.

19 DECEMBER 1921

Labor In the case of *Truax v Corrigan*, the Supreme Court finds the Arizona state law banning injunctions against picketing invalid on the basis of the due-process and equal-protection clauses of the Fourteenth Amendment.

22 DECEMBER 1921

Agriculture In passing the Russian Famine Relief Act, Congress appropriates $20 million to purchase corn, seed grain, and milk products for Russia. This move also seeks to alleviate the nation's ever-worsening agricultural depression.

OTHER EVENTS OF 1921

Science/Technology In Los Angeles, the Metropolitan Theatre is the first structure in the nation to receive a 'scientific air distribution' system, provided by Carrier Engineering Corporation.

Industry Construction-firm owner Henry Kaiser moves his headquarters to Oakland, California. During the 1930s and early 1940s, Kaiser will help build Boulder, Bonneville, Grand Coulee, and Shasta Dams; during World War II, his West Coast plants will provide numerous military planes, ships, and other vehicles.

Western Lore Bat Masterson, a legendary figure of the Old West, dies. A former gambler, lawman, and associate of Wyatt Earp, Doc Holliday, and Buffalo Bill Cody, Masterson attained respectability in his later years as a New York journalist.

11 JANUARY 1922

Montana The state supreme court declares unconstitutional the 21-year-old bachelor tax law. This poll tax had been levied on all males from 21 to 60 years of age who were not heads of families, to encourage population growth.

17 JANUARY 1922

Indians Members of the Umpqua, Clackama, and Rogue River tribes arrive in Portland, Oregon, to sue the Federal Government for $12.5 million for tribal lands that were annexed with no subsequent compensatory payment.

19 JANUARY 1922

National In Washington, DC, Idaho's political maverick and Republican Senator William Borah introduces a resolution to outlaw war. In 1924 Borah will become chairman of the Senate Foreign Relations Committee and continue to promote this stance. He will remain a leading isolationist even in the face of World War II, although public sentiment is overwhelmingly pro-war after Pearl Harbor.

CHRONOLOGY

24 JANUARY 1922
Life/Customs In Onawa, Iowa, Christian K Nelso patents the first 'Eskimo Pie,' a frozen snack food consisting of ice cream encased in a chocolate covering.

15 FEBRUARY 1922
Arts/Culture In San Francisco, Samuel Dashiell Hammett resigns from Pinkerton's National Detective Agency. Hammet has worked since 1915 as a professional detective for the agency, and his experiences will become the basis for his trend-setting hardboiled detective novels, several of which are set in Western locales. Butte, Montana, is the Poisonville of *Red Harvest* (1929), and *The Dain Curse* (1929), *The Maltese Falcon* (1930), and *The Thin Man* (1934) take place in San Francisco.

18 FEBRUARY 1922
Agriculture Congress passes the Cooperative Marketing Act, also known as the Capper-Volstead Act. This legislation permits farmers to buy and sell cooperatively, exempting them from anti-trust laws. This intended relief for the nation's hard-pressed farmers, over 300,000 of whom lose their property to mortgage foreclosures during the Harding Administration, does not solve the agricultural depression.

7 APRIL 1922
National The Teapot Dome scandal begins to heat up, as Interior Secretary Albert Fall secretly leases the Wyoming oil reserve to Harry Sinclair, owner of Mammoth Oil Company. Leases of the Elk Hills, California, reserve to Edward L Doheny follow on 25 April and 11 December. Later, a two-year Congressional investigation headed by Montana Senator Thomas Walsh discovers that in 1921 Doheny gave Fall an interest-free and collateral-free 'loan' of $100,000. In 1923 Sinclair will make a similar $25,000 loan to Fall. Suspicions first arise when Fall begins to make expensive improvements to his New Mexico ranch.

9 JULY 1922
Sports At an Alameda, California, swimming meet, Ilinois athlete Johnny Weissmuller is the world's first swimmer to cover 100 meters free style in less than one minute. He later wins national attention as the star of the Tarzan films.

21 SEPTEMBER 1922
Agriculture In a return to protectionism, Congress passes the Fordney-McCumber Tariff, which places high duties on imported farm products and other manufactured goods. This trend began with the Emergency Tariff of 27 May 1921. Congress also passes the second Grain Futures Act, succeeding the similar act of August 1921 which the Supreme Court had declared unconstitutional. This act regulates the trade in grain under federal powers over interstate commerce.

Athlete Johnny Weismuller as Tarzan.

1 OCTOBER 1922
Science/Technology Idaho native Philo T Farnsworth establishes a San Francisco laboratory, where he will develop an electronic scanning system leading to television transmission suitable for home sets.

21 NOVEMBER 1922
Ideas/Beliefs As the Ku Klux Klan continues its activity, Kansas begins a state supreme court suit to oust the KKK from the state. Meanwhile, in Oregon, KKK-influenced legislators lead an attempt to do away with Catholic parochial education in the state. On 31 March 1924, the US Supreme Court will declare the Oregon position unconstitutional.

18 DECEMBER 1922
Finance In a robbery at Colorado's Denver Mint, three men rob a Federal Reserve truck being loaded with $200,000 in $5 bills. The four guards open fire, but the robbers escape with the money. One is later found dead in a nearby garage in the bullet-riddled getaway car.

OTHER EVENTS OF 1922
New Mexico Discovery of the Hogback and Rattlesnake oil fields on Navaho Indian lands in San Juan County assures New Mexico's position as an important oil-producing state.
Science/Technology Researchers at Iowa State College develop cornstone or maizolith – a material made of corncobs and cornstalks that is

several times harder than the hardest woods. It is intended primarily for structural uses. At the University of California in Berkeley, Drs Herbert M Evans and Katherine C Bishop identify the compound they call Vitamin E.

Agriculture Henry A Wallace and Simon Casady of Des Moines, Iowa, develop a cross-fertilized variety of hybrid corn which will produce yields 25 to 30 times higher than those of the previously open-pollinated varieties. Hybrid seed corn for commercial use becomes available two years later. This success leads to the hybridization of wheat and rice, eventually resulting in the 'green revolution' of the 1960s. Wallace, a talented agriculturalist, becomes a controversial political figure, as Secretary of Agriculture and Vice-President in the Roosevelt Administrations and Secretary of Commerce in the Truman Administration.

Western Lore Paul Bunyan, the occupational hero of lumberjacks, and later the patron saint of oil fields, cowboys, and farmers, is firmly established in Western mythology with the publication of W B Laughead's *The Marvellous Exploits of Paul Bunyan*. The oral tradition is also set down in James Stevens's *Paul Bunyan* (1925) and *The Saginaw Paul Bunyan* (1932).

Conservation Representatives from Arizona, California, Colorado, Nevada, New Mexico, Utah, and Wyoming sign the Colorado River Compact. The plan calls for construction of dams on the Colorado River and its tributaries to control erosion and flooding and to produce hydroelectric power and water for irrigation. The major dams eventually built include the 1936 Hoover Dam, the 1938 Imperial Dam, the 1938 Parker Dam, the 1949 Davis Dam, and the 1963 Glen Canyon Dam. They prove an inestimable boon to the industrial growth and agricultural development of the Southwest.

3 FEBRUARY 1923
Environment Two earthquakes occur in the South Pacific and California's Lassen Peak, currently the nation's only active volcano, erupts for 12 hours. Five tidal waves sweep Hawaiian ports and inundate at least one village.

22 FEBRUARY 1923
Industry The nation's first successful chinchilla farm is established in Los Angeles, with 11 chinchillas imported from Peru and Chile. The farm is later moved to Inglewood, California, to accommodate 1300 of the animals, whose skins are used to make fur coats.

4 MARCH 1923
Agriculture Congress passes the Intermediate Credit Act to assist crop financing by creating 12 intermediate federal credit banks, under jurisdiction of the Federal Farm Loan Board. Loans may also be made to co-operatives and marketing associations.

5 MARCH 1923
Social Change Montana and Nevada enact the nation's first old-age pension laws. Montana septuagenarians will receive $25 per month.

4 JUNE 1923
Education In the case of *Robert T Meyer v State of Nebraska*, the US Supreme Court nullifies laws in Iowa, Nebraska, Ohio and 18 other states that make it illegal to teach foreign languages in private and public schools.

27 JUNE 1923
Transportation At Rockwell Field in Coronado, California, the first successful mid-air refuelling of an airplane takes place.

8 JULY 1923
National Arriving at Metlakahtla, President Harding is the first US president to visit Alaska while in office. As the Teapot Dome scandal comes to a boil, Harding sets out on a tour of the West.

15 JULY 1923
Alaska In Nenana, President Harding drives the golden spike completing the Alaskan railroad, the first railroad operated by the Federal Government. The 538-mile route, connecting Seward, Anchorage, and Fairbanks, does not stimulate widespread development, but will help in carrying military supplies during World War II.

2 AUGUST 1923
National President Harding dies in San Francisco after contracting ptomaine poisoning on 28 July. At 2:30 AM the following day, Vice-President Calvin Coolidge is sworn in as the nation's thirtieth president by his father in Plymouth, Vermont.

8 AUGUST 1923
Industry New oil discoveries have been driving down prices. South Dakota gas stations cut gasoline prices in a war on private dealers. On 22 August gas sells for six cents a gallon in Los Angeles.

10 SEPTEMBER 1923
Transportation In a re-enactment of the Pony Express of the 1860s, the old record from St Joseph, Missouri, is broken by 42 hours when Will Tevis rides into a San Francisco race track. The 75 participating couriers have covered 2180 miles at an average speed of 13.75 miles per hour. The riders were on the road for over 158 hours. The best average speed of the 1860s riders was 10.7 miles per hour.

15 SEPTEMBER 1923
Oklahoma Governor Walton places the state under martial law to curtail the terrorist activities of the Ku Klux Klan.

CHRONOLOGY

17 SEPTEMBER 1923
Environment Fire starting in the hilly underbrush sweeps Berkeley, California, destroying 1000 residences and wiping out three small towns. Many are killed and injured, and losses are estimated at $10 million.

19 NOVEMBER 1923
Agriculture The US Supreme Court rules that aliens in California and Oregon cannot own stock in land-owning corporations or make crop leases.

OTHER EVENTS OF 1923
California The state reaches the peak of its boom, based on oil and film industries, as 12 annexations of surrounding communities bring in 19,000 acres of new land to give Los Angeles a total area of 450 square miles. The city is at the height of its construction boom, with 800 new mercantile buildings, 400 new industrial buildings, 130 new schools, 700 new apartment houses, and 25,000 new houses. The doubling and quadrupling of land prices makes many rich. The city's annual oil production – at 38 million barrels in 1922 – will rise to 176 million barrels in 1929.
Science/Technology Physicist Robert A Millikan of the California Institute of Technology wins the Nobel Prize for determining the electrical charge of electrons. On 11 November 1925, he will announce the isolation of cosmic rays.
Industry Texas-born Howard Hughes inherits the Hughes Tool Company, which holds rights to a revolutionary oil drill. Hughes will expand the company and go on to become a record-setting aviator, a film producer, a Nevada real estate magnate, and one of the world's richest men.
Ideas/Beliefs Oklahoma is the first state to bar the teaching of evolutionary theory in schools.
Arts/Culture Architect Frank Lloyd Wright erects four pre-Columbian style textile-block houses in the Los Angeles area. They are the Millard House, the Storer House, the Freeman House, and the Ennis House. By the end of the decade, Los Angeles architecture is a fantastic melange of Spanish colonial, art deco, Hollywood-influenced Egyptian and Chinese movie palaces, medieval castles, and the like. Up the coast, a group of Oakland painters known as 'The Six' issues a manifesto exalting 'abstraction.' In the literary realm, Western novelist Hamlin Garland publishes *The Book of the American Indian*, short stories exploring the unjust treatment of Indians, and rancher James Henry Cook issues the classic Western autobiography *Fifty Years on the Old Frontier*, a wry account of his days as a cowboy, Indian fighter, army scout, and buffalo hunter. The San Francisco Opera Company is founded, becoming the second oldest (after New York's Metropolitan) continuing opera company in the nation. Hollywood produces the first of the great Western epics, *The Covered Wagon*, voted one of the year's ten best films. Western myth is also perpetuated in the film

Wild Bill Hickok, starring one of the era's greatest cowboy actors, William S Hart.
Conservation New Mexico's spectacular Carlsbad Caverns are declared a National Monument.

16 JANUARY 1924
Agriculture As the crisis worsens, the McNary-Haugen Farm Relief Bill is introduced in both houses of Congress. Proposing a federal farm board to purchase surpluses to sell abroad, or to store until prices rise, with an equalization fee to be paid by producers, the bill suffers successive defeats until 1927 Congressional approval. At that time, however, President Coolidge vetoes the legislation.

21 JANUARY 1924
Conservation Legislation creates the Mount Hood National Forest out of the Oregon National Forest.

FEBRUARY 1924
Transportation Regular passenger service by steamship line around the world begins as SS *President Harrison* of the Dollar Steamship Line sets sail from San Francisco. Previously, such trips had been made by cruise steamers once a year.

8 FEBRUARY 1924
Life/Customs The first use of lethal gas in an execution occurs in Carson City, Nevada, with the death of Gee Jon, convicted of the murder of a rival Chinese gang member.

6 APRIL 1924
Transportation Another aviation first occurs as the first round-the-world flight sets off from Seattle, Washington. The trip will end on 28 September.

26 MAY 1924
Immigration Sponsored by California Senator Hiram W Johnson and Missouri Senator James A Reed, the Johnson-Reed Act, also known as the New Quota Law, passes Congress. In response to the fears of labor leaders that high immigration could undercut recent wage gains by American workers, the act severely limits immigration quotas to 2 percent of each national group's total population in the US as of 1890. The law does not apply to immigration from Canada and Latin America, but it bars the Japanese entirely. On 10 April 1924, the Japanese ambassador warns the United States of grave consequence if the Japanese are excluded. Because of widespread controversy, the act is not implemented until 1929.

1 JUNE 1924
Immigration Authorized by the Act of 28 May 1924, the Border Patrol is established under the Immigration and Naturalization Service.

2 JUNE 1924
Indians The Snyder Act declares that all Indians born within the nation's territorial limits are US citizens. Beginning in 1855, various tribes had been granted citizenship: the Snyder Act extends the right to all. A Pueblo Land Board is also established in June to settle non-Indian claims to land within or in conflict with Pueblo land grants. The final determinations will be made in 1933.

4 JULY 1924
National At the convention of the Conference for Progressive Political Action, Wisconsin Senator Robert La Follette is nominated for president, with Montana Senator Burton Wheeler as his vice-presidential running mate. The new Progressive Party is an uneasy alliance of farm groups and left-wing labor. La Follette's radical campaign proposals are ahead of their time, but many, in altered form, will become law during the New Deal of the 1930s.

23 OCTOBER 1924
Science/Technology The first national radio network broadcast is received on the Pacific Coast, by stations in Los Angeles; Portland, Oregon; and Seattle, Washington: President Coolidge delivers a 45-minute speech at the dedication of the US Chamber of Commerce Building in Washington, DC.

1 NOVEMBER 1924
Life/Customs In Cromwell, Oklahoma, 71-year-old Marshal Bill Tilghman is murdered by a drunken Prohibition agent. Tilghman, a legendary lawman of Kansas and Oklahoma Old-West days, had been a Dodge City Marshal, a state senator, and an Oklahoma City police chief.

4 NOVEMBER 1924
National Calvin Coolidge is elected president by a sizeable margin. Progressive Party candidate Robert La Follette, who comes in third, surprisingly receives 4,823,000 popular votes. In the Western states two women are elected governors. In Wyoming, Nellie Tayloe Ross is elected to fill the unexpired term of her husband, William Bradford Ross. She takes office on 5 January 1925, becoming the nation's first woman governor. In 1933 she becomes the first woman director of the US Mint. In Texas, Miriam Amanda (Ma) Ferguson defeats the KKK candidate. She is inaugurated on 10 January 1925, but her husband, a former Texas governor impeached in 1917, will govern in all but name. Both the Fergusons will continue to oppose the Ku Klux Klan, which has been a problem since 1920. The KKK issue is also a leading factor in other Western state elections. In Kansas, Emporia's influential newspaper editor and writer William Allen White runs, unsuccessfully, as an independent candidate for governor on an anti-Klan platform.

MIRIAM A W 'MA' FERGUSON, 1875-1961

Miriam Amanda Wallace Ferguson was a placid political wife who found herself the second woman governor in the United States. Born to a comfortable farming family of Bell County, Texas, on 13 June 1875, she married up-and-coming lawyer James Ferguson in 1899. In 1915 he was elected governor of Texas, with a strong appeal to poor farmers and businessmen, but in 1917 charges of corruption led to his impeachment. He evaded jail, but was forbidden to hold office again.

The resourceful Jim Ferguson, who had been a lifelong opponent of women's suffrage, decided to run his wife for governor, with the understanding that he would be the real power. Running as 'Two Governors for the Price of One,' the Fergusons were elected in 1924. It was in that race that Mrs Ferguson's first two initials were joined to form 'Ma' – a folksy contraction that she hated, but which endeared her to the voters. Her first term was undistinguished, though her administration did reduce the power of the Ku Klux Klan in the state. Much of her time was spent, unsuccessfully, in trying to clear her husband's name. After losing the 1927 election, the Fergusons were returned to office in 1933. As a strong Roosevelt supporter, Mrs Ferguson was able to bring copious New Deal funds into Texas. After her second term, she made one more unsuccessful bid, followed by a long retirement until her death in 1961.

---

22 NOVEMBER 1924
Sports The first football game to attract an audience of 100,000 is played by the University of California and Stanford University in Memorial Stadium, Berkeley, California. While 76,000 fans are in the stadium, 24,000 more view the game from 'Tight Wad Hill.'

OTHER EVENTS OF 1924
Science/Technology The era's most important archaeologist, Alfred Vincent Kidder, who introduced stratigraphic techniques to field work, publishes his notable text *An Introduction to the Study of Southwestern Archaeology*.
Arts/Culture The West is featured in literature, as Edna Ferber publishes *So Big*, which will receive the 1925 Pulitzer Prize. Ferber goes on to write other best-sellers on Western themes – *Cimarron* (1929) and *Giant* (1952). Robinson Jeffers publishes his first important volume, *Tamar and Other Poems*. The Californian poet, who leads a reclusive life in Carmel, uses the craggy Pacific coastline and the primeval redwoods as a symbolic setting for these and subsequent poems.
Conservation Idaho's 48,004 acres of volcanic remains, which resemble telescopic views of the moon, are established as the Craters of the Moon National Monument. In southeastern Arizona, 10,480 acres featuring huge monoliths of volcanic rock eroded into fantastic formations are named the Chiricahua National Monument. The Apaches who once roamed this arid region have now given it one of their tribal names.

CHRONOLOGY

8 JANUARY 1925
Texas When three regular members of the state supreme court are disqualified from serving on the case of *W T Johnson et al vs J M Darr et al*, Governor Pat Morris Neff appoints a special court composed entirely of women. The new judges, who are sworn in on this day, form the first such court in the nation.

2 FEBRUARY 1925
Alaska Dog-sledder Gunnar Kasson arrives in Nome, blind and nearly dead from exposure, in the final relay of a heroic dog-sled team effort to rush in anti-diphtheria serum to fight an epidemic of the disease.

4 MARCH 1925
National Calvin Coolidge is inaugurated president, to serve his first elected term in office. A proponent of government economy and the free market, he will resist aid to farmers while favoring tax cuts that assist business. His is the first presidental inaugural address broadcast by radio; there are now 24 stations in the transcontinental network.

10 MARCH 1925
Texas The legislature passes a bill granting amnesty to former governor James Ferguson, who was impeached in 1917. Ferguson's wife was inaugurated governor on 10 January.

14 MAY 1925
National Prohibition proves difficult to enforce, but the Federal Government extends the war on 'rum runners' to the Gulf and Pacific Coasts, and along the Canadian border.

Popular humorist Will Rogers (right).

31 MAY 1925
Industry Congress ratifies a treaty with Great Britain for the preservation of the halibut fisheries of the northern Pacific Ocean, including those of the Bering Sea.

29 JUNE 1925
Environment In California, an earthquake partly destroys the city of Santa Barbara. The earth tremors, which began on 27 June, also affect Montana, Washington, Idaho, and Wyoming.

28 NOVEMBER 1925
Arts/Culture In Nashville, Tennessee, the Grand Ole Opry, under its original name of Barn Dance, begins its run as a 4½-hour Saturday night broadcast on radio station WSM. The popular series concentrates on the presentation of cowboy music, country ballads, and mountain music.

DECEMBER 1925
International Mexico adopts oil and land laws disadvantageous to American investors. Two years of State Department negotiations are to follow.

12 DECEMBER 1925
Life/Customs The nation's first motel, the Motel Inn, opens in San Luis Obispo, California. The hostlery can accommodate 160 guests in individual chalets with bathrooms, telephones, and garages.

OTHER EVENTS OF 1925
Colorado A Federal Reserve branch bank is

established in Denver; the state's petroleum industry benefits with the opening of Wellington Dome near Fort Collins and the oil fields near Craig.

Science/Technology One of the founding fathers of the new science of anthropology, University of California Professor Alfred Louis Kroeber, publishes his seminal *Handbook of the Indians of California*. His 1928 textbook, *Anthropology*, will become the standard work in the field.

Arts/Culture Swiss-born composer Ernest Bloch becomes director of the San Francisco Conservatory. In 1928 he will compose an 'epic rhapsody' titled *America*, evoking his appreciation for his new country. The pioneering modern dance company, the Denishawn Dancers – founded by Ruth St Denis and Ted Shawn – sets out from Los Angeles for a tour of the Orient. The noted modern dancers Martha Graham, Doris Humphrey, and Charles Weidman get their start with this group. In Hollywood, Charlie Chaplin produces a classic film of the golden age of comedy, *The Gold Rush*, a satirical re-creation of the 1898 Alaskan Klondike. The trailblazing California architect Julia Morgan completes William Randolph Hearst's $30 million castle at San Simeon. Magnate Hearst controls an empire of sensationalist newspapers in Los Angeles, San Francisco, Seattle, San Antonio and elsewhere. Thwarted in his own political ambitions, he helps Roosevelt to attain the presidency in 1932. Orson Welles bases his 1941 film masterpiece *Citizen Kane* on Hearst's life.

Conservation Two more national monuments are designated – Alaska's Glacier Bay National Monument near Juneau, and northern California's Lava Beds National Monument.

3 MARCH 1926

National In another attempt at Prohibition enforcement, the Senate ratifies a convention with Mexico to prevent the smuggling of narcotics, liquor, and aliens across the border. This remains in effect through 28 March 1927.

6 APRIL 1926

Transportation Varney Air Lines becomes the nation's first domestic air-mail contractor by flying a single-engine Swallow biplane between Pasco, Washington, and Elko, Nevada.

9 MAY 1926

Exploration Rear Admiral Richard E Byrd and aviator Floyd Bennett make the first successful flight over the North Pole.

14 MAY 1926

Exploration The dirigible *Norge* anchors in Teller, Alaska, completing a 71-hour, 2700-mile trip from Spitzbergen by way of the North Pole. Roald Amundsen, Lincoln Ellsworth, and other members of the expedition arrive in Nome, Alaska, two days later.

THE KING FAMILY

The popular image of the limitless Texas ranch, with millions of acres, countless livestock, and tentacles reaching around the world, is more or less the reality of the King Ranch. Its founder, Richard King, was born in Orange County, New York, on 10 July 1825. Running away from home at the age of eight, King worked on steamboats in Alabama before becoming a pilot himself. In that capacity he went to Texas in 1847 to help Zachary Taylor during the Mexican War. Having pursued various shipping endeavors, King bought 75,000 acres of wild land, the Santa Gertrudis tract, in 1853, intending to take up ranching.

Over the next 32 years of his life, King fought the Indians and the desert to forge a ranch that finally encompassed some 1.27 million acres, 40,000 cattle, 1200 sheep and goats, 6600 horses, and more. On King's death in 1885, his widow Henrietta King took over management of the ranch and expanded it into the world's largest. Their son, also Richard King, developed an adjoining ranch and carried on ably in his parents' tradition. He died in 1922, Henrietta in 1925, but the ranches remained in family hands. In the 1940s over 400 producing oil wells were drilled on the property, and by the mid-1970s King interests owned millions of acres in Australia, South America, and Africa.

---

15 MAY 1926

Indians In Washington, DC, five Arizona Hopi Indians transform the Capitol Plaza into a scene of the Far West before a 5000-person audience that includes Vice-President Charles Dawes and two Supreme Court justices. They present four tribal religious dances to demonstrate that they are not cruel rites.

18 MAY 1926

California In Los Angeles, Aimee Semple McPherson, 'the world's most pulchritudinous evangelist,' disappears mysteriously. Later she claims she was kidnapped, but in fact she enjoys a secret tryst. Her immense and vulgar Angelus Temple, dedicated on 1 January 1923, has attracted numerous converts to her Foursquare Gospel Creed with the aid of spectacular sound and lighting effects.

20 MAY 1926

Transportation Congress passes the Air Commerce Act to promote, safely regulate, and provide navigation aids, as the era of the stunt pilots known as barnstormers gives way to federal control over civil aviation. The West, with its relatively ideal climate, is the site of much of the nation's aviation industry and experimentation.

2 JULY 1926

National Congress creates the Army Air Corps. Military pilots, many of whom die in crashes in the Southwest during the 1920s and 1930s, play an important role in aviation history by making the first nonstop transcontinental flight (1923), the first round-the-world flight (1924), and pioneering flights to South America (1926) and from California to Hawaii (1927).

12 JULY 1926

Ideas/Beliefs In Texas, evolutionary theory is declared deleted from school biology textbooks, in compliance with the 16 October 1925 demand of the State Textbook Commission. This action placates religious fundamentalists, who actively oppose any teaching of evolutionary theory. On 21 July 1925, a Tennessee court found biology teacher John Scopes guilty of breaking state law by teaching evolutionary theory.

15 AUGUST 1926

International US agents from San Diego arrest, near the California/Mexico border, General Enriques Estrada, a former Mexican Secretary of War, and 200 followers preparing to begin a revolution in Baja California. On 19 February 1927, the general and 12 of his followers are convicted in Los Angeles of violating US neutrality laws, as the decades-long Mexican Revolution periodically spills over the border.

25 OCTOBER 1926

Education The site of the University of California is dedicated in Los Angeles.

1 NOVEMBER 1926

International Queen Marie of Rumania, on a lengthy visit to the United States, talks with farmers, sees a rodeo, at Medora, and at Mandan is adopted into the Sioux Nation as a 'war woman.'

OTHER EVENTS OF 1926

Iowa The state legislature adopts a constitutional amendment admitting women to the general assembly.

Industry The Greater Seminole oil field is developed, resulting in serious overproduction in the oil industry. In 1928 another major discovery follows with the opening of the Oklahoma City oil field.

Texas In Corpus Christi, the ship channel and deep-water port are completed, permitting large-scale shipping of oil, grain, and cotton. The 400-foot-wide and 40-foot-deep Inland Harbor connects with the Intracoastal Canal.

Science/Technology The 'father of modern firearms,' Utah-born John Moses Browning, dies. The inventive genius and holder of 128 patents had his designs manufactured by Winchester, Colt, Remington, Savage and others; by the 1960s, some 30 million weapons based on his designs had been produced. Experimental horticulturalist and plant breeder Luther Burbank dies on his Santa Rosa farm. Burbank, who came to California over 50 years ago, had been inspired by Darwin's evolutionary theories to develop such hybrids as the Burbank potato, the Shasta daisy, the plumcot, and about 1000 other new plant varieties.

Industry Joseph P Kennedy, father of the future thirty-fifth president, gains control, with an investors' syndicate, of the Film Booking Office, a movie company noted for low-budget Western films, with such actors as Tom Mix and Richard Talmadge under contract. Film-making, based in Hollywood, is now the nation's fifth largest industry, grossing $1.5 billion per year and accounting for 90 percent of the world's film output. There are now 14,500 movie theaters nationwide, and in the past year Hollywood has produced some 400 films.

Arts/Culture Cowboy writer and illustrator Will James publishes his most engaging book, *Smokey,* the story of a cow horse told in colloquial style and recounting vignettes of day-to-day range life. Novelist O E Rölvaag publishes *Giants in the Earth,* a saga of the pioneering hardships suffered by the first Norwegian immigrants to the Dakota Territory. The book is based on the author's own farming experiences in North Dakota. The influential painter, sculptor, and illustrator Charles M Russell dies. His work exhaustively documented the Old West, recording his own early life as a cowboy, as well as the Indians and historic episodes of the nineteenth century.

Western writer and illustrator Will James.

JANUARY 1927
Arts/Culture In Hollywood, the Academy of Motion Picture Arts and Sciences is founded. The 231 original members include actors, producers, directors, writers, and technicians. The academy will begin to bestow its awards, nicknamed Oscars, in 1929. The film *The Jazz Singer* is the first to introduce sound successfully in 1927.

2 FEBRUARY 1927
Arts/Culture On the New York stage, Harry Tierney's lively musical comedy *Rio Rita* opens. According to the lighthearted plot, a Texas Ranger meets the girl of his dreams while pursuing a Mexican bandit.

12 FEBRUARY 1927
Ideas/Beliefs South Dakota Governor Bulow vetoes the capital-punishment bill recently passed by the state legislature. According to the governor, 'Thou shalt not kill' must be the ruling principle for ethical social as well as individual behavior.

21 FEBRUARY 1927
Hawaii The US Supreme Court declares the 1920 law regulating foreign-language schools an unconstitutional invasion of the rights of the resident Japanese, who oppose the legislation.

24 FEBRUARY 1927
Kansas The US Supreme Court refuses to support the Ku Klux Klan in ruling on a Kansas court decision that bars the KKK from the state until it complies with Kansas corporation law.

25 FEBRUARY 1927
Agriculture President Coolidge refuses relief to the nation's farmers in vetoing the McNary-Haugen Bill, on ground that it benefits special groups and promotes price-fixing. In 1928 the bill passes Congress again, but Coolidge vetoes it.
Ideas/Beliefs The Oklahoma legislature defeats, 46 to 30, a law that prohibits the teaching of Darwinian theory in public schools.

28 FEBRUARY 1927
National The Teapot Dome scandal winds down with a unanimous decision by the Supreme Court that the Elk Hills oil reserve lease to Edward Doheny by former Interior Secretary Albert Fall is illegal and fraudulent. The court also decides that Doheny is not entitled to credit for the $11 million he expended, because everything done by his company was done fraudulently. Hence the Hawaiian oil tanks at Pearl Harbor, storing 1.5 million barrels of oil for the US Navy, now belong to the Federal Government. On 10 October 1927, the court invalidates the Teapot Dome oil-reserve lease made to Harry Sinclair's Mammoth Oil Company. On 17 March President Coolidge returns the naval oil and gas reserves in California, Colorado, and Utah to the jurisdiction of the Navy.

Charles Marion Russell, 'the Cowboy Artist.'

3 MARCH 1927
Agriculture President Coolidge signs a bill prohibiting the practice by sales people, cold-storage proprietors, and dealers in foodstuffs of destroying farm produce and related goods received in interstate commerce for the purpose of keeping up prices.

7 MARCH 1927
Black Experience In a ruling on *Nixon v Herndon*, the US Supreme Court invalidates the Texas law forbidding blacks to vote in Democratic primary elections.

8 MARCH 1927
Black Experience President Coolidge cuts 18 months off the 30-year sentences of 20 blacks, former members of the 24th Infantry, who originally were sentenced to death or life imprisonment for participation in race riots in Houston, Texas, on 23 August 1917.

27 APRIL 1927
Science/Technology Following the interruption of communications on the Alaska cable earlier this month, a repair ship discovers a 20-ton whale entangled in the cable. The whale had chewed completely through the cable's iron-shielded core in eight separate places. An 80-foot replacement of cable restores communication.

21 MAY 1927

Transportation Charles Lindbergh makes his historic nonstop New York-Paris flight in the *Spirit of St Louis,* a monoplane built by T Claude Ryan of San Diego, California. A 1925 graduate of the US Army flying school in San Antonio, Texas, Lindbergh has already set a California-New York speed record with his flight to New York.

27 MAY 1927

California A group of armed men overpowers guards stationed along the Los Angeles Aqueduct and dynamites a large section of pipe carrying water to supply the metropolitan district. More damage is done on 28 May, 5 June, and 19 June at Diaz Lake. On 16 July two aqueduct explosions shut off the city's main water supply.

13 JUNE-9 SEPTEMBER 1927

National President Coolidge and his party leave Washington, DC, for South Dakota's Custer State Park, where they settle in for a lengthy residence in the 'Summer White House.' On 25 June the president dedicates Mt Coolidge, formerly Mt Lookout. On 4 July, dressed in cowboy regalia, he celebrates Independence Day and his own fifty-fifth birthday; the following day he views the Tri-State Rodeo. On 12 July, in a Pony Express re-enactment, a relay of Western horsemen arrive with an invitation to visit Cheyenne, Wyoming. The 27 riders cover the 270-mile distance in 13 hours. On 2 August Coolidge conveys to newspaper reporters in Rapid City the message, 'I do not choose to run for President in 1928.'

SUMMER 1927

Science/Technology Near Folsom, New Mexico, archaeologist J D Figgins finds proof of prehistoric man in America by discovering a Stone-Age spear point in the skeleton of a bison that became extinct 10,000 years ago. Previously, it had been believed that human life in North America dated back only 4000 years, and that Ice-Age man had never even appeared on the continent.

26 JUNE 1927

Science/Technology Radio communications open between San Francisco and the Philippines.

28 JUNE 1927

Transportation In the longest over-water flight attempted to date, a Fokker piloted by Lieutenant Lester Maitland, with Lieutenant Albert Hegenberger as navigator, takes off from Oakland, California. They land safely at Wheeler Field in Hawaii, 2025 miles and 25 hours 50 minutes later.

7 JULY 1927

Transportation In Colorado, the 6.4-mile Moffatt Tunnel under the Continental Divide, to provide

Opposite: *Aviator Charles Lindbergh in Paris.*

INDIANS IN THE TWENTIETH CENTURY

Mistreatment of the Indians, paternalistic federal policy, and continuing land frauds persisted into the early twentieth century. Following World War I, however, increasing Indian agitation finally forced changes. The 1924 Snyder Act granting Indians US citizenship would be succeeded by the pivotal 1934 Indian Reorganization (Wheeler-Howard) Act, which returned reservation lands to the tribes. This legislation concluded the decade of activism led by Bureau of Indian Affairs Commissioner John Collier and marked recognition of heroic World War I Indian soldiers. The Reorganization Act also established a credit system for Indians, gave them the right to form business and other organizations, provided for vocational education, gave them the right to conserve and develop Indian resources, and granted certain rights of home rule on reservations. The act was a turning point in that it sought to reverse nineteenth century Indian policy: the New Deal tried to strengthen and enlarge the tribal land base, and reinforce tribal and cultural authority to let the Indians determine their own way of life.

This enlightened attitude came to an end in 1954 with the Termination Acts, which sought to remove the Federal Government from administration of Indian affairs, allowing tribes to go their own way without governmental support or guidance. The result was disastrous, as few reservation Indians were prepared either socially or economically to survive on their own. This policy was reversed in the 1960s. At the same time, the militant activists of the American Indian Movement (AIM) and other Indian nationalists began to demand a greater role in policy-making, while seeking further tribal autonomy. They publicized their cause with the 1969 occupation of Alcatraz and the 1973 Wounded Knee occupation. In the 1980s conditions on many reservations were still a national shame – their inhabitants were among the nation's poorest citizens, with substandard health care and high crime, suicide, alcoholism, and infant-mortality rates. (Some reservations possessing mineral wealth, mainly in the Southwest, are the exception.) The United States has yet to deal fairly with the original inhabitants of the West.

---

better rail connections between the eastern and western Rocky Mountain slopes, is completed at the cost of $18 million.

10 AUGUST 1927

Arts/Culture In South Dakota, President Coolidge dedicates Mount Rushmore, as Idaho-born artist Gutzon Borglum begins work on the national memorial by sculpting the massive heads of four US presidents – George Washington, Thomas Jefferson, Abraham Lincoln, and Theodore Roosevelt – from the living rock with a jackhammer. Coolidge is able to get partial govenment funding for the project, setting a precedent for the widespread New Deal financing of public-works projects during the 1930s. When Borglum dies at the age of 70 in 1941, his son Lincoln Borglum completes the memorial.

CHRONOLOGY

17 NOVEMBER 1927
International The Mexican Supreme Court rules that the limitations placed on foreign oil concessions by the January 1927 Petroleum Law are unconstitutional. This decision is a success for Dwight Morrow, appointed in September as US Ambassador to Mexico. Morrow helps to arbitrate several long-standing disputes with Mexico, generally improves relations between the two nations, and succeeds in securing wider Mexican concessions on oil lands developed by American investors before 1917.

24 NOVEMBER 1927
Life/Customs The increasing national prison unrest affects Western states. In the California State Prison at Folsom, several hundred convicts, some with smuggled-in arms, barricade themselves in a cell block. Over 300 National Guardsmen and 100 police attack. When the convicts surrender the following day, two prison guards and nine convicts are dead.

12 DECEMBER 1927
Oklahoma In Oklahoma City, Governor Henry S Johnston calls out troops to secure the state capitol and to prevent entry of legislators called to hear impeachment charges against him. Meeting elsewhere, the assembly votes charges against the governor, and the troops are withdrawn two days later. Johnston is finally impeached in March 1929.

15 DECEMBER 1927
Arts/Culture In the premier performance by the Cleveland Orchestra of his symphony *Horizons*, composer Arthur Shepherd conducts the four movements representing scenes of the American West – 'Westward,' 'The Lone Prairie,' 'The Old Chisholm Trail,' and 'Canyons.'

OTHER EVENTS OF 1927
Science/Technology Former rancher Henry H Cazier establishes the first completely automatic hydroelectric system in Nevada, as well as the region's first rural electrification system.
Agriculture John Daniel Rust and Mack Donald Rust invent the mechanical cotton picker, a valuable tool for the Western cotton belt, which extends from Texas to California. In North Dakota, the radical farm movement known as the Farmers Union begins as a powerful co-operative to control grain sales and the purchase of supplies.
Arts/Culture Architect Frank Lloyd Wright erects the Arizona Biltmore Hotel in Phoenix, marking the state's emergence as a center of tourism. Pulitzer-Prize-winning novelist Willa Cather publishes her second major Western novel, *Death Comes for the Archbishop*, the story of a pioneer-era missionary in New Mexico.
Social Change Denver, Colorado, judge and social reformer Ben Lindsey and co-author Wainwright Evans publish *The Companionate*

Marriage, which proposes a trial period in marriage. Lindsey, who also advocates more humane treatment of juvenile delinquents and compulsory sex education, becomes a target of the Ku Klux Klan and loses his judgeship the next year. In 1934 he is elected a judge of the California Superior Court.

1 JANUARY 1928
Science/Technology In San Antonio, Texas, the Milam Building officially opens. The 21-story structure is the world's first air-conditioned office building in which air conditioning is part of the original construction. Population of the Southwest will increase dramatically as this becomes commonplace.

4 MARCH 1928
Sports In the first cross-country foot race, 274 men start out from Los Angeles. On 26 May 55 runners reach New York's Madison Square Garden, with Andrew Payne, a Cherokee Indian from Claremont, Oklahoma, winning with a time of just over 573 hours for the 3422.3-mile distance.

13 MARCH 1928
Environment St Francis Dam, 50 miles from Los Angeles, collapses, spilling 12 billion gallons of water through Los Angeles and Ventura counties, causing $12 million damage and 451 deaths.

Isolated Guernsey, Wyoming, west of Laramie.

6 APRIL 1928
Arts/Culture The Boston Symphony Orchestra plays the premiere performance of *California*, festival scenes by composer Frederick S Converse.

19-20 MAY 1928
Life/Customs In Angel's Camp, Calaveras County, California, the frog-jumping jubilee takes place: the frog 'the Pride of San Joaquin' defeats 50 other contestants with a jump of 3 feet 4 inches. The annual contest commemorates Mark Twain's famous 1865 short story, 'The Celebrated Jumping Frog of Calaveras County.'

29 JUNE 1928
National In Houston, Texas, the Democratic Party nominates New York Governor Alfred E Smith as its presidential candidate. On 26 July in Omaha, Nebraska, the Bull Moose Progressive Party selects Dr Henry Hoffman as its candidate, with social reformer Jane Addams as his vice-presidential running mate (in 1931 she will receive the Nobel Peace Prize). The Republicans nominate Herbert Hoover.

11 SEPTEMBER 1928
Transportation The Yelloway Bus Line begins transcontinental Los Angeles-New York service with three 26-passenger buses departing daily on each coast, and covering 3433 miles in 5 days 14 hours. The Los Angeles bus manufacturer Pickwick Stages, Inc, produces 'nite coaches' with sleeping facilities.

15 SEPTEMBER 1928
Conservation South-central Utah's scenic wilderness area is established as 36,010-acre Bryce Canyon National Park.

28 NOVEMBER 1928
Exploration An expedition led by Richard Byrd reaches the South Pole. The party spends the winter in its first 'Little America' base camp on the Antarctic Ross Ice Shelf.

21 DECEMBER 1928
National Congress passes the Boulder Canyon Project Act, mandating construction of Boulder (later renamed Hoover) Dam on the Colorado River at the Nevada-Arizona border. With this project, the Federal Government begins decades of construction of large multipurpose water works in the West and elsewhere.

OTHER EVENTS OF 1928
Transportation A seven-mile-long tunnel under the Rockies, connecting Denver and Salt Lake City, by rail is completed with public financing.

CHRONOLOGY

Arts/Culture Architect Bertram Goodhue's Nebraska State Capitol building is finished. Designed in a classical modern style – a restrained version of art deco – it becomes a prototype for civic and governmental projects during the 1930s, among them the new Louisiana, North Dakota, and Oregon state capitols. Goodhue's Los Angeles Public Library also helps to popularize the style. Franz Boas's *Primitive Art* is published in the United States. Featuring the tribal arts of the Northwestern Coastal Indians, the book's hundreds of illustrations reveal the richness of the native American heritage.

Indians The Rockefeller Foundation-sponsored Meriam Report is published. Assessing the condition of the Indian, the report echoes 1927 Senate investigation calls for reform. Reforms are eventually instituted in the areas of health care and education.

13 JANUARY 1929
Life/Customs Legendary Dodge City and Tombstone marshal Wyatt Earp dies in Los Angeles. In his last years, he advised makers of Western movies, but was not compensated.

4 MARCH 1929
National Stanford University-educated Californian Herbert Hoover is inaugurated the nation's thirty-first president. Also sworn in is Kansas-born Charles Curtis, the first vice-president of American Indian ancestry.

30 MARCH 1929
International The Mexican situation remains uneasy, as Mexican rebels drop bombs on Naco, Arizona, wounding one person. Naco is attacked again on 6 April, as 75 bombs are found strewn along the tracks of the Southern Pacific Railway. On 12 April Mexican rebel General F R Manzo, with 15 of his staff, crosses into US territory at Nogales, Arizona; all are interned.

27 MAY 1929
Agriculture At the Chicago Board of Trade, wheat falls under $1 per bushel for the first time in 14 years. All grains, cotton, and many stocks slump. High money rates, bumper 1929 crop prospects, and large unsold 1928 surpluses are to blame.

15 JUNE 1929
Agriculture In an effort to bring relief to the farm community, President Hoover signs the Agricultural Marketing Act, which establishes the Federal Farm Board with a $500-million revolving fund to assist farmers' co-operatives, and authorizes stabilization corporations to buy up farm surpluses to maintain prices. The Grain Stabilization Corporation is chartered on 10 February 1930, and the Cotton Stabilization Corporation follows on 5 June 1930. Despite these moves, grain and cotton prices drop steadily.

11 AUGUST 1929
Arts/Culture At Interlochen, Michigan, composer Leo Sowerby conducts the premiere performance of his symphonic poem *Prairie*, inspired by Carl Sandburg's poem. The pioneer era and the West provide subject matter for many artists.

29 OCTOBER 1929
National On the day known as 'Black Tuesday,' the New York stock market crashes: a several-week price plunge culminates in the panic sale of over 16 million shares and inaugurates the Depression of the following decade. The burgeoning prosperity of the 1920s, and the small margin of 10 percent required for stock purchases, has encouraged many ordinary wage earners to join large investors in Wall Street speculation. This catastrophe causes so much misery to so many that only federal intervention by the Roosevelt Administration New Deal agencies can keep the nation going in the 1930s.

DECEMBER 1929
Science/Technology Dr Andrew Elliott Douglas announces development of the science of dendrochronology – the dating of wood by examination of the annual rings of trees – based on his Arizona studies of sunspot activity and tree-ring growth. In so doing, he pushes back the horizon of American prehistory to AD 700, based on a continuous, overlapping tree-ring chronology of 1229 years. By this method he is able to date accurately some 40 Pueblo ruins. In California, where there are older trees, other researchers will be able to push the regional tree-ring chronology back to 5200 BC.

OTHER EVENTS OF 1929
Arts/Culture In Salt Lake City, Utah, the Mormon Tabernacle Choir begins its weekly broadcasts over national radio, and eventually becomes world famous. In the literary realm, novelist and anthropologist Oliver La Farge publishes his Pulitzer Prize-winning novel *Laughing Boy*. La Farge, who worked on New Mexico archaeological expeditions to study Navaho culture, seeks to explore Indian life from an Indian point of view, rather than to present romanticized or sentimentalized portraits of the 'noble savage.' In the visual-arts area, William Henry Jackson retires as one of the most famous photographers of the West and turns to painting of Western scenes. In the 1870s, he was the official photographer for the Hayden Surveys: his photographs of Yellowstone help to establish the area as a national park. When Jackson finally dies in 1942, he is among the last of the era's Civil War veterans. The modernist painter Jackson Pollock, who was born in Cody, Wyoming, and who grew up in Arizona and California, leaves the West Coast for New York, where he will become, in the 1950s, the world's most famous abstract expressionist. Pollock acknowledges the influence of American Indian art and sand painting on his

own development. Modernist painter Georgia O'Keeffe arrives in Taos, New Mexico, as the guest of Mabel Dodge Luhan, a former New York socialite who settled in Taos in 1917 and married a Pueblo Indian. Luhan attracts a small but important coteriè of artists and writers to the region: among them are D H Lawrence, Marsden Hartley, Stuart Davis, and John Marin. After years of seasonal visits, O'Keeffe buys a house in Abiquiu in 1945 and settles permanently. Many of her rhythmic paintings incorporate the distinctive landscape, architecture, flora, fauna, bleached animal skulls and other phenomena of the American Southwest.

Conservation In Wyoming, the 310,443-acre Grand Teton area is established as a national park. And in eastern Utah near Moab, the Arches, a 34,250-acre park of dramatically eroded vertical redrock slabs, is declared a national monument; it becomes a national park in 1972.

25 JANUARY 1930

Immigration In Watsonville, California, race riots result in the death of one Filipino and the beating of others who had come to the US to work on Western ranches. Similar beatings occur in San Francisco, and on 29 January the Filipino Center in Stockton is bombed. The pattern of discrimination against low-paid immigrant labor is repeating itself.

Top: *An abandoned Oklahoma farm in the 1930s.*
Above: *Northern Pacific's engine 'Minnetonka.'*

CHRONOLOGY

18 FEBRUARY 1930

Science/Technology At Flagstaff, Arizona's Lowell Observatory, astronomer Clyde William Tombaugh discovers a ninth planet beyond Neptune – Pluto. The search for Pluto was based on the late Dr Percival Lowell's calculations, and the discovery is not officially announced till 13 March 1930, the anniversary of Lowell's birth and of Herschel's discovery of Uranus.

4 MARCH 1930

Science/Technology Near Globe, Arizona, former President Coolidge dedicates the Coolidge Dam – the world's highest multiple-dome dam to date. The Gila River barrier provides irrigation for some 100,000 acres and abundant hydro-electric power. Its completion ends 55 years of opposition by Apaches who fear destruction of their tribal burying grounds (an $11,000 concrete slab was laid over the site). The San Carlos Reservoir created by the dam also covers Geronimo's old camp. After the dedication, as the reservoir slowly begins to fill, humorist Will Rogers remarks, 'If this was my lake, I'd mow it.'

10 MARCH 1930

Life/Customs As President Hoover continues to press for Prohibition enforcement, hundreds of persons in Oklahoma, Tennessee and other states are reported suffering the symptoms of alcohol poisoning – swollen feet, paralysis of the legs and arms, blindness. The culprit is home-made alcohol from stills with such ingredients, in the Southwest, as creosote or crude carbolic acid (used as a sheep-dip). On 26 July the Prohibition Bureau reports that some 15,000 people nationwide suffer similar complaints.

17 APRIL 1930

Arts/Culture Composer Charles Sanford Skilton's one-act opera *The Sun Bride* receives its premiere performance on New York radio. The libretto is based on a tale from American Indian folklore, and Skilton also draws on Indian themes for many of his other works.

1 MAY 1930

California The Los Angeles Metropolitan Water District takes over the planning of the Colorado River Aqueduct Project.

9 MAY 1930

Black Experience In Sherman, Texas, a lynch mob burns the Grayson County Court House, killing George Hughes, a black on trial there for an attack on a white woman. Later, a mob attacks National Guard troops and storms the jail. Frequent racist incidents and lynchings occur in Texas and neighboring states during the 1920s and 1930s.

17 JUNE 1930

National President Hoover signs the Smoot-Hawley Tariff Act, an ill-fated attempt to shelter farmers from foreign competition by imposing record-setting protectionist tariffs on imported agricultural goods and manufactured products. The controversial bill results in retaliatory tariffs by US trading partners abroad, which in turn have a disastrous effect on US foreign trade – plunging the nation even deeper into economic depression. (On 7 May a petition signed by some thousand economists had been made public; the signators had protested the passage of such a law and urged Hoover to veto it if Congress passed it.)

Left: *Evangelist Billy Sunday.*
Opposite: *Novelist Willa Cather.*

30 JUNE 1930
Transportation Near San Antonio, Texas, Randolph Field, the 'West Point of the Air,' is dedicated. One of the largest such airfield/military complexes in the world, it is home to the Army Air Corps flying schools until 1938, when additional bases are established.

1 JULY 1930
Transportation At the Mare Island Navy Yard in Vallejo, California, the nation's first naval streamlined submarine, the USS *Nautilus*, is commissioned, following its 15 March launch. The 2730-ton vessel is 371 feet long.

13 AUGUST 1930
Agriculture As unprecedented summer drought besieges farmers, the Federal Government instructs drought-relief agencies to guard against profiteering in food products; the Justice Department is to curb speculation in agricultural goods. The Department of Agriculture assures the nation that there is no danger of food shortages, and therefore no need for hoarding. On 20 December 1930, the Drought Relief Act appropriates $45 million.

17 SEPTEMBER 1930
Industry Near Las Vegas, Nevada, construction begins on Boulder Dam, later renamed Hoover Dam. Henry Kaiser's company will complete the project two years ahead of schedule in 1936. During the decade, California-based Kaiser does so much work for the government that he becomes known as 'the New Deal's businessman.'

28 DECEMBER 1930
North Dakota Fire destroys the state capitol building in Bismarck, with a monetary loss of about $1 million and an incalculable loss of state documents.

OTHER EVENTS OF 1930
Science/Technology Physicist and rocket pioneer Dr Robert Goddard moves to the desert near Roswell, New Mexico, to experiment with advanced propulsion rockets. In 1935 he successfully tests a rocket that flies faster than the speed of sound. He leaves in 1942 to become director of research in the Navy's Bureau of Aeronautics.
Arts/Culture Noted Texas folklorist, collector, and writer J Frank Dobie gains national attention with the publication of two books, *A Vaquero of the Bush* and *Coronado's Children*. Shortly before his 1964 death, Dobie receives the Presidential Medal of Freedom from his old friend President Lyndon Johnson. His Paisano Ranch later becomes an endowed writers' retreat. Another literary event is the publication of *Frontier Trails* by former Texas lawman, desperado and Johnson County War veteran Frank M Canton. The book is an account of Canton's colorful past. In the area of visual arts,

Iowa painter Grant Wood's *American Gothic* brings him unexpected and widespread fame, and leads to the founding of the 1932-3 Stone City artists' colony. Here Wood and his students paint typical scenes of the rolling prairie and corn fields of Southeastern Iowa. Photographer and ethnologist Edward S Curtis completes a 30-year project of documenting 80 Indian tribes from Canada to Mexico in over 40,000 photographs with publication of the twentieth volume of his epic series *The North American Indian*. The musical world benefits as Oklahoma-born and California-educated composer Roy Harris returns to the United States from Paris, where he studied with Nadia Boulanger. Among his compositions, which combine American folk themes with classical forms, is his 1941 Western-inspired *Cimarron*.
Sports Rodeo champion Ed Bowman retires from the circuit at 44 undefeated as the greatest 'strap and cinch' relay man. His later interest in rope-working horses leads to a National Cutting Horse Association Championship, and in 1962 he is elected to the National Cowboy Hall of Fame.
Conservation Near Flagstaff, Arizona, the extinct volcano known as Sunset Crater and the surrounding 3040 acres of picturesque volcanic debris are declared a national monument.

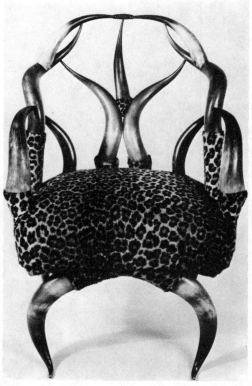

Western horn chairs were popular in the 1930s.

JANUARY 1931

Arts/Culture RKO releases one of the most popular and spectacular Western films to date, *Cimarron*, based on Edna Ferber's best-selling saga of the Oklahoma land rush days; it goes on to win the Academy Award as the year's best picture.

2 FEBRUARY 1931

Arts/Culture Modern dance pioneer and choreographer Martha Graham premieres *Primitive Mysteries*, a dance inspired by Indian and Spanish colonial rituals of the American Southwest. Later dances based on a similar theme are her 1932 *Ceremonials* and 1940 *El Penitente*. The Western experience reappears in her 1935 *Frontier* and 1936 *Horizons*. Graham, who dances the lead role in most of her creations, leads her New York-based company on transcontinental tours.

19 MARCH 1931

Nevada Governor Fred B Balzar signs into law a bill legalizing gambling, which had been legal from 1869 to 1910, when a reform movement succeeded in banning it. During the 1930s, gambling grows slowly in the state, but during World War II and afterward it becomes an essential source of revenue. It also attracts such underworld figures as mobster Bugsy Siegel, who is murdered in Los Angeles in 1947. On the same day, Governor Balzar signs a law requiring only six weeks of residence for divorce, effective 1 May. Reno becomes the nation's divorce capital.

22 JULY 1931

Agriculture As Kansas harvests a bumper wheat crop of 240 million bushels, wheat prices collapse. Many counties declare a tax moratorium to assist farmers, who are receiving the lowest prices in history.

DANIEL GUGGENHEIM, 1856-1930

The sons of emigrant businessman Meyer Guggenheim were told by their patriarch to 'be as one.' Five of them took that advice, co-operating to build an extraordinary business empire based in mining. The brains of that operation was Daniel Guggenheim, who was born in Philadelphia on 9 July 1856. After working in Meyer's lace importing concern, Daniel, with four of his brothers, became involved in their father's mining business in Colorado. By 1901 the Guggenheims had taken over the rival American Smelting and Refining Company. They were to extend that company's operations around the world, making it the basis of a network of corporations under Guggenheim control.

Daniel Guggenheim led the way in the innovative approach of the companies – especially in integrating every aspect of the mining business from exploration to smelting and refining. The brothers became industrial imperialists, spreading their operations into Africa and South America. In labor relations the Guggenheims were liberal for their time, making peace with various labor-protection laws and with organized labor. Daniel was also an active philanthropist, establishing funds and foundations in the arts and sciences. Having built the world's largest concern in nonferrous metal mining, Daniel Guggenheim died near Port Washington, New York, on 28 September 1930.

---

26 JULY 1931

Transportation By injunction, a federal court ends the armed Texas-Oklahoma quarrel over the toll and free bridges crossing the Red River at Durant. Both bridges are finally opened on 6 August.

The Coca Cola Bottling plant at Los Angeles.

CHRONOLOGY

27 JULY 1931
Agriculture South Dakota, Nebraska, and Iowa are scourged by a plague of grasshoppers.

12 AUGUST 1931
Agriculture The Federal Farm Board asks the governors of the 14 cotton states to urge growers to plow under one-third of the crop now growing, in order to increase prices. The suggestion is not accepted.

13 AUGUST 1931
Life/Customs To prevent Americans from participating in all-night gambling in Mexico, the US Customs Bureau orders closure of all Texas-border bridges from 9 PM to 8 AM.

17 AUGUST 1931
Industry Oil industry executives predict higher prices for mid-continent crude and possible stabilization of the national petroleum industry. At the same time, the East Texas oil fields placed under martial law by Governor Ross Sterling cease production. And in Oklahoma, Governor William 'Alfalfa Bill' Murray shuts down oil wells in an effort to stabilize prices. The Texas and Oklahoma moves cut daily output by one million gallons. On 12 December 1932, the US Supreme Court rules Governor Sterling's action unconstitutional.

30 AUGUST 1931
Idaho The governor declares martial law in Boise Valley and Idaho County, sending in the state militia to quell an outbreak of forest fires set by arsonists.

SEPTEMBER 1931
Finance Confidence in the banks begins to erode, as Great Britain goes off the gold standard. Americans start to withdraw money and hoard gold. The panic causes 305 banks to close in September, and 522 in October.

1 SEPTEMBER 1931
Science/Technology The nation's first anthropology laboratory opens in Santa Fe, New Mexico, under Jesse Logan Nusbaum.

22 SEPTEMBER 1931
Agriculture In Iowa, 2000 state troops back state veterinarians in enforcing the tuberculin test on Cedar County cattle. The Tipton Cattle War focuses national attention on farm problems, as the farmers oppose the state law on the testing of cattle for tuberculosis and the killing of infected animals.

22 NOVEMBER 1931
Arts/Culture In Chicago, Paul Whiteman and his orchestra perform the premiere of Ferde Grofé's *Grand Canyon Suite*, the movements of which include 'Sunrise,' 'Painted Desert,' 'On the Trail,' 'Sunset,' and 'Cloudburst.' Fittingly, Whiteman himself hails from Colorado.

7 DECEMBER 1931
National In Washington, DC, hundreds of 'hunger marchers' with an employment-seeking petition are turned away from the White House. As breadlines form around the nation, the jobless and homeless build the tarpaper-shack communities known as 'Hoovervilles' on the outskirts of major cities, from Seattle, Washington, to New York.

8 DECEMBER 1931
Arts/Culture In New York, Ernest Carter's three-act opera *The Blonde Donna, or The Fiesta of Santa Barbara* has its first full stage production. The libretto recounts the story of an 1824 Indian mission uprising in Santa Barbara, California.

DECEMBER 1931
Texas Lyndon Baines Johnson, on leave from his high-school teaching post, arrives in Washington, DC, as legislative secretary to Texas Congressman Richard Kleberg, heir to the legendary King Ranch. Kleberg, filling a vacancy, prefers the social scene to the political, so Johnson assumes almost complete responsibility for the office. Learning quickly, he develops a political talent that attracts the patronage of powerful Texas Congressman Sam Rayburn, and later of President Roosevelt, whose New Deal programs he supports. In 1936 Johnson is elected to Congress, and in 1948 to the Senate.

OTHER EVENTS OF 1931
Arts/Culture The Theatre Guild production of *Green Grow the Lilacs* by Cherokee-born poet and playwright Lynn Riggs is voted one of the 10 best plays on Broadway. Rodgers and Hammerstein later adapt it for their 1943 hit musical *Oklahoma!* A major exhibit of Indian tribal arts opens at New York City's Grand Central Galleries – the first time they are treated as works of art in their own right, rather than as ethnographic artifacts. Included is a section of contemporary paintings by Kiowa Indians.

Conservation The northeastern Arizona Canyon de Chelly, an 83,840-acre area within the Navajo Indian Reservation, is declared a national monument. It includes some 300 archaeological sites, among them 138 major ruins – some of the largest prehistoric cliff dwellings in the state.

22 JANUARY 1932
National In signing the measure creating the Reconstruction Finance Corporation, President Hoover makes his most dramatic move to combat the Depression. Federally funded at $500 million and authorized to borrow up to $2 billion more, the agency provides emergency financing for banks, insurance companies, railroads, and farm

mortgage associations. The RFC begins operation on 2 February, with 1925 Nobel Peace Prize winner and former vice-president Charles Dawes as its head. This federal lending body, which exists until 1957, is condemned as 'socialistic' by some conservatives, and as a 'bank for bankers' by liberals who see it as saving large firms at the expense of small ones.

MAY 1932

Agriculture The Farm Holiday Association, a militant group of farmers organized in 1931 to prevent farm mortgage foreclosures and to combat low agricultural prices, decides to inaugurate the 'Farm Holiday' program, with the motto 'Stay at Home – Buy Nothing – Sell Nothing.' The object is to drive up prices by withholding produce. The farmers, who are now selling well below the cost of production, rally under the leadership of Iowan Milo Reno. They block roads to prevent strike-breaking farmers from hauling goods to market, dump milk, carry placards with such slogans as 'In Hoover we trusted, now we are busted,' and prevent farm foreclosure sales by intimidating outside bidders and using the tactic of 'penny sales' to buy up personal property at very low cost and turn it back to the owners. On 16-31 August, when 1000 farmers picket highways outside Sioux City and Des Moines, Iowa, some farmers ship by rail to avoid the strikers. The movement, which spreads to neighboring states, remains active for several years.

27 JUNE-2 JULY 1932

National The Democratic convention, meeting in Chicago, chooses New York Governor Franklin Delano Roosevelt as presidential candidate, with Speaker of the House John Nance Garner of Texas as his running mate. On 10 July the Farm Labor Party nominates Jacob S Coxey for president.

16 JULY 1932

Colorado The 1878 Central City Opera House, originally the opulent centerpiece of a gold mining camp and once one of the state's leading theaters, reopens after 50 years of silence. Authentically restored by the University of Denver, the theater begins its first annual play festival with *Camille*, starring Lillian Gish. Future events feature Walter Huston in *Othello* and Ruth Gordon in *A Doll's House*. A summer opera festival will emerge from this and eventually commission such original works as Douglas Moore's *The Ballad of Baby Doe* (1956).

21 JULY 1932

National President Hoover signs the Relief and Construction Act, broadening the powers of the Reconstruction Finance Corporation by increasing its debt limit to $3 billion, funding state and local public-works projects and relief programs, and increasing assistance to agriculture.

WATER AND THE WEST

The population of the West has for some time been running ahead of Western resources: millions of Americans, for example, have moved to the Southwest, where water supply can remain adequate for human needs only if ecological risks are taken. Two cases from different Western areas illustrate the dilemma. In a farming area about 75 miles southwest of Spokane, Washington, regional power companies were swamped with a surplus of cheap hydroelectric power during the 1960s. They agreed with farmers who would install deep-well, electric-powered irrigation systems to sell them all the power needed at a discount. The irrigation system would triple the farmer's yield and boost profits. What happened? Aluminium refineries and other industries flocked to the Northwest, the water surplus disappeared, and power companies began building expensive coal-fired plants and nuclear reactors. The price of electricity soared, and farmers were caught in a bind.

It is Arizona, however, that epitomizes population growth and threatened ecology. Beginning in 1927, the subsiding water table caused cracks as deep as 400 feet to appear in the Arizona earth; by 1983 there were more than 100 such fissures. The population of Arizona has boomed since air conditioning was introduced in the early 1950s. To support the new people, and their burgeoning agriculture, the Colorado River has been dammed from top to bottom, and now trickles to a sad end in the Mexican desert. The Central Arizona Project will consist of a 400-mile system of aqueducts and dams to divert a yearly 1,200,000 acre-feet of the Colorado River to the Phoenix and Tucson areas. Ninety percent of the water will be used for agriculture but it will also serve as an insurance policy for the so-called oasis cities. However, the question remains: has prosperity brought the Southwest to the point where its ecology is a house of cards?

---

30 JULY-14 AUGUST 1932

Sports Vice-President Curtis opens the tenth modern Olympic Games in Los Angeles, with 2000 athletes from 50 countries. The United States scores the highest team total. Among the stars are Texas paragon Mildred 'Babe' Didrikson who establishes new world's records in the women's hurdles and javelin, and wins a silver medal in the high jump. Clarence 'Buster' Crabbe (later Hollywood's Flash Gordon) wins a gold medal in the 400-meter freestyle swimming event, and Eleanor Holm wins a gold in the 100-meter backstroke. Total attendance is estimated at 1.75 million.

26 AUGUST 1932

Finance As more and more Americans have trouble meeting their home mortgage payments, the Controller of the Currency orders a moratorium on the foreclosure of first mortgages.

31 OCTOBER 1932

Nevada The governor proclaims a 12-day banking holiday to save the state's banks.

CHRONOLOGY

F D Roosevelt campaigning in 1932.

8 NOVEMBER 1932

National As Democrat Franklin D Roosevelt wins the presidential election by a landslide, several influential Westerners also gain office. Nevada Democrat Pat McCarran is elected to the Senate, where he will oppose New Deal programs except for those that directly benefit Nevada. A future chairman of the Senate Judiciary Committee and a promoter of the Civil Aeronautics Act, he is also a committed anti-communist, responsible for the 1950 Internal Security Act and the 1952 McCarran-Walter Act, the restrictive cold-war immigration measure. In Kansas, millionaire oil man and progressive Republican Alf Landon is elected to his first term as governor; four years later he will oppose FDR in the presidential race. And in North Dakota, William Langer becomes governor and leads an aggressive fight against farm foreclosures, also placing embargoes on wheat.

OTHER EVENTS OF 1932

Arts/Culture Laura Ingalls Wilder publishes her *The Little House in the Big Woods*, a largely autobiographical account of pioneering days. This book is followed by *The Little House on the Prairie* (1935), and others in the children's series. In Oakland, California, the association of art photographers known as Group F 64 is founded by Edward Weston, Ansel Adams, Willard Van Dyke, Imogen Cunningham, Sonya Noskowiak, John Paul Edmonds, and Henry Swift. Other regional photographers associated with the group are Dorothea Lange, Peter Stackpole, Alma Lavenson, and Brett Weston. They hold their first formal exhibition at San Francisco's M H de Young Memorial Museum.

Conservation In Arizona, the Grand Canyon is declared a national monument; in Colorado, 34,980 acres of the nation's most magnificent sand dunes are established as the Great Sand Dunes National Monument.

Indians A landmark publication is *Black Elk Speaks*, the oral biography of the Oglala Sioux holy man recorded in 1930 by Nebraska poet John Neihardt. Wyoming's Black Elk, a cousin of Crazy Horse, had fought as a teenager in the battle of Little Big Horn and later had toured the United States and Europe with Buffalo Bill's Wild West Show. In a powerful mystical vision, Black Elk sees the Sioux tragedy as resulting from the tribal fallaway from a life of harmony with nature, coinciding with an increasing concern with material things. By recounting his story, he hopes to preserve Sioux tradition and to help the Sioux regain spiritual well-being. As the last living bearer of such knowledge, Black Elk later details the Sioux religion for anthropologist Joseph E Brown in *The Sacred Pipe* (1953).

3 JANUARY 1933

North Dakota Minnie Davenport Craig, a member of the Republican National Committee, is chosen the first woman Speaker of the House in the state legislature. Her term of office extends for one session, through 31 March.

15 JANUARY 1933

Social Change In Iowa's utopian community the Amana Colony, money changes hands for the first time since its 1855 foundation. Beset by economic hard times, the 30,000-acre colony of seven villages comprising farms, stores, bakeries, and woolen mills votes to abandon the communal life and reorganize on a capitalist basis, with each member receiving stock in the newly created corporation. The Amana ventures – also including handcrafted furniture, refrigeration units, meat shops, and wineries – eventually become a thriving empire.

19 JANUARY 1933

Finance Iowa Governor Clyde Herring issues a proclamation asking mortgage holders to refrain from foreclosures until the state legislature has had time to enact new economic emergency laws. On 30 January New York Life Insurance Company announces suspension of foreclosures pending legislation, not only in Iowa but also in the other states and Canada. (On 4 January a company agent at a Le Mars foreclosure sale had been forced to raise his bid to cover the remaining mortgage by a mob of farmers who threatened to hang him.) Other companies also adopt the moratorium.

11 FEBRUARY 1933

Conservation By proclamation, President Hoover establishes 2981 square miles of the nation's

The magnificent Grand Canyon of the Colorado.

hottest and lowest dry land, in California and southwestern Nevada, as Death Valley National Monument. Other areas thus established in 1933 are southeastern Arizona's Saguaro National Monument, featuring the monumental saguaro cactus; southwestern Colorado's Black Canyon of the Gunnison National Monument, featuring a spectacular geological display in a deep gorge; New Mexico's White Sands National Monument, featuring the largest of the region's rare gypsum deserts; and southwestern Utah's Cedar Breaks National Monument, featuring a colossal natural amphitheater eroded into colorful limestone cliffs.

4 MARCH 1933

National Franklin Delano Roosevelt is inaugurated the nation's thirty-second president, with Texan John 'Cactus Jack' Nance Garner as his vice-president. In his First Hundred Days, Roosevelt moves quickly to combat the Depression by creating a remarkable series of New Deal 'alphabet agencies.' Among his appointees is Utah executive and former governor George Henry Dern who, as Secretary of War, enlarges and motorizes the nation's army. FDR, whose favorite song is 'Home on the Range,' also names former Arizona Congressman Lewis Douglas to direct the Bureau of the Budget, and Iowa's Henry Wallace becomes Agriculture Secretary.

10 MARCH 1933

Environment The nation's second-most-destructive urban earthquake to date, centered in Long Beach, California, kills 118 and leaves property damages of $60 million. The catastrophe leads to changes in Los Angeles and other southern California building codes, with building heights limited to 150 feet.

27 MARCH 1933

Agriculture Roosevelt issues an executive order abolishing the Federal Farm Loan Board and consolidating the federal agricultural credit agencies into a new single agency, the Farm Credit Administration. On 16 June Congress passes the Farm Credit Act, designed to help agricultural production and marketing by refinancing farm mortgages at low interest rates for longer periods of time.

12 MAY 1933

Agriculture FDR signs the Agricultural Adjustment Act, designed to provide federal assistance to farmers, who are to restrict production of some crops to reduce surpluses and to receive cash payments for the uncultivated acreage. This act, which establishes the Agricultural Adjustment Administration, sets parity prices for specific basic commodities. Enthusiastic farmers plow under corn, cotton, and other crops, and butcher millions of pigs, whose meat goes to the needy or is turned into fertilizer. This legislation will bring the New Deal its harshest criticism.

WILLIAM H ('ALFALFA BILL') MURRAY, 1869-1956

In the course of a busy and adventurous lifetime, Bill Murray had much to do with bringing Oklahoma into the Union and, as its governor, guiding its course as a state. Murray was born in Grayson County, Texas, on 21 November 1869, and left home at 12 to work as a laborer in various menial jobs. Becoming ambitious, he studied here and there and by 1889 had earned a college degree in Texas. After starting a newspaper in the state, he took up law and in 1898 moved to Indian Territory (later Oklahoma) to begin practice.

Murray thrived as a lawyer, and within a few years was involved with Indian causes – a lifelong interest – and with the delegations that shepherded Oklahoma to statehood. Defeated for the governorship in 1910, he went to Congress for a term; by then he was already a tireless advocate of growing alfalfa for fodder, whence his nickname. Thereafter he traveled in South America, finally settling for six years in Bolivia. He returned to Oklahoma in 1930 to run for governor again and was elected by a huge majority, despite the opposition of every major newspaper in the state. His four years as governor were marked by efforts to alleviate the effects of the Depression and to promote states' rights, as well as bringing Oklahoma out of debt. In 1936 he retired to farm and to write on questions of politics, dying in Oklahoma in 1956.

---

27 JUNE 1933

Sports The California legislature legalizes horse racing and betting on races. The first licensed track in Los Angeles County is Santa Anita, which opens 25 December 1934. It is immensely successful, drawing business away from illegal bookies and from the Mexican-border area tracks at Agua Caliente and Tijuana.

23 JULY 1933

Transportation Aviator Wiley Post, a former Texas farmer and Oklahoma oil driller, arrives at New York after circling the earth in 7 days 19 hours. In becoming the first solo flier to circumnavigate the globe, Post shaves just over 21 hours off the previous record, established by himself and Harold Gatty in 1931 in the same purple-and-white monoplane, *Winnie Mae*. On the flight, Post averages 127 miles per hour, makes 10 refueling stops, and passes over Siberia and Alaska.

18 October 1933

Agriculture FDR establishes the Commodity Credit Corporation by executive order. The agency is organized under the Agricultural Adjustment Administration with an initial capitalization of $3 million, which it lends to farmers on their crops, thus supporting farm prices. Average past prices determine present payments; if market prices fall, farmers can turn over their crops to the corporation for disposal, with their government absorbing the loss. If prices rise, farmers can sell their crops, repay the loans, and keep the profit.

5 NOVEMBER 1933

Agriculture The end to farmers' problems is not yet at hand. Near Lawton, Iowa, farm strike picketers, said to be predominantly communists from Sioux City, stop an interstate cattle train and release the animals. They then burn a railway bridge six miles north of Sioux City.

11 NOVEMBER 1933

Environment A major dust storm sweeps across South Dakota and reaches Albany, New York, two days later. Over the 1930s, dust storms sweep topsoil away from farms from Texas to the Canadian border. Decades of overplanting and overplowing have made the soil so powdery that some 150,000 square miles of western farm land become a near desert.

5 DECEMBER 1933

Life/Customs Utah is the thirty-sixth state to ratify the Twenty-first Amendment, making the repeal of Prohibition official.

15 DECEMBER 1933

Arts/Culture Serge Koussevitzky conducts the Boston Symphony Orchestra in the premiere performance of Emerson Whithorne's *Moon Trail*, a suite of four symphonic sketches impressionistically evoking a landscape of the American West.

DECEMBER 1933

Life/Customs In a scheme to solve the Depression, Long Beach, California, physician Francis Townsend proposes an old-age pension plan to help the elderly poor, by which the government would pay $200 per month to those over 60. Recipients are required to spend the whole amount in the United States within the month; this will stimulate the national economy toward recovery. Although economists dispute the plan's effect, the idea catches on: over the next two years, some 2.5 million people join Townsend Clubs to press for legislative passage of the plan. Several variations are defeated in Congress, and with the 1935 passage of the Social Security Act, the Townsend movement loses urgency.

OTHER EVENTS OF 1933

International The United States and Mexico ratify a treaty to regulate the course of the Rio Grande River from El Paso to Fort Quitman, and to build a dam at Caballo to control flood waters.

National Utah becomes the thirty-sixth state to ratify the twenty-first Amendment to the Constitution, repealing Prohibition, the 'noble experiment,' which had been in effect since 1920.

Former boom town Carson City, Nevada.

CHRONOLOGY

Science/Technology Zoologist and geneticist Thomas Hunt Morgan, of the California Institute of Technology, wins the Nobel Prize for his studies of the mechanism of heredity by experimenting with the common fruit fly. In Laguna Beach, California, teenager Howard Wilson finds a prehistoric skull. In an attempt to identify it, he sends it to various American and European experts, who are mystified. Not until 1967 does a University of California radiocarbon analysis of the skull – suggested by anthropologist Louis Leakey – date it at between 18,620 and 15,680 years old. The Laguna skull is the oldest direct evidence to date of prehistoric man, or woman in this case, in North America.

31 JANUARY 1934
Agriculture Congress passes the Farm Mortgage Refinancing Act, establishing the Federal Farm Mortgage Corporation (FFMC) under the Farm Credit Administration. The FFMC is to issue up to $2 billion in bonds that will be exchanged for consolidated farm loan bonds, thus facilitating the refinancing of farm debts.

23 FEBRUARY 1934
Agriculture In passing the Crop Loan Act, Congress sets aside $40 million to be lent by the Farm Credit Administration to farmers in 1934 for planting and harvesting crops.

6 APRIL 1934
Arts/Culture In Philadelphia, the Monte Carlo Ballet premieres *Union Pacific* by composer Nicolas Nabokov, who adapts American Western songs for local color.

16 APRIL 1934
Oklahoma The National Guard carries out the governor's order to stop delinquent-tax sales of real estate.

23 APRIL 1934
National North Dakota Senator Gerald Nye becomes chairman of the Senate Munitions Investigation Committee. Public hearings through 1936 reveal the large profits reaped by World War I-era arms manufacturers, and consequently increase isolationist influence, particularly in the face of World War II.

9 MAY 1934
Labor The summer of 1934 will witness an epidemic of strikes. The Houston, Texas, longshoreman's strike of 30 April – termed a 'waterfront reign of terror' – is followed by a walkout of 12,000 of San Francisco's maritime workers on the issue of an open shop. As the strike continues, 2000 National Guardsmen move in on 5 July; the protest also spreads to Portland, Oregon, and Seattle, Washington. On 16 July supporters of the maritime workers begin the nation's first general strike, as 100,000 union workers leave their jobs. Nearly all San Francisco restaurants close, and some food stores are looted, while National Guard tanks and machine guns are placed at strategic points. In Oakland, citizen-vigilantes guard food and milk supplies. Labor leaders call off the general strike on 19 July; on 31 July the longshoremen finally return to work in San Francisco and other Pacific Coast ports.

23 MAY 1934
Western Lore Outlaws Bonnie Parker and Clyde Barrow are gunned down outside of Plain Dealing, Louisiana, by Frank Hamer, one of the last of the great Texas Rangers, and his men. During their heyday, since 1932, the youthful pair have killed at least 12 persons, 9 of them law officers, while robbing numerous banks in the Southwestern states.

12 JUNE 1934
Agriculture Congress adopts the Farm Mortgage Foreclosure Act, allowing the Land Bank Commission to make loans to foreclosed farmers so they can regain control of their properties.

17 JUNE 1934
North Dakota Governor William Langer and four others are convicted of soliciting federal employees for political contributions. Langer refuses to resign, and a few days later is renominated in the primaries. Replaced as governor on 19 July, he is later vindicated, re-elected governor in 1936, and elected to the US Senate in 1940, where he serves until 1959 as a leading isolationist.

18 JUNE 1934
Indians The Indian Reorganization (Wheeler-Howard) Act returns to various tribes reservation lands that had been for sale.

19 JUNE 1934
Finance A victory for the Western populist-free money faction comes with passage of the Silver Purchase Act. Chiefly benefiting farmers who call for additional inflation and silver producers, the act permits an increase in the monetary value of the Treasury's silver holdings, nationalization of silver stocks, and federal purchases of US and imported silver. On 9 August the Treasury begins to buy all US silver at a set price, concurrently issuing about $80 million in silver certificates.

28 JUNE 1934
Agriculture The Taylor Grazing Act sets aside 8 million (later up to 142 million) acres of public land under jurisdiction of the Interior Department for livestock grazing purposes.

23 JULY 1934
Agriculture In drought areas of Oklahoma and Kansas, the Federal Government is buying and

shipping 200,000 cattle for resale or to slaughter-houses. In other plains states, the earth is scorched, crops are damaged, and cattle are perishing. In Texas drought areas, cattle are being shot at the rate of 1000 per day. Deep wells are being drilled, and about 1.6 million people are receiving support from federal relief programs.

29 JULY 1934
Environment Forest fires sweep large tracts in Montana, Idaho, and Washington, also destroying thousands of acres of grain and pasture land.

AUGUST 1934
Transportation In Houston, Texas, the opening of the Intercoastal Waterway gives shippers access to Mississippi River traffic, eventually making Houston the nation's third largest port. The Intracoastal Canal connects the Sabine River to Galveston Bay.

3 AUGUST 1934
National At Bonneville, Oregon, after his return from Hawaii, President Roosevelt visits the site of the proposed $31-million hydroelectric and navigation dam, pledging the government to greater hydroelectric development and to shifting control over such projects to local authorities. FDR tours the drought states on his way back to Washington, DC.

6 AUGUST 1934
Finance It is revealed that the government is transferring all of the gold from the San Francisco Mint – some $3 billion in bullion – to the Denver Mint. The move is completed by 31 August.

22 AUGUST 1934
Agriculture In Arizona's Salt River Valley, American-born farmers threaten the forcible expulsion of Japanese and Hindu farmers who cultivate land mostly under lease from American owners, in violation of the state law forbidding aliens to use or possess agricultural lands.

28 AUGUST 1934
California The novelist, muckraker, and eccentric socialist Upton Sinclair wins the Democratic nomination for governor on the radical platform of 'End Poverty in California,' or EPIC. He narrowly loses the November election.

30 OCTOBER 1934
Colorado In Denver, hunger marchers are clubbed and dispersed by the police, with many injuries on both sides.

6 NOVEMBER 1934
Nebraska The legislature adopts a unicameral nonpartisan form of government, ending 20 years of discussion, in an attempt to eliminate the delays and deadlocks of a two-house body. The new sys-

A California ghost town.

tem is more economical in that fewer members are elected after redistricting, but it also does away with checks and balances, making the body more susceptible to outside influence. This experiment makes the state a focus of interest for public officials and political scientists.

12 NOVEMBER 1934
Arizona A threat of war over the Parker Dam site ends as the Federal Reclamation Bureau stops construction on Arizona territory. Opposing the diversion of Colorado River water to California, Governor E B Moeur had proclaimed martial law and called out the National Guard to prevent the dam's construction. After several weeks, the soldiers are withdrawn, and the Supreme Court subsequently renders a decision against the Arizona position on water rights.

16 NOVEMBER 1934
Arts/Culture Leopold Stokowski conducts the premiere of Harl McDonald's *First Symphony*, subtitled *The Santa Fe Trail*. The composition impressionistically evokes the frontier era and landscape of the American West.

16 DECEMBER 1934
California Work begins on the All-American Canal from the Colorado River to west of Calexico.

CHRONOLOGY

20 DECEMBER 1934
Arts/Culture The New York Philharmonic premieres Philip James's symphonic overture *Bret Harte*, inspired by Harte's Western adventure stories.

OTHER EVENTS OF 1934
Arts/Culture Texan John Lomax is appointed the first honorary curator of the Library of Congress Archive of American Folk Music. A lifelong collector and recorder of such music, Lomax published the 1910 landmark collection *Cowboy Songs*, which included for the first time such tunes as 'Git Along, Little Dogies,' and 'Home on the Range.'
Conservation Work begins on the Yuma-Gila reclamation project in Arizona.

11 JANUARY 1935
Transportation Kansas-born Amelia Earhart leaves Honolulu on the first solo flight by a woman between Hawaii and California. Some 16 hours later she lands in Oakland.

SPRING 1935
Agriculture Socialist Norman Thomas organizes the Southern Tenant Farmers Union to procure government benefits for tenant farmers and to halt their eviction by land owners who receive federal payments for fallow fields. The resulting violence spreads to Colorado sugar beet harvests, the Arizona lettuce fields, and California's orange groves.

25 APRIL 1935
Oregon Fire destroys the 60-year-old capitol building in Salem. The structure will be replaced, with the aid of federal funds, by an art-deco style capitol designed by Francis Keally.

27 APRIL 1935
Agriculture An Act of Congress establishes the Soil Conservation Service, under the Department of Agriculture, to prevent recurrence of the dust storms that have ravaged the Western states.

MAY 1935
New Mexico Governor Clyde Tingley appoints Dennis Chavez to fill a vacant US Senate seat, which he is to hold for the rest of his life. The most important Spanish American senator of his era, Chavez supports New Deal programs, higher education, agriculture, water development, and Indian causes. In 1966, the state honors him with a bronze statue in the capitol's rotunda.

1 MAY 1935
Alaska The first party of federally sponsored settlers leaves San Francisco for Alaska, to be allotted lands in the Matanuska Valley, near Anchorage, for dairy and crop production. Among the 300 are 64 children and 100 women; the ship also carries lumber for the settlers' houses.

WESTERN ART AND THE NEW DEAL

The job-creating programs of the Roosevelt Administration also put artists back to work, and the result was a remarkable and enduring testament to Western Americana. The nation's first such completed project was San Francisco's Coit Tower, a Telegraph Hill memorial to the city's firemen, which opened to the public on 14 October 1934 amid a storm of protest. The tower's murals, by some 20 regional painters who depicted scenes of agriculture and labor, among other subjects, included several controversial details, among them a hammer and sickle, which were finally painted over. Similar government-supported mural projects provided work for unemployed artists throughout the West. The one that received the most favorable national notice was the series of murals Grant Wood created in 1934 for Iowa State Library at Ames. The Public Works of Art Project also employed about 70 Southwestern and Plains Indians. The Kiowa erected murals recording tribal rites at two state colleges, and in the state historical society building in Oklahoma. New Mexico's Santa Fe and Albuquerque Indians also painted murals, crafted textiles, and made pottery for such Indian Service buildings as schools, hospitals, and community centers. Public-arts patronage also inspired a Kansas newspaper campaign led by editor William Allen White, resulting in the offer of a $20,000 commission to native Kansan and nationally known regionalist painter John S Curry to paint a series of murals in the state capitol. The majority of the public murals in Western post offices and other civic buildings depicted the idealized history and mythology of the West – the pioneers, Pony Express, miners, and cowboys – as an inspiring example to struggling Westerners of the Depression era.

Dawes Glacier, one of Alaska's many ice fields.

25 MAY 1935
Agriculture Wheat farmers in 37 states vote on whether the government should continue its efforts to control their production. Over 86 percent of the vote favors continuance. A similar vote occurs on 26 October, when farmers in 16 corn- and hog-growing states vote 6 to 1 for continuation of Agricultural Adjustment Administration programs.

22 JULY 1935
Agriculture In South Dakota, 19,000 heads of families are removed from the state relief rolls in a move to force them to seek employment in the harvest fields. On 7 August able-bodied Texans are ordered to quit relief rolls for cotton-picking jobs. On 29 November the federal dole, in effect since May 1933, ends after paying almost $3.7 million in benefits.

15 AUGUST 1935
Life/Customs The nation is shocked as Will Rogers and Wiley Post die in a plane crash off Point Barrow, Alaska. One of the era's most famous public figures, Rogers, born in Oklahoma of Cherokee ancestry, was revered as an entertainer, Western humorist, newspaper commentator, and political satirist. He starred in 15 films, wrote 7 books, published over 1000 newspaper articles, was active in charity work, and was an enthusiastic promoter of commercial aviation. On 4 November 1938, the Will Rogers Memorial Museum is dedicated in Claremore, Oklahoma.

26 AUGUST 1935
Indians Congress grants Indian tribes the right to obtain judicial review by the US Court of Claims in cases of treaty violation. Previously, Indians had been unable to sue in the courts and had to rely instead on legislative determination of their claims.

2 OCTOBER 1935
California In San Diego, from the deck of the cruiser *Houston*, President Roosevelt watches the largest tactical maneuver in US naval history, as every arm of the services demonstrates the part it would play in a modern battle – 129 warships, 449 planes, and 50,000 men execute a mock attack.

22 NOVEMBER 1935
Transportation With the departure of the *China Clipper*, Pan American Airways inaugurates trans-Pacific air service from San Francisco to Manila.

OTHER EVENTS OF 1935
Washington The 'blanket primary' replaces the closed primary, so that voters can cast their ballots for any candidate, regardless of party affiliation.
Indians On South Dakota's Rosebud Reservation, a repayment cattle program designed to put Indian families into ranching, begins. Young men

receive cattle with the stipulation that as their herd increases, they return part of the increase until full repayment is made in cattle. These returned cattle are given to other Indians, who follow the same procedure. By 1948 the number of cattle owned by the reservation Indians increases from 3144 to 17,338.

29 FEBRUARY 1936
Agriculture As a substitute for the invalidated Agricultural Adjustment Act, Congress passes the Soil Conservation and Domestic Allotment Act. Crops are still restricted, but on the basis of soil conservation. Participating farmers are paid for leasing their fallow acres to the government, and tenant farmers and sharecroppers are to receive part of the payments.

10 APRIL 1936
International General Plutarco Elias Calles, former Mexican president, is arrested and deported to the United States by the order of President Lazaro Cardenas. He arrives by plane, along with others arrested by Mexican military authorities, in Brownsville, Texas.

9-12 JUNE 1936
National The Republican national convention choses Kansas Governor Alfred E 'Alf' Landon as presidential candidate. The Socialists choose Norman Thomas, and the Communists Earl Browder. On 19 June North Dakota Congressman William Lemke announces his candidacy on the ticket of the Union Party, a new populist coalition formed by followers of the Reverend Charles Coughlin, Francis Townsend, and Gerald L K Smith. Father Coughlin's National Union for Social Justice will hold its own conventionon 14 August and endorse Lemke, but his new movement wins little support.

17 JUNE 1936
Alaska Temperatures as high as 110 degrees Fahrenheit are recorded, as a wide area of the far north continues to experience unusual heat.

1 JULY 1936
International At Nuevo Laredo, Mexico, Vice-President Garner and General Eduardo Hay, Mexican Minister of Foreign Affairs, ceremonially open the International Bridge, also opening to traffic the $17-million highway linking the Texas border and Mexico City.

AUGUST 1936
Nebraska Near Omaha, Boys Town, also known as Father Flanagan's Home for Homeless Boys, is incorporated as a village. Contributed to by William Randolph Hearst, Jack Dempsey, Will Rogers and others, the 320-acre community accommodating 275 boys receives nationwide publicity for its techniques of teaching self-reliance and character.

CHRONOLOGY

9 AUGUST 1936
Colorado In Breckenridge, Governor E C Johnson unfurls the US flag and declares American sovereignty over 1300 square miles of mountain territory extending for nearly 70 miles. The tract has been 'no man's territory' since the 1803 Louisiana Purchase.

9 OCTOBER 1936
Science/Technology Flashing 266 miles across mountain and desert, electric power from Boulder (later Hoover) Dam comes to Los Angeles, flooding the city with light. The dam, the world's highest to date, creates 115-mile-long Lake Meade, whose water will irrigate one million acres in California, Arizona, and Nevada. A colossal aqueduct also brings drinking water to 10 million people in the Los Angeles areas.

3 NOVEMBER 1936
National In a Democratic landslide, President Roosevelt and Vice-President Garner are elected to a second term. In Western races, Texan Lyndon Baines Johnson wins a congressional seat, and in South Dakota, liberal Democrat George McGovern is the only Democrat elected to Congress between 1936 and 1970.

12 NOVEMBER 1936
Transportation The $77-million San Francisco-Oakland Bridge, the longest to date over navigable waters, is dedicated by California Governor Frank Merriam, as President Roosevelt presses a button in Washington, DC, opening the span to traffic.

21 DECEMBER 1936
Sports In Sun Valley, Idaho, the nation's first luxury ski resort opens to snowless slopes near the old mining town of Ketcham. Developed by W Averell Harriman for the Union Pacific Railroad, the resort thrives through publicity and glamorous patrons and becomes the model for others – including Colorado's Aspen and Vail, and California's Mammoth Mountain. Skiing will become an important component of the Western tourism industry.

OTHER EVENTS OF 1936
Conservation A spectacular southeastern California desert area of 504,720 acres is established as the Joshua Tree National Monument.

18 MARCH 1937
Texas In New London, a natural gas explosion destroys the public school, killing 43 students and 14 teachers. The blast, caused by a leak, lifts the roof, which falls into the building.

29 MARCH 1937
Labor In the Washington State case of *West Coast Hotel v Parrish*, the US Supreme Court upholds the principle of minimum wage for women.

11 APRIL 1937
Labor In Galena, Kansas, nine men are shot down in front of the headquarters of the International Mine, Mill and Smelter Workers Union, a CIO affiliate, climaxing a day in which 4000 area miners of the tristate lead and zinc mining district oppose CIO organization efforts in a pick-handle-wielding demonstration.

14 APRIL 1937
Arts/Culture In Provo, Utah, composer William F Hanson conducts the premiere of his three-act opera *The Bleeding Heart of Timpanoyos*, based on an Indian theme and musical techniques.

23 APRIL 1937
Labor In Stockton, California, 50 persons are injured in a riot by cannery workers. Police use shotguns and tear gas to enforce a truce. Work at the Ford Motor Company's plant at Richmond, California, is halted by 600 sit-down strikers. Following nationwide strikes by United Automobile Workers and sympathizers, the plant finally reopens on 7 June. (On 7 February 1939, the Supreme Court declares sit-down strikes unconstitutional.)

1 JULY 1937
Transportation While on a round-the-world flight that left Oakland, California, on 17 March, Amelia Earhart sends her last radio message after leaving Lae, New Guinea. Earhart reports that she is over the Pacific with a half hour's fuel supply and no sight of land, 'position doubtful.' From 2 to 18 July, US warships and planes conduct a search, but Earhart and her navigator, Fred Noonan, are never found.

22 JULY 1937
Agriculture The Bankhead-Jones Farm Tenant Act creates the Farm Security Administration (FSA) to oversee the Resettlement Administration. The Act also establishes a loan program to assist tenant farmers, sharecroppers, and farm workers in acquiring farms of their own, and regulates wages and working conditions of migrant labor.

28 SEPTEMBER 1937
Industry President Roosevelt dedicates the $81.8-million Bonneville Dam on Oregon's Columbia River. Wartime industry, centered in Portland, will rely on cheap hydroelectric power for ship building, chemical and metallurgical processing plants, and public construction.
Arts/Culture On the same day, FDR dedicates the Mt Hood recreational center called Timberline Lodge, constructed by WPA craftsmen and artists. It opens to the public on 4 February 1938.

OTHER EVENTS OF 1937
Industry Andre Gagnon, 'the Father of Modern Sawmills' and inventor of the Gagnon bandsaw, dies at 93 in Portland, Oregon.

Amelia Earhart at Lockheed's Burbank plant inspecting her plane.

Arts/Culture Conrad Richter publishes *Sea of Grass*, an elegaic novel of the conflict between cattlemen and farmers for control of the open range. His 1953 *The Light in the Forest* is based on stories of whites captured by Indians. Edward Weston receives the first Guggenheim Fellowship ever awarded to a photographer: he produces the book *California and the West*. Near Scottsdale, Arizona, architect Frank Lloyd Wright builds his winter headquarters, Taliesin West, of desert rubblestone.

Life/Customs Ronald Reagan, a sportscaster from Des Moines, Iowa, begins a Hollywood acting career that brings him roles – usually as the good guy who loses the girl – in 50 films, most of them grade B.

Conservation In southern Arizona, a 328,691-acre tract of the Sonora Desert featuring rare species of plant and animal life is declared the Organ Pipe Cactus National Monument. In southern Utah, Capitol Reef National Monument is established.

LYNN JOSEPH FRAZIER, 1874-1947

In a long career of tireless labor on behalf of farmers, Lynn Frazier was branded a radical, a socialist, a Communist, and worse. He was also one of the first state officials in American history to be recalled. Born in Steele County, Minnesota, on 21 December 1874, Frazier graduated from the University of North Dakota and pursued small farming and teaching for a few years. In 1915 he became a member of the Nonpartisan League in North Dakota, which promoted the interests of farmers and leaned toward socialist solutions. A dynamic gift for leadership and devotion to the cause brought Frazier the League nomination for governor in 1916, and he was swept into office.

Over the next seven years, Frazier promoted a flurry of progressive legislation, including women's suffrage, a state bank, state control of utilities, state farming operations, and farmers' insurance. But in 1921 bankers and other business elements managed to get Frazier and two others recalled in a special election. Next year the voters relented and sent Frazier to the Senate, where he remained until 1940. His efforts there were mainly on behalf of farming bills and disarmament. Frazier died in Maryland in 1947.

CHRONOLOGY

21 JANUARY 1938
Washington In Seattle Harbor, a peace activist drowns in an attempt to blow up the Japanese steamer *Hiye Maru* with a time bomb that fails to detonate.

16 FEBRUARY 1938
Agriculture The second Agricultural Adjustment Act seeks to curb continuing farm surpluses and price declines by limiting production and use of parity payments. The act also creates the Federal Crop Insurance Corporation (FCIC) as an Agricultural Department agency to insure producers, initially of wheat, against crops losses due to weather or disease.

18 MARCH 1938
International The Mexican Government nationalizes the properties of foreign oil companies. Financial settlements are not made until 1941.

20 MARCH 1938
National Following close upon Hitler's 13 March annexation of Austria, the US Navy's second large-scale war game in the mid-Pacific sector within a year is underway, beginning with the fleet's departure from San Pedro, California. An armada of 150 fighting ships and 500 aircraft, manned by 3600 officers and 55,000 men, has been maneuvering along the 5000-mile line from Alaska to Samoa by way of Hawaii to test the strength of the fleet and Hawaii's capability as the nation's westerly outpost. On 17 May the Vinson Naval Act commits the United States to a billion-dollar naval expansion over the next ten years.

Above: *Barges near Bonneville Dam, Oregon.*
Opposite: *Jeanette MacDonald and Nelson Eddy in the film* Girl of the Golden West.

26 MAY 1938
National Headed by Texas Congressman Martin Dies, the House Committee on Un-American Activies is established to investigate Communist, Nazi, Fascist and other organizations. New Deal agencies, labor unions, and the movie industry also come under HUAC scrutiny.

29 JUNE 1938
Conservation Washington State's Olympic National Park is established after a long struggle between the Interior Department, which sought to preserve the area's natural state, and the Forest Service, who sought to open the area to commercial lumber and mineral development. President Roosevelt, visiting the area in 1937, worked out a compromise between the factions. Also declared a national monument in 1938 are the Channel Islands, a wildlife refuge off southern California. The Pacific Northwest will be in the vanguard of conservation efforts for decades, along with California, which leads the way.

16 OCTOBER 1938
Arts/Culture In Chicago, the Ballet Caravan premieres the one-act ballet *Billy the Kid*, with music by Aaron Copland and scenario by Lincoln Kirstein. The score incorporates such cowboy songs as 'Git Along, Little Dogies,' 'Old Chisholm Trail,' and 'Bury Me Not on the Lone Prairie.'

CHRONOLOGY

Popular Western novelist Zane Grey.

OTHER EVENTS OF 1938

Arts/Culture The classic Western novelist Owen Wister dies. His 1902 book *The Virginian* has sold over 1.5 million copies by now, and is adapted to film (four times), Broadway, and later television. In the book he introduced such now-familiar motifs as the laconic hero, the mail-order bride, and the dude who goes West and comes to terms with frontier life. Wister, himself an Easterner, spent his summers in Wyoming, where a Grand Teton peak is named in his honor.

Indians In Wyoming the Shoshone tribe is granted nearly $6.4 million in claims against the Federal Government for land in the Shoshone reservation occupied by the Arapaho for six years. The decision clears the title to 2.3 million acres of Wyoming land, and gives legal status to the homes of over 1000 Arapaho.

16 FEBRUARY 1939

Arts/Culture In Denton, Texas, the short opera *Cynthia Parker* by Julia Smith premieres. The opera, which incorporates Indian music and dances, recounts the story of a girl abducted by Indians in Old Texas.

18 FEBRUARY 1939

California The Golden Gate International Exposition opens on man-made Treasure Island in San Francisco Bay. It celebrates completion of the Golden Gate Bridge on 27 May 1937. After the exposition, the 400-acre island is taken over by the navy as a training camp and embarkation point.

MARCH 1939

Arts/Culture In the greatest year for the film Western, John Ford's classic *Stagecoach* opens in New York's Radio City Music Hall. Hollywood has been producing 500 films a year, 100 of them frontier tales.

3 SEPTEMBER 1939

World War II The conflict begins, as Great Britain and France declare war on Hitler's Germany, which is invading Poland. US involvement is strongly opposed by the vocal isolationist faction, which includes such Westerners as Idaho's William Borah, Montana's Burton Wheeler, and Nebraska's George Norris. The interventionists are led by Kansas newspaper editor William Allen White. Although he officially asserts US neutrality, President Roosevelt asked for a $1.3-billion defense budget on 5 January, steps up military production, in January 1940 sends military supplies to Great Britain, and signs the 11 March 1941 Lend-Lease Act to provide vital assistance to the Allies.

9 DECEMBER 1939

Arts/Culture In Seattle, Washington, the surrealistic composition *Imaginary Landscape No. 1*, by California's avant-garde composer John Cage, receives its first performance.

OTHER EVENTS OF 1939

Science/Technology The Nobel Prize in physics goes to South Dakota-born Ernest O Lawrence for his 1930 development of an atom smasher, the cyclotron, at the University of California. Lawrence will go on to play an important role in the development of the atomic bomb.

Arts/Culture In South Dakota, the first annual summer production of the Black Hills Passion Play takes place at Spearfish. A number of important literary events occur. Californian John Steinbeck receives the 1940 Pulitzer Prize in Literature for *The Grapes of Wrath*, a novel of dust-bowl migrants. Steinbeck, who will receive the 1962 Nobel Prize, uses California as a setting for such important works as *Tortilla Flat* (1935), *Cannery Row* (1945), and *East of Eden* (1952). California playwright and novelist William Saroyan wins the 1940 Pulitzer Prize for his drama *The Time of Your Life*, set in a San Francisco waterfront bar. Many of Saroyan's exuberant stories and plays are also set in California. Nathanael West publishes *The Day of the Locust*, a bitter satire of Hollywood life based on his own experiences as a scriptwriter. Mystery writer Raymond Chandler publishes his first big novel, *The Big Sleep*, introducing the tough wise-cracking detective Philip Marlowe, and making effective use of a seamy 1930s Los Angeles setting. Novelist Vardis Fisher will receive the Harper Novel Prize for his *Children of God*, an exposé of Mormon bigotry. Popular Western novelist Zane Grey dies, leaving behind 78 books, of which 17 are published posthumously. The best-known of

HOLLYWOOD IN THE 1930s AND 1940s

By the 1930s movie-making had become a fantastically profitable industry. Action-packed Westerns remained an enduring favorite, not only in the form of Grade-B films and serials, but also in such classic icons as *Stagecoach*, and such increasingly complex views of morality and history as *The Ox Bow Incident* and *Red River*. Characteristic of the Depression era were such genres as extravagant musicals starring Nebraska-born dancer Fred Astaire, or choreographed by Busby Berkeley; airy, glamorous comedies; and stylized gangster films: all provided escapist entertainment for millions of hard-pressed Americans. The 1934 imposition of a ratings system by the Roman Catholic Legion of Decency did little to dim the attraction of films, but as the US began to come out of the Depression, the film industry slumped: its overseas markets closed because of the war, and some of the familiar forms, such as musical comedy, had worn out their welcome. Meanwhile, however, hard times had brought literary lions like F Scott Fitzgerald

John Ford's classic Western Stagecoach.

and William Faulkner to screenwriting jobs in Hollywood.

When America entered World War II, Hollywood rallied to support the national effort, with war-bond selling tours by stars – comedienne Carol Lombard died in a 1942 plane crash near Las Vegas, Nevada, during such a tour – and by producing patriotic, flag-waving war movies – some 80 of them in 1942. Some of the classics included *Mrs Miniver, Casablanca*, and *Watch on the Rhine*. By 1944 many male stars – among then Clark Gable, James Stewart, Tyrone Power, Robert Taylor, Mickey Rooney, and Ronald Reagan – had joined up, as had directors Frank Capra, John Ford, William Wyler, and John Houston. Other film stars helped keep up morale by entertaining the troops at home – in such settings as the Stage Door Canteen – and abroad. Hollywood, the epitome of the glittering West, had gone to war.

his sentimentalized, moralizing works are *The Riders of the Purple Sage* (1912) and *The Thundering Herd* (1925).

Conservation Arizona's Bartlett Dam and New Mexico's Conchas Dam are completed.

15 MAY-NOVEMBER 1940
New Mexico The state celebrates the 400th anniversary of explorer Francisco Vásquez de Coronado with a folk festival, rodeo, series of concerts, and the historical play *Coronado Entrada*, which is also performed in Texas and Arizona.

24-28 JUNE 1940
National The Republicans nominate Wendell Willkie as presidential candidate, with Oregon Senator Charles NcNary as his vice-presidential running mate. On 15-19 July the Democrats renominate Roosevelt, this time with Iowan and former Secretary of Agriculture Henry Wallace as vice-presidential candidate.

27 AUGUST 1940
Arts/Culture Composer Meredith Willson conducts the San Francisco Symphony Orchestra in a

CHRONOLOGY

performance of his *Second Symphony*, subtitled *The Missions of California*. Also performed is the world premiere of his *Prelude to the Great Dictator*.

16 OCTOBER 1940
National Following the 16 September signing of the Selective Training and Service Act, the first call goes out for draft registration. As later reported, most of the able-bodied members of the Navaho tribe arrive in Gallup, New Mexico, on horseback, carrying rifles, packs, and food. The warriors are prepared to begin fighting Hitler, whom they call 'the mustache smeller,' immediately.

7 NOVEMBER 1940
Transportation In Tacoma, Washington, the Narrows Suspension Bridge collapses into Puget Sound after it is weakened by wind vibration.

15 NOVEMBER 1940
Labor In Downey, California, a 12-day airplane plant strike begins, halting $50-million worth of plane construction. On 23 December 1941, labor and industry unite to declare a no-strike policy in war-related industries.

DECEMBER 1940
Transportation In California, the first unit in a system of modern express highways through an urban region is inaugurated with the opening of the Arroyo Seco Parkway between Los Angeles and Pasadena. By the late 1950s, Los Angeles will have more automobiles per capita than any other city in the world.

OTHER EVENTS OF 1940
National Texan Sam Rayburn becomes Speaker of the House, a post he will occupy longer than any politician to date. A supporter of New Deal legislation, he will later help develop the principle of bipartisan foreign policy.
Arts/Culture In his novel *The Ox-Bow Incident*, Walter Van Tilburg Clark examines both frontier justice and the nature of fascism.
Conservation In California, King's Canyon is established as a national park. Fort Peck Dam is completed in Montana, part of a major hydroelectric project.

4 MARCH 1941
Arts/Culture Composer Wesley La Violette conducts the San Francisco Symphony Orchestra in the premiere performance of his symphonic poem *Music from the High Sierras*, which adapts old regional Spanish chants.

1 AUGUST 1941
California The Colorado Aqueduct brings water from Arizona's Parker Dam 240 miles across the Mohave Desert and the San Bernadino Mountains to the cities and towns of the Los Angeles Metropolitan Water District.

Albert Einstein's theories changed man's world view.

24 NOVEMBER 1941
California In *Edwards v California*, the Supreme Court finds the state 'anti-Okie' law, which bars penniless migrants, invalid.

7 DECEMBER 1941
World War II Japanese forces attack the US naval base at Pearl Harbor, Hawaii, sinking the battleships *Arizona, California, Oklahoma,* and *Utah,* and disabling much of the US Pacific fleet. Hawaii is immediately put under martial law.

8 DECEMBER 1941
World War II Congress votes to declare war on Japan. The sole dissenting vote is that of Montana Representative Jeannette Rankin, a pacifist who also voted against US entry into World War I on 6 April 1917.

OTHER EVENTS OF 1941
National Texan Tom Connally becomes chairman of the Senate Foreign Relations Committee, where he will play a pivotal role in supporting Roosevelt and Truman foreign policy through 1946.
Science/Technology In Topeka, Kansas, pioneering psychiatrist Karl Menninger establishes the Menninger Foundation, which will help transform the provincial city into a major center for training and research in the science of psychiatry. A professor at the University of Kansas, Menninger is also active in prison reform. In northwestern

Grand Coulee Dam, Washington State, part of the Columbia River Basin irrigation system.

Washington State, Grand Coulee Dam, the world's largest concrete dam to date, is completed after eight years of work.

Arts/Culture Singing cowboy Gene Autry is included among the box-office top ten. In Los Angeles, Igor Stravinsky conducts the premiere of his *Danses Concertantes*. Los Angeles becomes an international artistic and intellectual community with the arrival of such European émigrés as Thomas Mann, Franz Werfel, Alma Mahler, Bertolt Brecht, Aldous Huxley, and Arnold Schönberg.

19 FEBRUARY 1942
World War II By executive order, President Roosevelt authorizes the War Department to exclude some 110,000 Japanese-Americans from California, Oregon, Washington, and Arizona by moving them to inland relocation camps.

23 FEBRUARY 1942
World War II During FDR's 'fireside chat' via radio, Japanese submarines fire 12 to 15 shots in a 20-minute period at the Barnsdall Oil Refinery, 12 miles west of Santa Barbara, California. No one is hurt, and the only direct hit causes $500 damage. As the reality of war comes to US shores, anti-aircraft guns begin to rise around Los Angeles and San Francisco.

Cowboy singer and film star Gene Autry.

The Japanese attack on Pearl Harbor, Hawaii, 7 December 1941.

CHRONOLOGY

2 MAY 1942
Arts/Culture Composer Ernest Bacon conducts the premiere of his four-scene opera *A Tree on the Plains*, the saga of a Southwestern family that includes such Americanisms as a chewing-gum ballad.

21 NOVEMBER 1942
Transportation The 1523-mile Alcan Highway officially opens: it runs, through Canada to Fairbanks, Alaska, and serves as a military supply route.

OTHER EVENTS OF 1942
Arts/Culture Nebraska historian Mari Sandoz publishes *Crazy Horse*; an important later work will be his 1953 *Cheyenne Autumn*. A Creek Indian who has become rich through Oklahoma and Texas oil holdings establishes the Thomas Gilcrease Foundation: its Tulsa Museum (1949) will house one of the world's largest collections of Western painting and sculpture, Indian artifacts, and archaeological material.

3-21 JUNE 1942
World War II The Japanese occupy US Alaskan territory by taking Attu and Kiska in the westernmost Aleutians.

21 JUNE 1942
World War II A Japanese submarine ineffectively shells Fort Stevens on the Oregon coast, near the mouth of the Columbia River.

1-9 AUGUST 1942
Arts/Culture The world's leading composers – among them, Bela Bartok, Darius Milhaud, Frances

---

GEORGE SUTHERLAND, 1862-1942

In his time, conservative Supreme Court Justice from Utah George Sutherland was called 'the living voice of the Constitution.' With his insistence that laws must conform to the Constitution regardless of fairness or practicality, he became leader of a group of justices who resisted most of Roosevelt's New Deal legislation. Sutherland was born in Buckinghamshire, England, on 25 March 1862, and emigrated with his family to Provo, Utah, as an infant. Receiving a law degree in Michigan in 1883, he practiced in Utah for some years, becoming one of the most prominent lawyers in the state. He then mounted a ladder of political posts – state legislature, Congress, and the Senate in 1905-17 – that led to his Supreme Court appointment by President Warren G Harding in 1922.

With the coming of the Roosevelt administration, Sutherland and his cohorts rejected the constitutionality of the administration's efforts in union protection, labor and business regulation, social security, and retirement benefits. After weathering Roosevelt's threat to pack the court, Sutherland, in his last months before retirement in 1938, voted in favor of some of Roosevelt's laws on their second time around. He died in Massachusetts in 1942.

Poulenc, Ernest Bloch, Carlos Chavez, and Paul Hindemith – present new works at the 19th Festival of the International Society for Contemporary Music in Berkeley, California.

1 OCTOBER 1942
Transportation Robert Stanley pilots a successful test flight of the XP-59, the first US jet plane, at California's Muroc Army Base.

16 OCTOBER 1942
Arts/Culture In New York, the Ballets Russes de Monte Carlo premieres Aaron Copland's one-act ballet *Rodeo*.

24 MARCH-15 AUGUST 1943
World War II In the Aleutians, US forces use the new tactic of 'leapfrogging' from one island to another to retake Attu on 11 May and to reoccupy Kiska – already abandoned by the Japanese – on 15 August. This strategy will be effective in the Pacific war.

31 MARCH 1943
Arts/Culture The longest-running musical to date, Rodgers and Hammerstein's *Oklahoma!*, opens on Broadway. It will receive a special 1944 Pulitzer award.

JUNE 1943
Life/Customs In Los Angeles, the 'zoot suit riots' rage, as thousands of servicemen from San Diego and San Pedro attack anyone wearing a zoot suit – a stylish, wide-shouldered jacket topping balloon-shaped trousers. Most of the victims are Hispanic and black youths, and the violence began after repeated muggings of servicemen. Leading the police effort to control the unrest is black officer Tom Bradley, who becomes mayor of Los Angeles 30 years later.

19 JULY 1943
Industry The 'Big Inch,' the world's longest oil pipeline, running 1254 miles from Texas to Pennsylvania, is dedicated.

14 OCTOBER 1943
Arts/Culture Andre Kostelanetz conducts the premiere of Paul Creston's symphonic piece *Frontiers*, which evokes the westward trek of the pioneers.

OTHER EVENTS OF 1943
Arts/Culture Folk singer and dust-bowl survivor Woody Guthrie publishes his autobiographical *Bound for Glory*. Guthrie, who writes over 1000 folk songs, patterns his 'illiterate style' after Will Rogers'.

31 MARCH 1944
World War II Despite military opposition, Federal Judge D E Metzger lifts martial law in Hawaii.

Japanese residents of California are interned.

3 APRIL 1944

Black Experience In *Smith v Allwright*, the Supreme Court rules that blacks cannot be denied the right to vote in Texas Democratic primaries.

6 JUNE 1944

World War II Under Supreme Commander General Dwight D Eisenhower, the long-awaited invasion of Europe begins on D-Day, as the Allies land some 176,000 men on the Normandy coast of France.

12 JUNE 1944

Conservation In western Texas, the 708,221-acre Big Bend region is established as a national park.

17 JULY 1944

Black Experience In the California naval base at Port Chicago, an enormous explosion destroys two transport vessels loading ammunition and the base itself, damaging the nearby town, shattering windows 20 miles away, and lighting up the San Francisco sky. In this, the worst home-front disaster of the war, some 320 naval personnel – 200 of them black ammunition handlers – die instantly. These casualties point up the widespread racial discrimination practiced within the armed forces: most black GIs are shunted into menial jobs. The relatively few who are given combat roles, notably the all-black 761st Tank Battalion and the airmen of the 332nd Fighter Group, perform with distinction. Civilian blacks work in defense industries, thanks to Executive Order 8802, barring racial discrimination in government-funded employment.

AGRICULTURE

In the twentieth century, Western farmers and ranchers underwent a tumultuous upheaval. A 1920s agricultural depression ended the World War I boom, as ever-increasing production sent prices plunging. The 1930s New Deal programs attempted to end the epidemic of farm foreclosures and the rock-bottom prices farmers were receiving for their produce. The Agricultural Act of 12 May 1933 set the pattern by limiting production. On 28 July 1933, a White House ceremony marked the first payment under the Act, as President Roosevelt handed Nueces County, Texas, farmer William E Morris a $517 check as 'adjustment' pay for the 47 acres of cotton he had plowed back into the ground. Morris also received an option on 23 bales at 6 cents per pound.

As the New Deal sought to aid farmers by establishing a necessary balance between supply and demand with such radical legislation, critics ridiculed the destruction of produce while millions in the nation went hungry. The weather soon began to assist in limiting production. A single dust storm on 11 May 1934 blew away an estimated 300 million tons of topsoil. That spring, drought and storms had destroyed winter wheat at the rate of one million bushels a day. Some 60 percent of all the inhabitants of the Dust Bowl counties of South Dakota, Kansas, Nebraska, Colorado, Oklahoma, and Texas had to leave their homes during the decade. Discouraged farmers or 'Okies' – some 350,000 in all – headed toward California, where many became migrant farmworkers living in shantytowns. Their plight was vividly documented by such Farm Security Administration-sponsored photographers as Dorothea Lange, Walker Evans, Ben Shahn, and Arthur Rothstein. Only the 1940s war boom finally absorbed the Okies, and restored the Western farmer to prosperity for several more decades.

CHRONOLOGY

20 JULY 1944
World War II In San Diego, California, President Roosevelt views 10,000 amphibious troops in a landing exercise. The following day he leaves by cruiser for Hawaii, where he meets with Admiral Chester W Nimitz and General Douglas Mac-Arthur to plan Pacific War strategy. In a Honolulu naval hospital, he visits the amputee ward in the wheelchair necessitated by his polio paralysis. The cruiser then takes FDR to Adak, in the Aleutian Islands, where he proposes Alaska as a new frontier for settlement by returning soldiers once the war is over. This trip gives rise to the rumor that FDR sent back a destroyer at enormous cost to retrieve his dog, Fala, who had been left behind in the Aleutians. On 23 September, in one of his more memorable radio speeches he humorously denounces the story as a libelous fabrication by Republican opponents. Those who have been worried about FDR's health are thereby reassured that he has the strength to make still another presidential campaign.

OTHER EVENTS OF 1944
Arts/Culture Western novelist Max Brand dies as a war correspondent in Italy. Raised in California, the prolific Brand's best-known book was *Destry Rides Again*. The Rabelaisian writer Henry Miller, author of *Tropic of Cancer*, settles near Carmel, California: his 1957 *Big Sur* describes his life there. Ansel Adams publishes *Born Free and Equal*, a photographic essay documenting the Manzanar Japanese relocation camp in Owens Valley, California.

Above: *Open house at the Santa Fe Railway – 1938.*
Opposite top: *Mount Rushmore, South Dakota.*

12 APRIL 1945
National President Roosevelt dies, after beginning an unprecedented fourth term. Harry S Truman succeeds him.

18 APRIL 1945
International The Senate consents to a treaty guaranteeing Mexico rights to water from the Colorado River, in return for which the United States can divert water from the Rio Grande and Tijuana Rivers.

25 APRIL-26 JUNE 1945
International Delegates from 50 nations assemble in San Francisco to draft the charter for the United Nations, in an attempt to prevent another world war.

5 MAY 1945
World War II Near Lakeview, Oregon, a woman and five children die when they try to drag a Japanese balloon out of the woods and the bomb it is carrying explodes. The Japanese have been releasing such balloons for some time, but this is the only one that does harm.

7 MAY 1945
World War II Germany surrenders unconditionally, ending the war in Europe.

Controversial author Henry Miller in the 1930s.

WORLD WAR II AND THE WEST

Despite strong isolationism and the official neutrality of the Roosevelt Administration, the United States began to prepare for war in 1938, when the Army Air Corps established Colorado's Lowry Field as a technical school, with over 64,000 acres for practice bombing. It also took over Fort Logan, opened Buckley Field, and allotted the British RAF a field at La Junta. Also in 1938 a key agricultural event had occurred: a self-propelled version of the combine – which cuts, threshes, and cleans grain – was developed, replacing the tractor-driven combine. This flexible machine helped the West to meet the worldwide food needs of the wartime era. In March 1942 the government granted Henry Kaiser a $100 million loan to construct the first Pacific Coast integrated steel mill at Fontana, California. This permitted expansion of Los Angeles's aircraft factories, shipyards, and related industries to a state of intensified war production, providing well-paid jobs for hundreds of thousands hitherto unemployed. Kaiser also constructed six shipyards on the West Coast, and his pioneering prefabrication techniques produced Liberty ships in 4½ days and a new aircraft carrier per week.

The war had a vast impact on the West. Not only did the government set production and distribution goals – in October 1942, for example, the government suspended gold mining to concentrate on the mining of such strategic metals as lithium, manganese, tungsten, and uranium – but in a short time an enormous physical plant was constructed in the West – airfields, military training camps, prisoner-of-war camps, munitions and military equipment plants, and

research facilities. The Denver, Colorado, area got the Rocky Mountain Arsenal – the major US chemical warfare plant – as well as the Denver ordnance plant. Arizona got some of the largest fighter-pilot training centers – Luke Air Force Base and Williams Air Force Bomber Base. In Texas, Fort Bliss became the nation's air defense center. Pasadena's Jet Propulsion Laboratory and Sunnyvale's Ames Research Center were established in California. Los Alamos, New Mexico, became home to the Manhattan Project, which ultimately developed the atomic bomb.

CHRONOLOGY

Roy Rogers, Western singer and cowboy-movie star.

16 JULY 1945
World War II The first atomic bomb explodes near Alamogordo, New Mexico, marking success for the Manhattan Project at Los Alamos. The plutonium for the bomb was developed in a secret plant in Hanford, Washington. The bomb is then detonated over Hiroshima, Japan, on 6 August and over Nagasaki on 9 August. The Japanese sign surrender documents on 2 September.

25 SEPTEMBER 1945
World War II German prisoner of war Georg Gaertner escapes from Camp Deming, New Mexico. Using a false name, he works in Colorado, California, and Hawaii for 40 years, until he surrenders in September 1985 as the last fugitive POW in the United States. During the war, some 425,000 German POWs are jailed in 500 camps, mostly in the West.

25 NOVEMBER 1945
Arts/Culture Arturo Toscanini conducts the NBC Orchestra in the premiere of Elie Siegmeister's *Western Suite* – its five movements are 'Prairie Morning,' 'Round-Up,' 'Night-Herding,' 'Buckaroo,' and 'Riding Home.' This year Ernest Krenek composes the *a cappella* choral piece *The Santa Fe Time Table*.

OTHER EVENTS OF 1945
Arts/Culture Singing cowboy Roy Rogers makes the box-office top ten. He stars in films with his wife, Dale Evans, his horse, Trigger, and character actor Gabby Hayes.

7 MARCH 1946
Settling By executive order, President Truman reopens all public lands in the United States and Alaska, except those with uranium deposits, to homesteading.

16 MAY 1946
Arts/Culture In New York, Irving Berlin's musical comedy *Annie Get Your Gun* opens. It is based on the life of Annie Oakley, star of Buffalo Bill's Wild West Show.

2 JULY 1946
World War II A rousing New York reception greets the return of 500 members of the Japanese-American 442nd Regimental Combat Team. During three years in Italy and France, the Nisei outfit received more citations and decorations than any US Army unit of comparable size.

16 JULY 1946
Conservation The Bureau of Land Management comes into being, with responsibility for all surface and subsurface resources of US and Alaskan public lands.

30 JULY 1946
Science/Technology A captured German V-2 is the first rocket to reach a height of 100 miles at White Sands Proving Grounds in New Mexico. In 1945 Werner von Braun and other German missile scientists had arrived at Fort Bliss, Texas.

1 AUGUST 1946
Environment Tidal waves towering to 100 feet, and traveling 300 miles per hour, sweep a vast area in the Pacific from the Aleutians to Hawaii and the US West Coast. In Hawaii, 113 die. A series of underwater earthquakes centered near Dutch Harbor, Alaska, are the cause.

13 AUGUST 1946
Indians The Indian Claims Commission is established to settle all remaining Indian claims against the government since the nation's inception. This year, in *US v Tillamooks*, the Supreme Court rules in favor of several Oregon tribes who claim an involuntary and uncompensated loss of lands to the white man.

5 NOVEMBER 1946
California Attorney and naval officer Richard M Nixon enters politics by winning a Congressional seat. He will emerge as a strong anti-communist in his vigorous prosecution of the 1948-9 Alger Hiss case.

Above: *USS* Indianapolis *off Mare Island.*   Below: *PT boats patrol Alaska's Inside Passage.*

OTHER EVENTS OF 1946

Science/Technology   A Nobel Prize goes to geneticist Hermann Joseph Muller for the discovery of X-ray-produced mutations. (He conducted his studies on fruit flies at the University of Texas in the 1920s.) In Alaska, an international glaciological and environmental research program is established on Juneau Icefield. Earlier in the decade, the US Naval Arctic Research Laboratory was established in Barrow to study sea ice and other conditions.

Life/Customs   The ranch style house becomes popular with returning GIs and their new families.
Conservation   Montana's Custer Battlefield, on the Little Big Horn River, is declared a national monument.

18 JANUARY 1947

Arts/Culture   Leopold Stokowski conducts the New York Philharmonic in the premiere of Elie Siegmeister's *Prairie Legend.*

CHRONOLOGY

16 APRIL 1947
Texas In Texas City, the French freighter *Grand Camp* explodes while being loaded with fertilizer. The city is leveled and 500 die.

22 MAY 1947
Science/Technology At White Sands Proving Ground, New Mexico, the first ballistic missile, the *Corporal*, is tested. It flies 63 miles and responds successfully to guidance commands.

24 JUNE 1947
Ideas/Beliefs Airline pilot Kenneth Arnold reports sighting near Washington state's Mt Rainier nine unidentified flying objects 'like saucers.' Flying saucers capture the public imagination and lead to extensive inconclusive studies by the Air Force and by the 1952 Tucson, Arizona, Aerial Phenomena Research Organization. During the 1950s, UFOs inspire numerous quasi-religious cults such as the Brotherhood of the White Temple in Sedalia, Colorado; the Universarium Society of Portland, Oregon; and the Aetherius Society of Los Angeles.

14 OCTOBER 1947
Transportation At California's Muroc Air Force Base, Chuck Yeager is the first to break the sound barrier in the experimental Bell X-1 jet.

20 OCTOBER 1947
Ideas/Beliefs The House Un-American Activities Committee opens public hearings on alleged communist infiltration in Hollywood. Among the film stars called to testify is Screen Actors Guild president Ronald Reagan, who denies that leftists ever controlled the guild and refuses to name any communists. Many are blacklisted and become unemployable.

2 NOVEMBER 1947
Transportation Howard Hughes pilots the *Spruce Goose* – a colossal eight-engine plane with a 700-passenger capacity – in its only flight. Produced by Hughes and Henry Kaiser on a wartime contract, the plane is then stored in Long Beach, California. The Senate investigation damages Hughes's reputation as an aircraft designer, and he becomes a recluse.

8 NOVEMBER 1947
Agriculture The Friendship Train leaves Los Angeles on a cross-country tour to collect food for Europe. California's 1947 farm output exceeds that of almost any other state, even though a virus strain had almost destroyed the citrus industry several years earlier. Domestic restrictions remain in force, as US agriculture attempts to feed the starving peoples of the postwar world.

OTHER EVENTS OF 1947
Science/Technology Willard Libby and his University of California/Berkeley research team develop radiocarbon dating, to determine the age of fossil and archaeological remains. Libby will receive the 1960 Nobel Prize in Chemistry for this work.
Conservation In the North Dakota Badlands, 70,436 acres are declared the Theodore Roosevelt National Memorial Park.

12 JANUARY 1948
Black Experience With *Sipeul v University of Oklahoma*, the Supreme Court begins to strike down segregationist policies in higher education. Its decisions in the Texas *Sweatt v Painter* case and in *McLaurin v Oklahoma State Regents* (5 June 1950) continue this trend. On 30 July 1948, President Truman's Executive Order 9981 bars segregation in the armed forces; on 1 October the Court invalidates a California law barring interracial marriage.

APRIL 1948
Arts/Culture Oklahoma-born of Osage descent, Maria Tallchief becomes the leading dancer of the New York City Ballet, where her work (to 1965) makes her the most famous US ballerina of the era.

John Wayne and Montgomery Clift in Red River.

Maria Tallchief dances The Nutcracker.

3 JUNE 1948
Science/Technology At California's Mt Palomar Observatory, the world's largest reflecting telescope to date is dedicated.

2 NOVEMBER 1948
National In the election, President Truman unexpectedly defeats Thomas E Dewey, whose vice-presidential running mate is California Governor Earl Warren. Progressive Party candidate Henry Wallace receives one million popular votes. Oklahoma oilman Robert Kerr wins a Senate seat, as does Lyndon Johnson, after one of the narrowest primary victories on record. Johnson becomes the Democratic whip in 1951.

OTHER EVENTS OF 1948
Science/Technology The largest known single stone-mass meteorite falls in Norton County, Kansas.
Ideas/Beliefs In Tulsa, Oklahoma, controversial revivalist Oral Roberts founds the Oral Roberts Evangelistic Association, forerunner of the 1963 Oral Roberts University.
Arts/Culture Utah-born Bernard De Voto wins the Pulitzer Prize for *Across the Wide Missouri*, a history of the Rocky Mountain fur trade. Evelyn Waugh publishes *The Loved One*, a satire on bizarre California life styles and the systematic denial of death in American culture. Television's first hit series is *Hopalong Cassidy*; *The Lone Ranger* is also popular.

CHRONOLOGY

11 JANUARY 1949
Environment For the first time in weather-recording history, a heavy snowfall blankets Los Angeles, San Diego, Palm Springs, and Pasadena: California's citrus crop suffers heavy losses. On 24 January the Air Force begins Operation Haylift to drop feed to millions of starving cattle and sheep in Nevada, Colorado, Utah, South Dakota, Wyoming, and Nebraska. Some 79 people die in the month-long snow and ice storms, the worst ever known.

OTHER EVENTS OF 1949
Colorado After the USSR detonates its first atomic bomb, government policy makers seriously consider making Denver an alternate national capital, since it is less vulnerable to nuclear attack than Washington, DC.
Ideas/Beliefs In Los Angeles, Billy Graham achieves a sensational success in his Canvas Cathedral evangelistic crusade, converting 6000 of his 350,000-person audience. Promoted by the Hearst Newspapers, he will become a confidant of presidents.
Arts /Culture Walter Paepcke establishes the Institute for Humanistic Studies in the former silver mining camp of Aspen, Colorado, making Aspen a summertime cultural mecca.
Conservation Iowa-born ecologist Aldo Leopold's *A Sand County Almanac*, essays promoting a balance of nature and synthesis of science and morality, is published posthumously.
Indians The northern Arizona Navaho reservation is revealed as the nation's number-two source of uranium.

1 JULY 1950
International The United States begins active involvement in the Korean War by landing its first ground troops in South Korea.

OTHER EVENTS OF 1950
Agriculture In order to meet a growing demand, Congress permits 250 Basque sheepherders to enter the United States. Growing herds in California, Nevada, Wyoming, and southern Idaho lead to the authorization of 500 more Basques on three-year contracts in 1952.
Arts/Culture A B Guthrie's *The Way West* wins the Pulitzer Prize.
Sports The Associated Press name Texan Babe Didrikson Zaharias as the Woman Athlete of the Half Century. After her 1932 Olympic feats, she became a pioneering golf champion.
Indians Arizona surpasses Oklahoma for the first time as the state with the largest Indian population (65,761). On South Dakota's Cheyenne River Reservation, some 25,000 acres of tribal lands are leased for oil exploration.

JANUARY 1951
Life/Customs A Los Angeles construction com-

pany conducts a public ground-breaking ceremony for one of the nation's first undergound family fallout shelters. Business is brisk during the decade.

27 JANUARY 1951
Science/Technology The atomic bomb is exploded at the new Nevada test site, Frenchman and Yucca Flat, some 65 miles northwest of Las Vegas: the flash is seen as far away as San Francisco. During the atmospheric tests, which continue for six years, ground troops are stationed as close as 2500 yards from ground zero and moved even closer soon after the blast. Fears of radioactive fallout will lead to underground testing in 1957.

17 APRIL 1951
National After President Truman fires him for insubordination in the conduct of the Korean War, General MacArthur arrives in San Francisco to a tumultuous hero's welcome. Truman is burned in effigy in San Gabriel, California and Oklahoma, and the California legislature censures the president.

12 JULY 1951
Agriculture Truman signs a bill allowing the hiring of Mexican farm workers, or *braceros*, to meet US labor demands.

Above: *Traveling on the 'California Zephyr.'*
Opposite: *Los Angeles pioneered the freeway system.*

CHRONOLOGY

Square dancing dates back to rural England.

OTHER EVENTS OF 1951

Science/Technology At the University of California/Berkeley, Glenn Seaborg and Edwin McMillan share the Nobel Prize in Chemistry for discovering plutonium and other transuranic elements – americium, curium, berkelium, californium.

Arts/Culture Roscoe Carlyle Buley wins the Pulitzer Prize for his frontier history *The Old Northwest*. In New York, Lerner and Loew's musical comedy set in the Gold Rush era, *Paint Your Wagon*, opens.

17 APRIL 1952

California The Supreme Court declares the state's alien land law unconstitutional. On 17 October the state supreme court voids the University of California's loyalty oath and orders reinstatement of the 18 teachers fired because they refused to sign it.

4 NOVEMBER 1952

National In the presidential election, Texas-born, Kansas-raised Dwight D Eisenhower breaks the 20-year Democratic hold on the White House. California Senator Richard M Nixon, who saved his place on the ticket with his 23 September 'Checkers' television speech, will become vice-president. The only new Democrats to win Senate seats are Washington's Henry 'Scoop' Jackson, who will support a strong defense policy, and Montana's Mike Mansfield, who will become the

Senate's longest-serving majority leader to date. Also elected to the Senate is Arizona's conservative Republican Barry Goldwater.

12 NOVEMBER 1952

Conservation A 2745-acre site in southeastern Arizona is declared the Coronado National Monument. Arizona's Davis Dam, the last of four major barriers on the lower Colorado River, is dedicated this year.

18 FEBRUARY 1953

Arts/Culture Composer Leroy Robertson's oratorio *The Book of Mormon* premieres in Salt Lake City's Mormon Tabernacle.

11 APRIL 1953

National President Eisenhower names Oveta Culp Hobby, a Texas publisher and the first director of the Women's Army Corps, to the post of Secretary of the Department of Health, Education and Welfare, established on 1 April. Among his other appointments are Utah's Ivy Baker Priest as the nation's thirtieth Treasurer, and California Governor Earl Warren as Chief Justice of the Supreme Court.

22 MAY 1953

National After a prolonged political and legal battle between Texas and the Federal Government,

Shirley Jones and Gordon MacRae in Rodgers and Hammerstein's Oklahoma!.

President Eisenhower signs the Submerged Lands Act, transferring to coastal states the federal rights within the three-mile limit.

OTHER EVENTS OF 1953

Arts/Culture In San Francisco, poet Lawrence Ferlinghetti co-founds the City Lights Bookstore, a landmark of the Beat generation, which includes nonconformist writers Allen Ginsberg, Kenneth Patchen, Gregory Corso, and Kenneth Rexroth. The movement's archetypal work is Jack Kerouac's 1957 novel *On the Road,* which reflects a fascination with drugs, alcohol, sex, jazz music, Eastern religions, and a nonconformist life style. Louis L'Amour achieves his first big success with *Hondo.* The North Dakota-born Western novelist will have over 160 million copies of his 92 books in print by 1985.

1 APRIL 1954

National President Eisenhower signs the bill establishing the Air Force Academy, which will receive its first class on 11 July 1955 at Lowry Air Force Base, Denver, Colorado. In 1958 the academy moves to its permanent location near Colorado Springs.

17 MAY 1954

Black Experience In *Brown v Board of Education of Topeka, Kansas,* the Supreme Court makes the historic ruling that segregation in public schools is unconstitutional and mandates changes in state laws. In the West, segregation is required by law in Oklahoma and Texas schools, and is allowed in Arizona, Kansas, New Mexico, and Wyoming.

17 JUNE & 13 AUGUST 1954

Indians The Termination Acts sever certain tribes from federal Indian Affairs jurisdiction, allowing them to make their own way without federal support or guidance. In general, this program proves to be a failure.

23 SEPTEMBER 1954

Oregon President Eisenhower dedicates the McNary Dam on the Columbia River, a part of the extensive system of dams and locks which have harnessed the river's power for man.

3 NOVEMBER 1954

Science/Technology The Nobel Prize in Chemistry goes to the California Institute of Technology's Linus Pauling for his study of the structure of proteins and other molecules.

17 JUNE 1955

Life/Customs In Anaheim, California, Disneyland – an elaborate theme park inspired by Copenhagen's Tivoli Gardens – opens. Walt Disney's 1954 television series 'Davy Crockett' sets off a nationwide fad for coonskin hats.

24 SEPTEMBER 1955
National While on a Colorado vacation, President Eisenhower suffers a heart attack. He recovers in a Denver hospital for nearly three weeks.

18 OCTOBER 1955
Science/Technology University of California scientists discover a new nuclear particle, the antiproton.

2 NOVEMBER 1955
National President Eisenhower names Rear Admiral Richard Byrd as US head of Antarctic affairs.

11 NOVEMBER 1955
Arts/Culture In Oklahoma City, Governor Raymond Gary and Will Rogers, Jr dedicate the site of the Cowboy Hall of Fame, supported by 17 Western states.

OTHER EVENTS OF 1955
Arts/Culture On television, Westerns are the most popular fare. Among the hits are 'Gunsmoke,' 'Maverick,' 'Wyatt Earp,' 'Lawman,' 'Colt .45,' and 'Texas Rangers.'
Indians Iwo Jima war hero Ira Hayes, his glory days over, dies as an alcoholic suicide on Arizona's Pima Reservation.

11 APRIL 1956
Conservation With the Upper Colorado Project Act, Congress grants $760 million for the largest and most controversial Reclamation Bureau project.

28 MAY 1956
Agriculture The Agricultural Act of 1956 sets up the soil bank program.

30 JUNE 1956
Transportation In the worst commercial aviation disaster to date, two airliners collide over the Grand Canyon, killing 128.

7 JULY 1956
Arts/Culture Colorado's Central City Opera House presents Douglas Moore's folk opera *The Ballad of Baby Doe*, based on a silver-mining era episode. Another key event of this year is the establishment of the Santa Fe Opera Association, which will achieve worldwide renown with its outdoor performances in the Sangre de Cristo mountains.

11 FEBRUARY 1957
Arts/Culture In Dallas, Texas, Ernest Bacon's symphonic poem *Great River (The Rio Grande)* has its premiere.

1 JULY 1957-31 DECEMBER 1958
Science/Technology International Geophysical

Year begins with a rocket fired from California's San Nicholas Island by the Naval Research Laboratory to study the effect of solar radiation on communications.

OCTOBER 1957
Sports The West will gain two baseball teams, as the New York Giants decide to move to San Francisco, and the Brooklyn Dodgers to Los Angeles. California's first World Series win comes in 1959, when the Dodgers are victorious.

13 APRIL 1958
Arts/Culture Texas pianist Van Cliburn wins first prize in Moscow's Tschaikovsky Competition.

19 MAY 1958
International Canada and the United States establish the joint North American Air Defense Command (NORAD) with headquarters in Colorado Springs.

29 JULY 1958
Science/Technology The United States enters the space age, as President Eisenhower signs the bill creating the National Aeronautics and Space Administration (NASA) which will be centered in Houston, Texas.

3 AUGUST 1958
Exploration The US Navy's atomic submarine *Nautilus* makes the first undersea crossing beneath the North Pole.

OTHER EVENTS OF 1958
Science/Technology California Institute of Technology's George Beadle is a co-winner of the Nobel Prize in Physiology and Medicine.

3 JANUARY 1959
Alaska The territory of 586,412 square miles, over twice as large as Texas, becomes the nation's forty-ninth state.

21 AUGUST 1959
Hawaii The Pacific islands become the nation's fiftieth state, with war hero Daniel Inouye as the nation's first US Congressman of Japanese ancestry and Hiram Fong as the first of Chinese ancestry.

19-22 SEPTEMBER 1959
International On his historic visit to the United States, Soviet Premier Nikita Khrushchev tours the West – viewing a Hollywood film set, accusing Walter Reuther and other union officials of being 'agents for capitalists' in San Francisco, and tramping through an Iowa cornfield.

15 OCTOBER-1 DECEMBER 1959
International At a 12-nation conference, the United States and other participants sign a 34-year

pact freezing territorial claims and reserving the Antarctic for peaceful purposes.

9 NOVEMBER 1959
Agriculture The government warns that the Washington State cranberry crop may be contaminated by cancer-causing herbicides.

18-28 FEBRUARY 1960
Sports In Squaw Valley, California, 30 nations participate in the eighth Winter Olympic Games. US skaters Carol Heiss and David Jenkins, and skier Penny Pitou, make the nation the unofficial team champion.

23 APRIL 1960
Arts/Culture Composer Ferde Grofé conducts the San Francisco Symphony Orchestra in the premiere of his *San Francisco Suite*, which includes a percussion reprise of the 1906 earthquake.

2 MAY 1960
Ideas/Beliefs Convicted of robbery and sexual assault, Caryl Chessman loses a 12-year legal struggle when he dies in the gas chamber of California's San Quention Prison. The controversial case helps to bring the issue of capital punishment to the center of national debate.

11 JULY 1960
National In Los Angeles, the Democratic National Convention nominates John F Kennedy as its presidential candidate. Washington's Henry Jackson is a leading vice-presidential contender, but when he fails to deliver the bloc of Western delegates, Kennedy turns to Lyndon B Johnson for a running mate. Stewart Udall, who delivers the Arizona delegation, will be appointed Interior Secretary in the Kennedy Administration.

Railroads enabled the mining industry to develop Western mineral resources.

19 OCTOBER 1960
International Canada and the United States sign the Columbia River pact for joint development of hydroelectric power and flood control in the Northwest. On 24 October the United States and Mexico agree to joint construction of the Armistead Dam on the Rio Grande.

20 JANUARY 1961
National John F Kennedy is inaugurated president.

CHRONOLOGY

23 FEBRUARY 1961
National President Kennedy makes a speech on natural resources, setting forth the principles of retention and multiple use: public land is now regarded as a valuable natural resource which should be retained in federal ownership and administered under the principle of multiple use and sustained yield of surface resources.

24 MARCH 1961
Science/Technology President Kennedy asks Congress for a supplementary appropriation of $60 million for conversion of a plutonium reactor at Hanford, Washington. The Kennedy Administration plans to convert the reactor into the world's largest atomic power plant. The House rejects the plan on 13 July, but the Senate approves it on 18 July. Hanford has been a site for nuclear operations since the end of World War II. Between 1940 and 1980, the population of the Tri-Cities area adjacent to the Hanford Nuclear Reservation has risen from approximately 400 to 115,000. Meanwhile, the Hanford area becomes the largest nuclear dump in the world. It contains enough waste to 'eliminate human life from much of this continent if it ever got loose in the air and water,' according to Northwest specialist A Robert Smith.

16-18 APRIL 1961
International West German Chancellor Konrad Adenauer visits Texas at the conclusion of his visit to the United States. Adenauer flies to Austin on 16 April and is feted at a public barbecue at the Gillespie County Fairgrounds near Vice-President Lyndon Johnson's ranch. On 17 April the chancellor addresses the Texas legislature in Austin.

23 APRIL 1961
Finance The Commerce Department reports that the state of South Dakota had the highest percentage rise in income for any state in 1959-60 – 28 percent.

6 SEPTEMBER 1961
National The National Wilderness Preservation System, which would set aside 9,100,000 acres of forest as public land, is approved by the Senate but shelved in the House, due to opposition of mining and other commercial interests. The bill is not passed until September 1964.

27 SEPTEMBER 1961
California Former Vice-President Richard M Nixon announces at a news conference in Los Angeles that he will not be a candidate for the presidency in 1964, but that he will run for governor of California in 1962.

10 OCTOBER 1961
Science/Technology A nuclear explosion is set off deep underground at the test site in Nevada. On 29 October a 'low-yield' nuclear device is also tested.

Test firing, White Sands Missile Range.

3 MARCH 1962
Black Experience A 35-day sit-in begins in suburban Monterey Park, Los Angeles, after Robert Liley, a black physicist, attempts to buy a home in the neighborhood and is rebuffed. Conducted by Mrs Liley and several others, the sit-in is successful when another developer buys the land and invites Mrs Liley to be his first customer.

21 APRIL 1962
Life/Customs A World's Fair, Century 21 Exposition, opens in Seattle. The fair has been seven years in the making, and is the first to be located in the United States since 1940. The theme is 'Man in the Space Age.' The fair covers 74 acres, and has exhibits from 59 countries. President Kennedy makes an inaugural speech by telephone. The 600-foot Space Needle, which has a revolving restaurant on top, is a popular attraction. Most of the buildings are constructed for permanent use, and the city is left with a grand $90 million legacy – the Seattle Center, which becomes the cultural and recreational heart of the city. Another holdover is Seattle's monorail, which takes a passenger from the Seattle Center to downtown Seattle in 95 seconds.

6 JULY 1962
Science/Technology The second US explosion of a thermonuclear device for non-weapons purposes is set off at the proving grounds in Nevada. On 9 July a thermonuclear explosion equal to about 1,400,000 tons of TNT is set off at an altitude of 250 miles over Johnston Island, 800 miles south of Honolulu.

4 September 1963

25 OCTOBER 1962
Arts/Culture California writer John Steinbeck receives the Nobel Prize for Literature for a body of work that includes the novels *The Grapes of Wrath*, *East of Eden*, *In Dubious Battle*, *The Long Valley*, *Cannery Row*, *Of Mice and Men*, *Sweet Thursday*, *Tortilla Flat*, and *The Wayward Bus*. Elements of Western social history on which Steinbeck focuses include the Great Depression, social prejudice, religion, prostitution, and, above all, various forms of labor.

6 NOVEMBER 1962
National Former Vice-President Richard M Nixon loses his bid for election as governor of California. In an emotional press conference, Nixon tells reporters that his political career is over. Daniel K Inouye, a Hawaiian-Japanese who served with the US Army in Italy during World War II, is elected to the Senate from Hawaii. Senator Frank Church, an environmentally conscious, liberal Democrat from Idaho is re-elected to the Senate. Church will lead the fight for the National Wild Rivers System and sponsor legislation to create the Sawtooth National Forest and the 2,300,000-acre River of No Return Wilderness.

OTHER EVENTS OF 1962
Environment Author/scientist Rachel Carson publishes *Silent Spring* which raises the specter of a world made uninhabitable by indiscriminate use of pesticides and other harmful chemicals. The book makes a passionate plea for strict curbs on the use of such poisons while their side effects are closely studied. On 15 May 1963, a presidential science advisory committee issues a cautionary report on the use of pesticides.

8 FEBRUARY 1963
Science/Technology The underground testing of nuclear weapons resumes in Nevada. Suspension of tests had been ordered on 20 January during the test-ban talks with the Soviet Union.

16 MARCH 1963
International The United States formally protests to the USSR the flight of two Soviet reconnaissance planes over Alaska on 13 March, the first 'clearly established incident of a Soviet overflight of the USA.'

3 JUNE 1963
National The Supreme Court settles a 40-year controversy over apportionment of water from the lowest basin of the Colorado River. Arizona – which had brought the case forward in 1952 with the complaint that California was diverting more than its share – benefits from the seven-to-one decision. The Court also rules 5-3 for a provision that allows the secretary of the interior to allot water in times of below-normal flow.

2 AUGUST 1963
Arts/Culture Author/anthropologist Oliver La Farge dies at 83. He had worked for the welfare of the Indians, and his first novel, *Laughing Boy* (1929), was a sensitive and accurate description of the Navajo culture and psychology.

4 SEPTEMBER 1963
Black Experience The public schools of Fort Worth, Texas, desegregate with the uneventful entry of 20 black students into the first grade.

The Jeffrey Pine, Yosemite National Park, California.

CHRONOLOGY

22 NOVEMBER 1963
National One of the most dramatic days in American history centers on Dallas, Texas, where President and Mrs Kennedy have gone to mend political fences between the liberal and conservative wings in Texas politics. At 12:30 PM the President and Governor John Connally are shot while their motorcade moves into Dallas. Rushed to the hospital, Kennedy is pronounced dead at 1:00 PM (Connally survives his wound). Dallas police capture Lee Harvey Oswald, the suspected assassin; he will be charged with shooting Kennedy and Connally from the sixth floor of the Texas School Book Depository. At 2:30 PM Vice-President Lyndon Johnson of Texas is sworn in as president.

24 NOVEMBER 1963
National As Lee Harvey Oswald is removed from police headquarters in Dallas to a safer jail, he is shot fatally by Jack Ruby, a Dallas nightclub owner. A backlash against violence in Dallas brings the election of Erik Jonsson as mayor in February 1964; he will lead the city toward a more moderate image.

17 DECEMBER 1963
International The Senate consents to the Chamizal Treaty, which cedes a small disputed section of El Paso, Texas, to Mexico.

25 JANUARY 1964
Science/Technology Echo II, the first American-Soviet co-operative space program, is launched from Vandenberg Air Force Base, California. Echo II sends messages around the world by reflecting radio signals from one point on earth to another.

27 MARCH 1964
Environment A severe earthquake in Alaska kills 66 persons, and causes damage of $500 million. Seismic waves caused by the earthquake race across the Pacific, hitting coasts as far away as Midway Island, Siberia, Japan, and Hawaii, and sweep the North American coast from British Columbia to southern California. The epicenter is near the entrance to Prince William Sound, 105 miles east of Anchorage, which is hit hard, with buckled streets and shattered buildings. The quake is measured at a magnitude of 8.4 on the Richter scale, compared to 8.25 for the 1906 San Francisco earthquake.

28 MARCH 1964
National Presidential Johnson declares Alaska a major disaster area, following the earthquake of the previous day.

2 JUNE 1964
Black Experience The Oklahoma city council adopts an ordinance forbidding public businesses to refuse services or facilities to persons because of race, religion, color, creed, ancestry, or national origin. This is Oklahoma's first public accommodations ordinance. Hundreds of blacks from several cities throughout the state march around the capital on 6 June, demanding that the next session of the state legislature in 1965 adopt a statewide public-accommodations law.

13-17 JULY 1964
National Senator Barry M Goldwater of Arizona is nominated for the presidency at the Republican Party convention in San Francisco.

31 AUGUST 1964
Population The Census Bureau announces that California has become the most populous state in the nation. Alaska has the lowest population; the second lowest is that of Wyoming.

2 SEPTEMBER 1964
Black Experience Seven hundred blacks attend integrated classes at the start of the fourth year of desegregation in the Houston school district. Two white children enroll at an all-black school in Fort Worth on 8 September, the first recorded instance in the state of whites voluntarily attending a black school.

3 SEPTEMBER 1964
Conservation The National Wilderness Preservation System is established. Over nine million acres of national forest lands which have been designated as 'wild,' 'wilderness,' or 'canoe' areas become part of the system. Other lands are to be added after review by the executive branch.

12 SEPTEMBER 1964
Conservation President Johnson signs a bill establishing the Canyonlands National Park, 257,000 acres along the Green and Colorado Rivers, in Utah.

10-12 OCTOBER 1964
National President Johnson campaigns over 4400 miles in the West. Starting in Austin, he moves to Phoenix, Arizona, the hometown of Barry Goldwater, thence to Los Angeles and on to five other states. Meanwhile, Barry Goldwater campaigns in Texas, his home state of Arizona, California, Utah, Washington State, and Oregon.

22 DECEMBER 1964
Environment Oregon and four counties in northern California are declared disaster areas because of heavy snow, rain, and floods.

1964-1965
Ideas/Beliefs The 'Free Speech' movement ushers in an era of protest on American campuses. The movement's origins are credited to students at the University of California at Berkeley, who protest the lack of a student role in shaping goals.

Top: *The Kennedy assassination in Dallas, Texas.*
Above: *Lyndon B Johnson is sworn in as president*
(left) and Jack Ruby is shot.

Conservation The Army Corps of Engineers proposes to build Rampart Dam on the Yukon River.
The object is to produce 4,700,000 kilowatts of
electricity at an estimated cost of $2-3 billion.
Yukon Power for America, an Alaska-based
citizens' group, is in favor of the project, but those
opposed to the dam quote the Fish and Wildlife
Service to the effect that 'Nowhere in the history of
water development in North America have the fish
and wildlife losses anticipated to result from a
single project been so overwhelming.' The conservationists win the controversy.

20 JANUARY 1965
National President Johnson is inaugurated. The
assassination of President Kennedy in November
1963 has had an effect on security – bullet-proof
glass surrounds three sides of the stand on which
Johnson is sworn in. Johnson says in his address
that 'Our destiny in the midst of change will rest
on the unchanged character of our people – and on
their faith.'

9 APRIL 1965
Sports President Johnson is among the guests at
the inauguration of the Houston Astrodome. The
baseball players – Houston Astros versus New
York Yankees – are troubled by glaring light
transmitted by the plastic dome, which is later
painted over.

César Chavez seeks support for migrant workers at a mass rally.

10-11 JUNE 1965
Environment A cloudburst over Sanderson, Texas, sends water streaming through the normally dry Sanderson Canyon. A flash flood sends water through Sheep Creek Canyon on the Utah-Wyoming border, and the swollen South Platte and Arkansas Rivers overflow their banks on 17-26 June, bringing heavy damage to parts of Colorado, Kansas, Wyoming, Montana, New Mexico, and Nebraska. President Johnson declares Colorado a major disaster area, and more than 20,000 people are removed from their homes during the course of the floods.

11-16 AUGUST 1965
Black Experience Watts, a black district of Los Angeles, is the scene of a major race riot. Initiated by a minor incident, the upheaval expands to looting, burning, and 34 deaths – not to mention $40 million in damage. Governor Edmund Brown appoints a committee to investigate. According to blacks, police brutaility is the key issue. The violence at Watts foreshadows the serious summer riots in Newark and Detroit in 1967.

28 OCTOBER 1965
Life/Customs The steel Gateway Arch in St Louis is completed. The 630-foot parabolic arch commemorates the Louisiana Purchase and the role that St Louis played in westward movement.

2 DECEMBER 1965
Science/Technology A 13,200-square-mile area with about one million people, 50 cities, and four military bases in southwest Texas, southern New Mexico, and Ciudad Juarez, Mexico, is blacked out for two hours as the El Paso Electric Company experiences a power failure.

4-5 JANUARY 1966
Environment Twenty days of heavy rain and snow cause major flooding in northern California and Western Oregon. Residents of Orick, California, flee the rising Redwood Creek; 1000 are stranded temporarily by flood waters.

23 FEBRUARY 1966
Conservation President Johnson calls for projects to clean the nation's waterways, federal grants to preserve historical landmarks, and financing for pollution-control research. On 3 November Johnson will sign the Clean Waters Restoration Act.

10 MARCH 1966
Arts/Culture Mari Susette Sandoz, novelist and historian of the old West, dies in New York City. Born in Sheridan County, Nebraska, in 1901, Sandoz wrote *Crazy Horse, Cheyenne Autumn, Buffalo Hunters*, and *Love Song to the Plains*.

15 MARCH 1966
Black Experience Rioting breaks out in a 12-block area of the black Watts district of Los Angeles. There are two deaths. Governor Edmund Brown

WESTERN-STYLE POLITICS

In the political life of the modern West, many names are immediately recognizable; Barry Goldwater, Lyndon Johnson, Richard Nixon, Ronald Reagan, Dixy Lee Ray, Jerry Brown have all made national headlines with their determined, sometimes controversial policies. These politicians flourish especially in the states that have large electoral-vote counts, such as California and Texas. The Reagan-Bush presidential ticket in 1980 was aided immensely by its claim to the California and Texas constituencies.

On the local and regional level, Western politics is confronted with immediate and sometimes revolutionary social change. During the 1970s and early 1980s, blacks, women, Hispanic-Americans, and homosexual populations exerted considerable influence on state and municipal elections in the West (*e.g.* Tom Bradley of Los Angeles, Dixy Lee Ray of Washington, some 3000 Hispanic-Americans holding office in 1985). The voting power of the Hispanic-American population in the Southwest will continue to grow, as more immigrants cross the Rio Grande River into the United States.

It is dangerous to predict any sure winner in Western politics, however, because of the changeability of Western voters, of which there are numerous examples. For instance, Dixy Lee Ray was unceremoniously dumped in the Democratic primary when she ran for re-election in Washington State in 1980. Mercurial California has produced politicians as distinctive and disparate as Jerry Brown and Ronald Reagan – both were governors – S I Hayakawa, Ronald Dellums and, of course, Richard Nixon, a true 'native son' of California before his move to New York City. Perhaps what unites Western politicians is a sense of immediacy: aware that they may soon be replaced, they can urge and promote policies that might be regarded as drastic in the East or the Midwest. Exciting and controversial new legislation may be anticipated from the West in the future – perhaps laws on population quotas or social change.

Texan Lyndon Baines Johnson at his LBJ Ranch.   *President Ronald Reagan, first elected in 1980.*

outlines a pilot program getting underway in California to make available all state services 'under a single roof.' Brown is reacting both to the immediate violence and to the tragedy at Watts of August 1965.

6 APRIL 1966

Labor The National Farm Workers Union, led by Cesar Chavez, has been out on strike against California grape growers since 8 September 1965. The union scores its first important victory when it is recognized as the bargaining agent for the farm workers of Schenley Industries, a major grape grower.

11 JULY 1966

Science/Technology Nebraska and parts of South Dakota and Wyoming are hit by two major power failures. The Nebraska public power system attributes the blackouts to the overdemand on cooling systems.

SEPTEMBER-OCTOBER 1966

Ideas/Beliefs Controversy surrounds the iconoclastic views of the Reverend James Albert Pike, the retired Episcopalian bishop of California. In his final sermon at Grace Cathedral in San Francisco on 4 September, Pike says that he cannot affirm the existence of an 'all powerful, all good, all

NASA's Johnson Space Center, Houston, Texas.

knowing' God. The possibility of a heresy trial develops. After debate, the house of bishops adopts a resolution on 27 October: 'Christian truth requires constant rethinking and restating at every age.' Pike is not tried by his church.

15 OCTOBER 1966
Conservation President Johnson signs bills establishing parks or similar recreational areas in the Bighorn Canyon National Recreation Area (Montana and Wyoming), Guadalupe Mountains National Park in western Texas, and Point Reyes National Seashore near San Francisco.

7 NOVEMBER 1966
National President Johnson signs a bill which authorizes the Army Corps of Engineers to construct 40 water projects in 25 states. The two most costly projects are Knights Valley (Russian River) and Marysville (Yuba River) California.

3 DECEMBER 1966
International President Johnson inspects the $78 million Amistad Dam on the US-Mexican border. The dam's cost is shared equally by the two countries

15 DECEMBER 1966
Life/Customs Walt Elias Disney dies at 65 in Los Angeles of acute circulatory collapse, after an innovative career as an animated cartoonist, motion-picture and television producer, founder of Walt Disney Productions Inc (1926), and creator of the Disneyland amusement park in California in 1955.

3 JANUARY 1967
Texas Jack Ruby, the assassin of Lee Harvey Oswald, who was believed to have killed President Kennedy on 22 November 1963, dies suddenly while awaiting a second trial, after he had originally been sentenced to death on 14 March 1964.

20 JANUARY 1967
Education The California board of regents votes to dismiss Clark Kerr from the presidency of the University of California, effective immediately. Kerr's ouster climaxes a dispute over university finances, which had been set off by Governor Ronald Reagan's proposals to reduce the university's operating budget and impose tuition fees for state residents – ending most free college education in California. These proposals have sparked protest, and reaction to Kerr's removal is widespread. On 24 January Governor Reagan holds a news conference in Sacramento to deny that Kerr's dismissal was a political move.

25 APRIL 1967
Social Change Colorado Governor John A Love signs the most liberal abortion law in the United States. The law permits therapeutic abortions when a three-doctor board of an accredited hospital licensed by the state department of health unanimously consents to the termination of the pregnancy. After the signing of the bill, Colorado doctors begin to receive inquiries from pregnant women throughout the country.

5-11 JUNE 1967
Hispanic Americans Some 40 armed Hispanic Americans raid the Rio Arriba County Courthouse in Tierra Ararillo, New Mexico, and free 11 'rebels' previously arrested; the raiders exchange shots with the police and wound two. Taking two hostages, they flee into the mountains, where they exchange more shots with state troopers and the National Guard, as one hostage escapes and the second is released. On 10 June the group's leader, Reies Lopiz Tijerina, is captured at a roadblock. Most of the others are captured later, and all will be arraigned in Santa Fe on 22 June. Meanwhile, on 9 June, responding to statements from some leaders of the Hispanic American community in the Southwest that these people do in fact live in great poverty, President Johnson names a cabinet-level committee to study the problems. The rebel group's name is Political Confederation of Free City States, and their immediate demands center around their claim to some 2500 square miles of land in nothern New Mexico that they believe to be their inheritance.

15 JULY 1967
Labor A strike of some 37,000 workers in the AFL-CIO United Steelworkers of America halts about 90 percent of the nation's copper production. The strike is against the Kennecott Copper Corporation, Anaconda Company, Phelps Dodge Corporation, and American Smelting & Refining Company, which have facilities in 12 states, primarily in Arizona, Utah, Nevada, New Mexico, and Montana.

30 JULY 1967
Black Experience Oregon governor Tom McCall places 500 National Guardsmen on standby alert after an outbreak of rock-throwing, firebombing, and vandalism in Portland's Albina district, home to 14,000 of the city's 18,000 blacks. The disorder follows a meeting at which a speaker had blamed whites for the poor conditions endured by blacks.

28 OCTOBER 1967
International President Johnson and Mexican President Diaz Ordaz meet in El Paso for ceremonies to transfer to Mexico the 437-acre border of El Chamizal, separated from Mexico in the 1850s when the Rio Grande River changed its course.

29-30 NOVEMBER 1967
War: Vietnam Students at the University of California at Berkeley participate in a 'mill-in' at Sproul Hall and virtually halt all operations in the administration building. The demonstration is held in protest against the suspension of two students for participating in anti-draft rallies in October.

4 DECEMBER 1967
National The Supreme Court rules that about 26,000 acres of possibly submerged land in the Gulf of Mexico belongs to the Federal Government, not to Texas, which has claimed off-shore land extending for nine miles from its coasts. The court rules that the state must measure from the natural shoreline (the coastline of Texas in 1845) and not from the tip of artificial jetties built out into the Gulf.

10 JANUARY 1968
Transportation A US Marine Corps C-54 transport plane en route from Denver to Seattle crashes and burns in a blizzard, 32 miles north of Battle Mountain, Nevada. All 17 US Marines and Navy personnel aboard are killed.

19 JANUARY 1968
Social Change The Colorado health department announces that 120 legal abortions have been reported for 1 May-31 December 1967, following Governor Love's 25 April signature of the new permissive abortion law. Only 29 of the 120 women involved were from outside of Colorado. Nine of the women were victims of rape, two were described as suicide risks, and psychiatric reasons were given in 50 cases. In 22 other cases, physical danger to the woman or child was cited. No reason was given in the case of 37 therapeutic abortions. Groups like Planned Parenthood favor abortion on demand.

18 APRIL 1968
Science/Technology The Army concedes that testing of nerve gas at the Dugway proving grounds on 13 March has killed at least 6400 sheep in western Utah's Skull and Rush Valleys. The gas reportedly had been blown to the sheep's grazing area, 30 miles southwest of the test grounds, by an unexpected wind shift.

28 MAY 1968
National Senator Eugene McCarthy defeats Senator Robert Kennedy in the Oregon Democratic presidential primary, making the California primary (4 June) crucial for both men. McCarthy is favored by college groups because of his opposition to the Vietnam War.

4 JUNE 1968
National Robert Kennedy learns that he has won the Democratic presidential primaries in both California and South Dakota. His victory in California, with 46 percent of the vote, is attributed to a heavy vote for him by minority groups – blacks and Hispanic Americans – and labor. That night Kennedy tells a crowd of supporters at the Ambassador Hotel in Los Angeles that 'We can end the division within the United States, the violence.' As Kennedy leaves the meeting and walks through a kitchen passageway, he is fatally wounded by a shot fired (at 12:08 AM) by a Jordanian immigrant, Sirhan Bishara Sirhan. Kennedy dies the next day.

30 SEPTEMBER 1968

National President Johnson signs the Colorado Basin Act, the largest reclamation program ever authorized in a single piece of legislation. The act authorizes construction of the Central Arizona Project to divert water from the Colorado River to Phoenix and Tucson, and other parts of central and southern Arizona.

6 NOVEMBER 1968

National Richard M Nixon, in a remarkable political comeback, wins the presidential election after losing the presidential election of 1960 and the California gubernatorial race in 1962.

OTHER EVENTS OF 1968

Alaska The state of Alaska chooses 26 million acres of land including the oil-rich Prudhoe Bay area for its use. Under the statehood act of 1959, the state is authorized to select 103 million acres, but on 17 January 1969, Interior Secretary Walter J Hickel agrees to maintain a Johnson Administration freeze of land selection until the land claims of native Alaskans are settled.

20 JANUARY 1969

National Richard M Nixon is inaugurated president. The ceremonies are marked by massive security precautions and demonstrations against the unpopular Vietnam War.

Los Angeles police confront the Black Panthers.

5 FEBRUARY 1969

Environment A huge oil slick off the coast of Santa Barbara closes the city's harbor.

Education California Governor Ronald Reagan declares a state of extreme emergency at the University of California at Berkeley, following clashes between police and striking students of the Third World Liberation Front who demand an ethnic-studies program relevant to other minority-group students as well as to blacks.

23 APRIL 1969

California After nearly 12 hours of deliberation, a Los Angeles jury condemns Sirhan Bishara Sirhan to death in the gas chamber for the shooting of Senator Robert F Kennedy on 5 June 1968.

25 APRIL 1969

Science/Technology A meeting of the Geophysical Union in Washington, DC, hears evidence that earthquakes are being triggered by underground atomic tests in Nevada. The two largest underground tests are said to have caused earth tremors and faults as far as 1200 miles from the test site, up to a month after the blasts. These reports contradict previous statements on the problem. In a related development, an earthquake measuring 6.7 on the Richter Scales strikes the Aleutian Islands (14 May), 100 miles from Amchitka, Alaska, where the Atomic Energy Commission has decided to locate a new atomic-testing site.

1 January 1970

A Great Northern freighter along Puget Sound.

10-18 MAY 1969
Labor Cesar Chavez leads a grape strikers' march from Indio, California, to the Mexican border. Chavez announces that his union, the United Farm Workers Organizing Committee, wants migrant workers to join.

24 MAY 1969
Science/Technology The first steam-driven rocket airmail service is launched in Las Curces, New Mexico, but proves impracticable.

22 JUNE 1969
Industry Plans are announced for a 2080-miles natural gas pipeline to carry natural gas reserves from Alaska's North Slope to US and Canadian markets. The first section of the pipeline will reach from Canada's Northwest Territories to the US border. A second extension, to be completed by 1978, will carry the line to Prudhoe Bay, Alaska.

9 AUGUST 1969
Crime Film actress Sharon Tate, 26, and three others are found brutally murdered in Tate's house in Benedict Canyon, California.

10 SEPTEMBER 1969
Alaska The state of Alaska receives bids of over $900 million from a group of petroleum companies competing for oil and gas leases on the mineral-rich North Slope.

2 OCTOBER 1969
Science/Technology The Atomic Energy Commission explodes a 1.2-megaton hydrogen bomb underground on the island of Amchitka in the Aleutians, despite widespread concern that the test may cause an earthquake.

20 NOVEMBER 1969
Indians Seventy-eight Indians representing more than 20 tribes seize Alcatraz Island in San Francisco Bay and say that they want an Indian cultural and educational center established there.

9 DECEMBER 1969
Crime A Los Angeles County grand jury hands down indictments against Charles M Manson – leader of a clan of young drifters – and four of his followers for the murder of actress Sharon Tate and five others on 9 August.

OTHER EVENTS OF 1969
Life/Customs The first live television programming is made available to Alaska.

1 JANUARY 1970
National The National Environmental Policy Act of 1969 makes protectioon of the environment a matter of national policy. The act requires all federal agencies to consider the effect on the environment of all major activities, and to include in every recommendation for legislation an impact statement – a written analysis of those effects, as well as alternatives to the proposal.

CHRONOLOGY

8 JANUARY 1970
Transportation The Civil Aeronautics Board approves an Alaska Airlines request to fly 10 charter flights to Siberia during the summer of 1970, the first scheduled flights to that region from any part of the United States.

22 APRIL 1970
Conservation 'Earth Day' is observed nationwide, at the suggestion of Senator Gaylord Nelson of Wisconsin, as a means of focusing public attention on ecological problems. Millions of Americans participate in environmental teach-ins, anti-pollution protests, and various clean-up projects. This marks the peak of national harmony on environmental issues. Thereafter, enthusiasm begins to diminish with realization of the economic costs entailed.

16 MAY 1970
War: Vietnam Anti-war demonstrations occur nationwide on this Armed Forces Day. Police break up scuffling between 500 anti-war demonstrators and 75 counter-demonstrators in Killeen Texas, near Fort Hood.

28 JUNE 1970
Education The *Washington Post* reports that 3-6000 elementary school children in Omaha, Nebraska, have been receiving behavior modification drugs prescribed by local physicians to improve their personal conduct and capacity for learning.

A 4-H Club show at the Nebraska State Fair.

19 JULY 1970
Science/Technology The Air Force announces that missiles capable of delivering independently targetable re-entry vehicles (MIRVs) have been deployed at Minot, North Dakota.

23 OCTOBER 1970
Science/Technology Gary Gabelich sets a land speed record by averaging 622.4 miles per hour in two runs at the Bonneville Salt Lake Flats in Utah, driving the Blue Flame – a rocket-powered vehicle using liquid natural gas as fuel.

10-11 NOVEMBER 1970
Indians Peter MacDonald is chosen tribal chairman of the 129,000-member Navajo Nation, the largest Indian tribe. MacDonald will be the first college graduate to lead the Navajos, who possess an estimated $267 million in assets and live on a 25,000-square-mile reservation covering parts of New Mexico, Arizona, and Utah. On 2 November 1982, MacDonald will be unseated, following stories of abuses of his position.

15 DECEMBER 1970
Indians Forty-eight thousand acres of land in the Blue Lake area of New Mexico are returned to the Taos Pueblo Indians, who consider the area a shrine whose religious value was destroyed when it was put to multiple use after being taken from the Indians by the Forest Service in 1906.

OTHER EVENTS OF 1970

National During the period 1781-1970, a total of 1,144,000 acres of public land were disposed of by the Federal Government. On 23 June 1971, a commission will make recommendations for use of the 775 million acres that remain in government hands.

Indians The American Indian Movement is founded. It soon emerges as the most militant spokesman for radical reform of federal Indian regulations.

9 FEBRUARY 1971

Environment Southern California is rocked by a severe earthquake, which buckles freeways, causes major damage to almost 1000 buildings, and results in 62 deaths.

29 MARCH 1971

Crime Charles Manson and three female associates are sentenced to death after being found guilty of murder in the gruesome Tate-LaBianca slayings in Los Angeles on 9-10 August 1969.

13 APRIL 1971

Social Change Patricia Sewell Latting, sworn in as the mayor of Oklahoma City, becomes the first woman mayor of a city of more than 200,000 persons.

2 JUNE 1971

Crime Juan V Corona, a 37-year-old farm labor contractor, is arraigned and pleads not guilty to murder charges in connection with the slaying of 25 men, whose bodies have been found buried in peach orchards in Yuba City, California. Almost all the bodies are believed to be those of itinerant farm workers. Corona has a history of mental illness; he is linked to the slayings by two sales receipts found in a victim's grave. Corona is found guilty on 18 January 1973. He will appeal, be retried, and found guilty again in 1982.

23 JUNE 1971

National The Public Land Law Review Commission presents a 343-page report, *One Third of the Nation's Land*, to President Nixon and Congress. Stringent controls over the environment are recommended for the 755 million acres of federal land. More than 350 specific recommendations provide guidelines for overhauling outmoded laws and unsnarling conflicting regulations governing the use and sales of public lands.

18 DECEMBER 1971

Indians Forty million acres of federal lands and nearly $1 billion are given to 53,000 Eskimos, Indians, and Aleuts under provisions of the Alaska Native Land Claims Act.

OTHER EVENTS OF 1971

Alaska The state of Alaska claims 76,600,000 of

True Grit, *one of John Wayne's last films.*

the more than 100 million acres of vacant public-domain lands, on which the state holds options for community, recreational, and commercial uses. Previously, 24 million acres had been claimed. The newly claimed lands constitute 70 percent of Alaska's territory.

Conservation Conservationists present a case in court opposed to construction of any more paper-pulp mills, which have been built at Ketchikan and Sitka, Alaska, since the early 1960s. The pulp and paper industry is utilizing the forest resources of the Alaska Panhandle.

Finance The state legislature of Montana approves the first minimum-wage legislation for that state.

18 FEBRUARY 1972

California The California State Supreme Court holds that the death penalty is cruel and unusual punishment. One hundred and seven condemned convicts, among them Sirhan Bishara Sirhan (the assassin of Robert Kennedy) and Charles M Manson, will be spared by this ruling.

21 APRIL 1972

War: Vietnam Army chief of staff General William C Westmoreland is hit by a tomato during a demonstration by civilians and some servicemen in El Paso Texas. Next day, 30-40,000 protesters against the war in Vietnam march in San Francisco, while another 10-12,000 take part in a Los Angeles march.

2-3 MAY 1972

Disaster A smoldering fire erupts savagely at the 3700-foot level of the Sunshine Silver Mine near Kellogg, Idaho (the largest and the richest such facility in the United States). Flames, smoke, and carbon monoxide fumes block a crucial exit route for miners who are working in a large shaft. At least 35 miners are killed immediately; by 9 May the death total climbs to 91. Spontaneous combustion or an electrical failure are suspected. Sunshine officials say that elaborate security pre-

cautions were taken beforehand, but on 3 May a published report from the Bureau of Mines shows that the company had failed to correct numerous hazards found during an inspection in November 1971.

20 MAY 1972

Indians By executive order, 21,000 acres of land in Washington are returned to the Yakima tribe, for whom the area has a religious significance. The acreage had been incorporated in the Mount Rainier Forest Reserve in 1908 in the mistaken belief that it was public land.

6 JUNE 1972

Montana A new state constitution, which stresses populist, environmental, and consumer-protection values, is approved in Montana: the voters thereby replace the state constitution written in 1889. The new law provides for annual sessions of the legislature in place of biannual sessions, single-member legislative districts, open state-government meetings, election of the governor and lieutenant governor as a team, and a legal basis for a statewide property tax. The constitutional convention leaves the unicameral question to the electorate, which decides to retain the bicameral, or two-chamber system, leaving Nebraska the only state with a unicameral legislature. Montana has long been an economic dependency of the Anaconda Copper Mining Company, but that company's market value fell from $1,400,000,000 in 1969 to $260,000,000 in 1972. In 1974 the Montana Strip Mine Reclamation Act will emerge as the strongest in American history, and become a model for other states.

9-10 JUNE 1972

Environment Heavy rains in the Black Hills of South Dakota create flood conditions in Rapid City and the surrounding area, killing 235 persons and causing $100 million in damage.

17 JULY 1972

Indians The Federal Government offers to turn over to the Navajo tribe control of all Bureau of Indian Affairs operations in its area, including the $110,000,000 annual Navajo budget. The offer is made by Anthony Lincoln, director of the bureau's Navajo affairs, directly to tribal chairman Peter MacDonald, and is seen as a victory for the self-determination forces within the bureau. (Only two other tribes have acquired complete control of all programs affecting their reservations to date: the Miccosuke of Florida and the Zuñi of Arizona. Neither reservation compares in size with the 25,000-square-mile Navajo reservation.

28 JULY 1972

Social Change A University of California demographer announces that California's five-year liberalized abortion law is curtailing the state's birth rate and reducing the number of children on welfare. The number of abortions in California rose in 1970 to 65,000, quadruple the number in 1969.

4 SEPTEMBER 1972

Life/Customs The first horse race with a purse of more than $1 million takes place at the All-American Futurity in Ruidoso, New Mexico.

Previous pgs: *Union Pacific Railroad complex, Omaha.* Below: *New Mexican Zuñi at their tribal gathering.*

2-8 NOVEMBER 1972

Indians The American Indian Movement occupies the offices of the Bureau of Indian Affairs in Washington, DC, demanding the rights and property guaranteed to Indians by treaties made in the past.

OTHER EVENTS OF 1972

Conservation The Forest Service makes recommendations on those of its land holdings that might qualify for addition to the National Wilderness Preservation System, as stipulated in the Wilderness Act of 1964. The process, called Roadless Area Review and Evaluation (RARE), recommends 12,300,000 acres for wilderness designation, but a public outcry leads to another study, RARE II, released in 1979, which recommends 15,400,000 acres. In 1982 a legal challenge from the state of California will force yet another examination. The legacy of RARE II becomes apparent in 1984, when Congress passes and President Ronald Reagan signs laws designating 8,600,000 acres of new wilderness area.

27 FEBRUARY 1973

Indians About 200 armed supporters of the American Indian Movement seize control of the hamlet of Wounded Knee, South Dakota, and remain barricaded in confrontation with about 250 law officers. The Indians demand Senate investigation of specific problems: that Senator Edward M Kennedy begin an investigation of the Bureau of Indian Affairs, that Senator William Fulbright investigate 371 treaties between the United States

President and Mrs Richard M Nixon at the Great Wall of China – 1972.

and various Indian nations, and that the 'Oglala Sioux be allowed to elect their own officers,' rather than accept Bureau of Indian Affairs 'puppets.' The Indians barricade themselves in a Roman Catholic Church. Russell Means, an American Indian Movement leader, says in a telephone interview that the Indians have rifles, shotguns, explosives, and hand grenades, and that the government must either attack or negotiate. Wounded Knee was the scene of an 1890 battle in which some 300 Indians – including women and children – were massacred by a US Cavalry unit. The siege this time will last until 8 May.

26 APRIL 1973

Environment An earthquake in Hilo, Hawaii, causes more than $1 million in damage.

8 MAY 1973

Indians Members of the Oglala Sioux tribe and federal negotiators reach an agreement to end the siege at Wounded Knee, South Dakota, which began on 27 February. The agreement calls for a meeting between tribal leaders and White House representatives to discuss charges that the United States has consistently violated Indian treaty rights, particularly the treaty of 1868 with the Sioux. The 70-day confrontation ends with the surrender of about 120 remaining occupiers. After Wounded Knee, Indian militancy as seen in the 1960s and early 1970s will decline.

CHRONOLOGY

29 MAY 1973
Black Experience Thomas Bradley wins a runoff election to become the first black mayor of Los Angeles. A city councilman for 10 years, and a police lieutenant before that, Bradley says that the election proves 'People will listen to a candidate and make their judgement on merit instead of race or creed.'

11 JUNE 1973
National Environmentalists win a victory when the Supreme Court upholds a lower court decision that states may not permit the quality of their air to deteriorate below current levels. The suit has been filed by the Sierra Club and three other environmentalist groups seeking a strict interpretation of the Clean Air Act of 1970; it has been opposed by the Environmental Protection Agency, the US Chamber of Commerce, utility and mining interests, and the states Arizona, California, and Utah.

22 JUNE 1973
Indians The secretary of the interior is ordered to pay the $106,197 in legal costs incurred by the Paiute Indians in their successful 1972 suit blocking the Interior Department's attempt to divert water from Pyramid Lake in Nevada.

The Apple Computer complex, Cupertino, California.

13 JULY 1973
Indians The New Mexico Supreme Court rules that the state cannot impose taxes on the reservation income of Indians living on a reservation. This decision is based upon the principle that the Federal Government has exclusive jurisdiction over Indian activities on reservations.

30 AUGUST 1973
National The Interior Department reports that the fuel potential of oil in shale deposits will offset the environmental damage caused by exploitation of such deposits. This report is the final environmental-impact statement on the department's proposal to lease six tracts of federal lands for a prototype construction project. The tracts total 30,000 acres in Colorado, Utah, and Wyoming.

16 NOVEMBER 1973
Industry President Nixon signs the Alaska Pipeline Act. Following five years of controversy between environmental groups and elements of the oil industry, construction of the pipeline is authorized; it could ultimately carry up to 2 million barrels of crude oil per day from Alaska's North

A drilling pipe shipment through Texas on the Santa Fe Railway.

Slope to the ice-free port of Valdez on the Gulf of Alaska, to be transported by tanker to the US. To prevent further court challenges by the environmentalists – a ruling on 9 February of the US Court of Appeals, District of Columbia Circuit, blocking construction has been upheld on 2 April by the Supreme Court – the act provides that all actions necessary for completion of the pipeline be taken without further delay under the National Environmental Policy Act of 1969. Judicial review is restricted to constitutional grounds. The Aleyeska consortium, builder and operator of the pipeline, is to be held liable for the full costs of controlling and removing any pollution caused by the pipeline. Spokesmen for Aleyeska predict that if there are no more court delays, oil deliveries could begin by late 1977.

17 JANUARY 1974
Industry The Interior Department announces that it has accepted a top bid of $210 million from Standard Oil Company of Indiana and Gulf Corporation in an equal-interest, joint venture for the development of a tract of oil-shale land in Colorado. The announcement signals the federal government's move toward long-term development of federal energy resources in Western states.

24 JANUARY 1974
Indians Shirley Plume becomes the first American Indian to be appointed superintendent of a Bureau of Indian Affairs Agency.

7 MAY 1974
Social Change The voters of Boulder, Colorado, defeat an amendment of the city charter that would prevent job dismissal on ground of homosexuality.

CHRONOLOGY

9 AUGUST 1974

National President Richard M Nixon's resignation becomes effective at noon. Following his return to national politics in 1968, and his re-election in 1972, Nixon had become involved in the Watergate scandal. The President had wanted to fight the issue and remain in office, but resigned when even such conservative Republican leaders as Arizona's Barry Goldwater assured him that he would be impeached and convicted unless he left office. At 12:03 PM Gerald R Ford is sworn in as President. Nixon leaves by plane for California.

22 AUGUST 1974

International A joint Soviet-American expedition which has been working for two months on Anongula Island, off Alaska, announces discovery of 9000-year-old artifacts. The relics, which include tool blades matching implements previously discovered in Siberia, are further confirmation of the theory that the original inhabitants of North America came from Siberia via the Bering Strait.

16 SEPTEMBER 1974

Indians A federal court judge strongly criticizes government conduct of its case against militant Indian leaders Dennis Banks and Russell Means. The charges – assault on government officials, conspiracy, and larceny – stem from the February-May 1973 Indian occupation of Wounded Knee, South Dakota. Earlier in the trial, the Federal Bureau of Investigation was found to have suppressed documents showing that testimony by a prosecution witness was false. Testimony by FBI agents about wiretaps during the Wounded Knee siege was also shown to be false. The charges against Means and Banks are dropped.

6 NOVEMBER 1974

Social Change Janet Gray Hayes wins the mayoral election in San Jose, California. Hayes is the second woman mayor of a major city in the United States.

9 JANUARY 1975

Life/Customs The Interior Department announces that the grizzly bear is now on the list of 'threatened species.' Hunting of the grizzly bear is now restricted to Alaska and Montana; if the bear had been placed on the 'endangered species' list, all grizzly hunting would have been prohibited.

6 MAY 1975

International Former South Vietnamese Premier Nguyen Cao Ky arrives in the United States and settles temporarily in a refugee camp at Camp Pendleton, California. Like the majority of Indochinese refugees, Ky will eventually settle permanently in California. Other Indochinese will settle in Louisiana, along the Gulf of Mexico, where they can pursue their customary way of life as fishermen.

21 MAY 1975

Social Change Oregon Governor Bob Straub signs a new rape law that prohibits introduction of evidence about a rape victim's prior sexual relationships with persons other than the defendant. This is a victory for the women's movement in Oregon.

23 MAY 1975

International Former South Vietnamese Premier Nguyen Cao Ky completes his processing and is released from Camp Pendleton, California. Ky intends to organize a farming community for several thousand refugees. He reports having received several offers of assistance, including one from movie actor John Wayne, who has written Ky a letter offering 17,000 acres in Arizona as a base for the farming community.

26 JUNE 1975

Indians Two FBI agents have been sent to the Oglala Sioux Indian Reservation at Pine Ridge, South Dakota; according to the FBI's version, they are there simply to serve warrants on members of the American Indian Movement who are alleged to be holding people against their will. Allegedly, the FBI agents are met by a hail of rifle fire, and although they radio for help, they are both killed. Four Indians will be indicted, but only one, Leonard Peltier, a member of the American Indian Movement, will be found guilty – on 18 April 1977 – and sentenced to life imprisonment. Peltier's case will elicit a great deal of support, for many believe his claim that he is being framed for his membership in the AIM.

2 SEPTEMBER 1975

Social Change Students in the Omaha public school system begin classes under the first stage of a court-ordered desegregation plan.

5 SEPTEMBER 1975

Crime Lynette Alice Fromme, 26, a follower of Charles M Manson, points a gun at President Gerald Ford while the president is shaking hands with the public in Sacramento, California. A Secret Service agent subdues Miss Fromme, and no harm comes to the president. The incident is viewed on national television. Secret Service protection for the president is increased. The nation has not forgotten the traumatic public assassination of President John F Kennedy in 1963.

12 OCTOBER 1975

International Japanese Emperor Hirohito concludes a visit to the United States by attending a Hawaiian luau in Honolulu.

29 NOVEMBER 1975

Industry President Ford visits a construction site of the Alaska pipeline. The president hails the pipeline as an 'outstanding example of how our ecology can be preserved while energy needs are met.' Not all agree with this optimistic statement. Alaska is the focus of a growing controversy about what to do with the final land frontier. Among the differing groups are the native Alaskans, Alaskan citizens, such environmentalist groups as the Wilderness Society, oil companies, and the national government.

31 DECEMBER 1975
Conservation President Ford signs a bill to establish the Hells Canyon National Recreation Area, 662,000 acres in Oregon, Idaho, and Washington, following a 68-mile stretch of the Snake River.

OTHER EVENTS OF 1975
Utah Arab oil money reaches Utah, as Saudi Arabian brothers Adnan and Essam Khasshogi take a liking to Salt Lake City and begin to pour nearly $1 billion into various development projects, including a $450 million industrial park near the airport and a $410 million downtown complex. Named the Triad Center, the complex boasts twin 40-story office towers, condominiums, and a hotel.
Environment Several utility companies plan to build a 3000-megawatt coal-fired electric plant on the Kaiparowits Plateau in Utah, less than 100 miles from Bryce Canyon and Zion National Parks. The plant is eventually cancelled, and environmentalists attempt to protect the area's vistas with passage of the Federal Surface Mining Act in 1977.

4 FEBRUARY 1976
Conservation The Senate approves a bill that imposes a four-year moratorium on mining in three areas of the National Park System and bars new mining claims in Death Valley National Monument, California; Organ Pipe National Monument, Arizona; and Mt McKinley National Monument, Alaska.

10 FEBRUARY 1976
Montana Former Montana governor Tim M Babcock loses his appeal of a four-month prison term for his part in an illegal campaign contribution in 1972.

31 MARCH 1976
Industry Congress passes a bill that provides for commercial production of oil from three reserves that had been set aside for the US Navy early in the century. The bill directs the Navy to begin production of petroleum from the reserves at Elk Hills and Buena Vista in California, and the Teapot Dome reserve in Wyoming. The oil may be sold commercially or – at the President's discretion – stored to form a strategic petroleumm reserve. The legislation also directs the Navy to transfer jurisdiction of the North Slope petroleum reserve in Alaska to the Interior Department by 1 June 1977. Production of the 100 million barrels of oil there is barred until Congress grants specific approval.

15 APRIL 1976
Environment Thirteen men drown when a survival capsule launched from a sinking oil rig capsizes during a storm 30 miles into the Gulf of Mexico off Corpus Christi, Texas.

5 JUNE 1976
Environment The Teton River Dam in Idaho collapses, resulting in at least nine deaths and the loss of 4000 homes. An estimated 40,000 people are evacuated from the region. The dam, which burst as it was filled for the first time, had been challenged by environmentalists and geologists. On 6 January 1977, an independent investigation will atttribute the collapse to deficiencies in the dam's design rather than to its location, which had been the subject of earlier criticism.

8 JUNE 1976
Science/Technology California voters reject Proposition 15 by a two-to-one margin. The measure called for full assumption of financial liability for nuclear accidents. It would have barred new plant construction and cut back operating plants to 60 percent of full power output, phasing them out unless a two-thirds majority of the state legislature approved plant safety.
National Democrat James (Jimmy) Carter assures his nomination to the presidency by winning in Ohio, even though he loses the California primary to Governor Jerry Brown. Ronald Reagan's primary victory in the winner-take-all California Republican primary keeps alive his attempt to take the nomination from President Ford. Reagan's political career has been ascendent since his tenure as Governor of California.

10 SEPTEMBER 1976
Industry The Transportation Department releases an evaluation of the state of progress on the Alaska pipeline. On 21 May the Interior Department had disclosed that it was reviewing nearly 4000 'problem welds' that joined the sections of pipe. The new study raises 'serious doubts' as to whether the pipeline will be operational in mid-1977, as originally planned.

21 OCTOBER 1976
Conservation President Ford signs the Federal Land Policy and Management Act, which mandates a review of all Bureau of Management lands for potential additions to the Wilderness System. The bureau holds 284 million acres of land, all that remains of the original 2,100,000,000 acres for public domain after withdrawals for parks, forests, grasslands, wildlife refuges, monuments, defense installations, land grants to states, colleges, canal companies, railroads, creation of the Indian Reservation System, and sale and dispersal through hundreds of land laws over 200 years. The 'leftover lands' now have their own organic act. The result is that 25 million acres of Wilderness

CHRONOLOGY

Study Areas are set aside, with the Bureau of Land Management to make wilderness recommendations by 1991.

20 JANUARY 1977
National Jimmy Carter is sworn in as the thirty-ninth president.

26 JANUARY 1977
Finance Great Western United Corporation agrees to refund nearly $4 million in cash to the 14,000 homesite buyers at three land development projects in California, Colorado, and New Mexico. Great Western neither admits to, nor denies, the charges of land fraud brought by the Federal Trade Commission – that the company had misrepresented the land as a good investment, the nature and extent of the developments, and the amounts of water available at the developments.

Country and Western singers (clockwise from top left) Merle Haggard, Dolly Parton, Johnny Cash Hank Williams Jr.
Opposite: Emmylou Harris.

20 FEBRUARY 1977
Environment Interior Secretary Cecil D Andrus meets with the governors of Washington, Oregon, Idaho, and Montana to discuss the extremely dry weather affecting California and the Pacific Northwest. Andrus concedes that the drought is 'real, immediate,' and potentially 'devastating.'

17 MARCH 1977
Labor A bullet-riddled body found by rock hunters about 40 miles southwest of Las Vegas, Nevada, is identified as that of Al Bramlet, 60, president of the Nevada AFL-CIO, considered one of the most powerful men in the state.

WESTERN CHIC

How is 'the West' perceived in the late twentieth century; what is its image in the eyes of most Americans and the world? Since the Western has almost vanished as a genre, at least temporarily, from the films and television – although it still has its following in reruns and rereleases – perhaps advertising is the best reflector of the persistence of the ideal West. If the advertisements are to be believed, the West is the place where the beer is colder, the trucks are ruggeder, and the cigarettes are still satisfying.

On Madison Avenue West, the male is still a rugged loner, closer to nature than to society. Women are always in pursuit of these men, but apparently they'd rather be off by themselves quaffing beer or puffing smoke. In this updated West, the men are no longer violent gunslingers: they all look slightly dreamy, staring off at limitless horizons. True to the traditional image of the Cowboy, they seem more comfortable with horses than with newfangled machinery. In any case, in Marlboro Country there are no ecological crises, no socio-economic problems, no missile bases, no female politicians.

There are other manifestations of the West, of course. Some are closely related to the Cowboy tradition: blue jeans are popular around the world. Cowboy boots come in and out of fashion, as do Stetson-style hats and the draw-tie. A short-lived fad for mechanical bucking broncos contrasts with a longer-running trend for Western automotive 'brands': Mustang, Maverick, Cougar, Lynx, and the like. Western music retains its popularity. There is also the Palm Springs and Aspen West: a place where well-heeled people golf and ski perpetually. And the 'Dallas' and 'Dynasty' realm, where wealthy Westerners connive and romance in more or less equal proportions. California sports two sub-variants: the Rodeo Drive-Show Business Strain and the Tanned & Blond Surfer Strain.

Do all these images from the West have anything in common? For one thing, all try to recapture the traditional man's world. The life portrayed is closer to nature, somehow more genuine than that of the urban complex. The authorities can be ignored: cigarette smoke doesn't seem to affect anyone adversely in this West, despite the Surgeon General. In short, it is a world of rugged individualism, with few social constraints or issues – the Old Frontier repackaged.

8 APRIL 1977

International Customs officials estimate that 27-30 airplanes loaded with marijuana currently cross the 1945-mile border with Mexico daily. Using new advanced flight techniques and ground-surveillance networks, smuggler pilots are landing on isolated airstrips in the deserts of New Mexico, Arizona, and Texas. Hundreds of pounds of marijuana are unloaded in minutes at these drop-off points. Arizona is known to be the major corridor for drug smuggling between Mexico and the United States.

4 MAY 1977

Environment The Geological Survey reports that the prolonged water shortage in California is the worst drought on record. Rivers and streams in California are measured at as much as 87 percent below normal flow.

CHRONOLOGY

16 JUNE 1977
Environment Moderate to extreme drought conditions persist in areas of the West despite heavy May rains. The dry spell continues in western Wyoming and Colorado, eastern and southern Oregon, eastern Washington, and throughout most of Idaho and California. The rainstorms have, however, produced nearly normal conditions in the wheat belt extending from Montana to Texas.

18 JUNE 1977
Environment A forest fire engulfs 12,000 acres of New Mexico's northern and central timberland. At one point the flames spread to within 800 yards of an explosives storage unit at the Los Alamos Scientific Laboratory, a major nuclear research facility. Reportedly ignited by sparks from a motor bike, the fire is eventually contained by the efforts of some 1100 firefighters.

20 JUNE 1977
Industry Oil from the Prudhoe Bay field on Alaska's North Slope begins to flow through the Trans-Alaska pipeline system. The petroleum is expected to reach the other end of the line, 789 miles away at the ice-free port of Valdez, in 30-40 days. Once filled with nine million barrels of oil in late July, the pipeline will be tested with gradually increasing rates of flow. By the fall of 1977, some 1,200,000 barrels of oil will be delivered to Valdez daily. The *Wall Street Journal* reports that the pipeline has been completed almost precisely on schedule in part because the builders cut corners on environmental safeguards. According to the *Journal*, the results are water pollution, massive oil spills, uncontrolled erosion of the frozen tundra, and damage to fish-spawning beds.

24 JULY 1977
Indians Elders of the Comanche tribes and the Ute Nation formally end a 200-year-old feud over hunting rights. More than 2000 persons attend the ceremony in Ignacio, Colorado.

13 DECEMBER 1977
Environment The cancer branch of the National Center for Disease Control reports that two cases of leukemia are linked to observation of a nuclear bomb test in Yucca Flats, Nevada, in 1957.

28 FEBRUARY 1978
International The Carter Administration reports that the Soviet Union has questioned US adherence to the terms of the 1972 Strategic Arms Limitation Treaty. Specifically, the USSR charges US concealment of missile silos, deactivation of obsolete Atlas and Titan I intercontinental ballistic missiles, dismantling of a radar system in Montana, and the legality of a radar station in Alaska. The case has been settled to the satisfaction of both the United States and the Soviet Union.

22 APRIL 1978
Indians A tribal council announces that non-Indians will no longer be permitted on the Fort Hall Reservation in Idaho. The action is taken in response to a Supreme Court ruling that non-Indians who break laws on reservations cannot be tried in Indian courts for criminal offenses without congressional consent. Previously, the Snake River and other areas on the reservation have been used by non-Indians for hunting, fishing, and trapping.

29 APRIL-1 MAY 1978
Ideas/Beliefs Opponents of nuclear power stage a protest demonstration at the Rocky Flats nuclear weapons facility in Golden, Colorado, which manufactures the plutonium triggers used in hydrogen bombs.

9 MAY 1978
Social Change By a margin of over four-to-one, voters in Wichita, Kansas, repeal a city ordinance that prohibited discrimination against homosexuals. On 23 May Eugene, Oregon, rejects a similar ordinance by a two-to-one margin – a backlash in the trend toward homosexual civil rights.

11 JUNE 1978
Social Change Joseph Freeman Jr becomes the first black ordained to the priesthood of the Mormon Church in Salt Lake City.

The Chugach Mountains of Alaska.

21 JUNE 1978
Indians Aleuts of the Pribilof Islands are awarded $11,200,000 in a 27-year-old claim against the Federal Government. The damages are granted as compensation for poor treatment the Aleuts received from the government and its lease-holders in the fur-seal monopoly between 1870 and 1946.

28 JUNE 1978
Social Change In a landmark ruling, the Supreme Court decides that Allan P Bakke most be admitted to the University of California's Medical School. Bakke had sued on the grounds that he had been passed over for acceptance because the university had a quota for black and other minority applicants, who were less qualified than he. While supporting Bakke and setting aside strict racial quotas, the Court does invite educational institutions to consider racial origins as one of several factors when accepting applicants.

29 OCTOBER 1978
Life/Customs James Schelich wins the first slot-machine payoff of $275,000 in Las Vegas.

30 OCTOBER 1978
Industry Some $500,000 worth of damage done to the three giant electrical generators of the Grand Coulee Dam in Washington has indefinitely delayed completion of that hydroelectric plant.

1 DECEMBER 1978
Conservation President Carter brings 56 million acres of Alaska land into the national park system to protect the territory from development until Congress makes a decision on the land's status. Acting under the Antiquities Act of 1906, Carter withdraws the land from commercial exploitation by designating various parts as national monuments. The action more than doubles the size of the existing national park system. Carter declares: 'Among the treasures to be preserved are the nation's largest pristine river valley [the Noatak River Basin], the place where man may first have come into the New World [the Bering Land Bridge], a glacier as large as Rhode Island, and the largest group of peaks over 15,000 feet in North America.'

6 MAY 1979
National As the nation begins to experience its second oil shortage, Càlifornia begins to ration gasoline by employing the odd-even license plate plan (for odd-even calendar days).

16 MAY 1979
Conservation The House of Representatives approves an Alaska land bill favored by conservationists. The measure would set aside 126 million acres – larger than all of California – for 13 national parks, 21 wildlife refuges, 12 wild and scenic rivers, and two national forest wildernesses. Representative Don E Young, Alaska's only house member, opposes the bill, on ground that it deprives the people of Alaska of the use of lands they had been promised at the time of statehood. In answer, Representative Morris K Udall of Arizona points out that the 400,000 people of Alaska still retain an area twice the size of California to use as they will, and that all 220 million Americans are entitled to preserve Alaska lands as 'the last great area of world beauty left in the United States.'

13 JUNE 1979
Indians The US Court of Claims awards the Sioux Nation $105 million as compensation for the Black Hills of South Dakota, which the US Government took from the Indians in 1877, after Lieutenant Colonel George Armstrong Custer discovered gold there in 1874.

13 JULY 1979
National The 'Sagebrush Revolt' begins. Nevada enacts emergency legislation to appropriate 49 million acres from the Bureau of Land Management. At stake ultimately is 68 percent of all US land west of the one-hundredth meridian. Nevada (87 percent of which is owned by the Federal Government) hopes to provoke a legal skirmish that will lead to the Supreme Court. Operating against that possibility is a doctrine known as 'sovereign immunity,' which means that a state cannot sue the Federal Government unless the

government agrees to a suit. The argument over management of Western lands is seen as an indication of the growing hostility in the West toward Federal Government policies. The Carter Administration is coming under pressure to open up more federal lands in the West to development, and to grant the West more of a say in that development.

18 JULY 1979
Immigration Health services in San Francisco are strained beyond capacity by an influx of Indochinese refugees. In June President Carter had doubled the number of Indochinese allowed into the United States each month (7-14,000). The refugees suffer from much higher rates of tuberculosis, leprosy, and parasites than do local residents. A public-health-service team is sent to Asia to improve health screening there, and refugees are checked upon their initial arrival in Honolulu.

4 OCTOBER 1979
Environment Governor Dixy Lee Ray of Washington closes the Hanford nuclear waste-disposal site after improperly packaged waste material is found in trucks bound for the plant. On 15 November Ray will reopen the site for humanitarian reasons – medical research communities need a storage site for the low-level radioactive residue resulting from the newest methods used to help patients with cancer and leukemia.

28 NOVEMBER 1979
Idaho An investigative panel announces that poor filler soil highly susceptible to erosion contributed to the collapse of the Teton River Dam on 5 June 1976.

16 DECEMBER 1979
Science/Technology Stan Barrett drives the first rocket vehicle to break the sound barrier on land, at Edwards Air Force Base in California.

18 MAY 1980
Environment Volcanic Mount St Helens, in southeast Washington, erupts at 8:23 AM, killing at least 26 people and showering volcanic ash over the countryside for 120 miles. Scientists will later estimate that the eruption had a force 500 times as great as the atomic bomb dropped on Hiroshima in 1945. A massive ash fallout of some 4 billion tons turns the sky black and is seen as far away as Montana. The eruption is a vivid reminder to Western residents that the mountains of the Pacific Northwest are not settled, but are a region still very much in the process of formation. Mount St Helens, which had last erupted in 1857, will produce a series of lesser eruptions in subsequent months.

7 JUNE 1980
Science/Technology The first solar-cell power plant is dedicated in Utah.

19 AUGUST 1980
Conservation The Senate approves an Alaska lands bill that will preserve about one-third of the state for wildlife refuges, national parks, and other conservation areas.

30 SEPTEMBER 1980
Industry The Atlantic Richfield Company (ARCO) closes the smelter in the town of Anaconda, near Butte, Montana, citing sagging world copper prices. The firm claims that the cost of meeting pollution and safety regulations would be $400 million. ARCO turns over the property to the city and leaves a $3 million community adjustment fund. It is difficult to attract new industry, however, and the smelter smokestack – largest in the world – remains the overwhelming physical presence in Anaconda.

21 NOVEMBER 1980
Disaster Eighty-four people die in a fire at the MGM Grand Hotel in Las Vegas. Partial responsibility lies with Clark County, Nevada, which had not required automatic fire sprinklers in high-rise buildings.

2 DECEMBER 1980
Conservation President Carter signs the Alaska National Interest Lands Conservation Act, which adds 56 million acres of Alaska to the preservation system. The bill is a masterpiece of legislative compromise in giving both conservationists and commercial interests less than they want. It opens up some areas to mining, logging, and oil exploration. Most people in Alaska oppose the bill; they resent President Carter and 'East Coast liberals'' efforts to bar the way to so much natural wealth. Alaska actually creates a statehood commission; it is the first time since the Civil War that any state's people have asked to re-examine their relationship to the Union. In 1982 the commission will report that although the Federal Government has gone back on promises made in the Statehood Act, secession is not a realistic alternative.

OTHER EVENTS OF 1980
Hispanic Americans The census finds 14,228,383 persons of Spanish origin in the United States, some 2,985,643 in Texas alone. Eighty percent of them are city dwellers. In 1961 Henry Gonzalez had become the first Mexican-American congressman in Texas history.

Population Western population grows by 24 percent since 1970. Florida, Texas, and California account for nearly half the nation's population gain of 23 million. Nevada grows by 63 percent – on top of 71 percent in the 1960s – Arizona by 53 percent, Utah by 38 percent, Alaska by 32 percent.

7-8 JANUARY 1981
National Controversy follows President-elect Ronald Reagan's choice of James Watt as secretary

of the interior. At his confirmation hearing, Watt stresses his deep roots in the West (he was born and educated in Wyoming) and his goal of achieving balanced development of federal lands. Watt's designation has drawn sharp criticism from environmental groups, but he is endorsed by witnesses representing ranchers, farmers, energy groups, and Indians. On 22 January the Senate confirms Watt as interior secretary.

20 JANUARY 1981

National Ronald Wilson Reagan is inaugurated the fortieth president. Reagan, the former governor of California, is also remembered as a movie actor in Westerns.

18 APRIL 1981

Indians Hopi and Navajo Indians have long been forced to share a 1,800,000-acre tract of land in Arizona, but the two tribes do not get along. The US Government has interceded and announces today that the land is to be divided equally between the two tribes: each will have to gather all its people into its acreage. This means that some 5000 Navajos will have to relocate, while only about 100 Hopis will have to move. Although the government tries to minimize the impact of this decision, it will still be resisted five years later.

26 JUNE 1981

Environment A federal judge in Spokane, Washington, rules that the state's ban on the shipment of out-of-state nuclear waste is unconstitutional. Nearly all the atomic waste at the Hanford site comes from out of state.

17 AUGUST 1981

Science/Technology Dr Philip Bjork, director of the Museum of Geology at South Dakota School of Mines and Technology in Rapid City, is called in to investigate a large clump of earth in Haystack Butte, South Dakota. Digging with ranchers and volunteers, Bjork finds a Tyrannosaurus Rex skeleton, buried some 65 million years ago. This is the sixth such discovery worldwide.

4 OCTOBER 1981

National The body of Lee Harvey Oswald is exhumed and positively identified in Fort Worth, Texas. Exhumation follows upon a British author's conjecture that the coffin contains the corpse of a Soviet spy who assumed Oswald's identity.

18 DECEMBER 1981

Conservation Conservationists are appalled at the Interior Department's decision to open recreational areas – Lake Mead, Arizona; Glen Canyon in Utah and Arizona; Whiskeytown in California; and Ross Lake in Washington – to mineral exploration. Equally objectionable to environmentalists is the allowance made for increased motorboat use in the Grand Canyon area.

OTHER EVENTS OF 1981

Indians Governor Theodore Schwinden of Montana adds to his personal staff the first Indian appointed to deal with state Indian affairs.

Finance The state budget of Alaska has risen from $124 million in 1969 to $1,800,000,000 in 1981, due largely to oil revenues. Alaska's population and economy are booming.

18 JANUARY 1982

Science/Technology Four Air Force jets practicing a stunt maneuver crash into the sand near the Indian Springs auxiliary airfield outside Las Vegas. All four pilots are killed in this accident, the worst in the history of the Thunderbirds since that precision Air Force flying team was established in 1953.

26 JANUARY 1982

Indians The Oglala Sioux tribe of South Dakota files a $6 billion suit against the Homestake Mining Company for operating a gold mine in the Black Hills for more than a century. The tribe wants title to the land, reparations, and an account of all gold taken from the mine since 1876.

15 JUNE 1982

Immigration The Supreme Court rules 5-4 that the children of illegal aliens are entitled to a tuition-free public education in the United States. The court's decision is aimed specifically at the state of Texas and its ongoing effort to deny public-school education to the children of illegal aliens.

18 JULY 1982

Life/Customs Don Bennet, a one-legged mountain climber, fulfills a 10-year-old dream when he ascends to the top of Mount Rainier in Washington State and plants a flag in the name of the handicapped. Bennet had climbed the mountain once before, in 1970, before losing his leg in a boating accident.

31 AUGUST 1982

National A possible land swap between the Federal Government and Alaska is disclosed. Interior Secretary James Watt is seeking to exchange some park lands in Alaska for state-owned land that is already within the national-park system. Watt says that he wants to obtain land considered crucial to the national-park system without spending large amounts of money.

2 NOVEMBER 1982

Indians In tribal elections, the Navajos choose Peterson Zah, 45, over incumbent tribal chairman (since 1970) Peter MacDonald, who has been considered the best Indian leader in modern times. (*Mother Jones* magazine has charged that MacDonald is growing rich, while the Navajo per-capita income is $2900 per year.) Zah, on the other hand, has founded and directed the reservation's legal-aid program, without having a law degree himself. The new leader pledges to stop and prevent exploitation of the reservation's natural resources. Zah is also expected to open negotiations with the neighboring Hopi tribe over distribution of land in northern Arizona.

22 NOVEMBER 1982
National President Reagan calls for deployment of 100 experimental missiles in a controversial 'dense pack' basing system, in silos at Warren Air Force Base, near Cheyenne, Wyoming. The MX missile was first approved for development in 1977 by then-President Carter. The original plan for a mobile-based system in the deserts of Utah and Nevada was cancelled by President Reagan in October 1981.

23 NOVEMBER 1982
Environment Hurricane Iwa strikes Hawaii, killing one person and inflicting $200 million in damages. On 27 November President Reagan declares Hawaii a disaster area, making the islands eligible for millions of dollars in federal relief funds.

23 JANUARY 1983
Alaska A study by the Alaska Statehood Commission urges the Federal Government to lift its ban on the export of Alaskan crude oil to other countries. The recommendation is part of a $1 million study of Alaska's relationship with the Federal Government, authorized by the voters in a 1980 referendum.

12-13 APRIL 1983
Conservation The House passes a bill that designates as federal wilderness some 2,330,000 acres of national forest land in California. The Senate passes several bills bringing national forest areas in Montana, Wyoming, and Missouri into the wilderness system. In Montana, 35,000 acres are set aside as a special province to protect the habitat of the grizzly bear.

26 JUNE 1983
Environment Twelve hundred persons are forced to evacuate their homes when the Colorado River bursts through a dike at Grand Junction, Colorado. The overflow is attributed to the heavy snowfall late in the season followed by extreme heat in May, and to government miscalculations of the effects of the unusual weather.

1 SEPTEMBER 1983
Washington Senator Henry M Jackson dies at 71 in his home town of Everett, Washington. Jackson served nearly 43 years in Congress, and was one of the most influential members on defense matters, as well as an architect of the nation's environmental policy.

7 SEPTEMBER 1983
Population The Census Bureau predicts that by AD 2000 the national population will reach 267,500,000 persons. The West will experience the fastest regional growth – a 45 percent increase in population – from 43,200,000 in 1980 to 62,500,000 by 2000.

28 SEPTEMBER 1983
National The White House attempts to quiet controversy sparked by a remark made by Interior Secretary James G Watt on 21 September. Long unpopular with environmentalists, Watt had made a denigrating comment on the personnel of a special commission studying the Interior Department's coal-leasing policies, in saying that the five-member group had 'every kind of mix you can have.... a black, a woman, two Jews, and a cripple.' Watt later apoligizes, but the remark costs him his position: he resigns on 9 October.

1983
Life/Customs It is estimated that the homosexual population of Houston, Texas, has risen to 250,000. The electoral power of the Houston Gay Political Caucus was demonstrated in the 1979 council elections, when a long time councilman was not re-elected after he used abusive language about homosexuals.

25 MARCH 1984
Environment Mauna Loa, the world's largest active volcano, erupts in Hawaii, spewing molten lava 150 feet into the air. It is the volcano's first major eruption since 1950. When nearby Kilauea volcano erupts on 30 March, it is the first simultaneous activity since 1868.

26 MARCH 1984
Arts/Culture Louis L'Amour, the author of countless Western novels that have sold in the millions over many years, is awarded the nation's highest civilian honor, the Medal of Freedom; the presenter of the medal is one of L'Amour's biggest fans – President Ronald Reagan.

6 APRIL 1984
Alaska William A Egan dies in Anchorage of cancer. The first governor of Alaska after admission to statehood, Egan served three terms and presided over Alaska's constitutional convention.

24 APRIL 1984
Environment An earthquake registering 6.2 on the Richter Scale hits northern California. Centered 12 miles southeast of San Jose, the quake is said to be the strongest on the Calaveran fault since 1911, and the fourth quake in the San Francisco Bay area to register more than 6.0 since 1906. There is growing concern that the heavily populated West Coast will be struck by an earthquake of devastating magnitude.

Indian child at a Sacramento tribal gathering.

26 JUNE 1984

National Walter Mondale (former Vice-President in the Carter Administration) and Gary Hart (US Senator from Colorado) announce that they are united in the Democratic Party effort to defeat incumbent President Ronald Reagan. Mondale has interviewed prospective candidates for the vice-presidential nomination, including San Francisco Mayor Diane Feinstein, and Los Angeles Mayor Tom Bradley, but Mondale eventually chooses Representative Geraldine Ferraro, the first woman nominated for a place on a major-party presidential ticket. Ferraro is a member of Congress representing the Borough of Queens, New York City. She has achieved some recognition in this role.

17 AUGUST 1984

Industry President Reagan signs legislation that provides for 30 more years of low-cost hydro-electric power from Hoover Dam to consumers in Arizona, California, and Nevada. The measure has pitted Western against Eastern and Midwestern congressmen. At issue is whether public utilities in the three states will continue to receive power at low cost rather than at normal market rates. The rates charged for Hoover-generated electricity have remained the same for 50 years and are one-fourth to one-fourteenth the national average. Opponents of the bill call it a give-away that subsidizes Western development at the cost of conservation.

6 NOVEMBER 1984

National President Ronald Reagan wins re-election by a landslide over Democrat Walter Mondale. The incumbent president wins every state except Minnesota and the District of Columbia. CBS News declares that Reagan is the winner at 8:01 PM Eastern time. Polls in California do not close until 11 PM Eastern time – thus many Western voters hear that the election has been decided before they have voted. Both houses of Congress had passed resolutions earlier in the year urging the television networks to refrain from projecting a presidential winner until the polls had actually closed in the West.

11 JANUARY 1985

Indians The National Tribal Chairmen's Association – the main council of American Indian leaders – votes 84-18 to reject the proposals made in November 1984 by the Presidential Commission on Indian Reservation Economies. The commission's recommendations included: abolishing the Bureau of Indian Affairs; shifting Indian enterprises from tribal private hands; increasing outside investment in Indian reservations; subordinating tribal courts to the federal courts. Indian leaders reject these proposals as contrary to the traditions and best interests of their people.

APRIL 1985

Life/Customs Archaeologist Richard Fox and Doug Scott of the Park Service's Midwest Archaeological Center in Lincoln, Nebraska, publish the results of their interpretation of material unearthed during the summer of 1984 at the battlefield of Custer's Last Stand. More than 1000 battle-related artifacts – buttons, bones, spurs, bullets, cartridges, and arrowheads – were uncovered. The analysis provides illuminating details on the historic confrontation.

SUMMER 1985

Disaster Beginning in late June and continuing for much of July, fires sweep across large areas of 11 Western states – California, Oregon, Washington, Idaho, Montana, South Dakota, Utah, Nevada, Nebraska, New Mexico, and Arizona. Most of the fires are in forested areas, but some – believed to have been set by arsonists – destroy millions of dollars worth of homes. Thousands of firefighters, including volunteers from all over the country, fight the fires for weeks. This same summer, several Western states – Idaho, Montana, Utah, Wyoming, Colorado, western North Dakota, and parts of South Dakota – suffer one of the most severe grasshopper plagues in recent years.

Life/Customs Convinced that Americans are ready to support another revival of the Western film genre, Hollywood releases two major Westerns this summer – *Pale Rider*, with the immensely popular Clint Eastwood, and *Silverado*. Both do only moderately well at the box office.

19 AUGUST 1985

Hispanic Americans *US News & World Report* estimates that the Hispanic population of the United States has increased by 60 percent, to 18 million, since 1970. More than 3000 Hispanic Americans hold office, including 13 members of Congress, the governor of New Mexico, and the mayors of San Antonio and Denver. Thousands of Hispanic Americans cross the 1950-mile border with Mexico each day. The border area in Texas, New Mexico, Arizona, and California is taking on a life of its own – a blend of American and Mexican elements.

1985–

Life/Customs Levi Strauss & Company, which went on the stock market in 1971 to raise capital for its dramatic expansion, has become the largest apparel business in the world. Still a family-run concern, Levi Strauss employs about 37,000 persons in over 100 plants in the United States and abroad. It was the official outfitter for US teams in the Olympics, Pan American Games, and other international sporting events. In addition, the original line of Double X blue-denim 501 'jeans' has become a genuine artifact of Americana. The long-wearing riveted pants – invented by an immigrant tailor – have taken their place with the sewing machine, telegraph, and electric light as an American contribution to the world community. The original version is now on display at the Smithsonian Institution in Washington, DC.

THE FRONTIER THESIS

At a meeting of the American Historical Association held at the Chicago World's Fair in July 1893, a young history professor from the University of Wisconsin, Frederick Jackson Turner (1861-1932), read a paper entitled 'The Significance of the Frontier in American History.' In this seminal paper, Turner rejected the prevailing interpretation of American history, the so-called germ school of history, which held that democracy, self-government, and other institutions had been transplanted intact to England, and then to America, from the medieval institutions of Germanic tribes. Instead, Turner argued boldly that 'The existence of an area of free land, its continuous recession, and the advance of American settlement westward, explain American development.' As the American frontier moved westward in a succession of waves of settlement, men and women were forced to adapt themselves and their institutions to the new environment 'at the meeting point between savagery and civilization.' Out of this cauldron emerged a unique American character and experiment in democracy that, far from being a replica of Europe, steadily separated itself from Old World influence. 'The true point of view in the history of this nation is not the Atlantic Coast,' stated Turner, 'it is the Great West.' Turner sought to move the study of American history away from a focus on constitutional and political events east of the Alleghenies and replace it with a more dynamic, developmental approach that stressed underlying social and economic forces. Using this approach, Turner identified a series of successive kinds of frontier, which he called the trader's frontier, the miner's frontier, the rancher's frontier, and finally, the farmer's frontier, each blazing the trail for the one to follow. Each frontier produced a new kind of individual, and appropriate institutions.

Turner's essay drew little attention at first, but by the end of the century both Turner and his 'frontier thesis' had gained increasing acclaim. An entirely new generation of American historians – many trained by Turner himself – fanned out into universities and colleges across the nation, committed to studying the frontier and interpreting American development in relation to the settling of the West. By the early 1930s, however, Turner's thesis began to come under attack. Some critics, like Charles Beard, argued that the frontier did not 'explain' American development any more than any other single factor; they emphasized instead the struggle between capital and labor. Writers of the 1940s worried that a focus on the frontier would result in a preoccupation with America's rural-agrarian past at a time when the country was attempting to assume a leading role in world politics. Since then, the thesis has enjoyed a resurgence, as historians have modified it and placed it in the context of other factors shaping the course of American history. Like other powerful concepts and views of human history, it is still in the process of evolution, moving with the tide of events toward new syntheses. To this day, Turner's essay continues to exert a powerful influence on the study of American history, above that of any other single work, and his identification of the various types of frontier remains the standard framework for viewing America's westward expansion.

Index

Index

Index

Index

Index

Index

Picture credits

American Graphic Systems: 208, 219
Albany Institute of History and Art: 174 (top)
Apple Computer Inc.: 346
Associated Press/Wide World Photos: 307, 333 (top), 338
Association of American Railroads: 195 (right)
Coni Beeson: 357
Marcello Bertinetti: 176 (right center & bottom)
Bison Picture Library: 76–7, 81, 95, 97, 98, 103, 112, 113,
114, 120, 128, 129, 147, 154 (below), 156, 158 (below), 247,
250, 278, 282, 286, 291 (below), 309, 323, 325
Black Star/Tashi: 345
Anne S K Brown Military Collection, Brown University
Library: 169 (top), 209 (above)
Buffalo Bill Historical Center, Cody, Wy: 245 (above)
California State Library: 144
Chicago, Burlington & Quincy Railroad Company: 324
Coca Cola Bottling Co., Los Angeles: 295
Colorado Historical Society: 165 (top)
Comstock: 176 (bottom left)
Corcoran Gallery of Art, Washington, DC: 120–21
Country Music Foundation, Nashville, Tenn.: 313
(bottom), 320, 350 (top right and below), 351 (left)
Denver Public Library, Western History Dept: 9 (top)
Duquesne Club, Pittsburgh, Penna.: 168
Free Library of Philadelphia: 57
Thomas Gilcrease Institute of American History & Art,
Tulsa, Oklahoma: Front cover, 108, 165 (bottom)
Great Northern Railway: 339
Hopkins Picture Studio: 271 (bottom)
I & S Photographics: 164 (top)
Illinois State Historical Library: 124
Lyndon B Johnson Library: 333 (below left), 335 (left)
Kansas State Historical Society, Topeka: 215 (below)
Jack Kightlinger, The White House: 335 (right)
Kurz and Allison: 166-7, 182 (below)
Landesbildstelle: 312
Las Vegas (Nevada) News Bureau: 176 (top)
Library of Congress: 4–5, 15 (top), 18, 23 (top), 24, 25
(both), 26–7, 28 (bottom), 39, 40–41, 45, 50, 52, 58, 59,
62–3, 65, 67, 71, 72, 75, 79, 122–3, 125, 133, 142, 146, 151,
154 (top), 160, 161 (below left), 162 (top), 170 (bottom
left), 171 (below), 180, 182 (top), 196 (both), 199 (top),
200, 202, 203, 204, 205, 210 (both), 214, 216, 221, 223, 229,
230 (left & below right), 231, 234, 240 (both), 249 (above),
265, 271 (top), 272, 291 (top), 298, 319
Lowie Museum of Anthropology, University of California
at Berkeley: 235
Rick Marschall: 350 (top left)
Metropolitan Museum of Art, New York, NY: 245 (below)
Bequest of Jacob Ruppert (1939)
Montana Historical Society, Helena: 226
Museum of the City of New York: 161 (top)
Museum of Modern Art/Film Stills: 327
NASA: 336
National Archives: 37, 47, 88, 126–7, 183, 188, 189, 199
(below), 201, 209 (below), 211, 222 (below), 224 (below),
268–9, 288–9, 317, 321 (top)
National Film Archives Stills Library: 249, 257, 311, 322–3,
341

National Gallery of Art, Wash, DC: 164 (bottom left)
National Museum of American Art, Smithsonian
Institution: 111, 164 (bottom left)
National Park Service, US Department of the Interior: 172
(all), 299, 319 (top), 331, 352–3
National Railway Historical Society: 190
National Trust for Historic Preservation: 271 (center)
Nebraska State Historical Society, Solomon D. Butcher
Collection: 230 (top right)
Peter Newark's Western Americana: 333 (below right)
New Mexico State Economic Development/Tourism
Department: 344
New-York Historical Society, New York City: 77 (below),
90, 91
New York Public Library Picture Collection: 14, 16, 23
(below), 29, 31, 35, 92, 102, 138–9, 143, 161 (below right),
162–3 (all), 195 (left), 198, 212, 217, 218, 220, 222 (above,
both), 225, 243 (below), 252, 255 (below), 261, 263, 284,
285, 293, 310
New York Public Library Prints Division, I.N. Phelps
Stokes Collection of American Historical Prints: 141
New York Public Library, Rare Book Division: 21
Oklahoma State Historical Society: 231
Remington Art Museum, Ogdensburg, New York: 264
H. Armstrong Roberts, Inc: 2–3, 148–9, 157, 158–9 (top),
173 (J. Blank, top; M. Roessler, above); 173 (W.
McKinney, bottom); 175 (top), 181, 185, 187, 192–3, 194,
255 (top), 258 (left), 294, 301, 303 (W. McKinney), 313
(top)
Arthur Rothstein: 9 (bottom)
Southern Pacific Corp.: 207, 227, 232, 329 (below), 347
Shepler's, Wichita, Kansas: 351
Smithsonian Institution National Anthropological
Archives: 140, 214 (top), 224 (above), 237, 239
Sotheby-Parke Bernet, Inc.: 294
South Dakota State Historical Society: 233
Texaco: 175 (bottom), 258–9
The Title Guarantee Company: 23 (top)
Union Pacific Railroad: 191, 329 (top), 342–3
US Army Photo: 314–15, 330
US Department of Agriculture: 243 (above), 340
US Naval Historical Center: 321 (below)
US Navy Photo: 86–7, 89, 249
University of Wyoming, American Heritage Center: 206
The Wallace Collection/Crown Copyright: 15 (below), 137
Louis A. Warren Lincoln Library and Museum,
Springfield, Illinois: 108
Westport, Connecticut, Public Library: 334

Acknowledgments

The executive editor and publisher would like to thank
the following people who have helped in the preparation
of this book: Janet Bond, Samuel Crompton, David
Kotker, Sherry Marker, Raymond Quirnbach, and Eva
Weber, for contributing chronology and topic essays; Jan
Swafford for the biographies; Mike Rose, who designed
the book; Mary R Raho, who did the picture research;
Robin Langley Sommer, who edited the book; and
Cynthia Klein, who prepared the index.